THE FRENCH IN INDIA

HISTORY OF THE FRENCH IN INDIA.

(*New Edition.*)

NOTICES OF THE FIRST EDITION.

From the *Edinburgh Review*.

"Colonel Malleson has produced a volume alike attractive to the general reader, and valuable for its new matter to the special student. It is not too much to say that now for the first time we are furnished with a faithful narrative of that portion of European enterprise in India which turns upon the contest waged by the East India Company against French influence, and especially against Dupleix."

From the *Revue des deux Mondes*.

"Aussi M. Malleson a-t-il trouvé moyen de rectifier, chemin faisant, plus d'une opinion erronée. Il a rendu aux personages leur vrai caractère. Disons tout de suite que nos compatriotes sortent de cette épreuve à leur honneur. A voir en quelle estime l'auteur du livre que nous allons analyser tient les fondateurs des colonies rivales de celle de l'Angleterre, avec quelles couleurs il peint les grandes figures de Martin, de Dupleix, et de Bussy, on ne dirait pas que cette ouvrage a été écrit par un étranger."

From the *Friend of India*.

"Taking Colonel Malleson's book as a whole we do not hesitate to pronounce it to be one of the most important books connected with India which has appeared for many years. The author displays a power of exhaustive research, and expresses himself in vigorous language, which cannot fail to secure him a lasting reputation among all classes of readers; whilst as a contribution to the military history of India, as well as to the history of the French in this country, it is invaluable."

From the *Contemporary Review*.

"This important and most interesting work is in every way creditable to its author. That an English officer should undertake to illustrate the brief but brilliant period of French rule in India, to render due honour to the great men who are all but unknown in England, and most unjustly estimated by France, is a gratifying circumstance to the world in general, while the manner in which Colonel Malleson has done his work is equally praiseworthy in itself, and advantageous to our literature. It is impartial, appreciative, thorough in its details, and written in an easy, able, and attractive style."

From the *Times*.

"Colonel Malleson's work exhausts all that can be said respecting this episode. His book possesses an independent interest in the literature which relates to the European occupation of India."

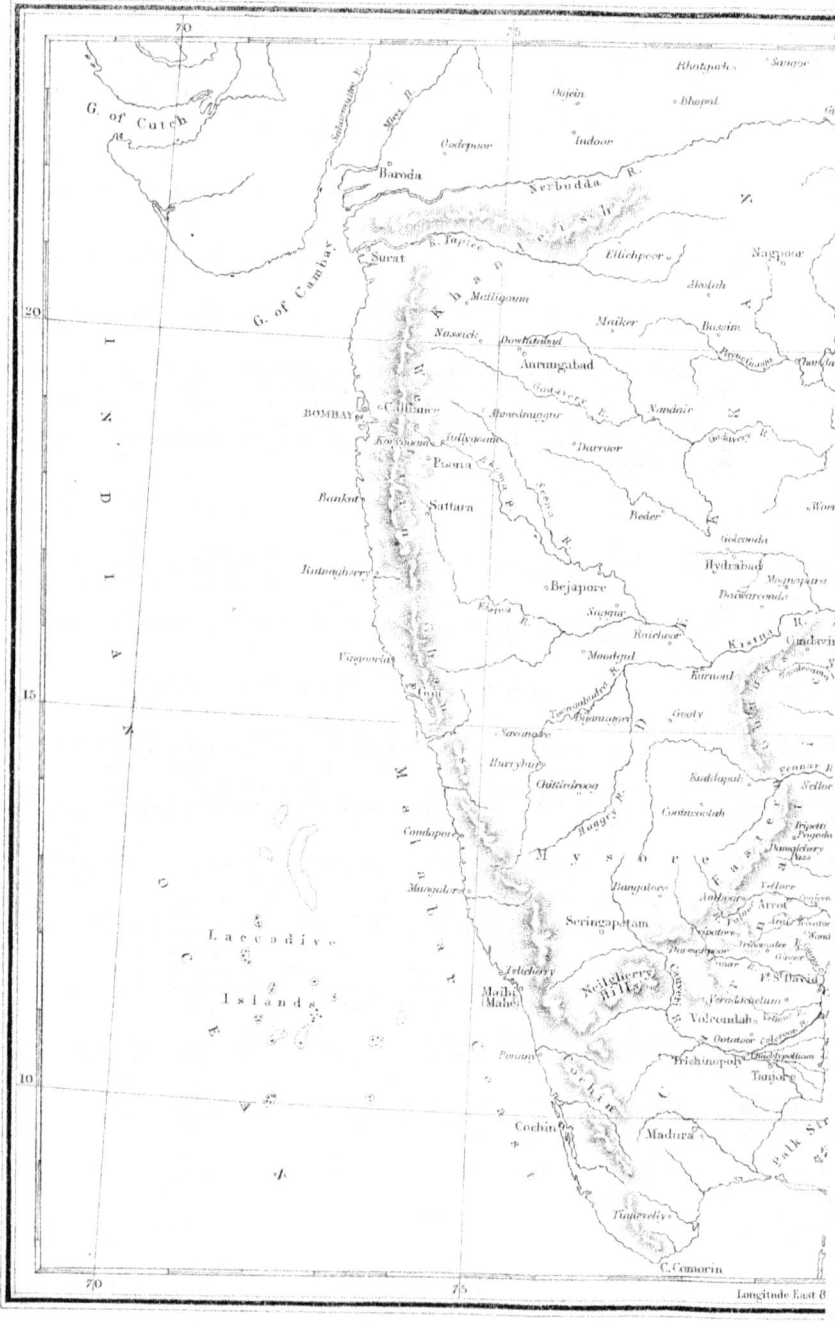

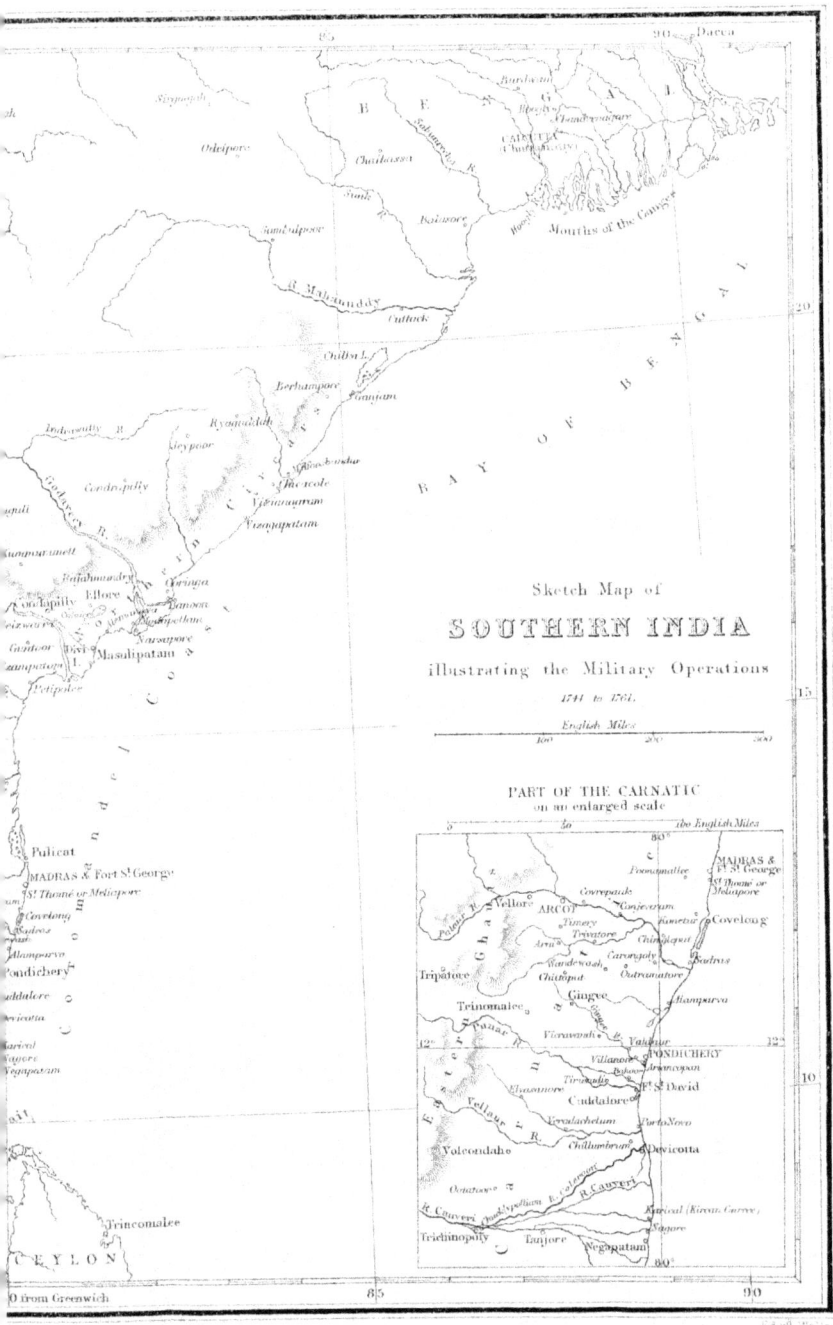

HISTORY

OF THE

FRENCH IN INDIA

FROM THE FOUNDING OF PONDICHERY IN 1674
TO THE CAPTURE OF THAT PLACE IN 1761

BY

COLONEL G B MALLESON C.S.I.

AUTHOR OF "THE HISTORY OF THE INDIAN MUTINY," "LIFE OF LORD CLIVE,"
"THE DECISIVE BATTLES OF INDIA"

NEW EDITION, CAREFULLY COMPARED AND REVISED

"On admire beaucoup et l'on cite souvent l'ANGLETERRE pour avoir résolu ce grand problème de gouverner, à quatre mille lieues de distance, avec quelques centaines d'employés civils et quelques milliers d'employés militaires, ses immenses possessions de l'INDE. S'il y a quelque nouveauté, quelque hardiesse et quelque génie politique dans cette idée, il faut reconnaître que l'honneur en revient à DUPLEIX, et que l'ANGLETERRE qui en recueille aujourd'hui le profit et la gloire, n'a eu qu'à suivre les voies que le génie de la FRANCE lui avait ouvertes."—INDE, *par M. X. Raymond.*

The Naval & Military Press Ltd

Published by

The Naval & Military Press Ltd
Unit 5 Riverside, Brambleside
Bellbrook Industrial Estate
Uckfield, East Sussex
TN22 1QQ England

Tel: +44 (0)1825 749494

www.naval-military-press.com
www.nmarchive.com

In reprinting in facsimile from the original, any imperfections are inevitably reproduced and the quality may fall short of modern type and cartographic standards.

PREFACE TO THE NEW EDITION.

A QUARTER of a century has passed away since I first offered this volume to the British public. During that time it has made the tour of Europe. It has been translated into French; quoted largely by Italian writers; read with avidity in Germany; and has procured for the author appreciative letters from distinguished men. Within the last three years the demand for it has been so continuous that I have been asked to edit a new edition. This must be my excuse for once more introducing it to the public.

Since I brought out the book in 1868 I have largely prosecuted my studies in Indian history, especially in the history of the periods immediately preceding and running parallel to the events of which I treat in this volume. I am bound to add that the increased knowledge has not brought to light any errors of importance. The reasons for the conduct of La Bourdonnais after the capture of Madras, my account of which one writer challenged four years ago, have been found, after the most exhaustive examination, to have been correctly stated in the first edition. They, therefore, appear here unaltered. The curious reader who may care to examine the question for himself, will find the controversy fully set forth in the appendix. In almost all other matters the alterations I have made are purely verbal. The spelling I have adopted is mainly that favoured by the late Professor Blochmann; similar in almost every case to that employed in the late Sir Henry Elliott's "History of India by its own Historians," a work I have carefully consulted in connection with the revision of the present volume.

G. B. M.

London, 10th July, 1893.

PREFACE TO THE FIRST EDITION.

A COMPLETE and connected account of the doings of the FRENCH IN INDIA throughout the period embraced in this volume has never yet been given to the world. The student and the soldier whose curiosity and whose interest may have been alike aroused by the outline of the deeds of Dupleix and of La Bourdonnais, of Bussy and of Lally, given in the pages of Mr. Mill's *History of India*, and who may have felt anxious to learn something more of the policy and aims of those famous Frenchmen, have hitherto been compelled to fall back for such information upon the voluminous work of Mr. Orme. Of the historical value of this work there can be no doubt. Mr. Orme was a member of the Madras Council and had access to all the Madras records, besides enjoying, as a contemporary, the opportunity of conversing with many of the actors of that stirring period. Of the feelings of the English in Madras, of the principles which animated their leaders civil and military, of the movements of their fleets and armies, his history is a most full and detailed, and, I believe, generally a faithful, record. Yet, with all this, Mr. Orme's work, judged even from an English point of view, constitutes rather a compendium of information for others to use, than a history which in the present day would commend itself to the general reader. It is often diffuse even to prolixity, and brings into prominence actions not mainly affecting the current of the narrative, and such as in the present day would be interesting only to the student of individual character. At the same time, whilst it indulges in the fullest details regarding the exploits of the ensigns and lieutenants who assisted Clive and Lawrence in annihilating the schemes of Dupleix and Lally, it regards the French rather as accessories than as principals in the story, seldom entering at any length into the reasons of their military movements, never conveying to the reader any fixed idea of the policy by which the rulers of Pondichery were guided. Throughout the work, indeed, there is a natural but entire want of sympathy with French aspirations. Even Orme, therefore, full and explicit as he is regarding the doings of the English, would fail to satisfy the inquirer for a complete and connected account of the deeds of the French in India.

Nor is the omission supplied, so far as I am aware, by any French history. The most valuable of these that I have met with in my researches is the *Histoire des Indes Orientales* by the Abbé Guyon, published in Paris in the year 1744. The value of this work consists mainly in the long and copious extracts given by the author from the archives of Pondichery, and in the correspondence, also inserted, between M. Dumas and the Native Princes of India. The supplements to the memoirs of La Bourdonnais, of Dupleix, of Lally, of Bussy, of De Leyrit, of Moracin, and of many others, give at full length the official correspondence of the various periods. These, likewise, form an excellent basis upon which to found a history, but there are few who would take up such works for amusement, or who would consider the trouble of wading through so many bulky tomes, all of them more than a hundred years old, compensated for by the information they might impart.

The void then undoubtedly existing, I have written this volume to supply it. Led, in the first place, rather accidentally, to examine the career of Lally, the interest of the subject induced me to look more deeply into the history of the settlement with which he was so prominently connected. To this study I have devoted most of my leisure moments during the past two years and a half. My labours have, however, all along been greatly stimulated by the conviction that I have been able to throw some new light upon a most interesting period. The story of François Martin, the founder of Pondichery, is, I believe, unknown to, at all events it has been unnoticed by, English historians. A new and, I am satisfied, a correct version is given of the quarrel between Dupleix and La Bourdonnais ; the reasons for the conduct of the latter are fully set forth : and if this portion of the history be regarded as too overladen with detail, I trust it may be remembered that for a hundred years the historians of France and England have, in connexion with this very point, covered the memory of Dupleix with obloquy ; and that charges so weighty, so sustained, and so long uncontradicted, are not to be refuted without full and sufficient proof. I trust also it may be found that the reasons which guided Dupleix in his policy, the relations of Bussy with the Subadar of the Dakhan, and the cause of the fall of Chandranagar, have been placed in a clearer and more intelligible light than heretofore.

In executing the task which I set myself, I have naturally incurred many heavy obligations. I am anxious to express the great debt which I owe, in common with every other writer of the Indian history of that period, to Mr. Orme, the minute detail of whose work makes it invaluable to the historian. To the work of the Abbé Guyon, and to the various French memoirs to which I have referred, I am likewise greatly indebted. It is by means of these that I have been enabled to give the history of the period from a point of view entirely Indo-French, showing, I trust clearly, the plans and policy of the rulers of Pondichery. Colonel Lawrence's *Memoirs*, Mr. Grose's *Voyage to the East Indies*, Dr. Ive's *History*, and the *Sëir Mutakherin*, have also been consulted. Amongst others, of more modern date, I may mention Colonel Wilks's *Southern India*, Captain Grant Duff's *History of the Maráthás*, Professor Wilson's edition of *Mill*, M. Xavier Raymond's *Inde*, Baron Barchou de Penhoen's *Histoire de la Conquête de l'Inde par l'Angleterre*, and that most admirable, though, unfortunately, too little known volume, Broome's *History of the Bengal Army*. I take advantage of this opportunity also to express my obligations to the writer (unknown to me) of an article on 'Dupleix,' in the 15th volume of the extinct *National Review*, which not only displays ability and research of no ordinary character, but is also remarkable as being, so far as I am aware, the first attempt to do justice to that illustrious Frenchman. I beg also gratefully to acknowledge the courtesy of M. Bontemps, Governor of the French Establishments in India, and of M. Derussat, Chief of those Establishments in Bengal, in replying to the various questions with which I troubled them, and in forwarding to me extracts from the archives of their respective seats of Government. Nor can I close this long list of obligations without expressing the deep sense I entertain of the encouragement afforded me in the prosecution of this work by Lord Ellenborough—an encouragement which mainly induced me to expand the original sketch of Lally into the history of his countrymen in India—as well as by my honoured friend, Sir Henry Durand, one of the Members of the Supreme Council of India.

I may add, in conclusion, that this work originally appeared, in separate parts, in the pages of the *Calcutta Review*, though it has since been thoroughly revised and indeed partly re-written. It was my wish, before offering it in a complete form to the English public, to submit it to the ordeal of the criticism of those, some of whom, from their long experience of India and their close acquaintance with its history, were thoroughly competent to pronounce an opinion as to its merits. If I may presume to draw any conclusion from the recorded opinion of the Indian press on the work as it appeared in parts, I shall have no reason to regret the act which I am now about to take upon myself —of presenting it to my countrymen as a whole.

G. B. M.

SIMLA: *May* 24, 1867.

CONTENTS.

CHAP.		PAGE
	PREFACE TO THE NEW EDITION	v
	PREFACE TO THE FIRST EDITION	vii
I.	THE EARLY FRENCH IN INDIA	1
II.	THE PERPETUAL COMPANY OF THE INDIES	40
III.	THE RISE OF THE FRENCH POWER IN INDIA	64
IV.	LA BOURDONNAIS AND DUPLEIX	130
V.	THE FIRST STRUGGLE IN THE KARNATIK	188
VI.	FRENCH INDIA AT ITS ZENITH	231
VII.	THE STRUGGLES OF DUPLEIX WITH ADVERSITY	283
VIII.	BUSSY TO 1754	346
IX.	THE FALL OF DUPLEIX	385
X.	GODEHEU AND DE LEYRIT	432
XI.	CHANDRANAGAR AND THE DAKHAN	465
XII.	THE LAST STRUGGLE FOR EMPIRE	507
	APPENDIX A	587
	INDEX	599

LIST OF MAPS.

SKETCH MAP OF SOUTHERN INDIA, illustrating the Military Operations, 1744 to 1761 . . . . . *to face title-page.*
MAPS OF THE OPERATIONS BEFORE TRICHINAPALLI, *to face* pp. 289 and 389.

HISTORY

OF THE

FRENCH IN INDIA.

CHAPTER I.

THE EARLY FRENCH IN INDIA.

OF the five great European maritime powers of the sixteenth and seventeenth centuries, France was the fourth to enter into the race for commercial communication with India. The fifth power, Spain, never attempted the contest, and Portugal, Holland, and England had reaped considerable benefits from their enterprise before the attention of the French people had been sufficiently attracted to the trade. Nevertheless, though the French were the last to enter upon the venture, though entering upon it after the three powers we have named had obtained a firm and solid footing on the soil, their natural genius asserted itself in a manner that speedily brought them on a level with the most securely planted of their European rivals. The restless action that had made the France of the seventeenth and eighteenth centuries the fomenter of disturbances in Europe soon found in India a wide field for its display, whilst the ambition that had urged her most famous monarch to dream of universal dominion in the West, began, before very long, to form plans for the attainment of a French empire in the East. He was a French statesman who first dared to aspire to subordinate the vast empire of the Mughal to a European will. He was a French statesman who first conceived the idea of conquering India by the aid of Indians—of arming, drilling, and training natives after the fashion of European soldiers, thus forming the germ of that sipáhí army which has since become so famous. They were French soldiers who first demonstrated on the field of battle the superiority of a handful of disciplined Europeans to the uncontrolled hordes of Asia. As we contemplate, indeed, the great achievements of France on the soil of Hindustan; as we read the numerous examples of the mighty conceptions, the heroic actions, the mental vigour, and the indomitable energy displayed there by her children, we cannot but marvel at the sudden destruction of hopes so great, of plans so vast and deep-laid. There may be, indeed there always are, many excuses for ill-success. Sometimes failure is to be attributed solely to the superior skill, genius, and force of character of an adversary. Sometimes, the hostile intervention of a third party, or his failure to keep engagements made with a principal, tends to the same result. But there are other fluctuating causes, which are often more influential still. An acute attack of a prostrating disease prevented the destruction of the Russian army at Borodino, and thus caused the annihilation of the soldiers of Napoleon in the snows of Russia. A careless movement on the part of Marshal Marmont, induced by a feverish desire to monopolise to himself the glory of expelling the English from Spain, brought on that battle of Salamanca which was the turning point of the Peninsular war. The storm on the afternoon and night of June 17 materially affected the movements of the French Emperor at Waterloo, and contributed to the actual result of that famous battle. The misdirection of a despatch brought on the battle of Navarino; and it is believed in Vienna that the accidental absence of the Austrian General from his post alone prevented the capture of Napoleon III. at Magenta. There are thus many causes, some natural, some dependent on the constitution of an individual man, some not to be foreseen, and in no way to be calculated upon, which affect the fortunes of a people. It is not that all the genius, all the strong character, all the valour are on the side of the conquerors. Genius, indeed, has been compelled to succumb to a combination of incidents apparently insignificant, and impossible to have been guarded against. There suddenly appear, when least expected, influences, apparently small, and yet really so powerful, that all calculations are upset, and we are compelled to acknowledge the might of that Providential superintendence, which, working with its own instruments and for its own designs, fashions and directs the destinies of nations.

But there is, nevertheless, always a great deal that is to be accounted for and explained on natural grounds. The character of the governing or directing body as a body, and the characters of the instruments used to carry out their policy, are sufficient to explain many results. In this respect the history of the French in India presents a most interesting and instructive lesson. That lesson is interesting, because the great deeds of great men always charm and excite the imagination : it is instructive, because we see in it a great deal of individual action, and obtain a great insight into individual character. The scene is laid at period so distant from the present, that whilst we have the actors before us conducting their skilful intrigues and engaged in their complex negotiations we have in addition, what their rivals had not, a clear view of the motives that prompted them, of the causes that urged them on. So rich in detail is this eventful period that the history possesses all the interest and excitement of a romance. Yet in no romance that was ever penned did any of the characters dare to entertain plans so wide-spread and so deep-laid as were cherished by many of the actors in this real drama. It is yet another peculiarity of this eventful history that the actors in it did not only dare to build up vast plans; they brought them to the very brink of success; they failed, too, only to let those plans fall into the lap of another and a rival nation, which, bewildered by their vastness, long refused to entertain them, and only consented at last, when the force of events had convinced them that there was no middle course between the prosecution of those plans and their own destruction.

It is strange that this story, with all its wonders, has almost faded away from the tablets of history. There exists, indeed, a record, published in the last century, of the facts connected with the rise and progress of the French East India Company, but since its appearance a flood of light has been shed upon events which were then dark and mysterious. Yet even this record has, until very recently, been almost a sealed book. Glimpses of the deeds accomplished by the French on Indian soil are occasionally to be found in old accounts of famous voyages, in forgotten French histories of India, and more recently in those English histories which are devoted to the glorification of the triumphs of our own countrymen. Occasionally, too, in some old biographic memoir, or in the notes to some graver history, we meet with curious accounts of men, who, when their prospects as a nation had been annihilated, strove, and strove earnestly in the service of native princes, to prevent the development of the fortunes of their successful rivals. We have sometimes wondered why a more modern history of this eventful episode has never been undertaken by the French. It cannot be because a brilliant career culminated in disaster. It was a disaster which at all events reflected no discredit on the soldiers of France. What discredit there was is directly to be imputed to the effete administration of the most effete and degraded representative of a House which France herself has expelled. Much, also, is due to the fact, that the mighty gulf of the French revolution intervenes between the times of which we are writing and the present; that the military history of modern France begins with the wars of 1792; and that, however much France may regret that the great Eastern prize did not fall into her hands, she cares little for the details of a struggle which occurred before the period at which she conquered the great nations of the continent, and constituted herself, for a time, mistress and arbitress of continental Europe.

We have stated that three of the maritime powers of Europe had effected permanent settlements in India, before the attention of France had been sufficiently attracted to the advantage of the trade. That this was so was attributable far more to the distractions of her government, than to any want of enterprise on the part of the French people. A period in which foreign wars alternated with civil dissensions, was certainly not favourable to fostering commerce with far distant countries. Yet, despite the turbulence of the period, and the inherent vice of their government, the desire for Eastern traffic displayed itself at a very early period amongst the French. In the reign of Louis XII., in the year 1503, two ships were fitted out by some merchants of Rouen to trade in the Eastern seas. But it is simply recorded of them that they sailed from the port of Havre in the course of that year, and were never afterwards heard of. The successor of Louis XII., King Francis I., issued to his subjects, in the years 1537 and 1543, declarations in which he exhorted them to undertake long voyages, and placed before them the pecuniary and national advantages which would result from their following his counsel. But the records of the reign of Francis abound in accounts of exhausting wars, and it is owing probably to this cause that we do not find that his wishes in respect of distant navigation were attended to. Probably the constant civil dissensions which occupied the reign of Henry III. neutralised any effect which an edict of his, to the same effect as those of his grandfather, dated December 15, 1578, might have had in less troublous times. The peaceful and prosperous reign of Henry IV. opened out, however, new prospects. On June 1, 1604, a Company was established under the King's letters patent, granting it an exclusive trade for fifteen years. But, though the services of Gerard Leroy, a Flemish navigator, who had already made several voyages to the Indies in the employ of the Dutch, were engaged, disputes amongst the proprietors, and the paucity of funds, hindered the action of the Company, and the design came to nothing. Seven years later, however, the project was renewed under Louis XIII., but owing to the same causes, nothing was undertaken during a period of four years. But in 1615, two merchants of Rouen, disgusted with the inactivity of the Company, petitioned the King for the transfer to them of the privileges accorded to it, expressing at the same time their readiness to fit out ships that very year. This petition was opposed by the Company. The King, however, after hearing the arguments on both sides, decided in favour of a coalition between the contending parties; and on this being effected, he issued (July 2, 1615) letters patent conferring the former privileges on the thus united Company.*

This Company quickly proceeded to action. In the following year (1616) it fitted out two ships, the command of the larger of which was given to Commodore de Nets, an old naval officer; and of the smaller to Captain Antoine Beaulieu, who had already made a voyage to the coast of Africa. Of the expeditions to the Indies, Beaulieu has written an interesting account.†
The first one, though not in itself to be called positively

---

* Relations de diverses Voyages curieuses, par M. Thevenot.
† Voyages des Indes, par Tavernier.

successful, was yet deemed so in that age, inasmuch as it was not absolutely a failure. It appears that the navigators met with considerable opposition from the Dutch at Java, and as there happened to be a considerable number of Dutch sailors amongst their crews, they were considerably inconvenienced by an order of the President of the Dutch possessions, by which all servants of the republic were required instantly to leave the French vessels. This neceesitated the sale of Beaulieu's ship, and the transfer of himself and the remainder of the crew to that commanded by Commodore de Nets. They succeeded so far, however, in their trading negotiations, that, notwithstanding the loss of one ship, the voyage entailed no actual loss.

Encouraged by the result of this first effort, the Company equipped another expedition of three ships in 1619, giving the chief command to Beaulieu, whom they created commodore. The names of the ships were the " Montmorenci," of 450 tons, carrying a hundred and sixty-two men, and twenty-two guns; " L'Espérance," of 400 tons, carrying a hundred and seventeen men, and twenty-six guns; and " L'Hermitage," an advice boat, of 75 tons, thirty men and eight guns. They were all victualled for two years and a half. This expedition sailed from Honfleur on October 2, 1619, and, after a prosperous voyage, reached Achin in the island of Sumatra. At Java—whither they subsequently proceeded—Beaulieu had the misfortune to lose one of his ships—" L'Espérance "—not without strong suspicions, amounting in his mind to conviction, that it had been sunk by the Dutch. But, whatever the immediate cause, it is certain that she foundered off Java with all her crew, and cargo valued at between seventy and eighty thousand pounds sterling. After experiencing this loss, Beaulieu returned to Havre, and arrived there, with his vessel well laden, on December 1, 1620.

For upwards of twenty years after this second attempt to open out a trade with the East, the Company effected nothing. A few desultory efforts, by individual traders, to make a settlement in Madagascar, produced no definite result. The powerful Minister, who then virtually ruled France, was occupied during the greater part of his tenure of power in firmly establishing his master's authority over the resisting nobles, and he could ill spare any considerable portion of his time even to foster large commercial undertakings. In 1642, however, Richelieu was master; he had triumphed over every enemy, and he at once addressed himself to the revival of commercial intercourse with the East. Under his auspices a new Company was formed, for the avowed purpose of trading to the Indies. Letters patent, dated June 24, 1642, accorded to it exclusive privileges for twenty years, and its Directors, designating it "La Compagnie des Indes," and began to make serious preparations to justify their right to the title. Their first ship had scarcely started on its expedition when Cardinal Richelieu died. This event, however did not at all affect the resolution which had incited the French Company to devote their energies, in the first instance, to the development of the large and fertile island of Madagascar.

We are not in a position, judging even by the light of subsequent events, to pronounce this determination to have been unwise. It appears, on the contrary, to have been dictated by a sound and far-seeing policy. The advantage of a resting-place midway between Europe and the Indies, had been illustrated in the possession of the Cape of Good Hope by the Portuguese. This was an example which the French, embarking for the first time seriously on a distant trade, were too prudent to neglect. Nor was it, in its consequences, an unsuccessful venture. For though the French were forced, after several trials, to abandon their hold on Madagascar, it was only as we shall see, to seize and secure the smaller islands contiguous to it, the possession of which from 1672 to 1810 proved to them a tower of strength in their wars with England; a festering thorn in the sides of their maritime rivals.

Madagascar, originally discovered by Marco Polo in 1298, and subsequently lost sight of, had been reopened to European enterprise by the Portuguese under Fernan Suarez, one of the officers of Lawrence Almeida, in 1506. It was visited the following year by a Portuguese squadron under Tristan de Cunha; but that celebrated navigator, after a minute examination of the topography of the place, the customs of the inhabitants, and the productions of the soil, thought it inexpedient to form a settlement there, and continued his voyage eastward. Two years later, however, the Portuguese Government resolved to occupy a post on the seaboard of the island. A settlement was accordingly made on its northern part, but those who formed it had been massacred by the inhabitants before the period of the French expedition of 1642.

The first French vessel equipped by the French India Company reached Madagascar in the summer of 1642, and landed the settlers at a point near the southern extremity of the island. Their landing was opposed, though ineffectually, by the natives of the country. They forthwith attempted to carry out a regular scheme of colonisation, and to this purpose they devoted all the resources of the Company. They soon found, however, as the wise Tristan de Cunha had foreseen, that, though in appearance rich and fertile, the soil of the island could not produce, in any great quantity, those articles which entered the most into European consumption. When they began to make inroads into the interior, they found still greater difficulties awaiting them. They came in contact, then, with a numerous and warlike race, detesting strangers, and preferring savage freedom to foreign domination. By the bulk of these, the French settlers were received, from the very outset, with marked hostility. This feeling was increased to absolute hatred in consequence of the treacherous seizure and deportation to the neighbouring island of Mauritius, as slaves, of a number of natives who had voluntarily entered the limits of the French territory. This act was ruinous in its consequences to the French settlers. Not content from that time with repulsing every effort of the French to penetrate into the interior, the inhabitants, gaining boldness from success, assumed the offensive, and began in their turn to attack the wretched wooden stockades which the colonists had erected with infinite labour and expense, and had dignified by the name of "Forts." So numerous were the islanders, and so determinedly hostile, that the French experienced very great difficulty in offering to them an effectual resistance. The time and the labour employed in so doing drew them away almost entirely from cultivation; and, though they were ultimately successful in defending their forts, it was a success which was as costly as a defeat; for it sank all the large sums which had been expended on the enterprise without the chance of a return. It would be surprising that, under these circumstances, and though the French India Company relinquished their claims to the island in 1672, the French Government should have continued to maintain their hold of the seaboard several years longer, were it not for the fact that the retention at all costs of a portion of the country, was considered eminently desirable as forming a resting-place and a shelter in the long voyage to India.

The ill-success of this enterprise was not, however, at once recognised in France, although for a time there appeared no desire to renew it. The long minority of Louis XIV., the ministry of Cardinal Mazarin, with its wars of the Fronde and its contests with Spain, were not favourable to commercial enterprise. Mazarin, however, died in 1661. His successor, Colbert, was one of those men who stamp their name on the age in which they live. Colbert was one of the glories of France. Born in the middle rank of life, the son of a merchant, himself educated as a banker, and having, in that capacity, been charged with the management of the affairs of Cardinal Mazarin, he had gained so entirely the confidence of that Minister, that, on his dying bed, the Cardinal recommended him to his master as a man of immense capacity, strict fidelity, and unwearied application. Colbert succeeded him, first only as Controller of Finances, but not long after he was invested with the entire administration of the country. Under his guiding hand, France quickly assumed in Europe a position such as she had never before held. Her finances, commerce, industry, agriculture, art, all felt the impulse of his strong will and firm direction. Colbert made the French navy. In a few years after his accession to power, France possessed a hundred vessels of war, and there were 60,000 sailors inscribed on the rolls. He created the naval ports of Brest, Toulon, and Rochefort; he bought Dunkirk from the English, and he commenced Cherbourg; and " binding together industry, commerce, and the marine in one common future, he founded French colonies to assure outlets to industry and commerce, and an employment of the navy in time of peace."

Colbert had been neither blind nor indifferent to the great advantages which had accrued to the Portuguese, the Dutch, and the English from their possessions in India, and he made it one of his greatest objects to encourage the formation of a grand Company, somewhat on the English model, to open out a regular traffic with that country. He held out to it promises of the strongest support of the administration. He offered it a charter granting it the exclusive right of commerce with India for fifty years; it was to be exempted from all taxation; and the Government agreed to engage to reimburse it for all losses it might suffer during the first ten years after its formation. On these conditions, in the year 1664, the French " Compagnie des Indes " was formed. Its capital was 15,000,000 " livres tournois," equivalent to about 600,000*l.*; but as, even under the conditions mentioned, the entire sum was not subscribed for, a fifth of the amount, 3,000,000 livres, was advanced by the Treasury. This example had a great effect upon the nobility and rich courtiers; and these at once became eager to join an undertaking which the Government seemed to cherish as one of its most favoured projects.*

The prospects of the Company on its formation were thus brilliant. Starting under the auspices of a monarchy which had not attained the height of its power, but was then fast rising to it, which, in its capabilities for offensive operations and for the display of real strength, contrasted favourably with the other European states, this Company seemed to require but firm and steady direction to become a great success. Nevertheless, its first movements were neither well considered nor fortunate. Full of the recollection of the attempt made in 1642 upon Madagascar, a settlement in which was still regarded as an indispensable preliminary to a voyage to the unknown Indies, the Directors of the new Company conceived the idea that, by transporting simple colonists to that island, they might yet realise some of the results of the labours of their predecessors. Their first expedition was accordingly directed to Madagascar. On March

---

* Louis XIV. himself, under the influence of Colbert, endeavoured to reconcile his nobility to a participation in the enterprise, by declaring that trade to *India* was not derogatory to a man of noble birth.—*Édit du Roi*, Août, 1664.

7, 1665, four large ships, equipped for war as well as trade, and carrying five hundred and twenty men, sailed from Brest harbour, and reached Madagascar on July 10th following. The first act of the colonists was to change the name of the island from St. Lawrence, as it had been called by the Portuguese, to Isle Dauphine, in honour of the heir-apparent, then four years old. It proved to be but a poor compliment to the Dauphin, They soon discovered that, instead of profiting by their predecessors' mistakes, they had themselves fallen into those predecessors' errors. The new colonists, like those who went before them, found that their labour was hindered by three causes, by climate, by the nature of the soil, and by the hostility of the natives. This last-mentioned cause produced yet another, for it exposed the unfortunate emigrants to constant exposure and constant fatigue. To such an extent did they suffer, and disclose by their sufferings the hopelessness of the undertaking, that the Company, although for a long time it continued to reinforce the colonists with supplies of men, resolved ultimately to give up all thoughts of permanently colonising Madagascar, and to divert their energies to another quarter. The movements of the colonists were however quickened by the action of the natives, who succeeded, in 1672, in surprising Fort Dauphine, and massacring the majority of those who were within its walls. Of the baffled colonists, some proceeded ultimately to India; others, however, contented themselves with the formation of a small settlement in the island of Mascarenhas, lying with Cerné a little to the east of Madagascar. These islands, under the names of the Isles of France and Bourbon, and again as the Islands of Mauritius and Réunion, have since become well known. The Isle of Mauritius, or Cerné, had been early discovered, and abandoned, by the Portuguese; occupied in 1598 by the Dutch, who, in honour of Prince Maurice of

Nassau, called it Mauritius; abandoned by them at some time between the years 1703 and 1710; and occupied later, between that period and 1719, by the French, who changed its name to the Isle of France. Bourbon, or Mascarenhas, called so after a Portuguese nobleman, was absolutely desolate when the French, touching there on the way to Madagascar in 1649, took possession of in the name of the King of France. It remained uncolonised till 1654, when eight Frenchmen and six negroes emigrated to it from that island, but deserted it again four years later. The island continued uninhabited till 1672, when, on the collapse of the Madagascar enterprise, an inconsiderable number of the colonists took possession of it, and formed the nucleus of a settlement which was one day to be powerful.

But the French India Company had not wasted all its resources in their attempts on Madagascar. In 1666 another expedition was fitted out, and the command of it bestowed upon one Francis Caron, a man who possessed at that time considerable reputation for experience in Eastern undertakings. Caron, though of French origin, had been born in Holland, and he had spent many years of his life in the service of the Dutch republic. At a very early age, he had obtained a situation as a cook-mate on board a Dutch man-of-war bound for Japan; but during the voyage he showed such intelligence that he was promoted to the post of chief steward. This office gave him a little leisure which he devoted to the study of arithmetic. On the arrival of the vessel at Japan, he at once applied himself to the study of the language of the country. Having acquired this knowledge, he was able to make almost his own terms with the agents of the Dutch Company, and he was soon appointed a member of the general council of administration, and director of commerce. But, little satisfied with this, he applied for a post of still higher importance in Batavia.* He was refused. Whereupon, Caron, listening only to his anger, abruptly resigned his appointment under the Dutch, and tendered his services to Colbert. Colbert closed eagerly with the offer, and Caron soon after received letters patent nominating him Director-General of French commerce in India. Associated with Caron was a Persian named Marcara, a native of Ispahan, from whose local knowledge of India many advantages were anticipated.

The expedition sailed from France in the beginning of 1667, and made a fair voyage to Madagascar. But, on arriving there, Caron found the French establishments on the coast in a condition so deplorable, and the prospect of being able to effect an amelioration so discouraging, that he determined not to waste any of his resources in the attempt, but to proceed at once to India. He directed his course, accordingly, towards Surat, a place which the enterprise of the other maritime powers of Europe had made familiar to traders to the East. On December 24, he touched at Cochin, where he was well received. Thence he continued his voyage, reached Surat in the beginning of 1668, and established there the first French factory in India. The negotiations into which he entered were at first successful. A very valuable cargo was quickly transmitted to Madagascar. And this result was no sooner known in

---

* It is stated by some authorities that, when Caron was in charge of the Dutch agency at Japan, he made an audacious attempt to establish himself on the coast. Having ingratiated himself with the King, he obtained permission to build a house close to the Dutch factory. Knowing the Japanese to be ignorant of fortification, he built this house in the form of a tetragon—made it, in fact, a regular fortification. He then applied to the Governor of Batavia to send him along with casks of spices, casks of the same size containing guns, and filled up with cotton or oakum. This was done, but, unfortunately for Caron, in rolling the casks up the beach, one of them fell in pieces, and a brass gun made its appearance. This discovered the deception. Caron was at once seized, sent to Jeddo, and confronted with the King. Being unable to offer any excuse, he was sentenced to have his beard pulled out hair by hair; to be dressed in a fool's coat and cap; and to be exposed in that condition in every street in the city. After this he was shipped back to Batavia.— *Recueil de Voyages du Nord*, vol. iii.

This story is not credited by later writers.

CHAP. I.
1667.

France, than, as a reward for his exertions, and possibly to incite him to others, the King at once conferred upon the Caron the riband of St. Michel.

In the following year an extension of operations was resolved upon. Marcara was directed to proceed to the court of the then independent king of Golkonda, with the view of obtaining from him the privilege of trading throughout his dominions, and of establishing a factory at Machhlipatan (Masulipatam). To procure this, Marcara had not only to fight his way through those obstacles peculiar to an oriental court, but he had to meet also the opposition of the English and of the Dutch. However, he triumphed over all difficulties, and on December 5, 1669, obtained a firman which permitted the French Company to undertake negotiations in the dominions of the King, without payment of duty, import, or export; a license was granted him at the same time to establish a factory at Machhlipatan. Thither, accordingly, Marcara proceeded.*

It is curious, that the one fatal feeling which attended all the efforts of the French to establish themselves in India, and which contributed very greatly to their failure, should have shown itself at this early epoch. This feeling was jealousy. It seldom happened that a man, high in office, could endure that any great feat should be accomplished by another than himself. Rarely could a sense of patriotism, a love of country, an anxiety to forward the common weal, reconcile a servant of the French Company to the success of a rival. We shall see, as we proceed, what golden opportunities were lost, what openings were deliberately sacrificed to the gratification of feelings as mean and paltry in themselves, as they were base and even treasonable in men who had been sent to advance the fortunes of their country in a distant land.

The French had not been two years in Surat before

* Mémoires du Sieur Marcara; Histoire des Indes Orientales.

this feeling evinced itself. Caron, though he could boast of great achievements himself, could not endure the idea that one of his associates should obtain the sole credit for deeds in which he could claim no share. The success of Marcara then, so far from being to him a source of joy, as to a patriotic Frenchman it ought to have been, awakened feelings of envy. He at once removed all the friends of the Persian from employ, and represented his conduct in a most unfavourable light to the French Minister. Marcara, however, on receiving an account of these aspersions, transmitted to Colbert a statement of his proceedings. This statement was so precise, and was so well supported by facts, that, after a full inquiry, Marcara was declared to have cleared himself of every charge brought against him. The contest, however, between the two principal officials in India did not tend to the stability of the rising settlements.*

Caron, however, was bent upon effecting some results of greater importance. He accordingly represented to the Minister that, to obtain a firm footing in the country, it was necessary to hold some place in absolute possession, unassailable by the natives of India, and to use it as a stronghold whence commercial operations could be carried on with the inhabitants of the mainland. Following the idea of Albuquerque, he suggested, for this purpose, the occupation of an island, and he indicated the seaboard of Ceylon, then partially occupied by the Dutch, as well adapted to the end in view.†
He did not fail to point out the great commercial advantages which must accrue to France from an immediate participation in the spice trade, and he

---

* In consequence of his quarrel with Caron, Marcara, unable any longer to work with him, embarked with his adherents on board a French ship, and sailed to Java. Arriving at Bantam, they established factories there, of which, however, they were dispossessed by the Dutch some ten years after (1682).
† Journal du Voyage des Grandes Indes.

intimated he had sounded the King of Kandy on the subject of the dispossession of the Dutch, and that the enterprise would meet with his support. The project was approved by Colbert, and a fleet under the command of Admiral Lahaye—a man of some reputation,* who had quitted high civil employment to gratify his passion for warlike operations—was placed at the disposal of Caron to carry out the design. Lahaye made his first attempt towards the end of the year 1672 on Point de Galle. But either the place was too strong, or the jealousies on board the French squadron were too great: for the French were unsuccessful. They were more fortunate at Trinkámalí, which they took and garrisoned. But they had hardly landed the guns necessary to defend the fortress, when a Dutch fleet of at least equal force, under Commodore Rylckoff van Goens, came in sight.† Lahaye declined an encounter, and leaving the garrison at Trinkámalí to shift for itself, make sail to Malaipur, then known as St. Thomé, on the Koromandel coast. Though this place had been well fortified by the Portuguese, from whom it had been taken by the Dutch some twelve years before, the French commander managed to occupy it in a very short time with the loss of only five men.

This solitary result of an expedition, from which so much had been hoped, gave little satisfaction to the French Ministry. Trinkámalí had had to surrender with all its garrison to the Dutch fleet, and now of their conquests—for at Surat and Machhlipatan they had but factories—St. Thomé alone remained. As is common in such cases, the first outcry was against the projector, and every possible fault was at once attributed to

---

* It would appear that Lahaye's reptuation was far greater than could be justified; not only had he, when Governor-General of Madagascar, abandoned the colonists there when they were pressed hard by the natives, but his conduct in the attack upon Ceylon, and subsequently, appears to have been utterly unworthy of a man occupying his high position.

† Annales des Provinces Unies.

Caron. Some were jealous of his position; others detested his imperious character, and declaimed against his grasping disposition. Had Caron succeeded, but little perhaps would have been heard of these faults, but having failed, they were made use of to procure his recall. The French Directors, who likewise looked very keenly to results, were so much mortified at the ill-success of this costly expedition, that they also petitioned the Minister to recall Caron, in order, they said, that they might inspect his accounts. The petition was complied with, and, to prevent the chance of any evasion of the instructions, the order sent to Caron did not convey his absolute recall, but directed him, in complimentary terms, to return to France, that he might be personally consulted with regard to some new enterprise. Caron at once obeyed, and, embarking all his wealth, of which he had amassed a great deal, he set sail in 1673 for Marseilles. He had already passed the Straits of Gibraltar, when he learned from a stray vessel the real intentions of the French Government regarding him. He at once altered his course and proceeded towards Lisbon. But, on entering the harbour, the ship struck on a rock, and almost immediately foundered. The only survivor of the disaster was one of the sons of Caron.*

In the expeditions undertaken against Ceylon and St. Thomé, a very prominent part had been taken by one Francis Martin, a Frenchman, who devoted a long career, in singleness of heart and with great success, to the furtherance of the designs of France in the East. Little is known of him prior to the year 1672, beyond the fact that he, too, had commenced his career in the service of the Dutch East India Company, and that he had left it at an early age to join the French. He had probably made the acquaintance of Caron when they

* Histoire des Indes Orientales, vol. iii.

were both serving under the Dutch flag. This is certain, that he was known at Surat as a man on whose energy and discretion Caron had the greatest reliance; and he was regarded, at the time of its being carried out, as the soul of the enterprise undertaken against Point de Galle and Trinkámalí. Some, indeed, have asserted that the attempt on Point de Galle failed, because Martin, who had the direction of the attack, had applied for, and been refused, the governorship of that place. But this statement, which was but little credited at the time, is refuted by the whole of his subsequent career. It is no slight proof of the confidence which he had inspired in those under whom he served, that although he was the trusted subordinate of Caron, he was regarded with equal favour by those in whose hands the departure of that official left the direction of affairs in 1674. These were Admiral Lahaye and M. Baron.

The position in which these gentlemen found themselves was by no means enviable. They had provoked the hostility of the Dutch by attacking their possessions, and the Dutch were now masters of the seas, and inflamed against them with a particular animosity. They had retaken Trinkámalí, and the French could scarcely hope that they would allow them to retain peaceable possession of St. Thomé. With a view, therefore, to provide themselves with a place of refuge in case of evil days, the two French Directors ordered Martin to place himself in communication with Sher Khán Lodí, the Governor of the possessions of the King of Bíjápur in Tanjur and the Karnátik, for the grant of a piece of land which they might call their own. Martin obeyed, found the Governor accessible, and was allowed to purchase a plot of ground on the sea-coast in the province of Jinjí, near the mouth of the river of that name, considerably to the north of the river Kolrún.

This arrangement concluded, Martin returned to St. Thomé. He there found the two Directors not at all doubtful regarding the intentions of the Dutch. It was no longer a secret that the Government of Holland, highly incensed at the attack upon its possessions in Ceylon, was by no means satisfied with the recapture of Trinkámalí, but had sent out pressing instructions to its agents to drive the French likewise from St Thomé. Possessing the power, that Government determined to exercise it by striking out the French from the list of its rivals in the Indian trade. Whilst, therefore, showering rewards upon Admiral van Goens for the energy with which he had acted with reference to Trinkámalí, it urged him to follow up his blow, and, by a well-aimed stroke, to put a final end to the ambitious projects of the French in the East.

The Dutch agents immediately set to work to carry out these instructions. Their first care was to provide themselves with native allies. They, therefore, represented to the King of Golkonda that the capture of St. Thomé by the French was a deliberate and wanton attack upon possessions which they held only in vassalage to him; that the newcomers were an enterprising and energetic race, who would not be content with merely a port on the sea-coast; and that it concerned his safety, as well as his honour, to expel them. They acted, in fine, so much on the jealously and fears of Abul Hásán, the last representative of the House of Kutb-ul Mulk, that he detached a considerable force to besiege St. Thomé by land, whilst the Dutch should attack it by sea.

The combined force made its appearance before St. Thomé in the beginning of 1674, but for a considerable time they failed to make any impression upon its defences. The place was garrisoned by nearly six hundred men, the remnants of the expedition which two years before had sailed with such alacrity against Point de

CHAP. I.
1674.

Galle. Now, though reduced in numbers, they were animated by the best spirit, and they were under the immediate direction of a man who never knew what it was to be discouraged. Such was the energy of their defence, that, finding, at the expiration of some weeks, how little had been accomplished towards the reduction of the place, the Dutch resolved to land a considerable body of men to co-operate with the Golkonda army. By this means they were enabled to subject the garrison to a strict blockade. These proceedings were effectual. Unable to procure fresh supplies, and having consumed their last stores, the French were compelled to surrender. The conditions granted to them were favourable; for they were allowed to march out with all the honours of war, and to proceed in whatever direction they might perfer.* If it had been the object of the Dutch to expel the French from India, they had much reason to complain of the agents who granted a capitulation containing such a clause. But these had little idea, in all probability, of the use that would be made of it.

To a small but resolute minority of the French garrison, this capitulation, if a blow, was a blow which they had expected, and for which they were prepared. Having been allowed to choose their own destination, they at once selected the territory which they had purchased north of the Kolrún. Thither, accordingly, marched some sixty of them, under the orders of Francis Martin, and there they arrived in the month of April, 1674. They had everything to do, and their resources were at a very low ebb. The remainder, who constituted a large majority, determined to return at once in the ships that remained to them to Surat. Amongst those who adopted this course were the two Directors, Messrs. Lahaye and Baron.†

* Annales des Provinces Unies, vol. ii.   † It would appear that both Lahaye and Baron visited the plot of

The supreme authority now remained with Martin. He had with him sixty Europeans, including the crew of the "Vigilante" frigate, which alone remained in the roads at his disposal. He had likewise all the effects which had been brought from St. Thomé, and a considerable sum in ready money. His first care was to obtain permission from the native ruler on the spot to erect such buildings as should be necessary to secure his people and their property from desultory attack. He had entered into such relations with this chieftain that this permission was granted without much difficulty. The command of the sea by the Dutch had forbidden him to think of opening a trade with Europe, and as Sher Khán Lodi was in want of funds, and he had those funds lying idle, he had thought it good policy to lend them to him at the then moderate interest of eighteen per cent. The character of Sher Khán Lodi enabled him to do this without much risk; and, contrary to the old proverb, the transaction made of the borrower a fast friend.* Under his protection, the slender defences and the houses within them sprang up rapidly; and by the wise dealings of Martin with the natives, a little village, containing the native population who worked for the factory, soon grew up under its walls. The whole formed a sort of town which was at first called by the natives "Philcheru," but was gradually altered to the designation, which it bears at present, and by which it has always been known to Europeans, of "Pondichery."†

The measures adopted by Martin for regulating his commercial transactions were characterised by the same

ground on which Pondichery was afterwards built *en route* to Surat. From Surat Baron wrote to the Company that "next to St. Thomé, the site selected by Martin was better fitted for their purposes than any other on the Koromandel coast."— *Mémoire dans les Archives de la Compagnie des Indes.*

* Mémoires dans les Archives de la Compagnie des Indes.

† Browne's Carnatic Chronology. The native historians of those times and of the times that were to follow invariably write of the French settlement as "Phúljari," vide Elliott's History of India, vol. viii., page 391.

prudence. In those days India supplied Europe with piece-goods, and it was to the opening of a trade in this commodity that the attention of the little colony was at first directed. So successful were their efforts that in about two years after their arrival, Martin wrote to the Company that he would be able to send them an annual supply to the value of 1,000,000 livres or more. He added a full description of the place; stated that he considered it as well adapted as any other on the coast for the purpose of a French settlement; that the roadstead in front of it, which prevented the near approach of men-of-war, rendered it secure against any sudden attack; that it was fairly sheltered from the monsoon; that it was healthy and well situated for commercial purposes. This report, and the intelligence which accompanied it, so different from the accounts which the fall of St. Thomé had led them to expect, were received with the greatest satisfaction by the Directors.

It must not be imagined that the colonists were entirely free from troubles and alarms. Pondichery was, in fact, founded and nutured amid the clash of arms and the clamour of falling kingdoms. The Sultanat of Bijápúr from which the ground on which it was built had been obtained, ceased in 1676 to be ranked as an independent sovereignty. Twelve months later, Golkonda, which had assisted in the expulsion of the French from St. Thomé, had itself fallen a prey to the insatiable ambition of Aurangzéb. At the same time, the enemy of all established authorities— Síváji—was engaged in levying contributions wherever he could obtain them, in annexing towns and provinces, and in laying the foundation of that predatory power which his successors carried to so great a height. In such a time, the only chance of safety, especially for a community comparatively rich, was to be well armed, and well capable of offering resistance. None felt this more than Martin. As, then, he noticed the periodical increase of his manufactories, he felt that he had need of more numerous defenders than the few Europeans who formed his party. He accordingly, in 1676, applied to his friend Sher Khán Lodí, for permission to entertain some native soldiers for the purposes of defence. Sher Khán willingly assented, and made over to him three hundred of his own men. Martin used these men not only as soldiers, but colonists. He gave each a piece of land, and encouraged them to build houses, and to employ themselves profitably in the manufacture of tissues and other articles for export.

For some time everything went on well, and the settlement continued to increase in prosperity. But in the seventeenth century peace and tranquillity were rare in India; and the turn of Pondichery came at last. In 1676, Síváji, having in the four preceding years possessed himself of many places on the Malabar coast, and been crowned King of the Maráthás, proceeded to Golkonda, and, after having made an alliance with its ruler for the protection of his own territories during his absence, poured like a torrent on the Karnátik. In May, 1677, he passed by Madras, then occupied by the English, and appeared before Jinjí, regarded as inaccessible. Jinjí, however, surrendered, owing, it is stated, to a previous understanding with the commander. Proceeding further south, he was met by Martin's friend, Sher Khán, at the head of five thousand horse, but Sher Khán was defeated and taken prisoner. Síváji then invested Vellur, took Arni, and threatened to overwhelm the settlement established by the French, on the ground of their being dependents of his enemy Sher Khán.

The situation was critical. Martin's three hundred soldier-workmen were powerless in such an emergency, even supported by the entire European community. Resistance, therefore, was out of the question. But Martin had before dealt with Asiatics, and he knew that there was one argument against which few of them were proof. For greater security, however, he took the precaution, in the first instance, to send all the property of the Company by sea to Madras. He then requested one of the petty native chieftains in his neighbourhood,* who had made his own submission to the irresistible Maráthá, to represent his perfect readiness to acknowledge the authority of Síváji, and to pay the necessary sums for a license to trade in his dominions. This request, accompanied by a handsome offering, did not fail of success. Síváji, never very ready to attack Europeans, had, on this occasion, no personal animosity to gratify, and he granted all that was asked of him on the sole condition that the French should take no part against him in military operations. The negotiation was scarcely terminated, when the news of the invasion of Golkonda by the Mughals called him away in a northerly direction, and Pondichery was the safer for the danger that had threatened it.

After this, affairs went on for some time quietly. But subsequently to the invasion of Síváji, Sher Khán, the old friend and protector of the rising settlement, appears to have been engaged in constant warfare, a warfare that did not always end in success. It became therefore an object to the French that he should repay, whilst yet he was able, the sums that had been advanced to him in 1674, amounting to eight thousand rupees. To him therefore, in a friendly manner, Martin signified his wishes. Sher Khán, unable to pay, granted him, instead, the revenue of the lands in the district of Pondichery, and made the cession of that place itself absolute, an arrangement very advantageous to French interests. Thus secure of a fixed revenue, Martin began with greater vigour than ever to carry out his improvements. His

* Guyon speaks of him as a Brahman living in Pondicherry; he was probably a small landowner.

sixty Europeans had been reduced to thirty-four; but he did not despair. He continued to build houses, magazines, and stores; and in the beginning of 1689, he obtained likewise, though with much difficulty, the permission of Sambají, son of Síváji, to make of the defences he had erected a regular fortification.*

In that year, however, war broke out between France and Holland, and the Dutch appeared determined to take advantage of the opportunity to repair the fault they had committed in 1674, when they granted the French a free retreat from St. Thomé. The prosperity of Pondichery alarmed them. The occasion was propitious. The French navy was too much occupied in Europe to be able to assist its possessions on the Koromandel coast—which, indeed, had been systematically neglected from the outset. The Dutch, on the contrary, had a strong force in the eastern seas; and, free from all fear of opposition, they resolved to use it to nip in the bud the young French settlement at Pondichery.

In accordance with these views, a fleet of nineteen sail of the line, exclusive of transports and smaller vessels, appeared before Pondichery at the end of August, 1693. It was one of the most imposing armaments that had ever sailed on the Indian seas. It had on board fifteen hundred European troops, and two thousand European sailors, besides some native Cingalese in Dutch pay; it had sixteen brass guns, six mortars, and a siege train. Nevertheless, scarcely satisfied with their own means, the Dutch had previously written to Rám Rájá, who, on the death of Sambají, had been appointed ruler of the Maráthás, offering to buy from him the district of Pondichery. The reply of Rám Rájá deserves to be remembered. "The French," he said, "fairly purchased Pondichery, and paid for it a valuable consideration; therefore all the money in the world would never

---

* It is a tradition of Pondichery that these defences were planned and carried out by a Capuchin monk, Father Louis.

tempt me to dislodge them.* But when the Dutch fleet appeared before Pondichery, the high-souled Marátha was no longer able to exert his influence in their favour. He was shut up in the fortress of Jinjí, on the capture of which Aurangzéb had set his heart. The surrounding country fell during this siege under the influence of the preponderating power of the Mughals, and these did not hesitate, on an application from the Dutch, to sell to them the district of Pondichery for fifty thousand pagodas, and even to detach a body of men to support them.

To resist this formidable attack, Martin had literally no resources. The French Company, on taking stock in 1684, had been terribly alarmed by finding that, instead of gaining by their commercial enterprises, they had actually lost one-half of their capital. They were therefore little in the mood to send out any material assistance to Martin, especially as they had all along regarded his undertaking as foolhardy and impracticable. Martin had been therefore from the very outset left to himself. We have seen what he had accomplished; how he had built and fortified a town, established a trade, gained the confidence of the natives, princes as well as people, and laid the foundation of an enduring prosperity. And now all this promising fabric was to be overthrown. In the course of one of those contests, in which the country was always engaged, his native allies were temporarily on the losing side. From them, therefore, he could expect no assistance. He had six guns, thirty to forty Europeans, and some three or four hundred natives, and he was attacked by a fleet and army strong enough to take possession of all the European settlements in India.

It must have been a sad day for Martin when he beheld this storm breaking over his head, and destroying

---

* Mémoire dans les Archives de' la Compagnie des Indes; Grant-Duff's History of the Maráthás.

the tangible evidences of his wise and skilful policy. Nevertheless, he brought to bear against it all the resources of a mind habituated to calm and cool judgment. He had taken the precaution to move the idlers out of the town, and he prepared for a vigorous defence. The Dutch, however, gave him no respite. They landed their troops at the end of August, cut him off at once from the inland and from the sea, and plied their attack with such energy that, on September 6, having then offered a resistance of twelve days' duration, Martin had no hopes of being able to prolong the defence, and demanded a parley. This resulted in a capitulation, signed on September 8, and consisted of thirteen articles, the principal of which were, that the place should be given up to the Dutch East India Company; that the garrison should march out with all the honours of war; that the native soldiers should retire whither they pleased; but that the French should be sent to Europe, either that year or the beginning of the next. These conditions were implicity complied with.*

Thus ended, apparently for ever, the attempt of the French to establish themselves permanently on the Koromandel coast. Of all the efforts ever made by that nation to form a settlement in India, this one had been undertaken under the most gloomy auspices, and with the smallest resources; and yet up to the time of the capture of Pondichery, it had succeeded the best. Formed of the remnant of the garrison of St. Thomé, composed originally of but sixty Europeans, never regularly reinforced, but receiving only stray additions, it had not only maintained itself for seventeen years, but it had made itself respected by the natives of the country. What it had accomplished in its internal arrangements, we have already recorded. As we ponder over the story of these seventeen years of occupa-

* Mémoire dans les Archives de la Compagnie des Indes, in which the capitulation is given in full.

tion, the question cannot but arise, how it was that this handful of men, left to themselves, accomplished so much, whilst other expeditions, upon which all the resources of the Company had been so exuberantly lavished, failed so signally? We can only reply by pointing to the character of the leader. Everything was due to Francis Martin. His energy, his perseverance, his gentleness with the natives, his fair dealing, formed the real foundations of Pondichery. Never was there an adventurer—if adventurer he can be called— who was more pure-handed, who looked more entirely after the interests of France, and less after his own. In this respect he was the very opposite of Caron. Caron was avaricious, grasping, jealous of others' reputation. Martin was single-minded, liberal, large-hearted without a thought of envy or jealousy, and a true patriot. Such are the men who found empires, and who are the true glory of their country! The foundations which Martin laid were not, it is true, destined to be surmounted by an imperial edifice, but they only just missed that honour. That they were worthy of it is his glory; that those that followed him failed, cannot reflect upon him. We see him now with all his hopes baffled, his seventeen years of expectation destroyed, a poor man, sailing to France with nothing to show as the result of all his labours. Was there indeed nothing? Aye, if experience of a distant country, if successful management of mankind, if the ability to make for one's self resources,—if these be nothing, Martin returned to his country destitute indeed. But in that age such acquirements were more highly considered than they sometimes are now; and no long time elapsed before Martin was to feel that they had gained for him the confidence of his country to an extent that enabled him to repair the losses of 1693, and to rebuild on the old foundation a power whose reputation was to endure.

Before, however, we proceed to record the further

THE DEPENDENCIES OF PONDICHERY.

attempts of the French to establish themselves on the southern Koromandel coast, it is necessary that we should glance at their proceedings in other parts of Hindustan.

We have already alluded to their establishment at Surat.* This was strengthened in the year 1672 by the transfer to it of the head authority from Madagascar,—the Company's settlements in which were abandoned in that year, and Madagascar nominally transferred to the French crown.† Some of the Madagascar settlers proceeded, as we have seen, to the Isle of Mascarenhas, afterwards known as Bourbon; others came on to Surat. But the establishment at Surat did not prosper. The wretched condition of the affairs of the parent Company naturally affected their servants, and prevented them from carrying on trade with the vigour or success of the Dutch and the English. Politically, the location there of the factory was of no advantage to the French, and its commercial value lessened with the rising importance of Pondichery and Chandranagar. For many years therefore the trade at Surat languished, and the place was finally abandoned in the beginning of the eighteenth century. It was abandoned, however, in a manner little creditable to the French Company. Their agents left behind them debts to a very large amount, and such

---

* Grand Duff records that when Surat was plundered for the second time by Síváji (Oct. 3rd, 1670), "the English, as on the first occasion, defended themselves successfully, under the direction of Mr. Streingham Masters, and killed many of the Maráthás; the Dutch factory, being in a retired quarter, was not molested; but the French purchased an ignominious neutrality, by permitting Síváji's troops to pass through their factory to attack an unfortunate Tartar prince, who was on his return from an embassy to Mekka."

Ignominiously avoiding a combat is not characteristic of the French nation; and, considering that on this occasion Síváji's force consisted of fifteen thousand picked troops, whilst the French were few in numbers, and occupied a weak position it is scarcely astonishing that they entered into an engagement which secured to them their property. The plunder of the Tartar prince can scarcely be considered a consequence of this engagement. Surat was for three days in the possession of Síváji's troops; and the Tartar prince would have been plundered under any circumstances.

† Edict Louis XIV. 12th November, 1671.

was the effect on the native merchants that when, a few years afterwards (1714), a company, formed at St. Malo, despatched ships to trade at Surat, the ships were seized and sequestered on account of the debts of the French India Company, with which that of St. Malo was in no way connected. In dealing with the French intercourse with this place we have advanced beyond the main point of the narrative; but it is of the less consequence, as we shall have little further occasion to make any reference to Surat.

The French factory at Machhlipatan was, as we have seen, founded by the Persian Marcara, in 1669, under a patent obtained from the King of Golkonda. Its trade at the outset was extremely flourishing; but the expulsion of the French from St. Thomé, by the aid, it will be remembered, of the Golkonda army, was a heavy blow to its prosperity. It exerted for a long time after little political influence on the march of affairs. It revived, however, with the rise of Pondichery. In 1693, the French obtained permission to build a square, which is still in existence, and is known by the name of France *pata*. Machhlipatan became later one of the most important of the minor French settlements. To the circumstances connected with its rise we shall have occasion to refer further on.

In the year 1663, Sháyista Khan, the maternal uncle of the Emperor Aurangzéb, having been driven out of the Dakhan, and compelled to flee for his life by Síváji, whom he had been sent to repress, was appointed, to compensate him for his humiliation, Subadár of Bengal. It was during his vice-royalty* that a French fleet entered the Hugli, and disembarked a body of settlers at the village of Chandranagar. This village was ceded to those settlers by an edict of Aurangzéb in 1688. Eight years later, Subhán Singh, a landed proprietor of

---

* Stewart, in his History of Bengal, says "about the year 1676."

Bardwán, rebelled against the authority of the Subadár Ibráhim Khán, the successor of Sháyista Khán, and rallying to his standard the Orísca Afgháns and other malcontents, plundered Hugli, and carried devastation to the very gates of the European settlements. In this crisis, the English, French, and Dutch traders pressed upon the Subadár the necessity of their being permitted to fortify their respective settlements—a favour which had been before asked and refused. The Subadár would only tell them in reply to provide for their own safety. This was regarded as a tacit permission to fortify, and was acted upon accordingly. Nevertheless, the French at Chandranagar never attempted to be anything more than traders. For a long time their efforts in that respect were not very successful. All French writers speak of their trade there, for many years, as languishing. By letters patent, dated February, 1701, Chandranagar, with the other French possessions in the Indies (Baléshwar, Kásimbazár— an offshoot from Chandranagar—and Machhlipatan), was placed under the authority of the Governor of Pondichery. It was not, however, till nearly thirty years later that the trade received an impulse which converted Chandranagar into one of the most flourishing settlements of the Company. To that change and its causes we shall refer at the proper time. The factory at Baléshwar (Balasore) was insignificant, and was virtually abandoned at an early period.

It will thus be seen, that of all the places in India in which the French had made a settlement, Pondichery was in 1693 the most advanced and most promising. And now they had lost Pondichery. The Dutch knew well the value of their conquest. Its situation, sheltered for nine months in the year from the monsoon, the inconsiderable surf, and the fact of there being a little river falling into the sea navigable for flat-bottomed boats, rendered it superior as a settlement to any other place on the Koromandel coast. They therefore determined to make it worthy to be the capital of Dutch India. Their first care was to strengthen its defences. They built new walls, supported by bastions, and rendered it the strongest fortress possessed by an European power in Hindustan. They endeavoured also to cement their relations with the natives, and to establish with them the same cordial intercourse which had existed with the French. It was an end towards which they strove that as in their wars with the Portuguese they had permanently retained the fortified places they had taken from them in India, so, after this contest with the French, peace when it came might once more confirm to them the possession of their Eastern gains.

Meanwhile, Martin and his companions had arrived in France. The reception they met with was encouraging. The Minister and the Directors were equally pleased to honour a man who had effected so much with so little. The King himself conferred upon him the dignity of Chevalier of the order of St. Lazare. On the other hand, his description of Pondichery and its advantages imparted vitality and excitement to Directors who had had to experience nothing but losses. They began for the first time to appreciate the importance of the place which they had hitherto so neglected, and which, owing to that neglect, had been lost to them. Just then, however, nothing could be done. France was fighting single-handed against Spain, Germany, England, and Holland; and of these England and Holland were her successful rivals in the Indies. There was nothing for it but to wait for peace.

Peace at last came. On September 21,* 1697, the treaty of Ryswick was signed. One of the articles of that treaty engaged that there should be a mutual

---

*All dates given in this volume are according to the new style.

restitution of all places taken on both sides, both in and out of Europe; and at the close of that article was a clause in which the fortress of Pondichery was particularly mentioned, with an especial proviso, that its fortifications should not be destroyed, but that it should be delivered up in its then condition.

Pondichery thus recovered, the French Company resolved that it should not easily again slip from their possession. Martin was at once appointed to the command of the place, and instructions were given him to add still further to its strength. It was agreed to reimburse to the Dutch 16,000 pagodas, which they asserted they had expended on the fortifications. A squadron was at the same time sent out to India, having on board two hundred regular troops, several engineers, a large supply of military stores, several heavy and field-guns, and materials in abundance for the use of the settlement.

On arriving at his destination, Martin commenced the work of improvement. He enlarged and strengthened the fortifications, and collected a garrison of between seven and eight hundred Europeans; he laid out a plan for a large town, the erection of which he commenced. In little more than a year, a hundred new houses had been erected, and the place presented such an improved appearance, that, it is stated, a person who had only seen it in 1693 would not have recognised it. Nor did he omit to renew his relations with the natives. By the same course of gentleness and straightforward dealing which he had formerly followed, he attracted them in great numbers to the settlement, so much so that on his death, in 1706, the native town was computed to contain nearly forty thousand inhabitants.

We have stated that on the abandonment of Madagascar in 1672, the supreme French authority in India was transferred to Surat. But, in 1701, less than three years after the re-occupation of Pondichery, the trade at

CHAP. I.

1697.

Surat had become so unprofitable that it was resolved to abandon the factory there. How the factory was abandoned, we have already seen. But, prior to that not very creditable episode, letters patent had been issued, by which the Superior Council of the Indies, as it was called, was transferred from Surat to Pondichery, and this place was made the seat of the Director or Governor-general, with supreme authority over the other French factories in any part of India. Almost immediately afterwards, Martin was appointed President of the Superior Council, and Director-general of French affairs in India.*

Meanwhile, the affairs of the French Company in France, always badly managed, did not reap much advantage from the peace. Unable, from paucity of funds, to fit out trading expeditions of their own, they were compelled to have recourse to the system of selling trading licenses to others. With funds and good management in Paris, and a Martin at Pondichery, the French might have established an inland trade in India, which it would not have been easy to destroy, and which would have immensely aided the ambitious projects of some of the successors of Martin. But at the close of the seventeenth century, the resources of the French Company were nearly exhausted. They struggled on, indeed, by means of the shifts to which we have adverted, for some time longer. But the material aid which they afforded to the settlement at Pondichery was of the slightest description. The traders who purchased their licenses made fortunes; whilst the Directors of the Company which granted those licenses were just able by their sale to realise sufficient to keep their servants from starving. This was an immense misfortune at a time when the affairs of the Company were being managed in India by a man

---

* Letters patent signed by Louis XIV., dated February, 1701.

of conspicuous ability and of rare integrity. Whilst the town of Pondichery was increasing, and its native inhabitants continued enormously to augment, merely by reason of the good government that they found there, the connexion with the parent Company was becoming every day more precarious and uncertain, and the Superior Council could not but fear that the time would shortly arrive when Pondichery, like Madagascar and Surat, would be abandoned.

Whilst affairs were in this uncertain position, Martin died—December 30, 1706. Upon the plot of ground which he had occupied just thirty-two years before with sixty men, there had risen up under his auspices a large and flourishing town. He himself, its founder, had not only amassed no riches, but he died poor—poor but honoured. He had devoted all his energies, private as well as public, to his country. Pondichery, at his death, although still in its infancy as a city, had an air of prosperity which it was impossible to mistake. There was a fine palace for the Governor, built of brick, and other houses and shops of the same material. Keeping in view the rising importance of the city he had founded, Martin had been careful to lay out the streets in such a manner that those who built houses could not but contribute to its regularity and beauty. The fruit of his excellent rules was fully realised in the time of his successors, and is to be seen at the present day.

Nearly ten years had elapsed since the Dutch had restored Pondichery, and they had been years of peace and growing prosperity. The French enjoyed in those days a great reputation at the courts of the various native princes for qualities the very opposite of those they were wont to display in Europe.[*] The power and resources of France, the sacredness of the persons of her sons, were subjects which the French in India

[*] Historie des Indes Orientales.

never dwelt upon. They were careful, on the contrary, to pay the utmost deference to the wishes of the prince with whom they were brought in contact, and to attempt to gain his confidence by a recognition of his power and authority. Their policy, in fact, was to adapt themselves as much as possible to native habits, whilst not departing from those strict principles, an adherence to which alone can beget confidence. In this respect, the ruler of Pondichery had something to repair, for the discreditable departure from Surat had materially affected French credit. Though it was left unavoidably to the successors of Martin to atone for that blot, yet, by the fairness of his own dealings, he brought his relations with the natives to such a point, that he and his French were not only trusted, but personally esteemed and regarded. In this way he laid the foundation for that intimate connexion with native powers, which the most illustrious of his successors used with such effect to build up a French empire in India. Perhaps it was, that, left so long to his own resources in the presence of contending powers, any one of which was strong enough to destroy him, he deemed a policy of conciliation his only safe policy. But, even in that case, to him the credit is undoubtedly due of being able to dive so well into the character of the natives as to use them for his own purposes by seeming to defer to their wishes; to turn the attack of Síváji into a claim for Marátha protection, and to convert the loan to Sher Khán Lodi into the means of obtaining a fixed and perpetual revenue.

It is a remarkable result, too, of Martin's skilful policy that the progress of Pondichery caused neither envy nor apprehension to any of the native rulers of the country. It is a result which can only be ascribed to the confidence which that policy had inspired. The guns on the ramparts were regarded, not as threatening to a native power, but as a means of defence against one of the rival nations of Europe. When a native prince visited Pondichery, he was received as a friend; he was carefully waited upon; he was pressed to stay. The idea of regarding the natives as enemies was never suffered by any chance to appear. Acknowledging them as the lords paramount of the country, the French professed to regard themselves as their best tenants, their firmest well-wishers. Pondichery rose, therefore, without exciting a single feeling of distrust. It was freely resorted to by the most powerful princes and nobles in its neighbourhood. The good offices of the French were not seldom employed to mediate in cases of dispute. Thus it happened that they gained not only toleration but friendship and esteem. They were the only European nation which the natives regarded with real sympathy. Evidences of this regard were constantly given; that it was real, subsequent events fully proved.

This cordial understanding with the children of the soil—the solid foundation upon which to build up a French India—was, with much more that we have described, the work of that Martin whom the latest* French account of French India dismisses in half a dozen lines. Was it his fault that his successors risked and lost that which he had secured with so much care, with so much energy, with so much prudence? The most fervent admirers of Dupleix, the most determined defenders of Lally, the most prejudiced partisans of Bussy, cannot assert that. Was it not rather that the very facility of Martin's success opened out to the most ambitious of his successors that splendid vision of supreme domination which is especially alluring to those who feel within themselves the possession of great powers? To answer that question, we must turn, in an inquiring spirit, to their careers.

* Inde, par M. X. Raymond.

CHAPTER II.

THE PERPETUAL COMPANY OF THE INDIES.

CHAP. II.

1714.

EIGHT years after the death of Francis Martin the fifty years' monopoly of the Company of the Indies, granted by Louis XIV. in 1664, came to an end. It was indeed time. For several years the Company had been unable, in consequence of its numerous debts and its want of funds, to use the privileges with which it had been invested for its own advantage. Even so far back as 1682, being unable to purchase a sufficiency of goods wherewith to load its vessels, it had permitted private speculators to forward merchandise to India, on the sole condition that such merchandise should be despatched on board the vessels of the Company, and that it should be paid for as freight. In 1708, it allowed a M. Creuzat to equip two vessels under the name of the Company, on condition that he should pay it fifteen per cent. of the gross sum realised by the sale of his wares, and two per cent. on the product of the captures his vessels might make beyond the Line. The Company reserved to itself at the same time the right of retaining for its agents in India ten tons of the wares of Pondichery for the home voyage. These expedients, however, failed to produce such a return as would enable the Company either to pay its debts or to re-enter upon its legitimate trade. To such an extent did resources fail, that, in 1712, two years before the expiration of its charter, the Company was compelled to abandon entirely even the attempt to despatch vessels to the Indies, and to content itself with giving up its rights in this respect to the merchants of St. Malo, in consideration of an annual payment. Thus it happened that when, in 1714, it petitioned the King for a renewal af its privileges, it was actually unable to avail itself of those privileges, but maintained a lingering existence solely by letting them out to others.*

It can easily be imagined how this state of things re-acted on Pondichery. Wanting money, no longer even receiving ships belonging to the parent Company, the first successors of Martin, MM. Dulivier and Hébert,† were able to do but very little. The carrying trade passed gradually from their hands into the hands of other merchants and companies, and from this time to 1722, the commerce and credit of Pondichery alike continued to decline. The debts contracted at Surat remained unpaid, and this fact alone was sufficient to affect the credit of the town to which the Government had been transferred from that place. It was a hard time indeed for those agents of a bankrupt Company. They strove nevertheless to do what they could to second the paltry efforts which the Directors made from time to time to increase their trade. But it was in vain. Fortunately during the entire period they were left unmolested by the native Powers. Though all India resounded with the clash of arms that followed the death of the Emperor Aurangzéb in 1707, though warlike operations were taking place in the Dakhan and on the Malabar coast, Pondichery remained unthreatened. It was a period indeed which a rich parent Company in France, supported by active agents on the coast, might have used with immense advantage to French interests. But under the actual circumstances of the case it was

---

* Histoire des Indes Orientales, par M. l'Abbé Guyon.

† M. Dulivier succeeded Martin on January 1, 1707, but continued as Governor only till the arrival of the Chevalier Hébert in July, 1708. Hébert continued to administer the affairs of the colony till October, 1713, when Dulivier re-assumed the office. He held it for nearly two years, when he was again succeeded by Hébert, who continued as Governor till August 19, 1718.—*Extract from the Archives of the Company, forwarded to me by M. Bontemps.*

fortunate for Pondichery, neglected and impoverished, that she was able, for the fourteen years that followed the death of Martin, to drag on a feeble existence, hoping for better times. There was little in that interval to call for the remark of the historian. The interest of the period is rather concentrated in the change that took place in the fortunes of the parent Company, and which, at the expiration of the fourteen years we have alluded to, enabled the rulers of Pondichery to make a real start in the race for wealth and prosperity. We propose therefore to return to the affairs of the Company in Europe.

That Company had in 1714 applied, as we have already stated, for a renewal of the privileges which would lapse in that year. The state of its affairs was well known to the mercantile world of France as well as to the Ministers, and a strong opinion was expressed against the policy of granting to the Company privileges of which it could only make use by transferring them to others. But notwithstanding public opinion, in those days feebly expressed, the Directors had sufficient interest to carry their point. On September 29, 1714, a Royal edict was issued, directing the continuance to the Company for ten years of all its privileges, dating from January 1, 1715, with the sole proviso, that thenceforth, one-tenth of the product of the captures made by the Company's vessels beyond the Line should revert to the Great Admiral of France.

It appeared then that for another ten years the affairs of French India were doomed to languish, and perhaps even to perish of atrophy. But on September 1, 1715, an event occurred which changed for a time the current of affairs in France and her dependencies. On that day Louis XIV. died, leaving behind him a public debt of 2,412,000,000 francs, and the revenue mortgaged for years to come. Misery and disease reigned amongst the population, commerce and industry were in an extraordinary state of depression, national bankruptcy appeared inevitable. The Duke of Orleans, brother of the King, upon whom had devolved the office of Regent, whilst he almost despaired of the means whereby to extricate the country from the calamity by which it was threatened, was yet determined to resort to any expedient rather than declare bankruptcy. Whilst yet meditating on the courses open to him, there suddenly appeared in Paris, within a month after the death of the King, a young Scotchman named Law, who, addressing himself to the Regent, declared his ability to rescue the country from the financial abyss into which it had fallen, and to restore to it credit and prosperity.

To understand the revolution which overtook the affairs of the East India Company at this juncture, it will be necessary to give here a brief outline of the measures adopted by Law, under the sanction of the Regent. In pursuance of his demands there was created, by letters patent dated May 2, 1716, a bank of deposit and discount, authorised to issue notes payable to the bearer in coin of the current value of the day. The capital of this bank, styled the General Bank, consisted of 6,000,000 francs, in 1,200 shares of 5,000 francs each, payable in four instalments, one-fourth in specie, and three-fourths in Government notes. One great object of the establishment of bank was thus to relieve the public credit, by accepting at par, for the payment of its shares, Government notes which were then scarcely saleable at 70 or 80 per cent. discount. At the same time that it did this it declared its own notes payable in cash to the bearer at the current value of silver. The sudden establishment of a bank on such principles, and with a comparatively low rate of discount, at a period when confidence had disappeared, had an electric effect. Instantly there was a strong demonstration in its favour, and a rush to partake of the advantages it offered. The confidence in its stability became so strong, that, although it possessed a capital of but six millions, Law saw himself enabled, within a short time of its establishment, to issue notes to the value of fifteen or twenty millions. The credit of the bank was further augmented by the publication, on April 15, 1717, of a decree, which commanded all the agents intrusted with the management of the Royal revenues, to receive the notes of the bank as money, and to cash such notes at sight to the extent to which cash was available.

The success of the bank had already greatly relieved the State credit, for it being a condition of the purchase of bank shares that they should be paid for, three-fourths in Government notes, a run had ensued upon these securities, and they had risen greatly in favour. The revival of credit stimulated the other industries of the nation, and commerce and trade, shortly before so depressed, began to resume the position natural to a state of prosperity.

But this was only a beginning. Its success stimulated Law to propose, and the Regent and the public to accept, the more speculative schemes which were formed by his teeming brain. The district of Louisana in North America, discovered in 1541, and traversed by M. de Salle in 1682, seemed to Law to offer a basis upon which to erect a scheme which would secure immense commercial advantages to France, and at the same time benefit her finances. The idea itself was not new, for one Antoine Crozat, a speculative merchant, had already attempted the task of colonisation, and had failed. He was too willing therefore to make over his privileges to Law. But if the idea was not new, the treatment proposed by Law was startling by its novelty. He declared it would be necessary to raise a Sovereign Company, rivalling the companies of England and Holland, and depending on a large capital. This capital, he proposed, should be not less than 100,000,000 francs, divided into 200,000 shares of 500 francs each, payable in Government notes. As these were still at a discount, the proposal was regarded with wonder, and at first, with some distrust. But Law was confident. It was his object to cause by the success of his scheme a further run upon the Government notes, so as to raise them to par.

The scheme was presented to the public in August, 1717. Letters patent, bearing that date, conferred upon the Company of the West, as it was called, for twenty-four years, the privileges of a monopoly of the entire trade with Louisiana and Canada. Every right of the citizen and the trader, and of the absolute owner of the soil, was comprised in these privileges. They were made dependent solely upon the condition of rendering fidelity and homage to the King of France in token of vassalage. But though presented to the public in August, 1717, some time elapsed before Law saw fit to take the scheme, as it were, by the hand, and to push it into public favour. Measures, hostile to himself and his plans, were being hatched at the time under the auspices of the Parlement of Paris, M. d'Argenson, President of the Council of Finance, and the brothers Pâris. He deemed it more prudent therefore to await the moment when he could act with a certainty of success.

It is only necessary to state here that in the contest of the Regent with the Parlement the Regent triumphed. Profiting by this victory, he caused to be issued, on December 4, 1718, a royal proclamation by which the General Bank was declared attached to the State, under the designation of the Royal Bank, with effect from January 1, 1719. The King, *i.e.*, the State, thus became security for the notes. The change was effected by the purchase by the State of the twelve

CHAP. II.
1718.

hundred shares which constituted the original capital of the bank. These shares were paid for in cash. It will be recollected that the original shareholders had paid for each share of 5,000 francs only, the first fourth of 1,250 francs in cash, and the remainder in Government notes, then at 70 or 80 per cent. discount. The transaction then was most favourable for the shareholders. It seemed at first scarcely so for the State. So greatly indeed did the notes of the bank multiply that Law found it would be impossible to act up to the rule which had made the fortune of the General Bank, and which provided for the payment in specie, to the bearer, of the amount of the note at the current value of silver. Under his auspices, then it was decreed that thenceforth the amount represented by the note should be paid in "*livres tournois* of a fixed and unvarying value whatever might be the after variations of coined money;" and that only notes under 600 francs should necessarily be paid in cash, it being optional to the banker to give change for notes above that amount in notes or cash, as he might consider most convenient.

This interference with the free trade of currency, this upsetting of the ladder by which Law had made his first reputation, was undoubtedly a great mistake. The General Bank, however, had been so successful a project, that the public were slow to perceive the error, and before it could be exposed, Law had launched, in all earnestness, that commercial and financial operation, which is so intimately connected with the subject of our history. We have alluded to the formation of the Company of the West. Pending the conversion of the General into the Royal Bank, Law had left this scheme, as it were, to itself, and the shares, consequently, paid for in depreciated notes, had fallen to the value of one-half. He then suddenly conceived the idea of uniting to this new Company, the old East India Company founded by Colbert, as well as the Companies of China and of Senegal, neither of which was in a very flourishing condition. To the thus united Company would fall, he fondly hoped, the trade of France with the East as well as with the West. The Regent entered fully into the scheme. With his sanction a royal decree was issued dated May, 1719, to carry it into effect. In this decree the failure of the Company founded by Colbert was admitted and dwelt upon; the cessation of its trade, its abandonment of its privileges to others, were adverted to, and attributed to its bad management; the continuation of its charter for ten years, by the late King, from January 1, 1715, was admitted: "but," the decree went on to state, "in place of fulfilling its legitimate duties (the payment of its debts), the Indians have carried to us reiterated complaints that the Company will pay neither interest nor capital, and that for more that sixteen years it has not sent any vessel to Surat." After a further reference to the inevitable consequence of such management, the decree continued thus: "We have considered it proper for the welfare of our Kindgom to re-establish and increase the commerce of the French with the Indies, and to preserve the honour of the nation by paying to these people the debts contracted by the Company. To carry out this design we have resolved to suppress the privileges accorded to the Companies of the Indies and of China, and to unite them to that of the West." After this preamble there followed twelve decrees, revoking the privileges of the old Companies, and conferring on the Company of the West the sole right of commerce to the countries east of the Cape, including, besides the African Islands and the Indian Seas, the Red Sea, Persia, the territories of the Mughal, Siam, China, Japan, as well as the Straits of Magellan and the seas to the south. To the same Company was likewise granted possession " of the lands, islands, forts, houses, magazines, property movable and immovable, revenues, ships, barks, munitions of war and provisions, negroes, animals, merchandise, and, in fact, everything that the Companies of India and China have been able to conquer or acquire, or which has been conceded to them in France, in the Indies, or in China, on condition of paying to the French, as well as to the Indians, all the lawful debts of the Companies of India and of China." The commercial advantages granted to the Company were very great. It was allowed the exclusive right of importing from the countries indicated all products not prohibited in France, and facilities were accorded to it of selling the prohibited articles to foreign countries. By the 11th decree it was directed that thenceforth the Company should be styled the "Company of the Indies," and should assume the arms of the Company of the West.

But perhaps the most important of the decrees promulgated on this occasion related to the mode in which the funds necessary for carrying on the business of this great Company should be raised. The part of the sixth decree, which settled this point, ran thus: "We have permitted and do permit it to issue new shares to the value of twenty-five millions of francs to be paid for in ready money only, and at the rate of 550 francs for each share. These will be of the same nature as the 100 millions of the Company of the West, which are before the public, and their numbers will follow immediately that of the last share of the 100 millions; and in consideration of the ten per cent. which the purchasers will pay above the par value, it is our will that these shares shall be on the same footing as the others."

Law had thus at his disposal 50,000 shares of the nominal value of 500 francs each, but for which the purchasers were required to pay ten per cent. in excess of that value. But his scheme comprehended something far more extensive than the simple project indicated in the decree from which we have quoted. Just prior to the amalgamation of the Companies he had gone into the market and had bought up all the shares of the Company of the West that were to be had. This proceeding brought them up to par, even to a premium. But it was after the amalgamation had been decreed that he made his great *coup*. Acting under his influence, the Regent caused to be decreed on June 20 following, that, to insure an equal chance to all, without favour to any, no one should be eligible to become a purchaser of the new shares, who did not possess in the old shares (of the Company of the West) a value four times greater than that for which he now wished to become a subscriber. Now it is curious to mark the consequence of this edict. The old shares had been issued at 500 francs each, payable in four instalments in Government notes, then at, perhaps, 70 per cent discount. Of this sum the first instalment only had been called up; that is to say, possession of each of these shares had been obtained by a cash payment of less than 40 francs.* Now the effect of Law's new proposal to forbid the sale of shares in the new Company to all who did not possess four times the amount in the old was to cause an extraordinary run on the old shares. They rose consequently to an enormous premium. The original holders, and those who, like Law and his friends, had purchased before the amalgamation, made thus very great profits. The Parisians, with their usual felicity of nomenclature, styled the old shares *mères*, and the new shares *filles*, appropriately remarking that these latter always brought with them their dower; for such was the hourly increasing rage for speculation that a purchaser could almost immediately realise double or treble the amount he had invested.†

---

* Supposing that Government notes were then at 70 per cent. discount, the value of 125 francs in notes could be purchased by 37½ francs in cash. Now, 125 francs in notes represented the first call made on the shareholders of the Company of the West.

† Law, *son Système et son Époque*.

THE PERPETUAL COMPANY OF THE INDIES.

CHAP. II.
1719.

Another impulse was soon after given to the shares of the Company of the Indies. The profits of the coinage for nine years were made over to it, on the payment to the King of fifty millions of francs, by regular instalments, in fifteen months. To raise this sum a new issue of shares became necessary. Consequently authority was decreed to the Company to issue 50,000 new shares at a nominal value of 500 francs each. But at that time the first issue of shares, the *filles*, had risen from their issue value of 550 francs to 1,000 francs each in the market, or nearly cent. per cent. To profit itself by this rise, the Company decreed that though issuing these new 50,000 shares at a nominal value of 500 francs each, they would be purchasable only at the current rate of the other shares, or 1,000 francs each. But in addition to this, and still further to increase the value of the old shares, Law caused it to be notified that to obtain these shares at their advanced rates, it would be necessary to own paper of five times the amount applied for, in old shares, and to pay for them, not in specie, but in notes of the Royal Bank. This, the latest issue of shares, received at once from the public the name of *petites-filles*. The desire to obtain these increased not only the value of the *mères*, but made everyone anxious to exchange his coin for notes of the Royal Bank. This measure, as it were consummated the first part of the financial revolution inaugurated by Law. The Government notes, which, in 1715, had been at 70 to 80 per cent. discount, rose actually to par,* and the shares of the Company of the Indies were quoted at 200 per cent premium.

In the same year the Company made a most important purchase, for it proved to be almost the only

---

* When Law, in introducing to the public the scheme of the Company of the West in 1717, boasted that one of its effects would be to raise the depreciated Government notes to par value, the public, incredulous, declared that if he were to accomplish this, he would be worthy of having statues raised to him all over France. Yet he did it.

one of those that survived the golden reign of Law, and contributed in later times even to the prolongation of its existence. They acquired from the Government, for 4,020,000 francs, the monopoly of tobacco. The value of this monopoly increased to such an extent, that in after years it brought in an annual revenue of eight millions, a sum almost sufficient, at 8 per cent., to pay the total interest on the capital of the Company, as it was fixed in 1725. There was granted to it about the same time the farming of the salt mines of Alsace and Franche Comté.

But great as had been the previous measures of Law, and unexampled as had been their success, he was prepared to go still further. It was his great ambition to extinguish, by means of the Company, the public debt of France. This debt amounted at that time to from 1,500 to 1,800 millions of francs, and its yearly interest to 80 millions. Law believed it possible, in the then state of confidence and excitement, to substitute for the public debt, the shares of the Company of the Indies. He offered then to lend to the State twelve hundred millions, a sum afterwards increased to fifteen hundred millions, at 3 per cent. per annum, on the condition of receiving authority to issue shares to that amount, and of being intrusted with the collection of the public taxes. On the 2nd of September the Government officially accepted these offers. The Company at once created 324,000 new shares, bearing the nominal value of 500 francs each, but as the value of the other shares had by that time risen to 1,000 per cent.—each share being thus worth in the market 5,000 francs—it was at first determined to offer them to the public at that rate. Subsequently, however, it was resolved to sell them, in series, by public auction, in front of the magnificent palace which the Company had just then purchased at the corner of the Rue Vivienne. Here, and in the neighbouring streets, crowds were wont to sit through

E 2

the long nights, caring neither for cold nor hunger nor thirst, each man armed with his heavy bag of coin or well-filled pocket-book, anxious only to secure or to maintain a good place, from which to bid for the coveted shares. At this public auction the Company realised for the 324,000 new shares no less a rate than a thousand per cent. on the nominal value of each share. Taking stock in November, the Directors ascertained that whilst they had issued 624,000 shares, representing 312 millions, for which they were responsible, they had sold them for 1,797,500,000, francs, representing the enormous profit of 1,485,500,000 francs. Unfortunately but a small portion of this was realised.

It is impossible to describe the eagerness and alacrity with which all classes entered into this race for wealth. Men who had been beggars became suddenly rich beyond previous calculation. A cobbler made for some time two hundred francs a day by establishing a stall for the supply of pen and paper for the calculations of the speculators. Men made a trade of lending their backs as desks upon which speculators might write, and gained thereby considerable sums. The Duke of Bourbon realised twenty millions of francs, and the Duke of Antin twelve. Nor was their example a solitary one. Luxury increased in proportion to the establishment of wealth. Unheard of prices were paid for furniture, carriages, and articles of dress. It seemed as though the age of gold had dawned. The principal advantages, however, were realised by those who happened to be in the confidence of Law. To obtain his friendship, even his acquaintance, was the aim of every man's ambition. Princesses vied with duchesses for the honour of an introduction to this disburser of fortunes,* and when this was impossible,

---

* The dowager Duchess of Orleans wrote: "Law is so pursued that he has no rest night or day. A duchess has kissed his hand before everybody. And if Duchesses act thus, how will other woman kiss him?"—Cochut, *Law, son Système et son Époque.*

they did not hesitate to have recourse to all sorts of artifices to obtain an opportunity of speaking to him. All this time, the great mart of business, the Rue Quincampoix, was crowded by "nobles and footmen, bishops and clergy, men of the sword and shopmen, magistrates and pickpockets, marquesses and servants, Frenchmen and foreigners," all animated by but one object, the scramble for wealth. So entire was the confidence in Law's paper, that it was actually preferred to coin, which was then regarded as but a clumsy sort of circulating medium.* Law himself was nominated, on January 5, 1720, Controller-General of Finances, having paved the way for the assumption of that high office by embracing the Roman Catholic faith.

But though Law was apparently at the summit of his ambition, the crisis was at hand. Many of those who had realised fortunes from their speculations were clear-headed enough to perceive that it would be wise to invest a portion of their gains in land. This movement, adopted almost simultaneously by very many, threw a number of shares into the market and cheapened the price of all. Even at the end of 1719 shares had indicated an inclination to fall. Law, however, threw himself manfully into the gap. By a series of measures he endeavoured to make the possession of paper-money still more advantageous to the public than specie. He offered increased facilities to small capitalists and annuitants to invest in the scheme. At the same time he showed a bold front to the public by directing the employés of the Royal Bank to display the utmost readiness to exchange specie for notes. But, in February, 1720, the rage for speculation had been superseded by the rage for realising. Men of all sorts hastened to exchange their notes for silver, and for the most part to invest this silver in tangible property. To such extravagance, in its turn, was this system carried, that after

* Cochut, *Law, son Système et son Époque*.

the shops of the jewellers and upholsterers had been exhausted, people invested their realisations in groceries and even books. Any investment was preferred to the now discredited paper. To so great an extent had it fallen, in an incredibly short space of time, in public estimation, that in March, shopkeepers advanced their prices 50 and 100 per cent. when paper was presented to them for payment.

Meanwhile Law, still confident, endeavoured, by fresh artificial and arbitrary measures, to keep up the value of paper and to lower that of specie. To effect this purpose edict followed upon edict. It was forbidden to employ silver in making payments above ten francs, or gold above three hundred. The wearing of diamonds, pearls, and precious stones was forbidden, and the manufacture of articles of gold and silver was confined to the narrowest limits. A decree of the 28th January directed a lowering of the standard of the coinage above a certain value, with a view to recall all such pieces in circulation into the Treasury. Another, of the 27th February, forbade the possession by anyone of more than 500 francs in silver, and directed that all payments above 100 francs were to be made in bank-notes. On March 11, gold was entirely recalled from circulation from May 1 following, and the use of silver, the small pieces excepted, forbidden with effect from August 1. In the same month, to prop up the Royal Bank, Law united it to the Company of the Indies. The saleable value of the shares of this latter was fixed, irrevocably, at 9,000 francs each, and two offices were opened for the conversion of shares into bank-notes, and *vice versâ*, at this rate. The office for the conversion of shares into bank-notes was at once crowded. Taking the notes, men rushed to sell these at a depreciated value for cash, or sent them for sale in the provinces where they were still accepted. The proceeds they invested in any sort of tangible property.

THE COMPANY RE-ORGANISED.

These contrivances did not prevent the downfall of the entire scheme. The prohibitory clauses brought indeed great stores of specie into the bank from the untitled classes, but they were powerless against the higher nobility, who, in those days, were above the law.* But though they brought in money, they absolutely destroyed confidence, and the depreciation continued. Law, after other minor experiments, which proved inoperative, endeavoured to stop the depreciation by the issue of a decree on May 21, by which the value of the shares was to be gradually decreased to 5,000 francs each, at the same time that the bank-notes were reduced to one-half their actual value. The measure, in consequence of the debasement of the coinage, would, had confidence existed, have been beneficial to the shareholders. But in the actual state of affairs they regarded it simply as a depreciation of nearly one-half of their property. The panic, therefore, increased so greatly in intensity that Law was forced, on May 27, to issue another edict withdrawing that of the 21st. But this wavering on his part only increased the want of confidence. Shares fell to a mere nominal value; tumults took place in the streets; capital disappeared; the misery of the populace for want of a purchasing medium increased daily; the Royal Bank was crowded with poor wretches anxious to exchange their small notes for silver; a guard was placed over Law, nominally to prevent his escape, really for his protection. Everything foreboded a catastrophe. At this crisis the Company of the Indies came forward, and offered to take up all the depreciated notes of the Royal Bank and to extinguish them at the rate of fifty millions a month for a year, provided its commercial privileges

---

* As soon as the decree was issued the Prince of Conti drew from the bank three carts full of crown pieces. The Duke of Bourbon withdrew twenty-five millions. Others, of lower rank, were unable thus to defy the law. In the house of one shopkeeper, fifty thousand marks in gold and silver were seized by the State, on account of his non-compliance with the edict.—*Law, son Système et son Époque*

were made perpetual. This offer was accepted by the Government; a decree, dated June, 1720, was issued, and thenceforth the Company which ruled French India from the Rue Vivienne is known in history under the designation of the Perpetual Company of the Indies.

But this measure, which the Parlement refused to confirm, did not stop the panic. In October of the same year it was therefore determined to effect a return to cash payments. The union between the Royal Bank and the Perpetual Company of the Indies was therefore dissolved, and that Company was reorganised on the footing of a commercial association independent of the State, the value of its shares being reduced to 2,000 francs each. About the same time the contract, which secured to it the right of coining money and collecting the revenues of the State, was cancelled. Shortly after, Law having been forced to retire from France, its shareholders were declared responsible for all the engagements it had contracted and for all the notes it had issued; its property was sequestered, and a provisional board, composed of officials denominated *Régisseurs*, was appointed by Government to carry on its affairs. The investigations and cancellings to which this Board had recourse resulted in leaving the Company, in 1723, a private commercial association, with a capital of 112,000,000 francs in 56,000 shares of 2,000 francs each. Two years later the number of the shares was reduced by 5,000 representing 10,000,000 francs. Of all the great privileges conceded to the Company during the administration of Law, there then remained only the inheritance bequeathed to it by the old Company, founded by Colbert, and the monopoly of tobacco.*

Meanwhile, the Company of the Indies had not forgotten, in the midst of its vast speculations, one of the

---

* In this account of Law, the following works have been consulted: *Law, son Système et son Époque*. Cochut. *Histoire du Système des Finances sous la Minorité de Louis XV*. Duverney. With these have been compared the various edicts issued during the Regency.

main objects of its being. Confident in the permanence of its prosperity, and anxious to draw from it every possible advantage, it had equipped and despatched to Pondichery, in 1720, three vessels richly laden, not only with the merchandise of Europe, but with gold and silver. These vessels reached their destination in 1721. Lenoir, the ablest of the successors of Martin, had just then succeeded temporarily to the office of Governor, in the place of M. de la Provostière,* who had died. He was a steady, plodding merchant, shrewd, hard-headed, and well fitted to be the chief of a peaceful community. But the arrival of these three vessels took him completely by surprise. We have already seen how, since the year 1712, the Company had been absolutely obliged to give up its commerce, and to abandon it, on certain considerations, to the merchants of St. Malo. The sudden arrival then of ships laden, not only with merchandise but with specie, was an event for which Lenoir was by no means prepared. It was, nevertheless, a most acceptable arrival. The non-payment of the debts originally contracted at Surat had long lain heavily upon French credit in India. Other obligations too had, in the state of destitution in which the establishments had been left since the death of Martin, been unavoidably entered into at Chandranagar, Baleshwar, and other places. Lenoir, correctly judging that good credit was the foundation of mercantile success, determined to invest the greater portion of the money he received in payment of the debts of the old Company, rather than, leaving these unpaid, to purchase return cargoes for the vessels. This course accordingly he adopted, with, however, the unavoidable result that the Company received but a very poor immediate return for a very large outlay.

* M. de la Provostière was appointed *ad interim* successor to M. Hébert on August 19, 1718. He died in October, 1721, and was succeeded temporarily by Lenoir.—*Extract from the Archives of the Company.*

Meanwhile, as we have seen, the system having collapsed, and the notes of the Company having been suppressed, before the close of 1720, it no longer possessed the funds to equip ships for India. None were sent, therefore, in 1721 or the year following. In consequence of this, the settlement of Pondichery was reduced in 1722 and during the greater part of 1723 to the direst straits. The local Government had neither merchandise, nor money, nor resources, and became, on that account, a butt for the ridicule of its rival traders to the Hugli and the Koromandel coast. But this was not the worst result of the collapse. Lenoir had, naturally enough, regarded the advent of the three ships and the specie in 1721 as a type of what was to follow. He had, in fact, been assured by his Directors that a similar supply should be sent him yearly. In anticipation, then, of the arrival of the fleet of 1722, he had made great preparations to open out new markets for the expected cargoes. But when, not to speak of the cargoes, he was unable to welcome even a ship, he felt utterly overwhelmed. His credit had been pledged, and it was upon its credit with the natives that the prosperity of the little settlement at Pondichery at this epoch mainly depended. But it is on such occasions that the real character of a Government is most surely tested. In this crisis the French settlers reaped the advantage, not less of the system of good faith adopted by Martin, than of the act of the previous year, by which Lenoir had devoted his sudden accession of wealth to the payment of the debts of the Company. The rich natives with whom he had contracted, knowing the cause of his failure to fulfil his engagements, were content to wait for better times. It was by their aid and forbearance alone that Lenoir was enabled to save the credit of the colony in this dire necessity.

We have already noticed how in 1723 the restrictions imposed by the French Government on the Com-

ADMINISTRATION OF LENOIR.

pany were removed, and it was left in that year a private Company with a capital of 112,000,000 francs. In consequence of this arrangement there were despatched to Pondichery two ships lapen with merchandise. One of these brought out likewise the nomination of M. Beauvallier de Courchant to the office of Governor in room of Lenoir. M. Beauvallier assumed office on the 6th October of that year, without, however, in any way interfering with the system of his predecessor. The cargoes of the two ships of 1723 did little more than satisfy the claims which two years' of neglect had produced in the French settlement, and they were able to carry back but a poor return in the shape of merchandise. Nevertheless, from that date to 1726 the Company continued to despatch each year three or four vessels to Pondichery, and by the aid of these the nearly extinct commerce began gradually to revive. Subsequently to 1726 it made still greater progress. The many years of peace, which, with but a slight intermission, signalised the administration of Cardinal Fleury, were of the greatest advantage to the Company and its settlement. Lenoir, who replaced M. Beauvallier as Governor for the second time on September 4, 1726, had thought it an immense advance on previous transactions, when he was able to transmit to Europe in October, 1727, and January, 1728, merchandise valued at 2,234,385 francs, nearly 9,00,000 rupees; but in September, 1729, and January, 1730, he sent home cargoes worth 5,404,290 francs, or nearly 2,170,000 rupees; and although this was an exceptionally good year for the colony, it testifies to the great commercial progress made by the settlement, and to its entire recovery from the state of nullity and depression into which it had fallen in 1722 and 1723. The capital of the Company had been reduced, as we have seen, in 1725, by the withdrawal of 5,000 shares, representing 10,000,000 francs, which were, by a royal decree,

CHAP. II.

1723.

publicly annulled and burnt in that year. The interest on the remaining capital at 8 per cent. was provided by the sum paid to the Company by the farmers-general for the tobacco monopoly. The Company was able, therefore, to hope for additional profits from the mercantile operations we have recorded. But its expenses were considerable. It had laid out large sums on Port L'Orient, and had made it one of the finest harbours in France; it had been compelled to place upon an efficient footing its marine establishments there and in India;* to build large ships, purchase lodges and *comptoirs*, and to erect magazines; it had been forced likewise to expend 15,000,000 francs on the swamps of Louisiana. Still, until exhausting wars, with their consequent ruin to commercial traffic and their large calls upon the Company for assistance, increased expenditure, and cut off all prospect of receipts, the Perpetual Company of the Indies occupied a position, which if insignificant when compared with that it had assumed in the golden era of the Controller-Generalship of Law, was still considerable and promising.

To revert to the colony. With its prosperity Governor Beauvallier had begun, and, after him, to a far greater extent, Lenoir had carried on, those improvements in the town which had been in contemplation ever since the time of Martin. As in the course of years the number of its inhabitants, drawn thither by the increased traffic, had greatly augmented, it was resolved, first of all, to surround the city with a wall. For this purpose a tax was laid upon the inhabitants, equal to one day's pay per mensem. This moderate impost produced a sufficient sum to enable the authorities to commence the work, and even, after a considerable time, to complete three sides of the town. It was reserved for Dupleix, under a very pressing emergency, to erect the side, in his day the most

* Dictionnaire de Commerce, vol. ii.

important of all, looking towards the sea. About the same period too, commenced, on a great scale, the embellishment of the town. Under the auspices of Lenoir and his successor this made great progress. On the west side of the Governor's house a beautiful garden was laid out, planted with fine avenues, which served as public walks. In the midst of this garden was a large and well-furnished building, destined to be the residence of foreign princes and ambassadors. Near this was the college of the Jesuits, containing twelve or fifteen priests, to whom was committed the care of the education of the youth of the colony. There was a house also for the foreign missions, containing two or three priests, and another near it, for the Capuchins, with seven or eight. One of the conditions on which the land had been granted to the French required toleration of the Hindu religion; consequently the two pagodas, or temples, which they found there, still remained. All the streets were regularly traced out, broad and at right angles, and the houses joined one another. The sea face of the town was distant about a hundred yards from the sea, which at full tide had never more than two feet of water. The largest ships were forced to ride about three miles distant from the shore. Its fortifications, as made after the restoration of the town by the Dutch, and added to by Lenoir and Dumas, were sufficient to keep out a native enemy, but it was not until the war of 1743 that Dupleix succeeded in making them sufficient to repel European attack. The native town was divided from the European town by a canal; the houses in this were solidly constructed of wood and chunam—the latter being a composition made of shells ground to powder, and wrought into a kind of paste, which, by exposure to the air, becomes as white, and almost as hard, as stone.

The Government of Pondichery consisted of a Supreme Council composed of not less than five members, presided over by the Governor. In their hands was the entire administration. Justice was administered and the laws were enforced in the name of the King, but the Governor and the Councillors were the servants of the Company, liable to removal without any reference to the Sovereign or his Ministers. All the colonial offices, judicial and other, were in the gift of the Council, and to it were likewise subject the subordinate chiefs of the other French *comptoirs* or settlements in India.* It is curious to read the account of the state observed by the Governor in those primitive days of Indian occupation. Attending upon him on great occasions, it is stated, are "twelve horse-guards clothed with scarlet laced with gold, and an officer, with the title of Captain, commands them. He has also a foot-guard of three hundred men, natives of the country, called peons, and when he appears in public, he is carried in a palanquin very richly adorned with gold fringe." Such, however, was in those early days the economy of the administration that, except on public or particular occasions, these guards were employed in the commercial service of the Company, and earned all the wages they received. At the time of the accession of M. Dumas, the native population is computed to have exceeded seventy thousand.

All the institutions dependent on the action of the local Council received their full development during the incumbency of the successors of Martin, more especially of Lenoir. Theirs was indeed a system of peace. It would perhaps have been happy for the colony had it been able much longer to adhere to the policy of non-interference with native princes. But though its rulers were, for a long time, animated by the very best intentions, circumstances were ultimately too strong for them. But a few months before Lenoir assumed the Governorship for the second time, an event had

* Histoire des Indes Orientales, par M. l'Abbé Guyon.

occurred which introduced prominently on the scene a man who was destined, some years later, to act no inconsiderable part in the contests which were then to ensue for existence or for empire. That event we propose now to describe.

CHAPTER III.

THE RISE OF THE FRENCH POWER IN INDIA.

CHAP. III.

1725.

In the year 1725, a small French squadron under the command of M. de Pardaillan, acting under the orders of the Government of Pondichery, came to opposite the little town of Maihi,* just below Tellicheri, on the Malabar coast, and summoned the place to surrender. The Governor refused. The situation of Maihi indeed seemed to place it out of all danger. On high ground rising up from the sea, and washed on its north side by a little river, the entrance into which, as it ran into the sea, was closed by rocks for even the smallest boats, Maihi seemed to be able to bid defiance to any enemy who should attack it on the side of the sea. So at least thought the Governor, and so, apparently, seemed to think the French commodore. He, at all events, was hesitating as to the course he should adopt under the circumstances, when the captain of one of his ships submitted to him a plan which he begged he might be permitted to carry himself into execution. The name of this captain was Bertrand Franccis Mahé de La Bourdonnais.

As this is a name which will occupy considerable space in these pages, it may be as well to take the earliest opportunity of describing who and what manner of man this was, the earliest trace of whose action in the Indian seas we have just adverted to. La Bour-

---

* But little is known of Maihi prior to the attack upon it by the French. It formed nominally a part of the possessions of the petty Rájá of Cherakal, but, in all probability, was practically independent. The attack recorded in the text was made in pursuance of orders from the Directors, with the view to secure, on the Malabar coast, a post that would indemnify the French for the loss of Surat. For this purpose Maihi was well suited.

donnais was born at St. Malo in 1699. When not ten years old he was entered as a common sailor on board a merchant ship bound for the South Sea. Returning thence, he made, in 1713, a second voyage to the East Indies, and to the Philippines. During this voyage, a Jesuit on board taught him mathematics. In 1716 and 1717, he made a third voyage to the North Sea, and in the following year a fourth to the Levant. In his twentieth year, he entered the service of the French India Company, as second lieutenant in a vessel bound to Surat. In 1722, he was promoted to be first lieutenant, and in that grade made a third voyage to the Indies. He occupied his leisure hours during the passage out in composing a treatise on the masting of vessels. But he had an opportunity of showing on the return voyage, that he was as daring in action as he was prompt and ready in suggestion. His vessel, the "Bourbon," on her arrival off the Isle of Bourbon, was in a sinking state and in want of everything. No ship was in sight, and no aid was procurable from the island. In this extremity, La Bourdonnais proceeded in one of the ship's boats to the Isle of France, to search there for a vessel to render assistance to his charge. His search was successful, and the "Bourbon" was, by this daring exploit, saved from destruction.

La Bourdonnais had scarcely returned to France, when he found himself under orders to proceed to the Indies as captain commanding a frigate. During his previous voyages, he had acquired a knowledge of navigation, of carpentering, of everything that related to the construction of a ship, and of gunnery. But in this, under the able instruction of M. Didier, an engineer in the Royal Service, he devoted himself to engineering, and soon became a proficient in that science. On arriving at Pondichery, he was attached to the squadron of M. de Pardaillan, just starting for the conquest of Maihi. It is under the orders of this commodore,

F

CHAP. III.

1725.

hesitating regarding the attack of the place, that we now find him.

The plan which La Bourdonnais submitted to the commodore, was to land the troops on a raft of his own designing, in order of battle, under cover of the fire of the squadron. He pressed also that he might be permitted to lead them himself. M. de Pardaillan, struck with the ingenuity of the plan, and with the energy and quickness of decision evinced by the young officer, gave his consent to the scheme. It was carried out almost instantly. The raft was made, the troops were placed upon it, and, piloted by La Bourdonnais, were landed, with dry feet and almost in order of battle, at the foot of the high ground. This difficulty being surmounted, the place was stormed. As an acknowledgment of the skill and enterprise of his young captain, the commodore, by a slight alteration of the letters which went to form the name of the captured town, transformed it from the Indian Maihi or Mahi into the French Mahé —the first name of La Bourdonnais. This new name not only took root, but it gradually effaced the recollection that the town had ever borne another.*

The order of events, as they occurred at Pondichery, will not allow us to proceed for the present with the career of La Bourdonnais. Him, we shall meet again, a little later on the scene. Meanwhile it will be necessary to advert to the proceedings of one whose influence upon French India was destined to be even more direct, more commanding, more enduring;—whose brilliant genius all but completed the work which Francis Martin had begun;—who was indebted for all that he did accomplish to his own unassisted energies; who owed his failure to carry through all his high-soaring designs

---

* We are indebted to the Carnatic Chronology of Mr. C. P. Brown, late Madras C. S., for the information regarding the origin of the name "Mahé." It was evidently unknown to Mr. Mill, and equally so to the authors of the "Indian Gazetteers."

to that system of universal corruption, which, during the reign of Louis XV., consumed the very vitals of France, ruled in her palaces, and tainted all her public offices. We need scarcely say, that we advert to Joseph Francis Dupleix.

This illustrious statesman was born at Landrecies, in the province of Flanders, in 1697. His father was a wealthy farmer-general of taxes, and a Director of the Company of the Indies The young Dupleix displayed, at a very early age, a strong passion for the exact sciences, and particularly for mathematics. To the mercantile life, to which his father had destined him, he showed a decided aversion. To cure him, therefore, of his speculative habit of thought, and to plunge him at once into practical life, the old farmer-general sent the thoughtful and retiring student, then just seventeen, to sea. The result corresponded entirely to his hopes. Dupleix returned from voyages in the Atlantic and Indian oceans, cured of his love of abstract sciences, anxious to mix with the world, eager to put in force theories he had formed on the subject of commercial enterprise. It was in the power of his father to comply at once with his wishes. Director of the Company of the Indies, and a man of no small importance in the direction, he was able to nominate his son, then only twenty-three, to the second position at Pondichery. This was the office of First Councillor and Military Commissioner of the Superior Council. Dupleix joined his appointments in 1720, and at once began to put in force the theories which had formed the subject of his speculations. He found the colonists absorbed by the contemplation and care of the trade between Europe and Pondichery. His idea was to develop and foster a coasting trade and inland traffic. He desired to open out large schemes of commercial exchange at the various towns on the coast, and with the large cities in the interior. It did not seem sufficient to him, that Pondichery should be the exporter merely of her own manufactures and the manufactures of the country in the immediate vicinity; he would make her the emporium of the commerce of Southern India. The Government of Pondichery was not pecuniarily in a position, at the outset, to embark in the undertaking, although the Governor, Lenoir, regarded its execution as desirable, and eventually practicable. But this formed no bar to the prosecution of the plan by Dupleix. On the contrary, private trading being permitted by the Company, he was glad of an opportunity of showing the European residents of Pondichery, who were mostly clerks of the Company, how they might, by legitimate means, enrich themselves. Anything which could open out to them an independent position would tend to give them a higher interest in the country and in the prosperity of the settlement. He himself did not scruple to set a bold example, and to embark his fortune in the trade. The results were such as he had anticipated. He speedily realised a very handsome return, and the knowledge of this had more effect than all his theories in inducing his fellow-countrymen to follow in his footsteps.

Since the formation of the Perpetual Company of the Indies, the control of the Directors in Paris over their agents in Pondichery had become far more stringent and direct than it had been prior to 1720. Details were interfered with, regarding the proper management of which the Home Government could have no knowledge, and the most arbitrary, and often ill-judged, orders were issued. These orders led to misunderstandings and dissensions, and it resulted from one of these, M. Lenoir being at the time Governor-General, that in the month of December, 1726, Dupleix was suspended from his office by order of the Directors. But, though offered a free passage to France, Dupleix determined to await in India the result of an appeal he at once proceeded to make against that decision. At the end of nearly four years, the result he had striven for occurred. The sentence of suspension was removed (September 30, 1730), and, as a compensation for the injustice he had suffered, he was appointed very soon after Intendant or Director of Chandranagar, a junior officer previously appointed by Lenoir being removed to make way for him.

From the period of its first occupation in 1676, to the time when Dupleix assumed the Intendantship, Chandranagar had been regarded as a settlement of very minor importance. Starved by the parent Company in Paris, it had been unable, partly from want of means, and partly also from the want of enterprise on the part of the settlers, to carry on any large commercial operations. The town, as we have seen,* had been fortified in 1688. Lodges, or commercial posts, dependent upon Chandranagar, had also been established at Kásimbazár, Jugdiá, Dháká, Báléswar, and Patná. But their operations were of small extent. The long stint of money on the part of the Company of the Indies had had, besides, a most pernicious effect upon the several intendants and their subordinates. The stagnation attendant upon poverty had lasted so long that it had demoralised the community. The members of it had even come to regard stagnation as the natural order of things. It had thus deprived them of energy, of enterprise, of all care for the future. The utmost extent of their efforts was limited to an endeavour to surmount a pressing emergency. That once accomplished, they relapsed into the *far niente* mode of life that had become habitual to them. The place itself bore evidence to the same effect. It had a ruined and forlorn appearance; its silent walls were overgrown with jungle; and whilst the swift stream of the Húglí carried past it

* Chapter I.

Eastern merchandise intended for the rivals who were converting the mud huts of Chattánati into the substantial warehouses of old Calcutta, the landing-places of Chandranagar were comparatively deserted.

To govern a settlement thus fallen into a state of passive and assenting decrepitude Dupleix was deputed in 1731. But, decaying and lifeless though he found Chandranagar, Dupleix regarded its situation with far other feelings than those of anxiety or dismay. He saw, almost at a glance, the capabilities of the place, and, conscious of his own abilities, having tried and proved at Pondichery his ideas regarding the power of trade, he felt that the task of restoring the French settlement would, under his system, be comparatively easy. The office of intendant had for him this great recommendation, that there was something for a man to do, and he felt that he was the man to do it. Little time did he lose in deliberation. He at once set in action the large fortune he had accumulated, and induced others to join in the venture. He bought ships, freighted cargoes, opened communications with the interior, attracted native merchants to the town. Chandranagar soon felt the effect of her master's hand. Even the subordinates, whom he found there, recovering under the influence of his example from their supineness, begged to be allowed to join in the trade. Dupleix had room for all. To some he advanced money, others he took into partnership, all he encouraged. He had not occupied the intendantship four years, when, in place of the half-dozen country boats which, on his arrival, were lying unemployed at the landing-place, he had at sea thirty or forty ships, a number which increased before his departure to seventy-two, engaged in conveying the merchandise of Bengal to Surat, to Jeddo, to Mocha, to Basrá, and to China. Nor did he neglect the inland trade. He established commercial relations with some of the principal cities in the interior, and even opened communications with

Tibet. Under such a system Chandranagar speedily recovered from its forlorn condition. From having been the most inconsiderable, it became, in a few years, the most important and flourishing of the European settlements in Bengal. Its revival caused the greatest satisfaction in France. The Government and the Directors thoroughly appreciated the advantage of having at the head of the settlement a man who had such confidence in his own plans, and who cared so little for responsibility, that he never hesitated to advance his own funds for public purposes. Dupleix was always ready to do this, whilst he traded at the same time on his own account. Thus it happened that his fortunes and the fortunes of Chandranagar grew up side by side. If his own gains were great, a comparison of the Chandranagar of 1741 with the Chandranagar of 1731 would have shown that the gains of the dependency which he governed were certainly not in smaller proportion.

Meanwhile M. Lenoir, whose second administration of Pondichery and its dependencies lasted nine years, had been succeeded as Governor-General on the 19th September, 1735, by M. Benoit Dumas, then Governor of the Isles of France and Bourbon. Up to this period, since the death of Francis Martin, the relative position of Pondichery to the native chieftains in the neighbourhood had but little varied. But with the advent of M. Dumas appeared the first symptoms of a new order of things, less attributable to the character of that gentleman, than to the character of the events of which the province of the Karnátik was about to become the scene. It is therefore necessary that we should record the events of the government of M. Dumas with some minuteness.

M. Dumas had been a servant of the old Company of the Indies. He had entered the service at the age of seventeen, in the year 1713, and had proceeded direct

CHAP. III.
1735.

to Pondichery. Here he displayed so much ability and aptitude, that, five years later, he was made a member of the Supreme Council, and, in June, 1721, Attorney-General. Transferred thence to the Isles of France and Bourbon as a member of the Supreme Government, and filling there in turn the offices of General Director for the Company of the Indies and of President of the Supreme Council, he was finally appointed Governor of those islands. This position he held till 1735, when he was nominated to succeed M. Lenoir as Governor-General of the French possessions in the Indies.* The new Governor was a shrewd, calculating, prudent man —one not given to risk much without having in view a very tangible result; brave, resolute, jealous of the honour of France, thoroughly acquainted with native ways, holding fast by the traditions of Francis Martin, a lover of peace, and anxious, above all, to extend the French territories in India by smooth means.

M. Dumas, it may be imagined, was just the man to carry out a mild and peaceful policy. Certainly under his sway Pondichery lost nothing of its attractiveness to the independent native rulers. Indeed, almost immediately after his accession to office a circumstance occurred which served to knit, even more closely, the bonds of friendship that existed between the French and the most powerful of their neighbours, Nawwáb Dost Ali Khán, ruler of the Karnátik.

In 1732 Nawwáb Saadat-ulla Khán, then ruler of the Karnátik, one of the most enlightened native noblemen of that period, died. His nephew and nearest of kin, Dost Ali, at once occupied the vacant *masnad*, without, however, obtaining the sanction of his immediate superior, the Viceroy of the Dakhan. It may have been partly on that account that Dost Ali showed very early a disposition to lean upon European support, and

---

* The account of the previous services of M. Dumas is taken from the letters patent issued by Louis XV., dated September 4, 1742, confirming the ennobling of M. Dumas on the occasion of his return to France.

it was not long before he established very intimate relations with the courteous, hospitable, and friendly people who had established themselves at Pondichery. With M. Dumas, in particular, he formed an intimate friendship. Dumas, anxious to turn this to the advantage of the settlement, pressed upon Dost Ali the advisability of procuring for him the permission to coin money—a permission which had been granted to the English, but, by them, after a short trial, neglected. The Nawwáb forwarded the request, with his own strong recommendations, to Delhi, and he succeeded, at the end of 1736, in procuring a firman, issued by Muhammad Sháh, and addressed to the Nawwáb of Arkát, authorising the coinage by the French of the current coin of the realm, in gold and silver, bearing, on one side the stamp of the Mughal, and on the other the name of the place at which the money was coined.*

The advantages which the French derived from this permission were very great indeed. The reputation of the Indo-French money became in a short time so great that it was the cause of establishing a very profitable trade in bullion. But, in addition, the actual profits were large. The annual amount struck off did not fall short of five or six millions of rupees,† and the profits on the coining of this amount were considered equal to an income of 200,000 rupees annually;—a very great consideration in a settlement, which, like that of Pondichery, was left almost to shift for itself by the Directors in Europe.‡

---

* The following is a translation of an extract from the letter addressed on this occasion by Dost Ali to M. Dumas: " The reputation you have acquired of being a true and faithful friend is known everywhere. In the view, therefore, to gain your friendship, I grant you permission to coin rupees at Pondichery of the coinage of Arkát, conformably to the Parwana which I send you."—*Guyon.*

† The French rupee was a little broader than an English shilling, and very much thicker. In point of fineness it was superior to the English standard. The gold coin was called the " pagoda," equal in value to about nine shillings. Three hundred and twenty rupees were considered equal to one hundred pagodas; hence an Indo-French rupee was worth more than two shillings and ninepence, reckoning a rupee at two shillings.

‡ As a reward for the success of his negotiations in this matter, M. Dumas was made Knight of the Order of St. Michel, and received patent letters of nobility.—*Guyon.*

But the intimacy with Dost Ali was productive of more important results. Dost Ali had two sons, of whom the elder was Safdar Ali, and several daughters, one of whom was married to his nephew, Murtizá Ali, and another to a more distant relation, Chanda Sahib. Of these Safdar Ali, whilst he did not altogether share his father's liking for the French, had a very great respect for their power, and especially for the fortifications of Pondichery; Chanda Sahib, on the other hand, carried his admiration for the foreigners to a very high pitch. Alone, perhaps, amongst his countrymen, he understood them. Born himself without wealth, but possessing great capacity, considerable energy, and unbounded ambition; brought, moreover, by his marriage with the daughter of Dost Ali, into a position, in which, whilst he dared openly aspire to nothing, he might secretly hope for almost anything; yet possessing but a small personal following, and being ever in the presence of relatives whose claims and whose power were superior, and whose ambition was equal to his own; he had been for a long time sensible that he must look for support beyond the circle of his own family. The position of the French had early attracted him. He appears even then to have detected their latent desire to increase their territory. It is certain, at all events, that he took the first opportunity to proffer his aid to bring fresh lands under their rule. That he did this with the view to obtain for himself French support is scarcely to be doubted. Ever since his connexion with Dost Ali, he, of all the native allies of M. Dumas, had been the most frequent visitor at Pondichery, and had attracted, more than any other, the personal regards of the high officials in that city.

It had happened that at the end of the year 1735, the Hindu Rájá of Trichinápalli had died without issue. A contest for power immediately arose between his widow, the Rání, and a relation of the deceased prince.

CHANDA SAHIB TAKES TRICHINÁPALLI.

In her distress, the Ráni appealed to Dost Ali for assistance. The opportunity was too tempting to be foregone. Dost Ali despatched a force, of which his son Safdar Ali was the nominal, his son-in-law Chanda Sahib the real, commander, to take possession of the disputed territories. The kingdom was soon overrun; the capital alone bade defiance to the invaders. Of this, however, Chanda Sahib obtained possession the 26th April, 1736, on taking an oath,* that his troops should be employed only in the service of the Ráni. But he kept this oath only until Trichinápalli was in his power; he then imprisoned the Ráni, and being invested by Safdar Ali, who returned to Arkát with plenary powers, he assumed the government as lieutenant for his father-in-law. While in that position he continued to maintain intimate relations with the French.

Adjoining Trichinápalli, lying between it and the Koromandel coast, lay the Hindu kingdom of Tanjur. This was bounded on the north side by the river Kolrún, which falls into the sea about thirty miles below Pondichery. Tanjur, one of the conquests of Sháhjí, father of the famous Síváji, had been bestowed in perpetuity by the latter on his brother Venkají. Venkají was succeeded by his son Tukají. This latter, dying in the month of February 1738, left behind him three sons—Bábá Sáhib, and Sahují, legitimate, the third, Partáb Singh, the offspring of a concubine. Bábá Sáhib succeeded to the sovereignty, but died, the same year, without issue. After a short interregnum, during which Sa'id Khán, the Muhammadan commandant of Tanjur, raised two candidates only to cause them immediately to disappear, the surviving legitimate son, Sahují, obtained possession of power. But in a very short time Sa'id Khán brought

CHAP. III.
1736.

---

* Orme states that the people of the country believed that the Ráni had fallen in love with Chanda Sahib; but the story is improbable. Chanda Sahib may have considered himself free from the responsibility of the oath, because he had taken it upon a brick instead of upon the Kurán—the brick having been wrapped up in the usual covering of the Kurán.

CHAP. III.

1738.

forward Sidují, a pretended cousin of Sahují, and endeavoured to effect a revolution in his favour. Suddenly collecting their friends, they seized on the palace and on the strong places in Tanjur. Sahují had barely time to save himself on horseback. Accompanied by a few friends, he passed the Kolrún, and took refuge in the pagoda, Chelambram, a very strongly fortified position about six miles north of the Kolrún, and only twenty-four distant from Pondichery. From this place Sahují opened negotiations with M. Dumas. He offered to make over to the French the town of Kárikál, and the fort of Kirkangarhí, ten villages in the country adjacent, and all the lands depending upon them, if M. Dumas would afford him material aid in the recovery of Tanjur. The offer was the most tempting that could have been made. The French had been long engaged in endeavouring to effect an arrangement which would secure to them a footing in the kingdom of Tanjur, but up to that time they had been thwarted by the jealousy of the Dutch at Nágápatan, a settlement a few miles south of Kárikál. Now, however, all that they desired was offered to them. The risk was but little, for they had but to supply one of the contending parties with material aid to ensure an easy victory. M. Dumas did not hesitate. He at once entered into an engagement with the envoys of Sahují, by which he bound himself to supply that prince with a lakh of rupees in silver, to furnish him with arms, gunpowder and other warlike stores, and to render him all other assistance in his power. In return for this engagement, Sahují sent him a formal cession of the town of Kárikál, of the fort Kirkangarhí on the river Kárikál, of the ten villages, and of the lands dependent upon them. In pursuance of this engagement, M. Dumas despatched two ships of war, the "Bourbon" of sixty guns and the "St. Géran" of forty, with troops, artillery, and warlike stores, to take possession of Kárikál, and to afford the promised assistance. These ships anchored before Kárikál in the month of August of that year (1738).*

Meanwhile Sahují had been using other methods more congenial to him than force. By dint of bribes and promises he had gained over the principal nobility of Tanjur, and amongst them the all-powerful Sa'id. A plan of operations was agreed upon, in pursuance of which, the usurper, Sidají, was suddenly seized in his palace. Intelligence of this was at once dispatched to Chelambram, and Sahují immediately mounting his horse, returned in triumph to Tanjur.

This was the intelligence that greeted the captains of the "Bourbon" and the "St. Géran," when they anchored in the roads of Kárikál. It was accompanied by an intimation that the French succours were not wanted; that Kárikál was occupied by between three and four thousand troops under Khán Sáhib, a trusted officer of Sahují; and that any attempt to land would be considered as a hostile act, and would be met accordingly. In consequence of this intimation the senior French captain determined to suspend action pending instructions from Pondichery.

But whilst Sahují had transmitted instructions of the nature we have recorded to Kárikál, he had written in a somewhat different strain to M. Dumas. To him he declared his perfect willingness to surrender Kárikál, but the impossibility of doing so immediately. He was, he said, scarcely secure in his own capital, and he was threatened at the same time by Chanda Sahib from Trichinápalli. He pointed out the impossibility of surrendering, under such circumstances, resources which were essential to his safety.

These excuses, plausible though they were, did not deceive M. Dumas. Yet there can be no doubt that

* The account of the expedition against Kárikál has been taken mainly from the statement communicated by Dumas to the Abbé Guyon, and from a very old paper entitled. *Mémoire particulière sur l'aquisition de Kárikál.*

CHAP. III.
1738.

the slipping from his grasp of this much-coveted place just at the moment his hand was closing upon it, caused him great mortification and annoyance. He was well aware that with the force in the two ships of war before Kárikál, it would be easy to take possession of the place, and that, to a less prudent man, would have been a very great temptation. But M. Dumas' great characteristic was prudence. He would not risk, even for so valuable a prize, the character gained by the French as a non-aggressive nation. He preferred to wait for the opportunity which he felt sure would, sooner or later, present itself, satisfied that he had made a great step in advance in having secured from the Rájá of Tanjur the legal cession of Kárikál and its dependencies. He therefore recalled the ships to Pondichery.

The opportunity he waited for soon came. No sooner did the intelligence reach Chanda Sahib that Rájá Sahují had refused to fulfil his engagement regarding Kárikál, than he realised that the moment had arrived for him to cement his alliance with the French. He accordingly wrote to M. Dumas, informing him that he was at war with Sahují, and offering to march his own troops upon Kárikál, to conquer it, and to make it over, in full sovereignty, to the French. From them he asked no assistance: he would employ, he said, none but his own soldiers.

Chanda Sahib, it will be recollected, was son-in-law of Dost Ali, Nawwáb of the Karnátik, and feudal lord of the territory to the north of the French possessions; he himself, as Dost Ali's lieutenant, held the country on the south-west; that on the south-east alone was held by the Rájá of Tanjur. It was clear then that Chanda Sahib's offer to conquer a portion of that Rájá's possessions involved no risk to the French; it did not even invoke the suspicion of a greed for territorial extension. It was the offer of a powerful Indian potentate to compel a weaker ruler to adhere to his agreement. M.

Dumas then violated no principle of his predecessor's policy by accepting that offer. This he did almost as soon as it was made.

No sooner had Chanda Sahib received this authority to act, than he detached four thousand horse, commanded by Francisco Pereira, a Spaniard in his service, but who was entirely attached to French interests, to Kárikál. The Tanjur forces fell back at their approach, and Pereira arrived at Kárikál, February 6, 1739, without meeting with any opposition. He found, however, the fort of Kirkangarhí, on the river Kárikál and about a mile and a half from the town, occupied by about four hundred Tanjurians. He immediately attacked this fort, stormed it the same day, and hastened with the news to Pondichery. M. Dumas, delighted with the prompt success, at once equipped a small vessel of a hundred and fifty tons burden, and despatched her with all the troops and stores she could carry to Kárikál—Pereira accompanying them. They reached their destination in four and twenty hours. Then Kárikál, the fort of Kirkangarhí, and the adjacent territory, previously ceded by Sahují, were made over to the French by Pereira. This cession bears date February 14, 1739. A few days later, on receiving an account of the French occupation, M. Dumas despatched to Kárikál a ship of war, laden with everything necessary to place the settlement in a state of security.*

The effect of these forcible measures upon Rájá Sahují was such as might have been expected from a man of his weak and unmanly nature. He was completely overawed. He at once sent messages to Pondichery, casting all the blame of the previous hostile conduct on the evil counsels of the Dutch at Nágápatan;

---

* Full details of these occurrences are given in Guyon's *Historie des Indes Orientales*, and in the *Mémoire particulière sur l'acquisition de Kárikál.*

stating that he had always intended to cede the territory at the proper time; and professing his readiness now to execute in full the treaty of Chelambram. As a proof of his sincerity, he sent at the same time two instruments, dated April 25, 1739, one of which contained a ratification of the former treaty, and the other, an order to the inhabitants of the districts he had yielded, to acknowledge and obey the French in future as their masters. It is probable that the complaisance of Sahují in this matter was quickened by the fact that one of the clauses of the treaty of Chelambram contained a stipulation for the payment to him of 100,000 rupees—a stipulation which the French, now in possession, might, according to oriental notions, have been inclined to evade. Before, however, his propositions reached Pondichery, a domestic revolution hurled Sahují from his throne. But his successor and half-brother, Partáb Singh, not only confirmed the agreement of Chelambram, but added to it a greater extent of territory. In a personal interview he held with M. Dumas in the beginning of the year 1741, Partáb Singh even recommended him to fortify the towns in his new possessions. From this date, the district of Kárikál may be regarded as an integral portion of the French possessions in India.*

But meanwhile events of great importance had occurred. The Muhammadan conquests in the south of India had aroused the jealousy of the Maráthás, and an army of 50,000† men of these famous warriors had

---

* The ceded districts consisted of the town of Kárikál, the fortress of Kirkangarhí, ten villages on the sea-coast, and a tract of country fifteen or sixteen miles in extent, very fertile in rice, and producing also cotton and indigo, inhabited by ten or twelve thousand people, and yielding a yearly rent of ten thousand pagodas, equal to about £4,500 sterling. The town of Kárikál, at the time of cession, contained 638 houses of stone and brick, and upwards of 5,000 inhabitants. The fort of Kirkangarhí was about gunshot distance from Kárikál. Both are on the river Kárikál, a branch of the Kolrún, navigable for vessels of about 200 tons burden. Kárikál is 75 miles south of Pondichery and 12 miles north of Nágápatan.

† Grand Duff (*History of the Maráthás*).—Captain Duff took the numbers from Marátha manuscripts; they differ somewhat from those given by Orme and other writers.

DOST ALI DEFEATED AND SLAIN.

assembled under the orders of Raghují Bhonsla—serving under whom, his first campaign, was the afterwards famous Murarí Ráo—and had marched eastward with the avowed intention of plundering the long-untouched Karnátik. But Dost Ali was not prepared to grant them an easy ingress. Learning, towards the end of 1739, that they were approaching by the Damalcheri pass in the northern Arkát district, he occupied that strong position with the only troops at his disposal, amounting to about 10,000 men, and sent pressing orders to his son, Safdar Ali, and to his son-in-law, Chanda Sahib, to hasten to his assistance. But both Safdar Ali and Chanda Sahib were prosecuting their conquests in the south of India, and though they professed their readiness to obey the summons they had received, they moved, especially Chanda Sahib, with slow and unwilling steps. Before they could arrive, the Maráthás had approached the pass. This, as the most important, was held by Dost Ali in person, but there was a gorge, or opening, to the south of his position, the defence of which he had intrusted to one of his commanders, a Hindu. This latter had allowed himself to be seduced from his allegiance, and permitted the Maráthá army to march through the gorge he was guarding on the night of the 19th May. The Maráthás thus secure of their prey, moved swiftly at daybreak the next morning on the rear of the position occupied by Dost Ali. This chieftain, noticing the approach of cavalry, imagined that his son, Safdar Ali, had arrived to reinforce him, and was only undeceived when their movements indicated undisguised hostility. Driven to bay, however, he determined to sell his life dearly. The battle which ensued was, notwithstanding the disparity of numbers, contested most desperately, and it only terminated when Dost Ali himself and his second son, Hásán Ali, lay dead upon the field, and his first minister, Mir Asad, had been taken prisoner. Almost all

CHAP. III.

1739.

G

the principal officers were killed or trodden under foot by elephants, and the slaughter was unprecedented even in that age. No rout could have been more complete.

The account of this defeat spread dismay and consternation in the Karnátik. Safdar Ali, the son of the deceased Nawwáb, received the news when he had advanced as far as Arkát; he immediately, for greater security, moved at the head of his forces to Vellur, which was better fortified, there to wait the course of events. Chanda Sahib, more dilatory, had not moved beyond the boundary of his satrapy. The intelligence he received determined him to remain within it, and to place its chief city in the best possible state of defence. He returned, therefore, to Trichinápalli.

On one important matter, however, the two brothers-in-law acted as though they had been inspired by one brain. Regarding the result of the contest with the Maráthás as extremely uncertain, they bethought them of the protection which the fortifications of Pondichery might be able to offer, and they determined to consign, the one his father's family, the other his own, with all the valuables that could be lightly carried, to the courtesy of M. Dumas.

M. Dumas was placed, by the result of the battle, in very much the same position as that in which M. Martin had found himself after the defeat of Sher Khán Lodi, by Síváji. On that occasion, as on this, the Maráthás had completely defeated the actual rulers of the country —the allies and protectors of the French. There was, however, this difference, that the Pondichery governed by M. Dumas was far more capable of offering an effective resistance than the infant city under the rule of Francis Martin. But M. Dumas, notwithstanding his confidence in the defences of Pondichery, was very well aware of the difficulties of his position, and he prepared to act with his usual prudence and judgment. He greatly strengthened, with all the means at his disposal, the west fortifications of the place. For fifteen days carts and beasts of burden were seen pouring into Pondichery laden with grain and other stores. M. Dumas superintended himself all the arrangements for procuring and storing this grain, and of ordering the defences. No point was neglected; his industry was untiring. At the same time, the natives of the surrounding country, who had anything to lose, arrived in vast numbers, bringing with them their stores and valuables. But other and greater guests were approaching. On May 25th, five days after the battle, whilst the preparations we have above alluded to were still progressing, a grand cortége was seen moving towards Pondichery. This proved to be the widow of Dost Ali Khán, with her children, her dependents, her jewels and other property, under the escort of a large body of cavalry. Arriving before the walls, she at once sent a message to the Governor, praying for admission into the city.

None knew better than M. Dumas, that if anything would most certainly draw down upon himself the power of the Maráthás, and would infallibly induce them to move upon Pondichery, it would be the knowledge of the fact that the city contained within its walls the most valuable property of the late Nawwáb. It is certain that under any circumstances, the chivalrous feelings natural to a real man would have incited him to throw wide open the gates to one who was not only a woman, but a woman in distress. But there was no occasion for him to act from mere feeling. It was in his eyes more politic to run the risk of bringing the Maráthás upon Pondichery, than to undergo the certainty of being dishonoured and contemned throughout India. Safdar Ali also was still unsubdued, and the refusal to admit his mother would undoubtedly make an enemy of one, who had even then the best chance of becoming the feudal

CHAP. III.
1740.

lord of the country about Pondichery. However, before replying to the request of the widow of Dost Ali, M. Dumas summoned a Council. He told the members that, in his opinion, honour, gratitude, humanity, and policy, all pointed to the admission; he added his reasons, pointed out the risks, and then asked for their opinion. The Council approved his arguments, and a decision was at once arrived at to admit the cavalcade.

This was done with great state and ceremony. The garrison was placed under arms, the ramparts were manned. The Governor himself, in a magnificent palanquin, and followed by his horse and foot guards, went down to the Valdávar gate. The gate was then thrown open. Immediately there entered the widow of the Nawwáb, her daughters and relations, in twenty-two palanquins, followed by fifteen hundred cavalry, eight elephants, three hundred camels, two hundred bullock-carts, and two thousand beasts of burden. The entrance of the principal personage was saluted by a discharge of cannon from the ramparts, and she was conducted by M. Dumas in person to the apartments he had provided her.* A similar hospitable reception was accorded a few days later to the wife and son of Chanda Sahib.† Meanwhile the Maráthás, taking advantage of their victory, had marched upon Arkát, and had occupied it without opposition. Thence they sent detachments to pillage the country. But though the devastation they caused was ruinous and often wanton, the actual receipts fell far short of their expectations. The inhabitants of the Karnátik had taken advantage of the first rumours of war to remove all their valuables into fortified places. Some had fled to Madras, some to Vellur, some to Pondichery. The

---

* These details, together with the account generally of M. Dumas' administration, are taken from the extracts given in the Abbé Guyon's work already referred to.

† Orme states that the wife of Safdar Ali also took refuge in Pondichery, but it appears from the correspondence of M. Dumas with the Maráthás that she joined her husband at Vellur.

consequence was, that though the Maráthás gleaned every blade of grass, there was but little else to gather, and they were beginning to feel that, looking at it with the eyes of marauders, the campaign had been a failure.

That was a frame of mind which would willingly have listened to offers of payment for retiring from so barren and desolated a country, and such offers they did receive at the proper time. They had liberated Mir A'sad, first minister of the deceased Dost Ali, and he, betaking himself to Vellur, prevailed upon his new master to make proposals of peace to the invader. Mir A'sad was a bitter enemy of Chanda Sahib, and he had succeeded in imbuing the mind of Safdar Ali with suspicions as to the designs of his brother-in-law. He had easily convinced him also that the sacrifice of Chanda Sahib would lighten the conditions likely to be imposed upon himself. This being agreed upon as a basis, negotiations were opened, and after a short interval, a treaty was signed in the month of August, 1740, by which it was arranged that Safdar Ali should be recognised as Nawwáb of the Karnátik in place of his father; that he should pay by instalments ten millions of rupees to the Maráthás; that he should join his troops to those of the Maráthás to drive Chanda Sahib from Trichinápalli; and that all the Hindu princes on the Koromandel coast should be reinstated in possession of the places they held prior to 1736. The two last articles, however, were kept secret, and the better to prevent their existence being suspected, the Maráthás at once retired from the Karnátik.

Some information, however, regarding the secret clauses of this treaty reached M. Dumas, and he did not fail to take advantage of it. He had already been threatened by Raghují Bhonsla, and a correspondence, not tending at all to accommodate matters, had ensued between them. He had been asked to pay tribute, and he had refused; he had been called upon to give up the

CHAP. III.
1740.

wife and son of Chanda Sahib with their treasures, he had replied that all the French in India would die first; Pondichery had been threatened with the fate of Bassein, then recently captured by the Maráthás from the Portuguese, he had answered that if the Bhonsla came against Pondichery, he would try to deserve his esteem by successfully defending it.* In this state of the

---

* The following are extracts from the correspondence between Raghují Bhonsla and M Dumas: From Raghují Bhonsla. "Forty years have elapsed since our sovereign gave you permission to establish yourselves at Pondichery; nevertheless since our army has arrived in these parts, I have not received a single letter from you.

"Our sovereign, persuaded that you were deserving of his friendship, that the French were people of their word, who would never fail in their engagements towards him, made over to you a considerable territory. You agreed to pay an annual tribute, which you never have paid. At last, after a considerable time, the army of the Maráthás has arrived in these districts. It has beaten the Musalmans, puffed up with pride, and forced them to pay tribute. We need not tell you this news. We have now orders from the Maharájá to take possession of the fortresses of Trichinápalli and Jinjí, and to put garrisons in them. We have also orders to collect the tribute due from the European towns on the sea-coast. I am obliged to obey these orders. When we consider your conduct, and the manner in which the King has favoured you, in allowing you to establish yourselves in his territory, I cannot hinder myself from saying that you are wrong in not paying this tribute. We had consideration for you, and you have acted against us. You have given refuge to the Mughals in your town. Was that well done? Again, Chanda Sahib has left, under your protection, the treasure chests of Trichinápalli and of Tanjur—the precious stones, elephants, horses, and other things of which he possessed himself in those kingdoms, as well as his family—was that, too, well done? If you wish that we should be friends, you must give up this treasure, these jewels, these horses, these elephants, as well as the wife and son of Chanda Sahib. I send my cavalry to whom you can make them over. If you decline to do so, we shall be compelled to force you to it, as well as to the payment of the tribute which you have kept back for forty years.

"You know how we have treated the town of Bassein. My army is very numerous, and it wants money for its expenses. If you do not act in conformity with my demands, I shall know how to draw from you wherewith to pay my whole army Our ships will arrive in a few days. It will be better for you to terminate the matter quickly. I rely upon your sending me, in conformity with this letter, the wife and son of Chanda Sahib, with his elephants, horses, jewels, and treasure."

Extract from the reply of M. Dumas: "You tell me that we have owed for forty years past a tribute to your King. Never has the French nation been subject to any tribute. It would cost me my head, if the King of France, my master, were informed that I had consented to pay tribute to any one. When the princes of the country gave to the French a piece of land on the sands of the sea-shore, upon which to build a fortress and a town, they required no other conditions, but that the pagodas and the religion of the people should be unmolested. Although your armies have never yet appeared in our neighbourhood, we have always faithfully observed these conditions. * * * * * * * *

"You say that you have orders to take possession of the fortresses of Jinjí and Trichinápalli. Well and good, so long as that does not oblige you to become our enemy. As many

correspondence, the intimation he had received regarding the secret clauses was of great importance. He continued, with the same ardour, the repair of the fortifications at the same time that new defences were erected. He formed a body of European infantry 1,200 in number, and supplemented them by four or five thousand Muhammadans, whom he armed and drilled in the European fashion—the germ of the sipáhi army—and who were found most useful in performing the routine duties of the garrison. He brought into the town also, all the crews of the ships in the roads, and exercised them in the various operations of land warfare. Stores of all sorts he likewise continued to accumulate.

Whilst these preparations were going on, the new Nawwáb, Safdar Ali, paid a visit to Pondichery. The avowed object was to thank M. Dumas for the protection he had afforded to the female members of his father's family. None knew better than Safdar Ali, how galling to the Maráthás had been the knowledge that the families and valuables of his late father and of the Mughals as have been masters here have treated the French with friendship and distinction. From them we have received only favours. In virtue of this friendship, we have given shelter to the widow of the late Nawwáb, Dost Ali Khán, with all her family. Ought we to have shut our gates and leave them in the country? Men of honour are incapable of such cowardice. The wife of Chanda Sahib has also come hither with her mother and her brother, and the others have proceeded to Arkát.

"You have written to me to make over to your horsemen this lady, her son, and the riches she has brought here. You, who are a nobleman full of bravery and generosity, what would you think of me, if I were capable of such baseness? The wife of Chanda Sahib is in Pondichery under the protection of the King of France, my master, and all the French in India would die rather than deliver her to you. * * * * "You threaten me finally that if I do not comply with your demands, you will send your armies against me and lead them hither yourself. I am preparing myself to the utmost of my ability to receive you well, and to deserve your esteem, by showing that I have the honour of commanding the bravest nation in the world, who know how to defend themselves with intrepidity against those who attack them unjustly. Above all I place my confidence in Almighty God, before whom the most powerful armies are like the light straw which the wind blows away. I hope He will favour the justice of our cause. I have heard what has happened at Bassein, but that place was not defended by Frenchmen."—*Mémoire dans les Archives de la Compagnie des Indes.*

Chanda Sahib were in safety behind the walls of Pondichery. He was well aware that Raghují Bhonsla, their leader, had expressed his determination to make the French suffer for their audacity; and he, in common with the other chiefs of the Karnátik, had been struck with admiration at the quietly defiant attitude assumed by M. Dumas. His object in visiting him now was to thank and to reward him. He was quickened in this also, by a message his mother sent him from Pondichery, desiring to see him. Chanda Sahib, who knew little of the storm that was brewing against him, and who had already at Arkát offered homage to his brother-in-law as Nawwáb of the Karnátik and his liege lord, accompanied him on this occasion to Pondichery.

There they arrived on the evening of September 1, 1740, and were received with great demonstrations of friendship and respect by M. Dumas, in a tent, splendidly adorned and illuminated, without the walls. After resting there some time, Safdar Ali was conducted to the house which had been set apart for his mother and sisters in the public gardens. Here he remained for two days in mourning and seclusion. On the 4th, Safdar Ali paid a visit of state to M. Dumas. He thanked him repeatedly for the courtesy and hospitality extended to the members of his father's family, at a season of great difficulty and danger; declared that it should never be forgotten, and that henceforth the French should be as much the masters of the Karnátik as he himself was. Although these words were merely the expression of the oriental form of gratitude, and were doubtless only taken as such, the Nawwáb had evidently deemed it sound policy on his part to conciliate M. Dumas by some practical proof of his esteem. Simultaneously with the announcement of his arrival at Pondichery, he had delivered to the French Governor a parchment conferring upon him personally lands bordering on the southern territory of Pondichery, bringing in a yearly revenue of 10,000 rupees. This cession was soon afterwards confirmed by a firman from the Court of Delhi.

After a stay of several days in Pondichery the visitors left, Safdar Ali with his father's family proceeding to Arkát, Chanda Sahib, leaving his wife and family with their jewels in Pondichery, making his way alone to Trichinápalli. To the immediate fortunes of this chieftain we must now turn our attention.

That M. Dumas had a strong idea that all danger from the Maráthás had not passed away, is evident from the fact that even after their departure, he continued to labour at the fortifications and to store supplies. That he had communicated these suspicions to Chanda Sahib, and had induced him, on the strength of them, to leave his family and valuables at Pondichery, is extremly probable. Yet it is certain that Chanda Sahib had no sooner quitted Pondichery than he began to act in a manner entirely inconsistent with the idea that he had any fear of a second Marátha inroad. During the first invasion, he had taken the precaution to store Trichinápalli with grain, under the conviction that with ample supplies within the walls, the fortifications were strong enough to keep out the Maráthás for an indefinite period. But no sooner had he returned from his visit to Pondichery, than, as though he felt assured of the future, he sold the grain, and so far from thinking that any necessity to defend his own territories could arise, he began to entertain a design of adding to them, and sent for that purpose his brother, Bárá Sahib, to Madura. This was in the end of November. An account of the movements of Bárá Sahib and the unprovided state of Trichinápalli was quickly conveyed to Raghují, who at the head of his Maráthás, had retired only to Sivágangá, some eighty miles in a southerly direction from the capital. The news was that for which Raghují had been waiting. Without an hour's loss of time, he assembled his forces, made forced marches upon Trichinápalli, and sat down before it, before Chanda Sahib had taken any steps to replenish his empty stores.

Nevertheless, though taken by surprise, Chanda Sahib resolved to defend himself with resolution. He had hopes from his brother, Bárá Sahib, and to him accordingly he sent a message urging him to march to his relief. Bárá Sahib at once complied, and collecting supplies, escorted them, at the head of three thousand horse and seven thousand foot, towards Trichinápalli. The Maráthás, however, had knowledge of all his movements, and on his approaching to within about fifteen miles of the city, they detached a superior force— amounting to about 20,000 men—to intercept him. A desperate encounter ensued, Bárá Sahib fighting with all the energy of despair. A chance shot, however, hurled him from his elephant, and his followers, missing the inspiration of his presence, at once gave way. The body of Bárá Sahib, which was found on the field of battle, was carried to the camp before Trichinápalli, clothed there in rich stuffs, and sent in to Chanda Sahib, to announce to him, as under similar circumstance the head of Hasdrubal had announced to Hannibal, the futility of depending upon his brother for aid.

Thus driven to depend upon his own resources, Chanda Sahib continued to display unflinching resolution and determined courage. At last, after defending himself for upwards of three months, having exhausted all his money, stores, almost all his ammunition, and having lost some of his best troops, he had no alternative but to surrender. The terms were hard, his life only being secured to him, but they were the best he could obtain. On the 21st of March, after a siege of more than three months, he opened the gates of the city, and surrendered himself a prisoner. He was at once sent off under a strong guard to Satára, whilst the

Maráthás appointed Murári Ráo as Governor of the fortress, with 14,000 men to support him.

Whilst engaged in the siege of Trichinápalli, Raghují Bhonsla had not ceased to lavish his threats upon M. Dumas. His demands even increased. They now embraced the immediate payment of 6,000,000 rupees, a regular annual tribute, and the delivery to him of the wife and son of Chanda Sahib, with their elephants, horses, and jewels. To these demands M. Dumas continued to oppose a steady refusal. He took, however, the precaution of despatching a special messenger to the Isles of France and Bourbon, requesting the early transmission of as many men as could be spared thence to reinforce his garrison. The Maráthá, however, was bent upon intimidating him. In this view, whilst still himself before Trichinápalli, he despatched a force of about 16,000 men to beat up the coast. These marched upon Portonovo, a town about thirty-two miles south of Pondichery, and then used as a depot by the Dutch, French, and English. This they plundered, though little to the detriment of the French, who had taken the precaution to move the greater part of their property within Pondichery. They next moved upon Gudalúr, an English settlement twelve miles from Pondichery, and pillaged it. Marching then to within five miles of the French settlement, and halting there, they sent in threatening letters to M. Dumas, whilst they detached small parties to ravage the country and to collect plunder. At the same time, in pursuance of advices received from the Bhonsla, they organised an expedition on the western coast to attack the French settlement of Mahé.

M. Dumas was not appalled by these letters, nor by the still more threatening visit of one of the chief officers of the Maráthá army, sent to inform him that the fate of Trichinápalli was reserved for Pondichery. On the contrary, he received this officer with the utmost politeness, showed him the supplies he had stored up, the guns bristling on the ramparts, the drilled Europeans, the armed sipáhis; he hid, in fact, nothing from him. He then calmly informed him, that so long as one Frenchman remained alive, Pondichery would not be evacuated. With reference to the demand of the Marátha general for tribute, he sent a message to him through the envoy that the territory occupied by the French possessed neither mines of gold nor mines of silver; but that it was rich in iron, and that those who occupied it were ready to use that iron against any assailants. The envoy left immensely impressed with the power and resources of the French settlement, and with the resolute bearing of its governor.

It happened that on taking his leave, the Marátha envoy had received from M. Dumas, under the name of cordials, a present of ten bottles of liqueurs. Some of these he made over to his general, Raghují Bhonsla, and he, in his turn, gave them to his wife, who found them so much to her liking that she insisted upon others being procured, whatever might be the cost. The influence of woman is proverbially powerful. Raghují was most unwilling, after all his threats, to abate one iota of his demands against Pondichery. Yet the Nantes cordials had given the French an ally against which he was but a child. These cordials were to be obtained by any means, and it seemed they could only be secured by friendly communication with M. Dumas. The determination to possess them led, therefore, after a good deal of circumlocution, to negotiations, which ended finally in a pacification. Raghují was so charmed by the opportune present of thirty bottles of these cordials, that he soon became disposed to forget all his previous anger against the French. He prohibited any pillaging in the neighbourhood of Pondichery, and he began to listen without anger to the reports which were made to him that in attacking Pondichery he had everything to lose and nothing to gain. He accordingly withdrew his demands for the payment of a sum of money, as tribute, and for the surrender of the family of Chanda Sahib, and retired without any further demonstrations, fortified by cordials, to the western coast.

The expedition against Mahé, to the organisation of which we have alluded, resolved itself into a blockade, which lasted eight months, when it was put an end to by M. de la Bourdonnais in a manner to which we shall presently refer.

The conduct of M. Dumas on this occasion—his bold and resolute refusal to deliver up his guests; the coolness with which he had defied the conqueror of Trichinápalli—procured him, amongst the nations of southern India, the reputation of a hero. Congratulations and thanks poured in to him from oll sides. The Subadar of the Dakhan, Nizámu-l-Mulk, wrote to him a letter of thanks couched in terms of the highest respect, and transmitted to him, at the same time, a dress of honour. Safdar Ali, as a mark of esteem, sent him the armour of his deceased father, richly adorned with gold and precious stones, together with three elephants, several horses, many swords and jewelled weapons, and accompanied by a letter carried by his favourite minister. The Emperor of Delhi, Muhammad Sháh, on hearing of this successful resistance to Marátha presumption, conferred upon M. Dumas the rank of Nawwáb, with the title of Mançabdár of 4,500 horse, 2,000 of whom he was allowed to keep about his person in time of peace, without being at any charge for their maintenance. On the application of M. Dumas the title and command were declared transferable to his successor.

Shortly before the receipt of these honours, M. Dumas had intimated to his masters his wish to return to his native country. His resignation had been accepted, and Joseph Francis Dupleix, the successful Intendant of Chandranagar, had been nominated to succeed him.

CHAP. III.
1741.

M. Dupleix arrived at Pondichery in the month of October, 1741, and took at once the oaths as Governor-General, at the same time that he caused himself to be acknowledged as the Mughal's Nawwáb, and Mançabdár of 4,500 horse, in succession to his predecessor.

The records of the six years' administration of M. Dumas show with sufficient clearness that he was no unworthy successor to Francis Martin. His administration was signalised by the display of tact, prudence, courage, and skill. He understood the native character thoroughly. So well did he make use of that knowledge that though all his allies were beaten, he managed to reap advantage, in the most legitimate manner, from their misfortunes. So adroit was his conduct that the territory which he coveted he gained without drawing the sword; he even accepted it as a favour to his native friends, instead of asking for it as a benefit to himself. Under his rule the dominions of the French on the Koromandel coast increased very greatly in extent and value, whilst the prestige of the French power attained in the eyes of the natives, a height which, even to us who look back at it, appears perfectly astounding. It seemed, indeed, when Dumas left Pondichery, that it would be only necessary for his successor to continue the same cautious and prudent, yet daring and acquisitive policy, to make Pondichery the most powerful and important city in Southern India.

That successor, as we have seen, was Dupleix. We left him last engaged in restoring the credit and fortunes of Chandranagar. This he had succeeded in accomplishing beyond his most sanguine expectations. It could not be expected that, occupying as he had the position of Intendant or Director-General of Chandranagar, nominally under the orders of the Governor and Superior Council of Pondichery, yet practically irresponsible—daily and hourly forced, in fact, to act upon his own responsibility—he should not sometimes

DUPLEIX ASSUMES THE REINS.

have run counter to the ideas of his immediate superior. The very promptness of Dupleix's acts must have made them often appear rash and precipitate in the eyes of men of prudence and caution. Difference of opinion on these points had latterly arisen between himself and M. Dumas, and Dupleix, chafing under a control which he felt to be unwise, and believed to be unauthorised, had requested M. Godeheu, a member of his Council, who was returning to Europe, to explain, more fully than he could write, the exact state of affairs. The Directors at Paris entered fully into the views of their agent at Chandranagar, from whose daring yet practical genius they had so largely benefited, and, on the resignation of M. Dumas, they appointed Dupleix to succeed him at Pondichery. He was installed there in the month of October, 1741.*

He left Chandranagar, which he had found almost a ruin, the most important European settlement in Bengal, possessing two thousand brick houses, an extensive trade, and unsurpassed credit. He had made for himself, by private trade—a proceeding not only allowed but encouraged by the Directors—an enormous fortune. In the early part of the year in which he was appointed to Pondichery, Dupleix had married the widow of one of his councillors, Madame Vincens,† a lady who had been born and educated in India, but whose strong yet devoted character and brilliant intellect made her an admirable companion for the far-sighted and deep-scheming politician. Her proficiency in the native languages rendered her aid invaluable to Dupleix in his confidential dealing with native princes. She likewise

---

* Neither Mr. Orme nor Mr. Mill gives the exact date of the appointment of Dupleix. The writer of the article on Dupleix in the *National Review*, and the *Nouvelle Biographie Générale* give 1742, but the *Archives de la Compagnie des Indes* give the month of October, 1741, as the precise date; and this is undoubtedly correct. The fact that Dupleix visited Chandranagar in 1742 may have misled the other authorities.

† She was the daughter of a M. Albert, a Frenchman. Her mother belonged to the Portuguese family of De Castro. By M. Vincens, her previous husband, she had six children.

added to that proficiency a quickness of comprehension and zealous devotion to his interests, such as form, when united, an inestimable endowment.

On assuming the Government of Pondichery, Dupleix found the settlement suffering from the effects of the Marátha invasion. These marauding warriors, where they had not eaten up the land, had, by the fact of their presence, prevented its being tilled, and now the misery of famine had succeeded to the desolation of war. Added to this, the Karnátik was in a condition bordering upon anarchy. Safdar Ali had only rid himself of the anticipated rivalry of Chanda Sahib to fall into the real clutches of Nizámu-l-Mulk, the Subadar of the Dakhan, who loudly called upon him for the arrears of revenue, due by him as a vassal of the Mughal. The fortifications of Pondichery, too, however formidable they might have appeared to a native power, were quite insufficient for defence against an European enemy, and there were no funds available to enlarge or to repair them, notwithstanding that, even at this date, the rumours of the probability of war between France and England were brought out by each sailing vessel.

But Dupleix was equal to the occasion. Convinced that Pondichery had now attained such a stage of development as to require that the power of France should be recognised and acknowledged, he at once assumed, with an ostentatious publicity, the dignities that had been conferred upon him by the Mughal, receiving homage from those petty chieftains in the neighbourhood who were of a lower order of nobility. He at the same time set himself to work to inquire into the causes of the increasing public expenditure, to check corruption among the subordinate officers of the administration, and to examine the state of the defences. On these several points, with the mode in which they should be remedied, he transmitted full reports to the Company. Having thus set everything in train, he proceeded to Bengal to be installed as Nawwáb at Chandranagar. When the ceremony, which was conducted with great pomp, was concluded, he went in state to Húglí for the purpose of paying a visit of respect to the Muhammadan Governor. But this latter, recognising the superior rank of Dupleix, insisted upon making the first visit himself.* The honours with which he was received, and the state which he assumed, appear to have made a deep impression upon the natives, prepared as they were to regard with favour everything that was French, and to have rendered his relations with them of a still more intimate and agreeable character.

On his return to Pondichery from these visits, Dupleix at once assumed a greater state than had been indulged in by any of his predecessors. It was a part of his policy to impress upon the native princes in his vicinity that he too was an officer of the Mughal; that he owed his rank to the King of Delhi. He, therefore, would not permit a single sign or symbol which rightfully belonged to his rank to be omitted or neglected. Situated at Pondichery, far away from the reach of the distracted court of the descendant of Akbar, he was able to avail himself of the credit which his position as an officer of that monarch gave him amongst the natives, without in the smallest degree confining his own action, or making any infringement on the duties he owed to his sovereign. He, in fact, was absolute master of the situation, and he simply used the power given him by his title to strengthen and confirm his position.

Just at this moment, whilst engaged in this laudable design, and preparing at the same time to make Pondichery really as impregnable as the natives believed it to be, Dupleix received from the Company one of those strange despatches so often written by narrow-minded

* Histoire des Indes Orientales, vol. iii.

officials holding supreme power, to cripple and thwart their more capable agents on the spot. In this despatch, dated September 18, 1743, he was informed by the Directors that, in consequence of the approaching prospect of a war between France and England, they were compelled to restrict the number of vessels for India to four, two of which were destined for Pondichery, and two for Bengal; they then proceeded to press upon him, as the greatest and most important service he could render, (1) the reduction of all the expenses in India by at least one-half; and (2) the suspension of all expenditure on account of building and fortifications. To carry out this service, they added their belief, "that this operation cannot be intrusted to better hands than yours, whose wisdom and zeal are known. It is that which determines it"—the Company—"to charge you alone with the sole execution of this operation, free from consulting with the Council regarding it."*

The announcement in this despatch, that a war with their great European rivals in India and on the seas was impending, and the injunction which accompanied it to spend no money on the fortifications—the unsatisfactory condition of which was, nevertheless, known to the Company—must have sounded strange in the ears of Dupleix. Not only were the fortifications in bad order, but on the front facing the sea there was a space of a thousand toises—nearly a mile and a quarter—which was absolutely open. Regarding this in connexion with the intimation he had received of the prospect of an European war, in which the enemies of France might obtain the mastery of the Indian seas, he felt that his duty as Governor of Pondichery—a place for which he was responsible to his sovereign—was paramount to every other. The orders which he received he therefore boldly disregarded. He caused a

* Mémoire pour Dupleix.

solid rampart to be erected along the entire length of the open space, with a broad and deep ditch in its front. On this, night and day, workmen were employed; yet with all their vigilance, the rampart was not completed until nearly two years' after war with England had broken out, and it required the exercise of all the genius and talent of Dupleix to prevent an attack, by a powerful English squadron, on the unfinished defences. The expenses of this undertaking Dupleix supplied by his purse and by his credit. From the same sources he furnished cargoes to the two vessels which, in pursuance of the notification, came out to Pondichery, and which otherwise would have been forced to return empty. The other point, that of reducing the public expenditure, he carried out with a firm hand. The difficulty of his situation in this respect was enhanced by the fact that he alone was intrusted with the execution of the order; that he was thus not only deprived of the support of his Council, but its members might cast obstacles in the way of the carrying out of a requisition, in which they were so lightly treated. Abuses were put down, corruption was strangled, salaries were reduced, until, in spite of murmurs on all sides, which, however, were not directed against him personally, the necessary reductions were effected.*

These proceedings on the part of Dupleix were most agreeable to the Company. His very disobedience of their order, in repairing and completing the fortifications of Pondichery, seems to have met with their approval. No wonder, perhaps, considering that the expense of those repairs and of that completion had fallen upon himself! We find them writing to him a letter, dated November 21, 1744, regarding the provision of cargoes for the two ships they had sent out: "The Company, as you will see by this letter, has been very much pleased

* Mémoire pour Dupleix.

at the zeal which you and the Councils of Pondichery and Chandranagar have displayed for its interest in procuring cargoes for our two ships, the 'Fleury' and the 'Brillant,' sent from the Isle of France. As it is by your endeavours that this operation was completed, it is proper that you, especially, should enjoy the honour of it."

With respect to the fortifications, they wrote, under date November 30, 1746 : — "The promptitude with which the town of Pondichery has been enclosed on the side facing the sea, has given us real pleasure ; we are under a great obligation to you on that account"— for this disobedience of their orders! Further on— "we have not seen with less satisfaction all the measures you have taken, both to provide, notwithstanding your poverty, cargoes for the ships, the sailing of which we had announced to you, and to second M. de la Bourdonnais in the operations which he was planning."*

But before the receipt of this second letter war between France and England had been declared. This war had been long threatening. The death of the Emperor Charles VI. without male issue, had tempted France, Prussia, and Bavaria to combine to despoil his heroic daughter of the possessions she had inherited. In this war, the King of England, George II., soon found himself involved as Elector of Hanover. Without any declaration of war on the part of England, he had, in 1743, transported a combined army of English, Hanoverians, and Hessians into the valley of the Main, to co-operate with the Austrians. On the 27th June of the same year, when in danger of being compelled to surrender with his whole army to the French general, the Duc de Noailles, the mad impetuosity of the Duc de Gramont not only saved him from that calamity, but enabled him to gain a great victory before even the two nations were professedly at war. But this was too

* Mémoire pour Dupleix.

much for the endurance of France, and in the month of March, 1744, she formerly declared war against England.

It will thus be seen, that the event which now took place had been long expected, that the breaking out of war had been regarded as a mere question of time. We have seen how Dupleix prepared himself to meet those hostilities when they should come. We have now to regard him in a different aspect, to notice how earnestly and indefatigably he strove to ward them off altogether.

When the Directors of the Company of the Indies intimated to their Governor-General at Pondichery, that war with England was inevitable, they apprised him at the same time that they had instructed the Governor of the Isle of France, M. de la Bourdonnais, to proceed with a squadron to his assistance, but they especially urged upon him to endeavour to bring about a treaty of neutrality with the Governor of the English settlement, and to arrange with him that the commercial operations of both countries with India should continue without molestation from either. Those instructions found Dupleix in the very mood to comply with them, though very little hopeful of success in the negotiation. Of the movements of La Bourdonnais he had no positive knowledge. Even before the declaration of war, the English cruisers had spread themselves over the Indian seas, ready to carry devastation into French commerce.*
Yet from stray vessels, and from other sources, intimation had reached him that a squadron under Commodore Barnet was on its way out, especially charged with the entire destruction of the French settlement.

Nevertheless he made the attempt, earnestly, almost beseechingly. But Mr. Morse, the Governor of Madras, and his Council, had precisely the same reasons for

* The French commerce with the Indies had made great progress since the time of Lenoir. In 1740 the Company possessed forty large ships fitted for the Indian trade. Ten or twelve of these were sent every year to the Indies.—*Histoire des Indes.*

wishing for war, by which Dupleix was influenced in his desire for peace. The squadron under Commodore Barnet was, he well knew, in the Eastern seas, engaged in intercepting the French traders between China and Europe; it was shortly expected, with its prizes, at Madras; letters had been received some time previously, announcing its proximate arrival, and those letters contained the instructions for the annihilation of French commerce to which we have just alluded. To the urgent requisition of Dupleix, Mr. Morse pleaded therefore the orders he had received from England.†

Another disappointment awaited the French Governor. He had hoped that, should these negotiations fail, he might derive some assistance from the promised squadron of La Bourdonnais. But, just about the time that the unfavourable reply was received from Mr. Morse, intimation reached him that in obedience to instructions received from Paris, La Bourdonnais had sent back his squadron to France, and was apparently powerless to assist him. Ignorant, as he was then, of the undaunted energy and persistent resolution which so eminently characterised the Governor of the Isle of France, Dupleix felt himself at that moment absolutely cast upon his own resources. He had but himself to depend upon. With a garrison of 436 Europeans, the fortifications of Pondichery progressing, but not then finished, with but one small ship of war at his disposal, he had to meet the threatened attack of three men-of-war and a frigate, subsequently increased to six vessels of war, whose cannon alone, playing upon the unfinished rampart from the roadstead, could demolish the French town. Even the one vessel at his disposal he despatched to the Isle of France, with an urgent requisition to La Bourdonnais to come to his aid. This was a situation to test in the most searching manner the capacity of a man. Was it possible, under such circumstances, to escape the

† Dupleix, Orme, Cambridge.

threatened danger, and even to turn it to his own profit? It did not seem so certainly, yet Dupleix proved that it could be done. It was when the European enemy appeared most threatening, that the policy adopted from the commencement—the system inaugurated by Martin and carried on by his successors—the system of treating the natives of India as friends and as equals, bore its natural fruits. From the menaces of Mr. Morse, Dupleix appealed to the friendship of the successor of Sher Khán Lodi and of Dost Ali. The reply he received showed that the esteem, which the Nawwábs of the Karnátik had always professed to feel for the representative of the French nation, was no transient or fair-weather sentiment. Anwáru-dín Khán, the representative, though not the relative, of those chieftains, had inherited their traditions; he responded to the call made upon him with a fidelity to professions not always exercised in Europe, and Pondichery was saved. To render the account of subsequent events more clear and intelligible, it is necessary that we should state very briefly the principal events that had occurred in the Karnátik since we last left it.

The Karnátik suffering from the famine caused by the invasion of the Maráthás; Chanda Sahib a prisoner at Satárá; his brother-in-law, Nawwáb Safdar Ali, pressed by his feudal superior, the Subadar of the Dakhan, for arrears of revenue: such was the condition of the Karnátik in the middle of 1741. It was worse for the people than for the ruler. The people had been plundered and were starving. Safdar Ali, on the contrary, had had his treasures well guarded at Pondichery. Notwithstanding his professions, he had still abundance of wealth to pay up the arrears demanded by the Subadar. But he did not choose to pay them. The Subadar had not supported his demands by force, and Safdar Ali was resolved not to yield to a mere verbal request. He amused therefore the Suba-

CHAP. III.
1742.

dar with excuses, and, to be prepared for the worst, he took up his residence at Vellur, whilst he deposited his treasures in the custody of the English at Madras.* But a crisis was at hand. The assessment, which the stipulated payment to the Maráthás had compelled Safdar Ali to impose upon his nobility, had made him extremely unpopular, and had even caused a combination amongst some of his courtiers to resist it. The unsatisfactory nature of his relations with the Subadar had induced these conspirators to believe that his overthrow would not be regarded with disfavour in that quarter. Amongst those who had joined this conspiracy, was the other brother-in-law of Safdar Ali, Murtizá Ali by name, a man well known for his cowardice, his cruelty, his wealth, and his parsimony. On September 2, 1742, this man, taking advantage of the confidence inspired by the contempt which the Nawwáb felt for him, seized the opportunity of Safdar Ali being with but few attendants, first, to cause him to be poisoned, and, that proving ineffectual, to have him stabbed to death. He then proclaimed himself Nawwáb, and obtaining by artful representations possession of Vellur and acknowledgment from the troops, installed himself at Arkát. But the detestation of his crime combined with the contempt felt for his cowardice to make his tenure of office extremely brief. His principal officers appealed to Murári Ráo, Governor of Trichinápalli, and he declared war against him. The English were requested by the insurgent nobility to protect the family and treasure of Safdar Ali, whilst the army, the support of his power, suddenly made a tumultuous demand upon him for the payment of their

* Orme states that he transferred his confidence, in regard to the custody of his family and treasures, from the French to the English on the advice of his Prime Minister, Mir. Ásad, who suspected the connexion which existed between Chanda Sahib and M. Dupleix. This Ásad was, as has been already told, the bitter enemy of Chanda Sahib, and the author of all his calamities.

arrears. Murtizá Ali terrified at these demands, and not possessing spirit equal to his villainy, bent before the storm, and disguising himself in woman's clothes, fled in safety to the fort of Vellur. On his flight becoming known, the son of Safdar Ali, Sa'id Muhammad Khán, an infant who was with his mother at Madras, was at once proclaimed Nawwáb.

The appointment of an infant to this position did not tend to the tranquillity of the province. Every nobleman assumed an independent position. But, in the beginning of the following year, Nizamu-l-Mulk, the Subadar of the Dakhan, appeared upon the scene at the head of an army of 80,000, horse and 200,000 foot. He at once became the master of the situation. He put down upstart noblemen, threatening to scourge them, should they dare to assume the title of Nawwáb—a practice which had become common amongst them—and appointed one of his chief officers, Khoja Abdullah Khán, to administer the province. The Subadar then moved upon Trichinápalli, which the Maráthás evacuated without striking a blow in its defence. Having recovered this principality for the Mughal, he returned to Golkonda, taking Khoja Abdullah with him.

It had been intended by the Subadar that this officer should return to assume the regency of the Karnátik the following year, but on the very eve of starting, he was found dead in his bed. Anwáru-dín, known as a brave and experienced soldier, was appointed to succeed him as temporary governor and guardian to the son of Safdar Ali, until the latter should attain his majority.

But a few months, however, elapsed, before, at a wedding to which Murtizá Ali, the murderer of his father, had been invited, Sa'id Muhammad Khán was assassinated. In the confusion that followed Murtizá Ali took to his horse, and escorted by a body

CHAP. III.

1742.

1743.

of cavalry, escaped to Vellur. The immediate result was that Anwáru-dín, who was no relation of the old family, was appointed permanent Nawwáb of the Karnátik.

This was the man to whom, in the difficult circumstances in which he was placed, the Governor of Pondichery made his appeal. He reminded him of the longstanding frendship between his predecessors and the French nation; of the moral support and protection to the families of those predecessors given at the time of the Marátha invasion; he alluded to the conciliatory disposition always shown by the French; to their desire to be at peace with all around them; and he urged upon the Nawwáb to prevent, by his authority, the aggression of the other European nation occupying a portion of the seaboard of the Karnátik, upon those who had always been friends to his predecessors, and whose Governor was himself a high officer of the Mughal.

Anwáru-dín was not insensible to the force and reason of this appeal. Neither of the European powers on the Koromandel coast had shown up to that point any aggressive tendencies, nor had then the superiority of the European soldier in the field been demonstrated in any way. It was natural that he should desire to maintain peace in his jurisdiction and its dependencies, and it is very probable—indeed, subsequent events proved—that he was not at all insensible to the marks of friendship and cordiality which the rulers of Pondichery had always evinced. He therefore sent a pressing message to the Governor of Madras, informing him that he would not permit any attack on the possessions of the French on the Koromandel coast. The despotic character of this resolution he endeavoured to soften by a show of fairness; for he informed Mr. Morse, at the same time, that should hereafter the French power preponderate, he would use the same authority to prevent any aggressive action on their part. Mr. Morse had no course but compliance.

But though he was thus saved from immediate attack, the situation of Dupleix was still particularly trying. The English squadron had come round to the coast, had even received reinforcements, and the vessels of which it was composed, cruising about, did their best to intercept and destroy the French merchantmen. The Company of the Indies, even before the outbreak of the war, had ceased to send any ships to Pondichery, so that Dupleix was dependent for his information on stray arrivals. Still, amid the doubt and despondency that surrounded him, he maintained a bold and resolute bearing. Though within all was anxiety, without, there was the security of apparent composure. He was, however, immensely relieved, when, in the month of May, 1746, he learned from a sure source, that the long-announced and long-despaired of squadron of M. de la Bourdonnais had been heard of at Mahé.

La Bourdonnais was last introduced in these pages as the skilful and enterprising officer who had devised the means by which Mahé—so named, it will be remembered, after himself—had been captured in 1725. We shall now briefly relate the course of his life during the nineteen years that had elapsed since that first brilliant essay of arms in India. Reduced by the peace, to which France at that period seemed disposed, to inactivity, La Bourdonnais, after the capture of Mahé, fitted out a ship on his own account, and traded for three or four years in the Arabian seas. The ascendency which he here speedily assumed over all with whom he came into contact, and which especially signalised itself on the occasion of a disturbance, that he succeeded in quelling, between some Portuguese and Arab sailors, in the harbour of Mocha, recommended him to the Governor of Goa, and induced that Viceroy to offer him the command of a ship of war under the King of

108 THE RISE OF THE FRENCH POWER IN INDIA.

CHAP. III.
1746.

Portugal—an appointment carrying with it several orders and titles. La Bourdonnais accepted the offer, and made an expedition to Mozambique, and several cruises in the Indian seas. But the situation of a foreigner in the service of another country can never be wholly satisfactory, and at the end of two years La Bourdonnais found that the annoyances to which he was constantly subjected were not compensated by either the pleasure or profit of his command. He therefore threw it up and returned in 1733 to France. There he married, and, in 1735, he was appointed to succeed M. Dumas as Governor of the Isles of France and Bourbon.

1710.

To understand all that La Bourdonnais accomplished in his new position, it is necessary that we should refer to the connexion of the French with those islands from the time of their earliest occupation. We have already* given a brief sketch of their history from their first discovery by the Portuguese to the occupation of Bourbon by a small number of the baffled colonists of Madagascar in 1672, and the settlement in the Isle of France at some period between 1710 and 1719. It is probable, that the remnants of the Madagascar colonists, never much caring for labour on its own account, would, had they been able, have taken an early opportunity of leaving an island, in which they seemed entirely cut off from association with the outer world. But they had escaped—a mixed crew of men and women—the latter, it is stated, being natives—in two canoes, and they had no means of proceeding in any direction. They betook themselves therefore perforce to the erection of huts, and to the cultivation of articles of food. Fortunately the nature of the soil was such that a very small expenditure of labour was sufficient to enable them to live in abundance. Soon after, their numbers were increased by the wreck upon their coast of a piratical

* Chapter I.

craft,* on board of which were many female prisoners. By degrees too they were joined by deserters from East Indian ships which touched there. These were for the most part attracted by the easy life which the fertility of the soil enabled its inhabitants to enjoy. The prosperity of the island increased in a greater degree than could be imagined, if the elements of which its society was formed were alone considered. Houses were erected, small trading vessels were built, many of them for piratical purposes, slaves were purchased, and articles fit for export were cultivated. So glowing indeed were the accounts of this prosperity taken home to France, by ships which touched at the island, that towards the close of the seventeenth or the beginning of the eighteenth century, the French Company put in their claim to its possession, and sent thither five or six families and a Governor.† The Governor was well received at first, but the descendants of the pirates and deserters soon found him an inconvenient incumbrance. They accordingly seized and imprisoned him, and kept him in a dungeon till he died. Their rebellion had no other result. A new Governor was sent with orders to punish the ringleaders, and to erect a fort for his protection—orders which he is stated to have carried out effectually.

In 1717, the population of the island was computed at two thousand nine hundred free men, and eleven hundred slaves. In the following year an event occurred

---

* It is stated that amongst other additions from various sources, the early inhabitants of Bourbon "received an increase by some English pirates, who came along with Avery, England, Condon, and Pattison, who, after acquiring considerable riches in the Red Sea and coasts of Arabia and Persia, quitting their way of life, settled on the island, and had a pardon from the King of France. Some of them were alive in 1763, and their descendants are numerous on the island."—*Dalrymple's Oriental Repertory*, vol ii.

† It would appear, however, from the *Calendrier des Isles de France et de Bourbon* that the inhabitants had had a regular succession of governors of their own since the formation of the settlement. Thus, it is recorded that "in 1675, Père Hiacinthe, Capuchin, arrived there in the quality of *Curé*, and took upon himself the right of Governor."

which gave an impetus to its trade, and which assured its future prosperity. This was the introduction of the cultivation of coffee, which thenceforth became the staple trade of the island. Two years prior to this, possession had been taken of the deserted Isle of France, although no earnest attempt at colonisation was made before 1721. An edict, dated November of that year, however, decreed the erection of a Provincial Council in that island dependent upon that of Bourbon, and in 1723, M. Dumas was appointed Governor of both islands. Great inducements were at the same time held out to the inhabitants of Bourbon to emigrate into the larger island. For this purpose grants of land were made to settlers, and sums proportionate to each grant were advanced to each settler by the Company. Yet for several years, it seemed as though the colonisation of the Isle of France was likely to be unprofitable, and its abandonment was constantly threatened. The colonists had been unable at the expiration of twelve years to set on foot a trade sufficient even to enable them to repay the sums that had been advanced them by the Company. But, in the crisis of the hesitation as to the line of action to be adopted, La Bourdonnais arrived in France. The fame of his skill, his energy, his indomitable resolution, had preceded him, and the Directors resolved to give one more chance to the new colony, by appointing as Governor of the Isles of France and Bourbon, one who had given so many proofs of the possession of great qualities.

La Bourdonnais went there. He found in Bourbon a fertile soil, a healthy air, and, comparatively, a settled community, He found the greater part of the Isle of France, on the other hand, still covered with almost impenetrable forests; possessing two harbours, one of which at all events, up to that moment unimproved and scarcely safe, might, with a little labour, be made excellent for all purposes; a soil less fertile indeed than that of Bourbon, but still capable of production; and a climate, mild, temperate, and healthy. The fact that it possessed a harbour gave to the Isle of France a great superiority in the eyes of La Bourdonnais over Bourbon, and he at once made it the seat of government.

But the people! Had La Bourdonnais been less of a real man than he was, he might well have been appalled at the task of making anything of a race to whom toil of any sort seemed the worst species of evil. Almost naked, defenceless, and starving, having preferred to be comfortless and miserable rather than to exercise even the small amount of labour which in such a clime would have amply supplied their necessities; dwelling in wretched cabins; possessing no energy, living in fear of their lives from the attacks of the Maroons—the free descendants of the slaves who had been kidnapped from Madagascar, and who had found refuge in the interior—endowed apparently merely with the animal love of existence—these so-called colonists were yet capable of combining to resist any lawful authority over them. But La Bourdonnais was not a man to be baffled. He taught them, in a hundred of instances, that he was resolved to be master. And yet, in doing this, he showed such tact, he was so gentle while so determined, his measures were so wise, and the benefits resulting from them so evident to all, that he forced these colonists, even whilst murmuring against him, to admit in their reasonable moods, that he was the wisest, gentlest, and best of governors, the only man who could have induced them to forego their old habits of indolence and sloth.

By his own personal teaching—whether as regarded the merest rudiments or the higher requirements of agriculture—the first principles of mechanical labour or the acquirements of the skilled artisan; by constantly impressing on the minds of these people the absolute necessity under which they lay to work, he succeeded before long in forming out of this unpromising raw material a civilised community. Under his influence, some took to planting, some to manufacturing, others to soldiering. La Bourdonnais assisted them in various ways. He imported negroes from Madagascar, and employed these as policemen, as cultivators, and as artisans. In a short time the island assumed a new appearance. In place of the uncultivated waste of the interior, and the wretched hovels scattered along the coast, he caused to be built substantial private dwelling houses, magazines, arsenals, barracks, fortifications, mills, quays, canals, and aqueducts. Of these last, one in particular is mentioned, built for the purpose of bringing down fresh water to the port and to the hospitals, as having been 3,600 toises (more than four miles and a quarter) in length. But his greatest efforts were directed to the sea-coast. There were, we have seen, two harbours, one on the south-east side of the island, open to the prevailing winds, the other on the noth-west side, sheltered from the wind, but only to be entered through a narrow channel. On this he bestowed all his efforts, and he very soon made it fit in every respect for the reception of thirty-five or forty ships. He provided it likewise with wet and dry docks, pontoons, canoes, yards, and timber. It became thus as easy to lay up and repair ships at Port Louis, for so he named the capital, as in any port in Europe. In 1737, eighteen months after his arrival, he was able to launch a brigantine; the following year, he built two good ships,* and put another of five hundred tons on the stocks. This, however, was but a portion of what he effected in that respect during his viceroyalty.

---

* As might have been expected, the first attempt at shipbuilding was not altogether a success. It is related of his first ship, that "after a great deal of trouble, time, and expense in building, she was found so heavy in launching, that they were obliged to haul her ashore again, and rip off a great deal of timber and put other in her place before she was fit for sea." This vessel, the "Insulaire," was lost in 1746, in the Ganges, on her way to Chandranagar after the action with Commodore Peyton.

His internal administration was equally energetic and judicious. He took very good care that the negroes were not unduly oppressed by the colonists. He compelled the landowners to lay out tapioca plantations, five hundred yards square, for each negro and family serving under them. He encouraged the cultivation of sugar, soon to become a great success, prevented the indiscriminate slaughter of cattle, and, until the breed should revive, he forced the ships' crews to live upon fish and turtle during their stay in port.*

Nor was he less successful in Bourbon, though that island, at the time of his arrival, was further advanced in civilisation than the other. His principal object was to administer the two islands, so that they should be valuable to France, and to make them fit to be the commercial station between France and India. To this end, it was necessary that they should be fortified. Though the means were apparently wanting, La Bourdonnais commenced the work, and in less than five years he succeeded in providing them with such fortifications as would have rendered an attack upon them by a small force extremely hazardous.

In 1740, La Bourdonnais returned to France. On his arrival there he learnt that complaints preceded him. Cardinal Fleury was then still Minister. A timid economist, with little breadth of view, Fleury had but one principle of external policy. This was the maintenance of peace, especially of peace with England, at any price. It was partly from a fear of giving umbrage to England, partly from his economic habits, that he starved the French navy, neglected the army, and gave no encouragement to commerce. Such a man could have little sympathy with a genius so fertile, an energy so buoyant, a desire to advance French interests so irrepressible, as were bound together in the person of La Bourdonnais. When therefore some of those

* Mémoire pour La Bourdonnais.—*Raynal's India.*

repressed speculators, and baffled ship-captains, whose gains and depredations had been lessened by the measures of La Bourdonnais, presented to the Minister and to the Directors of the Company a long list of their grievances, accompanied by insinuations common to their class, that La Bourdonnais was working mainly for his own interests, the narrow mind of the Cardinal did not repel the charges, and, worked upon at the same time by the Directors, he began to concert with them measures for his disgrace. It was partly the intimation of this, and the consequent desire to justify himself, that had brought La Bourdonnais from the scene of his labours.

Though narrow-minded to a degree, Fleury was not intentionally unjust. He received the great colonist with marked disfavour at the outset, but he did not remain long proof against the candour and frankness which characterised alike his demeanour and his statements. La Bourdonnais in fact insisted upon being informed of all that had been said against him, and, this done, he had little difficulty, not only in justifying his conduct, but in convincing the Minister and the Directors of the great value of the measures he had accomplished. The personal charges against him dissolved into air. He showed, in the course of his justifications, that he had never possessed a foot of land in the islands; that he had never traded for a single *livre;* and that so great had been the confidence of the colonists in his impartiality, that all the differences in the islands had been terminated by his arbitration, without recourse having been had, except in one solitary instance, to a lawsuit.

Released from the charges against him, and reinstated in the confidence of his masters, the fertile mind of La Bourdonnais began at once to revolve fresh schemes. At that time (1740-41), hostilities between France and England seemed imminent. The two nations had taken opposite sides in the war of the Austrian succession, and it was evident that not all the devices of Fleury would be able much longer to keep back a declaration of war. Under these circumstances, La Bourdonnais foreseeing that that nation which, on the breaking out of the war, should have an overwhelming superiority of force to the other in the Indian seas, would be able to crush its rival, advised that he should be allowed to equip and fit out a squadron of six or eight ships as vessels of war. With these he proposed to sail to the Isle of France, there to await the breaking out of hostilities. On that event occurring, he would be able, he said, to intercept and capture the English merchantmen, and then, steering to India, ruin the English settlements in that country.

This plan, practical, easy of execution, and, under an unfettered La Bourdonnais, certain of success, was nevertheless too grand in its grasp to commend itself to the timid and cautious policy of the Directors of the Company of the Indies. These therefore declared against it at once. But Fleury, timid as he was, had too much of the statesman in his composition, not to perceive the immense advantages that might accrue from its successful operation. La Bourdonnais too was on the spot, and La Bourdonnais was careful to point out to him, amongst other arguments, that his consent to the plan did not commit him to any overt act of hostility against England, that the squadron would patiently await in the harbour of Port Louis the first declaration of war. Fleury, convinced by these and similar arguments, gave in to the plan, merely altering some of the details; the opposition of the Directors he for the time silenced.

The alteration in the details of the scheme, as originally proposed, consisted in the idea of substituting at least two ships of the French navy for those which La Bourdonnais was to fit out. But, in France, in the reign of Louis XV., action seldom followed counsel. When the time came for the squadron to sail, the two King's ships, with which so much might have been effected, were

CHAP. III.
1741.

diverted to some unimportant purpose, and La Bourdonnais found himself reduced to the command of five vessels belonging to the Company. But these would have been sufficient for his purpose, had he been allowed to pursue that purpose to its end. They carried a considerable armament,* and they had on board 1,200 sailors and 500 soldiers. Yet even amongst these, he had difficulties to contend with. But few of the sailors had ever been at sea, and the soldiers had been but little instructed in military exercises. With both these classes, La Bourdonnais pursued the course he had found so successful with the colonists of the Isle of France. He taught them what their duties were, and he set them himself the best example of doing them. To train them to the various labours likely to devolve upon them, was his constant and unremitting business on the voyage; and to such an extent did he succeed, that the ships which left France on the 5th April, 1741, manned by landsmen as sailors, and carrying recruits for soldiers, arrived at the Isle of France on August 14th following, with crews as efficient as those which manned the King's navy, and soldiers as well trained in all their musketry exercises as those who fought at Fontenoy.

It was the sad fate of those heroic men who struggled to establish a French Empire in India, to find their chiefest and most redoubtable enemies in France itself. The genius of Clive, the persistent valour of Coote, and the almost forgotten gallantry of Forde,† might have struggled in vain to overturn a settlement which was based on the solid foundations on which the early rulers of Pondichery had begun to build up a French India, had France herself been true to her struggling children. But the France of Louis XV. more resembled the Medea of the ancient story than the tender and watchful mother.

---

* These ships were the "Fleury" of 56 guns, the "Brillant" and "Aimable" of 50 each, the "Rénommée" of 28, and the "Parfaite," of 16.

† Vide the "Decisive Battles of India."

Often did she, "with her own hands, immolate her offspring," and, failing this, she treated the best and bravest of her sons rather as enemies to be thwarted, baffled, persecuted, and driven to despair, than as men who were devoting all their energies, the every thought of their lives, to increase her dominions. In the course of this history it will be seen how opportunity after opportunity was missed; how the Indian interests were persistently neglected; when a well-timed effort would have secured the empire for which the sons of France on the spot were gallantly struggling.

And it was now that France betrayed her champion. She betrayed the man, who, but for the acts of the rulers of France, would have enjoyed the best opportunity of effectively establishing a French Empire in India, of rooting out every rival. La Bourdonnais had scarcely set sail, when those infamous intriguers and whisperers —the certain hangers-on of corrupt Governments—began to uplift the voices which in his presence had remained mute. Amongst the Directors, the cry was raised that this expensive armament was useless for the purposes of France; that it was intended to minister to the ambition of its promoter. They declared that a policy of neutrality in the Indian seas was the only sound policy, and they expressed a conviction that, in case of war, the English would be glad to accede to such an arrangement. From the Directors the cry rose to the Ministry. The weak Fleury, then ninety years old, and no longer under the influence of the spell of La Bourdonnais' presence, after a short struggle, gave way to the clamour. In an evil hour for France and for French India, this dispenser under Louis XV. of the fortunes of his country transmitted orders to La Bourdonnais to send back his ships to France, "even though they should have to sail without cargoes."*

Meanwhile, La Bourdonnais, unsuspicious of back-

* Mémoire pour La Bourdonnais.

CHAP. III.
1741.

stairs influence, had, as we have seen, arrived at the Isle of France. The intelligence which awaited him there, was of a nature to stimulate all his energies. He received the news, which had some short time before arrived, of the danger which threatened Pondichery from the anticipated attack of Raghují Bhonsla, and further that the authorities of the islands, obeying an urgent requisition from M. Dumas, had despatched their garrisons to India. Impressed with the necessity of saving Pondichery at all costs, La Bourdonnais remained only a week at the Isle of France, and sailed then for Pondichery. Arriving there on September 30, he found that the tact and skill of M. Dumas had warded off the danger from that settlement, but that Mahé was still beleaguered. Thither, accordingly, to the scene of his early Indian triumphs, he sailed, and arriving there speedily re-established French ascendancy. There being nothing more for him to accomplish in India, he sailed back to the Isle of France to carry out the scheme he had concerted with Fleury. It was on his return thither that he experienced the bitter pang which those alone can feel who, prompted in their actions by noble and generous sentiments, find themselves restrained and held back by men of inferior powers. Then for the first time the order reached him to send back his ships to Europe. He knew the full significance of that order; he felt that it was to give up, for the coming war, at all events, all hope of French preponderance in India; he felt that it would leave him a powerless spectator of the triumphs of the English—disarmed and defenceless, perhaps even a prey to their attacks; he felt that it destroyed the hope of his life, the object of all his toil, the certain accomplishment, but for that, of his legitimate ambition. But what was he to do? The order was imperative. He must obey it. With a pang, the bitterness of which few men can have experienced, and which must have been enhanced afterwards by the prompt realisation of all his anticipations, he sent back the fleet. With it, however, he sent his own resignation, with an earnest prayer that he might be speedily relieved.

Why did he obey? Surely it was not his fault that he did obey. But what cruel destiny was it that was weighing down the fortunes of France? A few favouring gales, a swift-sailing ship, an energetic captain, and the fate of India might have been changed! Scarcely had the first keenness of the disappointment caused by the departure of the fleet been obliterated in the energetic action which now found a vent in the care of the colony, when there arrived at Port Louis a French ship conveying a despatch from the Controller of the Finances and Minister of State, M. Philibert Orry, authorising La Bourdonnais to retain the fleet, and expressing a hope that he had disobeyed his previous instructions. Cardinal Fleury, in fact, was dying, Orry was virtual Minister, and taking in at once the great importance of La Bourdonnais' schemes, he had sent out this ship and these instructions. Too late, alas! for La Bourdonnais' hopes. The ships had gone, and there was no possibility of recalling them.

It is difficult to imagine the aggravation of disappointment which this message from the new Minister must have caused. How many it would have utterly crushed! How many it would have driven to despair! But La Bourdonnais was made of a very hard material. He was not proof against all the attacks of fortune, for he, too, as we shall have occasion to describe, had his weak side; but this disappointment neither crushed him nor stopped his action. Learning a little later that the Minister and Directors refused to accept his resignation, he calmly resumed his duties as Governor of the islands, and began at once to make preparations for a possible future.

The French Ministry refused to accept the resignation

of La Bourdonnais, but they did not immediately send back the ships. They informed him that he possessed all their confidence, and that it was to him they looked to take the supreme post in India in case of any accident happening to Dupleix. Meanwhile, Cardinal Fleury had died (January 29, 1743), war had been declared between France and England, and La Bourdonnais saw with pain the great rivals of his nation reaping the field which he had sown to gather.* That English fleet, under Commodore Barnet, of which we have already spoken, had come to cruise in the Indian seas, and French merchantmen were picked up in every direction. La Bourdonnais could do nothing to hinder their depredations. As if to add to his perplexities, he, at this time, when utterly powerless himself, received a pressing message from Dupleix, with whom he had been some time in correspondence, begging him to hasten, with all the force at his disposal, to the defence of Pondichery.

Then was seen, in full perfection, an example of the truth of the maxim that great difficulties are nothing more than obstacles which a real man may overcome. It would seem impossible that this man, left destitute himself, should have been able to carry assistance to a countryman in distress. But no axiom is more true than this, that nothing is impossible to a brave man— brave, we mean, not in the narrow view of personal courage, but in its widest and its broadest sense; brave to bear the reproach, the obloquy, the hatred, the discontent, of his fellow-men; brave to disregard the studied neglect, the insolent glance, the open attacks, of men whom accident has placed higher than himself in the social scale; brave still, despite of all, to go on straight to the end he has marked out to himself,

---

* "We are now executing against you," said Commodore Barnet to the captain of a French merchantman he had taken, "that which M. de la Bourdonnais had projected against us."

despite of jeers and taunts, of open opposition, and secret calumny. It was in that sense that La Bourdonnais was brave, and being thus brave, he conquered the impossible.

What was the impossible? Without ships, without sailors, without an army, the Indian Ocean covered by hostile cruisers, with no resources but those which he had made in the colony, he was asked to embark an army, to traverse the Indian Ocean, to avoid or encounter the trained fleet of the enemy, and to relieve the beleaguered capital of French India. Could he stamp upon the ground and bring into existence the men, the guns, the material, the ships, that he had not? Did it not seem a very impossibility? Yet, undeterred by this seeming, La Bourdonnais set to work calmly, patiently, steadfastly, to accomplish the undertaking.

To succeed in such an attempt it was especially necessary to greatly dare; to throw to the winds all dread of responsibility; to use to the utmost extent the powers at his disposal. La Bourdonnais thus acted. Every ship—and some, despite the English cruisers, did arrive—that touched at Port Louis, likely to be suitable for his purpose, he detained. The objections of the captains and of others interested in the vessels he peremptorily silenced. It was unfortunate that, in addition to other difficulties, the islands, owing to an unwonted scarcity caused by a total failure of the crops, were unable to supply sufficient food for the crews; equally so that a vessel laden with provisions from Europe, the "Saint Géran," had gone down at the very entrance of the harbour. Such was the scarcity, that the inhabitants of the islands were restricted by an order of the local council to daily rations of one pound of bread or rice for every European and freeman, and a pound and a half of rice for each negro. The necessary requirements for the equipment of the ships, carpenters and smiths and tailors to work upon them, sailors sufficient to man them, and soldiers to be conveyed by them, were alike wanting. But La Bourdonnais determined to make what he had not. He himself, carpenter, engineer, tailor, and smith, constructed with his own hands the model of all the articles that were required. Under his own personal superintendence, some men were trained to act as tailors, to cut out and prepare sails; others, as carpenters, busied themselves with gun-carriages, and fitted the vessels to receive them. Some were set to work to prepare materials for building ships, others to put together those materials. Then, again, the sailors were trained to work together, to serve the guns, to scale walls, to fire at a mark, to use the grappling hook. Finding their number insufficient, he recruited from the negroes, and formed the whole into mixed companies. Working in this way, he soon found himself at the head of a body of men, well taught and well disciplined, and ready to undertake any enterprise he might assign to them.

Nor was he less painstaking and energetic regarding the supply of provisions. He had already detained and had begun to equip five vessels, including the twenty-six gunship which had brought him the pressing requisition from Dupleix, when he received intelligence from France that a squadron of five ships had started from L'Orient, and would be with him in October of that year (1745). The arrival of this squadron would cause a double strain upon his slender stock of provisions. He therefore arranged that, so soon as a ship should be equipped, she should sail at once for the coast of Madagascar, and there lay in supplies of rice and other articles of food that might be procurable. In this way he managed to over-ride that which otherwise would have been an insurmountable difficulty.

The squadron, promised in October, 1745, arrived in January of the following year. It consisted of one ship of war of seventy guns, the "Achille," and of four unarmed merchantmen.* To arm and equip these latter, and to reconcile their officers to the displacement of their several cargoes,† tasked all his resources. However, he succeeded. The armament consisted almost entirely of eight and twelve pounders, a calibre insignificant when compared with that of the guns ordinarily found, even in those days, on board a man-of-war. Even of these he had an insufficient number, and almost all his improvised fighting ships were pierced for a greater number of guns than they actually carried. However, one by one, partially equipped as they were, they left the island for the rendezvous at Madagascar. When all had taken their departure, he himself, brimful of bright hopes and enthusiasm, set sail to join them.‡

This was on March 24. Scarcely, however, had he sighted his squadron, when one of those tempests which periodically sweep over the Indian Ocean burst upon him. His ships were driven from their anchoring ground, and for three days were tossed about by the storm. One of them foundered;§ the admiral's ship, the "Achille," lost her three masts, and many of the others suffered equally. At last, however, they found a safe refuge in the Bay of Antongil, on the north-eastern coast of Madagascar. In this bay, laying off a

---

* La Bourdonnais' expression regarding these vessels runs as follows: "It is proper to observe regarding these vessels that they were very badly off for crews. The 'Achille' alone was fitted out as a ship of war. The others were no more armed than simple merchant ships."—*Mémoire.*

† The armament of these vessels necessitated the landing of all the merchandise with which they were laden, to the great loss of the owners.

‡ We subjoin a list of the names of the vessels forming the squadron and their respective armaments. The "Achille" of 70 guns; the "Bourbon" pierced for 42, carrying 34 guns; the "Phenix," pierced for 44, carrying 38 guns; the "Neptune," pierced for 36, carrying 30 guns; the "Saint Louis," pierced for 36, carrying 26 guns; the "Lys," pierced for 36, carrying 24 guns; the "Duc d'Orléans," pierced for 36, carrying 24 guns; the "Rénommée" pierced for 28, carrying 24 guns; and the "Insulaire" of 30, carrying 20 guns. —*Mémoire pour La Bourdonnais.*

§ The "Neptune des Indes," of 34 guns, not included in the above list.

desert island within it, the work of refitting was undertaken. Perhaps never was such a work begun under so many accumulated disadvantages. The island was marshy and insalubrious; the periodical rains had begun; the ships had suffered fearfully, and their crews were knocked up by fatigue. There was no landing-place; the forest whence wood was to be procured was on the mainland, upward of two miles distant; between it and the shore was a marsh three miles in circumference; a winding river, with sufficient water to render the frequent crossing it wearisome, but not sufficient to float the logs down to the sea; and, even when in the sea, they were yet three miles from the shipping. But these difficulties, great as they were, were all overcome. He built a quay of the stone which the island produced, he erected workshops for the construction of masts, ropes, and other appliances; he threw a road across the marsh; he caused the logs to be dragged along the bed of the river, and constructing rude canoes, he launched them at its mouth, and by their aid paddled the logs to the side of the disabled vessels. To choose these logs, he penetrated into the pestilential forests, in order that he might be sure that he had the advantage of the best species of wood procurable. His example stimulated the whole fleet. Those who, at first, had been inclined to show discontent, could not long resist his magic influence. But a short time elapsed before all worked with an energy of which before they had scarcely seemed capable. At the end of forty-eight days they had repaired every damage, though at a loss, from climate and exposure, of ninety-five Europeons and thirty-three negroes. The fleet, however, was saved, and was once more ready to sail for the long-wished-for goal.*

At length, on June 1, it started. It consisted now of but nine ships. Besides the "Achille" of seventy

---

* Mémoire pour La Bourdonnais.

ENCOUNTERS THE ENGLISH FLEET.

guns, one vessel carried thirty-eight guns, one thirty-four guns, one thirty guns, one twenty-six, three twenty-four, and one twenty guns. He had on board 3,342 men, of whom nearly one-fourth were Africans. Sailing with a fair wind, constantly exercising and encouraging his crews, La Bourdonnais arrived off Mahé at the end of the month. Here he learned that the English fleet had been last heard of off Nágápatan, below Kárikál; that though inferior in the number of ships, and slightly inferior in the number of crews, it was much superior in weight of metal, being armed with 24-pounders, and that it was waiting at Nágápatan to intercept him. Summoning his captains on board his ship, La Bourdonnais at once held a council of war. He was resolved to fight, but he wished first to test the temper of his subordinates. To his delight he found in them an eagerness almost equal to his own, a desire to gain, if possible, the empire of India on the sea. His mind entirely at ease on this point, he altered his course, and a few days later arrived off Trinkámalí.

It is time now that we should turn to the proceedings of the English fleet. We left Commodore Barnet, prevented by the interdiction of the Nawwáb Anwáru-dín from attacking Pondichery, reduced to the necessity of confining his operations to sea. Taking up a position at Mergui, near the entrance of the Malacca Straits, he had employed himself industriously in intercepting French traders, and in effectively stopping French commerce. Hearing some rumours in the early part of 1746 of the intended expedition of La Bourdonnais, he had returned to the Koromandel coast, and anchored off Fort St. David. Here in the month of April he died, and the command of the squadron devolved upon Commodore Peyton.

This squadron consisted of one ship of sixty guns, three of fifty, one of forty, and one of twenty guns, six ships in all.* But they carried mostly 24-pounders, and were armed with their full complement of guns. A daring commander would have been able, with such a force, to cause terrible destruction amongst the lightly-armed vessels of La Bourdonnais.

Intelligence had been conveyed to Commodore Peyton of the appearance of a French fleet off Ceylon, and he was cruising off Nágápatan to intercept it. Early on the morning of July 6 it was descried. The discovery was made about the same time on board the French vessels, and the hostile squadrons began at once to manœuvre, the English to preserve the advantage of the wind, the French to gain it. La Bourdonnais, knowing his inferiority in weight of metal, and his superiority in men, had felt that his only chance of success lay in a hand-to-hand encounter, and his great object was to board. But the skill of Commodore Peyton, who divined his enemy's object, defeated this intention, and at half-past four o'clock in the afternoon that officer had gained a position which enabled him to open fire at a safe distance on the French.

This distance was all in favour of the English. With their 24-pounders they inflicted great damage on the French ships, which these latter, with their 8 and 12-pounders and musketry, were very partially able to repay. Three of their ships were disabled at the beginning of the action—one, indeed, completely dismasted —and had not La Bourdonnais, coming up with the "Achille," the only ship of his squadron that carried its proper complement of heavy guns, drawn upon himself for half an hour the whole fire of the English, the squadron could not have escaped defeat. As it was,

---

* Subjoined are the names of the vessels and their commanders:—The "Medway," Commodore Peyton, 60 guns; the "Preston," Captain Lord Northesk, 50 guns; the "Harwich," Captain Carteret, 50 guns; the "Winchester," Captain Lord T. Bertie, 50 guns; the "Medway's Prize," Captain Griffith, 40 guns; the "Lively," Captain Stevens, 20 guns. The total number of the crews amounted 1,660 men.—*Grose's East Indies.*

night separated the combatants before a decisive advantage had been gained on either side.

Day broke showing the French squadron formed in line, the advantage of the wind still being, as on the previous day, with the English. It rested with the latter, therefore, whether the contest should be renewed. There were very many weighty reasons in favour of prompt and vigorous action. The English had had but sixty men killed and wounded* the previous day, and one only of their ships had received any considerable damage from the enemy's fire; they were all ships of war; eight of the French ships were but imperfectly and lightly armed; the English fleet had been stationed off Nágápatan to obstruct the advance of the French fleet; to abandon the field, therefore, was to leave Madras a prey to the enemy.

But in 1746 the English were not accustomed to regard the empire of the seas as their own. Some of those on board that squadron might, perchance, have recollected the time when the English channel had been scoured for weeks, unopposed, by the victorious fleet of de Tourville—the English fleet having sought refuge in the Thames.† Certain it is, that Commodore Peyton acted as English commodores of the time of the revolutionary war never would have thought of acting. Because one of his ships was leaky he deemed the attack too hazardous to be made. A council of war having confirmed this view, he made sail to the south, bound for Trinkámalí, leaving the way open to Pondichery—deserting that Madras which he had been sent to protect.

If ‡ La Bourdonnais was relieved by the departure of

---

* The English lost fourteen men killed and forty-six wounded; the French, twenty-seven killed and fifty-three wounded.

† After the battle off Beachy Head, June 30, 1690.

‡ La Bourdonnais states in his memoirs that it was with extreme regret he saw the English escape him. He adds, that being without provisions, and having on board a great number of sick and wounded,

his enemy, he did not show it. On the contrary, he made an appearance of pursuing the English. But it was only an appearance. He must, in reality, have been greatly relieved by their sheering off. He had expended a great portion of his ammunition, he had provisions but for twenty-four hours longer. The disappearance of the English left him free to accomplish his object. His dismasted ship, the "Insulaire," he ordered to Bengal to be repaired; then, quickly collecting the remainder of his squadron, he resumed almost immediately his northerly course, and on the following evening cast anchor in the Pondichery roads.

One portion of his seemingly impossible task had thus been accomplished. Pondichery was safe, the French fleet mistress of the Indian seas, Madras uncovered. The positions of the contending rivals had been exactly reversed. It would now be for the French to threaten, for the English to sue for neutrality. What will be the result? Will the Nawwáb of the Karnátik, standing neutral between the contending parties, extend to the English the same protection he had accorded to their rivals? If not, it would seem as though their case were almost desperate. Abandoned by their fleet, with but three hundred Europeans within its walls, Madras presented far fewer means of defence than Pondichery. Governor Morse, too, was neither a Dumas nor a Dupleix. On the other hand, the French had at their head two masters, both men of genius, of energy, of ambition; the one a master in council, an adept at statecraft, skilled in all the wiles of a subtle policy, but himself unacquainted with war and its

---

he was constrained to renounce their pursuit. In his letter to Dupleix, however, he says nothing about the disappearance of the English, but writes thus:—"The fear of missing Pondichery, the large amount of money for you on board, and, more than that, the scarcity of food, of which many ships had only four and twenty hours' supply, made me contemplate the frightful situation in which I should be, if I were to fall to the leeward of the place: this determined me to bear up for Pondichery."

details; the other, a man great in action and prompt in council, accustomed to command, accustomed to see his will obeyed, to bear down every obstacle; but whether equally fitted to carry out the will of another, as yet unproved. The uncertainty in this respect formed the only cloud in the horizon of the fortunes of French India. Would the active genius, who had "conquered the impossible," who, by the sheer force of his will had created the soldiers and the sailors, the ships and the guns, wherewith he has relieved Pondichery, would he now subordinate that will to the will of another man, his superior in position, but whom he has yet only heard of as a successful trader? Up to the moment of casting anchor at Pondichery not a shadow of a contest had arisen. Hitherto each had acted independently of the other. The communications between the two Governors had been most friendly. "The honour of success," wrote Dupleix in the early part of the year, "will be yours, and I shall hold myself lucky in contributing thereto through means that owe their value entirely to your skill." "We ought," wrote La Bourdonnais on his side, "to regard one another as equally interested in the progress of events, and to work in concert. For my part, Sir, I devote myself to you beforehand, and I swear to you a perfect confidence." But circumstances had altered. Success had now been attained; the two men were about, for the first time, to come in contact. Which of them was to take the lead? It was in the chance of some disagreement between those strong natures, both conscious of the possession of genius, both accustomed to command, that lay the best chance of Governor Morse and Madras.

CHAPTER IV.

LA BOURDONNAIS AND DUPLEIX.

THE eight ships which formed, after the repulse of the English fleet, the squadron commanded by La Bourdonnais, anchored off Pondichery on the evening of July 8, 1746. The meeting between the governor and the victorious admiral was cordial.* There was no reason why it should not be so, for they were striving alike after the same object—an object which could be attained only by their mutual co-operation. La Bourdonnais held an independent command, but on the continent of India he was subordinate to the Council of Pondichery.† In the contemplated expedition, however, against the English, Dupleix was very willing to give up the entire control of the operations to La Bourdonnais. He was mainly anxious to see that the operations themselves were well-matured, but he was naturally resolved to hold in his own hands the supreme political power. The correspondence between the two had been conducted, as we have seen, in the most cordial manner. Dupleix had declared that the honour of success would belong to La Bourdonnais; that he would use every effort in his power to contribute to that success. He had added: "I shall esteem myself

---

* La Bourdonnais asserts in his memoirs that he was received in an unbecoming *(peu décente)* manner; but even if it were the case, which we doubt, it does not appear, if we may judge from the correspondence, to have affected the friendly terms upon which he consorted with Dupleix for the first few days after his arrival.

† The order sent from Paris to La Bourdonnais in 1741 provided, that whilst under all circumstances he was to command on the seas, his control over the land forces, in any French settlement beyond the limits of the Isles, was dependent on the authority with which the local Councils might invest him.—*Extrait des Ordres du Ministre*, 16 *Janvier*, 1741.

happy to have contributed to it by causes which will only derive merit from your conduct and its happy results, for which I am ardently desirous. I hope that my previous assurances, as well as this one, will convince you of the light in which I regard the question. I feel too much the importance of our union, not to give myself entirely to bring it about. Have no fears, therefore, on the score, but count on me as on yourself."* La Bourdonnais had replied in similar terms: "Be assured," he wrote from the Malabar coast on June 21, "that my conduct will be guided as much as possible by your counsels. I burn with impatience to embrace you, and to consult with you measures for repairing our losses." There certainly seemed no reason why these two men should clash.

And yet there was seen here, what the world has seen so often since, an example of the extreme difficulty with which men of action, accustomed to command—to plan as well as to execute—submit to a superior authority. They will obey, it is true, a man of acknowledged genius, in whose hands is vested irresponsible power. Thus Masséna and Ney, Soult and Suchet, acknowledged and obeyed genius and power combined in the person of Napoleon. But away from the influence of his presence, Ney chafed and grumbled when placed under the orders of Masséna, and even Suchet, able as he was, refused to make a movement which would have given to the French army a great superiority over Lord Wellington, when, as a consequence of it, he would have been brought under the orders of Soult. Perhaps it was, at Pondichery in 1746, that La Bourdonnais, conscious of his own abilities, felt a revulsion which he could not control at being called upon to work under one who was known to fame chiefly as a successful merchant and trader, and whose skill as a manager of men he had had no opportunity of testing.

* Dated, April 23, 1746, and received by La Bourdonnais at Mahé.

This is certain, that La Bourdonnais had not been long on shore before he began to adopt a line of conduct entirely inconsistent with his well-known character for enterprise, to show doubt, hesitation, and uncertainty, to refuse to move on an expedition without positive orders from the Council, of which, in virtue of his commission as admiral, he was a member, to decline even to make an election of the two alternatives which were presented to him—to go in search of the English fleet, or to sail at once for Madras.

The taking of Madras had been all along regarded by the two French leaders as the first fruits of a decisive victory at sea. A very few days after his arrival at Pondichery, La Bourdonnais addressed a lengthy letter to Dupleix on the subject of his plans, and he thus alluded to the project regarding Madras: " At the time of our former squadron of 1741, you know what designs I had formed upon Madras. Encouraged by M. Dumas, to whom I had communicated my project, I begged him to communicate it to you, at the time of your installation. You approved of it, and made preparations which the continued peace rendered useless. Since the outbreak of war, persisting in my first design, I have imparted it to you, begging you at the same time to add to your former preparations, others to facilitate our success. . . . . My plan is to destroy or disperse the English squadron, if it be possible; the capture of Madras must result."*

The reply of Dupleix was couched in the same spirit. " Your idea regarding Madras," he wrote,† " is the only one which can indemnify the Company for all its losses and expenses, restore the honour of the nation, and procure for this colony a more solid footing than hitherto. This enterprise is very easy, and your forces are more than sufficient to carry it out, but it cannot be

* Dated July 17, 1746. † Dated July 20, 1746.

attempted with safety, before the English squadron is destroyed or beaten." As to the treatment of Madras, in case it should fall into his hands, La Bourdonnais had thus, on July 17, addressed the Governor-General: "If fortune favours you," he wrote, "what do you think we ought to do with Madras? My idea is to take possession of and carry off all the merchandise we may find there, and to ransom the remainder; for if we should raze every stone in the town, it would be rebuilt in a year, and Madras would be much stronger than it is now." The answer of Dupleix on this point deserves to be remembered. He replied, on June 20 :—" I cannot say at present what it would seem good to do with Madras; if you should have the good fortune to take it, circumstances will decide as to the fittest course to be adopted. But I beg you to recollect, that so long as Madras remains as it is, Pondichery will languish, and commerce will fall off. It is not sufficient to think only of a present, and, perhaps, an uncertain advantage; we must look forward to the future. I am not of the opinion that this town, once dismantled, could be restored in a year. It has taken very many years to make it what it now is, and the facilities and means for re-establishing it are less than they were for making it."

In the letter from which we have extracted, La Bourdonnais had given an exact statement of the condition of the armament of his fleet, and had requested Dupleix to supply from the arsenal of Pondichery the deficiencies under which he laboured. He had indented upon Dupleix altogether for forty-four eighteen, and fourteen twelve-pounders. It was not in the power of Dupleix to comply literally with this demand, without weakening to a dangerous extent, the defences of Pondichery. But he supplied instead a larger number of guns than were asked for. In place of forty-four guns of eighteen, and fourteen of twelve, he sent him twenty-eight of eighteen, twelve of twelve, and twenty-two of eight, and offered to change those which were only slightly damaged. He accompanied this offer with an explanation so frank and courteous, that it seems surprising that his conduct in this respect should ever have been made the subject of animadversion.*

Yet notwithstanding the supply of guns, ammunition, provisions, and men,† La Bourdonnais could not make up his mind to set sail. The idea that the English fleet might keep out of sight until it were reinforced from Europe, and that, thus reinforced, it might take him at a disadvantage when before Madras, seemed at first greatly to weigh upon him. To obviate this risk, and to draw the English within fighting distance, he proposed, on August 10, that a force should proceed to Gudalur, twelve miles south of Pondichery, to attack Fort St. David, built by the English in its vicinity. If the English fleet were to bear up to assist that fort, he would then attack it; but if it should not, it would be a proof that it had been very severely handled in the former

---

* After enumerating the necessity that Pondichery should be a strong place, under whose walls French vessels might always find a secure refuge, and alluding to the probable increase to their naval enemies by the chances of a war with Holland, Dupleix adds: "This augmentation of enemies, the only thing we have to apprehend ought to render me more circumspect with regard to a place so considerable; the safety of which depends entirely on others:" (the victorious course of the French fleet). "A thousand mishaps, to which sea forces are subject, might disappoint this place for a long time of the guns which you wish to take from it. The Minister has given me orders to assist you, and I obey willingly orders so deserving of respect. But I cannot persuade myself that his intentions are that I should risk the safety of Pondichery. I believe, on the contrary, and I flatter myself that he will be better pleased, that I should not place it in jeopardy. Nevertheless, to act up to his orders and your demands, I am ready to make over to you twenty-eight eighteen-pounders, twelve of twelve, and twenty-two of eight, and to change those which are but slightly damaged, and which, after being repaired, can be made serviceable These guns will make a great gap, but the word of honour you give me to return them, and the moral certainty I feel of your victory over the enemy, permit me to take the step of dismantling the walls with less disquietude."— *M. Dupleix à M. de la Bourdonnais, July,* 20, 1746.

† The reinforcements furnished by Pondichery consisted of 200 Europeans, 100 topasses or Indio-Portuguese, 300 sipâhis, besides officers, in addition to lascars, as well as 170 sailors and 50 European soldiers belonging to the garrison already serving on the fleet.

action, and he would have no difficulty in taking Fort St. David.*

Against this plan, as an alternative to the long-meditated attack upon Madras, Dupleix strongly protested. "Gudalur and Fort St. David," he wrote on the 12th, "are not worth the powder and shot you will expend upon them." He pointed out that their capture would very probably range the Nawwáb on the side of the English, and that this would save Madras. "The enterprise against Madras," he added, "is the only one which can indemnify us, and do honour to the nation in India, and I cannot agree with you in your plan of abandoning that project for one which merits neither your attention nor mine, and of which the consequences will be costly and injurious to us." He continued to urge upon him, in a lengthened argument, that two principal objects had brought him to India—the destruction of the English squadron and the taking of Madras—and that abandoning one of those, he ought to attach himself with his whole heart to the other. The day after this correspondence, La Bourdonnais took advantage of a favourable breeze to go in search of the English squadron. He arrived off Kárikál on August 13, and there obtained, with some difficulty, positive information of the enemy. They had been descried on the 10th, six vessels in number, a little to the north of the northernmost point of Ceylon, about fifteen miles off the coast. To the Dutch officer who boarded them they stated that they had been repulsed by the French, but that they were only waiting the arrival of reinforcements to renew the attack. All their damages had been repaired. Satisfied, then, as he stated, that he was free from all attack on that side, La Bourdonnais

---

* It is in this letter that La Bourdonnais informs Dupleix of the sickness caused on board his squadron, and from which he himself especially suffered, from drinking the water taken in at Pondichery. In his memoirs, he makes of this a charge against Dupleix, insinuating that it was a part of the general scheme to annoy him.

CHAP. IV.
1746.

resolved to return at once to Pondichery, and, arriving there on the 19th, to embark the soldiers, sipáhis, and troops awaiting him, and to proceed immediately with the grand design against Madras. He added in his letter, however, that his health was greatly enfeebled, and that not for all India would he stay on the coast after October 15, when the monsoon would set in. Instead, however, of acting upon this plan, which he had communicated to Dupleix through M. Paradis, the commandant of the Kárikál garrison, La Bourdonnais suddenly changed his mind and went in search of the English. He found them off Nágápatan, and endeavoured to bring them to action. But though he hoisted Dutch colours to deceive them, they fled before him, he reported, in a manner that soon took them out of sight.* Thinking that they might return to Nágápatan, he waited there two days; but not meeting them, he again put out, and on the evening of the 25th anchored off Pondichery.

This escape of the English, and the uncertainty whither they had proceeded, completely changed the views of La Bourdonnais. He who, on the 14th, when he knew the English fleet to be below Nágápatan waiting for reinforcements, had declared his readiness to proceed with the utmost haste to Madras, had become on the 26th, after that fleet had sailed he knew not whither, hesitating and doubtful. He dwelt on the difference between commanding King's ships and vessels belonging to the Company. "In the former," he said, "one hazards everything for glory, in the latter one must look to profit;" and he stated his opinion that his squadron was insufficient for the double task of

---

* Mr. Orme states that "the English, perceiving the addition of cannon with which the enemy had been supplied at Pondichery, avoided an engagement." Mr. Mill simply remarks that the English fled. The reason given by Mr. Orme would not, we think, be considered sufficient by any English admiral of the present day. The English ships were mostly armed with 24-pounders, whereas the French had only taken on board twenty-eight 18-pounders, and others of smaller calibre.

attacking Madras, and beating off the English squadron reinforced by its expected ships. In this difficulty he appealed to the Superior Council for its advice.*

An extraordinary meeting of the Pondichery Council took place to consider this appeal. There were present at it thirteen members, and they came to a very decided opinion. This was contained in a letter addressed to La Bourdonnais bearing the same date.† In this letter, after recapitulating the preparations that had been made, the time that had been lost, the change in the opinions of the admiral, they set before him the choice of two alternatives. " Either, "they said, " you should go to Madras and attack it, or you should go and drive the English fleet from these seas. At present they are," they said, "in a position in which they can intercept every vessel coming from Europe, whilst you are here, effecting nothing now, and talking of leaving us to the mercy of the English fleet in October." They concluded with these words: " We are bound to add also that it would be shameful and disgraceful for the nation to abandon these two means, whilst we have a moral certainty that the treasure and the vessels which we expect from Europe will be taken by the enemy's squadron, and an equal certainty that you can succeed in one of the two. It is equally important not to render useless the strength of your squadron, and the money spent upon it. What reproaches will you not have to make yourself, if at the same time that you abandon the project which would serve to indemnify us, our enemies take possession of the vessels we are expecting from Europe, almost within sight of your squadron."

It is strange the transformation which a forced subordination to authority can sometimes make in the entire character of a man! Who would have believed that the daring, energetic leader, who had " conquered

---

* M. de la Bourdonnais à M. Dupleix, 26 Août, 1746.

† Lettre du Conseil Supérieur du 26, Août 1746.

the impossible " at the islands, who had there made ships and sailors, and soldiers and guns, who had sailed across the ocean with his untried crews, and had met and scattered the war-ships of the enemy, that the man whose motto was "action," should have suddenly so changed as to call forth an incitement to action couched in the terms we just given? Yet we have seen in our own day how blind to all perception of right, how oblivious even of the ordinary obligations of politeness, how open to the malignant suggestions of whisperers and sycophants, wounded vanity will make even those who, in other respects, soar far above the common run of their fellowmen. Up to the time of the despatch of that letter, Dupleix and the Council had met every requisition on the part of La Bourdonnais in the most obliging spirit. They had made over to him the particular officers he had asked for, of whom Paradis was one, all the stores, ammunition, and, as we have seen, all the guns they could spare. They had only pressed upon him to act. But the feeling that he was thus under control, that he, who had always impressed his own will upon all around him, should be subject to the will of another, had changed the heart and the blood of La Bourdonnais. The burden of all his letters was, that he could not attack Madras, because the English squadron had not been destroyed; that the English squadron had not been destroyed, because he could not bring it to action, and that he could not stay on the coast later than October 15. The meaning was that he would do nothing till then. Even the letter of the Superior Council failed to move him. Plain as were its terms, that he should either attack the English fleet or Madras, he had the boldness to declare that its contents prevented him from moving, because it did not prescribe precisely which of the two courses he was to adopt. Taking the letter in his hand, he declared publicly to all who would listen to him, that the

WOUNDED VANITY OF LA BOURDONNAIS.

Superior Council was the only obstacle to action on his part. This proceeding thoroughly roused Dupleix. He re-summoned the Council on the 27th, and put before it, for consideration, the course adopted by the Admiral.

The deliberations of the Council at this crisis were short, prompt, and to the point. They resolved to serve on La Bourdonnais a summons, calling upon him, " on the part of the King and the Company, to make choice of one of the two plans which had been presented to him on the 26th—the only plans we consider practicable, suitable to present circumstances, to the glory of the King, the honour of the nation, the interests of the Company, the force of his squadron, and the weakness of our enemies by sea and land; in default of doing this—of the choice of which he is left master—he is to be held responsible in his own name for all that may happen in consequence, as well as for all the expenses which his project on Madras, so long meditated and conducted to the point of execution, has occasioned the Company. If hindered by sickness from acting himself, as there is no time to lose and moments are precious, the Council consider M. de la Portebarré, of whom the capacity and prudence are known, to be very capable of executing whichever of the two plans he may select."

The reply of La Bourdonnais was short: " I have received," he wrote, " the citation and its contents. I consulted the Council of Pondichery only regarding the affair of Madras. It rested with it to give its opinion for or against that. As to the destination of my squadron, it has no right to interfere with it. I know what I ought to do, and my orders have been given for it to leave Pondichery this evening."*

The fleet accordingly sailed under M. de la Porte-

---

* À Messieurs du Conseil Supérieur de Pondichery, 27 Août, 1746.

CHAP. IV.
1746.

barré,* La Bourdonnais himself alone remaining behind on account of his sickness. The squadron sailing along the coast succeeded in capturing two small vessels in the Madras roads. It then returned to Pondichery. The health of La Bourdonnais, meanwhile, had improved, and his announced determination to attack Madras seems to have improved his relations with the Council. On the evening of the 12th, accordingly, he embarked to proceed on this long-meditated enterprise. On the 14th, approaching the shore, twelve miles south of Madras, he landed 500 or 600 men, with two pieces of cannon. Sailing slowly, parallel within these troops, on the 15th, he arrived at midday within cannon-shot of of the town. He then landed with 1,100 Europeans, 400 sipáhis and 400 Africans, and summoned the place to surrender. He had still from 1,700 to 1,800 men on board his squadron.

1639.

Fort St. George, and the town of Madras, of which it formed the defence, had been built upon a plot of ground,† which a petty rájá subject to the last of the Hindu rulers of Bíjanagar had made over to the English in 1639. Fourteen years later, the little settlement had been raised to the rank of a Presidency, and

---

* Mr. Mill states, that Dupleix carried his "unfriendly proceeding" so far as to command La Bourdonnais to "re-land the Pondichery troops." It is very true that on August 27, knowing only, by the reply of La Bourdonnais to the citation, that the fleet was to leave, but ignorant of the direction it was to take, or the object on which it was to be employed, Dupleix directed the re-landing of 250 soldiers and 100 sipáhis with their officers, assigning the following as a reason: "The distance which your squadron may find itself from this place by some event which God alone can foresee, and *these troops being useless in your vessels,* I beg you to disembark the troops above referred to, in order that I may be in a condition to answer to the King for the place which he has confided to me, &c." But it is not less true that on receiving in reply from La Bourdonnais a letter of the same date, informing him of the destination of the squadron, that it was "to sweep the Madras roads." and that it would not be absent for more than eight or ten days, he withdrew from the squadron only 125 Europeans and 50 sipáhis retaining those for the defence of Pondichery.

† Mr. Wheeler ("Early Records of British India") thus gives the story of its purchase: "A certain Mr. Day bought the strip of ground from the Hindu rájá of Chandragheri. The English agreed to pay a yearly rent of 1,200 pagodas, nearly £600 sterling for this piece of land."

it constituted for a long time afterwards the principal emporium of the English in India. It was not very well situated for that purpose. On a bluff point of the coast, where the current was always rapid, and exposed to all the violence of the monsoon, and the inconvenience of a surf which made navigation for English boats impossible, it would have been difficult to find a position less adapted for commercial purposes than Madras.

The roadstead was dangerous during some months of the year, especially from October to January, so much so, that on the appearance of anything approaching to a gale during those months, vessels were forced to slip their anchors, and run out to sea. Nor did the fertility of the neighbouring country compensate for these disadvantages. The soil was hard, dry, and barren; the population poor and sparse. In those days, however, it was apparently the custom of the different European nations to select, as their settlements, points on the coast in as close a contiguity to one another as was possible. And the situation of Madras probably owed its value in the eyes of Mr. Day, the English merchant who negotiated for the land, to the fact that it was but four miles from the Portuguese settlement of St. Thomé.

But notwithstanding its unfavourable situation, the industry and enterprise of English settlers soon brought prosperity to Madras. In 1768, the native population, attracted thither by the protection and opportunities of traffic they enjoyed under the English flag, amounted to 300,000, and the revenue, derivable from taxation, was estimated, nine years later, at about 160,000 rupees, equal, allowing for the probable increase of population during that period, to a capitation tax of eight annas. In 1696, Mr. Thomas Pitt, the grandfather of the great Commoner and possessor of the famous Pitt diamond, became Governor, and held the office for eleven years. It was during his administration that Madras first came into hostile contact with the native princes of the country. Dáud Khán, Nawwáb of the Karnátik under the Emperor Aurangzéb—a chief noted for his fondness for the strong waters of Europe—made a sudden demand upon Mr. Pitt (1702) for 10,000 pagodas, about 40,000 rupees. Mr. Pitt endeavoured by civilities and sumptuous entertainments to amuse the Nawwáb into forgetfulness of his demand. But if Dáud Khán loved cordials much, he loved rupees even more. Finding his requests evaded, he subjected Fort St. George to a strict blockade, cut off all supplies from the country, seized all the goods coming into the place, and only raised the siege when Mr. Pitt consented unwillingly to a compromise. In addition to Madras, and subordinate to it, the English possessed at this time, on the Koromandel coast, the settlement of Fort St. David, close to Gudalur, sixteen miles south of Pondichery, and the factories of Porto Novo, Pettaipoli, Machlipatan, Mádápallam, and Vioshákpatan. It does not appear that the history of Madras was marked by any other incidents of importance till the period of which we are treating. In the year 1744, Mr. Nicholas Morse was appointed Governor of Fort St. George. Morse was an old Company's merchant, ignorant of politics, caring little for them, a quiet, easy-going, sedate sort of man, who ever carried out, with a literal obedience, and regardless of any changes that might have occurred in the interval, the orders of his masters in England. Thus it was, that when, shortly after his accession to office, he received overtures from Dupleix to preserve neutrality in India during the coming war, Governor Morse, well convinced, all the time of the wisdom of the measure, excused himself from entertaining it, on the ground of the instructions he had received from the Company.

We have seen how little these instructions had availed the English. Although they had the command of the seas when the war broke out, they had, nevertheless, been prevented by the interest of M. Dupleix with the Nawwáb Anwáru-dín, from profiting to the full extent from their advantage. A positive prohibition had been placed upon them with reference to the French settlements on the coast, and they had been compelled to confine their operations to the capture of stray merchantmen on the seas. The Court of Directors, deeming themselves secure of conquest, had never contemplated the possibility of Madras being in danger. They had, therefore, altogether neglected to supply soldiers for its defence; nor does its appear that the contingency of defence being necessary ever presented itself to Governor Morse. When, therefore, the news in quick succession reached Fort St. George, that La Bourdonnais' squadron had left the Isle of France, that it had engaged and repulsed the English squadron off Nágápatan, that it had arrived at Pondichery, and was making preparations for an attack upon Madras itself, the surprise and consternation which prevailed amongst its residents may perhaps be imagined. The defences of Fort St. George were certainly not very formidable. The fort itself was an oblong, 400 yards by 100, surrounded by a slender wall, defended by four bastions and four batteries, very slight and defective in their construction, and unprovided with outworks. The English garrison consisted of 300 men, of whom 34 were Portuguese vagabonds or deserters, or negroes; of the remainder only 200 were fit for duty. The officers were three lieutenants, two of whom were foreigners, and seven ensigns who had risen from the ranks.*

In his extremity, Governor Morse applied to the Nawwáb of the Karnátik. It will be recollected that when this nobleman had forbidden the exercise of hostilities by the English against any place in the possession of the French on the Koromandel coast, he had

* East India Chronicle.

accompanied his order by a promise, that should the French at any future time obtain the superiority, he would place similar restrictions upon them. The event, which had then seemed so improbable as to be impossible, had now happened. The French were preparing to attack the English settlements on the Koromandel coast. Governor Morse, therefore, claimed at once the interference of the Nawwáb.

It cannot be supposed that a man possessing the Indian experience of Governor Morse was unacquainted with the formalities necessary for approaching an Indian ruler. It is, nevertheless, certain that he managed the mission to the Nawwáb—a mission, on which the very existence of the English at Madras seemed to depend —in such a manner as to militate very much against its chances of success. It is a time-honoured custom in Eastern Courts that an envoy should never go into the presence of the Prince to whom he is accredited empty-handed. Whether the custom is good or bad is not the question. It is a custom, the form of which is kept up by the English even in the present day; to neglect it, in the days of which we are writing, was regarded as nothing less than an intentional insult. But Governor Morse, in his blunt English way, as though he had been dealing with his own countrymen, did neglect this precaution. He sent his messenger empty-handed into the presence of the Nawwáb, to remind him plainly of his promise, to claim for the English that protection which he had so recently accorded to the French messenger, well provided with presents, and who had returned to beg the Nawwáb's permission to punish his rivals. It thus happened that, when the English messenger arrived, he found the Nawwáb apparently undecided, and though that nobleman declined to give any formal permission to the French to attack Madras, he refrained, equally to their advantage, from giving utterance to a direct prohibition.

LA BOURDONNAIS ATTACKS MADRAS.

Governor Morse was under the influence of the disappointment attending his negotiations with the Nawwáb, when, on August 29, the fleet of La Bourdonnais appeared in the roadstead. The unskilful manner in which the squadron was handled made it evident, however, to the garrison of Fort St. George, that the famous admiral who had brought the ships from the Isle of France was not with them.* Seeing nothing of the English fleet, and finding the way open, the officer commanding the squadron, M. de la Portebarré, contented himself, as we have seen, with making prize of two merchantmen he found in the roadstead, and then returned on September 5 to Pondichery. Eight days after, La Bourdonnais embarked, and arriving before Madras on the 15th, summoned it, as already recorded, to surrender.

Up to this point, Governor Morse had been partially sustained by the hope, that Commodore Peyton would yet be prepared to strike a blow for the preservation of the principal English settlement on the Koromandel coast. But these hopes were destined to be disappointed. Almost simultaneously with the arrival of the French fleet, he received the disheartening intelligence, that the Commodore with all his ships had appeared on September 3 off Pulikat, and had then borne up for Bengal. That leaky sixty-gun ship was again assigned as the reason for the desertion of Madras, the excuse for avoiding a trial of strength with the battered squadron of La Bourdonnais.†

Meanwhile, La Bourdonnais, having landed his troops on the 15th, prepared, on the evening of that day and during the 16th, to erect batteries which should play upon the town. On the 17th the native portion of the garrison made a sortie, but they were easily repulsed, and the French, following up their success, took possession of the Governor's house—about half-musket range

* Orme.   † Orme.

from the walls of the town—and fortified themselves in it. On the 18th, early in the morning, they commenced the bombardment from their land batteries, and as soon as night fell, the three vessels of the squadron possessing the strongest armament opened fire on the town. A circumstance occurred in the course of the night of the 18th, which shows how easy it would have been for Commodore Peyton, commanding as he did a squadron which sailed better than that of the French, to have saved Madras. On September 17, four ships were sighted off Pondichery. Dupleix conceiving they might be part of the English squadron, wrote off hurriedly to La Bourdonnais with the information. To him this news was most startling. Had it been true, it would have been but a confirmation of the views which he had so often pressed upon Dupleix, that to attempt the siege of Madras before the English fleet had been destroyed, was the height of rashness. He himself declares that he felt, under these circumstances, that but one path lay before him, and that was to push the siege with the utmost vigour. Mr. Orme, indeed, asserts, though upon what authority we know not, that "the report caused so much alarm in the French camp, that they were preparing to re-ship their heavy cannon." However this may have been, this at least is certain, that had Commodore Peyton borne up at that moment for Madras, and attacked the half-manned French fleet in the roadstead, he would have inflicted upon it very great damage, even if he had not compelled the raising of the siege.

But on the morning of the 19th, an express arrived from Dupleix, stating that the information regarding the strange ships was incorrect. Relieved on this point, yet not knowing how soon a hostile squadron might appear, La Bourdonnais pushed the siege with vigour, and with such effect, that in the evening he received a letter from Mrs. Barneval, the daughter of Madame Dupleix, and married to an English gentleman in Madras, offering on the part of Governor Morse to treat.

The reply of the French Commander being favourable to such a course, Messrs. Monson and Hallyburton presented themselves on the following morning in the French camp. They proposed to enter into negotiations to pay a certain sum to induce La Bourdonnais to retire from before the town. This, however, in unmistakable terms, the Frenchman refused, and the deputies returned to demand fresh instructions from the Governor. On the departure of the deputies, the fire recommenced, and continued till three o'clock. Between that hour and eight o'clock in the evening, however, no one appeared on the part of the English, except a foreigner in the service of the Nawwáb, without powers or authority to negotiate. At eight o'clock, therefore, La Bourdonnais reopened the fire, and maintained it throughout the night both from the land batteries and the ships. The reappearance of the English deputies on the following morning caused it to cease.*

This time, these latter were armed with full powers to capitulate. After some discussion, they agreed to the conditions, of which the following are a free summary. They agreed, first, to make over to M. de la Bourdonnais at 2 P.M. on that day, September 21, Fort St. George and the town of Madras with their dependencies. All the garrison, and generally all the English in the town, to become prisoners of war. All the councillors, officers, employés, and other gentlemen in the service of the Company to be free on their parole, to go and to come as they wished, even to Europe; provided only they did not carry arms against France, offensively or defensively, without being exchanged.

The articles of the capitulation having been signed, it was arranged that those regarding the disposal of the

* The French did not lose a single man in the siege: the English only five.—*Grose's East Indies.*

place should be regulated in a friendly way by M. de la Bourdonnais, the Governor, or his deputies, the two last engaging on their part to deliver faithfully to the French the goods and merchandises received or receivable from merchants, the books of account, the arsenals, ships, provisions of war and supplies, together with all the property appertaining to the English Company, without reserve; besides materials of gold or silver, merchandises, goods, and any other effects whatever, contained in the fort or town, to whomsoever they might belong, without exception.

The garrison was to be conducted to Fort St. David, as prisoners of war. But should the town of Madras be ransomed and restored, the garrison might be allowed to re-occupy it, as a means of defence against the natives. But in this case, an equal number of French prisoners (made elsewhere) were to be restored to the French.

The sailors were to be sent to Gudalur, and their exchange begun with those actually in Pondichery, the remainder to proceed in their own ships to England. But they might not carry arms against France until regularly exchanged, either in India or in Europe.

On the same day that this capitulation was signed, La Bourdonnais wrote a few hurried lines to Dupleix. His first letter, dated 2 P.M. on the 21st, simply states that he had just entered Madras at the head of 500 men, and that the white flag had been hoisted on the ramparts. The second, dated 8 P.M. of the same day, is more important, as showing the view which La Bourdonnais entertained at the time regarding the conditions he had granted. In this he says,—" The haste with which I informed you of the taking of Madras did not allow me to enter into any detail; I was too much occupied in relieving the posts of this place. The English surrendered to me with even more precipitation than I wrote you. I have them at my discretion, and the capitulation which they signed has been left with me, without their having dreamt of demanding a duplicate."

Two days later, the 23rd, he wrote a long report, in which he discussed the whole question of the future. This letter began thus: "At last Madras is in French hands. The conditions on which it surrendered, place it, so to say, at my discretion. There is, nevertheless, a sort of capitulation signed by the Governor, of which I subjoin a copy; but it does no more, as you will see, than authorise me to dispose of the place."

It would appear from these extracts, and from the tenor of the capitulation itself, that Madras had surrendered at discretion; that the town, the fort, and everything belonging thereto, had become absolutely French property. It is equally clear that there had been some discussion between La Bourdonnais and the English deputies regarding a ransom, but that it was finally resolved to leave this question for future adjustment.*

---

* La Bourdonnais thus describes in his memoirs the engagement he entered into regarding the ransom: "The next day, the 21st, the deputies returned for the second time and agreed at last to surrender on the conditions which had been proposed to them the previous evening, that is to say, on the condition of being permitted to ransom the town. Immediately the articles of capitulation were written out, Mr. Hallyburton took them to the Governor, who having examined them, sent them back by the same Mr. Hallyburton, with orders to represent to M. de la Bourdonnais, that neither the Governor nor the Council ought to be regarded as prisoners of war so long as the question of the conditions of ransom should be under consideration. Upon this representation, M. de la Bourdonnais, who wished the Governor and his Council to remain prisoners of war until these conditions should be agreed upon, contented himself with assuring the deputies that he would give an act of liberty to the Council and the Governor, as soon as they should agree with him regarding the ransom. The deputies having then demanded that this proposition should be inserted in the capitulation, M. de la Bourdonnais consented, and it was made an article. The deputies then took back the capitulation to the Governor, who signed it. In bringing it back again, they asked M. de la Bourdonnais for his parole, as an addition to the promise regarding the ransom. 'Yes, gentlemen,' replied he, 'I renew to you the promise I made you yesterday, to restore to you your town on condition of a ransom, which we will settle in a friendly way, and to be reasonable regarding the conditions.' 'You give us then your word of honour,' answered the deputies. 'Yes,' said he, 'I give it you, and you may be assured that it is inviolable.' 'Very well,' replied the two Englishmen, "here then is the capitulation signed by the Governor; you are now master of the town, and you can enter it when you like.'"

It must always be borne in mind, however, when reading the memoirs of La Bourdonnais, 1stly, that they were written some time after the

CHAP.
IV.
1746.

Meanwhile, the intelligence had reached the Nawwáb Anwáru-dín that the French had really carried out their intentions, and had laid siege to Madras. Inclined as this prince undoubtedly was to French interests, nothing was further from his intention than to permit their establishing themselves in the territories of their European rivals. He, therefore, at once despatched a messenger on a swift dromedary to Dupleix, the bearer of a letter, in which the Nawwáb expressed his surprise at the events passing at Madras, and threatened that unless the operations against that place were instantly put an end to, he would send an army to enforce obedience to his commands. But Dupleix thoroughly understood Asiatics. Determined not to forego his designs upon Madras, yet unwilling to bring down upon himself the hostility of the representative of the Múghal, he devised a plan whereby, as he thought, Madras would be lost to the English for ever, even if it

events described, and, 2ndly, that they were written with the view of exculpating himself from specific charges brought against him. Now, the question of the ransom, and especially the question as to whether any absolute engagement was entered into at the time of the surrender, formed one of these specific charges. On such a point, therefore, it is necessary to read La Bourdonnais' own statement with the greatest caution. The official correspondence is a far surer guide. Let us see what that says. We have given all that relates to the proceeding relative to the surrender, in the text. From this we find, first, that no mention is made of any promise regarding a ransom. In the letter dated 8 P.M. of the 21st, written only six hours after the interview he describes above, La Bourdonnais says:—" The English surrendered to me with even more precipitation than I wrote you, have them at discretion." Not a word about ransom. In the more elaborate letter written two days later he writes:—"The conditions on which it surrendered, place it, so to say, at my discretion. There is, nevertheless, a sort of capitulation signed by the Governor, of which I enclose a copy; but it does no more, as you will see, than authorise me to dispose of the place." Again, not a word of the solemn and reiterated promises recorded at such full detail in the memoirs!

If, further, we examine the capitulation itself, we shall find everything conditional. There had undoubtedly been some discussion regarding a ransom, but the question had been referred for further deliberation; that it was a doubtful one is, we think, shown by the words employed in the fourth article, in which it is stated, that "if the town is restored by ransom, then the English, &c., &c."

However this may be, it is certain that there was no occasion for La Bourdonnais to make such an offer, Madras being completely at his mercy; and, likewise, that it was entirely opposed to the views which he knew that Dupleix, his superior officer on Indian soil, entertained. *Vide* also appendix A.

were not gained to the French. In accordance with this idea, he sent instant instructions to his agent at Arkát, to inform the Nawwáb that he was conquering Madras for him, and that it was his intention to make it over to him on its surrender.

Well acquainted with the vague ideas regarding the ransom of Madras, to which La Bourdonnais had given utterance in previous correspondence, it became imperatively necessary for Dupleix to make known to the admiral the engagement into which he had just entered. At 8 p.m., on the evening of the 21st, therefore, he despatched to him a special messenger conveying a letter, in which La Bourdonnais was informed of the negotiations with the Nawwáb, and was specially warned to entertain no proposals for the ransom of Madras after its capture, "as to do so would be to deceive the Nawwáb, and make him join our enemies."*

This letter reached Madras on the night of the 23rd. Before its arrival La Bourdonnais had, as we have seen, sent to Dupleix a copy of the capitulation, together with a long letter, in which he entered fully into the subject of the reasons by which he had been actuated. Three courses he stated were before him. He might either make Madras a French colony; he might raze it to the ground, or he might treat regarding its ransom.†

* The perusal of this letter will leave no doubt on the reader's mind of the sincerity of Dupleix's negotiations with Anwáru-dín. He writes:—"I have informed the Nawwáb through my agent at Arkát, that as soon as we are masters of the town of Madras, we will make it over to him, it being well understood, in the state in which we may think fit," meaning, he would first raze the fortifications. He adds:—"This information ought to determine you to press the siege vigorously, and *not to listen to any propositions which may be made you for the ransom of the place after its capture, as that would be to deceive the Nawwáb and make him join our enemies*; besides, once masters of the place, I do not see with what the English will be able to ransom it. So long, too, as Madras remains as it is, it will always be an obstacle to the increase of this place. I beg you to weigh well these considerations."—*Dupleix to La Bourdonnais, dated Pondichery, September* 21, 1746, 8 P M.

† The fact that, in this letter, which accompanied the capitulation, La Bourdonnais expressly considers himself at liberty to decide upon one of the three courses indicated, two of which would have rendered the ransom of the place impossible, proves conclusively that up to the 3rd he had entered into no binding engagements to ransom Madras, and that the story related in his memoirs was manufactured afterwards.

CHAP. IV.
1746.

The first he did not consider advisable, because it was not, in his opinion, for the interests of the Company that they should have on the same coast, and in close vicinity to one another, two rival establishments. He added: "By the first orders received from the Minister, I was forbidden to keep any conquests;* it is certain

---

* As this is the only place in the entire correspondence in which La Bourdonnais alludes to the prohibition on the part of the French Ministry to keep any town or settlement conquered from the enemy, and as, nevertheless, he uses it in his memoirs as a principal justification of his conduct; as, moreover, Mr. Orme, Mr. Mill, and other writers of Indian history down to the latest, Mr. Marshman, have adopted without examination the assertions of La Bourdonnais on this point, it becomes necessary to subject those assertions to the test of critical inquiry.

It is perfectly true that the French Ministry had sent to La Bourdonnais an order prohibiting him "from taking possession of any settlement or *comptoir* of the enemy for the purpose of keeping it;" but even independently of the circumstance that such an order did not render necessary the restoration of the captured place to the enemy, it is a fact that this order bore no reference to the campaign in which La Bourdonnais was engaged in 1746. It is true, that in his memoirs, he places it among other orders issued in 1745 and 1746, to all of which the date is attached, but he has curiously omitted to assign any date to this one. The fact is, it was issued in 1741, at a time when La Bourdonnais had just been placed at the head of a combined fleet of King's and Company's ships to cruise in the Eastern seas, the moment hostilities should break out. But, even under those circumstances, it was not intended to be prohibitory in its action. As Professor H. H. Wilson justly remarks (Wilson's Mill, vol. iii. p. 49, *note*):—"The letter to the proprietors explains the purport of M. La Bourdonnais' instructions more correctly (than Mr. Mill had stated). He was not to form any new settlement, and the only alternatives in his power with regard to Madras were to restore or destroy it. The object of the French East India Company was to improve their existing settlements, at least, before new ones were established." Thus, even when originally issued, the real purport of the order was very different to that which La Bourdonnais assigned to it. But the circumstances of 1746 were far different from those of 1741. In 1746, he was acting on territory, which the moment it became French by conquest, fell at once under the sway of the Governor-General of French India. It was clearly beyond his authority to maintain that because, when conducting an independent cruise five years before, he had been restrained from making conquests that were to be permanent, he was, therefore, restricted from carrying out then the instructions of one who had supreme authority on all Indian soil that had become or that might become French. The following extract from the commission borne by Dupleix shows very clearly that his powers were of that extensive nature. He was nominated "Governor of the Town and Fort of Pondichery, and of the places subordinate to it, President of the Superior Council, to command there, not only the inhabitants of the said places, the clerks of the Company and other inhabitants established there, but all Frenchmen and foreigners who may establish themselves there hereafter, of whatsoever quality they may be; likewise all officers, soldiers, and *gens de guerre* who may be there or in garrison." Further he was ordered "to do generally whatever he might consider proper for the preservation of the said *comptoirs* and commerce, and the glory of our name, and to be entitled for the said charge to the accustomed honours, authority pre-

THE POLICY OF LA BOURDONNAIS.

that at the peace, the surrender of this place would form one of the articles of the treaty, the King will restore it, and the Company will have no advantage from it."

Against the second plan, the destruction of the place, he argued, that it would be impossible to prevent the English from establishing on the coast some other emporium equally fit for their purpose, and at a less expense than they would now willingly pay for the ransom of Madras. He then added that his opinion was strongly in favour of that plan, and that there would be no difficulty in carrying it out, as Governor Morse was ready to give bills on England for the amount demanded, and to make over eight or ten hostages till payment had been made. This letter, with the capitulation accompanying, was sent to Pondichery by M. Paradis, then commanding the Pondichery contingent. On the following day, La Bourdonnais wrote a short note to Dupleix, summarising his arguments, and begging that he might be furnished with the idea of the Governor-General as to the manner in which Madras should be treated;* and on the 25th, he sent a formal reply to a letter he had received from the Superior Council of Pondichery thanking him in the name of the nation for the difficulties, the cares, the labours, the fatigues, he had experienced and overcome—which contained this remarkable expression: " I have received the gracious letter you have done me the honour to write me on the subject of the taking of Madras; after the thanks you have to render on that account to the

eminence and prerogative, and to all the appointments ordered by the Company." Further, all the officers and servants of the Crown and clerks of the Company were ordered to recognise the said Sieur Dupleix in the said quality of Governor and President of the Superior Council, and to obey him, without contravention in any sort or manner on pain of disobedience." The orders of October, 1745, were even more categorical in their assertion of the supreme authority of the Governor of Pondichery on Indian soil.

* Dated September 24, 1746. The actual words were " Faites moi donc, Monsieur, un plan suivi de la façon dont vous pensez que je doive traiter cette ville;" a request which shows very plainly that no positive engagements to ransom the town had been entered into on the 21st.

God of armies, it is M. Dupleix who deserves your gratitude. His activity, his attentive care in supplying me with all that I needed for the siege, were the chief causes of its success."

We have thus alluded in detail to the course pursued by La Bourdonnais after the taking of Madras, in order that no doubt may exist as to the actual occurrences of that much canvassed period. We think it is clear, firstly, that La Bourdonnais had, as commander of the expedition, no right to conclude any definite treaty with the English, without the consent of the Governor-General of French India; secondly, that up to September 25, the fifth day after the capitulation, no such definitive treaty had been entered into, although there had been some conversation regarding a ransom; and, thirdly, that, up to that date, the feelings of La Bourdonnais, gratified by success, had been most friendly towards the Pondichery authorities. He had even gone out of his way, as we have seen, in a letter to the Superior Council, to render justice to Dupleix.

We have now to refer to that action on the part of Dupleix and the Pondichery Council which changed that friendly feeling into one of fierce and bitter hostility, ruinous alike to the cause and to the leader. But before doing this, we must examine at some length the motives which influenced Dupleix, in the responsible position which he occupied, in deciding upon his course of action.

There can be no doubt but that at this period the main object of the policy of Dupleix was the expulsion of the English from the Koromandel coast. The experience of the three preceding years had taught him that the safety of the one European power could only be assured by the expulsion of the other. It had tasked all his energies, he had had to draw upon all his resources, to preserve Pondichery from the dangers which had threatened it in 1744. But the prohibition given by the Nawwáb Anwáru-dín, the French settlements must then have been destroyed. But that was a reed upon which it would not be wise to lean for ever. The successor of Anwáru-dín might not be animated by the same sentiments; another incursion of the Maráthás might render powerless the representative of the Múghal; or anarchy might again prevail, as it so recently had prevailed, throughout the Karnátik. That he could not depend upon the French Ministry, or on the Directors of the French Company the events of the last few years had fully convinced him. With a three years' warning of the hostilities that were pending, the men who governed French India from Paris had literally starved their most important dependency. They had sent it neither ships of war, nor money, nor even good information. Hesitatingly and fearfully they had despatched two merchant vessels in as many years, with most inadequate supplies. Nay more, when another enterprising Governor had proposed a plan, whereby, at the smallest amount of risk, the ascendency of France in the East could be secured, and had wrung from the aged Minister an assent, they had taken the earliest opportunity to cancel the scheme, and had deprived the Governor of the means by which he had hoped to carry it into execution.

From France then Dupleix had little to hope. On the other hand he beheld England thirsting to destroy him, England strong in the energy of her sons, the resources of the India Company, and, more than all, in her comparative good government. He had seen that in the year which was now going on, England had acted as La Bourdonnais had proposed to act, and had thereby reaped the most important results. That stroke on the part of England, but for the interference of the Nawwáb, would have destroyed him. The superior energy and good direction of the England of the eighteenth century over the France of Louis XV., could not then have failed to impress him with the belief, that, in all probability, an opportunity would be afforded to the English of renewing the attempt under more favourable conditions.

What then formed his chance of success at such a conjuncture? Surely there was but one. It was to adopt that policy, even then consecrated by genius, the policy of Alexander, of Hannibal, of Gustavus—to carry the war into the enemy's country, and to use the means, which had been so wonderfully, so unexpectedly, placed at his disposal, to crush him at once and for ever. Madras in his hands, Fort St. David could scarcely hold out, and then, secure of the Koromandel coast, it might be possible to despatch a fleet to Bengal, to destroy the colony which had rivalled, and was now threatening to surpass, his own tenderly nursed settlement of Chandranagar.

Such being his views, his mortification may be well conceived, when he learned that notwithstanding his previous warnings, notwithstanding the positive arrangement he had made with the Nawwáb, La Bourdonnais was still harping upon the ransom of the place which he had conquered. The result of this he felt could only be, that the moment the English fleet should recover its former superiority in the Indian seas—an event daily dreaded alike by Dupleix and La Bourdonnais—an attempt would promptly be made to subject Pondichery to the fate of Madras, an attempt of which, if successful, the English would undoubtedly take the fullest advantage.

Impressed with these ideas, he wrote on September 25, a letter to La Bourdonnais, in which, whilst reminding him that according to the orders of the Minister, he was subject to the authority of the Superior Council of Pondichery, he pressed upon him the necessity of abandoning all notion of ransom. "The ransom which you are thinking of demanding from

Madras," he said, "is only a momentary, and, at the most, an uncertain advantage. All the hostages which you may have will not bind the English Company to accept the bills which the Governor may give you, and he, now a prisoner, will probably say that he has acted under compulsion to procure his freedom, and the Company will say the same." The same post conveyed to La Bourdonnais an official letter from the Superior Council on the same subject.

This letter, and the tone of superiority which pervaded it, seem to have decided the action of La Bourdonnais. It would appear that up to, and during, September 26, he had been engaged in discussing with Governor Morse and the English deputies the terms of ransom. On the morning of the 26th he wrote to Dupleix to state that he had almost agreed with Mr. Morse regarding the conditions; that there remained only a few slight differences to adjust, and to arrange the terms of payment. But during the 26th he received from Dupleix not only the letters to which we have alluded, but another from the Council, dated the 24th, in which he was informed that Messrs. Dulaurent and Barthélemy would arrive that day from Pondichery to congratulate him on his success, and to form with MM. Desprémesnil, Bonneau, Desforges, and Paradis, all Pondichery men, a Council, over which he was to preside. Instantly his part was taken. He states in his memoirs that from that moment he could not doubt the views of Dupleix; that he saw that he was resolved to be master of Madras and of the ships, to dispose of all as he wished. The assumption of such superiority he resolved at once to dispute.

Although the ransom-treaty was not then signed, he wrote to Dupleix as though it had been: " I wish with all my heart," he said, " that the deputies had arrived five or six hours earlier; there would have been time then to inform them of all that passed between the

English Governor and myself. But all had been concluded at the time of their arrival." He added: "if nevertheless these gentlemen wish to employ themselves during their stay in this town, I will find them employment." At the same time he addressed the Council, taking up high ground; acknowledging that all the then French establishments in India were under the Governor-General of Pondichery, he claimed the right of disposing of Madras, because he had conquered it. He disavowed, in fact, all subordination to Pondichery. The next morning he put the seal to his declarations, by sending to Madras the copy of an unsigned convention with Governor Morse, by which he bound himself to restore Madras to the English on receiving bills for 1,100,000 pagodas, payable at certain dates not very distant.*

Then ensued between the two men a contest injurious to the cause which they had equally at heart, to the country to which they belonged, and fatal in its result to the fortunes of one of them. Dupleix, feeling that this restoration of Madras was in effect to leave Pondichery open to attack, the moment La Bourdonnais and his squadron should have sailed to the islands, determined to maintain the authority which the King and the Company had conferred upon him. La Bourdonnais, on his side, unwilling to submit to any authority, and impatient of all control, declared that the Minister having left to him, as admiral, the sole conduct of his operations, he was even on Indian soil independent of the Government of Pondichery. Admitting that the phrase, "master of his operations," used by the French Minister to La Bourdonnais, seemed to convey to him an independent

---

* Equal to four lakhs and forty thousand rupees or £421,666 sterling. The terms were 500,000 pagodas, payable in Europe at six months' sight, in five letters of exchange of 100,000 each; and 600,000 in three equal payments of 200,000 pagodas each, the first payment to be made one month, and the second one year, after the arrival of the ships from Europe. A pagoda is worth nearly nine shillings.

authority, we regard it as clear that it could never have been the intention of the French Government thus to establish a second supreme authority, an *imperium in imperio*, within a few miles of the seat of their Government. Yet La Bourdonnais cared little for such considerations. Although, before starting on this expedition from Pondichery, he had carried his recognition of the authority of the Council to such an extent as to refuse to act without a positive order from them; he now, when the victory had been achieved, and when he was required by them to carry out their instructions, as emanating from an authority paramount to his own, daringly disavowed his subordination, and refused to recognise their supremacy.

It may not be out of place to inquire here what it really was, what was the motive reason that prompted him to this insubordination, to this sacrifice of the best interests of his country? Was it solely because he deemed his own policy to be the correct policy? That could hardly be. No one had felt more strongly than La Bourdonnais, that it would be impossible for him to remain on that coast, with any degree of safety, later than the second week in October. His plan had been to send two or three of his ships to winter at Achín, and to bear up with the remainder, laden with cargoes, for the islands, *en route* to France. Yet, it was not once or twice, but many times, that Dupleix had explained to him that, under those circumstances, Pondichery would be in the greatest danger; unprotected by a squadron, having incurred the wrath of the Nawwáb, and invited the retaliation of the English, nothing but the return of La Bourdonnais in the spring, with an overwhelming force, could have long saved the French capital, situated as it was between two English settlements—Fort St. George and Fort St. David—from capture. The ransom of Madras, then, not for cash, but for bills of exchange not then accepted, with the vision looming in the future that Madras shortly being in a position to demand a ransom from Pondichery, could not have seemed, even to La Bourdonnais, a sound policy for France.

But there is another light in which it is necessary to regard the transaction. Let us inquire whether, though it was not a sound policy for France, it did not seem a sound policy for the private interests of La Bourdonnais. And here we meet with some revelations which cannot fail to startle. We have seen in the course of the preceding narrative, that during the six days, from the 21st to the 25th of September, a negotiation had been going on between La Bourdonnais and Governor Morse, as to the amount and the terms of the ransom. But besides the question of public ransom for Madras, there was the other, the perhaps equally weighty question, of private present to La Bourdonnais. That he did receive* a considerable present is undeniable, and, though such a transaction accorded with the customs of India in those early days, this acceptance of money must in almost every case, have considerably influenced the conduct of those who received it. With the knowledge of this fact before us, the refusal of La Bourdonnais to entertain the statesmanlike plans of Dupleix becomes at once intelligible. Knowing, as we know now, that of the three measures which he himself submitted to Dupleix, viz., the occupation of Madras by the French, its destruction, and its ransom—that of the ransom was the only one which would bring him in material advantage, all the mystery that enveloped his conduct disappears. He stands robbed of much of his glory—of that bright halo of pure disinterestedness with which historians have sought to encircle him—but he is at least an intelligible being. We can watch his acts now, morally certain that we have our eyes on the secret spring by which all those acts were directed.

But we would not be understood to assert that this was

---

* *Vide*, Appendix A.—"The private present to La Bourdonnais."

the sole motive which influenced him. We even conceive it possible that La Bourdonnais himself did not fully realise the consequence of his actions. Even great men are very often unconsciously acted upon. More especially was this likely to be the case with a man who chafed so fretfully against superior control as did La Bourdonnais. Determined not to subordinate his will to the will of Dupleix, he may have been himself unaware of that secret influence, which, notwithstanding, most powerfully moved him. What can be more probable than that the two motives, powerfully assisting one another, so worked upon and mastered his reasoning powers, that he was but faintly, if at all, aware of the real moving and guiding power within him, but persuaded himself that he was influenced by considerations of duty—the selfish and sordid views which lay at the root of his conduct being kept entirely out of sight? However that may be, we have in this place to judge of the man by his acts. And in looking at those acts, we cannot but take advantage to the full of any circumstances which tend to throw light on the motives that prompted them. Hitherto, no consideration has been paid to those motives. In the contest between Dupleix and La Bourdonnais, the former has been ruthlessly condemned—condemned, we are satisfied, without a full and fair inquiry—without having been heard by means of public documents in his own defence. Yet, it is surely something in the question between them to inquire, whether there were any secret motives besides those that have been assigned, which might have tempted either of them to overstep his powers. In the case of Dupleix, we see the avowed reason—the determination to root out the English at any cost from the Koromandel coast—based upon the powers which as Governor-General of French India he believed himself to possess—but we can find no trace of any other. He had no personal objects to gain by refusing to ransom Madras. It appeared to him so plain that the restora-

M

tion of that place involved two dangers—hostility from the Nawwáb, and renewed hostility from the English—to Pondichery which might be defenceless: the reason of his conduct is, in fact, so plain, so apparent, that we search in vain for any secret motive, least of all for any which might have been beneficial to his private fortunes.

But it is not so with La Bourdonnais. It is now clear that up to September 26 he had entered upon no positive engagements to ransom his conquests. It is, we think, certain that on that 26th he agreed to terms with Governor Morse, one of those terms stipulating for a private present to himself of the equivalent of about £40,000; that, receiving on the same day convincing intimation from Pondichery, that Dupleix and the Superior Council would be no party to any scheme for a ransom, he suddenly resolved to break with them, to assert his own independent action. Is it too much to infer that the alarmed private interests stimulated, perhaps unconsciously, his jealous and easily roused ambition to a revolt against the better feelings of his nature?

To return to the narrative. We left La Bourdonnais on the evening of the 26th and on the morning of September 27, refusing to acknowledge the authority of the agents sent to co-operate with him by the Superior Council, sending to Pondichery for ratification a copy of the treaty of ransom, and yet—strange inconsistency—asserting his entire independence of the control of that Council.

But before this actually happened, some intimation that it was about to happen had reached Pondichery. Amongst the officers of the besieging army—the commandant, in fact, of the Pondichery contingent—was M. Paradis, a Swiss by birth, and a man of a bold, energetic, daring nature. He had previously been known to La Bourdonnais, and the latter had, even before his arrival at Pondichery, made a special application for his services. Placed in command of the Pondichery contingent, and second only, on land, to La Bourdonnais himself, he had behaved in a manner to give the greatest satisfaction to his chief, and until the time of the capitulation, the relations between the two had been of the most cordial nature. On the 26th, we learn for the first time that some difference had arisen on a point connected with the command of the troops, and that Paradis had left Madras for Pondichery on the 23rd, armed with letters from La Bourdonnais for Dupleix. It seems probable that Paradis, from his position in the force, had been made acquainted with the nature of the negotiations that were progressing at Madras, and that he had pointed out to the Superior Council that, unless they asserted their authority, none would remain to them. The Council were probably influenced by these considerations when they sent MM. Desprémesnil, Dulaurent, and Barthélemy to Madras. But on the 28th, they received the defiant letters of La Bourdonnais. They at once wrote to him a letter, in which they recapitulated the arguments they had used against the restoration of the place to the English; told him that M. Desprémesnil, the second member of Council, and then at Madras, would be authorised to take over from him the command of the place, with the Pondichery contingent under him; and concluded with a formal protest against all the engagements he might contract without the knowledge and confirmation of the Superior Council. On the following day, Dupleix despatched to him a letter written with his own hand—most touching, most entreating in its terms, conjuring him as a brother, as a friend, to give up all idea of ransoming the place, and to enter heartily into the designs he was nursing for the uprooting of the English. After dwelling upon the worthlessness of a ransom agreed to by prisoners, and adducing examples from history to prove that conditions made under such circumstances had never been considered binding, he added: "in the name of God; in the name of your children, of your wife, I conjure you to be persuaded of what I tell you. Finish as you have begun, and do not treat with an enemy, who has no object but to reduce us to the most dire extremity. Such are the orders which the enemy's squadron executes wherever it is able. If it has not done more, it was because it could not do more. Providence has been kinder to us than to them. Let us then profit by our opportunity, for the glory of our monarch, and for the general interests of a nation which will regard you as its restorer in India. Heaven grant that I may succeed in persuading you, that I may convince you of the necessity of annulling a treaty which makes us lose in one moment all our advantages, the extent of which you will recognise, immediately, if you will pay attention to my representations."

Meanwhile, the three Councillors, MM. Desprémesnil, Dulaurent, and Barthélemy, finding their powers disavowed by La Bourdonnais, transmitted to him on the 27th, a formal protest against his usurpation of authority, as well as against the restoration of Madras to the English; they sent also to the various commandants of troops copies of the King's orders conferring supreme authority in India upon Dupleix—a step to which, they said, they had been driven by the measures adopted by M. de la Bourdonnais in opposition to the orders he had received from Pondichery. On the 30th, the three Councillors made a second protest, and announced their intention to withdraw to St. Thomé, there to await further orders from Pondichery.

This was only the prelude to other and stronger measures. On October 2, a Commission, composed of the Major-General de Bury, M. Bruyère, the Procureur-General, and M. Paradis, arrived at Madras, armed with powers to execute the orders with which they were intrusted by Dupleix, as representative of his Sovereign in the East Indies. They carried a declaration made by Dupleix on behalf of the King and the Company of the Indies, which they were instructed to read publicly at Madras, setting forth, amongst other terms, that the treaty of ransom had been made "by the simple act, without lawful authority, of M. de la Bourdonnais, with prisoners who were unable to engage others on their account, especially in an affair of such importance; that it was null and void, and to be regarded as never having been executed." A second declaration, issued by Dupleix, on behalf of the King, and carried by them, created a Provincial Council of Fort St. George, "to render justice in the name of the King, civil as well as criminal, to all the inhabitants present and to come." Of this M. Desprémesnil was appointed President, and MM. Dulaurent, Barthélemy, Bonneau, Desforges, Bruyère, and Paradis, members. By another declaration M. Desprémesnil was nominated Commandant and Director of the town and fort of Madras, "to command in it, under our orders, the officers of land and sea forces, the inhabitants, the clerks of the Company, and all other Frenchmen and foreigners, established in it, of what condition soever they might be." They carried with them, besides, two requisitions, one from the Superior Council of Pondichery, the other from the principal inhabitants of the town, both alike protesting against the usurpation of authority on the part of La Bourdonnais, and against the restoration of Madras to the English, as a measure injurious to the national interest, and fraught with danger to Pondichery.

Early on the morning of October 2, six* of the members of the newly appointed Provincial and Executive Councils, accompanied by their chief clerk, entered Madras, and proceeded to the head-quarters of La Bourdonnais. By him they were received and conducted to

* They were, MM. Desprémesnil, Paradis, Dulaurent, Barthélemy, Bruyère, and General de Bury.

CHAP. IV.
1746.

the large hall. Here the business of the day was commenced by General de Bury handing over to La Bourdonnais a letter from the Superior Council, stating that he, the general, was authorised to reply to his letter of the 27th ultimo. The chief clerk then read aloud, in the presence of a large concourse of people, who were attracted by the rumours of some extraordinary scene, the several declarations and protests we have enumerated above.

Whilst this reading was going on, officers of all grades came crowding into the hall, the great majority of them belonging to the troops who had come with La Bourdonnais from the isles. As soon as the clerk had finished, La Bourdonnais replied. He stated that he would recognise no authority in India as superior to his own; as the orders which he had received from France concluded with a special proviso, leaving him "master of his operations." * M. Desprémesnil replied, that the authority just quoted in no way invalidated the powers conferred upon the Governor-General, and, in fact, bore no reference to the subject. La Bourdonnais, however, was obstinate, and seeing himself supported by a number of his own adherents, he assumed a haughtier tone, and threatened to cause the buglers to sound the assembly, and get the troops under arms. Immediately a cry was raised in the assembly against taking up arms against one another. Upon this La Bourdonnais assembled in the next room a council of war, composed of the officers who had come with him from the islands, and after a short sitting, communicated the result to the deputies from Pondichery. This was, in effect, that they con-

* Undoubtedly this was the case, and this was recognised by the Council of Pondichery, when two months before they had pressed upon him the necessity of a decision regarding them. La Bourdonnais had then refused to act, unless the Council prescribed to him a positive course. It may be observed in addition, that the fact of his being master of his operations, while it left him the choice of action, did not relieve him of subordination to the authority of the representative of his Sovereign in territories subject to that Sovereign.

sidered he ought not to go back from the promise he had given to the English. Upon this the deputies retired.*

La Bourdonnais having thus repulsed the demands, legally preferred, of the Pondichery deputies, proceeded without delay to deprive them of every chance of executing them by force. Spreading a report that the English fleet had been seen off Pulikat, he issued a general order to send fifty men on board each vessel. He at the same time privately instructed his trusted subordinates to assign this duty to the troops of the Pondichery contingent. This was executed on the morning of October 4, and he found himself then, at the head of troops entirely devoted to him, absolute master of his movements.

The members of the Provincial Council did not the less attempt to establish their lawful authority by legal means. Discovering during the day the ruse which La Bourdonnais had employed so well, apparently for his own interests, they resolved to place him under a moral restraint. For this purpose, General de Bury, accompanied by MM. Latour and Largi, proceeded to his headquarters, and delivered to him a written document, addressed to him as commandant of the French squadron, forbidding him to leave Madras with the French troops, without a written order from Dupleix. But the time had passed when it was necessary for La Bourdonnais to dissemble his resentment. He had rid himself of the Pondichery troops, and he was determined to use his usurped authority with the utmost rigour. He at once placed the three deputies under arrest, and when Paradis, hearing of this indignity, hastened to remonstrate with him, he charged him with being "a marplot who had brought them all within two fingers of destruction," and sent him to join his associates. He declared at the

---

* There are two accounts of this interview—one a *procès verbal* drawn up at the time by Desprémesnil and his colleagues; the other the account written three years afterwards by La Bourdonnais. The latter abounds with personal imputations which we have omitted.

CHAP. IV.
1746.

same time that he would leave them prisoners to the English on October 15—the day on which he had covenanted to restore Madras to that nation.

We will not attempt to describe the feelings of Dupleix on receiving a report of these proceedings. To carry through the darling object of his policy, the destruction of the English power in the Karnátik, he had employed entreaty, advice, persuasion, menaces, and moral force—and all in vain. The determined pertinacity of his rival left him stranded. Not a single resource remained to him. His authority denied, his soldiers sent on board the admiral's ships, his deputies arrested and confined in Madras—his entreaties answered by cold refusals, his assertions of authority by a contemptuous denial of it—what remained for him to do? It was vain to appeal to Paris. Thence no reply could arrive within fifteen months, and La Bourdonnais could not stay fifteen days longer, without extreme risk, upon the coast. He was irritated and annoyed, not only at the dissipation of the vast schemes which he had formed, but at his powerlessness to prevent any act which it might please the infuriated chief of the forces, naval and military, to carry out. The utmost that he could do was to protest. This he did, in a temperate and dignified letter,* so soon as intelligence of the proceedings at Madras reached him.

---

* Dated Madras, October 6, 1746. From the Superior Council of Pondichery to La Bourdonnais. "We learn by the letter of the Council of Madras of the 4th current, that you have caused to be arrested MM. Bury, Paradis, Latour, Largi, and Changeac. Our former letters, and that which M. Bury intimated to you, would have informed you that the Pondichery contingent not being under your orders, we had nominated a Commandant at Madras, and had established a Council there. Things being upon this footing, we might have demanded of you by what right, and by what authority, you have caused them to be arrested. But we feel the inutility of such a demand. We can now take no part with reference to all that you may do, but to wait tranquilly the issue of your proceedings.

"We confirm the order to the Council of Madras, to the officers and troops of Pondichery, not to evacuate Madras, and not to embark on board the ships, at least, until you forcibly compel them. But we tell them, nevertheless, to obey all your orders for the performance of the garrison duties of the place. We permit ourselves to hope that a ray of light will induce you to reflect very seriously."

Nor was La Bourdonnais himself at all at his ease. The month of October—a month famous for the storms and hurricanes which it brings upon the open Koromandel coast—was now well upon him. He had felt and had always declared that it would be dangerous to stay in the Madras roadstead after October 15. Yet, so intent had he been on this quarrel with Dupleix, that he had done very little in the way of embarking the property of which he had made prize. Not even an inventory had been made out. To leave Madras, too, on the 15th, as he had intended, with a treaty unratified by the Superior Council of Pondichery, would be to make over his conquest to Dupleix without conditions, as to lose for himself and for France the ransom-money he had been promised. That defiance of the Pondichery authorities which had apparently succeeded so well, what would it profit him, if, after his departure, those authorities should choose to ignore all his proceedings, and should deal with Madras as a conquest of which they alone had a right to dispose? And yet what was more probable than that they would thus act? Relying upon the physical force of which he disposed he had contemned their orders, refused to acknowledge their authority, arrested their generals, and put them to open scorn. It would have been contrary to all his experience of men to imagine, that the physical force being on their side, they would acknowledge any of the arrangements which, in open defiance of their instructions, he might have made.

At the moment then of his apparent triumph, La Bourdonnais felt all the hopelessness and helplessness of his position. Unless he could come to terms with Dupleix, all his plans would be subverted, the bills for public ransom and private gratitude would not be worth the paper on which they were written. Yet, how to come to terms with those whom he had slighted and scorned, seemed of all tasks the most impossible. To bend his haughty spirit to sue for the amity which, when pressed upon him " as a brother, as a friend," he had rejected, was a course which La Bourdonnais, of all men, would have scorned. Something, nevertheless, must be done. Dupleix could afford to wait for the future. It was from La Bourdonnais that the overtures must come.

He made them. Not, indeed, in that open, straightforward way, which would have acknowledged his error, and which would have caused the immediate renewal of cordial relations with Dupleix, but in that tortuous, indirect manner which those adopt, who, having committed an error, and finding that the consequences of that error are recoiling on themselves, are yet too much the slaves of a false pride to make a candid confession.

This was the plan he adopted. He commissioned Paradis, the Commandant of the Pondichery contingent, and whom, it will be remembered, he had placed in arrest, to sound Dupleix as to whether he would agree to the treaty of ransom, provided the restoration of Madras were deferred from October to January or February, with a view, ostensibly, to make a proper division of the spoils. If he could agree to that, Paradis added, La Bourdonnais would leave behind 150 of his own troops to reinforce those of Pondichery.

This proposition came upon Dupleix just immediately after his authority had been insulted and defied, when he, the civil power, had had flaunted before him, by the chief military power, the irresistible argument of brute force. He had divined some, if not all, of the motives of La Bourdonnais, and he had made up his mind to keep no terms with him. Openly to break off all correspondence with one who wielded the physical force of the colony would be however, in his opinion, conductive neither to French interests in general, nor to the interests of Pondichery in particular. But on receiving this indirect overture from Paradis, he saw in it a means of getting rid of one who refused to carry out himself, and who prevented others from carrying out, the views which he deemed essential to French interests. He resolved, therefore, to adopt that policy which the weak in all ages have deemed a legitimate weapon when battling against the strong, and to dissemble. He, accordingly wrote, on October 7, to La Bourdonnais, stating that he would entertain the project. But on the following day a circumstance occurred which immensely strengthened the hands of Dupleix. Three ships of war, long expected, the "Centaure" of 74 guns, the "Mars" of 56, and the "Brillant" of 50, having on board 1,520 men,* anchored that morning in the Pondichery roadstead. They brought out startling intelligence. M. Orry had been, in December, 1745, replaced as Controller-General by M. Machault d'Arnonville—a member of the Council of State—of no experience in finance, but devoted to Madame de Pompadeur. The Company informed Dupleix of this, as well as of the fact that war between France and Holland was imminent, and that he would, therefore, have to arrange to meet a new enemy in his neighbourhood. They also forwarded to him, in anticipation of his being joined by La Bourdonnais, specific instructions as to the relations to himself which the Commander of the French fleet would bear.

As this was the very point upon which La Bourdonnais had based his resistance to the orders of Dupleix, this document had naturally very great interest for the Pondichery Council. It was dated October 6, 1745, and was thus worded: "The Company considers it right and proper that the Commander of the squadron should be present at the meetings of the Superior Council; that he be summoned to it when any military expedition, in which this Commander is to bear a principal part, is under consideration; and that he have in it a deliberate

* Grose's East Indies, vol. ii. chap. 29.

voice. But it requires also that the conclusion, which shall be arrived at after discussion, whatever be the nature of the affair, be carried out by him without opposition, even though it should concern the disposing of all the ships of the Company which he may command." These orders appeared to Dupleix to be too clear to be disputed; he, therefore, sent a copy of them the same day to La Bourdonnais with the additional intimation, that they had been approved of by the new Minister.*

---

* The date of this letter—October 6, 1745, a date exactly two months antecedent to the appointment of M. Machault as Controller-General—together with the statement made by Dupleix that its contents "had been approved by the new Minister," afforded an opportunity to La Bourdonnais, of which he took full advantage, to contest its validity. "How is it possible," he observes in substance in his memoirs, "that *the new Minister* should have sent M. Dupleix orders, dated October 6, when his appointment dates only from December 6, and I myself received by the same opportunity letters from M. Orry, the old Minister, dated November 25?" He proceeds, on this, to speak of it as a "pretended letter." But this reasoning, plausible as it is, has no foundation. It is perfectly true that M. Machault's appointment as Controller-General dates only from December 6, 1745, but it is no less so, that for several months prior to that date he had been designated as the successor of Orry, who was in disgrace, and that he had been consulted on all the arrangements that were under discussion. Dupleix merely states in his letter, that the orders he had received from the Company had been "approved of" by the new Minister. What was more natural than that such important orders had been submitted, before transmission to a distant settlement, to the man who was virtually, though not actually, Minister, and who would be intrusted with their execution? That such was the practice is certain, and the very word used by Dupleix implies that the practice was carried out on this occasion. The very ships which carried out the orders sailed from France before the actual nomination of Machault; it would have been a transparent falsehood—for which there was neither necessity or excuse — for Dupleix to have employed the expression which he did use, if it had not been founded upon fact. Of the authenticity of the order there can be no doubt. But there is another point. La Bourdonnais adds that the letter of Orry to him was a confirmation of his independent authority in the Indian seas, and he quotes two garbled extracts from it to prove this. We give here, entire, the two first paragraphs from which those extracts are taken, believing that they strongly confirm the view we are supporting. It must be remembered that the letter is addressed to La Bourdonnais, as Governor of the Isles of France and Bourbon, and that at the time it was despatched Orry had not the smallest idea that La Bourdonnais would have been able to succeed, before its receipt, in fitting out a fleet for the Indies. He believed him, in fact, to be still at the Isle of France. The letter runs thus:—" The Company will send you this year, sir, six of its vessels, of which five will sail at the beginning of next month, and the sixth in the course of February. It has determined to address them all to you, leaving you master, to dispose of them according to circumstances, and the news you may receive from the Indies. It ought, however, to be your chief duty to send to Pondichery, at a proper sea-

LA BOURDONNAIS OFFERS CONDITIONS.

CHAP. IV.
1746.

But the shifts to which a wilful nature, working for a definite end, is able to resort, were not yet exhausted. La Bourdonnais, in his reply, thus referred to the instrutions of the new Minister: "With respect to the extract you have sent me, you may depend that I shall always conform to the orders of the Minister after I shall have received them. But he no longer writes to me here, and the extract you have sent me concerns the Company's captains and not me."* He added that he had received but one letter from the Company, and begged Dupleix to have the others sought for. This despatch had scarcely been sent off, when the missing letters arrived. Whether or not they contained any reference to the orders sent to Dupleix, it is impossible to say,† but this is certain, that from the date of their receipt the tone of his letters changed. In that of the 10th he announced to Dupleix that he would wait the receipt of his views till the 13th, and assured him that there was no condition he would refuse, if it did not involve the forfeiture of his word. The same evening he received the reply of Dupleix to the overtures made through Paradis, and he at once transmitted to Dupleix the conditions on which he would make over Madras to the Pondichery authorities, and depart.

---

son, the number of vessels which may be necessary to convey to it, in safety and with promptitude, the money and the troops, the ammunitions of war and the supplies, which are destined for that settlement."

"I do not dictate to you the manner in which you ought to act, to succeed in this expedition, of which you will yourself feel all the importance, persuaded as I am that you will do all for the best. Your chief point of view ought to be the preservation of the town of Pondichery, and of the other establishments which the Company possesses beyond the Cape of Good Hope and in India. This object ought to be preferred to all other enterprises. You should come to an understanding on this point with M. Dupleix, and should send him all the assistance he may demand of you, and for which he will look to you."—Dated November 25, 1745.

Now, this letter gives very large powers to the Governor of the Isles of France and Bourbon, but it in no way authorises that official to assume authority in the country of the Governor, for whom some of the assistance was intended. And yet that was the strained interpretation La Bourdonnais put upon it.

* La Bourdonais to Dupleix, dated Madras, October 10, 1746.

† He writes in his letter of October 10, to Dupleix thus:—"I have just received the letters of the Minister; they, in no way, affect my previous orders." But the letters are not given.

CHAP. IV.
1746.

The principals of these conditions were, a promise that the treaty he enclosed should be rigidly observed; that the Governor should be taken from his officers, and not from Pondichery; that Madras should be evacuated on January 1, 1747. The treaty contained articles very favourable to the English, especially when it is remembered that Madras, with its weak garrison, was incapable of further defence when it surrendered. The second article provided that one-half of the munitions of war should be returned to the English; the fourth, that the residue of the supplies, of which the quantity was large, after the re-victualling of the French squadron, should be restored to them; the other articles related to the ransom and matters previously noticed. On the following day, the 12th, he sent another letter, in which he stated that as M. Desprémesnil had assured him that Dupleix would agree to the conditions, he was now impatient to depart. He enclosed five articles, the two principal of which provided that Madras should be evacuated, at the latest, at the end of January, that it should not be attacked by either nation before that period, and that as long as it should remain in the hands of the French, the roadstead should be accessible to the ships of both nations. The Superior Council replied to these letters on the 13th and 14th. With reference to the conditions insisted upon by La Bourdonnais, they agreed to keep the engagement entered into with the English, provided the English kept theirs; but they required that La Bourdonnais should leave them 150 of his troops as he had promised Paradis, that Desprémesnil should be Commandant, assisted by a Council of four, two of whom might be named by La Bourdonnais, subordinate to Pondichery; and that the place should not be evacuated till a complete division of the prize property should have taken place. In their letter of the 14th,* the Council positively refused to agree to evacuate the

* In reply to La Bourdonnais of the 12th.

place by the time proposed, and entered into reasons which showed how dangerous it would be to French interests to accede to the other conditions proposed.*

But before this letter reached La Bourdonnais, an unforeseen event had cut the more than Gordian knot which neither party could agree to untie. In his letter of October 11 addressed to Dupleix, La Bourdonnais had remarked—" What we have most against us, is the monsoon ; I can stay here very well till the 20th, perhaps even to the 25th, if the weather continues favourable." On the following day he wrote—" Already the northerly wind has set in, then follows, as you know, the decided necessity of quitting the place. . . . I am writing to-day to each captain, giving them such orders, that in case the new moon and bad weather should compel them to put to sea, they may regain the coast afterwards." The next day, the 13th, was a lovely day, one of the finest of the season. During the night, however, there came on one of those hurricanes which periodically cause ruin and devastation along the Koromandel coast. The French vessels, with the exception of three—the "St. Louis," the "Lys," and the "Renommée"—which had been sent to Pondichery with a portion of the spoils of Madras, were in the roadstead loading. In addition to their crews, they had on board

---

* We extract the most salient passages from this letter of the Superior Council, dated Pondichery, October 14, 1746 : " M. Dupleix has communicated to us your letter of the 12th, with some articles which we have examined very attentively. Many reasons prevent us from being able to accede to them. The time to which you limit the evacuation of the place is not sufficient to enable us to make a division of the artillery, rigging, and the supplies, and to take them away. All that we can promise you, is to work as promptly as possible. . . . .

" With respect to the hostages, letters of exchange, and bills, we are very willing to engage to receive them, on the understanding, that this acceptance on our part does not pass for an acquiescence in the articles which relate to them. . . . . The roadstead of Madras cannot be open to the English during the division of the prize property ; the English squadron has only to come there with five or six ships from Europe, as well as from India, and to disembark their crews gradually. It would thus be very easy, as you will see, for the English to take possession of Madras, at least to concentrate there a force of 2,000 Europeans. It is for this reason that we have inserted a paragraph that the roadstead of Madras must not be open to the English."

CHAP. IV.
1746.

nearly five hundred troops—the Pondichery contingent, which, it will be recollected, La Bourdonnais, to assure his own unquestioned authority in Madras, had embarked upon them. The storm, as usual with such storms, gave but little warning of its approach. Before, however, it attained anything like its greatest severity, the ships had all slipped their cables, and put to sea. All night long the hurricane raged with terrible fury. La Bourdonnais, who, at the first whistle of the storm, had busied himself in making preparations to meet every possible conjuncture of fortune, vainly strained his eyes, as the day slowly broke, to discover any trace of his fleet. Not a vessel was to be seen. The hurricane continued to rage furiously, and, at eight o'clock in the morning, appeared to be even augmenting in force. During the whole of that day his anxieties increased. But he was not idle. Here, again, the old qualities of the great organiser of the islands displayed themselves to their full perfection. He sent parties along the coast, with means and appliances to succour the crews that might stand in need of aid. At Madras itself, he made preparations on a large scale for the same purpose; he wrote letters to Dupleix, detailing his terrible anxieties, and asking news of the ships at Pondichery; besides this, all the boats having been destroyed, he detached catamarans,* at half past three in the afternoon, when the storm had begun to abate, with letters detailing the state of things at Madras, and asking for information from any vessel they might fall in with. No intelligence reached him, however, before eight o'clock, nor did a single sail appear in view. At that hour he learned that the "Marie Gertrude," an English prize, having many soldiers in her, had been lost with nearly all on board, between St. Thomé and Kóvlaon; that one ship totally dismasted, and another,

* A catamaran is composed of three or four pieces of wood, about twenty feet long, tied together, upon which a man stands with a paddle.

with all her masts standing, were anchored safely off St. Thomé; that a Dutch vessel had gone down near the same place, and that two small trading barks had met with a similar fate. All next day his anxiety was increasing. At nine o'clock he learned that the "Bourbon" was at anchor fifteen miles off, with only a foremast standing, and leaking terribly; that the "Achille" was almost in the same state, and that another ship, name unknown, had been descried totally dismasted. Every hour brought news of fresh disasters. At seven o'clock in the evening he reported to Dupleix that the "Bourbon" was lost beyond redemption,* and that it would be possible to save only a very few of the crew; that the "Duc d'Orléans" was lost, one man only being saved, and that another vessel, totally dismasted, was in sight.

On the 16th the weather moderated; but it was not till the 17th that La Bourdonnais became acquainted with the entire extent of his losses. Of the eight French vessels† anchored in the Madras roads on the evening of the 13th, the "Achille," after incurring great danger, losing two of her masts, and throwing over sixteen 18-pounders, anchored safely in the roadstead; the "Neptune" had been totally dismasted, had thrown over fourteen 12-pounders, and had seven feet of water in her hold. All her prize-cargo had been ruined. The "Bourbon" was saved by a miracle; she had lost her main and mizen masts, and been compelled likewise to throw over fourteen of her guns. She had received in other respects such damage as to make her quite unfit to put to sea. The "Phénix" was lost with all on board; the "Duc d'Orléans" underwent the same fate, eight only of her crew being saved; the "Princesse

---

* She was, however, eventually saved.

† These were the "Achille," the "Bourbon," the "Phénix," the "Neptune," the "Duc d'Orléans," fitted out as men-of-war, the "Princess Marie," an English prize, the "Marie Gertrude," and the "Advice," also prizes.

CHAP. IV.
1746.

Marie" was dismasted, and had seven to eight feet of water in her hold: the "Marie Gertrude" and the "Advice" had foundered. Of these eight vessels, then, four were lost; two of the others were rendered utterly unseaworthy, and the remaining two were so damaged as to require almost superhuman exertion to fit them for sea. The French squadron had, in fact, suddenly ceased to exist. The loss in men alone had exceeded 1,200.*

It was whilst in the midst of his troubles, before even he knew the full extent of his losses, that La Bourdonnais received the letter, dated October 11, from the Superior Council to which we have alluded,† and in which they declined to fix an absolute term to the time of the withdrawal of the French troops from Madras. He apparently had expected some such answer. "I have received from the Council," said he, in reply, "the answer which I expected regarding the affairs of Madras. I shall take that which I believe to be the simplest part, which is to leave you a copy of the capitulation, and to abandon to you the field, in order to devote myself entirely to saving the *débris* of our losses." Four days later, writing when his losses were fully known to him, he still expressed himself hopefully about the future, proposing to winter and repair damages at Goa, whilst the undamaged portion of the fleet should remain at Achín for the protection of Pondichery. He then added—"My part is taken regarding Madras; I abandon it to you.‡ I have signed the capitulation, it is for you to keep my word. I am so disgusted with this

---

* Besides sixty men of the English garrison who were on board the "Duc d'Orleans."—*Grose's East Indies*,

† *Vide* note to page 174.

‡ It is necessary to notice that this was not written until La Bourdonnais had made a vain attempt to bring under his orders the captains of the "Centaure," the "Mars," and the "Brillant," just arrived from France. They pleaded, in reply, the orders they had received to place themselves at the disposal of the Governor-General and Council of Pondichery. — *La Bourdonnais à Messieurs du Conseil Suprême de Pondichery, Octobre* 18, 1746.

wretched Madras, that I would give an arm never to have put foot in it. It has cost us too much."

The next day he signed the treaty—the same treaty which, on the 11th and 12th, he had forwarded to Pondichery, and to some articles of which, on the 14th, the Council of Pondichery had objected—he signed this treaty, stating in the preamble that he did so, because the Pondichery Council, by articles signed on the 13th, and by that same letter of the 14th,* had engaged itself to hold to the capitulation in those terms.

Having thus concluded, by an act not only unauthorised, but, under the circumstances, even dishonourable, that struggle for authority, and—would that we could omit the remainder—for his own private ends—for the securing to himself of the private sum which was additional to the public ransom—La Bourdonnais assembled the members of the English Council, and, reading to them the treaty in both languages, received their acceptance of its terms. Governor Morse and five of his† councillors then attached to it their signatures. The treaty was sent the same day to Pondichery, accompanied by an intimation from the admiral to the Council, that he would hold them responsible, individually and collectively, for all contraventions perpetrated against its conditions by the French.

In the interim, La Bourdonnais had made extraordinary exertions to repair and refit his vessels. Here he

---

* In a foot-note to page 174 we have given the most important extracts from this letter. If the reader refer to it he will find, that so far from giving La Bourdonnais authority to accede to the terms mentioned, it distinctly objected to two of the most important conditions — conditions which, nevertheless, are found unaltered in the treaty which La Bourdonnais, on the strength, as he says, of this letter, signed. La Bourdonnais, in his memoirs, declares that the previous letters of Dupleix, agreeing in general terms to his conditions, authorised him to act thus;—but why, then, did he not quote these in the preamble?

† Mr. Grose, who was a contemporary, and who naturally adopted the English view, writes:—"If the French had not perfidiously broken their engagement, the price of the ransom would have been a very favourable circumstance to the English Company." No doubt, and that is just why Dupleix opposed it, though he broke no engagement, having made none.

was in his real element. Nothing could surpass his energy, or the zeal and determination he instilled into his subordinates. In less than five days after the remnants of the shattered squadron had re-anchored in the Madras roads, he had succeeded in rigging the "Achille" with jurymasts; the "Neptune" and the "Princesse Marie" had been rendered seaworthy, and even the "Bourbon" had been patched sufficiently to make the passage to Pondichery. Having placed what prize property he could on board these vessels, La Bourdonnais, on the morning of October 23, ordered a grand parade of the troops, and formally made over command to Desprémesnil. As he did this, it came on again to blow, and the ships, fearful of another hurricane, at once made for the open sea. La Bourdonnais himself waited for the conclusion of the ceremony, then threw himself into a country boat, and amid a terrible storm put out to join them, thus bidding a last adieu, amid the conflict of the elements, to that Madras, with regard to which he "would have given an arm never to have set foot in it."

All, meanwhile, had been quiet at Pondichery. The storm of the night of the 13th and the two following days had not extended so far south as the French capital. The three ships arrived from France, as well as the three which had been despatched from Madras some time previously to the storm, had thus ridden calmly in the Pondichery roads, whilst their consorts at Madras had been damaged or sunk. No sooner had the terrible losses become known, than the Council assembled to concert measures to be adopted to meet the possible results of such a calamity. Little, however, could be done, as the demands made on Pondichery for the expedition to Madras had exhausted all its stores, and the ships where not in a condition to take the sea immediately. On the 22nd a Council was held, at which the captains of the ships assisted, to deliberate on the disposal of the fleet. After hearing the opinions of the captains, a resolution was arrived at that the six vessels then off Pondichery should proceed to Achín,* under M. Dordelin, the senior captain, there to remain till the 20th or 25th of December, when the squadron should bear up for Pulikat, to proceed thence, if circumstances were favourable, to Madras. These orders were sent sealed to M. Dordelin. Neither Dordelin nor any of his junior captains appear to have been men of energy or character. The authority in whose presence they found themselves at the moment, acted upon them with a force that to their feeble natures was irresistible. They had not been many hours at sea, when they received a letter from La Bourdonnais informing them of his departure from Madras, and directing them to proceed along the coast to join him. On opening at the same time their sealed orders, their perplexity was extreme. It was difficult for them to decide to whom their obedience was due. Whilst yet hesitating, they fell in with the maimed squadron of La Bourdonnais. His daring, decided spirit settled the question in a moment. Taking upon him the command of the united squadron, he ordered them to accompany him as he continued his course for Pondichery. In that roadstead he anchored on the 27th.

Once more at Pondichery, the contest between the two men recommenced. It formed part of the plan of La Bourdonnais, and there can be no doubt that, as a plan, it was able and well considered, to take round the squadron to the Malabar coast. Leaving the sound vessels cruising in the Arabian Sea, he would have taken the damaged ships into the neutral harbour of Goa, and have there completely refitted them. Buying then other

---

* Achín is a native state in the north-western part of the island of Sumatra. The chief town, bearing the same name, is situate on a river about three miles from the sea. The port is indifferent, but affords a safe anchorage during the north-west monsoon.

vessels at Goa and Surat, he would reunite his squadron, and return with a force, sufficient to counterbalance the English force, to the Koromandel coast. But to carry out this plan he required to draw upon all the resources of Pondichery.

He required to borrow from her all her soldiers, all her heavy guns, a great part of her ammunition, and the remainder of her all but exhausted stores. He demanded of Pondichery, in fact, to take upon herself all the risks which might possibly attend his cruise, remaining herself all the time open to the attacks of an enemy. This idea, however, quite mastered him for the moment, and he pressed it, with all his earnestness, upon Dupleix. "Aid me," he said, "with the same zeal with which you aided me for the taking of Madras, and we shall be able not only to recover ourselves, but to gain fresh advantages."

It is doubtful whether, even under any circumstances, the Governor of Pondichery would have felt himself justified in undertaking so great a risk, even with the prospect of gaining so important an advantage. Certain is it that, after the experience of the preceding four months, Dupleix felt no inclination to permit the safety of the colony to rest on the caprices of a man who, up to that time, had never ceased to thwart and oppose his best devised schemes. Considering that the squadron of Commodore Peyton was yet unconquered, he felt it was absolutely necessary for the safety of Pondichery, that the bulk of the fleet should proceed to an anchoring ground, whence it might be recalled on an emergency. Such a position did Achín, in the opinion of himself and his Council, offer. Although, therefore, the letters of La Bourdonnais making this proposal were couched in the most conciliatory language; although in them Dupleix was urged to forget the past, and give once more, as he had given before the expedition to Madras, all the resources of Pondichery, in aid of the new scheme, he felt constrained to refuse to entertain it. The fact is he could not forget the past; he could not forget the terrible trials of the preceding six weeks; the open defiance of his authority, the arrest of his agents, the disposal of the Pondichery contingent on board the ships of the squadron, the usurpation of an authority supported by physical force alone. These things, indeed, would have been very hard to forget. Especially were they so at the moment when he who had suffered most from such proceedings had upon his shoulders the sole responsibility of the future of Pondichery. To have again voluntarily placed the settlement in the power of one who had shown no respect for the authority of its Governor, would have been the height of folly. The honied phrases of La Bourdonnais fell, therefore, upon ears which thoroughly mistrusted both them and their author. The Superior Council declined to entertain his plan for a moment. La Bourdonnais himself had refused to land; they declined to proceed on board his ship, as he requested, to discuss matters together. Neither party, in fact, would trust the other. Under these circumstances, it is scarcely to be wondered at, that the tenor of the reply to La Bourdonnais' proposition went simply to reiterate the orders which had directed the squadron to proceed to Achín.

In the first letter* which La Bourdonnais addressed to the Superior Council after his junction with the squadron of M. Dordelin, he had promised that he would not interfere with their command over the Company's ships. This promise, on his new plan being rejected, he proceeded to fulfil. He had at his disposal seven vessels—four† in good order, three damaged and

---

* A Messieurs du Conseil de Pondichery, October 26, 1746.
† These were the "Centaure," the "Brillant," the "Mars," and the "St. Louis."

shattered.* Of these he proposed to form two squadrons, which, sailing together, should endeavour to gain Achín. If they succeeded, he would send thence the "Lys" and the "Sumatra" to the islands, and repairing the "Achille," would make, at the end of December, for Pulikat, there to carry out the orders of the Superior Council. But should he not be able to gain Achín with the two squadrons, the first under the command of M. Dordelin was to make for that place, there to act under orders from Pondichery, whilst he himself, with the damaged squadron, should bear up for the islands.

Upon this plan he acted. On October 29th, after a stay in the Pondichery roads—for he did not land in the town—of only two days, he set sail with the seven ships before indicated for Achín. The result he had anticipated happened. The three damaged ships were soon left out of sight by those of the uninjured squadron. These latter sailing their best, as had been ordered, reached Achín on December 6th. La Bourdonnais, despairing of being able to gain that anchorage with ships that had been so shattered as his own, gave up all idea of reaching it, and bore up for Port Louis. He arrived there, his ships in a miserable condition, on December 10th.

In this manner, after a short sojourn of four months, did La Bourdonnais leave those latitudes, to triumph in which had been the dream of his heart during the best years of his life. Yet, in those four months, what stirring events had been concentrated! Arriving in the Indian seas with a fleet which he had, for all the purposes of the expedition, extemporised himself, with crews he had trained, and soldiers whom he had taught and drilled, he first encountered and beat off an English

---

* The "Achille," the "Lys," and the "Sumatra." The "Sumatra" had come in a shattered condition from the islands. The other ships, the "Bourbon," the "Neptune," the "Renommée," and the "Princesse Marie," had been too disabled to make the voyage.

fleet, inferior, indeed, in the actual number of the ships, but far superior in weight of metal; then, refitting and re-arming at Pondichery, he sailed out to encounter once more the English squadron. Not daring to accept his challenge to an engagement, they fled before him, and he, having thus obtained the mastery of the seas, sailed then to attack the stronghold of the English on the Koromandel coast. Taking it without the loss of a man, he heard very soon afterwards of the arrival of a reinforcement of three ships, armed as ships of war, at Pondichery! What a position did that give him! Conquerer of Madras, master of the ocean, with no one to oppose his onward progress, with a Govenor-General at Pondichery who was constantly impressing upon him the necessity of rooting out the English from every settlement in India, he might have sailed up the Húglí, have conquered Calcutta, and have destroyed English commerce in the Indian seas. In acting thus he would have fulfilled the very purpose of his mission; he would have carried out the most cherished dreams of his life. Why, then, did he not effect this? The answer is to be found in the motives which we have unveiled. It was partly—we believe chiefly—because, though he had triumphed over difficulties such as would have baffled most men, though he had conquered enemies on shore, and driven every rival from the sea, he had not overcome himself. Yet there was another reason too, regarding which it is impossible to be silent. The price of the ransom-treaty of Madras, even if it had no acknowledged influence on his conduct, stimulated, nevertheless, by its demoralising power, that spirit of rebellious pride, which led him first to oppose every order which would have set aside the treaty that he had concluded, and afterwards to assume a position, as defiant as it was unbecoming, as baneful to the interests of France as it was prejudicial to his own character.

CHAP. IV.
1746.

He has now, at the epoch of which we are writing, gazed for the last time on the scene of his triumphs. No more was he to be called upon to strike a blow for French India. Arriving in the Isle of France in the beginning of December, he found a successor, M. David, installed there, with orders to leave to La Bourdonnais the command of the fleet, only in case he found the accounts of his government in proper order.

M. David having pronounced favourably in this respect, La Bourdonnais was placed in command of the squadron, and directed to proceed to France, taking Martinique on the way. A storm shattered his ships off the Cape of Good Hope, but he succeeded, with four of them, in gaining Martinique. Here he learned that the homeward route was barred by English cruisers, whom it would be impossible to avoid, and who were too numerous to contend against. Impatient, however, to arrive in France to justify himself, he proceeded under a feigned name to St. Eustache, converted all his property into jewels,* and took a passage to France in a Dutch ship. War, however, had been declared between England and Holland, and the Dutch vessel was taken and carried into an English port. Here La Bourdonnais was recognised, and was at once constituted prisoner of war.

We diverge for a few moments from the strict record of our history to bring his career to a conclusion. Regarded by the English, in consequence of his conduct at Madras, as the champion of their interests in India—a poor compliment to a French admiral—testimonies of esteem and regard were showered upon him from all sides. By the Royal Family, by the Court of Directors, and by the public, he was treated with the greatest distinction. The Ministry even permitted him, at his own urgent request, to return to France on his parole, his

* Madame de la Bourdonnais embarked in a Portuguese ship with most of these jewels, and arrived safely in Lisbon; thence she proceeded to Paris.

anxiety to answer the charges brought against him being irrepressible.

But his reception in France was unfavourable. Accusations were lodged against him of having disregarded the King's orders, of having entered into a secret understanding with the enemy, of having diverted to his own use the funds of the Company. On these charges he was thrown into the Bastille, and was for three years kept confined in that fortress, deprived of the visits of his family, debarred even from the use of pen and ink. When, at the expiration of this period, his innocence* of the charges brought against him was declared, he came out of prison only to die. By means, nevertheless of handkerchiefs steeped in rice water, of coffee dregs, and of a pen made of a piece of copper money, he had succeeded in writing his biography—and this, published at a time when the fate of Dupleix was trembling in the balance, contributed not a little to turn the popular feeling against that statesman. La Bourdonnais died shortly after his release, on September 9, 1753.

But we must turn now to Pondichery, where Dupleix remains undisputed ruler, master of Madras, master even for the moment of the seas. His policy has triumphed, but yet dangers seem to be rising on two sides of him. On the one, England, alarmed at the loss of Madras, is making superhuman efforts to retaliate on Pondichery. On the other, the Nawwáb of the Karnátik, jealous of French aggrandisement, is demanding with eager messages the surrender to himself of Madras, the renunciation by the French of further designs of conquest, threatening hostilities in case of refusal.

In out next chapter will be recorded the consummate skill by which, in this crisis, Pondichery was preserved, Madras retained, and which planned the first direct blow for a French Empire in India.

* It was in the power alone of the Directors of the East India Company and of the Madras Council to prove the charge of bribery. Both preferred, on every account, to be silent.

CHAPTER V.

THE FIRST STRUGGLE IN THE KARNÁTIK.

CHAP. V.

1746.

THE mode in which Dupleix had purchased the consent of the Nawwáb of the Karnátik to the prosecution of his plans against Madras has been already related. With one great end in view—that of wresting Madras from the English—he had, during a crisis which might otherwise have been fatal, sacrificed the less important portion of the scheme, and, renouncing extension of territory for his own countrymen, had promised the Nawwáb to resign to him the conquests he should achieve. We have given our reasons why we believe Dupleix to have been sincere when he made this engagement. In his letter on the subject to La Bourdonnais—a letter intended for no other eye—he had expressed his intention to resign the town to the Nawwáb after demolishing its fortifications, and he had used this as a reason why it would be impossible for him to agree to any terms regarding ransom with the English. We have seen how the obstinacy of La Bourdonnais had for a long time prevented the accomplishment of these designs—how, from the date of the capitulation, the 21st of September, to his departure from Madras on the 23rd of October, that impetuous and self-willed officer had kept Madras in his own hands, and how, therefore, during that time, and for a week subsequently, the entire attention of Dupleix had been devoted to obtaining possession of the place, which had been conquered only to be kept from him. We have seen too how fatal the delay had been to him in one respect—in the destruction of the fleet which had been at once his mainstay for defence and the power upon which he counted for future blows against the English. Yet, damaging as had been the result in that respect, it sank into apparent insignificance when contrasted with the effect it had upon the suspicious mind of the Asiatic who had trusted him, only, it would seem, to be deceived.

The fact indeed that upwards of five weeks had elapsed since the French flag had first floated over the ramparts of Fort St. George, and that there were no indications of lowering it to make way for the flag of the Múghal, was in itself a circumstance more than sufficient to justify the doubt which Anwáru-dín was beginning to display. The quarrel between Dupleix and La Bourdonnais would naturally appear but a shallow and transparent artifice, invented for the purpose of cheating him out of his promised gains. It was enough for him that Madras continued French; to the name of the Frenchman who commanded there he was indifferent. His engagement had been made with the governor of the French possessions in India, and to that governor he looked for its absolute and literal fulfilment.

When, however, day succeeded day, and week followed week, and he received, instead of Madras, excuses founded upon the alleged insubordinate behaviour of the French official in command at Madras, the patience of the Nawwáb began to give way. Who were these French, he asked, these foreigners who had been so submissive and compliant, that they should thus not only beard him to his face, but should use him as a tool wherewith to effect their purposes? Upon what force did they rely to enable them to carry out their daring resolves? If they had a few hundred European and two or three thousand native soldiers, he could bring into the field twenty men to their one, and, against the means which the possession of a few places on the coast might make available for them, he could wield the resources of the entire Karnátik. He would teach these faithless Europeans to know their place and to respect his power, and if they should hesitate longer to carry out their engagement, he would compel its fulfilment by force of arms. At this determination Anwáru-dín had arrived long before La Bourdonnais had made over his conquest to Desprémesnil. He had even sent a detachment of his troops to the vicinity of Madras, there to remain until it should be joined by the main body. This main body, in number about 10,000, and commanded by Máfauz* Khán, eldest son of the Nawwáb, followed very shortly after, and encamped under the walls of Madras about the same date as that on which La Bourdonnais bade a final farewell to the roadstead of Pondichery.

This then was the first great difficulty which it fell to the lot of Dupleix to encounter after the departure of his rival. Let us consider for a moment what was actually his position. He had promised to make over Madras to the Nawwáb, but he had resolved, at the time he made that promise, first to demolish its fortifications. The insubordination of La Bourdonnais had prevented the possibility of doing one or the other before the 23rd October, and on that date his lieutenant, Desprémesnil, found himself threatened by the troops of the Nawwáb. He was on the other hand embarrassed by the engagements into which La Bourdonnais had entered with the English, and with which, although he had not ratified them, it would now be incumbent on him to deal in a decided manner. There was thus presented to him a complication of difficulties such as might well appal a mere ordinary mortal. Yet Dupleix set himself to meet them in the clear and logical manner natural to his well-ordered intellect. Of the difficulties we have enumerated, that caused by the threatening attitude of the Nawwáb was the most

* Derived from the Arabic words, *Ma,* splendour, *Fauz,* victory.

pressing. This, therefore, he set himself in the first instance to encounter. No man was more sensible than he of the very delicate nature of the task which thus lay before him. He had, indeed, promised to make over Madras to the Nawwáb, intending as we know, to make it over in a dismantled state. But being now for the first time in a position to perform the promise, he was prevented from accompanying that performance by the dismantling which, in his opinion, was a most necessary adjunct to it, and the more so, because Madras was at that moment invested by the Nawwáb. To dismantle Madras in the presence of the army of Máfauz Khán, would have roused in the breast of the Nawwáb an indignation equal to that which had been already kindled by abstaining from surrendering it. To make over Madras, on the other hand, with its fortifications still standing, would, he considered, be an act of treachery to French interests. It would be in that case, he felt, in the power of the Nawwáb to make his terms with the English, and to re-sell them a place which the French had conquered with the view to the permanent expulsion of that nation from the Koromandel coast. To such a line of conduct Dupleix could never reconcile himself. In the temper of the Nawwáb, however, any other course was fraught with danger. That danger and the possible disaster consequent upon it were, however, in the eyes of Dupleix, less formidable than the certain danger and certain disaster attendant upon an abject submission to the threats of the Nawwáb. He resolved, therefore, to risk the fury of his wrath rather than surrender French interests to his mercy, and to retain Madras for himself, rather than make it over with its fortifications undestroyed. But while he came to this fixed resolution, he determined to employ every art, to exhaust every device, to induce the Nawwáb to forego his claim, and to avert those hostilities with the satrap of the Múghal, which now, for the first time, seemed to threaten the French colony. As to his promise, he considered himself absolved from its performance by the fact, that the Nawwáb was now endeavouring to obtain by force of arms that which Dupleix, if left to himself, would have been willing, on the earliest possible occasion compatible with his own security, to concede.

Having resolved on this course, Dupleix sent instructions to Desprémesnil to keep Madras at all hazards, but to refrain from any act of hostility towards the troops of Máfauz Khán, beyond those which would necessarily result from the defence of the place. The French troops who garrisoned Madras amounted to between five and six hundred Europeans, and about the same number of natives, disciplined in the European fashion. In obedience to the orders received from Dupleix, the Governor, Desprémesnil, withdrew the whole of these troops within the walls on the approach of the enemy, with the intention of confining himself strictly to the defence of the town. But as Máfauz Khán showed himself very earnest in his attack, and in the course of a few days reduced the garrison to some difficulties, by cutting off from them the only spring which supplied them with good water, Desprémesnil found it necessary to abandon this cautious policy, and to try the effect of a sortie. On the 2nd November, therefore, early in the morning, he detached a body of 400 men, accompanied by two field-pieces, to attack that portion of the enemy's army which had gained possession of the spring. As this handful of men advanced, the guns following close in the rear, to encounter, as it seemed, certain destruction from the overwhelming force of the Múghal, the enemy's cavalry hastily collected and galloped towards them with the intention of riding them down. Still steadily, undaunted by the imposing array of the squadrons charging towards them, the French advanced. When, however, they judged the enemy to have arrived within point-blank range, they opened out from the centre, uncovering the fieldpieces, and halted. The first discharge from the two guns went straight into the mass of the hostile cavalry, killing some of the foremost horses. This caused a temporary confusion and halt, which gave the French time to load again. The enemy, unaccustomed to such rapid firing, knowing so little of the European practice of artillery as to consider one shot in a quarter of an hour excellent practice, were confounded at this second discharge. Instead, then, of taking advantage of it to charge home, they halted to look on in mingled doubt, wonder, and fear. But when a third discharge succeeded a second, and a fourth a third, all carrying destruction into their ranks, they hesitated no longer. Terrified at this novel mode of warfare, they fled precipitately, leaving their tents and baggage a prey to the conqueror. They lost from this cannonade about seventy men, whilst amongst the French not a man was even wounded.*

Meanwhile Dupleix had not been less indefatigable at Pondichery. The accounts he received as to the reality and earnestness of the attack on Madras, had convinced him that persistence in a purely defensive line of action would be highly impolitic, and he had determined to effect a diversion by threatening the enemy's camp from the side of Pondichery, with the view of compelling him to raise the siege. The command of the detachment which was to effect this end, and which numbered about 230 Europeans and 700 sipáhis, he intrusted to Paradis, the most capable officer under his orders.

The news of the march of this detachment reached Máfauz Khán immediately after the defeat of his cavalry by the Madras garrison. He appears to have instantly taken a resolution worthy of a greater com-

* Orme, Dupleix.

mander. This was to march with the bulk of his force to intercept and destroy that small detachment, before an opportunity should be afforded it of opening communications with the garrison of Madras. With this view he marched to St. Thomé, and took up a position on the northern bank of the little river Adyár, which runs into the sea on its southern side, and which it would be necessary for Paradis to cross in order to communicate with Madras.

On the morning of November 4, Paradis came in sight of the host of the Nawwáb, numbering nearly 10,000 men, posted on the north bank of the river, their position covered by guns. He had no guns, but he was a man of a stern and a resolute nature, prompt in his decisions, and losing no time in carrying them into effect. He was little startled by the sight before him. His orders were to open communication with Madras, and these he could not carry out by either halting or retreating. He therefore resolved to cut his way through the enemy. Without waiting to reconnoitre, he dashed into the river, which he knew to be fordable, scrambled up the bank in face of the enemy's guns, then halting to deliver one volley, ordered a charge. The effect was electric. The enemy at once gave way, and retreated in terrible confusion into the town, from behind the defences of which they attempted to offer a new resistance. But Paradis was not the man to leave half his work undone. He followed the enemy with vigour, and halted in front of the town, poured in volley after volley on the masses jumbled together in the crowded streets. These had but one thought—to escape. Their very numbers, however, impeded their movement in any direction, and it was not until after many of them had fallen, that they succeeded in extricating themselves from their position. Hardly had they accomplished this, however, when they found themselves assailed by another enemy. The garrison of

Madras had hastened on the first intimation of the approach of Paradis to march to his aid. They arrived in time to intercept the retreating masses of the Nawwáb's army, and to convert their defeat into an utter and demoralising rout. Their general, Máfauz Khán, had fled on the first charge of the French; the body of men who formed his army, without a leader, and terror-stricken by their crushing overthrow, at once gave up all thoughts of gaining Madras, and did not halt till they had traversed many miles from that place in the direction of Arkát.*

It may be well asserted that of all the decisive actions that have been fought in India, there is not one more memorable than this. Not, indeed, that there has not since been displayed a daring equal to that of Paradis, or that numbers as disproportionate have not within the memory of the living achieved as great a victory. The circumstance which stamps this action as so memorable is that it was the very first of its kind, that it proved, to the surprise of both parties, the absolute and overwhelming superiority of the disciplined European soldier to his Asiatic rival. Up to that time the native princes of India had, by virtue of their position as lords of the soil or as satraps of the Múghal, of their numerous following, their acknowledged power, arrogated to themselves a superiority which none of the European settlers on the eastern coast had ever thought of disputing. With the French, as we have seen, it had been a maxim of settled policy to avoid even the semblance of hostility towards them. We have noticed how Martin and Dumas and Dupleix had toiled to effect this end. When at last Dupleix, to avoid a more dangerous contingency, accepted this dreaded alternative, he did so more in the hope that he might find some means of pacifying the Nawwáb whilst the siege was in progress, than in any expectation of

* Orme, Dupleix.

CHAP. V.
1746.

routing him in the field. And now suddenly, unexpectedly, this result had been achieved. From being the suppliants of the Nawwáb of the Karnátik,—the vassals whose very movements depended upon his license,—they in a moment found themselves in reality, his superiors. This action at St. Thomé, in fact, completely reversed the positions of the Nawwáb and the French Governor. Not only that, but it inaugurated a new era, it introduced a fresh order of things, it was the first decided step to the conquest of Hindustan by an European power. Whether that power were French or English would depend upon the relative strength of either nation, and even more on the character of the men by whom that strength should be put in action. The battle which introduced this change was one then that well deserves to be remembered ; and, in remembering it, let not us, who are English, forget to record that the merit of it is due, solely and entirely, to that great nation which fought with us the battle of empire on Indian soil, and did not win it.*

To Dupleix this victory presented the means of extricating himself from all his difficulties. He now found himself able to carry out the plans which he had conceived at the time of the capture of Madras by La Bourdonnais. The conduct of the Nawwáb in declaring war against him, in besieging Madras, and in endeavouring to intercept and destroy his little army, had quite cancelled the obligation under which he had placed himself to make over to him his conquest. That difficulty had been happily surmounted. Nor did the other bequeathed to him by La Bourdonnais, that of restoring

---

* Mr. Orme wrote on this subject: "It was now more than a century since any of the European nations had gained a decisive advantage in war against the officers of the Great Múghal. The experience of former unsuccessful enterprises, and the scantiness of military abilities which prevailed in all the colonies, from a long disuse of arms, had persuaded them that the Moors were a brave and formidable enemy ; when the French at once broke through the charm of this timorous opinion, by defeating a whole army with a single battalion.

Madras to the English, present any longer an obstacle. He had never ratified the unauthorised engagements into which La Bourdonnais had entered. To him they were as though they had never been made. Madras, he knew well, would have surrendered at the same time, or at the utmost a day later, had no reference been made to a ransom. The place was not at the time capable of further defence. He regarded it therefore as his conquest, as a lawful prize to French valour, and he determined, now that he possessed the power, to use it for the interests of France, regardless of those engagements into which La Bourdonnais had been lured, and which he had never sanctioned.

No sooner, then, had he received intimation of the utter defeat of the Nawwáb's army, and of the triumphant relief of Madras, than he appointed Paradis military governor of that place, instead of Desprémesnil, who, as a civilian, would not, he considered, exercise sufficient authority over the troops, and instructed him to issue a declaration proclaiming Madras to be French by right of conquest, and disavowing all engagements entered into by La Bourdonnais as null and void.

Paradis was not slow to act upon his orders. He had beaten the Nawwáb's army on November 4, and had entered Madras the same day. On the 9th he received his instructions, and on the 10th he issued his proclamation. In this, he annulled La Bourdonnais' ransom-treaty; declared all the merchandise, provisions, warlike stores, and horses to be French property, and ordered all the English residents who would not take the oath of allegiance to the French, to quit the town within four days. On the other hand, the English were permitted to dispose of their moveables, clothes, and jewels, and they were simply required not to serve against the French till they should be exchanged. Governor Morse and the other officials were conveyed as prisoners to Pondichery, where, however, they were treated with the greatest courtesy and consideration.* The entire English community, indeed, protested against the high-handed proceeding of Paradis, and some of its members even made their escape to Fort St. David. Amongst those who adopted this course was a young writer named Robert Clive.

Fort St. David, about twelve miles south of Pondichery, and about two north of Gudalur, had been purchased by the English in the year 1691, and had been, by degrees, fairly fortified. Its strength for purposes of resistance was increased by its proximity to Gudalur, which was fortified on three sides, the side facing the sea being alone undefended. It had now become, by the capture of Madras, the English seat of government, and those who occupied the chief places of authority were animated by a fixed determination to defend it to the last extremity,—even to invoke, for that purpose, the aid of the native chieftains.

It was indeed high time that they should do something, for Dupleix had resolved that their last place of refuge should be his next conquest. This great statesman, in fact, believed that now, after all the vicissitudes of his career, after all the trials he had been subjected to, he had at last found his opportunity. Madras was in his possession; he was free from all fear of effectual interference on the part of the Nawwáb, what was then to hinder him from carrying out his darling plan of expelling the English from that coast? To bring matters to their present point, he had risked the contest with La Bourdonnais, the fury of the ruler of the Karnátik, and now, having attained that end, he felt his hands free to

---

* Mr. Orme declares that the English prisoners were marched in ostentatious procession through the streets of Pondichery, but he gives no authority for his statement. The fact is that the English prisoners were treated with the greatest consideration. The story of the procession was invented by La Bourdonnais, who had left Pondichery long before the prisoners arrived. In vol. xv. of the now extinct *National Review*, art. "Dupleix," the true version is given on the authority, apparently, of the *Ariel Papers*.

push his advantage to its utmost limit, and to strike at Fort St. David. With his accustomed promptitude, he determined to carry out this plan without any loss of time,—a determination the more necessary, as he fully expected that a few months would deprive him of the advantage which he then possessed of the mastery at sea.

The command of this expedition Dupleix intended to intrust to the officer whom of all under his orders he considered the most capable. This was Paradis. To him, therefore, he sent instructions to return to Pondichery with all the troops he could spare, as soon as he should have settled the affairs of Madras. It was not before the first week of December, however, that Paradis was able to move. Leaving then the bulk of the garrison behind him, he marched at the head of 300 men, escorting the plunder of Madras, in the direction of Pondichery.

These proceedings on the part of the French did not escape the attention of the Nawwáb. The month that had elapsed since the defeat at St. Thomé had very much effaced the sharper stings of the lesson the Múghal had then received. Máfauz Khán, especially, burned with impatience to efface the galling recollection of that day's defeat. No better opportunity, he thought, would present itself than that which seemed now about to offer, when a body of three hundred men should be embarrassed by the numerous coolies laden with the plunder which they were escorting. Impressed with these ideas, he assembled a body of 3,000 foot and 2,000 horse, the flower of his army, and took up a position at the little village of Kuntur, thirty-two miles south of Madras, through which he knew that the French detachment must pass. Paradis was marching in a careless style, unsuspicious of the vicinity of an enemy. He had divided his force into two bodies, an advanced party and a rear guard, and between these were the coolies. Suddenly the cavalry of Máfauz Khán appeared upon the plain, and made as though they would attack the rear-guard. The attitude of the French, however, shook their resolution, and they contented themselves with hovering about in the vicinity, dashing at stragglers, and forcing the troops who composed the rear-guard to constant formations. Uneasy at this, and fearing to be overtaken by night before he should reach the Dutch settlement of Sadras, ten miles further on, Paradis at once altered his order of marching. Sending the coolies in front of the troops he covered them with the body that had formed his advanced-guard, and with it hastened on to that place. The rear-guard, meanwhile, had the task assigned it of proceeding at a more leisurely pace, so as to engage the attention of the enemy. This manœuvre answered all his expectations. The first detachment with the coolies reached Sadras without the loss of a man, whilst of the second, only twelve men were captured, and these more from a disposition to loiter than from the fault of the commander. Arriving at Sadras, Paradis halted until he should receive further reinforcements. On the arrival of these he marched without molestation to join the main encampment of the French army at Ariákupum, a mile and a half south-west of Pondichery. Here he arrived on December 17. Máfauz Khán having found it impossible to gain any material advantage over the French troops, had desisted from his attempts after the arrival of the French at Sadras.

The junction of Paradis completed all the preparations of Dupleix. With a force of about 900 Europeans, 600 natives, 100 Africans, six field-pieces and six mortars, he was, it appeared, absolutely master of the coast. The English garrison of Fort St. David numbered but 200 Europeans and half the number of natives. The French, too, had all the inspiration of recent victory. The success of the intended expedition seemed certain, far more certain in fact than the success of La Bourdonnais had appeared at the period of his attack upon Madras. No one knew better, however, than Dupleix that, in spite of all favourable appearances, one necessary element of success was yet wanting. He had the soldiers, the guns, the munitions of war, but had he the general? This was the one want without which the success which seemed to be his would yet slip from his grasp. He knew this well, and with his accustomed energy he set himself to supply it.

The Commander-in-chief of the French troops in Pondichery at this time was General de Bury, an officer not only old, but possessing the worst characteristics of age. To intrust the command of the expedition to such a man was, Dupleix felt, to insure its failure. Yet, as the senior, he had the right to command. On the other hand, there was Paradis, the hero of St. Thomé, an engineer by profession, and a man whose courage and capacity were established. In his hands the expedition would have the best chance of success. To give the command to Paradis, therefore, all the efforts of Dupleix were directed.

Unfortunately for France, and for himself, he did not succeed. There were other officers between Paradis and de Bury, and these protested against such a supersession. His Swiss birth, his inferior rank, the jealousy which his recent success had caused amongst the small-minded, all contributed to hinder the elevation of Paradis, and in the presence of the great discontent which the proposal excited, Dupleix was, at last, forced to abandon the idea.

Under the command of de Bury, therefore, the force marched on the night of December 19, crossed the river Panár the following morning with but little opposition, and took possession of a walled garden, about a mile and a half to the north-west of Fort St. David. Here, deeming themselves secure, and being fatigued and hungry from their march, the troops lodged their arms, and prepared to cook their dinners.

It is time now that we should turn to the movements of the English. Irritated by the high-handed proceedings of Dupleix at Madras, by the abrogation of the treaty, these had resolved to undergo any extremity rather than surrender. In addition to the garrison of 300 men, to which we have adverted, they had taken into their service 1,000 irregular native troops, known then by the name of peons, and, what was of more importance, they had entered into an intimate alliance with the Nawwáb. In concert with him, it had been agreed that, whilst the French should be engaged in the attack on Fort St. David and Gudalur, both of which they were determined to defend to the utmost, he should suddenly seize that opportunity to assail them, and place them between two fires.

It is probable that had the French been led by a general of even ordinary capacity this attack would have failed, but de Bury was wanting in all the qualities that go to form a general. In taking possession of the garden, and allowing his troops to disperse to cook their morning meal, he considered he had quite sufficiently acted his part. He took no care that pickets should be told off, or sentries posted. Not a single man was, therefore, on the look out. Carelessly giving himself to the repose which his age required, de Bury acted, and allowed his soldiers to act, as though he and they had just completed an ordinary march, in a time of peace, through a friendly country.

Rightly was he punished for this neglect. His men were dispersed, their arms grounded, he himself taking his repose, when suddenly the alarm was given that the enemy were upon them. A panic seized them. Grasping at the first weapon that was at hand, some indeed half-dressed, they rushed disorderly to quit a place which they might have defended against the Nawwáb's whole army. Their one thought was to reach and cross the river, and towards it they ran without order or array. But the enemy, who were 6,000 horse and 3,000 foot of the Nawwáb's army, commanded by his two sons, were there before them. Notwithstanding this, the French rushed recklessly into the river, impatient only to gain the opposite bank. Fortunately for them, their artillery, which was admirably handled, and to the troops composing which the panic had not extended, kept the enemy at a distance. More than that, its commander, not content with covering the disordered retreat of the infantry, deliberately transported his own guns, one by one across the river, in face of the enemy, and, when on the other bank, served them so as to keep the Múghals at bay. It was not until the French had retreated for upwards of two hours, that the natives could be prevailed upon to pursue them, and then only after they had been urged thereto by the English garrison of Fort St. David, which had arrived too late to take any part in the skirmish at the river Panár. The pursuit was fruitless in results. The French had long before recovered from their panic, and the attitude they presented on the approach of the enemy, made the Múghal princes think rather of their own safety than of an attack on their position. M. de Bury on his part was equally indisposed to expose his army to further risks. As soon, therefore, as the allied force of the English and Múghals commenced a retrograde movement towards Gudalur, he continued his retreat to Ariákupum, where he arrived the same evening, after having sustained a loss in this ill-conducted expedition of twelve men killed and a hundred and twenty wounded. A small quantity of muskets and stores, which had been left behind in the garden at Gudalur, fell likewise into the hands of the enemy. On their side the French could congratulate themselves only on the facts that they had saved all their guns, and that they had killed and wounded of the Nawwáb's army upwards of two thousand men.*

For three weeks after this fruitless expedition, the French army continued in its encampment. Dupleix, however, had not been idle. On the fresh outbreak of hostilities, he had despatched instructions to M. Dordelin, who, it will be remembered, commanded the squadron which had gone to winter at Achín, to hasten with his four ships† to the coast. In the expectation of the early arrival of these, he resolved to re-open negotiations with the Nawwáb, to point out to him the folly of extending further protection to a people, reduced, as were the English, to the last extremity, and the expediency of maintaining amicable relations with the European power, which, in Europe as in Asia, occupied the first position among nations. That self-interest might aid in inducing the Nawwáb to lend a willing ear to these proposals, he directed the commandant of Madras to undertake without delay measures to threaten Arkát with an attack from a French army.

The messengers of Dupleix found the Nawwáb tired of fruitless hostilities, and not altogether indisposed to enter into an accommodation with the French, though still demanding the execution of the original agreement. To induce him either to decide at once, or to render his decision of less importance, Dupleix determined to endeavour to surprise Gudalur. On the night of January 10, he embarked five hundred men from the camp at Ariákupum in boats for the purpose. The night was dark but fine, Gudalur was open on the seaside, and everything promised success. But the boats had hardly got through the surf, when a storm arose which forced them to return.

Ten days later, M. Dordelin's squadron arrived. It now seemed to lie in the power of Dupleix to make

* Orme, Dupleix.
† The "Centaure," the "Brillant," the "Mars," and the "St. Louis."

upon the English settlement a combined attack by sea and land such as must be fatal. It is difficult to say why the attempt was not made. The importance of it was undoubtedly obvious to Dupleix. It is probable, however, that he was hampered by the character of his naval and military commanders. Dordelin was feeble and unenterprising; de Bury, as we have seen, worn out and incapable.

But though he did not use the squadron for the purpose to which he might, under better auspices, have directed it, its presence on the coast was not absolutely resultless. The Nawwáb, struck by this accession of force, and learning at the same time that the country around Arkát had been ravaged by the French troops, could no longer resist the conclusion that he had engaged in a struggle which could but end in loss and dishonour to himself; that the English had evidently been abandoned even by their own countrymen, and that every consideration of policy prompted him to accept the offers of the French Governor. He no longer therefore continued to insist upon the fulfilment of the agreement regarding Madras, but signed at once a treaty, by which the French were confirmed in possession of all the territories which they then held, and the Nawwáb agreed to leave the English to their fate. This treaty was ratified by Máfauz Khán in person during a visit of ceremony which he paid to Dupleix at Pondichery, at the end of the following February.

Now, at last, the English were apparently in his power. Abandoned by everyone, numbering but three hundred, occupying a position little capable of prolonged defence, what could possibly save them? If, at this conjuncture, Dupleix had put into action that great principle of warfare,—a principle appliable alike to all transactions in which men ordinarily engage,—to bring the greatest force to bear on the decisive point of the scene of contest, he must have gained his great end.

CHAP. V.
1747.

Between the time of Dordelin's arrival, January 20, and the visit of Máfauz Khán at the end of February, there had been ample time to carry out an expedition, which must under ordinary circumstances have succeeded. In allowing his fleet and army to remain inactive during this period, we fail to trace the practical ability and fertile genius which so often guided the operations of the French governor. The inactivity is the more inexplicable as Dupleix well knew that Commodore Peyton's squadron in the Húglí was waiting only the arrival of reinforcements, then daily expected, to re-assert the predominance of the English power in the Bay of Bengal. It is possible, indeed, that this very knowledge may have contributed to his inaction. We have seen how in his correspondence with La Bourdonnais, he clung to the idea of keeping a reserve of French ships within call of Pondichery. Dordelin's squadron was all that remained to him, and it can be conceived that he hesitated to engage those four ships, under a commander so wanting in energy and steadfastness, against the batteries of Fort St. David, knowing, as he did, that the northerly breezes which at that season blew down the Bay might at any moment bring upon them the squadron of Peyton, reinforced by fresh ships from England. It is probable, likewise, that the same consideration urged him, as soon as his negotiations with the Nawwáb had been brought to a successful close, to despatch that squadron to the safe and neutral anchorage of Goa. This he did on February 19.

But whatever were his motives, whether he was influenced by the considerations we have suggested, or by others of which we have no knowledge,* it is certain

---

* In his memoir, Dupleix does not allude to the possibility of using his ships for the purpose of attacking Gudalur and Fort St. David, although Gudalur, at least, was open towards the sea. He seems to have been impressed by the idea that, as the superiority at sea was about to pass almost immediately to the English, he could not better employ his time than to endeavour to detach the native powers from their alliance.

that he lost a golden opportunity. He too was fated soon to experience the truth that such opportunities, once granted, are seldom vouchsafed a second time; that, when offered, therefore, they ought to be seized with a promptitude and used with a determination before which all other considerations should be made to give way.

He did not, however, at all resign the great object of all his political manœuvres. On the contrary, he was more than ever bent on the expulsion of the English from Fort St. David. No sooner then had the accommodation with the Nawwáb been completed, and the Múghal troops withdrawn, then he summoned a council of war, placed before it the situation in which he was, the daily expected approach of an English squadron, and the expediency of attempting once more the capture of Fort St. David. He urged at the same time the fitness of Paradis for the command, and pressed upon the assembled officers the necessity of suppressing all considerations of self-interest in the presence of a crisis, calling so much for self-denial and earnest co-operation for a great end, as that which then existed. This appeal to their patriotism was at once heartily responded to, and the French officers consented to acknowledge and obey Paradis as their general.

Before, however, all these preliminaries had been carried out, the garrison of Fort St. David had received a small reinforcement of twenty men, and a considerable supply of money. An English ship decoyed into the Madras roads at the end of November by the sight of the English colours flying over the fort, and then suddenly attacked, had managed nevertheless* to escape and make its way to Trinkámalí. There the captain received information of the actual state of affairs on the

---

* Other ships were not so fortunate. One especially, having on board £60,000 in bullion, besides stores of all sorts, was entrapped into the roadstead in the same manner and there boarded.—*Orme.*

Koromandel coast, and thinking he might be able to serve his countrymen, he gallantly resolved to bear up for Fort St. David. He succeeded in this, in spite of the four ships of war under the unenterprising Dordelin and conveyed to the English garrison a reinforcement of twenty men and £60,000 in silver. This was the more acceptable, as, shortly before, another English ship, carrying soldiers and bullion, and consigned to Madras, had touched at Fort St. David, where deeming the state of the garrison irretrievable, her captain had refused to land either soldiers or money, but had proceeded in all haste to Bengal.

The small reinforcement we have referred to reached Fort St. David on March 2. On the 13th, Paradis put his troops in motion, and marching along the coast, took up a position the same day on the north of the Panár, about a quarter of a mile from the river. The Panár, though in some parts fordable, was in others of a sufficient depth to make crossing in the face of an enemy a difficult operation. Knowing this, the English garrison wisely resolved not to wait for the French within the walls of the fort, but to oppose the passage of the river. They accordingly moved out, took up a position on the southern bank of the Panár, and commenced a brisk cannonade on the French with three field-pieces they had brought with them. Paradis, for the time, contented himself with replying, but in the evening he moved with the bulk of his force higher up the river, and crossed it without opposition,—the English volunteers, who had been sent to observe him, retiring on the loss of two of their number, and retreating with the main body within the fort. Paradis immediately took possession of the walled garden from which De Bury in the former expedition had fled so precipitately, and made his preparations for the attack on the fort on the following day.

Then was seen, with a clearness incapable of being

misunderstood, the terrible, the fatal effect of throwing away an opportunity. From December 10 to February 13, the French army had been idle at Ariákupum. Dordelin's squadron had arrived on January 20, and within ten days of its arrival, the Nawwáb had signified his intention of withdrawing his support from the English. Had Paradis been allowed to march even a month earlier, on February 13 instead of March 13, he must have been able, within those twenty-eight days, to force his way into Fort St. David. Even one week earlier, and his chances would have been considerable. Whilst Dordelin's squadron might have attacked the open face of Gudalur with a certainty of mastering it, he might have moved, with an equal confidence of victory, upon Fort St. David. That it would have fallen may be considered certain when we recollect how quickly it surrendered, after its defences had been greatly strengthened, some years later, to the attack of Lally. Had that been accomplished, the fleets of England would have found no resting-place for the soldiers they carried with them on the soil of the Karnátik, and the foundations of a French Empire might have been laid.

But it was not to be. The inaction of one month, unexplained, and to our minds inexplicable, threw away that great chance, lost that splendid opportunity. In this one instance, Dupleix acted as though he believed he could count for ever on the favours of Fortune. The fickle goddess showed him in return that she will never continue to help those who decline to help themselves. She aids the daring and skilful warrior, but she leaves him the exercise of his free will. Should he evince carelessness, indecision, or blindness, she leaves him then, and rightly leaves him, to the consequences of his own acts.

On March 14, Paradis was in the position, in which, had Dupleix willed it, he might have been early in

February. In February he would have had the English garrison, then having received no reinforcement and destitute of supplies, to deal with. But, on the morning of March 14, as, before making his advance against the fort, he cast his eyes over the sea, the sight of several vessels, evidently vessels of war, sailing from the north, met his anxious gaze. Who could these strangers be? Not Dordelin and his ships, for Dordelin, he knew, was well on his way to Goa. They could scarcely even be French, for the French had but one vessel in the Madras roads. Who could they be, he felt, but the reinforced squadron of Peyton? His uncertainty, if he felt any, did not last long. The hoisting of the Union Jack soon told him that the third expedition against Fort St. David had failed.

It was, indeed, the long expected, long dreaded squadron, reinforced by two ships, one of sixty, one of forty guns, and what was of equal consequence, strengthened by the arrival of a new commander. This officer, Admiral Griffin, learning at Calcutta the danger which threatened Fort St. David, had sailed without delay to its succour, and thus arrived in time to save it and the English garrison from the fate by which both were threatened. He brought with him as a permanent reinforcement a hundred Europeans from Bengal, but the sailors on board the squadron were capable of affording still more efficient aid.

Under such circumstances but one course remained to Paradis. The arrival of this fleet endangered the safety of Pondichery. His little army constituted the main strength of that place, as well for defence as for attack. Thither, accordingly, he must return. He made up his mind at once, and before the English had recovered from the reaction of joy which the arrival of their ships produced amongst them, he had re-crossed the Panár, and was well on his way to Ariákupum. There he arrived the same evening. A few days after, on the appearance of Admiral Griffin's fleet before Pondichery, he was recalled within the town.

It was now the turn of Dupleix to be cut off from the sea, to be left entirely to his own resources. Not only was a powerful English fleet in the Pondichery roadstead, but ships from England, from Bombay, Tellicheri, and other places, continued to bring reinforcements to the garrison of Fort St. David. The three hundred Europeans and natives of which it was composed in January, had increased in July to 2,000, including upwards of 600 sailors borrowed from the fleet. The friendship of the Nawwáb, he knew, would always go with the stronger power. Madras had but a small garrison, and any movement of the Nawwáb's troops would cut off the only possible communication,— that by land,—with Pondichery, whilst that city itself lay exposed to the bombardment, as well as to the blockade, of a powerful squadron. Yet Dupleix was born to shine in adversity. Never did his great qualities appear so great as when he was surrounded by dangers. Though cut off from all communication with the sea, he yet managed to send instructions to Dordelin to proceed, as soon as the monsoon should be over, to the islands, to join his squadron to any French ships that should be there, and to represent to the governor the necessity under which he was of speedy and efficient aid. He held himself, meanwhile, ready not only to defend Pondichery against all attacks, but even, should occasion offer, to retaliate on the enemy.

The possession of the Isles of France and Bourbon, midway between the mother country and India, gave the French a very great advantage over their English rivals in this early stage of the battle for empire. These islands formed, in fact, the base of the operations, naval and military, which the French undertook in India. They were believed to be secure against hostile attacks, and a French squadron could wait its opportunity in the commodious harbour of Port Louis; could re-fit and re-victual there; and could reckon, almost to a certainty, the chances of meeting or avoiding a hostile fleet. There single ships could be detained, as they had been in the time of La Bourdonnais, until a sufficient number should be collected; and even should that number prove insufficient for the purpose required, that man, full of energy and resources, had proved the possibility of providing ships from materials which were to be found in the islands. The English possessed no such position. It was only when allied, as they were on the occasion of which we are writing, with the republic of Holland, that they were able to make use of the Cape of Good Hope, and even to augment their armament from its resources. This uncertain and temporary advantage, however, liable at times to be rendered nugatory, was not to be compared with the permanent benefit resulting to the inhabitants of Pondichery from the possession of a solid *point d'appui* in the Indian Ocean.

It was to derive from these islands the advantages they were so well capable of affording that Dupleix despatched Dordelin on his mission. His arrival at the islands in December, 1747, was opportune. He found the Governor of Bourbon, M. Bouvet, well inclined to respond to the call, and possessing or expecting the means which would enable him to do so with effect. In fact one ship of fifty guns, and another of forty, had arrived some short time since from France, conveying reinforcements and treasure for Pondichery. They had subsequently proceeded on a cruise in search of prizes, but their return was shortly expected. Two smaller vessels were in Port Louis ready to sail.

Accidental causes deferred the departure of this squadron, consisting, by the return of the cruising vessels, of seven large ships* and two small ones, from

---

* There was one of 74 guns, one of 56, two of 50, two of 40, and one of 26 guns.

the islands, till the beginning of May. M. Bouvet then set sail, having a fair wind, arrived off Kárikál about the middle of June. There he learned the superiority in numbers of the English squadron,* and he resolved, instead of hazarding an engagement, the result of which might jeopardise and even ruin French interests in India, to manœuvre so as to delude the English admiral with the expectation of a contest, and to take advantage of the darkness of the night to run on to Madras. He carried out his plan with exceeding skill. Arriving off Fort St. David on the afternoon of the 21st, and descrying and being descried by the English squadron, with which, he being to windward, it was optional to him to engage, he altered his course to the south-west, as though he intended to wait for the morning to attack. The English admiral was so impressed with the idea that either this or a desire to gain Pondichery was his intention, that he took no more advantage of the land wind which blew from off the coast in the evening, than to maintain out at sea the latitude of Fort St. David. But night had no sooner fallen than the French admiral again altered his course, and stood up for Madras. Having reached it the following morning, he waited only to land 300 soldiers, including several that were invalids, and £200,000, in silver; this successfully achieved, he hastened back to the Isle of France, having completely deceived the English Admiral, and accomplished at least one great part of his purpose.

But the indirect effects of this expedition were greater even than those which were apparent. Ignorant of the course taken by the French fleet, Admiral Griffin left his position off Fort St. David to go in search of it. This intelligence had no sooner reached Dupleix than he determined to profit by it, and by a bold effort to surprise Gudalur. To this end he despatched on the

* This consisted of three ships of 60 guns, three of 50, three of 40, and one of 20 guns.

27th June a force of 1,800 men, of whom 800 were Europeans, to make such a détour as would bring them without being observed into the vicinity of that town, upon which they were to fall in the darkness of midnight. But Major Lawrence, who had arrived shortly before from England to command the English forces in India, was too well served by his subordinates. He was informed, not only of the approach of the French, but of their intentions. Not only did he make no secret of the knowledge, he openly used it to increase the confidence of the enemy. He ostentatiously removed the garrison and the guns from Gudalur, and gave out that he intended to confine himself to the defence of Fort St. David. No sooner, however, had night fallen than he threw a strong garrison into the place, and mounted all the guns he could spare upon the ramparts. The French, completely deceived by his movements during the day, made sure of their conquest, and neglected every precaution. At midnight they advanced carelessly towards the place, believing they would meet with only a nominal resistance. But they had scarcely planted their scaling ladders than they were received with such a fire of grapeshot and small arms as sent destruction and disorder into their ranks. Utterly confounded and panic-stricken they retreated in the utmost confusion, scarcely stopping for a halt till, baffled and humiliated, they reached Pondichery.*

Thus, for the fourth time, was Dupleix forced to renounce his designs upon the last refuge of the English. The fault on this occasion was certainly not his own. An experienced and resolute general at the head of such a force as that of which the French detachment was composed, would have made Major Lawrence bitterly regret his *finesse*. Had the French advanced against Gudalur as soon as they observed its walls dismantled

---

* We have been unable to ascertain the name of the officer who commanded the French troops on this occasion.

and its garrison retreating the chances in their favour would have been very great. Major Lawrence, and not the French, would then have been surprised; the tables would have been turned on the author of the stratagem. But to do this required a head to devise, a resolution to execute promptly and at the moment. These were wanting in the leader of the French force. A foolish confidence reigned where energy and watchfulness ought to have held sway, and the movement which might have been made fatal to the English was, without thought, without examination, tacitly and complacently permitted by the French leader to become the means of inflicting upon his army a terrible defeat—upon the French colony a danger that appeared to forebode almost inevitable destruction.

For, in ordering this last attack, Dupleix had a far different purpose than that by which he was prompted in sanctioning those that preceded it. Then he was fighting for empire—he was struggling to expel the English from the coast. But since the last attack for that object, made on March 14th of the previous year, had been foiled by the arrival of the English fleet, the aspect of affairs had changed. It was not only that Admiral Griffin still remained on the coast preventing French traffic, obstructing all communication with France: it was not alone that M. Bouvet had appeared off Madras only to land a few soldiers and to return to the islands; but since that attack, intelligence had reached Dupleix that the English had fitted out a most formidable fleet and army, larger than any that had yet appeared in the Indian seas, with the express object of laying siege to Pondichery, and of retorting upon that city the disaster which had befallen Madras. He knew, from letters received from the French Ministry, that that fleet and army had left England during the preceding November, and might be expected to appear at any moment in the Bay of Bengal. It was, then, in an entirely defensive point of view that he had designed his fourth attack upon Gudalur. Securing that place, and by its means Fort St. David, during the absence of Admiral Griffin, he would have deprived the English force of any base of operations on the shore, and would have compelled them to attempt, in the face of an enemy, a landing upon a coast which presented natural difficulties of a most formidable character. The carelessness of his officers defeated, however, this well-considered project.

Forced then, once again, to depend upon his own resources, to resign himself to defence, he began, with characteristic energy, to strengthen as much as possible, before the enemy should appear, the places which he yet held. Of these, next to Pondichery, the principal was Ariákupum, a small post a mile and a half from Pondichery, and the same distance from the sea. To this place Paradis was sent, in his capacity of chief engineer, with instructions to make it as capable as possible of defence. He executed his instructions in a most effective manner. The fort itself was a triangle, with but few defences exterior or interior. Paradis set to work to construct three cavaliers within the body of the place, a deep ditch, and a covered way. The care of the works thus fortified was consigned to a young captain, named Law, a nephew of the famous Scotch financier, whose influence on the affairs of the French India Company has been before referred to.

We have already recorded the noble manner in which Dupleix, in the early days of his administration, had devoted himself to the completion of the defences of Pondichery.* The fortifications facing the sea, on which he had laboured, with so much earnestness, consisted of two demi-bastions, one at each extremity of the face. On the three other sides the city was defended by a wall and a rampart, flanked by eleven

* Chapter III.

bastions. The entire works were surrounded by a ditch and an imperfect glacis.* The side opposite to the sea, facing the interior, was also defended by several low batteries, capable of mounting upwards of a hundred pieces of cannon, and commanding the approaches from that side. Besides these artificial defences was a formidable natural protection, consisting of a hedge of prickly pear, which, beginning on the north side at the sea, a mile from the town, continued a semicircle all round it, until it joined the river Ariákupum, close to the fort of the same name; from that point the river continued the line of defence to the sea. Within this enclosure were cocoa-nut and palm trees so thickly studded as to render the ground very difficult for the advance of an enemy. Of these fortifications, Paradis, after the completion of the defences of Ariákupum, was constituted chief engineer, and charged with the defence.

It will be recollected that, on the occasion of the attack upon the French at St. Thomé by the Dutch, in 1674, that enterprise owed its success principally to the fact that the Dutch admiral had succeeded in inducing the King of Golkonda to operate by a land attack at the same time; and that similarly, during the siege of Pondichery, in 1693, the Dutch had enlisted in their service a large body of native troops. Dupleix was now warned by the French Minister that these tactics would again be pursued, that immense efforts would be made to gain over the native princes to English interests, and that the English commandant was well provided with presents for that especial purpose.

Leaving, for a moment, the French governor devoting himself to the defence of the territories which he held

---

* The account of the fortifications of Pondichery, and of the siege generally, so far as relates to the operations of the English, has been taken from the journal of an English officer present at the siege, reprinted in the *Asiatic Annual Register* for 1802, and which Mr. Orme copied almost *verbatim*.

for his sovereign, and endeavouring, by all the means in his power, to counteract beforehand the effects which the presents of the English were, he well knew, only too likely to produce on the mind of the Nawwáb, Anwáru-dín, we must turn to the proceedings of that fleet, the departure of which from England had caused so much perturbation and excitement in the French settlement. It was true, indeed, that the English East India Company, indignant at the loss of Madras, had determined to spare no efforts for its recovery, and that the English Ministry, sharing the sentiments prevalent at the India House, had promised to aid it with a fleet and army. Of these, when all the other arrangements for their departure had been determined, the double command was bestowed upon Rear-Admiral the Hon. E. Boscawen, this constituting the second and final occasion, subsequently to the Revolution of 1688, in which two such commands were united in the same person.

Admiral Boscawen was a man of birth and character. A grand-nephew of the famous Marlborough, he had entered the navy at the age of twelve years, and, passing with credit through all the subordinate grades, had found himself, when only twenty-six years old, captain of a man-of-war. Two years later, the ship which he commanded formed a part of that fleet at the head of which Admiral Vernon took Porto Bello and failed at Carthagena. In these expeditions, only partially successful as they were, Captain Boscawen lost no opportunity of distinguishing himself, and he soon acquired a reputation for skill and enterprise such as, combined with his high birth, marked him out for future command.

This was not long in coming to him. When it was decided in England to make a great effort to deliver a counter-stroke for the capture of Madras, Boscawen, then only in his thirty-sixth year, was selected to command the expedition. The instructions he received were to endeavour to deprive the French of the base of their operations against India, by the capture of the Isles of France and Bourbon, and, succeeding or not in that, to deliver his main blow against Pondichery itself.

On this expedition, with eight ships of war,* and a convoy of eleven ships, having on board 1,400 regular troops, Boscawen left England on November 15, 1747. The greater number of his ships reached the Cape of Good Hope on April 9 of the following year. The remainder arrived sixteen days later, but it was not till May 19 that the admiral left Table Bay for the islands. He had recived here, however, a considerable accession of force in six ships and 400 soldiers belonging to the Dutch East India Company. The united force, with the exception of three vessels, sighted the French islands on the morning of July 4.

Had the Isle of France been in the same position with respect to its defences in which it was in 1735, the English admiral would have found little difficulty in gaining possession of it. But by the efforts of La Bourdonnais, during the first five years of his administration, fortifications had been erected all along the coast, such as rendered an attack upon it, especially at a season of the year when the wind blew strongly from the land, a matter of great uncertainty. Thus, although the garrison was small, consisting of only 500 regular troops and 1,000 sailors lent from the ships at anchor in the harbour, the defences had been so skilfully thrown up, and there appeared to be such a firm resolution to defend them with pertinacity, that the admiral, after three days spent in examination of the coast, and in futile efforts to obtain some information as to the strength of the garrison, felt constrained to call a

---

* The fleet was composed of one ship of 74 guns, one of 64, two of 60, two of 50, one of 20, a sloop of 14 guns, a bomb-ketch, with her tender, and a hospital-ship.—*Orme*.

council of war to deliberate on the expediency of an attack. At this council it was resolved, with the concurrence of the admiral, to avoid an encounter which might perhaps disable the fleet from attempting its greater undertaking, and to push on with all speed to Pondichery. It set sail for Fort St. David accordingly on the following day, and, parting company with the Dutch ships, arrived there on August 11, effecting a junction with Admiral Griffin's squadron.

This union constituted a force at the disposal of the English Commander the most powerful that had ever arrived in the Indian seas—far more so than that with which the Dutch had conquered Pondichery in 1693, and infinitely more effective than that which La Bourdonnais had led to the capture of Madras. In this case, moreover, the English admiral was at ease regarding his communications. There was no hostile fleet threatening to interfere with his plans, or to contest with him the supremacy at sea. He was in possession of such strength* that he was able to divest his mind of all fears of naval attack, and to flatter himself with a certainty of the conquest of Pondichery. To attempt this last he landed an army which, by its junction with the troops already at Fort St. David, and with 120 Dutch sent from Nágápatan, amounted to 6,000 men, of whom 3,720 were Europeans. Of this force he detached 700 Europeans, on the morning of August 19, to attack Ariákupum. We have noticed the preparations which Dupleix had made at this place—the outwork of Pondichery—to resist the enemy. So secretly had the plans of Paradis been carried out, that the English were entirely unacquainted with the additions that had been just made to its strength, and, like the French before Gudalur, they marched to its attack with a careless con-

---

* His fleet after the junction with the fleet of Admiral Griffin, who himself left for England, consisted of 30 ships, of which 13 were ships of the line.—*Orme*.

fidence, that seemed to betoken a certainty on their part of easy victory. Law, who commanded the garrison, allowed them to approach within forty yards of the works without firing a shot. Then, however, he opened upon them with grapeshot and musketry, making great havoc in their ranks. The English, completely surprised, without scaling ladders, unable to advance and unwilling to retreat, for a short time kept their ground. But as the fire of the enemy continued they became sensible of the folly of a further persistence in attack. They accordingly moved off, but not until they had lost 150 of their number killed and wounded. This success greatly inspirited the French garrison, and restored to its soldiers the confidence which their several repulses at Gudalur had taken from them. They had reason now to hope that a persistent defence at Ariákupum would contribute to save Pondichery. Impressed with this view, they proceeded at once to throw up a battery of heavy guns on the opposite side of the little river, to the north of the fort, by means of which an advancing enemy would be taken in flank and enfiladed. Upon this the English, after one or two failures, erected a battery covered by an intrenchment, to reply to and silence the enemy's fire, and manned it partly by sailors from the fleet. Law, however, resolved to take advantage of the enthusiasm which his recent success had excited amongst his garrison, and moved out of the fort with 60 cavalry and about 150 infantry, under cover of fire from the ramparts. Charging them at the head of his horse, he threw, first the sailors, and immediately afterwards, the regular troops, into disorder, drove them from the intrenchment, and took some prisoners, conspicuous amongst whom was Major Lawrence, whose defence of Fort St. David and Gudalur had given him a reputation which he was soon to raise to a far greater height.

Up to this point the French had great reason to congratulate themselves on the success which had attended their defensive operations. They began even to entertain the hope of keeping Ariákupum secure from the enemy. But, at this crisis, one of those accidents from which no army is absolutely secure occurred to dash their hopes. A large store of gunpowder within the fort was suddenly ignited and exploded. The effect was most disastrous. Nearly a hundred men of the garrison were killed and wounded, and, what was of greater importance, a conviction was produced in the mind of their leader, that the place could no longer be successfully defended. They accordingly blew up the walls and the cavaliers, and retreated at once within Pondichery.

Still, however, their success against the English had produced a great effect upon the garrison of that city. Their confidence too was increased by observing the caution of the English commander. Admiral Boscawen, indeed, occupied Ariákupum on its evacuation by the French, but, instead of moving at once upon Pondichery, he remained five days to repair the fortifications of a place which was useless to him, and which, in its dismantled state, could not be used to any purpose by the enemy.

On the 6th September, however, Boscawen moved on Pondichery, taking possession of a redoubt in the north-west angle of the prickly pear hedge. But it was not until the 10th that he opened ground, and then only at a distance of 1,500 yards from the covered way. The next day 150 men having been detached to make a lodgement about a hundred yards nearer, 1,200 men of the garrison* under the command of Paradis, made a sortie, attacking both trenches at once. But the fall of Paradis, who was mortally wounded early in the sally, threw the party into disorder, and it was repulsed with the loss of seven officers and a hundred men. The death of Para-

* The French garrison consisted of 1,800 Europeans and 3,000 sipáhis. —*Dupleix.*

dis, which occurred within a few days of his wound, was the greatest misfortune that could have occurred to Dupleix at this conjuncture. He was his most capable officer—the only man upon whose combined prudence, knowledge and daring he could absolutely rely. In his memoirs he describes him as "a man of intelligence, well acquainted with his profession, thoroughly familiar with the locality, and with all the defects of the place. He had prepared all manner of devices to offer opposition to the enemy, especially in the weak points of the defences." The loss of such a man was the greater, as there was no one within the walls to supply his place. That is, rather, there would have been no one, had not Dupleix himself showed that great genius is capable of universal application, and that the arts of the warrior are not beyond its attainment.

Another, though a lesser, misfortune befell him at the same time. True to the instructions he had received in England, Admiral Boscawen had not delayed to urge the Nawwáb of the Karnátik to pronounce decidedly against those French, whose destruction he announced to be certain. The admiral supported his requisition by presents of considerable value. Dupleix had little to offer on his part. Yet so great was the respect in which the French name was held, so high the opinion entertained of the great qualities of Dupleix, that, notwithstanding his apparently forlorn and helpless condition, the Nawwáb hesitated long before he gave way to the entreaties of Boscawen. It was only after the fall of Ariákupum, and when the French were shut up within the walls of Pondichery, that he agreed to the alliance pressed upon him, and promised to assist the English with 2,000 horse. He actually sent, however, only 300 men, and those towards the conclusion of the siege.

One consequence of the death of Paridis was that the management of all the details of the defence devolved upon Dupleix. To use his own modest expression, "the study of mathematics, and especially of fortification, which his father had impressed upon him, became now of great assistance to him; he was sufficiently fortunate to be able to recollect the knowledge of this nature which he had acquired, so that all his operations succeeded even beyond his hopes."* Fortunately for him, his efforts were seconded by the inexperience of the English admiral in military operations, and the consequent neglect by him of some of the first principles affecting the conduct of a siege. But even this incapacity would not have interfered with the ultimate success of the English, had the garrison been permitted to give way to the despondency which reigned among them, in consequence of the death of the chief engineer. It was Dupleix who prevented this. It was Dupleix who, calm in danger, maintained an outward serenity and confidence that became contagious; who, by the attention he paid to all points of the defence, by the skill with which he strengthened the weak places and repaired those damaged by the enemy's fire, speedily transferred to his own person a belief in his capacity that savoured almost of enthusiasm. It was, in a word, this civilian governor who became the life of the defence, the hope of the defenders, the one principal cause of the ill success of the besiegers.

From the 6th of September, the day on which Boscawen moved on Pondichery, to the 17th October, forty-two days of open trenches, the siege was pushed with all the vigour of which the English leader was capable. But his efforts were thwarted by the skill and gallantry of Dupleix. Constant sorties, more or less successful, always retarded and often effectually destroyed the approaches of the besiegers. The English having, after much labour, advanced to the trenches within eight hundred yards of the walls, found that owing to the existence of a morass, it was impossible to carry them

* Mémoire pour Dupleix.

further on that side, and that it had become necessary to raze the batteries that had been erected. When at last a heavy fire was opened on another part of the town, they discovered that owing to the skill and energy of Dupleix, the fire of the besieged at that point was double that of the besiegers. The ships of the fleet which were brought up, as a last resource, to bombard the town, were compelled to sheer off after receiving much more damage than they had been able to inflict.* So energetic, so determined, so successful was the defence, that the English admiral found, at the end of five weeks, that he had actually gained no ground at all; that he had lost some of his best officers and very many men; that the enemy had been able to concentrate on his several attacks a fire far more destructive than that which he had been able to bring to bear on their defences. Added to this, the periodical rains which began to fall at the end of September had brought sickness into his camp, and had warned him that the real difficulties of his position were only about to begin. Under these circumstances, acting under the advice of a council of war, he commenced on the 14th October the destruction of the batteries, and the reembarkation of the sailors and heavy stores. On the 17th, this vast army, the largest European force that had till then appeared on Indian soil, and which counted Clive† amongst its ranks, broke up and retreated to Fort St. David, leaving behind it 1,065 men, who had perished either from the fire of the enemy, or from sickness contracted during the siege.‡

---

* The author of the journal before referred to, naïvely remarks that "owing to the distance of the ships from the town, and the heavy swell of the sea, shots never successively struck the same object."

† The author of the journal writes as follows: "The celebrated Lord Clive, then an ensign, served in the trenches on this occasion, and by his gallant conduct gave the first prognostic of that high military spirit, which was the spring of his future actions, and the principal source of the decisive intrepidity and elevation of mind, which were his characteristic endowments."

‡ The loss of the French during

Q

Thus had Dupleix, by his firmness, his skill, the wonderful activity of his genius, baffled that great enterprise which was to bring destruction upon French India, to root out the French establishments from the soil of Hindustan. If we take a retrospective glance at all that had been accomplished during this first struggle in the Karnátik, we shall be utterly unable to refrain our tribute of admiration to the man who possessed the brain to conceive, the steadfastness to carry out, that long list of daring achievements. The capture of Madras, its preservation to the French, the determination to bear the brunt of the contest with the Múghal, the momentous political result that followed that determination, together with this crowning defence of Pondichery, were works of his conception; to him too is mainly due the merit of their execution. Even at the greatest crisis of his fortunes he found means to send efficient aid and support to the other settlements dependent on Pondichery—a wonderful feat, gratefully acknowledged as such by his masters.*

---

the corresponding period amounted to 200 Europeans and 50 natives. On their way to Fort St. David, the English wreaked a last vengeance on the fort of Ariákupum, by utterly destroying what remained of its defences.—*Orme, Dupleix.*

* "All that you have done up to that time ought, in truth, to have made us tranquil regarding the fate of Pondichery, and your last letters of the 28th August, written at the time that the English had commenced their attack upon your advanced posts, left us nothing to desire, either with reference to the precautions you had taken, or to the courageous dispositions which you had inspired in the garrison and in everybody. Ought then our demonstrations of joy to be less, when, on the 20th of last month, a courier despatched by Monsieur Durand, our agent in London, announced to the Court this new triumph of the national arms?

"If it has been already satisfactory for you, that the Company could declare that the capture of Madras was due to the succours which you had furnished to M. de la Bourdonnais; that it was your firmness, the wisdom of your measures, and the choice of the brave officers you had employed, which compelled the Múghals to sue to you for peace; that you would even have taken Fort St. David from the English but for the unexpected arrival of Admiral Griffin: and that finally, despite the difficulty of communications during the entire war, you had found means to provide for the subsistence and security of the settlements of Chandranagar, Karikal, and Mahé; what praises do you not deserve now, when by the glorious use of the succours sent you by M. David" (alluding to M. Bouvet's fleet) "you have repulsed the most powerful efforts of your enemies, and have preserved to the Company all their establishments."—*Lettre de la Compagnie des Indes*, 11 *Avril*, 1749.

If, on one occasion, owing to circumstances of which we have no knowledge, he failed to take advantage of a great opportunity that offered for the destruction of the last establishment of the English on the Koromandel coast, few will deny that he made up for that one mistake by the wonderful skill and energy, with which, as civil governor, as commandant, as engineer, he conducted the defence of Pondichery against a force that might well have been regarded as irresistible. Truly may we echo the language used on the occasion by the Directors of the Company of the Indies, and declare that if all his other achievements merited the thanks of that France whose interests he served so well, this crowning success placed him on a pinnacle far beyond the reach of ordinary applause.

We can well imagine—we who have traced Dupleix up to this point of his career, who have noticed the manner in which he seized every occasion of exalting the power of France in the eyes of the natives of India —how eagerly and effectively he used the opportunity offered by the retreat of the English army to increase and magnify its effects. Messengers were instantly despatched to Arkát, to Haidarábád, even to Delhi, to acquaint the native potentates how the most formidable foreign army that had ever landed in India had been shattered against the walls of Pondichery. The answers to these communications showed how thoroughly he had mastered the characters of those whom he addressed. Letters of congratulation poured upon him from all sides. He received the greatest compliments on his success. The English were regarded as an inferior, almost an annihilated, power; and the one result of this long-threatened attack was to invest Dupleix with an influence and an authority, such as had up to that time devolved upon no European leader on Indian soil.

The siege of Pondichery had been raised, as we

CHAP. V.

1748.

1749.

stated, on the 17th October. The English had retired in a state of deep dejection to Fort St. David, where for a time they occupied themselves more with thinking of their own safety than of attacking the possessions of France. Dupleix, on his side, made earnest preparations for the renewal of offensive operations. He received early in the following year (1749) further supplies of men* and money from M. Bouvet, who, despite the presence at Fort St. David of the still numerous English fleet, gained the Madras roadstead and landed the soldiers and specie without molestation. It was at this time, when Dupleix was planning new enterprises against the English, that orders from Europe reached both parties for a suspension of arms pending the result of negotiations which had been entered into at Aix-la-Chapelle. These were shortly afterwards followed by an intimation of the conclusion of the treaty which bears the name of that ancient city.

By one of the articles of this treaty a mutual restitution of conquests was agreed upon between France and England,—a condition which necessitated the abandonment by Dupleix of that Madras, gained by so much daring, and guarded with so much jealousy and vigilance. Bitter must have been the pang with which the French Governor received the order to make a restitution which he knew well would be the first step towards providing his hated rivals with a new foundation of greatly increased power; deeply must he have lamented the blindness of the Ministers, who, not possessing his vast *coup d'œil*, could look upon Cape Breton as a sufficient compensation for a place which, if retained in 1749, would, as we shall see hereafter, most certainly have given the French an overwhelming superiority, leading to empire, in Southern India. But Dupleix was there, not to remonstrate, but to obey. The orders he had received were without appeal, and in obedience to them

* 200 in number.—*Orme*.

he, towards the close of the month of August, made over Madras to Admiral Boscawen.*

Thus, after a contest of five years, the two nations found themselves, in outward appearance, in the position in which they were at the outbreak of hostilities. Yet, if apparently the same, in reality how different! The vindictive rivalry between both, exemplified in the capture of Madras, the attempts upon Fort St. David and Pondichery, had laid the foundation of an eternal enmity,—an enmity which could only be extinguished by the destruction of one or other of the adversaries. Then, again, the superiority evinced by the Europeans over the natives, in the decisive battle at St. Thomé, had given birth, especially in the mind of the French leader, to an ambition for empire which, if at first vague and indistinct, assumed every day a more and more practical shape. Added to this, the expense of keeping up the greatly increased number of soldiers sent out from Europe pressed heavily on the resources of both settlements, and almost forced upon them the necessity of hiring out their troops to the rival candidates for power in Southern India. Thus, during five years which elapsed between 1745 and 1749 their position had become revolutionised. No longer simple traders, regarded as such only by the rulers of the Karnátik, they were then feared, especially the French, by all the potentates in the neighbourhood, their alliance was eagerly sought for, their assistance an object of anxious entreaty. From vassals they had jumped almost to the position of liege lords.

A new era, resulting from this war, dates thus from the moment when the treaty of Aix-la-Chapelle restored the rival European powers to the positions which they had nominally occupied in 1745. By the East India

---

* In the first edition it was stated on the authority of the writers of that period that Madras, when restored, was in a very improved condition. But the recent investigations of M. Forrest have shown that this was not the case.

Companies in Paris and London this change was not even suspected. They fondly believed that the new treaty would enable their agents to recommence their mercantile operations. They hoped that the reaction after five years' hostilities would lead to a feeling of mutual confidence and trust. Vain dream! The peace that reigned in Europe, was it not then to extend to both nations in India? Alas! with ambition aroused, mutual jealousy excited, the temptation of increased dominion knocking at their doors, what had they to do with peace?

CHAPTER VI.

FRENCH INDIA AT ITS ZENITH.

THE peace between the Powers of Europe which had been signed at Aix-la-Chapelle afforded, as we have already stated, an opportunity for the introduction into India of a system, afterwards carried to a very considerable extent, whereby the European Powers, moved by promises of material advantage, lent out their soldiers to the native rulers. It is but right to add, that in almost every case the temptation came from the natives, and it should also be remembered that the treaty of Aix-la-Chapelle had been concluded at a time when an unusual number of the troops of both nations had been thrown on the Indian soil, and when therefore the employment of, and provision for, these soldiers, caused no little anxiety to the governors of the settlements. Dupleix, indeed, in a letter* which he wrote to the Company of the Indies at the time, expressly justified his recourse to such a line of conduct by the necessity under which he was to practise the strictest economy.

In this custom, however, the English set the example. The account of the expulsion of Rájá Sahuji from Tanjur has been given in a previous chapter.† The duplicity of that monarch, his double overthrow by his own people, and his final expulsion in 1749, in favour of Partáb Singh, will doubtless be recollected. It is necessary to refer to it here, because it was this same Sahuji, twice expelled from his kingdom, who, by his promises and entreaties, induced the English to lend

* Dated March 31, 1749. All the letters quoted are to be found at length in the *pièces justificatives* attached to the *Mémoire pour Dupleix*.
† Chapter III.

themselves to the principle of supporting expelled and wandering royalty—a principle which nearly ruined them on this occasion, and which, more than ninety years after, brought their army to destruction in the snows of Afghánistán. Eleven years had elapsed since Sahuji had been expelled, and during that time Tanjur had enjoyed a quiet and a prosperity to which, under his rule, it had been a stranger; yet the desire of governing, so strongly planted in the Asiatic breast, would not allow the dethroned monarch to be tranquil. Although his experience of the attraction of a crown had been such as would have been sufficient to deter a man of ordinary sense from again striving for the dangerous prize, although on one occasion he had barely escaped from his enemies' hands, and on the other had been seized by them in the midst of his own guards, to the imminent danger of his life, he never ceased to sigh for his departed grandeur. To attain that state of sensual existence which had once been his, he was ready not only to stake his life, but to consent to the dismemberment of his country.

When, therefore, the news of the meeting of the European plenipotentiaries at Aix-la-Chapelle caused a suspension of Arms in India, Sahuji, who had been struck with the great superiority evinced in the field by the European over the Asiatic soldiers, resolved to endeavour to enlist on his behalf the aid of some of those redoubtable warriors. It was, however, he well knew, useless for him to appeal to the French. Not only had he deceived them in 1738, but they had since lived upon good terms with his successor, Partáb Singh. His only chance was with the English, and to them, therefore, he made his demand.

He was extremely liberal in his offers. The payment of all the expenses of the war, and the cession of Dévikota, a town at the mouth of the Kolrún, a hundred and twenty-two miles south of Madras, with the territory attaching to it, formed a tempting bait to a people possessing a surplus of soldiers, and just resting after a war which had severely tried their resources. At any rate it was eagerly grasped at, and in the beginning of April, 1749, a force of 430 Europeans and 1,000 sipáhis, under the command of Captain Cope, was despatched to re-establish ex-Rájá Sahuji on his ancestral throne.

In a history relating mainly to the transactions of the French in India, it will be necessary to follow the movements of the English only in those instances in which an effect was thereby produced on the policy of their rivals. We do not propose, therefore, to enter into the details of this expedition against Tanjur. The results will be found chronicled hereafter. It is essential, however, that we should allude prominently to the fact of the enterprise, in order to make it clear that in the course which Dupleix adopted at this period, he but followed an example which the English had set him. The main difference between his proceedings and theirs was this,—that whereas in all his undertakings he had a settled purpose and design,—his smallest actions tending to one mighty end,—the English had. for long, no great principle of action, and it was only after a time that they instinctively adopted the policy of offering, on all occasions, a steady opposition to French aggression.

In a previous chapter* we have recorded the fate which befell Chanda Sáhib in his endeavours to defend Trichinápallí against the army of Raghují Bhonsla. Taken prisoner by that general, he had been sent off (1741) under a guard to Satára, and there kept for seven years in confinement. Vainly had he exerted his utmost endeavours to effect his release. Although during that period the Múghals had re-occupied Trichinápallí, although the office of Nawwáb of the Karnátik had

* Chapter III.

passed from the family of Dost Ali, to which he was related, to a stranger, he was kept rigorously a prisoner. Not indeed that the Maráthás had any state object in view in thus keeping him from his native province; it was simply a question of ransom. Chanda Sáhib was comparatively poor. Allied only by marriage with the house of Dost Ali, he had not exercised independent authority for a sufficiently long time to amass any very considerable wealth. The jewels which constituted the greater part of it were with his wife and family in Pondichery. The remainder had been taken when he lost Trichinápallí. For a long time, however, the Maráthás insisted upon the payment of a kingly ransom, as an essential condition of his release, and all this time Chanda Sáhib, unable to pay it, saw opportunities vanish, kingdoms pass into other hands, and he felt too that every year added to that forgetfulness of himself, which is the unvarying consequence of the absence of a leader from the scene of action.

At last, however, fortune seemed to unbend. In the month of April, 1748, Muhammad Sháh, King of Delhi, died.* His only son, Ahmad Sháh, succeeded him, but the first months of his accession were too much engaged in preparations to maintain himself against his namesake, the Abdálí, and other enemies, to allow him to turn his attention to the events that were occurring in the remote Dakhan. It was, however, just at this moment that the attention of the feudal lord of the empire was particularly required in those parts. A few months after the death of Muhammad Sháh (June, 1748) Nizám-ul-Mulk, Viceroy of the Dakhan, followed him to the grave at the ripe age of seventy-seven years.† The succession had become, through the weakness of the central authority, by custom rather than by consent,

---

* His death occurred on April the 15. He had reigned thirty years and twenty-seven days. See Elliott's *History of India*, vol. viii., pp. 111-12.

† So says Elphinstone: but other writers indicate 104 years as his age at the period of his death.

hereditary in the family. Now Nizám-ul-Mulk had left five sons. The eldest, Ghází-ud-dín Khán, was, however, high in the imperial service, and preferred pushing his fortunes at Delhi to striking for an inheritance which he felt could only be gained by the sword. The second son, Ahmad Khán, called also Násir Jang, had been engaged in constant rebellion against his father, but he was with him, having been recently released from captivity, when he died. The other three sons were looked upon as men of little mark, content to live a life of ease and pleasure at the court of Aurangábád. Besides these sons, there was a grandson, Muzaffar Jang, the son of a daughter, who had been always indicated by his grandfather as his successor. The consent of Muhammad Sháh to this arrangement had been previously obtained, and on the death of Nizám-ul-Mulk, a firman, it is said, was issued by the court of Delhi nominating Muzaffar Jang viceroy in his place.

When that event occurred, however, Muzaffar Jang was at his government at Bíjápur, whilst the lately rebellious son, Nasir Jang, was on the spot. This latter at once acted in accordance with the customs which had obtained from time immemorial under the Muhammadan sway in Hindustan. He seized his father's treasures, bought over the leading men and the army, and proclaimed himself Subadar of the Dakhan. The claims of Muzaffar Jang he derided, and set his person at open defiance.

Muzaffar Jang, however, was not inclined to give up his pretensions without a struggle, though for the moment he did not possess the means to support them. In this crisis he bethought him of the Maráthás, the hereditary enemies of Muhammadan authority, and he decided to go in person to Satára to demand their assistance. At Satára he met Chanda Sáhib, of whose reputation he was fully cognisant. The two men felt at once that they could be mutually serviceable to one

CHAP. VI.
1749.

another. They therefore soon came to an understanding. They agreed to endeavour to obtain material aid from the Maráthás, insisting also on the unconditional release of Chanda Sáhib.

A negotiation was accordingly opened. But whilst it was in progress, and seemed to promise well, Chanda Sáhib, who had little real wish to conquer the Karnátik by the aid of his old enemies, communicated full details of their plans to Dupleix, with whom he had maintained, through his wife, a constant correspondence. Threatened at the time by the English, Dupleix had no desire to add to the existing complications by bringing on the province a Maráthá invasion. The prospect, however, of placing on the viceregal throne of the Dakhan one who would thus be a protégé of his own, and over the province of the Karnátik a man so devoted to French interests as he knew Chanda Sáhib to be, was too alluring to be resisted. Pondering in his mind how this could be effected, the thought struck him that it needed only a daring and decided policy of his own to bring about such a result. He at once embraced the project with all the ardour of his impassioned nature; wrote to Chanda Sáhib to negotiate only for his release, and not for troops; engaged to the court of Puná to guarantee the ransom that might be agreed upon; and promised to both Muzaffar Jang and Chanda Sáhib all the influence and power which he, as ruler of French India, was capable of exerting. His despatch had the desired effect. On receiving a guarantee from Dupleix for the payment of 700,000 rupees, Chanda Sáhib was released and furnished with a bodyguard of 3,000 men to escort him to his own country.

One of the first acts of Chanda Sáhib after his release was to enter into an engagement with Dupleix, whereby he took upon himself the payment of about 2,000 natives, drilled in the European fashion, belonging to the Pondichery garrison. In consideration likewise of being assisted by 400 Europeans, he agreed to make to the French the cession of a small tract of land in the immediate neighbourhood of Pondichery. Whilst arrangements were in progress for these troops to join him, he had succeeded in making his way, after some changes of fortune, to the frontiers of the Karnátik, and in augmenting his force to 6,000 men. Here he was joined by Muzaffar Jang at the head of 30,000. Chanda Sáhib, who was by far the abler character of the two, resolved, so soon as he should be joined by his French auxiliaries, to march upon Arkát. A victory here would place the resources of the Karnátik at his disposal, and bring him into close association with the French. He could then make it, with every prospect of success, the basis from which to operate against Nasir Jang.

Towards the end of July the French force already indicated, under the command of M. d'Auteuil, and accompanied by the son of Chanda Sáhib, joined the latter at the Damalchérí Pass, which he had taken care to secure. Here they received information that Anwáru-dín and his two sons, at the head of 20,000 picked troops, including among them 60 European adventurers, had taken post at Ambur, about thirty miles to the south, prepared to give them battle. Thither accordingly they marched. The position taken up at Ambur was extremely strong, being defended on one flank by a mountain surmounted by a castle, and on the other by a large lake. The ground between these, constituting naturally a very strong pass into the Karnátik, had been further fortified by intrenchments. These were defended by guns served by the Europeans to whom we have alluded. Behind these was the main army of the Nawwáb.

It was on the morning of August 3 that the combined armies of Chanda Sáhib and M. d'Auteuil came in sight of this position. It was at once resolved to storm it, and d'Auteuil offered to lead the attack with his French. Such an offer was gladly accepted, and, at the head of his gallant countrymen, d'Auteuil advanced boldly to the assault. The Nawwáb's guns, however, were so well served by the Europeans in his service, that the assailants fell back with some loss. Indignant at this, d'Auteuil rallied his men, and led them himself, notwithstanding a heavy fire, up to the foot of the intrenchment. The breastwork was even mounted by some of them, but in the crisis of the attack, d'Auteuil was wounded in the thigh, and, in the confusion that followed, his men lost order and retreated. The command then devolved upon M. de Bussy,* and the troops, encouraged by him and the other officers, eagerly called to be led on for the third time. This determination on their part disheartened the defenders, many of whom had already fallen. Even had they stood more firm, however, they could scarcely have resisted the impetuosity of the charge. Led on by the gallant Bussy, the French reserved their fire till close to the intrenchments; then delivering a volley, they dashed over the breastwork, and the day was their own. Having lost this defence, the native portion of Anwáru-dín's army made but little resistance. Followed by the troops of Chanda Sáhib and by that leader in person, the French pushed on. It was in vain that Anwáru-dín, himself a very old man,† made the most gallant efforts to restore the fight. In the very act of singling out Chanda Sáhib for a hand to hand encounter, he was shot through the heart by an African soldier. A general disorder followed; the defeat became a rout; Máfauz Khán surrendered himself a prisoner, and the second son, Muhammad Ali, saved himself by an early flight. The camp, the baggage, sixty elephants, many horses, and all the artillery fell into the hands of the victors. But their

---

* Charles-Joseph Patissier, Marquis de Bussy-Castelnau, who will occupy a very prominent place in this history. He was born in 1718.

† The native chronicles assign him 107 years, but they probably exaggerate.

TRIUMPH OF THE ALLIES. 239

greatest prize was the province of the Karnátik secured to them by this victory. Of this they obtained an immediate gage in Arkát, the capital, which they occupied the next day. In this battle the French lost 12 men killed and 63 wounded. About 300 of their sipáhis were killed and wounded.*

The earliest act of Muzaffar Jang on his arrival at Arkát was to proclaim himself Subadar of the Dakhan, and to nominate Chanda Sáhib Nawwáb of the Karnátik.† Having secured the surrounding country by means of flying parties, the two governors proceeded to Pondichery, Muzaffar Jang to acknowledge the aid he had received, Chanda Sáhib to pour out his thanks for the protection, which, for so many years, and under such trying circumstances, the French governor had afforded to his family. They were received with the greatest pomp and ceremony. No one knew better than Dupleix the effect of display upon the Oriental mind. He took care, however, that accompanying the glitter of outward show there should be a simultaneous exhibition of that material power which, more than any other, is in Asia capable of insuring respect. The defences which had defied the English were dressed out for the occasion; the European troops, whose superiority had been proved at St. Thomé and Ambur, were conspicuously drawn up, the ships in the harbour displayed their brightest flags. No artifice was omitted to impress upon the minds of his guests, that the pomp and ceremony of their reception were but the natural consequence of a wealth and influence based upon a power that nothing in the South of India could resist. The effect was all that he could wish. Muzaffar Jang was captivated by

CHAP. VI.
1749.

---

* Chanda Sáhib presented the French Troops after the battle with 75,000 rupees, and M. d'Auteuil with land worth 4,000 rupees per annum. —*Dupleix.*

† One of the first to congratulate Chanda Sáhib on his elevation, and to acknowledge him as Nawwáb, was the Governor of Fort St. David, Mr. Floyer.—*Mémoire pour Dupleix,* p. 46.

the display; the gratitude of Chanda Sáhib was unbounded. In the first moments of his delight he conferred upon Dupleix the sovereignty of eighty-one villages, adjoining the ground of which Pondichery was the representative capital. Muzaffar Jang stayed eight days at Pondichery. His army, amounting to from 45,000 to 50,000 men, remained encamped meanwhile within twenty miles of the city.*

But amid all the festivities that followed the arrival of these two chieftains, Dupleix did not lose sight of the main object which had brought them into the field. We have already stated that though Muzaffar Jang held the higher rank, Chanda Sáhib was of the two by far the abler man. When then Muzaffar Jang, at the expiration of eight days, rejoined his camp, twenty miles from Pondichery, Dupleix retained Chanda Sáhib to settle the plan of the campaign. It was true that the possession of the Karnátik seemed to have been decided by the battle of Ambur. Anwáru-dín had been killed, his eldest son taken prisoner, and the younger, Muhammad Ali, had sought refuge in flight. Yet, so long as there remained a pretender to the dignity, Chanda Sáhib could not consider himself firm in his seat. It is beyond question that he had, both by hereditary descent and by imperial nomination, a greater right to the office than any of the family of Anwáru-dín. He was, in the first place, the representative of the family of Dost Ali, and, in the second, he had been nominated by Muzaffar Jang, whose title to succeed Nizám-ul-Mulk as Subadar of the Dakhan had been confirmed by a firman from the Court of Delhi.† But, in the distracted state of the Múghal empire, no right

---

* Extrait de la Lettre de M. Dupleix à la Compagnie, le 28 Juillet 1749 ; Copie d'un Extrait du Régistre des Délibérations du Conseil Supérieur de Pondichéry, 13 Juillet 1749 ; Mémoire pour Dupleix; Orme, Cambridge, Raymond, and others. It is upon these works and upon the correspondence and official documents contained in them that the statements in this chapter are based.

† Dupleix, p. 42. Seir Mutakharín.

could be considered secure that was not based upon a possession that could be maintained. Nor, at the same time, could any possession be regarded as perfectly tenable to which a pretender was in the field waiting for an opportunity to assert his claims. Dupleix, well aware of this, did not cease to press upon Chanda Sáhib the absolute necessity of insuring the submission of Muhammad Ali, before he resigned himself to the more peaceful cares of his government. Rapidity in his movements was, he pointed out, the more requisite as Muhammad Ali had taken refuge in Trichinápallí, the fortifications of which had been greatly strengthened since Chanda Sáhib had been compelled to surrender it to Raghují Bhonsla. He added the information that Nasir Jang, the pretender to the Subadárí of the Dakhan, was engaged in levying an army wherewith to crush his nephew and rival, and that it was, therefore, more especially necessary to clear the Karnátik and its dependencies of all foes, before this greater enemy should be ready to march upon it. The exhortations of Dupleix to Chanda Sáhib to march without any delay upon Trichinápallí were earnest and repeated.

One circumstance, however, served to hinder the native chieftains from moving. The battle of Ambur had been fought on August 3; Madras, in pursuance of the articles of the treaty of Aix-la-Chapelle, had been made over to the English at the end of the same month, but still Admiral Boscawen remained on the coast. More than that, he had taken advantage of the disordered state of affairs to possess himself of the little settlement of St. Thomé, upon which he had hoisted the English flag. It was known, too, that he was himself strongly impressed with the necessity of remaining to support English interests, and that he had declared he would remain, if he were publicly requested to do so.* It appeared then to Chanda Sáhib, that for him to move

* Orme.

on Trichinápallí, whilst Admiral Boscawen was still on the coast, would act as a final inducement to that officer to remain, and would impel the English to cast in their lot, whilst their forces were yet considerable, with his rival, Muhammad Ali. He, therefore, hesitated as to his action, preferring to wait at all events in the hope that the October gales might compel the departure of so dangerous an enemy.

Whilst he and his allies are thus watching their opportunity, it may be convenient for us to turn to the movements of the English, and to relate as briefly as may be the result of their expedition against Tanjur.

This expedition had been undertaken, as we have already stated, with the avowed object of re-seating upon the throne of that kingdom the twice expelled Rájá Sahuji, with the real purpose of gaining for themselves the possession of Dévikota. Consisting of 430 Europeans and 1,000 sipáhis, under the command of Captain Cope, this force had left Fort St. David in the early part of April, and, on the 24th, arrived on the bank of the river Vellaur, near Portonovo. On the following morning a terrific storm ensued, which caused great damage to the land forces, and greater to the fleet. Of the former, many of the carriage-cattle, and a large proportion of the military stores were destroyed; of the latter, the Admiral's flagship, the "Namur," of 74 guns, the "Pembroke," of 60 guns, and the "Apollo," hospital ship, with the greater part of their crews, were totally lost.* It thus became necessary to suspend for a time the progress of the undertaking.

When, however, after having made good his losses, Captain Cope renewed his march and arrived on the borders of the Tanjur territory, he found the actual state of things to differ very much from the representations that had been made him. Not only was there no

---

* Journal of an officer present at the siege of Pondichery.

THE ENGLISH MOVE ON DEVIKOTA.

disposition evinced by the Tanjurians to strike a blow for Sahuji, but their army was found posted on the southern bank of the Kolrún, ready apparently to oppose the passage of the English They had entertained, however, no intention of fighting; they hoped, rather, to entice Captain Cope into the difficult country to the south, where his destruction would be certain. But the direction taken by the English after the passage of the river showed very plainly the real object they had in view in espousing the cause of Sahuji. Their army marched in the direction, not of Tanjur, but of Dévikota, where they expected to find support from the fleet. But on their arrival that same evening within a mile of Dévikota not a ship was to be seen. Having with them no supplies, and finding the place too strong to be escaladed, they resolved, after cannonading it fruitlessly during the night, to retreat. This they effected without serious molestation, and on the second day reached Fort St. David. Had the real object of the English been that which they professed—the restoration of the ex-Rájá Sahuji—they had seen enough to be convinced that to effect this they must be prepared to employ all the resources of their Presidency in a war with a native power. They no longer, however, even pretended to have this in view. But Sahuji had promised them Dévikota,* and the advantages presented by that place were too great to be lightly given up. Whether they received it from Sahuji or Partáb Singh was to them immaterial. They were resolved to possess it at any price, and with this avowed object, throwing over Sahuji, they despatched by sea a second expedition, consisting of 800 Europeans and 1,500 sipáhis, under the command of Major Lawrence.

CHAP. VI.

1749.

* The river Kolrún, which runs into the sea near Dévikota, was believed to be capable of receiving ships of the largest tonnage. The only difficulty was presented by the sands, but it was thought that these, with a little labour and expense, might be removed.—*Orme.*

Without entering into the details of this expedition, it will suffice to state that it was successful. Dévikota, after a gallant resistance, was stormed, and Partáb Singh, to avert further hostilities, and anxious now to secure the alliance of the English against Chanda Sáhib, whom he regarded as the most dangerous enemy of the Tanjur kingdom, agreed to cede that fortress, together with so much of the surrounding territory as should produce an annual revenue of 36,000 rupees. The English, on their part, promised to abandon the cause of Sahuji, and even to keep him under *surveillance* at Madras, on condition of his receiving a life-pension of 4,000 rupees. Such was the result to him of his alliance with an European power.

The English were occupied with their new conquest, when they learned the success of Chanda Sáhib at Ambur. They hastened to acknowledge him at Arkát. Nevertheless, noticing his subsequent visit to Pondichery, his protracted stay there, and the intimacy which he vaunted with Dupleix, they were not deaf to the solicitations—poor as they considered his chances of success—of Muhammad Ali. They waited, however, the further proceedings of Chanda Sáhib before committing themselves to any definite action. When, moreover, they saw that that chieftain remained idle at Pondichery, making no movement against his rival, they hesitated still more as to the course they should follow. Admiral Boscawen, on his part, was eager to support Muhammad Ali, and even offered to stay on the coast, if he were officially requested to do so. But the Governor, Mr. Floyer, shrank from a line of policy which seemed to commit the Presidency to the support of a pretender *in extremis*. He therefore suffered the Admiral to depart on November 1, taking from him only 300 men as an addition to his garrison.

The departure of Admiral Boscawen constituted the opportunity for which Chanda Sáhib had been so long watching. All his preparations had been made. Dupleix, with that rare disinterestedness and care for the resources of the colony which so eminently characterised him, had advanced to this chief 100,000 rupees from his own funds, and had induced other individuals to contribute 200,000 rupees in addition.* He also supplied him with 800 European troops, 300 Africans, and a train of artillery, from the support of which Pondichery was thus freed, whilst the troops remained at the disposal of Dupleix. They were now with Chanda Sáhib, under the immediate command of M. Duquesne. On the very day after the departure of the English fleet, this united army marched upon Trichinápallí. There, as Dupleix pointed out to the leaders, they would find the end of all opposition. The only man who had the shadow of a claim to oppose to the pretensions of Chanda Sáhib was in that fortress. To take it, therefore, was to destroy the last stronghold of the enemy, and with it the only chieftain capable of offering any opposition.

It is indeed clear to us now, as it was clear to Dupleix at the time, that upon the capture of this place depended the permanent preponderance of French influence in Southern India. Had that been accomplished, there could have been no possible rival to Chanda Sáhib, the English would have had no excuse to refuse to acknowledge his supremacy. In fact that supremacy would have been so firmly rooted, so strongly established, that they would not have dared to dispute it; they would, in a word, have been forced to recognise the sway on the Koromandel coast of a governor who, by inclination, gratitude, interest, was bound irrevocably to the French.

Such, indeed, was the aim of the policy of Dupleix.

---

* These advances were secured on lands which were temporarily made over to the French.—*Dupleix.*

To carry it out he had brought every resource to bear on his native allies. He had given them money, men, guns, and officers, and they, on their part, had left Pondichery, under an engagement to pursue the course of action he had pressed upon them, as alike best suited to his interests and theirs, viz., to march direct upon Trichinápallí.

Yet this occasion afforded another instance of the uselessness even of great genius, when the tools which genius is compelled to employ are weak and vacillating. Surely Dupleix had a right to believe that his native allies, having been equipped and supplied by him, and having started on an expedition they had promised to carry out, would at least march to their destination. Once there, he relied on his own commander, Duquesne, to do the rest. His mortification then can be imagined when he learnt that, after crossing the Kolrún, they had diverged from the road to Trichinápallí, and had taken that to Tanjur.

The fact was that, during their stay at Pondichery, Chanda Sáhib and Muzaffar Jang had exhausted on their own pleasures the money Dupleix had intended for the expenses of the army, and they found themselves, after crossing the Kolrún, in an enemy's country with an empty treasure chest. In this emergency Chanda Sáhib bethought him of the Rájá of Tanjur—a prince whose riches were proverbial, and whose arrears of tribute to the Múghal, Muzaffar Jang, as Subadar of the Dakhan, considered himself entitled to receive. In the hope of compelling this monarch to pay such a sum as would place them at ease regarding their expenditure, and in the belief that with the aid of their French allies the task would be easy of execution and short in its time of duration, they, without even consulting Dupleix, turned aside from the road leading to Trichinápallí, and took that to Tanjur.

This city, situated in the delta of the Kolrún and the

Kávarí, was defended by two forts, the greater and the lesser. The former was surrounded by a high wall and a ditch, but the fortifications were too inconsiderable to resist the attack of a vigorous enemy. The lesser fort, a mile in circumference, was far stronger, being surrounded by a lofty stone wall, a ditch excavated from the solid rock, and a glacis. Within this was a pagoda surpassing in magnificence all the buildings of Southern India, and believed to contain countless riches. The allied army arrived before this place on November 7, and at once summoned it to surrender. The Rájá, Partáb Singh, with a view to gain time, expressed at once his willingness to negotiate, whilst he sent pressing messages to the English and to Nasir Jang, demanding assistance. The English, who had already despatched 120 men to aid Muhammad Ali at Trichinápallí, ordered twenty of these to proceed to Tanjur. How Nasir Jang responded to the summons we shall see further on. On receiving the reply of the Tanjurian, Duquesne, the commandant of the French contingent, urged upon Chanda Sáhib not to waste his time in vain negotiations, but to compel compliance with his requisitions by force. This was undoubtedly the direct and proper course to pursue. But Chanda Sáhib, who wanted only the money, and who believed the rájá was in earnest about paying it, begged Duquesne to abstain from all appearance of hostilities so long as negotiations should be going on. In Partáb Singh, however, he met a man more wily and cunning than himself. For six weeks he suffered himself to be duped by protestations and promises, fruitless though they were of any result. In vain did Dupleix press upon him the superior advantage of Trichinápallí; to no purpose did he point out to him that he was giving time to Muhammad Ali to strengthen his position, and to Nasir Jang to march upon his communications. Chanda Sáhib was infatuated with his negotiation. To such an extent did he carry this feeling, that Dupleix, seeing the gathering storm, and apprehending not only the failure of his hopes, but danger to French interests, sent positive orders to Duquesne to break off the negotiation, and to attack Tanjur. Duquesne obeyed; and his vigorous measures had a decisive effect. On December 26, he captured three redoubts about 600 yards from the walls; three days later, after some fruitless negotiations, he assaulted and carried one of the gates of the town. This so intimidated the rájá, that he at once gave in, and on the 31st signed a treaty whereby, amongst other stipulations, he agreed to pay to Muzaffar Jang and Chanda Sáhib 7,000,000 rupees; to remit from the French East India Company the annual ground rent of 7,000 rupees, which it paid him; to add to the French possessions at Karikal territory comprising eighty-one villages; and to pay down to the French troops 200,000 rupees. But, meanwhile, Nasir Jang had succeeded in collecting an enormous army, and was on his march to crush his nephew and rival. Intelligence of this had already been conveyed by the English to the Rájá of Tanjur, and this monarch had recourse to all the arts of which he was master to lengthen out the term of payment. By sending out, in satisfaction of the sum he had agreed to pay, sometimes plate, sometimes obsolete coin, sometimes jewels and precious stones, he detained Chanda Sáhib for some weeks longer under his walls, and it was not until a pressing message from Dupleix informed him that Nasir Jang had entered the Karnátik, that this chieftain renounced the hope of obtaining, even by those instalments, the promised ransom. Even then Dupleix recommended vigorous measures. He urged him to seize Tanjur at once, both as a means of punishing the faithless rájá, and of providing himself with a place of refuge. Chanda Sáhib was willing enough to act upon this advice, but his troops refused to follow him. They too had heard the rumours of the approach

THE ALLIES BAFFLED.

of the vast army under Nasir Jang, and, panic-striken at the report of its numbers, they broke up without orders, and fell back rapidly on Pondichery.

CHAP. VI.

1750.

Thus, by the weakness of the instruments he was compelled to use, were the great plans of Dupleix temporarily shattered. Nay more, the very men who had caused the defeat, and who by their want of energy had plunged themselves as well as him into misfortune, now came to beg him to extricate them from their difficulties. He made the attempt, not indeed with any great confidence in his allies—for the past three months had shown him their weakness—but yet with a steadfastness, an energy, an adaptation of means to the end, such as even at this distant day must challenge and command our admiration. He did not, as we shall see, succeed in the outset, but his patience, his perseverance, his energy, could not be long working without producing some advantageous result. Before however noticing the manner in which he acted, we propose to take a comprehensive glance at the situation.

The army of Muzaffar Jang and Chanda Sáhib, 40,000 strong, panic-stricken from the rumours of the vast force of Nasir Jang, and mutinous from want of pay, was under the walls of Pondichery. With it had come the French detachment of 800 men, now commanded by M. Goupil, its former leader, Duquesne, having died of fever at Tanjur. On the other side, the enormous army of Nasir Jang, said to consist of 300,000 men,* of whom one-half were cavalry, together with 800 pieces of cannon and 1,300 elephants, was marching on them from Arkát. On its way it was joined by Murári Ráo at the head of 10,000 Marátha horse, fresh from a skirmish with the allied army at Chelambram; whilst on reaching Valdavur, fifteen miles from Pondichery, Muhammad Ali, the pseudo-Nawwáb of the Karnátik, brought 6,000

---

* The number of trained soldiers did not probably exceed 40,000.

horse into the camp of Nasir Jang, and, what was of far greater consequence, he was strengthened a few days later—April 2—by the junction of 600 Europeans under Major Lawrence. The English, in fact, had resolved to take advantage of the check received by the protégés of the French at Tanjur, by using all their influence to support the rivals and opponents of those chieftains.

Against such a force what was Dupleix to do? There was but one course, which even to conceive, it was necessary that a man should have been born with a profound and daring intellect. Successfully to encounter this force it was absolutely necessary that the opposing army, however disproportionate in numbers and deficient in material, should oppose to it a bold and resolute front. Yet how to infuse the necessary courage into the panic-stricken and mutinous soldiers of his two allies? This was a problem which seemed hard to solve. Dupleix nevertheless attempted it. First of all he stopped their mutinous spirit. This he effected by advancing from his own funds a sufficient sum to pay up their arrears. Their courage he endeavoured to reanimate by showing that he was not afraid to support them by the entire available garrison of Pondichery. Goupil, who had succeeded to Duquesne, having himself fallen ill, Dupleix placed at the head of the contingent M. d'Auteuil, who had recovered from the wounds he had received at Ambur, and increased its strength to 2,000 men. The total force, encouraged and strengthened by these means, moved in a north-westerly direction from Pondichery, and took up at the end of March a strong position opposite the enemy's camp at Valdavur. At the same time Dupleix did not neglect those means which he had often used so successfully, of endeavouring by intrigues and secret communications to work upon the mind of Nasir Jang in favour of French interests. He was on the point of succeeding when unexpected events, impossible to have been guarded against, neutralised the effect of these negotiations, and brought down the fabric of his vast plans.

It happened, unfortunately for Dupleix, that a very bad feeling prevailed at this moment amongst the officers of his army. The sum of money received at Tanjur had been divided amongst those troops only who had participated in that service. Many of these had received leave of absence, and those who took their places, as well as those who joined with the fresh troops, grumbled most unreasonably at having been assigned a duty which would expose them to great risks without the chance of prize-money. For the moment Dupleix was powerless to punish the malcontents, so few were the officers at his disposal. He trusted, however, to their military honour to behave as soldiers and Frenchmen in the presence of an enemy. But in this hope he was disappointed. On the very evening of the day on which the two armies had for the first time exchanged a cannonade from their respective positions—April 3—thirteen officers of the French army went in a body to M. d'Auteuil, resigned their commissions, and refused to serve. This was not the least of the evil. Not content with refusing to fight themselves, these officers had done their best to induce the soldiers they commanded to follow their example. By a baseness happily unparalleled they had succeeded in sowing amongst the soldiers the seeds of disaffection and distrust. Even the sipáhis in the pay of France could not see unmoved the sudden withdrawal of those they had been accustomed to regard as their leaders. Doubt and hesitation pervaded their ranks, and d'Auteuil suddenly found, on the eve of a battle which, if it were unfavourable to him, would be ruinous to French interests, that he commanded an army which was utterly demoralised, which could not be relied upon to face the enemy.

Few men have ever found themselves in circumstances

more difficult, more requiring quick and prompt decision. To stay where he was, to meet with his demoralised force, and the native levies of his two allies, the vastly superior numbers of Nasir Jang, the Maráthás, and the English, was to court destruction for all. His men would not fight, and their retreat would draw with it the disorderly flight of the followers of Muzaffar Jang and Chanda Sáhib. It seemed, too, more than probable that such a rout would encourage the enemy to make another attempt upon Pondichery. On the other hand, the withdrawal of his troops during the night would save the French army for future operations, and would assure the safety of the French capital. But before taking any steps in the matter, d'Auteuil made one great effort to induce his army to sustain the part which best befitted them as soldiers. But his entreaties, his remonstrances, even his threats, were all in vain. The poison of mistrust had entered their ranks; the mutinous officers had persuaded the men that they were being deliberately sacrificed to superior numbers, and so firmly had they imbibed this idea, that all the reasoning of their commander was ineffective. They would not fight. Convinced now that his only course was to retreat, d'Auteuil sought an interview with his two allies, and laid before them the circumstances of the case. He showed them that he was forced to retreat, and he put it to them whether they would prefer to follow his fortunes, or to endeavour to make their own terms with the enemy. Then came out the difference in the character of the two men. Chanda Sáhib, whose long acquaintance and constant intercourse with the French had given him a high appreciation of their character and a confidence in their fortunes, declared unhesitatingly that he would cast in his lot with his European allies. Muzaffar Jang, naturally weaker, possessing little relf-reliance, and unable to believe that d'Auteuil had not some other motive for his conduct, determined, on the other hand, to trust to the tender mercies of his uncle.

In accordance with these resolutions the French contingent commenced its retreat at midnight, followed by Chanda Sáhib, who, with his cavalry, insisted upon taking the post of honour in the rear. So great, however, was the disorder in the French camp, so complete the demoralisation of officers and men, that no one communicated the intelligence of the intended movement to the gunners, who, to the number of forty, manned the batteries in front of the camp; these, therefore, with their eleven guns, were left behind.

Day dawned before the retreat of the French was discovered. But no sooner was it known than Murári Ráo, at the head of 10,000 Marátha horse, started in pursuit of them. He came up with them just before they reached the prickly pear hedge, which formed the outer defence of Pondichery. Noting his approach, d'Auteuil formed his men up in a hollow square, whilst Chanda Sáhib held his cavalry in readiness to attack him after his repulse. Murári Ráo, however, a splendid horseman, little acquainted with squares or European tactics at all, boldly charged and broke into the French formation. But at the same time Chanda Sáhib charged his cavalry, who were thus, with the exception of fifteen, prevented from following their leader. In this manner Murári Ráo was, with but fifteen men inside the French square, apparently lost. But the sullenness of the Europeans and his own daring saved him. He dashed at the other face of the square, and succeeded, with the loss of nine men, in cutting his way out. He then joined his cavalry, who were engaged with Chanda Sáhib. With him and with the French he kept up a running fight till they reached the hedge, when he thought proper to retire.

In this retreat the French lost nineteen men, in addition to the forty left behind; many of them were sabred by the natives, the remainder rescued from their clutches, and taken prisoners, by the English. It was, however, less the loss of men and of guns that afflicted Dupleix, than the destruction, by this misfortune, of his vast plans. We have said that he was on the point of succeeding in inducing Nasir Jang to enter into engagements with himself. He had even persisted in this attempt after he had become aware of the existence of the mutinous feeling amongst the French officers, and it is probable that had the army only maintained its position in the field during the next day, Nasir Jang would have signed the treaty which was being pressed upon him. But this mutiny spoiled all.

"It is easy to imagine," he says, writing in the third person in his memoirs, "what was the mortification of Dupleix, when he was informed of all the details of the conduct of our cowardly officers, and further, to complete his misfortunes, that Muzaffar Jang had been taken prisoner and placed in irons by Nasir Jang." This last information was but too true. Though Nasir Jang had sworn upon the Kuran to restore his nephew to the governments he had held, yet, in accordance with the customs not uncommon in Europe in the thirteenth and fourteenth and in India in the eighteenth centuries, he at once loaded him with irons. He thus became undisputed Subadar of the Dakhan, and one of his first acts was to appoint Muhammad Ali Nawwáb of the Karnátik. This was the destruction to which we have alluded of those great schemes, whereby Dupleix hoped to bring Southern India in entire subordination to French interests. No doubt his mortification was extreme, yet great as it was, it neither caused him to give himself to despair, nor even to abandon his plans. On the contrary, it impelled him to try new and bolder expedients to bring them to maturity.

He himself and the other inhabitants of Pondichery had received the first intelligence of the disgrace of the French army from the runaway officers themselves. These had hurried into the town on the morning of the retreat, and alarmed the inhabitants with the cry that the French army was beaten, and that the Maráthás were upon them. The first act of Dupleix, on receiving intelligence of a nature so different to that he had expected, was to arrest these cowards. He then hastened to meet the army, to endeavour, if possible, to weed it of the disaffected, and to revive the spirit of the remainder. To this end he had recourse to the most stringent measures. All the disaffected officers were placed under arrest; d'Auteuil even was brought to trial for retreating without orders. The soldiers were reminded that their retreat was in no way due to the enemy, but to the recreant behaviour of their own officers. This confidence in difficult circumstances did not fail to beget its like. The French soldiers felt in his inspiring presence that they had been indeed guilty, and to insubordination succeeded an irrepressible desire to be allowed an opportunity of recovering their name.

But whilst thus engaged in restoring the discipline of the army, Dupleix was equally prompt in dealing with the enemy. This could only be in the first instance by negotiation, and we shall see that here he exerted the skill of which he was so great a master. Instead of showing, in this hour of his extremity, by any abatement of his pretensions, how fallen were the fortunes of Pondichery, he directed his envoys to make demands little inferior to those which would have resulted from a French victory. They insisted, therefore, in his name, that no one of the family of Anwáru-dín should be appointed Nawwáb of the Karnátik, and that the children of Muzaffar Jang should be established in the estates and governments of their father. But they did not stop there. To favour their negotiations, they had recourse to those wiles which they had learned from the Asiatic princes, and which they now showed they could use more skilfully than their masters. Thus they took credit for the defeat of d'Auteuil, and exaggerated the loss experienced by Murári Ráo in his attempts to cut them off from Pondichery. All this time these same agents intrigued with the chiefs of the Subadar's army, especially with the Patán Nawwábs of Kadapah, Karnul, and Savanur, and succeeded in establishing with these and others relations of a confidential nature.

Nasir Jang himself refused to agree to the terms proposed by MM. du Bausset and de Larche, the envoys of Dupleix, and on the seventh day these two gentlemen returned to Pondichery. By this time a good feeling had been restored in the army; the officers who had disgraced themselves had been severely punished; others, less guilty, were only anxious by some brilliant achievement to wipe out the stain on their honour; d'Auteuil, who had shown very clearly that he had acted in the only manner possible for him to act under the circumstances, had been restored to the command. Now was the time to strike a blow; this the opportunity to show the ruler who had rejected his proposals that the French were yet, as an enemy, to be feared. No sooner then had the envoys returned than Dupleix sent instructions to d'Auteuil to beat up the camp of Murári Ráo, situated between Pondichery and the main body of Nasir Jang's army. On the night of April 12, only eight days after the retreat from Valdavur, d'Auteuil detached 300 men under the command of M. de la Touche to surprise the enemy. They marched about midnight, reached and penetrated the camp without being discovered, killed about 1,200 of the surprised and terror-stricken enemy, and returned to Pondichery at daybreak, having lost but three men of their party. This bold stroke had such an effect upon Nasir Jang, that trembling now for his own safety, he broke up his camp, and retired in all haste to Arkát, abandoning the English, who returned to Fort St. David.

Having thus caused the prestige of success to return to his colours, Dupleix resolved to follow up his blow. Nasir Jang, on reaching Arkát, had resolved on a movement, by means of which, whilst he himself should remain safely shut up in that capital, he might avenge himself of his enemies. He accordingly took forcible possession of the lodges and factories which the French had established at the town of Machlipatan, and at Yanaon, situated at the junction of the Koringa river and the Godávari.

But he did not hold them long. It had happened shortly before these occurrences that two ships, the "Fleury" and the "d'Argenson," bound for Bengal, had touched at Pondichery for the purpose of discharging a portion of their cargoes, and re-loading at that place. On hearing of the proceedings of Nasir Jang, Dupleix, without confiding in anyone, made the necessary preparations, and the night before these ships were to sail he embarked on board of them 200 Europeans and 200 native soldiers, with a battering train, and directed the commander to sail direct for Machlipatan, and take possession of the place. They arrived there on the evening of the third day. The commander at once landed his troops, surprised the town, and took possession of it without the smallest resistance, and without spilling a drop of human blood. The French colours were at once hoisted on the place, and preparations were made for its retention.

But it was in the neighbourhood of Pondichery that Dupleix resolved to strike his most effective blow. Very soon then after Nasir Jang had left for Arkát, and the English for Fort St. David, he ordered d'Auteuil to march with 500 men, cross the river Panár, and take possession of the fortified pagoda of Tiruvádí, only thirteen miles from Gudalur, and almost in sight of the army of Muhammad Ali. The object of this was to obtain a *point d'appui* on the Panár, which would

CHAP. VI.
1750.

give him command of the neighbouring country and its revenues. The expedition completely succeeded. D'Auteuil captured the place without resistance, and having garrisoned it with 20 Europeans, 20 Eurasians, and 50 sipáhis, began to make arrangements for pushing his conquests further. But Nasir Jang, alarmed at the loss of Tiruvádí, yielded now to the pressing solicitations of Muhammad Ali, and reinforced him with 20,000 men. At the same time the English, to whom the possession of Tiruvádí by the French was a standing menace, sent a force of 400 Europeans and 1,500 sipáhis under Captain Cope to join Muhammad Ali. This combined army took up a position on July 30, near the French force, which they found encamped on the river Panár, about seven miles from Gudalur.

Notwithstanding the overwhelming superiority of the enemy, d'Auteuil resolved to maintain his position. This was not only strong by nature, but it had been strongly fortified. To hazard an attack upon Frenchmen in a position defended by intrenchments did not suit the feeble nature of Muhammad Ali. Acting on Captain Cope's advice, therefore, he moved against Tiruvádí in the hope of drawing out d'Auteuil to its assistance. But d'Auteuil was too wary to be caught by so transparent a device, and Muhammad Ali, when he wished to change the feigned assault into a real one, found that his soldiers had the same objection to stone walls as to intrenchments, when both were manned by Europeans. He accordingly marched back to his position in front of the French camp, and, encouraged by Captain Cope, opened upon it a violent cannonade. The fire of the French was, however, so brisk, and their guns were served so efficiently, that at the end of six hours the allies had had enough of it, and retreated with a considerable loss in killed and wounded. The French loss was slight; but they were too few in numbers to venture in pursuit. They contented themselves with maintaining their position, ready to profit by the disagreement which, they felt sure, would be produced by this repulse between Muhammad Ali and his English allies.

So indeed it happened. As prone to be unduly depressed in adversity as to be inflated in prosperity, Muhammad Ali did not consider himself safe from the attacks of the French so long as he remained in the open country. He therefore proposed to retreat upon Arkát. The English, who wished to cut off the French from Pondichery, finding that Muhammad Ali would neither listen to their advice nor advance any more money, returned to Fort St. David. No sooner was Dupleix acquainted with this movement than he directed d'Auteuil to break up from his encampment, and march on Tiruvádí; there to join a corps of 1,300 Europeans and 2,500 sipáhis led by de la Touche, and 1,000 horse commanded by Chanda Sáhib. With this force he was to surprise the camp of Muhammad Ali. This Nawwáb, with an army of upwards of 20,000 men, of whom the greater part were cavalry, had taken up a position between Tiruvádí and Fort St. David, with the river Panár in his rear, and awaited there the instructions for which he had applied to Nasir Jang. But on the afternoon of September 1, the day after the departure of the English, he was attacked by d'Auteuil. The French army advanced in good order, the artillery in front, the cavalry on either wing. In this formation, in full view of the army of Muhammad Ali, the handful of men moved forward, halting occasionally to fire their guns. So long as they were at a distance, the gunners of the Nawwáb's army replied by an ineffective fire. But when, within two hundred yards of the intrenchments, d'Auteuil brought up his infantry, and ordered a general charge, the courage of the Asiatics gave way. Not an effort was made to defend the entrance into the camp; the intrenchments were abandoned

s 2

as the enemy reached them; and the French, quickly bringing up their guns, opened out from one end of the camp a tremendous fire on the masses now huddled between them and the river. Muhammad Ali showed neither courage nor presence of mind. Here, as at Ambur, he thought only of his own safety. His men, left to themselves, behaved, as might have been expected, like sheep without a shepherd. The 15,000 cavalry who were in the camp did not strike one blow for their master. How to cross the Panár in safety was the problem each man sought to solve for his own advantage. Victory they never had dreamt of; now even orderly retreat was out of the question. Fortunately for them the river was fordable. Yet, before it could be crossed by the fugitives, they had left nearly a thousand of their number on the field of carnage. They left besides, to fall into the hands of the French, a great quantity of munitions of war, immense supplies of grain and fodder, thirty pieces of cannon, and two English mortars. The French did not lose a single man in the engagement; a few sipáhis only were wounded by the explosion of a tumbril.

If battles are to be judged by their consequences, this action may truly be termed a great victory. By it the French more than regained the ascendancy they had lost by the disastrous retreat from Valdávur; Chanda Sáhib, their ally, resumed, in consequence of it, a position in which he could lay a well-founded claim to the possession of the Karnátik; whilst his rival, Muhammad Ali, who had but two months before been master of the whole of that province—the territories ceded to the French and English alone excepted—was forced by this defeat into the position of a beaten and baffled fugitive, fleeing with two attendants for refuge to Arkát. The English, on their part, sulky with Muhammad Ali, on the point of losing their commandant, Major Lawrence, who was about to embark for England, were likewise by the same means reduced to an almost compulsory inaction, for they were not at war with France, and the dispersion of Muhammad Ali's army had left them almost without a native ally whom indirectly to assist.

It was true indeed that Nasir Jang was yet exercising the functions of the office of Subadar of the Dakhan, and Nasir Jang was their ally. Sunk in debauchery and the pleasures of the chase, Nasir Jang, however, left the direction of affairs to his ministers and nobility, and the chief of these had already — thanks to the intrigues of Dupleix — been won over to the interests of France. Whilst the army he had given to his protégé, Muhammad Ali, was being destroyed in the field, he remained inactive at Arkát, not yet thinking himself in danger, not yet believing that the army which fled before him at Valdávur would dare to compete with him in the field. Of this inaction, which he had used all his efforts to secure, and of the consternation caused amongst the partisans of Muhammad Ali by the victory of d'Auteuil, Dupleix resolved to take the fullest advantage. He therefore sent instant orders to d'Auteuil to detach a sufficient force under M. de Bussy to attack Jinjí, a fortress, fifty miles inland, and the possession of which would, he thought, decide the fate of the Karnátik.

The town of Jingí, surrounded by a thick wall and flanked by towers, is situated at the base of three lofty ranges, forming the three sides of an equilateral triangle. Each of these mountains was defended by a strong citadel built on its summit, and by the sides, in many places naturally steep and in others artificially scarped, by which alone access was possible. A cordon of advanced works contributed likewise to make all approach a matter of extreme difficulty. It was no wonder then that in the eyes of the natives Jinjí was deemed quite impregnable. Even Sívají, the founder of the Maráthá power, had been forced, in 1677, to come to an understanding with its commander to effect its reduction, and Zulfikár Khán, the general of Aurangzeb, had brought about the same result by means of a blockade of the strictest nature. The belief in its impregnability made it always the refuge of defeated armies, and the scattered parties of Muhammad Ali's force, to the number of 10,000 or 12,000 men, had fled to it after the battle on the Panár for the protection which it was deemed so well able to offer. Against this—the strongest of all the fortresses of the Karnátik—Dupleix directed d'Auteuil to send a detachment with all possible speed, indicating at the same time Bussy as the commandant of whom he would approve for such a service. This is not the first time that we have met with this officer. He it was, it will be recollected, who, when the French troops had twice recoiled before the intrenchments thrown up by Anwáru-dín at Ambur, when their commandant, d'Auteuil, had been struck down, rallied the repulsed infantry, and led them, the third time, victoriously to the charge. But little is known of his early childhood—a strange circumstance when it is recollected that he occupies a principal figure, in the estimation of some the foremost figure, in the history of the French in India. This much, however, is ascertained, that he was born in 1718, at Buçy, near Soissons: that he had lost his father at an early age, and inheriting little beyond his pedigree,* he had come out to the Isle of France at the time that La Bourdonnais was governor, and had formed one of the expedition led by that famous admiral to India in 1746. When La Bourdonnais returned to Europe at the end of that year, de Bussy remained behind as an officer of the Pondichery army. Here he found himself constantly in contact with Dupleix, and, in their frequent meetings, he had not been less struck by the large views and

* He was named Charles-Joseph Patissier, Marquis de Bussy-Castelnau.

brilliant genius of the Governor-General than had been Dupleix by the frank nature, the striking talents, the desire to acquire knowledge, especially knowledge of India and its people, displayed by the young officer. He had given many proofs of adding to these qualities a courage, a daring, and a presence of mind which, when united in a soldier, inevitably lead him to fortune; and it was on this account that he had now been selected to lead a detachment of the French army on the most daring expedition on which European troops had yet been engaged in India.

The force placed at the disposal of Bussy consisted of 250 Europeans and 1,200 sipáhis, and four field pieces. They left the scene of the action with Muhammad Ali on September 3rd, and came in sight of Jinjí on the 11th. Here at the distance of three miles Bussy encamped, and here intelligence reached him that the remnants of Muhammad Ali's army, 10,000 or 12,000 strong, together with 1,000 sipáhis trained by the English, and some European gunners with eight field-pieces, were encamped on the glacis, and were about to take advantage of their overwhelming superiority of numbers to attack him. Immediately afterwards the enemy was seen advancing. Bussy waited for him till his men came within pistol-shot, when he ordered a general advance, the four guns opening at the same time on the hostile cavalry. This, as was usual, not only prevented the advance but threw the enemy into confusion. They had already broken when the main body of the French army under d'Auteuil was seen approaching the field. A general panic instantly ensued amongst all branches of the enemy's forces, and Bussy, taking advantage of it, advanced and secured their guns, killing or taking prisoners the Europeans who served them. He then pushed forward and drove the fugitives under the walls of Jingí, the cannon of which opened fire on the pursuers.

But it did not stop Bussy. Following the fugitives to the entrance of the town, he applied a petard to the principal gate and blew it in. He at once rushed forward, sword in hand, followed by his men, and engaged in a desperate hand to hand contest with the defenders. Nothing, however, could resist French gallantry. Before nightfall the place was their own, and it was occupied during the night by the remainder of the force under d'Auteuil. The situation of the victors was, nevertheless, still one of great danger. We have already stated that the town of Jinjí lies at the base of three high ranges, the summits of which were strongly fortified. From these summits there poured in now an incessant fire on the French in Jinjí. Small arms, grape, round shot, and rockets were used with all the vigour of which the garrison were capable. For some time Bussy replied by a fire from his mortars, keeping his men under cover. But no sooner had the moon gone down than he moved out three detachments of picked troops, all Frenchmen, to escalade the ascents to the three citadels at the same time. The way was steep; redoubt after redoubt hindered the progress of the assailants; a terrific fire rained upon them from all sides; but no obstacle was too great to be overcome by Bussy and his comrades. The storming of one redoubt filled them with the greater determination to attempt the conquest of another; their onward progress gave them fresh animating power, whilst the defenders after each loss became more and more discouraged. At last, mounting higher and higher, they came to the citadels. These too, just as day broke on the horizon, fell into their hands, and the victors could gaze and wonder at the almost insuperable difficulties which they nevertheless had surmounted.

It was indeed a wonderful achievement, great in itself, and calculated by its effect upon the people of Southern India to be much greater. They were no second-rate warriors who could, within twenty-four hours, defeat an army vastly superior in numbers, and storm a fortress reputed impregnable, and which for three years had defied the best army and the best general of the renowned Aurangzeb. Not lightly would such a feat be esteemed in the cities of the south. The fame of it would extend even to imperial Delhi on the one side, and to the palaces of Puná on the other. It was a blow which, by the intrinsic advantages resulting from it and by the renown it would acquire for those who had delivered it, would strike not only Muhammad Ali but Nasir Jang, would seat the nominees of Dupleix at Golkonda and Arkát, might eventually bring Delhi itself almost within the grasp of the French Governor. Well might Dupleix hope that, by following it up, by using carefully yet vigorously every opportunity, this capture of Jinjí might indeed be made the first stone of a French empire in India.

The immediate results of the capture on the minds of the natives were all that could have been expected. Nasir Jang, till then devoted to pleasure, now roused himself to action. Yet even he, the Subadar of the Dakhan, the disposer of an army of 300,000 men, was thunderstruck at the feat. These French, he felt, must be beaten or conciliated. It appeared to rest with him whether he should attempt the first, or accomplish the second, for almost simultaneously with the news of the fall of Jinjí intelligence reached him that d'Auteuil was marching on Arkát whilst he at the same time received peaceful overtures from Dupleix. The principal of these suggested the release of Muzaffar Jang and his restoration to the governments he had held in his grandfather's lifetime, the appointment of Chanda Sáhib to be Nawwáb of Arkát, and the absolute cession of Machlipatan to the French. It is probable that Nasir Jang would have made no difficulty regarding the second and third of these conditions, but the release of Muzaffar

Jang was tantamount to a renewal of the civil contest, and rather than assent to that, he preferred to try the fortune of war. Summoning then his chiefs to Arkát, he set out at the head of an army consisting of 60,000 foot, 45,000 horse, 700 elephants, and 360 cannon, in the direction of Jinjí. When, however, he had arrived within twelve miles of the French force—which, after making one or two marches in the direction of Arkát, had returned, on the news of the approach of the enemy, to Jinjí—the periodical rains set in with such violence that any movements in the face of an enemy became impossible. An inaction of two months' duration, from September to the beginning of December, succeeded, the French army remaining encamped about three miles from Jinjí, whence, for some weeks, it drew its supplies. When these had been exhausted it received others, thanks to the excellent arrangements of Dupleix, and despite the unsettled state of the country, direct from Pondichery. Nasir Jang, on his side, was forced to remain in a most inconvenient position, hemmed in by watercourses swollen by the rains, and able to obtain supplies only with the greatest difficulty.

But these two months of military inaction constituted a busy period to Dupleix. Corresponding secretly with the chiefs of Nasir Jang's army, he had succeeded in persuading many of them, especially the Patáns and the Maráthás, that it would be more to their interest to regard the French as friends than as enemies. Both these sections had several causes of dislike to Nasir Jang. His manifold debaucheries, the treatment, after his solemn promise to grant him liberty, of Muzaffar Jang, his constant refusal to entertain the propositions for peace, and the knowledge that, with Muzaffar Jang upon the viceregal seat, they would enjoy not only peace and alliance with the French, but an accession of honours and dignities, all conspired to whet their desire to be rid of him. On the other hand, their admiration, mingled with fear, of the French nation, and especially of the statesman who was so daringly guiding its fortunes in India, gave to the proposals of Dupleix a weight which they found it difficult to resist. A secret agreement was accordingly arrived at between the two parties, which stipulated that if Nasir Jang should refuse any longer to agree to the terms offered by Dupleix, but should decide upon marching against the French, the malcontent nobles should withdraw their forces from those of their feudal superior, and should range themselves, a short distance from them, under the flag of France. To such an extent were the details of this arrangement carried out that a French standard was secretly conveyed to the malcontents, to be by them on the proper occasion hoisted on the back of an elephant in the most conspicuous part of the field. Other secret arrangements were at the same time entered into between Muzaffar Jang and the conspirators, with which Dupleix had no concern. There can be little doubt but that the death of the Subadar and the distribution of his treasures equally between Muzaffar Jang on one side and the conspirators on the other were resolved upon.

But meanwhile better thoughts had come over Nasir Jang. The difficulties of his army, the fear of finding himself engaged in a long and doubtful campaign with an enemy whom he dreaded, and, above all, the deprivation of much loved pleasures which this campaign would necessitate, induced him to reconsider the terms repeatedly pressed upon him by Dupleix. To these he had given no reply. But when the fine days of the early December showed him that the time had arrived when action could not be avoided, he determined to give up everything, to set free Muzaffar Jang, to yield Machlipatan, to appoint Chanda Sáhib—to make any concession, in fact, so that he might be free to drain the cup of pleasure. He accordingly wrote to Dupleix,

CHAP. VI.
1750.

offering to agree to his terms. With this letter he sent three of his officers, provided with full powers to negotiate, for the purpose of signing the treaty. Dupleix, caring little with whom the treaty was made, provided only that his own propositions were agreed to, determined to accede to the offers of Nasir Jang, and wrote at once to the commander of the French forces to suspend all hostilities until he should receive further instructions. But his orders arrived too late. M. de la Touche, upon whom the command had devolved, in the absence of d'Auteuil, laid up with the gout, had, before this letter reached him, received from the conspirators the signal he had preconcerted with them to advance. They were, in fact, acquainted with the contents of the letter sent to Dupleix, and justly feared that, if time were allowed, it would interfere with their long-meditated plans. Hence the sudden resolution to bring matters to a crisis and their call upon the French general to perform his part. Ignorant of the negotiations going on at the time with Pondichery, de la Touche had no option. In compliance, therefore, with instructions which had been given him as to his action in the event of his receiving such a summons from the conspirators, he set out on the night of December 15 from Jinjí, at the head of 800 Europeans, 3,000 sipáhis, and ten guns, in the direction of the Subadar's camp, under the guidance of a native who had been sent for that purpose by the conspirators. After a march of sixteen miles, de la Touche, at four o'clock in the morning, came in sight of the enemy. Their advanced posts, which gave the alarm, were soon dispersed, and de la Touche found himself with his 3,800 men in front of an army of more than 25,000. By the skilful management of his guns, however, he succeeded in keeping at bay, and eventually throwing into confusion, the vast masses of cavalry which were constantly threatening to charge him. No sooner were these dispersed than he advanced on the infantry, and after a very severe contest succeeded in breaking them. But this had hardly been accomplished when he perceived a body of at least 20,000 men advancing on his left flank. At the sight of this new enemy the French began almost to despair of success, but as they advanced nearer de la Touche discovered to his joy the French standard displayed on the back of the foremost elephant: almost immediately afterwards a messenger from Muzaffar Jang conveyed to de la Touche the intelligence of the success of all the plans of the conspirators.

Nasir Jang, in fact, relying on the full powers with which he had accredited the envoys he had sent to Pondichery, would not believe that they were French who were attacking him. When it would no longer admit of a doubt, he sent orders to his generals to repulse "this mad attempt of a parcel of drunken Europeans,"* whilst, seated on his elephant, he took his station amongst his guns. Near him, on another elephant, was seated Muzaffar Jang, under the guarddianship of an officer who had received instructions to behead him on the first appearance of treason. In the midst of the action, seeing some of his men retiring from the field, the Subadar inquired and learned that the Patán Nawwábs, the Dalwai of Maisur, and the Maráthás, had ordered their troops to abstain from any participation in the action. Enraged at this, he started on his elephant to threaten them, first giving orders for the beheadal of Muzaffar Jang. The Nawwáb of Kadapah, whom he first met and upbraided, replied by a defiant answer, and directed his attendant to fire at the Subadar. As the piece, however, missed, he unslung his own carbine, and shot Nasir Jang through the heart. The Subadar's head was instantly cut off and

* Orme.

laid at the feet of Muzaffar Jang, whose own had just escaped a similar ceremony.*

This was the intelligence conveyed to M. de la Touche by the messenger of Muzaffar Jang, just after the French, to their delight, had beheld their national standard displayed on the foremost elephant of the advancing party. The first act of the French leader was to despatch his second in command, de Bussy—although he had been wounded in the fight—to congratulate the new Subadar on his elevation. Bussy found the newly-made potentate seated on the splendidly-caparisoned elephant of his late rival, acknowledged as Subadar, not only by the conspiring nobles, but by all but a very small minority of the army which but a few hours before had obeyed the orders of Nasir Jang. The same evening M. de la Touche himself, accompanied by his principal officers, paid a congratulatory visit to Muzaffar Jang, and received from him the commission to inform Dupleix that nothing would be undertaken without his advice, to obtain which he, Muzaffar Jang, proposed instantly to proceed to Pondichery.

Whilst matters had thus progressed in the field, Dupleix had been awaiting in Pondichery the return of the messenger he had sent to the army to direct the suspension of hostilities. But before that messenger could return, the intelligence of the great victory and its results reached the town.† The excitement, the joy, the enthusiasm may be imagined. That the French might have entered into a satisfactory arrangement with Nasir Jang had been hoped; but every bound of reasonable expectation was exceeded when it was ascertained that, owing to the exertions of 800 Frenchmen and 3,000 sipáhis trained by them, the protégé of France

---

* He simply owed his escape to the fact that the officer in whose charge he had been placed was one of the conspirators.—Dupleix.

† Mr. Orme states that it was conveyed in person by Chanda Sáhib to Dupleix.

had become the ruler of Southern India, the lord over thirty-five millions of people. Still greater was the national exultation when it became known, through a brief despatch from M. de la Touche, how modestly Muzaffar Jang bore his triumph; how deferentially he acknowledged his obligations to the French people; and how submissively he had announced his intention to do nothing until he should have communicated personally with the great ruler of French India. The fire of artillery, the chanting of *Te Deums*, illuminations, processions and durbars, announced all the joy which these occurrences inspired.

Well, indeed, might the French in India feel a pride in their success. Not seventy-six years had elapsed since Francis Martin, at the head of sixty Frenchmen, had bought the plot of ground on which had since risen the city of Pondichery, and we find his successor in a position to give laws to thirty-five millions of people! Though besieged and taken by the Dutch, though besieged but two years before by an immensely superior force of English, Pondichery had risen to see the decadence of one nation as a rival on Indian soil, and the compulsory inaction and loss of reputation—both indeed destined only to be temporary—of the other. The genius of the people had suited itself so well to the natural temperament of the children of the soil, that the French were regarded everywhere as friends; the increase of their territory excited no jealousy. Their policy had been a policy of fidelity and trust. The intimacy of Francis Martin with Sher Khán Lodi had been continued by his successors to the family of Dost Ali. Neither the overthrow of that Nawwáb, nor the captivity of his successor, had been able to shake it. To support that traditional alliance, M. Dumas had bade defiance to the threats of Raghují Bhonsla, and his, till then, irresistible Maráthás; Dupleix had, for seven years, fed the hopes of the im-

CHAP. VI.
1750.

prisoned Chanda Sáhib with the prospect of a throne. And now this policy had blossomed and borne fruit. Chanda Sáhib, released from captivity by the efforts of Dupleix, had made common cause with Muzaffar Jang, the claimant of the viceregal dignity in the south of India, and, after many reverses, the two friends—thanks to French generalship and French valour—seemed to have attained the summit of their very highest wishes.

The glory which M. Dupleix had acquired by this successful policy attained its most dazzling elevation when, on December 26, Muzaffar Jang and his followers arrived at Pondichery. Entering the town in a state palanquin, this ruler of thirty-five millions paid to the French Governor the homage and respect due to a feudal superior. He at once made over to him all the treasure, the jewels, the gold and silver ornaments found in the camp of his late rival, and requested him to assume the office of arbitrator between himself and his confederates, the Patán Nawwábs, with whom already misunderstandings had broken out. Dupleix in this trying position was true to the traditional policy of the French in India. It was a main portion of that policy to respect native customs, to conciliate native opinion, to rule by means of that rather than by force, to be liberal, generous, trustful, confiding. His position as the secret ruler of the Dakhan, directing all its resources, surely yet unostensibly, by means of its native ruler, keeping his own power, of the superior might of which he was assured, necessarily in the background, was in his opinion more strong and more really powerful than if he had claimed for himself the ostensible dignity, and with it a territorial extension such as would provoke the jealousy of those even who granted it. His first act, therefore, was to disclaim for his own part any share in the booty taken after the victory. This, he decided, in his quality of arbitrator, should be divided equally between

Muzaffar Jang on one side and the confederate Nawwábs on the other, reserving the jewels only without division to Muzaffar Jang. Any claim which the French might have upon the latter for the part they had played in helping him to his dignities, he left entirely to his own generous impulses.

Having thus, and by some other arrangements, which it is unnecessary to detail, effected an amicable settlement of all misunderstandings, Dupleix prepared for the solemn investiture of Muzaffar Jang as Subadar of the Dakhan, in the presence of his tributaries and vassals. This imposing ceremony—a ceremony noticeable as indicating the period when French power in India had almost attained its zenith—took place in a magnificent tent pitched in the great square of Pondichery. The splendours of that day, the honours granted to Dupleix, the high position he assumed, have scarcely yet been obliterated from the traditions of Southern India. Let us imagine, as we well can, either side of the gorgeously draped tent lined by the armed nobles of the Dakhan. Muzaffar Jang enters and takes his seat at the head of the assembly. Quickly behind follows the Governor of French India, and presents to the Subadar, as he salutes him, the offering due to his rank. Muzaffar Jang advances to meet the French Governor and places him on a seat designedly placed there, and betokening a rank equal to his own. To them thus seated, though nominally only to the Subadar, the assembled nobles offer their gifts. On the conclusion of this ceremony, the Subadar rises, and proclaims the honours he proposes to confer on his French ally. He declares him Nawwáb or Governor of the country south of the river Krishná up to Cape Kumárí (Comorin), including Maisur and the entire Karnátik; he bestows upon him as a personal gift the fort of Valdávur, about nine miles to the north-west of Pondichery, with the villages and lands dependent upon

T

it, as well as a separate jaghir of 100,000 rupees a year. He confers upon him the title of Mançabdar of 7,000 horse, with permission to bear the ensign of the fish, one of the highest honours in the Múghal empire. He directs that the Pondichery currency shall be the sole currency of Southern India; he confirms the sovereignty of the French Company over the newly-acquired districts of Machlipatan and Yanaon, and an extension of the territories about Kárikál. Then, turning to Dupleix with the air of a vassal to his liege lord, he promises never even to grant a favour without his previous approval, and to be guided in all things by his advice. Dupleix, on his side, is true to himself, to his policy, on this tempting and trying occasion. With a generosity which, if assumed, shows his political fitness in a still stronger light, he calls up Chanda Sáhib to his side, presents to the Subadar his old and tried companion, and urges that if he himself is to hold the nominal dignity of Nawwáb over the country south of the Krishná, the real sovereignty and emoluments of that part of it known as the Karnátik may be bestowed upon one who had shown so much steadfastness and fidelity. We can well imagine the impression that would be conveyed to the minds of an Oriental assembly by an act so generous and graceful. He who could thus give away provinces, who, in the height of his prosperity, could recollect and reward those who under all circumstances had been true to him, showed the possession of qualities which, in that rude day, the princes of Asia could admire though they could not imitate. From such an one, practising such lofty sentiments, there was nought, they would believe, for them to fear. That one act of abnegation was sufficient to make them acquiesce without envy, without the least hesitation or doubt, in the substantial acquisitions that had been made that day to Dupleix. He indeed was the hero of

SPLENDID POSITION OF DUPLEIX.

the day's ceremony. He emerged from that tent the virtual superior of the lord of Southern India.

We have not yet enumerated all the advantages which accrued to the French on the occasion of this visit. In addition to those promulgated by Muzaffar Jang at the time of his installation, one sum of 500,000 rupees was made over to Dupleix for the soldiers who had fought at the late battle; another of the same amount was repaid to the Company, on account of moneys that had been advanced, and security given for the amount remaining due. The increase of revenue likely to accrue to the French Company by the territorial cessions we have adverted to, was computed at little short of 400,000 rupees annually. To commemorate these great results thus obtained, Dupleix ordered the creation of a town on the site of the battle which had caused them, to be entitled Dupleix-Fathábád.* This design, founded on sound policy, being in strict conformity with those native usages by which alone the mass of the people were likely to be impressed, and not, as has been ignorantly charged against him, on ridiculous vanity, was not, it is true, destined to be realised. Events were too strong even for this strong man. He, the pioneer of European conquest and European civilisation, whose vast plans were not, as so many of his contemporaries believed, too vast to be accomplished, was destined to see them appropriated to a great extent by his rivals. It will be for us very soon to point to the single weak point in that strongly welded armour—the solitary defect in that almost consummate genius, by means of which one great adversary possessing the quality wanting to Dupleix, shattered the vast fabric of his plans ere yet they had been made proof against attack.

Not only the urgent and pressing instructions from the Company of the Indies, but his own conviction of

* Indicating "The place of the victory of Dupleix."

the necessity of the case, disposed Dupleix at this period to consolidate his conquests by a definite peace. Peace, however, was utterly impossible so long as the rival candidate for the governorship of the Karnátik, Muhammad Ali, was at large maintaining his pretensions. This chieftain, seeing that by the death of Nasir Jang, his chances of dominion had been reduced almost to zero, abandoned by the English, and without following, had fled, on the news of the defeat, to Trichinápallí, behind whose walls he had once before found refuge. Dupleix, who had on that previous occasion experienced the delays and difficulties attending the attack by a native army on a fortified town, was particularly anxious to induce the fugitive nobleman to enter into some arrangement, by which, in virtue of some concessions made to him, he would engage to recognise the new order of things. He was the more hopeful that negotiations to this effect might succeed, as Muhammad Ali was now literally abandoned by all the world. To his gratification and surprise the first overtures for this object came from Muhammad Ali himself. Rájá Jánují, one of the Marátha leaders who had been with Nasir Jang, and had subsequently transferred his temporary services to his successor, was charged by Muhammad Ali with a proposal to recognise Chanda Sáhib as Nawwáb of the Karnátik, and to make over to him the city of Trichinápallí and its dependencies on condition (1) that he should be put in possession of the treasures left by his father, no inquiry being made into his administration, (2) that the Subadar should engage to give him another government in the Dakhan. Dupleix eagerly embraced these terms, and requested Jánují to inform Muhammad Ali of his acceptance of them. This led to the opening of a correspondence between the French Governor and Muhammad Ali, throughout which the latter ardently expressed his desire to be reconciled to the Subadar.

This important matter being regarded as settled, Muzaffar Jang, not doubting that peace would thenceforth reign in the Karnátik, informed Dupleix of his intention to proceed to the northern part of his government, as well to consolidate his power as to settle divers matters which in consequence of the war had fallen into great confusion. But he represented at the same time to Dupleix that, in order to undertake, with safety and success, a journey across provinces which had been so recently hostile, it would be very desirable that a body of French troops, upon whom he knew he could rely, should accompany him. He expressed himself willing to defray all the charges connected with these troops, and, he added, he would not send them back before he had given to them, as well as to the Company they served, real marks of his gratitude.

This proposal chimed in exactly with the policy of Dupleix. It assured him against any change of policy in the councils of the Subadar. It made him virtually master of the Dakhan, ruling Southern India through the representative of the Múghal. He consented therefore to the proposal. Perhaps if he had known the secret intentions which Muhammad Ali still cherished, he might have delayed the departure of his troops until the affairs of the Karnátik and its dependencies had been quite settled. But he had excellent reasons for believing that Muhammad Ali had entered into his schemes; that he would resign Trichinápallí in favour of a government elsewhere. Had he not been satisfied with the assurances he had received on this head, it is certain he would not have detached so far from Pondichery a considerable contingent of his little army, and —what was of far greater importance—his best officer to command it. But believing peace re-established, anxious to have French interests powerfully represented at the court of the Subadar, and not indifferent to the financial considerations resulting from the transfer to another exchequer of all the charges connected with the troops thus detached, he agreed to send with the Subadar to Aurangábád, his capital, a force of 300 Europeans and 2,000 sipáhis, the whole under the command of Bussy. For such a purpose, or indeed for any office, political or military, a better selection than that of Bussy could not have been made; but in sending him, d'Auteuil being still incapacitated by sickness, and de la Touche having returned to France, Dupleix deprived himself of the one man upon whom he could depend, in the event of any unforeseen military disaster.

On January 7, 1751, Muzaffar Jang left Pondichery to join his army, and on the 15th, in pursuance of the agreement he had entered into with Dupleix, he was joined by Bussy and the French contingent. At the end of about three weeks they entered the territories of the Nawwáb of Kadapah, who was himself with the army. Here a tumult, apparently accidental, but really preconcerted, occurred between some troops belonging to the army of the Subadar and some villagers. The Nawwáb of Kadapah hastened to support his tenants, and attacked the rear-guard of the main body of the Subadar's army, that being the part of the force with which the ladies of his harem travelled. Muzaffar Jang, enraged at this insolence, determined to avenge it, but wished, in the first instance, to assure himself of the countenance and support of Bussy. The orders given to this officer had been to avoid, as much as possible, all appearance of hostility, and in accordance with these, he addressed himself to the task of bringing about an accommodation between the two angry chieftains. But it soon appeared that the Nawwáb of Kadapah had allied himself with the Nawwábs of Karnul and Savanur against their former confederate, Muzaffar Jang, and that, although anxious, if possible, to avoid hostilities with the French, they were resolved to seize the opportunity to effect the destruction of the Subadar.

MUZAFFAR JANG IS SLAIN.

Muzaffar Jang had no sooner satisfied himself regarding their plans than he ordered out his troops to attack them, calling upon Bussy to support him. This, Bussy, who considered himself bound to side with the Subadar against traitors, promised to do. But Muzaffar Jang, without waiting for the slower march of the infantry, at once attacked the confederates with his cavalry. An obstinate contest ensued, many being killed on both sides. The confederates, however, maintained the position they had taken up, until Bussy and the French contingent arrived on the ground. A few rounds from their artillery and a general advance of their infantry decided the day. The rebel army broke, fled, and dispersed, leaving the Nawwáb of Savanur dead on the field, and taking with it the Nawwáb of Kadapah, grievously wounded. Muzaffar Jang, indignant at the idea that he, the principal conspirator, should escape, outstripped his French allies to pursue him on his elephant. In his headlong course he came upon the third confederate, the Nawwáb of Karnul. A desperate hand to hand contest ensued, in the course of which the newly made Subadar, Muzaffar Jang, was thrust through the brain by a spear, whilst his antagonist, the Nawwáb of Karnul, was instantly afterwards hacked to pieces.

The death of Muzaffar Jang, Subadar of the Dakhan, was in itself a severe, and might have been fatal, blow to the policy of Dupleix. In his person was struck down the main defender of the French alliance, the man who had personally experienced advantages to be derived from French wisdom and French valour, the personal friend and protégé of Dupleix. No successor could occupy the position he had occupied with reference to French India. It was indeed possible that the government of the vast possessions he had inherited only to lose might devolve upon a minor, or a declared antagonist, who might repudiate all the engagements and cancel all the advantages to which Muzaffar Jang had agreed. Under these circumstances, Bussy displayed the greatest wisdom. Feeling that to secure French interests it was necessary for him to act, and act on the moment; that it was essential that the chiefs and the army should not be left in doubt as to their ruler, but that a man should be appointed equally agreeable to them and to the French, Bussy, with the concurrence of the principal officers of the army, set aside the infant son of Muzaffar Jang, and at once proclaimed the next brother, of the previous Subadar, Nasir Jang, Salábat Jang by name,* as Subadar of the Dakhan. From a throne to a prison, from a prison to a throne, constituted in those days a condition of affairs which might almost be termed normal. Salábat Jang was no exception to the rule. He was taken from confinement to rule over thirty-five millions of his fellow-creatures!

The first act of the new Subadar was to confirm all the concessions that his predecessor had granted to the French; his next was to add to them. In gratitude, we may suppose for his elevation, he joined to the French possession Machlipatan the towns of Nizámpatan, a town and port in the Krishna district; of Kondavír in the same district; of Almanáva, and of Narsápur in the Godávarí district, with the lands thereto attaching. He ordered the rebuilding of all the factories at Yanaon which his brother, Nasir Jang, had destroyed; and finally he presented to Dupleix the territory of Mafuzbandar in the district of Kríkákolam (Chicakol). A few days later the army resumed its route, stormed on March 18 the fortress of Karnul, the residence of the deceased rebel Nawwáb of that title; bought off the threatened hostilities of the Marátha, Báláji Báji Ráo, by a present of two lacs of rupees; reached Haidarábád on April 12; remained there a month, and finally made

---

* *Vide* Elliott's *History of India by its Own Historians*, vol. viii., p. 392. Salábat Jang was the third son of Asaf Jah (Nizámu-l-Mulk). His full name was "Amíru-l-Mamálik Salábat Jang," or, "the lord of kingdoms, Salábat Jang."

a triumphant entry into Aurangábád on June 29. Here Salábat Jang, in the presence of Bussy and all the nobles of the province, was solemnly invested as Subadar of the Dakhan, on the authority of a firman stated to have been received from the imperial court of Delhi, but regarding the authenticity of which there are very grave doubts. Here we must leave him, and with him for a time the indefatigable Bussy, revolving great schemes, which, had all gone well in the Karnátik, would undoubtedly have produced abundant fruit in their season.

We can leave them indeed with the greater satisfaction at this conjuncture, because, regard being had to the influence exercised by Dupleix, it constitutes the period at which French domination in India may be said to have attained its zenith. A glance at the map of India will show the enormous extent of country, which, in the spring of 1751, recognised the moral supremacy of Pondichery. The entire country between the Vindhya range and the river Krishná, exceeding the limits of the territory now known as that of the Nizám, was virtually ruled by a French general; for a French army occupied the capital, and French influence predominated in the councils, of the Subadar. South of the Krishná again, the Governor of French India had been constituted by the Muhammadan Subadar of the Dakhan Nawwáb of the entire country, a country comprehending, be it remembered, the Karnátik; and, theoretically, Maisur, the kingdoms of Tanjur, Trichinápallí, Kochin, and the provinces of Madura and Tinivelli. If indeed the French Governor did not hold these places under his own sway, it was mainly because it was a part of his settled policy to keep his authority in the background, and to govern through the Princes of the country. It was for this reason that he had made over the Karnátik to Chanda Sáhib, and contented himself with exercising a moral influence, amounting, in

CHAP. VI.
1751.

fact, to a real supremacy, over the others. But in the beginning of 1751, his power was so far established that there was nowhere a sign of opposition. Muhammad Ali, the rival of Chanda Sáhib, had promised submission and obedience, and had consented to retire from the stronghold of Trichinápallí. The English, thus deprived of all pretext for interference, were sulking at Madras and Fort St. David. Their presence, it is true, constituted a thorn in the side of the French ruler, but his hands were withheld from attacking them, and the utmost he could aim at was to bring about such a state of things in Southern India, a condition of such universal acquiescence in French arbitration, as would leave his rivals without consideration and without power. Armed with the promise of Muhammad Ali to agree to the conditions that had been proposed, he seemed almost to have brought matters to that point in the spring of 1751.

Whilst, then, Bussy is marching on Aurangábád—the dictator of the Dakhan—everything seems to smile on the daring statesman who, from his palace in Pondichery, directs all the movements on the board, and of him thus triumphant, of him who in ten years has made Pondichery the centre-point of Southern India, we cannot refuse the expression of our admiration of the soaring genius, the untiring energy, the vast and comprehensive intellect.

CHAPTER VII.

THE STRUGGLES OF DUPLEIX WITH ADVERSITY.

THE energetic measures taken by Bussy after the death of Muzaffar Jang had confirmed the ascendency which the French had attained in the counsels of the Subadar. All the promises, all the arrangements, made by the deceased Prince, had been at once ratified by his successor. Of these perhaps the most important at the moment was the engagement entered into with Muhammad Ali. It will be recollected that this noble, the representative of the family of Anwáru-dín, abandoned by everyone after the downfall of Nasir Jang, had taken refuge in the strong fortress of Trichinápallí. Here, at the instance of the Marátha, Rájá Jánují, he had opened with Dupleix negotiations, which had terminated in a promise on the part of Muhammad Ali to recognise Chanda Sáhib as Nawwáb, and to make over to him Trichinápallí and its dependencies, on condition of being himself secured in the possession of his father's treasures, free from all inquiry as to his administration, and of being intrusted with a subordinate government in another part of the Dakhan. It was in the fullest belief that this engagement would be adhered to, and that the matter was settled, that Dupleix had despatched Bussy to Aurangábád.

Yet, notwithstanding that Muhammad Ali had before the march of Bussy agreed to the terms proposed, and that Dupleix, on his part, had obtained and forwarded to him the sanction of the Subadar to their being carried out in their entirety, the matter seemed to hang fire. Whether it was that he distrusted the promises of Dupleix, or that he trusted to the chapter of accidents, this at least is certain, that Muhammad Ali delayed, on one pretext after another, compliance with the terms to which he had agreed. At last, driven hard by Dupleix, he declared that further concessions would be necessary before he could give up Trichinápallí. So anxious was Dupleix for a peaceful settlement of the question, that even this new demand did not exhaust his patience. He sent the letter of Muhammad Ali to Bussy, with a request that he would obtain from the Subadar the necessary authority to enable him to agree to the terms it contained. Considerable as they were, these new demands were in his opinion small in comparison with the consequences which, he believed, compliance with them would entail, viz. the evacuation of Trichinápallí, and, with that, the pacification of the Karnátik. The consent of the Subadar was easily obtained by Bussy; the proper documents were then forwarded to Muhammad Ali, to be considered valid only on the condition that he signed the treaty without further delay. Muhammad Ali, however, still hesitated. He had been in fact, throughout this period, urgently beseeching the English for their assistance; and it was only when, at the end of four months after he had received intimation of the Subadar's consent to the additional conditions he had required, he wrung from them a promise of substantive aid, that he boldly threw off the mask, and refused to surrender Trichinápallí on any conditions whatever.

Thus again was Dupleix, much against his own inclinations, much, as he well knew, against the wishes of his masters in Paris, forced into war. Thus again did the question of French domination in India depend upon the capture of the city of Trichinápallí. The army, which, in November, 1749, had marched from Pondichery with the intention of carrying out this purpose, had been unwisely diverted to another object.

But this time Dupleix was resolved there should be no such mistake. To the native army of Chanda Sáhib, consisting of from 7,000 to 8,000 men, he added therefore a European detachment of 400 men, a few Africans, and some artillery—the whole under the command of M. d'Auteuil. These left Pondichery in the month of March, 1751.

Meanwhile the English, recognising and rightly recognising that their only chance of safety lay in their sustaining the cause of the anti-French pretender to the government of the Karnátik, had resolved to support Muhammad Ali with all the means at their disposal. In the early part of February, therefore, they despatched Captain Cope at the head of 280 Europeans and 300 sipáhis to aid in the defence of Trichinápallí; at the end of March following, they ordered a force of 500 Europeans, 100 Africans, 1,000 sipáhis, and eight fieldpieces to march from Fort St. David, for the purpose of co-operating in the field with the troops that still adhered to Muhammad Ali, and which were expected from Trichinápallí. This force was commanded by Captain Gingens, and, serving with it as commissariat officer,—the second time we have met him,—was Honorary Lieutenant Robert Clive.

The first detachment,—that under Captain Cope,— had during the same month made an unsuccessful attempt to capture the city of Madura, held for Chanda Sáhib by Alím Khán, and had returned dispirited to Trichinápallí. Captain Gingens, for his part, having been joined in the middle of May by Muhammad Ali's troops, 1,600 in number, had at once marched on the pagoda Verdachelam, about forty miles from the coast, and commanding the communications between Fort St. David and Trichinápallí. Taking and garrisoning this, and having been joined by a further detachment of 4,000 men from Muhammad Ali, and 100 Europeans despatched to his aid by Captain Cope, he moved forward to intercept Chanda Sáhib and the French, of whom he had last heard as marching on Volkondah, about thirty-eight miles to the north-north-east of Trichinápalli, and on the high road to that place.

Volkondah was a considerable place, strong in its natural position, and, for a native town, very fairly fortified. The governor held it for the Nawwáb of the Karnátik, but as the rival forces approached it from different quarters, he was apparently undecided as to whether Chanda Sáhib or Muhammad Ali had the better claim to that title. It was evident that a battle was imminent, and uncertain as to its results, he feared the consequences which a premature declaration in favour possibly of the faction that might be vanquished, might have on the party that should prove victorious. He therefore judiciously declared that the cession of the place would depend upon the issue of the impending contest, whilst at the same time he lent an attentive ear to the offers that were made him by both parties.

The march of Chanda Sáhib had been so slow that the English had had time to take up a position to the south-west of Volkondah, before he had advanced beyond that place on his road to Trichinápalli. It had now become indispensable for him to occupy Volkondah, and to drive the English from the neighbourhood. To gain over the governor he spared neither persuasion nor promises. Whether these would, under other circumstances, have brought about the desired result may be doubtful, but this at least is certain, that the shifty conduct of the governor so wearied the English commander, —who had likewise tried him his on persuasive powers,— that after a fortnight's useless negotiation, he resolved to compel that which the other would not willing yield. On the evening of July 19, therefore, without apparently acquainting the governor with his intention, Captain Gingens marched a great portion of his force against the place, with the intention of taking possession of it.

The outer defences of the town, and the town itself, fell at once into the hands of the assailants; but this attack, and the burning of some houses outside, roused the garrison of the fort, and the English were compelled to recoil from its stone walls with considerable loss. Their ill-advised movement decided the governor. He threw himself at once into the arms of Chanda Sáhib, and summoned the French to his aid. Before daylight, consequently, d'Auteuil put his force in motion, and entering the fort with a portion of his troops, poured upon the English such a fire of artillery, that notwithstanding all the efforts of their officers they quitted the field in a panic, abandoning their native allies, and leaving six pieces of cannon, several muskets, all their camp equipage and stores of ammunition, as a prey to the conqueror. Had the French pursued with anything like vigour, the war would have been that day at an end. But a fatality seemed to attend all the operations that might have been decisive. D'Auteuil was laid up with the gout, and was quite unable to give his personal attention to details, nor had he a single officer with him upon whom he could rely. Instead, therefore, of taking advantage of the panic which had overcome the English, and of converting their defeat into an overthrow which must have been ruinous, the French and their allies contended themselves with maintaining a brisk cannonade on their enemy from the north bank of the little river Valaru, which he had crossed in his retreat. It has been said,* indeed, that Chanda Sáhib was hindered in his onward movements by the defection of one of his generals, in command of 4,000 horse. Desertions from a victorious to a vanquished enemy are not common, least of all among nations of the East. But, however, they may have been, it did not influence in the smallest degree the movements of the French. It was for them, on this as on previous occasions, to give

* Orme.

the cue to their native allies. All the accounts of their historians, the memoirs of Dupleix himself, record that they failed to do this, and that they failed because of the illness and apathy of their general, and the want of spirit of their officers.

Never before, indeed, had such an opportunity been offered them; never had such an opportunity been neglected. The force under Captain Gingens constituted, with the exception of 180 men under Captain Cope at Trichinápallí, and a few left to mount guard at Fort St. David and Madras,* the entire available force of English soldiers on the Koromandel coast. A little display of energy on the part of d'Auteuil and his officers would not only have insured the destruction of this force, but, as a necessary consequence, the fall of Trichinápallí, and the restriction of the few English who remained to the limits of their possessions on the coast. This is no idle supposition. It is capable of positive proof. So complete was the panic which possessed the soldiers of the little army under Captain Gingens, that they left their native allies to fight whilst they fled in confusion;† they heard without shame the taunts of a native chieftain on their cowardice; and notwithstanding that they were not pursued, they abandoned their encampment at midnight, and leaving behind them their guns, camp equipage, and munitions of war, fled precipitately in the direction of Trichinápallí. Can anyone doubt that upon men so panic-stricken, the vigorous pursuit of an enemy would have produced the most decisive effect? Can anyone believe that the consequences of such decisive action would not have been ruinous to the English?

But no pursuit was attempted that day; d'Auteuil contented himself with securing possession of Volkondah. On the following morning, however, finding that the enemy had disappeared, d'Auteuil followed on his

---

* The reinforcements to be subsequently alluded to did not reach Fort St. David till the end of July.
† Orme, Cambridge.

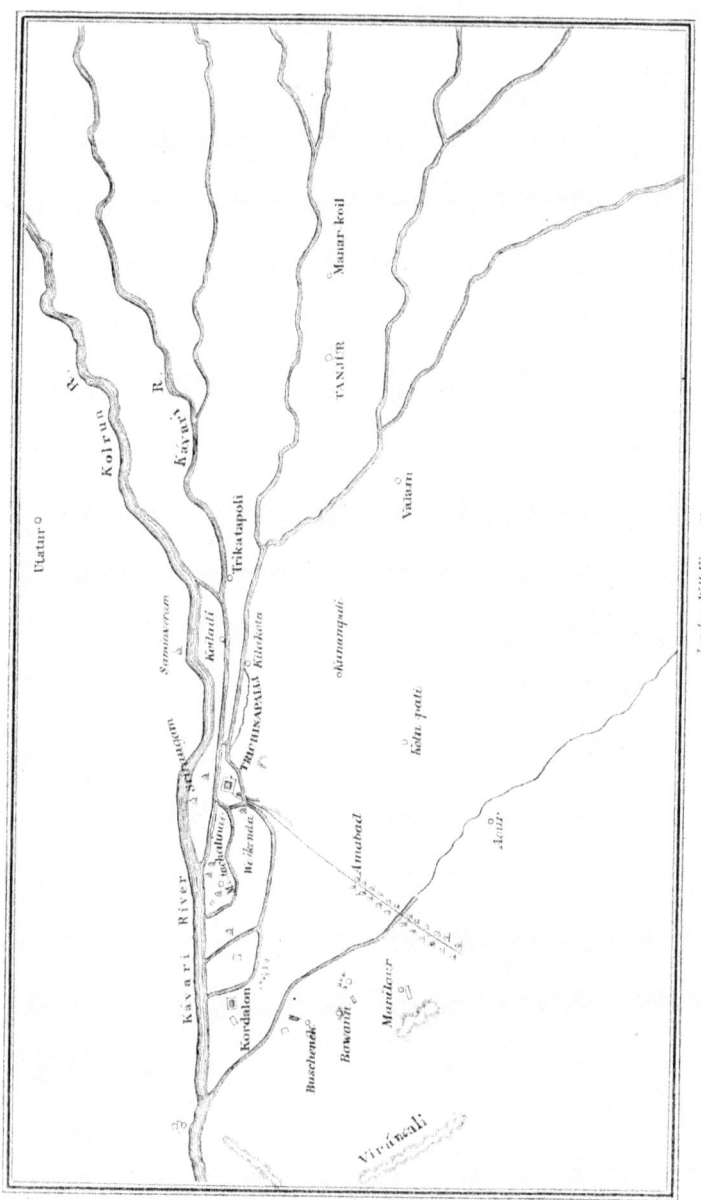

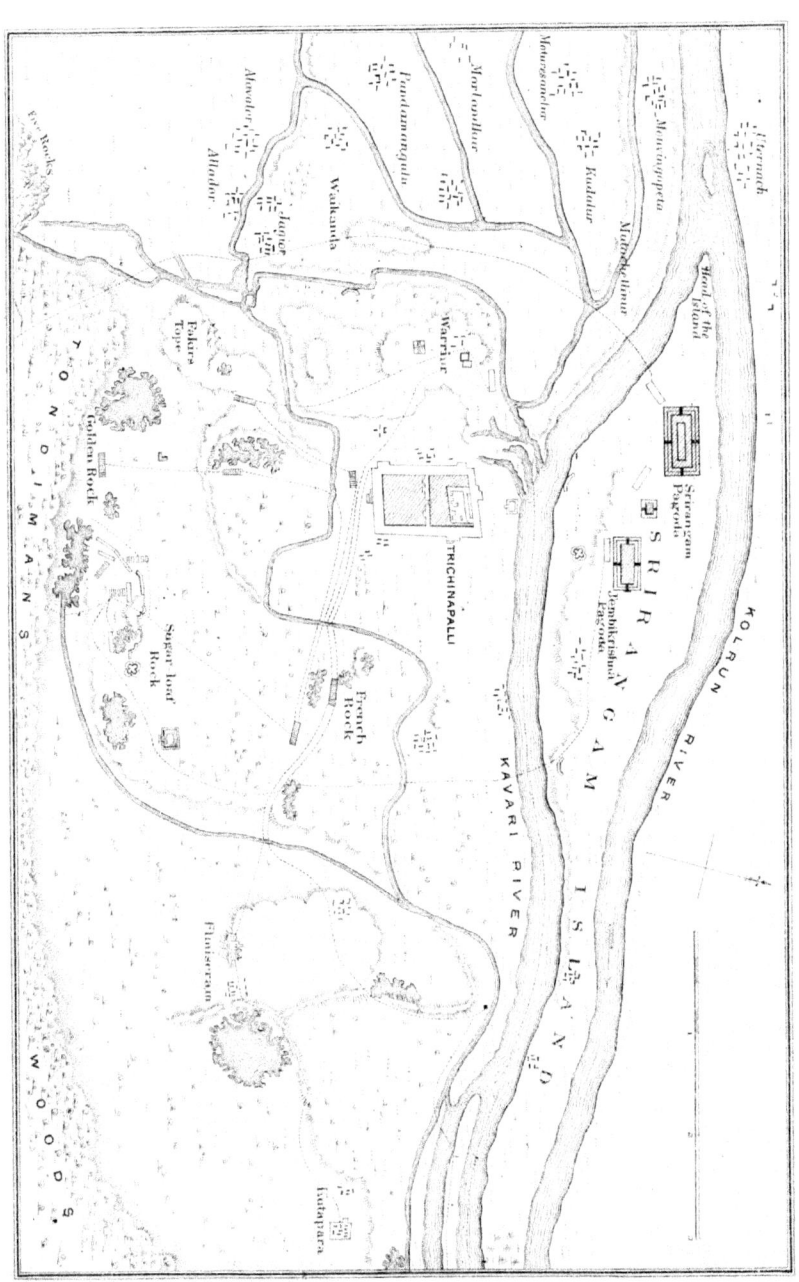

THE FRENCH INVEST TRICHINÁPALLÍ.

track, halting within a few miles of the position he had taken up in the hilly country round Utatur, about twenty miles north of Trichinápallí. Here during a halt of three days, several skirmishes ensued, in one of which the English fell into an ambuscade and suffered severely. On the third day, Chanda Sáhib attacked the English position, and although, owing to the non-arrival at the scene of action, at the time agreed upon, of the French contingent, he was repulsed, yet his attack made so serious an impression upon the English, that they retreated the same night to the banks of the Kolrún. They crossed this river, followed by Chanda Sáhib and the French, on the 25th, and took possession of Srirangam, an island formed by the division into two branches of the Kolrún and Kávarí rivers, but not deeming themselves even here secure, they abandoned this also and the pagoda upon it—a very strong position in which, supported by the troops in the city, they might have defended themselves against five times their number —and took refuge on July 28 under the walls of Trichinápallí.

The French and their allies meanwhile pushed on, and crossing the Kolrún took possession of Srirangam. First completing the conquest of this island by the capture of the mud fort of Koiládi, at its eastern extremity, they crossed the Kávarí, and encamped on the plain to the east of the town, near a position now known as the French Rock. From this they commenced a sort of bombardment of the place.

Trichinápallí* is situated on a plain which once was crowded with rich villages and plantations of trees. The town is in form of an oblong square, the longest sides of which are east and west. On the north runs the river Kávarí, less than half a mile from the fort. The town at the time of which we are writing was

* This description is taken from Colonel Lawrence's account of the war.

nearly four miles in circumference, with a double *enceinte* of walls with round towers at equal distances. The ditch was nearly thirty feet wide but not half so deep, and at different seasons was more or less supplied with water. The outer wall was built of greyish stone; it was about eighteen feet high, and four or five thick, without parapet or rampart; the inner wall, distant from it about twenty-five feet, was much stronger, and was thirty feet high. Its thickness at the bottom was thirty feet, and it gradually decreased as it ascended by means of steps, to a width of ten feet at the summit. In the middle of the old town stood a most extraordinary rock about 300 feet high. On the top of it was a pagoda " which," says Colonel Lawrence, " was of singular use to us the whole war; here was constantly stationed a man with a telescope, who gave us by signals and writings an account of all the enemy's motions." It remains to be added that the city is about ninety miles from the coast, the river Kávarí running something less than half a mile to the north-east of its northern face; beyond that, a little more than a mile from the south bank of the Kávarí, is the pagoda of Srirangam, and beyond that again the branch of the Kávarí known as the Kolrún.

The French had, as we have seen, taken post to the east of the city, and had opened fire on the walls. Before, however, much progress had been made in the siege, d'Auteuil, whom gout had utterly incapacitated, was, at his own request, relieved from his command, and returned to Pondichery. His successor was M. Law, nephew of the famous Scotch financier, and who had recently returned from France with strong recommendations from the Directors. We do not meet him here for the first time. He it was who, at the time of the attack on Pondichery by Admiral Boscawen, had been intrusted with the defence of the outpost of Ariákupum; a command in which he had displayed energy and vigour.

His past services and the character he then bore were sufficient to authorise the expectations which Dupleix had formed from his nomination. He was indeed destined to be disappointed. But Captain Law's case is not the only instance in which showy qualities have covered infirmity of purpose, or where pomposity and self-assertion in the council-chamber have been mistakenly regarded as indications of ability in the field.

Nevertheless, at the commencement of his proceedings, Law displayed no lack of energy. Finding that the English were resolved to defend Trichinápallí to the last, and deeming that its defences precluded the possibility of a successful assault, he determined to take advantage of the possession given him, by the recent French victory, of the neighbouring country, and to subject the town to a strict blockade. Everything seemed to favour such a proceeding. The great body of the English troops were shut up in Trichinápallí, the few that remained could not expect to cope successfully with the French in the field, still less to introduce supplies into the town: in the entire Karnátik but one place, the small fort of Verdachelam, on the road from Fort St. David to Trichinápallí, held out at this particular period for Muhammad Ali. The cause of the English seemed hopeless; the fall of Trichinápallí, if strictly blockaded and pressed vigorously, appeared certain.

Yet it was in these desperate circumstances, in this crisis of the fortunes of France and England, that there appeared upon the stage one of those men whose daring genius and power of original conception supply the want of armies. We have already stated that with the force led by Captain Gingens, to endeavour to intercept the march of Chanda Sáhib and the French on Trichinápallí, there served as commissariat officer Honorary Lieutenant Robert Clive. This officer had originally come out to India as a writer in the civil service of the Company in the year 1744, and had been in Madras when that place was taken by La Bourdonnais. On the departure of La Bourdonnais, and the disavowal by Dupleix of the terms of capitulation which he had unauthorisedly granted, Clive had escaped to Fort St. David. Here he enjoyed many opportunities of noticing the method of war adopted in the east, in the several attacks made upon Fort St. David by Dupleix and his allies, and in the movements of Anwáru-dín and his two sons to hinder their success. When, subsequently, the arrival of Admiral Boscawen secured for the English a preponderance on the Koromandel coast, and the siege of Pondichery was resolved upon, Clive obtained permission to join the besieging army in the rank of ensign. He is stated to have distinguished himself on this occasion by his daring courage, but the skill which was wanting in the leaders of the besieging army shone brilliantly within the walls of the town, and the enterprise miscarried. We next hear of Clive at Dévikota, as usual in the foremost rank; and shortly afterwards as commissariat officer of the expedition sent to intercept Chanda Sáhib. In the panic which followed the failure of Captain Gingens to possess himself of Volkondah, Clive showed considerable presence of mind, and attempted, though in vain, to rally the fugitives.* When the force retreated the following day towards Trichinápallí, Clive, disgusted at a leadership which did not lead, and which declined to accept advice, returned to Fort St. David, and arrived there just as a reinforcement of about 400 men landed from England. One detachment of these he accompanied to Verdachelam, and a second to Trichinápallí, increasing the English garrison in that place to 600 men. Clive himself did not remain in Trichiná-

---

* Orme states, "Captains Gingens, Dalton, Kilpatrick, and Lieutenant Clive endeavoured to rally them, but in vain."

pallí. What he saw there was not encouraging. The men were dispirited, and had lost all confidence in their leader. The French were superior in numbers, and seemed to be pushing their attack with resolution. The surrender of the last stronghold of Muhammad Ali appeared to him, therefore, to be inevitable, unless it were possible to infuse a sort of revolutionary energy into the counsels of the English. To attempt this at Trichinápallí would be, he knew, useless. The fate of the English must depend upon the action taken at the Presidency. To influence this action he left therefore Trichinápallí, and returned to Fort St. David.

The plan which Clive had revolved in his own mind as the plan absolutely necessary for the safety of his countrymen, was due doubtless rather to his inborn genius than to extensive reading or study. It was nevertheless the plan which the greatest military leaders have loved to pursue,—a plan which, adopted by a man possessing daring and prudence, must always be successful, except when opposed by immensely superior numbers, or by genius of a still higher order. There is this, too, with respect to such a plan; no one but a great captain ever has tried it, ever could try it. It is too much for the spirit, for the capacity, for the nerve of an inferior man. To him it seems too bold, too venturesome, too hazardous. It leaves too much at stake. And this,—though the plan is as safe as it is bold,—is safe because it is bold. We allude to the plan of carrying the war into an enemy's country. The inferior general who hesitates to do this, though he sees that if it could be done it would save him and ruin his enemy, does not calculate on the inevitable effect which such a movement must produce on the " morale " of the force opposed to him, especially when that force constitutes the principal, perhaps the entire, available army of the enemy. He does not consider that such a movement must paralyse the onward march of his opponent. Yet history abounds with such examples. Even Frederick II. of Prussia gave up, at a critical period, his movements in Saxony, when he found the Austrians were marching on Berlin. And if he, a consummate master of the art of war, would act thus, what may we imagine would be the effect of such a movement on men of inferior capacity? It must always be startling, almost always decisive.

Clive, we say, had arrived at such a conclusion by the mere force of his genius. He had the capacity to open the eyes of his mind, and see the result that must follow. He went, therefore, on his return from Trichinápallí, direct to the Governor, Mr. Saunders; pointed out to him how, if matters were allowed to take their sluggish course, Trichinápallí, and, with it, English interests, must fall; that Chanda Sáhib, having brought all his resources to bear upon the siege, had left his capital comparatively unguarded; that there was no force of his or of the French in the field; that Law was at Trichinápallí, Bussy at Aurangábád; that, therefore, a blow might be struck at the heart of the enemy's possessions, which, if successful, would either force him to leave his hold on Trichinápallí, or would open out a new field for military operations, success in which would compensate for the loss of that place. To add force to his proposition, he offered to lead himself the troops that might be destined to carry it into effect. Mr. Saunders, who had been appointed governor the preceding year, was a man who possessed the not inconsiderable merit of appreciating the large schemes of men whom he trusted. He cordially received the propositions made to him by Clive; ordered for field service a force of 200 Europeans and 300 sipáhis,— thus reducing the garrisons of Madras and Fort St. David to their lowest point,—and crowned the whole by nominating Clive himself as commandant, with the rank of captain, and with unlimited powers.*

Arkát, the place at which Clive aimed his blow, was the capital of the Karnátik,—the seat of the Nawwáb's government. It lies sixty-four miles south-south-west of Madras. At the time of which we are writing it was an open town possessing about 100,000 inhabitants. There was, it is true, a fort with the outward signs of fortifications, but these had long since fallen into decay. The ramparts were in a state of ruin, and the bastions were crumbling from age and want of repair. The garrison, entirely native, consisted of about 1,000 men, nearly one half of whom were cavalry; to the native gunners, however, had been attached two or three French artillerymen for the purpose of instructing them in the European method of rapid firing. These were at the time in Arkát.

To attack and take possession of this place, Clive, at the head of the force above detailed, left Madras on September 6; on the 11th, after halting one day at Kánchipuram, forty-five miles south-west of Madras, he arrived within ten miles of the capital. Thence he resumed his march, and, notwithstanding the unpropitiousness of the weather, which displayed itself in a thunderstorm of almost unprecedented violence, arrived the same day at the very gates of Arkát. The news of his march had preceded him, and the native garrison, terrified at the idea of opposing a man who could thus bid defiance to the elements, had hastened to evacuate the place. Clive therefore entered it without opposition, and, prescient as to the effect which its capture must have upon the enemy, proceeded at once to repair its fortifications.

This successful occupation of the capital of his native protégé and ally, whilst it surprised and vexed,

* Mr. Orme states that besides Clive there were but eight officers with this force, six of whom had never been in action, and four of the six were members of the mercantile service.

did not at all disconcert, the active-minded and energetic Governor of Pondichery. If Clive had calculated that his raid would lead at once to the abandonment of the siege of Trichinápallí, he found himself mistaken. Dupleix, in fact, looking at matters with the glance of a statesman and a general, saw that notwithstanding this diversion, the chances were still ten to one in his favour. It was by pressing more earnestly the siege of the strongly fortified Trichinápallí, the last refuge of Muhammad Alí, that he felt he could conquer Clive in Arkát. He therefore bent every energy of his mind to increase and render effective the force under Law. He sent him Europeans from Pondichery, a battering-ram from Karikál, and he urged both upon him and upon Chanda Sáhib the urgent necessity of permitting no consideration whatever to interfere with the pressing and absolute necessity of conquering Trichinápallí. This was the true policy for nullifying and defeating the daring action of Clive.

But, unfortunately for Dupleix, he was badly served. Law's action will be hereafter referred to. As for Chanda Sáhib, no sooner had he heard of the capture of Arkát, than he insisted on detaching 4,000 of his best troops to retake his lost capital. Dupleix, though regretting that the force before Trichinápallí had been thus weakened, strengthened this detachment, as it passed Pondichery, by 100 Europeans. It was further increased by other native levies to the number of 10,000 men. Thus augmented it marched under the command of Ráju Sáhib,* son of Chanda Sáhib, upon Arkát.

The siege which followed not only presents one of the most glorious pictures of Anglo-Indian history, but it may be considered likewise as the turning-point in the

---

* Orme and those who have followed his narrative call this prince "Rájáh Sáhib"; but "Rájá" is an impossible name for a Muhammadan. His name really was "Ráju," as stated in the text. Ráju is a good Muhammadan name. *Vide* Blochmann's *Ain-i-Akbari*, page 452.

Eastern career of the English,—the foundation-stone of their present empire. It was at Arkát that English officers taught their sipáhis to follow them with the implicit confidence which superior skill and energy alone can inspire; it was at Arkát that they learned the lesson, followed up afterwards with such magnificent results by their leader, that in Asiatic warfare the question of numbers is merely a secondary consideration; that discipline and the self-confidence born of it are of infinitely greater importance; and there is nothing which a capable general, one who can impress his spirit on his soldiers, may not prudently attempt against an undisciplined enemy. It was at Arkát in fine, that the Anglo-Indian army received its baptism of victory.

The incidents of that famous siege are well known to the readers of Anglo-Indian history. On October 4th Ráju Sáhib took possession of the town, and commenced the investment of the fort. On the 5th, the besiegers beat back a sortie headed by Clive in person. Fifteen days later their battering-train arrived, and on November 4, two 18-pounders from Pondichery. The garrison had been reduced to 120 Europeans and 200 sipáhis. A reinforcement of 100 Europeans and 200 sipáhis, sent from Madras and commanded by Lieutenant Innis, was attacked on the 5th at Tirupatur, and forced to take refuge in Punámallu. The garrison was thus left entirely to itself. Its stock of provisions, originally only a sixty days' supply, was more than half exhausted. On the 10th, a practical breach having been made in the walls, Ráju Sáhib sent to Clive a proposal to surrender, offering honourable terms to the garrison and a considerable sum of money to himself, and accompanying it by a threat to storm the fort and put the garrison to the sword, if his proposition were not acceded to. In reply Clive rejected the proffered terms, contemptuously as regarded the money, and tauntingly with respect to the threats.

CHAP. VII.
1751.

For some days Ráju Sáhib yet hesitated. He might still, had he been left alone, have forced the evacuation of the fort by a continued blockade, for he was well aware of the attenuated state of the supplies within its walls. But all this time Mr. Saunders, the Governor of Madras, had exerted himself with unsurpassable energy to deliver his young captain from his difficult position. First, by reinforcements to Lieutenant Innis, under a more experienced officer, Captain Kilpatrick, he had enabled the detachment to march from Punámallu in the direction of Arkát. Secondly, and with a far more important effect upon Ráju Sáhib, he had induced the Maráthás to take up arms on behalf of Muhammad Ali. A body of 6,000 of these, under the command of Murárí Ráo, had been for some time awaiting the course of events in the pass of Damalcheri. But, though nominally the allies of Muhammad Ali, the fortunes of that chieftain were at so low an ebb that they hesitated at first to commit themselves in his favour. The sturdy defence of Arkát, however, had not been without its effect upon these hardy warriors. In the handful of men who had defended its dilapitated fortifications against numbers so superior, they recognised soldiers worthy of their alliance. They determined, therefore, without further hesitation, to cast in their lot with the English.

The intelligence of this finally determined Ráju Sáhib. He had to choose between an encounter with Murárí Ráo in the field, supported by a sortie from the garrison, or an immediate assault. With correct judgment he chose the latter alternative, and, on the evening of the 24th November (new style), made his preparations for the storm. Unfortunately for the success of his plans, a deserter disclosed them to Clive. When, therefore, his troops advanced, early on the following morning, to the assault, they found that every possible preparation had been made to receive them, that cannon were pointed at the breach, that spare muskets were loaded and in readiness, and that the small garrison had, by the ability of its commander, been utilised so as to supply by the skilful disposition of the troops composing it the paucity of their numbers. Nevertheless, preceded by elephants to burst open the gates, the native troops of Ráju Sáhib advanced boldly to the attack. Unsupported as they were by the French contingent, which strangely kept aloof, they mounted the north-west breach, passed the first trench, and charged the English drawn up to receive them. They were, however, received with such a terrible and continuous fire, spare muskets lying handy for that purpose, that after vain efforts, in which they lost their gallant leader, a Muhammadan, they recoiled. The attack on the south-west, made by means of a raft thrown across the wet ditch, was equally unsuccessful, and at the end of an hour it became evident to Rájú Sáhib that his attack had failed. His loss amounted to 400 men, slain whilst gallantly attempting to storm a fortress defended mainly by Europeans, few indeed in number but strong in discipline, and commanded by a hero. No greater proof indeed could be given of the means at the disposal of the defenders than this, that, although not exceeding 200, including sipáhis, in number, they, besides serving five pieces of cannon, fired off during this hour's attack, not less than 12,000 musket cartridges! *

The following morning, Rájú Sáhib raised the siege, and retreated on Vellur, accompanied only by the French and the troops which had been sent from Trichinápallí, all the rest deserting him. Here we will leave him whilst we describe the effect of this repulse on the French leader himself.

We have already stated that Dupleix had never regarded the attack upon Clive as aught but a very

* Orme.

minor and subordinate part of his great scheme. He had strenuously opposed the weakening of the force before Trichinápallí for the purpose of aiding in any such enterprise. And when, owing to the fears of Chanda Sáhib, the native portion of that force was temporarily diminished, he had reinforced it by 100 Europeans, chiefly with the view of enabling it to contend, without certainty of defeat, against the English. His hope was that, thus reinforced, Ráju Sáhib might detain Clive in Arkát until Trichinápallí should be taken. It was a well-considered policy, the success of which was seemingly certain, provided only that skill and energy directed the movements before the walls of Trichinápallí.

We see then Dupleix, in this crisis, fully alive to all its dangers; detecting the able conceptions of Clive, and taking the measures which, properly carried out, would have thwarted them. We see him, so far from being deterred by Clive's march upon Arkát from prosecuting the siege of Trichinápallí, pressing that siege with greater eagerness than ever; at the same time that he offered to Clive's movement an opposition just sufficient to procure for himself time to carry out, unmolested, the great object of the campaign.

We left Law before Trichinápallí at the head of a force of about 400 Europeans. All the energies of Dupleix had been from the first directed to increase the number of these to a strength which should be irresistible. Every detachment that landed from Europe, every party that could be called in, was used for that end. They were all sent off to the plain before Trichinápallí. So energetic was Dupleix, so earnest and enthusiastic in all he did, that in an incredibly short space of time Law saw himself at the head of one of the largest disciplined forces that had till then operated in the interior of the Karnátik, amounting of all arms to nearly 900 Europeans and 2,000 disciplined sipáhis;

whilst, encamped beside him, aiding him in all his undertakings, was the native army of Chanda Sáhib, in number nearly 30,000, a very large proportion of whom were horsemen. Besides these he had a park of fifty guns, many of them of a large calibre. The most pressing orders were at the same time sent from Pondichery to push on the works, in order to capture the place before the operations of Clive should make themselves felt in the vicinity. Law, in consequence, made a great show of activity, and succeeded in submitting the garrison to a strict blockade. This, however, was all he did do. The man so bold and vaunting in council, whose pre-eminent object in life seemed to be to impress others with a sense of his great cleverness, showed himself, in command of an army, to be absolutely incapable. Overbearing to his officers, suspicious of everybody, haughty, vain, and obstinate, unenterprising himself and checking enterprise in others, Law gained no confidence and conciliated no opinions. Like an obstinate commander, deficient in vision, who, unable to see himself, distrusts the eyesight of others, and thus allows opportunity after opportunity to slip away, so did Law, headstrong and incapable, persist in measures that were useless, and reject counsels that might have led to easy victory. The English that garrisoned Trichinápallí were led by Captain Gingens of whose inferior abilities we have already spoken. They were animated by a spirit far less buoyant than that which had induced the soldiers of Clive to dare so many dangers and difficulties. They were dispirited by defeat, by retreat, and by being cooped up in a fortress which they appeared to have but small chance of defending with success. An assault on the part of Law would almost certainly have succeeded. This was pressed upon him from all sides, by Chanda Sáhib as much as by Dupleix. But, confident in his own cleverness, despising, or affecting to despise, the opinions of

CHAP. VII.
1751.

others, Law clung to his own courses, and adhered to the safe blockade which, he thought, would in the end pull him through.

Yet, even in this course, he showed singular blindness, and extraordinary deficiency in even the ordinary arrangements of his camp. The Dalwai of Maisur, encouraged by the resistance which Trichinápallí was making, and by the diversion of Clive, had sent a detachment of 500 cavalry to harass the besiegers. These not only defeated a small body of native horse, but were even successful, thanks to the want of order and arrangement in the French camp, and of spirit and enterprise on the part of the French leader, in entrapping sixty French dragoons into an ambuscade, and in destroying all but ten of that number: They were so encouraged by this success, that their leader, Innis Khán, proposed to Captain Gingens that he should march out with his English, and attack the united army of the besiegers. If Gingens would do this, and would undertake with his troops to engage the French, he promised, on his part, to encounter the entire cavalry of Chanda Sáhib, though outnumbering his own in the proportion of twelve to one. This was at first declined. But on receiving a reinforcement of 1,000 men, Innis Khán renewed his proposition. Captain Gingens being still unwilling, the Dalwai did not hesitate to tell him that he and his soldiers were of a very different nature from the men he had seen fighting so gallantly at Arkát.* Captain Gingens was apparently confirmed in his objection to active measures by the ill-success of a small force he had detached against the little town of Krishnawáram, thirty miles from Trichinápallí, occupied by the French,—the force having been repulsed with some loss, and their leader, Captain Cope, mortally wounded.

Thanks, then, to the incompetence of his opponent,

* Orme.

the measures of Law, unenterprising as they were, seemed to be on a fair way to success. But he forgot that there were other actors on the scene besides himself. He forgot that the time, with which he was trifling, might be used to good purpose by his opponents. He forgot, or, at least, acted as if he forgot, that his army and the fortress of Trichinápallí were not isolated from all the world; that, if he looked upon its capture as the final seal to French domination, others were determined to use every means in their power to prevent it. Thus it happened that he slumbered whilst others acted. When a little energy would have given him possession of the coveted prize, he was content to act with more caution and more reserve than might have been expected even from a Nicias; nay more, he absolutely threw away chances, courted defeat, and, by his conduct, gave to his rival that empire of the East, which, but for him, might have been gained, at least for a time, by the French. For whilst Law, disregarding the entreaties of Dupleix, slumbered before Trichinápallí, the daring energy of Clive was gaining for England advantages and resources of which the French were thus deprived. No sooner had the youthful victor of Arkát seen the besieging army of Ráju Sáhib melt away from before him, than, having received the reinforcement commanded by Captain Kilpatrick, and having made the necessary arrangements for the defence of the capital he had conquered, he set out in pursuit of the enemy at the head of 200 Europeans, 700 sipáhis, and three pieces of field-artillery. Notwithstanding that his Marátha allies, venturing too close to Vellur, had sustained a severe defeat at the hand of the French who were with Ráju Sáhib, and that a reinforcement of these from Pondichery had effected a junction with their countrymen, raising their number to 300, Clive did not hesitate to move in their direction. After a forced march of twenty miles he came up with them as they were preparing to cross the Arni. With their usual gallantry, the French turned to meet their rivals, but, though somewhat superior in numbers, they were absolutely deficient in that one necessity, the possession of which by the English made up for even greater disparity. The force under Clive consisted of 200 Europeans, 700 sipáhís, and 600 Marátha horse. With the French, 300 in number, were 2,500 foot, and 2,000 horse levies. But whilst they had no general, the English possessed Clive. The consequence was that the French badly posted, and having no competent commander, were completely out-manœuvred. Charged in their flank at a critical period of the action, they were forced to abandon the field, and with it their guns, to the enemy. They retreated thence hastily on Jinjí with a loss of 50 Europeans and 150 natives, killed and wounded. The English lost not one of their own countrymen and but eight sipáhis; of the Maráthás about 50 were missing.*

Encouraged by this success, Clive marched on Kánchipuram which had been meanwhile taken by the French, reduced it after a smart resistance, and then returned to Fort St. David to concert measures for the relief of Trichinápallí. Whilst engaged in this important design, intelligence reached the Presidency that Ráju Sáhib, taking advantage of Clive's absence, had recovered Kánchipuram, and had ravaged the country up to within a few miles of Madras itself. Determined to clear the province of this enemy before venturing on the greater enterprise, Clive left Fort St. David at the head of a force, which, though inferior to that of the enemy, was yet considerable. The terror of his name preceded him. Ráju Sáhib and his French allies at once abandoned the vicinity of Madras, and retreated to an intrenched camp at Vendalur. Here, however, they conceived the design of surprising Arkát, whilst Clive should be engaged

* Orme.

in the reduction of Kánchipuram. Strengthening this place, therefore, they moved by forced marches upon Arkát. The garrison of that place having refused their summons to surrender, they marched to the town of Kávarípák and occupied a position in front of it, so well covered that it was a veritable ambush. Here, under cover of the trees, they waited for Clive. Clive, who had been marching sixty-one miles with but little rest to his troops, fell into the ambush. It was dusk, and the enemy were so strongly posted that after a fight of two hours it appeared as though Clive would for the first time be forced to retreat. By means of one of his officers, however, who could speak French, the English leader, at the moment when matters seemed desperate, succeeded in deceiving the enemy's sentries, and in bringing a large force into their rear. These, suddenly firing a volley, caused such a complete panic amongst the French, that they hastily abandoned their position and their guns, and fled as they best could. Many of them were taken prisoners, and Clive, by this artifice, converted an impending defeat into a victory, till then the greatest of the war. Another proof, if any were required, that valour and strong positions are useless if there is a general to attack, and a fool to defend them.*

From the scene of this victory Clive marched to Arkát, and thence in the direction of Vellur. Whilst, however, contemplating the reduction of this place, which was held by Murtiza Ali on behalf of Chanda Sáhib, he received instructions to repair instantly to Fort St. David, there to undertake immediate measures for the relief of Trichinápallí, the garrison of which was suffering from the close blockade persisted in by Law. On his way to that place, he came upon the site of the victory gained by de la Touche over Nasir Jang,

* For a full account of this marvellous battle see *The Decisive Battles of India*.

on which the rising town of Dupleix-Fath-ábád* was already struggling into existence. Allowing for the moment his dislike of the great French statesman to stifle his more generous instincts, Clive razed the town to its foundations. He then marched in all haste to Fort St. David. Here he found that the governor had been unsparing in his exertions to make provision for the contemplated enterprise. So great, indeed, had been his energy that, in three days after his return, Clive found himself in readiness to march towards Trichinápallí.

This was on March 25, 1752. The 27th, however, brought once more to the shores of India the tried veteran, Major Lawrence. His arrival caused a delay of two days, as well as some change in the arrangement of affairs. On the 28th, however, all was in readiness, and a party of 400 Europeans and 1,100 sipáhis, with eight field-pieces, escorting military stores and provisions, set out that morning for Trichinápallí under the command indeed of Lawrence, but with Clive as his trusted subordinate.

It is time now that we should return to Dupleix. He it was who, at the time when he learned that Clive had proceeded to Fort St. David to concert measures for the relief of Trichinápallí, had, considering it no disgrace to learn something even from an enemy, instigated Ráju Sáhib to make that raid into the English territories, the results of which we have recorded. Though unsuccessful, it cannot be denied that it eminently deserved to succeed, that it had almost succeeded, when at the moment that victory was in his grasp, the carelessness of the French commander at Kávarípák threw it absolutely away.

---

* Mr. Orme speaks of this town as having been built to commemorate that detestable action, the death of Nasir Jang. The prejudices and passions of the hour may have disposed contemporary Englishmen thus to regard it, but the statement is incorrect. The town was built to commemorate the triumph of Dupleix's policy, brought to its crowning point by the victory of de la Touche. The death of Nasir Jang was an incident of that victory, for which the French were not responsible.

Dupleix was terribly mortified at this failure. For the moment indeed it entirely upset his plans. The defeat at Kávarípák had not only deprived him of soldiers whom he could scarcely spare, of field-artillery that was priceless; but it had cast down the spirits of his native allies to an unprecedented and even dangerous degree. No longer could he hope by their aid to effect a diversion in the northern part of the Karnátik. The English had not only gained territory, but with it, of more importance, the confidence of the military class. Desertion by wholesale had taken place from the French to the English standard. More than one important satrap had renounced his adherence to Chanda Sáhib, and taken the oath of fidelity to the besieged Muhammad Ali. And this was the consequence of the victories of Clive, of the repeated defeats sustained by the French, more especially of the fatal disaster at Kávarípák. To see advantages there so nearly gained, so carelessly abandoned, was more than even the composed spirit of Dupleix could bear. Those of his own officers indeed whom he could have made responsible for the disaster had either been captured or killed. Upon Ráju Sáhib, whose incapacity had been conspicuous, the weight, therefore, of his anger fell. For several days he refused to see him, and when at last they did meet, he showed towards the son of Chanda Sáhib a contempt, which it was impossible for him, practised as he was in dealing with native princes, to conceal.

But though mortified beyond measure at the ill-success of plans which so well deserved to succeed, Dupleix still adhered to that bold and daring policy which he justly regarded as more than ever necessary to the attainment of his vast plans. What had been lost in the northern Karnátik might be gained in the south. Trichinápallí might make amends for Arkát and Kávarípák. And now, Trichinápallí was apparently at its last gasp. Without money, with little ammunition, with deficient and failing supplies, with a European commandant devoid of ability, the English garrison and the Múghal soldiers and their leader had already begun a course of recrimination, which, occurring between allies, is the almost invariable precursor of disaster. A little more energy on the part of Law, and the place must have fallen. It was at this crisis that intelligence reached Dupleix of the measures that were being concerted at Fort St. David. The number of the men destined for the relief of Trichinápallí, the nature of the stores they were to escort, the probable date of their departure,— all were known to him. He instantly took a resolution worthy of himself. Detailing to Law the information which he had acquired, he sent him, at the same time, the most stringent orders to mass a great number of his troops, leaving only a few to maintain the blockade of Trichinápallí, in order to attack and intercept the enemy's convoy. These orders were reiterated in successive despatches. The very mode in which they could be carried out was indicated with a clearness which left nothing to desire. He sent him besides all the troops that had become available by the cessation of the campaign in northern Karnátik, enjoining upon him that upon this stroke depended the issue of the war,— that, the English beaten and the convoy captured, Trichinápallí must surrender, French influence must triumph; that, failing in this blow, France would have the mortification of seeing her power, her influence, her authority so dearly gained, and till then so vigilantly maintained, transferred to her hated rivals.

It was indeed a grand opportunity. Had there been a Bussy instead of a Law in the French camp, who can doubt how he would have executed the instructions of his superior? But unfortunately for the real interests of France, Bussy, the true soldier, was far away at Aurangábád, and Law, the pretender, was before Trichinápallí. It is vain indeed to speculate whether in the concussion between the rival and not unequal powers of Bussy and

Clive, the latter or the former would have come forth the victor. This at least is certain, that the youthful hero who laid the first foundations of English empire in India, though displaying on all occasions military talents and resources of the very highest order, never did meet on the field of battle an opponent of even ordinary merit.

We will now see how Law used his opportunity. The distance from Fort St. David to Trichinápallí being about 150 miles, and the route necessitating the crossing of eight considerable rivers, amongst which were the Valaru, the Kolrún, the Vellar, the Pudu-Kávarí, and the Kávarí, the latter three times, Law could calculate to a nicety the time and the means for best attacking and crushing the enemy. The necessity for the passage of so many broad and rapid rivers multiplied his opportunities for defending them. But he judged, it would seem wisely, that he would himself run less risk, and would insure the more complete destruction of the enemy, if he were to allow him to approach within an easy distance of Trichinápallí, and were then to engage him in a position in which his defeat would be certain. So far Law judged correctly and wisely. But in the execution of this plan he failed lamentably. Instead of detaching from his own force a body of troops sufficient in number to render success a matter of certainty, he sent to meet a party of 400 Europeans and 1,100 sipáhis commanded by such men as Lawrence and Clive, a force consisting of but 200 Europeans and from 300 to 400 natives. He did this too at a time when the troops at his own disposal, independently of the levies of Chanda Sáhib, consisted of 900 Europeans and about 2,000 sipáhis. Well could he have shared two-thirds of this number for the important service he had in view! Far safer would it have been for him to undergo the small risk of a sortie on the part of the English garrison, commanded, as it was, by a man whom recent experience had proved to be unenterprising, than to court defeat by sending against Lawrence a force which must be beaten. He might, under the circumstances, have safely left his camp under the protection of one-fourth of his army, and have marched with the rest to crush Lawrence. So would have acted a real general, but experience has abundantly proved that over-caution and incapacity in the field are the almost invariable accompaniments of superciliousness and self-laudation in the cabinet.

Having persuaded himself that he could only, with safety to his main force, detach 350 Europeans and 300 or 400 natives to crush 400 English, and 1,100 sipáhis, commanded by Lawrence and inspirited by Clive, Law sent them to occupy the fortified post of Koiládí, on the northern bank of the Kávarí river. The position was not ill-chosen, and, had it been occupied in sufficient force, would undoubtedly have proved a great obstacle to the advance of the English. A glance at the map will show the inherent strength of this position. The advance of Major Lawrence must necessarily take place between the two branches of the river Kávarí. Of these, the upper branch was defended by the fortified post of Koiládí on its northern bank, unassailable by the English. Between the northern and the southern bank the distance was less than half a mile. Possessing Koiládí, and having an equal or superior force available to occupy the ground between the two branches, it would have been easy for the French commander to have inflicted upon an advancing enemy a crushing defeat. As, however, the defending force did not nearly equal in number the advancing foe, its commander resolved not to attempt anything desperate. He considered, however, that as the ordinary road led directly within cannon shot of Koiládí, and that the English would probably follow it, he would be able, not only to inflict upon them considerable loss in men, but to capture or destroy a great portion of their convoy. Chance, at first, seemed to favour his designs. On April 7, Major Lawrence, misled by his guides, took his force even nearer to the upper branch of the Kávarí than would have been the case had he followed the ordinary route, and found himself all at once under the fire of the guns of Koiládí. These did considerable execution, and before he could move out of range, he had lost twenty Europeans, and his convoy and baggage had been thrown into great disorder. This was the time which the French force, had it been strong enough, might have used with crushing effect. But its commander had apparently imbibed the hesitating and unenterprising nature of his chief. Partly on this account, partly doubtless because he felt himself tied down by the orders he had received, he remained stationary in his stronghold. Major Lawrence therefore was able, not only to extricate himself from his position, but to safely convey that portion of the convoy* he had with him to within ten miles of Trichinápallí.

Thus failed, and failed deservedly, Law's first attempt to crush the advancing English. Like all the measures of weak men it was a half measure, and was therefore ineffective. Fearing to run the risk of an attack from the garrison should he detach a strong force to meet Lawrence, he sent only a weak one, and thus incurred the greater risk of losing his whole army. For he exposed his force, first, to the risk of being beaten in detail; secondly, to its being overwhelmed by the combined forces, superior in numbers, of Lawrence and Gingens. To avert a very small risk, therefore, he ran a very great one, and drew upon his force the destruction in which a bolder course of action would most probably have involved the English. It is a crisis of this nature which really tries a man, which tests the material of

---

* He had left the remainder the previous day at Triktápaltí, on the south of the upper Kávarí, a post belonging to the king of Tanjur.

which he is made. Law failed because, with all his pomposity and arrogance, he was essentially a man of a limited intellect and narrow views.*

His next measures appear to have been conceived in no abler spirit. Receiving intimation from the commandant of the detachment at Koiládí that he had been unsuccessful in preventing the advance of the English, it was even then possible for him, commanding as he did the high road from that place to Trichinápallí, as well as the country in its neighbourhood, to atone, by a combined attack, for his previous inaction. But, although he had for some time been well acquainted with all the movements of Major Lawrence, he had made no effort to mass his forces. They lay scattered in the various posts he had assigned them. When, therefore, the news reached him that the English had passed Koiládí, he was for the moment, thanks to his own negligence, entirely without the means of offering an instantaneous obstruction to their further advance. Seeing nevertheless the great advantage over him which the English would certainly obtain, should they effect a junction with the garrison of Trichinápallí, he hastily called in his scattered detachments, prepared, when too late, to risk a general action. Such a resolution, taken twenty-four hours earlier, might have saved his army, and even have gained Trichinápallí.

This movement could not be effected till the following morning. All that night the detachments moved into camp, and at daylight the force proceeded to take up the position assigned to it by Law, and upon which he fondly hoped the English general would march. Yet this position, although strong, was in a certain point of view almost necessarily ill-chosen. Law was too close

---

* We are well aware that Law, in his *Plainte contre le Sieur Dupleix*, attempts to justify himself; but admitting his facts, he must still be condemned. Had he, as he asserts, only 600 Europeans, he should have marched with those to crush Lawrence. Any course would have been preferable to that which he adopted. But it is clear from the number he had with him at the time of his surrender—nearly 800—that the number of his force of Europeans on April 7 is understated at 900.

to Trichinápallí to draw up his men so as to bar the road across which Lawrence must pass, for in that case he would have exposed himself to the serious danger of an attack on his rear from the garrison. He was compelled, therefore, to take up a position in which he could meet an assault from both parties on his front. In this view he drew up his forces in a line drawn obliquely from the village of Chakalpálam on the Kávarí to the French Rock, and extended thence still more obliquely to the almost inaccessible rock of Elmiseram. As the direct road to Trichinápallí lay between those two positions, Law was not without hope that the English would move upon them before attempting a junction with the garrison.

Major Lawrence, however, was far too wary. Marching early in the morning from Kilakota, where he had encamped the previous evening, he fell in, before he had gone more than a mile, with an officer sent by Captain Gingens to inform him of the disposition made by the French. Feeling that the game was too secure in his hands for him to risk the loss of it by a premature attack on a strong position, he made a *détour* round the point of Elmiseram in the direction of the Sugarloaf Rock, near which he was joined by 200 soldiers of the garrison, under the command of Captains Clarke and Dalton. At this place, therefore, the junction with the garrison may be regarded as having been virtually effected.

It was just this moment, when the English could no longer be assailed with advantage, when they might, in case of defeat, take secure shelter under the guns of the fort, that the incompetent Law selected to assault them. Feebly made on his part, though supported with great resolution by the levies of Chanda Sáhib, his attack did not succeed. The superiority of the French in artillery was neutralised by the superior energy of Clive, who led the English to the attack; and after an interchange of cannon shot, considered, whilst it lasted, to have been

CHAP. VII
1752.

hotter than any till then experienced on the plains of Southern India, the French retreated to their rock with a loss on their part of 40 men, on the part of their native allies of 300. Had not Major Lawrence, in consideration of the intense heat of the day, stopped the pursuit, they would have suffered far more severely.* Having repulsed this attack, the English marched without molestation into Trichinápallí.

No language can paint the anger and mortification of Dupleix when intelligence of these events reached him. This then was the result of confiding the conduct of an army to a man whose principal credentials consisted in the super-excellent opinion, which, he allowed all the world to perceive, he had formed of his own abilities. All his recommendations had been disregarded, inordinate caution had prevailed when the necessities of the hour peculiarly required dashing and daring tactics, and the English army, though encumbered by an enormous convoy, had been allowed to enter the beleaguered city virtually unmolested,—no serious attempt having been made to hinder them till they were under the walls of Trichinápallí! Was it for such a result that Dupleix had schemed and planned, that he had pledged the rising fortunes of French India to the support of native princes who should be but the puppets of France? Was it to see the superiority in the field passing from his hands to the hands of his hated rivals, to witness not only the loss of the capital of the Karnátik, but a repulse from the last refuge of Muhammad Ali? He was fated indeed to suffer disappointments more bitter even than these. But, up to the present moment, he had been so thoroughly buoyed up by hope; he had trusted that when the time came Law would show himself what he had always boasted himself to be; above all, he had counted so implicitly on the

* The English, who fought under cover, lost fourteen men only from the cannonade, seven however were struck down by the sun.—*Orme*.

capture of this convoy, on the destruction or, at least, the repulse of this relieving party. To this end he had devoted all his faculties. He had been to Law the eye to see, the ear to hear; it was not, alas for him, in his power to be the mind to conceive or the arm to strike. He had given Law all the necessary information; the rest, being soldier's work, he had left to him as a soldier to perform. The result showed that the mere donning of epaulets does not make a man a soldier: that if devoid of the intellect given by God to man, and not, as some would seem to think, implanted in the dress he wears, that very dress and the fancied knowledge attaching to it make the pedant more pedantic, the shallow-minded and narrow more vain, more obstinate, more contemptuous of the opinion of the many wiser men who wear it not.

Law had come out to Dupleix recommended by letters from the directors and by his own vauntings,— the latter probably the cause of the former. Had he, who boasted himself a soldier, acted even as a man of ordinary common-sense would have acted, it might have been pardoned him had he failed in fair fight before the genius of a Clive and the persistence of a Lawrence. But it is clear that he would have failed equally before men of far inferior capacity. It needed but for his opponent to be capable of advancing,—a rarer quality, however, than is generally supposed,—and Law would have succumbed. He did everything out of season; and the reason was, that although he wore a soldier's coat, he was not a soldier.

How keenly Dupleix felt the bitter disappointment can scarcely be described, nor will we attempt to describe it. We would rather dwell on the measures which, in spite of his disappointment, he adopted unhesitatingly, to remedy, as far as possible, the disaster. His was indeed no easy position. Where was he to find a general? Bussy, the only competent commander he had under him, was at Aurangábád with the Subadar; Law, helpless at Trichinápallí. Besides those two, there was but the infirm d'Auteuil, disabled by the climate, and by gout, incapable certainly of making head against the vigorous energy of Clive. It seemed almost preferable to maintain Law, who was at least still vigorous, in command, than to intrust the last remains of the army to d'Auteuil.

Before, however, he could take any measures in this respect, in fact the second day after he had heard of the entrance of Lawrence into Trichinapallí, Dupleix received from Law a despatch which threw him into even greater amazement. This was to the effect that, threatened by the English, and despairing now of gaining the place, he had determined to retreat at once into the island of Srirangam. The madness of such a scheme was patent to the far-seeing vision of Dupleix. It seemed to him indeed that for a general deliberately to move his forces into an island, where he would be cut off from all communication with his countrymen, was an act of which no one, who had not lost his head, could be guilty. There could not, he felt, be a more dangerous, a more incompetent commander at the head of an army than the man who should propose such a step. Under the influence of this feeling he instantly acted. Hoping that it might not possibly be yet too late to avert a great calamity, he sent strict orders to Law to retreat, if he must retreat, not into Srirangam, but upon Pondichery. With the view of aiding him in this undertaking, and to be prepared at all events for the worst, he strained every nerve to levy a fresh force to move towards Trichinápallí, and to endeavour to effect a junction with Law. His own funds, constituting the bulk of the private fortune he had amassed during his service, were freely spent for this purpose. No regard for his own interests stood in the way of the performance of his duty to his masters and to France.

LAW'S POSITION STILL STRONG.

Thus, by incredible exertions, he succeeded in raising a force of 120 Europeans, 500 sipáhis, and with four field-pieces. The command of it he made over to d'Auteuil, the only officer at his disposal, with instructions that, on effecting a junction with Law, he was to assume command of the combined army. The party left Pondichery the second week in April.

Meanwhile, however, startling events had occurred in the neighbourhood of Trichinápallí. Law, although repulsed on April 8 in his attempt to prevent the march of the English into that fortress, still occupied an extremely strong position. His right resting on the Kavarí, maintained his communications with Srirangam and with the country on the northern bank of the Kolrún; his centre was protected by the French Rock, whilst his left extended to the extremely strong post of Elmiseram, on the top of which cannon had been mounted. Chanda Sáhib with his troops occupied the line of the Kávarí, forming an obtuse angle with the French position. Had the resolution of Law then consisted in anything but words, he might have safely awaited here the attack of the combined English force; for, although he would then be fighting with a river in his rear,—a most unpleasant position,—yet the ground he occupied was so strong that had it been resolutely defended an attack upon it must have resulted in the defeat of the assailants. It would appear that the English commander, Major Lawrence, thoroughly recognised this fact; for he states in his memoirs that having sounded his native allies, and having ascertained that on one pretext or another they were evidently unwilling to aid him in an assault on the French position, he was extremely concerned as to the steps he ought to adopt to force Law to retreat.

Law, however, played his game most effectually. The English, not thinking themselves strong enough to attack the French position unsupported by their native allies,

CHAP.
VII.

1752.

had resolved to beat up the quarters of Chanda Sáhib. For this purpose, a detachment of 400 men under Captain Dalton moved out of Trichinápallí on the night of April 12, hoping to surprise the native levies. Unacquainted however with the road, they found themselves at break of day in front of the strongest part of the French position, between the French Rock and Elmiseram. Discovering at once the danger which they ran of being crushed by the entire French force, they endeavoured to retreat without being perceived. The morning light, however, warned the French of their presence before they were out of danger, and the chances seemed all to be in favour of their destruction. But the sight which would have lent vigour and energy to an ordinary man, which would have been used by Clive to make his own cause triumphant, added terror and dismay to the palsied faculties of Law. Far from regarding the retreating English as men whom by an energetic movement he could cut off and destroy, he looked upon their presence there as an indication that he and his force had been subjected to imminent peril, from which they had miraculously escaped. Instead then, of moving to attack them, he rejoiced at their retreating of their own accord. His apprehension indeed carried him so far as to direct that, as soon as the English should be well out of sight, preparations should be made for an immediate retreat across the Kávarí into the island of Srirangam.

It would appear, indeed, that this movement had been for a long time contemplated by Law, for he had often insisted upon its necessity to Chanda Sáhib, and had even mentioned it in his letters to Dupleix. But Chanda Sáhib, a better soldier than Law, had not only pointed out the insensate folly of the movement, but had absolutely refused to join in it; whilst Dupleix, though for a long time not regarding it as serious or possible, had pointed out, in the clearest terms, that such a movement would, more than any other, compromise his own force

LAW RETREATS INTO SRIRANGAM.

and the interests of French India. When finally he heard that it had been decided upon, he had replied, as we have already stated, by an imperative order to retreat upon Pondichery, and by the supersession of Law by d'Auteuil. It is difficult indeed to believe how a man in the possession of his senses could have persuaded himself that Srirangam was a proper place to retreat upon. It was, in the first place, actually within long cannon-shot of Trichinápallí. In the second place, the fact of a small force remaining in an island, the river surrounding which could be crossed, was surely to invite an enterprising enemy to cut it off,—to force it in fact, unless relieved, to a surrender. To attempt such a movement in the presence of a Clive was a species of folly which that man only could have committed whose nerves and whose senses had been utterly prostrated. Of all places that could have been selected for such a purpose, Srirangam was, without exception, that one which most completely shut the door of hope on the force occupying it, in the face of an enemy strong enough to act on both banks of the river.

CHAP. VII.

1752.

Yet this was the place to which Law had resolved, not by a sudden inspiration of folly, but after many days of painful consideration, to carry over the French army. Yet, though the matter had been long predetermined in his own mind, he had made no preparations for carrying his plan into effect. Perhaps he had hoped that after all it would not be necessary. This at least is certain that, up to the moment when the appearance of the English retreating from before his own position brought so vividly to his mind the idea of the dangers that might be in store for him on the right bank, not a single preparation for that retreat had been made. Nevertheless, bent on effecting it, he sent to Chanda Sáhib, and to him communicated his resolution. This faithful ally of the French received the intelligence with anger and disappointment. Not he alone, but his principal commanders, opposed it with all their eloquence. Better far, they said, to meet defeat and death in open action, than to retreat to a position in which surrender must be necessitated. But all their remonstrances remained without effect on the paralysed spirit of Law. He would retreat, he said; they might act as they choose; and he issued orders at once to carry out his resolution. Chanda Sáhib, though unconvinced, though despising the man, would not, at that dark hour, abandon the nation that had so long supported him. He might have escaped, but preferring to cast in his lot with the French, he accompanied them across the Kávarí.

Great was the confusion of the retreat. Not a single preparation had been made for it. The provisions, necessary for the support of the troops in Srirangam, were abandoned and burnt. Much of their baggage was left behind. The guns were with great difficulty transported. However, after infinite labour, the French troops and those of Chanda Sáhib found themselves in occupation of Srirangam, a detachment of the former only having been left to guard the rock of Elmiseram, which it would have been wiser to abandon with the rest of the position.

The natural consequences of this movement were soon apparent. First ensued the capture of Elmiseram, effected on April 13, by Captain Dalton, after a faint resistance. Next, the movement which Dupleix and Chanda Sáhib had alike foreseen, the detaching of a portion of the English army to the northern bank of the Kolrún, in order not only to cut off the supplies of the French, but to sever their communications with Pondichery. This measure was suggested to Major Lawrence by Clive, and the former, on consulting his native allies regarding it, found to his satisfaction that it met with their approval conditionally on the command of the English section of the force being intrusted to the conqueror of Arkát. This matter having been settled, a detachment consisting of 400 Europeans, 700 sipáhis, 3,000 Maráthás, 1,000 Tanjurian horse, with eight pieces of artillery, crossed the Kávarí and Kolrún on the night of April 17, and on the following morning took up a position at the village of Samiáveram, nine or ten miles north of Srirangam, and on the high road between that place and Pondichery. This masterly movement owed its success as much to the boldness of the English as to the nerveless despondency of the French leader. Had Clive been in the position of Law, what an opportunity here presented itself of placing the English in the position in which they had hoped to pin the French, by crossing the Kolrún, and taking them between the Srirangam force on one side, and that of d'Auteuil on the other. But all spirit and sense had apparently fled from the counsels of Law. He acted, as though he had but one object,—that of delivering himself and his allies, bound hand and foot, to the enemy.

Meanwhile d'Auteuil, who had left Pondichery on April 10 at the head of 120 Europeans, 500 sipáhis, and four field-pieces, reached Utatur, fifteen miles north of Samiáveram, on the 25th of that month. Here he learned the situation of affairs; that Law was cooped up in Srirangam, and that between Law and himself lay Clive at the head of a superior force. Though, infirm and gouty, d'Auteuil had still spirit enough left in him not to be disheartened by these tidings. He had been sent expressly to relieve Law, and he could not leave him to himself without at least an effort on his behalf. Accordingly, he resolved to make a *détour* so as to avoid Samiáveram, and thus to reach the Kolrún without molestation from the enemy. He sent intelligence to Law of his intended movement, but unfortunately for him, one of his messengers was captured by Clive.

CHAP. VII.
1752.

Ignorant of this, however, d'Auteuil set out on the evening of the 25th, taking a route to the westward; but he had not proceeded far before intelligence reached him that Clive, apprised of his movements, was on his march to intercept him; he accordingly returned to Utatur. Clive, learning this, moved back upon Samiáveram. Meanwhile, however, Law had learned from one of the messengers sent by d'Auteuil of his intended march. Certain information reached him, at the same time, of Clive's intention to intercept him. Here was a splendid opportunity. By making a forced march of ten miles from Srirangam with his whole force, he might seize Samiáveram whilst Clive should be engaged with d'Auteuil, and then press on to crush the former in the field. Of the many chances granted to the French leader, this was the last and not the least tempting,—not the least likely to lead to great and important consequences. To have even a probability of success, however, it was requisite that Law should move with the bulk of his force, and should move with the rapidity of lightning. But this unfortunate leader, though a little braced up by the intelligence of the approach of d'Auteuil, was still incapable of real vigour or energy. Instead of moving himself at the head of his force, he detached only 80 Europeans, of whom 40 were English deserters, and 700 sipáhis,* to carry out a scheme, upon the success or ill-success of which depended the domination of the French or English in India.

This detachment approached Samiáveram after Clive had returned from his fruitless search after d'Auteuil. Little thinking, from his experience of the character of Law, that there was the smallest fear of an attack from the side of Srirangam, Clive had made no preparations to meet one, and had gone quietly to bed. The French detachment, meanwhile, had arrived at the

* Orme.

gates, succeeded, by means of the deserters who formed a part of it, in persuading the English sipáhis on guard there that they had been sent by Major Lawrence to reinforce Clive, and they thus obtained entrance into the very heart of the English camp before the presence of an enemy was suspected there, and whilst Clive was still sleeping. Yet sleeping though he was, the presence of that one man on the side of the English alone made the difference between victory and defeat. Had he been the leader of the French none can doubt but that the latter would have that night crushed their enemies in their camp, and have recovered all the results that had been so wilfully thrown away. But Clive was the leader of those opposed to them, and never did he vindicate so completely his title to be a leader of men, a prince amongst his people, as on that eventful night. Never did anyone under such circumstances display a presence of mind more perfect, a courage more brilliant and ready. The circumstances were almost marvellous. The English force at Samiáveram occupied two pagodas, about a quarter of a mile distant from one another; round these were encamped the natives. Now, the French force had advanced through the natives, and had penetrated to the lesser pagoda, in an open shed close to which Clive was sleeping in his palanquin. Here, being challenged, they fired volleys into each of these places, one of them narrowly missing Clive, and most effectually awakening him. They then moved on, occupied the larger pagoda, and drew up their sipáhis in front of it,—these keeping up an incessant fire in the supposed direction of the enemy. Meanwhile, Clive, on the first alarm, had run to the greater pagoda, and marched up 200 of his Europeans to see what could have caused the disturbance, still considering it a false alarm of his own sipáhis, and never dreaming of an enemy. Approaching close to the lesser pagoda he went among the French sipáhis, still believing them to be his own, and ordered them to cease fire. He did not even discover his mistake when one of them, ascertaining him to be an Englishman, wounded him in two places, and then, when attacked by Clive, ran towards the lesser pagoda. Clive followed him, only however to find himself in the presence of six French soldiers, who called upon him to surrender. Then, for the first time, the whole truth burst upon him. Comprehending it all in a moment, he called upon the Frenchmen to yield in their turn; told them he had even come to offer them terms, and invited them to see for themselves his whole army drawn up to attack them. Completely deceived by his bold and ready artifice, three of the Frenchmen at once laid down their arms; the remainder communicated Clive's terms to the party in the larger pagoda. These, however, refused to surrender, and it was not till after a most sanguinary contest, in the course of which Clive had another narrow escape, caused mainly by the desperation of the English deserters, that they yielded to terms. The French sipáhis, meanwhile, had marched out of camp, but they were pursued by the Marátha cavalry and cut to pieces, it is said, literally to a man.

After this repulse the situation of the French in Srirangam became desperate indeed. Entirely to cut them off from all relief, as well as from all hope of escape, possession was taken by the Tanjurian allies of the English of Koiládi on May 7. There then remained only M. d'Auteuil with whom to deal. To rid that part of the country of him, Major Lawrence, on the 20th, despatched Captain Dalton at the head of 150 Europeans, 400 sipáhis, 500 Maráthás, and four field-pieces,— leaving Clive's detachment entire at Samiáveram.

Meanwhile, d'Auteuil, scared by the ill-result of his attempt to turn Samiáveram, and of the well-meant but ill-supported attempt of the Srirangam party to surprise that place, had remained quietly at Utatur waiting his opportunity. The opportunity came, but did not find him capable of taking advantage of it. In fact Captain Dalton's party after a skirmish in front of Utatur, which had no decisive results, had advanced at once upon that place. Late experience had shown the English that the surest way to victory was to move straight on,—to destroy by that advance the *morale* of the enemy, and thus to more than half beat him before the actual fight had begun. Acting on this plan, Dalton made such a display of his troops, maintaining only a few with his guns and sending the infantry to attack the enemy in flank, that d'Auteuil imagined that he had not simply a detachment, but the whole force of Clive before him. Having this impression, all his intellect fled, and he became the slave of his fears. Had he been as bold as Dalton, a resolute advance on the guns must have decided the action in his favour. But fear, not physical but moral, shutting his eyes and taking away his senses, he allowed himself to be deceived by this shallow device, and notwithstanding that he did actually repulse the English from Utatur, he abandoned that place in the night, and fled, unmolested, to Volkondah, thus leaving Law to his fate, to England a certain triumph.

Whilst this was going on, Law, noticing from the watchtower of Srirangam the march of Dalton's troops, concluded that they must belong to Clive's force, and, this time acting with boldness, crossed the river with the bulk of his army, hoping to gain Samiáveram. But Clive was not the man to expose himself twice to the chance of being surprised. He at once marched to meet him, and came up with him just as he had crossed the Kolrún. It was not for Clive, under the circumstances, to seek an engagement. The enemy was already in the toils. A battle alone could extricate him. On the other hand, every circumstance should have induced Law to court an action. It was, his only chance, and here the numbers were in his favour. But,—he did not fight;—he returned to Srirangam, only, alas for French interests, to surrender.

The capture of Pachandah, a fortified pagoda on the northern banks of the Kolrún opposite Srirangam, completed the investment of the French, and took away from them the opportunity, till then open to them, of communicating in any way with the direct road from Pondichery. This place having been gained, still further to deprive them of all hopes of reinforcements from d'Auteuil, Clive marched in search of that officer, and coming up with him on June 8, at Volkondah, the native commandant of which place had been secretly gained by the English, he compelled him with his whole force to surrender.

Thus deprived of his last hope, what was there for the unfortunate Law to do? He, poor man, knew well, in his heart of hearts, to what end recent events had been tending, and for some days past he had been well aware that there was no alternative between cutting his way out and a surrender. Under such circumstances great men act; small men, on the contrary, allow themselves to be acted upon by every vague rumour, no matter whence it may have arisen; nay, they go so far as to delude themselves into the belief that somehow—how they cannot say—all will in the end be well. Thus it was with Law. He allowed himself to be deluded by all kinds of vain imaginings; for a long time it was d'Auteuil's advance; then it was the hope of reinforcements from France; sometimes one thing, sometimes another. He appears never to have bethought him that a man's energy is given him to be employed; that there is no conjuncture, however trying, from which a man, by the exercise of that quality, may not extricate himself; that to depend on chance is altogether unworthy of a real man. Had he only dared to look facts in the face, he must have seen that he must surrender if he could not escape. His provisions were fast failing him, his native allies were deserting him in hundreds, but still he had his Europeans. In the beginning of June there yet remained to him 800 of these, in addition to about 2,000 trained sipáhis, and 3,000 or 4,000 native levies who still remained faithful to Chanda Sáhib. With these he might easily have taken advantage of the first fall of the Kávarí to attack Major Lawrence's camp on the south of the river, to the troops guarding which he was in numbers vastly superior. Overpowering this, he might have thence cut his way, without much chance of molestation, to Karikal. In vain did Chanda Sáhib over and over again implore him to have recourse to some such means. He could not make up his mind, he preferred to depend on accidents and chances,—and he was lost!

Nevertheless, it must not be supposed that he was so base as to be indifferent to the fate of that faithful supporter of French interests. Law knew full well that but one result to Chanda Sáhib would follow his surrender to the now triumphant Muhammad Ali. As for surrender to the English, that was absolutely out of the question, for France and England were not at war. In the contest between Muhammad Ali and Chanda Sáhib, the French and English were not principals, they were simply hired mercenaries engaged on opposite sides. Whichever party might be victorious neither then could claim the open direction of affairs. A proposition of surrender to the English could not, therefore, and would not, have been entertained. As for Muhammad Ali, it was not to be expected that, brought up as he had been to regard all means lawful to accomplish the death of a rival, he would hesitate as to the punishment to be meted out to one who had proved himself so persistent, so daring, so fertile in expedients as the French-protected Chanda Sáhib. Having rejected all bolder counsels, and having made up his mind to surrender, Law busied himself therefore to find the means of saving the life of his

CHAP. VII.
1752.

ally. For this purpose he entered into negotiations with Mánakjí, general of the army of the Rájá of Tanjur. This chieftain readily accepted the terms offered, and having received a stipulated sum of money in advance, with the promise of more to follow, having likewise sworn solemnly to protect the life of the fugitive Nawwáb, Mánakjí, on the night of June 11, sent an officer with a palanquin to escort him to his camp. No sooner, however, had the unfortunate man arrived there, than he was violently seized, loaded with irons, and placed under a guard. The next morning a conference was held to determine his fate, at which Major Lawrence was present. There can be no doubt whatever that a firm persistence on the part of that officer, more especially on the second day,—after the English had become, by the surrender of Law, absolute masters of the situation,—would have saved the life of Chanda Sáhib. Major Lawrence himself asserts that, in the course of the debate as to the manner in which Chanda Sáhib should be disposed of, he himself was at first silent, but subsequently proposed that he should be made over to the English. This, however, was objected to, and no resolution was arrived at. The second day after however, when Mánakjí inquired from him whether he seriously desired to have charge of the prisoner, the English commandant passed upon him virtual sentence of death, by declaring that he did not wish to interfere further in the dispute regarding his disposal.* A few hours later Chanda Sáhib was stabbed

---

* This indifference,—to use a light term,—of the English commander to the fate of Chanda Sáhib has been very gently treated by most English historians. The statement however of Orme, biased as that writer is against the French, shows how completely it was in the power of Major Lawrence to have saved Chanda Sáhib, had he chosen to stretch forth his hand. Orme, after alluding to the contest between Muhammad Ali, the Maisurians, and the Maráthás for the possession of the person of Chanda Sáhib, writes thus:—"Terrified at the commotions which would inevitably follow if he gave the preference to any one of the competitors, he (Mánakjí) saw no method of finishing the contest, but by putting an end to the life of his prisoner; however, as the Major (Lawrence) had expressed a desire that the English might have him in their possession, *he thought it necessary to know whether they seriously ex-*

LAW SURRENDERS.

to the heart by order of Mánakjí, and his decapitated head was sent to his triumphant rival.

But before this tragedy had been consummated, Law himself had surrendered. Resting on the broken reed of delusive expectations, he had allowed every opportunity to pass by, until at last the arrival of a battering-train from Dévikota placed it in the power of the English to compel him to submit to their own terms. After the usual amount of protests, and threats to defend himself to the last should those protests not be acceded to, he finally agreed that the French army should surrender prisoners of war; that the officers should be liberated on giving their parole never to serve against Muhammad Ali and his allies; that the English deserters should be pardoned; that all the arms, artillery, and munitions of war should be made over faithfully to the English commandant; and that the island itself should be surrendered. The conditions were faithfully carried out. On the morning of June 13, 35 officers, 785 soldiers, and 2,000 sipáhis laid down their arms and surrendered themselves prisoners to the English commander, this latter acting not on his own account but as representative of Muhammad Ali. There was given up at the same time forty-one pieces of cannon, and an immense quantity of ammunition.*

---

pected this deference; and accordingly, on the same morning that the pagoda surrendered, went to the Major, *with whom he had a conference, which convinced him that the English were his friends, and that they were resolved not to interfere any further in the dispute. He, therefore, immediately on his return to Chakalpalam put his design into execution, by ordering the head of Chanda Sáhib to be struck off.* (The italics are our own.) It is unfortunately clear from this, that Major Lawrence did connive at the death of the unfortunate prisoner. Professor Wilson states, in deprecation of this verdict, that at that period the English were not so well assured of their power, as to pretend to dictate to the native princes with whom they co-operated. It is clear that in the case now under notice it was not at all a question of dictation. It is too evident that a word from Major Lawrence to Mánakjí would have changed the fate of the victim. How can we avoid the simple conclusion to be drawn from the fact, that Mánakjí, satisfied that the English would not interfere to save the life of the prisoner, went straight from the presence of Major Lawrence to order the execution of Chanda Sáhib?

* Our authorities for the account of this short campaign are the history of Mr. Orme, the journal of Major Lawrence, the memoir of Captain Dalton, and the memoir and official letters of Dupleix.

Thus fatally ended, after intense labour and anxiety to its projectors, the expedition which, but eleven months before, had been despatched, full of the certainty of success, from Pondichery. What a termination to prospects which shone with such brilliancy in the outset, what a sequel to plans which seemed, at the time of their projection, to be proof against failure! Then there was but one barrier to French domination in the Karnátik. They possessed commanding resources, a ruler whose influence with the natives was unparalleled, and, above all, the prestige of victory. Opposed to them was a pretender deserted by his allies, but occupying a fortified town, and a mere handful of dispirited English. But at the end of eleven months what a different picture do we behold! The pretender has become the *de facto* ruler; the handful of dispirited English, the arbiters of the Karnátik; the victorious French army are prisoners of war. Whence this revolution? Can we discern in the steady mind of Dupleix any symptoms of faltering, any signs of decay? On the contrary. Never had he shown more unfaltering resolution; on no previous occasion did he manifest a more zealous energy. His orders to Law, his encouragement of Chanda Sáhib, his attempt to infuse energy into d'Auteuil, show the ardour of his spirit, the correct aim by which his views were guided. Had his orders been carried out, had even common prudence and energy been displayed by his commanders, his policy must have triumphed, the genius of France must have conquered.

If, then, we look for the causes of a contrary result, we must turn our eyes to another quarter. Dupleix was the civil governor, possessing a power of devising plans, even military plans, for there is nothing in military plans which genius, though not specially trained to warfare, is unable to master,—such as has been accorded to but few men in any age. His was the eye to see, the brain to conceive; but he possessed not in addition the arm to strike. To carry out his vast plans he was compelled to confide in others, and it happened, unfortunately for him, that whilst, at this period, those whom alone he was able to employ were men of singularly feeble intellect, deficient in energy and enterprise, dreading responsibilty, afraid to run small risks, and therefore exposing themselves to great dangers, his principal adversary was a man of vast and comprehensive genius, of an aptitude for war surpassing all his contemporaries, of a ready audacity and prompt execution in the field, such as have never been surpassed. Whilst then the designs for the French campaign were most masterly, being conceived in the brain of Dupleix,—their execution was feeble beyond the power of description, that execution being left to his lieutenants. The orders, the letters, the entreaties of Dupleix stand living witnesses in the present day of the exactness of his conclusions. Had they been obeyed,—and it is clear that obedience to them was easy,—Trichinápallí would have fallen whilst Clive was still besieged in Arkát; or, had untimely occurrences prevented that great triumph, a literal obedience to his instructions would have insured the interception and defeat of the relieving forces of Lawrence and Clive on the banks of the Kávarí. Who could have believed that imbecility and fear of responsibility would ever find the level reached in the manufacture of a Law,—imbecility and fear of responsibility so clear as to draw even from the English historian, jealous as he is on all occasions of the reputation of the English leaders, the remark, that "it is indeed difficult to determine whether the English conducted themselves with more ability and spirit, or the French with more irresolution and ignorance, after Major Lawrence and Captain Clive arrived at Trichinápallí?" *

To judge fairly and candidly the degree of merit or demerit attaching to Dupleix at this crisis of the

* Orme.

fortunes of French India, we propose to examine his conduct after the occurrence of the misfortunes we have recounted. In what a position was he then! Law, with the main body of the French troops, beaten and taken prisoners; d'Auteuil, with the relieving force consisting of the only French troops available for garrison purposes, beaten and taken prisoners; Bussy, with all that yet remained, far off at Aurangábád; Chanda Sáhib, his trusted ally, murdered, and his levies dispersed. To Dupleix then there remained at this crisis merely Pondichery, Jinjí, and the French possessions on the coast, without garrisons to defend them, still less with troops available for operations in the field. His enemies, on the contrary, triumphant, possessors now of the influence and of the material advantages for which he had toiled, had it in their power apparently utterly to overwhelm him. They had not only an army and numerous native allies, but a Lawrence and a Clive to command them. Dupleix had no longer an army, no longer an ally; since the departure of Bussy he had never had a general: he had to depend upon no one but himself,—and one other trusted and indefatigable councillor,—his own wife. Let us watch now how this man, thus overmatched, thus driven into a corner, made head against the enormous difficulties with which he had to contend.

His own experiences and alliances with native chieftains had satisfied Dupleix, that to such men there was no such disorganiser as victory. Prepared after defeat to sacrifice in appearance even their just claims, if by so doing they could retain a basis for future action, they would on a change of fortune, however occurring, show an absolute forgetfulness of past admissions, and increase their demands to a most exaggerated degree. If this were the case when a native prince might be in alliance with a European power, to a much more extended and dangerous degree would it occur when three or four native princes should occupy such a position. For then each ally would measure his own claims by the claims of his rival, and it would inevitably happen that such claims would often clash. Now in the war that had just then concluded, Muhammad Ali, the rival of Chanda Sáhib, had been aided by three native allies, —by the Rájá of Tanjur, the Rájá of Maisur, and the Maráthás. So long as it seemed certain that Muhammad Ali and his English allies would prove triumphant,—a conclusion which the imbecility of Law had made clear to the acute intellects of the natives at an early period of the contest,—it was evident to Dupleix that no attempts to bring them over to his side would have the smallest effect. Nevertheless he maintained native envoys at their courts, instructed by him from time to time to act as circumstances might render advisable. It was then, when victory declared itself against him, when he had no more any troops and not a single ally, that he put in action those arts of which no one better than he understood the use. His attempts were not at first made on Muhammad Ali. The English, he well knew, were acting in the name of that prince, and would be bound to attend mainly to his interests. Of the other parties to the alliance, the Maráthás were the most influential, and with these, at the moment when the power he represented lay lowest in the estimation of the world, he commenced his secret negotiations.

So well did he succeed that Muhammad Ali and his English allies soon found that almost the only profit they had derived from their victory was the surrender of Law and his army. In a moment, as it were, they discovered that the animosity of the Maisurians against Muhammad Ali, and of Murárí Ráo against both, would prevent that combined action in the field on which they had previously calculated; whilst the men of the Tanjur contingent, sick of service which seemed likely to bring little advantage, were clamorous to return to their own country. So pronounced were the secret intrigues and so undisguised the mutual suspicions, that, although Law's force had surrendered on June 11, it was not till the 9th of the following month that the Nawwáb and his English allies were able to leave Trichinápallí, and even then he was forced to leave 200 of the latter and 1,500 of their sipáhis as a garrison to protect the city against his former associates,—the Maisurians and the Maráthás.

The delay thus caused, and the disaffection in the enemy's camp were eminently serviceable to Dupleix. It so happened that in that very interval the yearly reinforcements of troops arrived at Pondichery from France. It is true that the men composing it were not of the best material,—indeed Dupleix himself asserts that they were a collection of the vilest rabble,—but they formed at least a basis upon which to work. To increase their number he landed the sailors from the fleet, and manned the vessels in their place with lascars. By these means he found himself provided with a body of nearly 500 European soldiers, able once more to present a respectable appearance in the eyes of the native powers. To effect all this he had freely drawn upon his private resources, and made his entire fortune subservient to the cause of his country. An opportunity soon presented itself still further to confirm the opinions entertained regarding the magnitude of his resources, and to intimate very clearly to the native princes that Pondichery was yet unconquered. Harassed by their native allies, and by the intrigues fomenting around them, the English had made but slow progress after leaving Trichinápallí. They took indeed Tiruvádí, held by a small garrison of French sipáhis, on July 17; but from that moment their counsels became as uncertain as had been those of the French two months earlier. Major Lawrence had left them on account of his health; Clive had been compelled to proceed to Fort St. David from the same cause; and the command of the troops in the field was left to the incapable Gingens. This officer remaining idle at Tiruvádí, instructions were sent him from Governor Saunders, contrary to the advice of Major Lawrence, to detach a portion of his force against Jinjí. Major Gingens obeyed these orders by sending, on August 3, 200 Europeans, 1,500 sipáhis, and 600 of the Nawwáb's cavalry under the command of Major Kinneer, an officer who had but just arrived from Europe.

Intelligence of the march of this detachment having been promptly conveyed to Dupleix, he determined to use it to strike a blow for the recovery of the prestige of the French arms. Sending orders, therefore to the commandant of Jinjí to hold that place to the last extremity, he organised from his new levies a force of 300 Europeans and 500 sipáhis, and sent them with seven field-pieces to occupy a position half way between Pondichery and Jinjí, and commanding the pass just traversed by the English on their route to the latter place.

Jinjí was a fortress on many accounts very dear to the French. Its almost marvellous capture by Bussy, on the 11th September, 1750, had raised the reputation of his countrymen to the highest point all over India: the victory gained near it by de la Touche over the forces of Nasir Jang, had seemed to consolidate and cement French power in the Karnátik. The possession of Jinjí alone gave them a prestige in the eyes of the natives, which it would have taken much to eradicate. Its natural inaccessibility, Dupleix was well aware, was sufficient to enable a well-commanded garrison to beat off a force five times the strength of that commanded by Kinneer. That officer likewise, he knew, was a stranger to the country and its people, and it seemed highly improbable that in the lottery of the distribution of commands, the English should draw a second Lawrence, still less another heaven-born genius of the stamp of Clive. His plan, therefore, seemed certain to succeed. Operating on the rear of the enemy, who, he was sure, would make nothing of his movement against Jinjí, he would induce him to attack the French in a position previously chosen and previously fortified, and he would then, it seemed certain, take his revenge for Srirangam.

It fell out just as he had anticipated. Kinneer arrived before Jinjí on August 6, summoned it, and met with a determined refusal. Appalled at its strength he was hesitating as to his action, when news reached him that the French had taken up a position at Vieravándi in his rear, cutting off his communications with Tiruvádi. With the spirit of a soldier Kinneer turned at once to attack this new enemy, and, rendered bold by the repeated successes of the English, he did not care to reconnoitre, but dashed directly on the French position. To draw on the English against the strongest part of this, M. de Kerjean, a nephew of Dupleix, who held the command, directed his men to retire. The English, on this, advanced with greater audacity, till they found themselves exposed to the full fire of the enemy's field-pieces, separated from them by a strongly fortified wall. At this moment Kinneer was wounded, the English sipáhis retreated, and even the English white troops began to waver. Just then Kerjean directed a movement on their flank. On this service 100 French soldiers started. The manœuvre was decisive. The English fell back after but a slight resistance, leaving forty of their men dead on the field of action.

Thus in less than two months after the terrible and seemingly irreparable losses caused by the incapacity of law, did Dupleix bring back victory to the French standards, and recover his influence amongst the native princes of the Karnátik. The effect was increased by the capture, shortly afterwards, of a company of Swiss mercenaries, employed by the English under the command of Captain Schauf on the high seas. The English denounced this action as opposed to the law of nations, the two countries being nominally at peace. But Dupleix triumphantly replied that he had as much right to capture English soldiers on the seas, as the English had to capture French soldiers on land; that on this occasion he was merely acting in self-defence, as these soldiers had been sent to sea that they might the more effectually attack the French possessions on shore. There can be no doubt as to the soundness and completeness of this reply.

It was about this period that Dupleix received from the Subadar of the Dakhan, Salábat Jang, a patent containing his formal appointment as Nawwáb of the Karnátik, and of the countries south of the Krishná, and as possessor of all the other honours conferred upon him by Muzaffar Jang. Salábat Jang also informed him that the Emperor Ahmad Sháh would shortly send an embassy with the imperial patents of confirmation. In consequence of the authority thus received, Dupleix appointed Ráju Sáhib, the son of the deceased Chanda Sáhib, to hold the appointment under him. Finding, however, that the young man himself preferred pleasure and sloth to the occupation of war, he entered into negotiations with Murtizá Ali, the surviving son-in-law and nearest relative of the family of Dost Ali. Murtizá Ali responded freely to the conditions, and agreed to advance a considerable sum of money, and to levy troops in support of his title. In the same month, likewise, the Directors of the Company of the Indies wrote to Dupleix to express their entire satisfaction with his conduct, and to inform him that the King of France had been pleased, in compliance with their solicitations, to confer upon him the title of

Marquis, with reversion in direct line to his descendants. From all the eminent public men in France he received by the same opportunity congratulations on the receipt of this well-merited honour, and expressions of entire concurrence in the policy he had adopted. Meanwhile, all his hopes raised by the success at Vieravándi, Dupleix renewed his negotiations with the Maisurians and Murárí Ráo, pressing them to declare openly in his favour. This they agreed to do, provided Dupleix should engage so to employ the main army of the English as to leave them free to prosecute their views upon Trichinapállí. In accordance with these views Dupleix reinforced Kerjean to the utmost extent possible, and sent him to enforce a blockade of Fort St. David, so as to prevent any possible co-operation by the English with their detachment at Trichinápallí. By this means Kerjean's force was increased to 400 Europeans, 1,500 sipáhis, and 500 native horse.

The news of this vigorous action aroused Major Lawrence from his bed of sickness. Proceeding to Fort St. David by sea he arrived there on August 27, and on the following morning moved out at the head of 400 Europeans, 1,700 sipáhis, and 400 troops belonging to Muhammad Ali, to reconnoitre the French position. Strong as it was he resolved to attack it on the following day. But Kerjean, not confident as to the result of an action, retreated during the night to Báhur, two miles from Fort St. David, and the following evening,—Major Lawrence still advancing,—to Valianur, within three miles from Pondichery.

At this time Dupleix was momentarily expecting the arrival of a ship called the "Prince," having on board 700 men, and, what was of equal importance, a tried commander on Indian soil,—M. de la Touche. As Major Lawrence was forbidden by his instructions to attack the French in their position on French soil, it would have been wise policy on the part of the French

LAWRENCE AGAIN DEFEATS THE FRENCH.

commander to remain where he was until the reinforcements should arrive. But it would appear that Major Lawrence was equally aware of the hopes entertained regarding the "Prince," and he wisely bethought him of trading on the ambition of M. de Kerjean, who could scarcely expect to retain his command on the arrival of an officer with the reputation of de la Touche. He resolved, therefore, to move back to Báhur, hoping that Kerjean would followed him. The result fully answered his expectations.* Kerjean followed the English major the next day, and early on the morning of September 6 received the shock of his attack. The action was obstinate and bloody. The French received the assault with great intrepidity, crossing bayonets with the enemy. Their sipáhis, however, who were stationed in the centre, could not support the English charge and gave way in disorder. Their centre thus pierced, the whole line fell back, and fled in confusion. Kerjean himself, 15 officers, and about 100 men were taken prisoners. The number of the killed and wounded on the part of the French is not recorded. The English, however, lost one officer killed, four wounded, and 78 men killed or wounded.†

The worst result of the action for the French was the unfavourable effect it had upon the Maisurian and Marátha leaders. Of the warriors of the latter nation, 3,000 under Innis Khán, who were on the march to join the French, at once transferred their allegiance to Muhammad Ali, and the Maisurians deferred for a short time their plans against Trichinápallí. The work of Dupleix, however, had been two well performed for a defeat of this nature to cause its permanent failure.

---

* Major Lawrence states that Kerjean was forced to act thus by the repeated orders of Dupleix, and by the threat that he would be superseded by de la Touche. No authority is given for this assertion, and it can only be imagined that Kerjean, who was taken prisoner in the action, wished to clear himself at his uncle's expense. The movement was exactly that which Dupleix would have wished to delay.

† Orme; Lawrence's *Memoirs*.

CHAP. VII.
1752.

He promised the Maisurians that, if they could only take Trichinápallí, it should be theirs. The magic of his influence, still all-prevalent in the minds of the natives, was confirmed by the inaction of Lawrence after his victory. Thus it happened that, within six weeks of that action, the Maisurians and the Maráthás abandoned the English alliance, and declared openly for the French.

Another advantage before the termination of the campaign of 1752 accrued to the French governor. The greatest of his opponents, Clive, was forced before the close of the year to abandon the scene of his triumphs, and to proceed to Europe for the benefit of his health. It is true that he signalised the few months prior to his departure by two achievements, showing not less energy, daring, and military talent than had distinguished his early victories. We allude to the capture of the forts of Kóvlaon and Chengalpat; the former on the sea coast about midway between St. Thomé and Sadras, 16 miles south of Madras; the latter on the river Palar, commanding the high road between Fort St. George and Pondichery, and about 40 miles from the English Presidency. The capture of these two places is memorable from the fact that the 200 troops who formed the European portion of Clive's little army were raw recruits,* the sweepings of the English jails, and so little disciplined that on a shot from the fort of Kóvlaon killing one of them all the rest ran away. Nevertheless, even upon this rabble, Clive exercised an influence so magical; he won their respect to such an extent by his own contempt of danger and personal daring, his failing health notwithstanding; that at their head and by their means he reduced Kóvlaon, defeated a force of

---

* Lord Macaulay, in his essay on Clive, states that the force was of such a description that no officer but Clive would risk his reputation by commanding it. Orme, however, who was Lord Macaulay's authority for this statement, simply remarks, it could hardly be expected that any officer who had acquired reputation would willingly risk it by taking the command of them.

700 sipáhis and 40 Europeans sent by Dupleix to relieve it, and then marching on Chengalpat, the strongest place next to Jinjí in that part of the country, forced the French garrison of 40 Europeans and 500 sipáhis to evacuate it. He then proceeded to Madras, and thence to England.

Notwithstanding these losses, however, a careful survey of the position of Dupleix at the close of 1752, and a contrast with the state to which he had been reduced by the surrender of Law and d'Auteuil but six months before, will show how much his vast genius had been able within that short period to accomplish. To do this completely, his relations to the Directors of the Company of the Indies must be borne in mind. This Company, not possessing one-fourth part of the wealth of the English Company, had deceived itself by the hope that the position of Dupleix, as master of the Karnátik, was too assured, too secure for him to require any special aid from France. The Directors looked rather to Dupleix to transport to France vast sums of money. No doubt even up to the end of 1751, the position of Dupleix justified the public men in France in the most sanguine hopes as to the future of French India. But that was the very reason why real statesmen would have aided and supported him with all the means at their disposal. The transport of 2,000 or 3,000 men to Pondichery in 1751, would almost certainly have given France absolute possession of Southern India. She herself would not have felt the loss of that insignificant number of her soldiers, whilst they could scarcely have failed to gain for her the coveted prize. But instead of support of this nature the Directors literally starved Dupleix. They sent him comparatively a small number of ships, and no funds; the few men to serve as soldiers —to gain for France an empire greater than herself— were the off-scourings of the jails and the sweepings of the galleys. When he asked them for a competent general they sent him a Law. It is true that, elevated by the hopes they had formed from the success of his large schemes, they vouchsafed him flattering letters and a marquisate. These, however, were but cheap rewards which Dupleix would gladly have bartered for a few hundred of those brave troops who were idling their time in the garrisons of France. Thus left to his own resources we see him evoking material strength out of the slightest materials, drawing to himself allies, when, as it would appear, there remained to him nought but destruction. He thus succeeded because, in the first place, he possessed a genius for organisation of the highest order; because, in the second, he considered no sacrifice too great to be made for the glory and interests of France. Bitterly personal as was the hatred borne to him in that day by contemporary Englishmen, seizing as they did every occasion to attribute to him motives of personal ambition and personal vanity, even they were forced to admit his genius and his devotion to his country. "To give Dupleix his due," writes Major Lawrence in his memoirs, "he was not easily cast down; his pride supported him, and at the same time his mind was full of resources." Mr. Orme likewise admits that the French would have been compelled " to cease hostilities after the capture of Srirangam, had not M. Dupleix been endowed (and this at least is much to his honour) with a perseverance that even superseded his regard to his own fortune, of which he had at that time disbursed £140,000, and he continued with the same spirit to furnish more." It was this disinterestedness, this abnegation of his own interests when the interests of France were concerned, that gave him influence and authority with his own people, that gained the lasting admiration and respect of all the native princes with whom he came in contact. In Dupleix they recognised a man not only thoroughly in earnest, but who was proof against the ordinary consequences of disaster.

Never was he more full of resources than when apparently the well of those resources had been dried up. The princes of India never felt safe when they were opposed to that versatile intellect, to that resourceful genius. So thoroughly did the English recognise his magic power, that they kept their puppet, Muhammad Ali, in the strictest seclusion. Dupleix contrived, nevertheless, to correspond with Muhammad Ali. It was only, however, to receive an answer begging Dupleix not to impute to him the fault of his conduct, "for," added Muhammad Ali, "you know that I am no longer master of my actions."

Never, perhaps, was his genius more eminently displayed than after the catastrophe of Srirangam. Without troops he was exposed to the full fury of the victorious army of Lawrence and Clive, and though these were forbidden to attack Pondichery, they had it apparently in their power to reduce the French settlement to the most insignificant dimensions, to deprive it of all real power in the country, of all influence with the natives. Yet by raising up enemies within their own camp, Dupleix delayed their march from Trichinapállí, rendered any decided action on their part impossible, gained for himself that which of all other things was most necessary to him,—time,—and actually succeeded in less than two months after that great disaster, in beating in the field the victorious English, and in determining the most powerful native allies of that nation to transfer their material aid to the French colony. But for the precipitancy of Kerjean, the advantages gained by the English at Trichinápállí would have been quite neutralised.

It was, it must be admitted, an immense misfortune to Dupleix, that whilst his own commanders in the Karnátik were men of the most ordinary ability, and even, as in the case of Law, of marked imbecility of character, there should have been opposed to him the

CHAP. VII.
1752.

greatest genius for war of that epoch. The strong, sharp, incisive blows of Clive were terribly effective on the besotted leaders of the French forces; they were met by no counterstroke, by nought, in fact, but weakness and indecision. With a rough and determined hand Clive broke down the foundations of French dominion, infused a confidence into the English soldiers that never afterwards left them, and showed the world that the natives of India, when well led and when possessing confidence in their commander, are capable of evincing the best qualities of real soldiers, alike of courage and constancy, heroism and self-denial. But for this one man no diversion would have been attempted on Arkát, the English garrison would have remained dispirited in Trichinápallí, and, it is more than probable, would have yielded that city to the superior numbers of Law. But it was Clive that broke the spell of French invincibility: he it was who first showed his troops and the natives of the Karnátik that it was possible to conquer even the soldiers of Dupleix. He transferred, moreover, to the English troops that opinion of their own qualities in the field, which till his coming had been monopolised by the French. It was a hard destiny that brought to the overthrow of the plans of Dupleix, a genius so warlike, a mastery over men so unsurpassed.

Yet, though unsuccessful, on the whole, in the Karnátik, the victories of the French troops in another part of Indian soil, more than compensated in the mind of Dupleix for the calamities they sustained near the coast. French influence was still paramount, the reputation of the French arms still supreme, the power of the French governor still unquestioned, at the court of the Subadar. To gain that influence, to maintain that reputation, to increase that power, Dupleix had not hesitated to deprive himself of the services of his best, his only, general, even to risk his supremacy on the

Koromandel coast. Certainly in those days it was considered, even by the enemies of Dupleix, that the gain at Aurangábád far outweighed the losses in the Karnátik. To see how that gain was achieved, how French influence was so consolidated as to be for many years proof against the overthrow of French power at Pondichery, we must now devote a few pages to the romantic career of the energetic and stout-hearted Bussy.

CHAPTER VIII.

BUSSY TO 1754.

CHAP. VIII.
1751.

THE vigour and energy displayed by Bussy at Ambur and Jinjí, his prompt action at Kadapah, alike on the field of battle as after the death of Muzaffar Jang, his subsequent march through the entire breadth of the Dakhan, and his triumphant entry into Aurangábád on June 29, 1751, have been already adverted to.* What there then remained to him to accomplish, and how he accomplished it we have still to record.

But in order that we may obtain a complete and comprehensive view of the situation—that, transporting our minds to the past, we may gaze at a panorama from which the light of the present is excluded, so as to see the India of that day exactly as India then was—we purpose in the first place to give a brief retrospective sketch of the country known as the Dakhan, defining its original connexion with, and its degree of dependence upon, the empire of the Múghals.

The term Dakhan, or more correctly Dakhin, though embracing in its literal meaning the whole of the southern part of India, was always held by the Muhammadans, and has been since held by ourselves, to comprehend only that portion of southern India lying between the Narbadá and the Krishná. After the extinction of the Tughlik dynasty in 1399, there arose from the ruins of the Delhi monarchy six independent sovereignties south of the Narbadá. These were the states of Golkonda, Bíjápur, Aurangábád, Bídar,

* Chapter VI.

Birár,* and Khándesh. Of these, in the course of time, Birár merged into Aurangábád, and the greater part of Bídar into Golkonda, the remainder being swallowed up by Bíjápur. But with the accession of the House of Taimur to the throne, there commenced a struggle on the part of its representatives to conquer these ancient appanages of the empire. Their efforts were so far successful that in 1599 Khándesh was incorporated by Akbar into his dominions. Thirty-eight years later, Aurangábád, till then governed by the Nizám Sháhí dynasty, and the capital of which had been captured by Akbar in 1600, was finally conquered by Sháh Jahán. The dynasty of Adil Sháh in Bíjápur succumbed to his son and successor, Aurangzeb, in 1686; whilst the dynasty of Kútab Sháh in Golkonda, offered a successful resistance to that monarch but a year longer. Thus it happened that, twenty years before his demise, the whole of the country—lost to the crown of Delhi on the dissolution of the empire under Muhammad Tughlik—had recognised the supremacy of Aurangzeb.

It must not be imagined, however, that every portion of the three fallen monarchies of Golkonda, Bíjápur, and Aurangábád, stretching as they originally did to the sea to the westward, and comprising the cities of Puná and Satára, as well as Bíjápur and Golkonda, was in an equal degree subject to that monarch. Before even their conquest had been achieved, there had appeared the first germs of a power destined to rival, and finally to overshadow even, that of the Múghal. Commencing as a robber and a freebooter, Siváji succeeded in baffling, sometimes even in defeating, the armies of the Emperor. Leaving the capitals of the Musalman

---

* The Birár of those days did not include nearly so much territory as the kingdom of that name governed by the Marátha family of the Bhonsla. Nágpur itself did not form a part of it, being the capital of the adjoining province of Gondwána. Its capital was Elichpur.

dynasties to be occupied by the Mughals, he filched whole districts for himself. So successful had he been in such enterprises, that on his death, in 1679, he left as an inheritance to his son the western or seaboard portion of the territories that owed allegiance to the rulers of Aurangábád and Bíjápur. The consequence of this, and of the subsequent contest of the Maráthás with Aurangzeb, was that on the death of that prince in 1707, the territory called the Dakhan, dependent on Delhi, comprised the ancient kingdom of Golkonda, a portion of the old kingdom of Aurangábád, with Aurangábád itself, and but a small slice of Bíjápur. Dependent on this, however, was the long slip of 560 miles of territory on the eastern coast, known as the Karnátik. The western coast, with the exception of the parts occupied by the English and Portuguese, but including the cities of Puná, Satára, and Bíjápur, had become permanently Maráthá.

Aurangzeb was himself exercising regal functions in the Dakhan when his last illness attacked him at Ahmadnagar. On his death—February 21st, 1707—the authority in that quarter devolved upon his son, Azím Sháh, with whom was the best officer of the late Emperor, Zulfikár Khán. When, notwithstanding the efforts of Zulfikár, Azím Sháh was defeated and slain by his brother Sultan Muazzam, at Agra, in June of the same year, the latter so highly appreciated the talents of his opponent's general, that he at once appointed him Subadar of the Dakhan, conferring upon him at the same time the title of Amír-ul-umará, or lord of lords. Zulfikár, however, preferred the intrigues of the Delhi court to an independent viceroyalty. He accepted, indeed, the appointment, but, leaving Daud Khán Pani as his deputy, he joined Muazzam, who had assumed the title of Bahádur Sháh. On the death of this prince, in 1712, a grand opportunity was offered to Zulfikár for the exercise of the adroit baseness that with him was habitual. He took full advantage of it, so full indeed, that he very speedily met with the ordinary fate of unprincipled intriguers. For, having betrayed the Emperor Jahándár Sháh into the hands of his nephew Farukh Siyar, he was at once strangled by order of the new sovereign. Zulfikár was succeeded in the governorship of the Dakhan by Chin Kalich Khán, created Nizám-ul-Mulk, a title which has gone down to his descendants, the present rulers of Haidarábád.

Nizám-ul-Mulk, at a later period honoured by the title of " Asaf Jah," the " pillar of state,"* was Subadar of the Dakhan when the first contest for supremacy between the French and English began in the Karnátik. We have seen how in the early part of those struggles he imposed his law upon the contending parties, by the appointment, after the murder of Said Muhammad Khán, of his trusted lieutenant, Anwar-ud-dín, as Nawwáb of the Karnátik. His death, and the consequences resulting from it—the succession of his son Nasir Jang, his alliance with the English, his murder at the battle of Jinjí; the installation of Nasir Jang's nephew Muzaffar Jang, his death at the moment of victory over the revolted Nawwábs; and, finally, the elevation in his place of Salábat Jang, the next surreviving son of Nizám-ul-Mulk, have been already recorded.† We have now to see what sort of an inheritance it was upon which Salábat Jang thus entered, the obstacles that lay in his path, the difficulties that seemed to increase with every movement that he made. The office of Subadar of the Dakhan had not been an hereditary office. It had lain in the gift of the Emperor of Delhi. Now, at the time of the death of Nizám-ul-Mulk, the imperial throne had just fallen into the nominal possession of Ahmad Sháh, but that

---

* Literally, "the Asaf of dignity." The word "Asaf" is a proper name, supposed to be that of the Wazir of Solomon, and indicates the possession of the highest wisdom.
† Chapters III. and VI.

monarch found himself too beset with difficulties of his own to pay much attention to the affairs of the Dakhan. It was in consequence of this, and of the increasing anarchy at Delhi in succeeding reigns, that the satrapy of Haidarábád—the appointment to the government of which still remained nominally with the Emperor— came to be regarded virtually as an appanage of the family of Nizám-ul-Mulk. It was, however, the knowledge that the real appointment was vested in the Emperor, which induced the various claimants of the family of Nizám-ul-Mulk to the Subadárí to fortify their pretensions by the publication of an imperial firman. It was by virtue of such a rescript, real or pretended, that on the death of Nizám-ul-Mulk, his son, Nasir Jang, set forth his claims to be his successor. Relying upon the same authority, the validity of which was equally doubtful, Muzaffar Jang disputed those claims. When death had removed these two competitors, and the French general, Bussy, had elevated the third son of Nizám-ul-Mulk, Salábat Jang, to the dignity, that nobleman, records Mr. Orme, " did not think it safe to appear in sight of the capital before he had acted the stale but pompous ceremony of receiving from the hands of an ambassador, said to be sent by the Great Mughal, letters patent, appointing him viceroy of all the countries which had been under the jurisdiction of his father, Nizám-ul-Mulk."

Salábat Jang, however, was but the third son of that famous viceroy. The elder brother, Gházi-ud-dín, had indeed, as we have stated, preferred, on the death of his father, to give a sullen acquiescence in the elevation of his second brother, Nasir Jang, to the Subadárí, rather than to plunge into a contest with one who had taken care to possess himself of his father's treasure. But time had changed the aspect of affairs. Nasir Jang had gone, Muzaffar Jang had gone, and in their stead reigned Salábat Jang—a man born in luxury, unused to govern, effeminate, slothful, and possessing an almost empty treasury. This state of things presented an opportunity for self-aggrandisement, which, in the decline of the Mughal Empire, few possessed sufficient virtue to resist. Gházi-ud-dín at least had not that virtue. Through the agency of Mulhar Ráo Holkar, he opened negotiations with the Peshwá, Báláji Bájí Ráo, and succeeded in inducing the great chief of the Maráthás to support his pretensions.

We have seen how the difficulty presented by this alliance had been momentarily overcome. A present of two lakhs of rupees, during his march to Golkonda, had induced the Marátha general to retire. Such presents, however, ever form but incitements to new attacks. From the date of his triumphant entry into Aurangábád—June 29, 1751—to the autumn of the same year, Salábat Jang had indeed lived unthreatened. During that interval, however, Gházi-ud-dín and Báláji Bájí Ráo had had time to cement their plans, and it soon became but too clear that the prospect of a larger bribe had combined with the promises of Gházi-ud-dín to determine the Peshwá to make a new and more formidable attack upon the Dakhan on the earliest and most convenient occasion. Affairs in that quarter being thus threatening, we may proceed to inquire how they were influenced by the conduct of Bussy; how, likewise, his presence in the capital of that division of the empire affected, or was likely to affect, the plans which Dupleix was evolving for the growth of a French empire in India.

The march of Bussy to Aurangábád in 1751, at the head of a force of 300 Europeans and 2,000 disciplined sipáhis, his overthrow during that march of the three conspiring Nawwábs, his prompt elevation of Salábat Jang to the office and dignity of Subadar, had had the primary effect of making the French absolute masters of the situation. Bussy had, indeed, been a consenting party to the payment of two lakhs of rupees to Báláji Bájí Ráo, as the price of his retreat, but solely because he considered, and rightly considered, that the possession of the capital, and the peaceful occupation of the country, in the first instance, were objects which could scarcely be purchased too dearly. Arriving at Aurangábád, he so ordered his conduct that, whilst nominally the faithful ally, he might really be the master, of the Subadar. To this end he selected as his own residence, and as the place to be occupied by his troops, a fortress at one of the extremities of the city, and completely commanding it. On the defences of this he mounted his guns, and disposed his detachment in such a manner that it might be ready for immediate service. He established amongst his men the most rigorous discipline. No soldier was permitted to leave the fort but at a fixed hour and at a fixed time, and not even then without the written permission of the commandant. Punishments, more or less severe, according to the offence, followed every infraction of discipline. The result was all that could be desired. There were neither bouts of drunkenness amongst the soldiers themselves, nor quarrels or altercations with the townspeople. The richest and most valuable goods were freely displayed under the protection of the French soldiery. Indeed, their conduct at Aurangábád was so exemplary, that the natives soon came to admire them for their courtesy, as much as they had before feared and esteemed them for their valour.*

Nor was Bussy for a long time less happy or less successful in his dealings with the Subadar and his courtiers. It was impossible that a man possessing any discrimination of character could be long associated with Salábat Jang, without noticing the weakness of

* The account of the proceedings of Bussy from 1751 to 1754 is based upon the memoir and correspondence of Dupleix, the histories of Orme, Wilks, and Grant Duff, and the "Sëir Mutákherin."

his nature. Few could fail to see that in a Government like that of the Dakhan—a Government quasi-independent, but which, notwithstanding, a powerful Emperor at Delhi might at any moment reclaim, a Government which, thus founded on no solid or permanent foundation, was exposed to the incessant attacks of the encroaching power of the Maráthás—everything must depend on the character of the ruler. If that ruler were weak and unstable; if he had no resources within himself, no mental energies upon which to fall back and to depend, it was certain that he must become the sport of fortune, the tool and instrument of the strongest mind that had access to him. Now, Salábat Jang, Bussy early divined, was that weak and unstable nature, and he determined that no one but himself should play the part of the strong-minded counsellor. In the force which he commanded he had one instrument upon which he could count to enable him to attain the desired position. It was not, indeed, that he displayed, or intended to display, his troops in an attitude of menace. He was far too wise for that. He shut them up, as we have seen, in a fortress, and drilled them into courtesy and gentleness. But the moral effect of that force was increased thereby tenfold. Whilst they excited no jealousy, not a man but knew what they had done, what they could do, what they were ready to attempt, at the slightest word from Bussy. His power of restraining such a force added greatly to the influence of its presence.

But it was not upon the force that he entirely relied. That was indeed the basis of his power; but a less able man might notwithstanding have used the influence given him by so strong a position to little purpose. Bussy trusted for the success of his plans to his own acquaintance with native character. Though frank, open, and conciliatory, he was in those days, before yet age and gout had begun to undermine his faculties, a

A A

model of resolution and tact. He had spent many years in India in close contact with the natives, more especially with those of high rank, and he understood them thoroughly. He had, too, the advantage of possessing a settled plan. Before leaving Pondichery he had concerted with Dupleix the manner in which he was to carry on his relations with Muzaffar Jang, and he anticipated no difficulty in following his instructions to the letter now that he had to deal with the more facile character of Salábat. A glance at the map of India, and a recollection of the history of that period, will show how vast, how gigantic, yet, under ordinary circumstances, how feasible was this plan. Separated by the Vindhya range from the disorganised empire proper of the Múghal, the possessor of the Muhammadan province of the Dakhan seemed to be in a position to be able to give law to the whole of south-eastern India. He commanded a large army, and ruled over a warlike population. He was the liege lord of the ruler of the Karnátik, and he wielded in that province itself the authority of the Mughal. He was thus the possessor of the moral and physical power; he had the right to use force, and the force ready to be used; and in those days, when the name of the Mughal was everything, and the reputation of the European settlers comparatively nothing, that double power was, if not an irresistible, yet a very potent, lever.

This being the position of the province known as the Dakhan, and this the power of its ruler, can we greatly blame that policy which at a moment when France had all but overcome her hated rival in the Karnátik, determined, without striking a blow, to make that position and that influence purely French? What a vista did it not hold out to a patriotic ambition! What dreams of empire, what visions of imperial dominion! Possessing the Karnátik, by this policy gaining the Dakhan, the minarets of the Jami Masjid, and the jewelled ornaments of the peacock-throne seemed near enough to excite the fancy and to stimulate to irresistible action! This tempting vision offered yet another advantage. It seemed so easy of accomplishment. Knowing the native character so thoroughly as did Dupleix, he was well aware that notwithstanding the obligations under which the reigning Subadar might be to the French, they would all be forgotten unless he were continually reminded of their power as a people—unless he had constantly before his eyes evidence of their superiority. It was therefore, primarily, not less to maintain French influence at the court of the Subadar, than to support the pretensions of Muzaffar Jang, that Bussy had been directed to accompany that prince to Aurangábád. Dupleix did not doubt that with the French troops under a soldier-diplomatist in occupation of his capital, engaged to support the Subadar; and, what was of more consequence, with the Subadar himself feeling that he could depend upon them alone to support him; the soldier-diplomatist, if he were skilful and able, would inevitably draw to himself the whole influence of the province, that he would shape its foreign policy, and inspire its political action—that he, in fact, would become the omnipotent mayor of the palace, the Subadar subside into the powerless automaton.

Thus to divide his forces and to lose the services of his ablest general in the presence of such an enemy as the English, who had the sea as their base of operations, was undoubtedly to run a great risk. Yet before we condemn Dupleix too harshly for running such a risk, we must point to the situation of affairs on the coast at that time. The two nations were nominally at peace. The entire Karnátik and Trichinápallí, with the sole exception of the town of that name, had acknowledged Chanda Sáhib as Nawwáb. The English had positively refused to assist Muhammad Ali in the defence of that city. But, even were he to succeed in persuading them to do so, it seemed as though Dupleix had nothing to fear from their efforts, for Lawrence, their ancient leader, was absent, the genius of Clive had not then been discovered, and Dupleix knew and rated at its real value the capacity of such men as Gingens and Cope. Could he foretell that out of that dispirited colony of baffled enemies, who, not even venturing to remove their seat of Government to Madras, remained cooped up in Fort St. David, idle spectators of his daring enterprise, there would arise one of the most consummate leaders of the age? Ought he to have acted as though such a contingency were possible? Yes, undoubtedly, if we are to judge men by the highest standard, if we are to make no allowances for human impulses and human passions, we are bound to declare that he ought so to have acted. Before sending Bussy to the Dakhan, he ought at least, as a measure of wise precaution, to have made sure of Trichinápallí, to have crushed the last rival of Chanda Sáhib. Had he done that—had he thus deprived the English of all pretext to interfere, and had he then been able to send Bussy to Aurangábád—the Karnátik would have been his, the Dakhan would have become his, and before long, all India south of the Vindhya range would have acknowledged the supremacy of the French.

Still, though it was a great, as it turned out, indeed, a fatal fault, who will assert, that in the presence of so great a temptation, and in the prospect, seemingly certain, of repose in the Karnátik—for, it will be remembered, Muhammad Ali had lulled the suspicions of Dupleix by promises to surrender—who, we say, will assert that such a fault ought to be imputed as a fatal mistake to the illustrious Frenchman? We must recollect that the moment was so opportune—Muzaffar Jang going to take possession of his government, the necessity that he should be accompanied by a body of Frenchmen so urgent, the peace of the Karnátik so assured—that there seemed but small necessity for the services on the spot of a Bussy. To Dupleix it must have appeared as if he incurred a very small and a very distant risk, in order at once to grasp a very present and very certain gain—a gain which must have an enormous effect on the result of any future struggles in the Karnátik. Can we even blame him much, if he, looking into the future with but human eyesight, decided to run that small risk? The prospect, indeed, was so peculiarly alluring to a brilliant imagination, that Dupleix would not have been Dupleix had he decided to neglect or to defer it.

As it was, everything seemed at first to favour the daring plans of the French governor. He could not certainly have been more fitly or more ably represented than by the clever and versatile Bussy. We have already noticed the skilful and unobtrusive manner in which this officer disposed his soldiers in Aurangábád. His own conduct was based upon the same principle. To appear as nothing, yet to be everything in the State; to show himself to the world as the commandant of the French contingent, maintaining in the eyes of the natives by his lavish expenditure and outward show the dignity of that office; to direct in secret all the foreign relations of the Government, to make all their acts chime in with French interests. In this manner he laid the foundations of an influence destined to survive the loss of power and prestige at Pondichery, and which, had that power and that prestige not fallen, would, in all probability, have worked with a most decisive effect on the events that were to follow. From the date of the arrival of Bussy in Aurangábád, on June 29, 1751, all his efforts were directed to the establishment of this occult influence. He entirely succeeded. Very little time elapsed before he had brought Salábat Jang to the persuasion that the safety of his person depended on the presence of the French troops at his capital, and that the security of his empire could be best assured by his following the counsels of the French general. The latter kept himself all this time studiously in the background. His secret influence, however, was exerted to appoint as ministers of the Subadar men whom he believed to be devoted to himself; and although he was more than once, as we shall see, deceived by the superior *finesse* of Asiatic intriguers, he never wanted the boldness and promptitude to repair every error, and even to use to the advantage of his country the opportunity afforded him by the attempts to weaken his influence.

Whilst Bussy was thus employed in laying the foundation of French power at the court of the Subadar, the intelligence reached him of the alliance between Ghází-ud-dín and the Maráthás, having for its object the expulsion of the French nominee, Salábat Jang. Whilst, in all probability, Bussy would have preferred to pursue that task of consolidation which would have enabled him to employ the resources of the Dakhan in aid of the French designs in the Karnátik, he can scarcely have regretted the opportunity, which this threatened invasion seemed likely to afford him, of teaching the warlike inhabitants of western India to respect French discipline and French valour. Whilst, therefore, the news, that Ghází-ud-dín himself was advancing from the north at the head of 150,000 and Báláji Bájí Ráo from the west with 100,000 men, spread consternation and dismay in the court of Aurangábád, whilst some counselled retreat, and others even entered into negotiations with the invader, Bussy himself remained calm and unmoved. When called upon by the Subadar for his opinion, he gave him advice of the same nature as that which Clive a little later gave to Governor Saunders— advice which stamped him at once as the man for the occasion:—"Care not," he said, "for the invading army, you will best preserve the Dakhan by marching upon Puná." It is a signal proof of his great influence at the court of the Subadar, that this bold advice was promptly followed. The better to make his preparations the Subadar had moved from Aurangábád to Golkonda. When, after many days, he ascertained that the allied enemies had begun their movements from two opposite directions upon Aurangábád, he, accompanied by Bussy, and in pursuance of the plan suggested by him, broke up from that place, and, leaving Aurangábád to its fate, marched upon Bídar,* the original capital of the ancient kingdom of that name. Besides the large but irregular army of Salábat Jang, Bussy had with him 500 French troops in the highest state of discipline, and 5,000 drilled sipáhis. Meanwhile, no sooner was the rainy season over, than Báláji Báji Ráo entered the Dakhan, and, proceeding on the true Marátha principle of making war support war, ravaged the country on every side. It is not to be imagined that he had any particular regard for Ghází-ud-dín, or any particular hatred of Salábat Jang. With him it was simply a matter of business. Whilst the two Muhammadans were fighting for the sovereignty of the province, it was for him to hold aloof until one was thoroughly beaten, and both were completely exhausted.

* Grant Duff and the author of the "Sëir Mutákherin" both state that Ahmadnagar was the town upon which the Subadar marched after leaving Golkonda. Mr. Orme on the contrary indicates Bídar. We are inclined to believe that in this instance Mr. Orme is correct. The Maráthás were marching on Aurangábád from Puná, and their natural route would take them through Ahmadnagar. Considering that Ghází-ud-dín was likewise marching upon Aurangábád, a movement of Bussy upon Ahmadnagar would certainly not have had the effect of alarming Báláji-Báji Ráo about the safety of Puná. On the other hand, Bídar lies in the direct route from Golkonda, where Bussy then was, to Puná, and it is the place whence the most telling attack could be made on the Marátha's territory. We can easily imagine how the intelligence of an expedition starting for Puná from that place, would inevitably bring down Báláji from the north to protect his capital. Elliott's *History of India by its own Historians* (vol. viii., page 318) states distinctly that Ghází-ud dín marched on and occupied Aurangábád, and that Salábat Jang, on hearing this, marched forth to meet him.

Action on his part, then, would give a large slice of the Dakhan to the Maráthás. Meanwhile, little dreading any movement on the part of Salábat Jang, he proposed to enrich himself and his followers by the plunder of the border provinces of the Dakhan. The bold march of Bussy upon Bídar, however, entirely disconcerted these plans. Still more was Báláji troubled when he saw that the enemy had no intention whatever of remaining at Bídar, but were moving thence direct upon his capital. Renouncing at once all thoughts of the invasion of the Dakhan, Báláji hastened to proceed to the defence of his dominions. He was at the head of a numerous army, confident in its leader, and in whom that leader reposed the fullest trust. Very often had he led them to victory, more than once indeed over this same army of the Dakhan, which now had the presumption to invade the sacred soil of the Maráthás. Could he doubt the result now? Of the foreigners who accompanied the army of Salábat he might indeed have heard, but the smallness of their numbers was sufficient to deprive them of any formidable character. They, besides, had never come in contact with a regular Marátha army; had never been called upon to repel those sweeping charges of cavalry, which had so often proved fatal to the armies of the Muhammadans.

Selecting then 40,000 of his best horse, and leaving the remainder to follow, Báláji hastened to bar the road to Puná, and, if possible, to destroy the enemy at a blow. The Subadar with his French allies had but just left Bídar *en route* to Puná, when they learned the approach of the Maráthás. In accordance with the Muhammadan tactics they formed up to await their attack. Bussy, however, so planted his guns, consisting of ten field-pieces, as to command the ground over which the enemy must charge. Having done this and placed his infantry in line of support, he calmly awaited the approach of Báláji.

It was indeed the first time that the Maráthás had regularly met a European enemy on the open field—for the Marátha contingent in the Karnátik had consisted of comparatively a handful, and they had there acted the part of auxiliary skirmishers rather than of an independent force. But Bussy had now before him the flower of the Marátha army—and of the Marátha army in its best form. The Maráthás were at that time the rising power of Hindustan. The warriors of that people had not then begun to depart from the traditions, an adherence to which had made them a nation. Their splendid horsemanship, their long endurance, their ability to move without tents, without baggage of any sort, without other supplies than those which each individual soldier carried upon his horse, had combined with their daring tactics to render them superior to those Muhammadan armies, which a long course of misgovernment and want of system had ruined. The luxurious equipments of the armies of Aurangzeb formed a striking contrast to the unostentatious camps of Akbar, and from the time of the death of Aurangzeb even the appearance of discipline had ceased. The Mughal armies, hopeless of victory, conscious of the incapacity of their leaders, half beaten before they had struck a blow, felt themselves unfit to make head against the new power that was gradually overwhelming southern India.

Bussy was well aware of this. Full well did he know that the issue of the contest that day depended upon himself and his soldiers, upon those French whom he had led almost across the continent; who, starting from the waters of the Bay of Bengal, were now straining their eyes to gaze upon the Arabian Sea. He waited for attack, however, full of confidence. At length it came. The clouds of dust, the loud tramp of countless horses, could forebode nothing else. It was clear that 40,000 of the choicest horsemen of the East were about that day to endeavour to surpass all their former deeds of valour. At full speed, though without order, with spear in rest, shouting victory, they charged. But the nerves of the little band of Frenchmen were not shaken. Standing at their guns, they waited coolly the order of their commander. When it came, discharges of grape and cannister, not single but continued, combined with a never-ceasing file firing from the infantry, told the Marátha horsemen what kind of enemy this was against whom they would have to contend for empire. The result was never doubtful. After a few rounds the Marátha horse could bear no more. They turned their horses' heads and disappeared.* Bussy was not the man to allow a victory to remain barren. He pursuaded the Subadar to march instantly towards Puná, not stopping to listen to the offers of the Peshwá for accommodation, but to move straight upon the capital.

There were, however, as is usual with an oriental army, wheels within wheels. Báláji Báji Ráo was on bad terms with Tárá Báí, the grandmother of the youthful Rájá of Satára, and she was even then disputing his right to govern for her grandson. With her, therefore, to weaken Báláji, the advisers of Salábat Jang had entered into communication. On the other hand, Báláji, recognising at once the value of the services rendered by the French contingent to the Subadar, endeavoured, by all those means so common at an oriental court, to excite amongst the the nobles of the Dakhan jealousy of the French leader, by attributing to him personal motives and private ambition. We shall see that both these efforts bore their fruit in their season.

Little caring for, probably ignorant of, these intri-

---

* The author of the "Sëir Mutákherin," a Muhammadan, thus writes of the battle, "Báláji Ráo, without suffering him (Salábat Jang) to come so far (as Puná), met him half way with an army of 50,000 horse, but was defeated; at which time the French with their musketry and their expeditious artillery drew smoke from the Marátha breasts."

gues, Bussy, still prevailing with the Subadar, moved on until he found himself once more in the vicinity of the Marátha army at Rájápur on the Gur river. The time was propitious for an attack. An eclipse of the moon had called all the Hindus to their devotions, and Bussy was resolved to take advantage of their superstition to beat up their quarters. It was a new thing to his Muhammadan allies to witness this attempt to fight the Maráthás with their own weapons—to attempt to surprise those who had owed a great part of their success to their own quickness and vigilance. So great was their opinion of the Maráthás that this attack seemed to them, witnesses as they had been of the flight of the cavalry of Báláji in the open field, to savour more of rashness than prudence. Nevertheless Bussy attempted it. Taking advantage of the moment when the eclipse of the moon would, as he believed, engross all the attention of the enemy, he moved upon their camp, and opened suddenly a fire of artillery and small arms. The surprise was complete. Báláji himself, who was "busy at his devotions, and naked, had hardly time to throw himself on an unsaddled mare, on which he saved his life by flying with all his might."* His example was followed by his entire army, and though the accounts of the slaughter vary,† it is certain that the Maráthás lost an immense quantity of booty, and that a heavy blow was dealt to their prestige as warriors. Proportionately, and even more than proportionately, did the victory increase the reputation of Bussy. It can easily be understood on how high an elevation those who had so dreaded Marátha dash and daring must

---

* Sëir Mutákherin.

† Grant Duff asserts, on the authority of Marátha accounts, that the surprise was incomplete, and that the Maráthás did not suffer materially. The author of the "Sëir Mutákerin" states, on the other hand, that the Maráthás "were set upon in the night, and with so much success, that they lost a vast number of men, whom the French consumed in shoals at the fire altars of their artillery." Grant Duff admits that this action had an immense effect in raising Bussy's reputation.

have placed the man who knew thus how to avail himself of their weaknesses.

The day following this exploit, November 23, 1751, Bussy advanced towards Puná, the Maráthás contenting themselves with hovering about his flanks, and endeavouring, though unsuccessfully, to impede his advance. On the 24th he attacked and destroyed the town of Taligaon. Two days later, Báláji made another desperate effort to recover his lost prestige. Some of the most famous Maráthá chieftains—amongst them the sons of Ránují Sindhiá and Kunir Trimbak Yekbuti—were chosen to lead a renewed attack on the allied camp. On November 27 this attack was made, the enemy charging the native troops of Salábat Jang, dashing through every obstacle and completely overwhelming them. It seemed for an instant as though it would be impossible to restore the day. The little band of Frenchmen all this time, however, maintained their position, threatened but not assailed. At last, noting the slaughter of his allies, Bussy changed his front and brought his guns to bear upon the masses of hostile cavalry with such effect, that they retreated from the field they had almost gained, and gave time to the troops of the Subadar to rally from their disorder. The next day the town of Korigaon on the Bhíma was occupied by Bussy, who thus found himself within twenty miles of the capital of the Peshwá.

It formed no essential part of the plan of Salábat Jang, however, to make any conquests from the Maráthás. His interests pointed rather to breaking up the confederacy between that people and Ghází-ud-dín, even, if possible, to forming an alliance with those who had been the allies of his rival. Swayed by the wise counsels of Bussy he had, in the presence of two armies, each superior to his own, succeeded not only in preventing a junction which would have overwhelmed him, but in forcing the one army to meet him on the ground he had chosen, and in so dealing with it as to convince he had chosen, and in so dealing with it as to convince its leader that it was for his interest to ally himself with him, rather than with his competitor for the rule of the Dakhan. Thus, after the last battle, the Peshwá began to consider whether it was necessary or advisable to continue the contest further. Any nearer approach to Puná or Satára might, he felt, give to the partisans of Tárá Báí a weight sufficient to endanger his own influence and power. He accordingly opened negotiations with Salábat Jang, and although these were protracted, owing to some difficulties raised by that nobleman, an armistice was concluded at the beginning of the year.

Salábat Jang was anxious to come to an understanding with the Maráthás, the more so as his own army, badly organised and worse officered, was almost in a state of mutiny. The men had some reason for their discontent, for their pay was considerably in arrear, and the officers, especially the superior officers, for the most part uneducated in their profession, were jealous of the credit gained by the French. They constantly insinuated that Bussy had ulterior objects in view which a prolongation of hostilities alone could procure for him. But there was another reason not less potent. Ghází-ud-dín was approaching Aurangábád, and it was an object with Salábat to deal with him whilst yet the recollection of the recent campaign should be fresh in the minds of the Maráthás. The advice given by Bussy, under these circumstances, was worthy of his reputation for tact and skill. The French leader had not been unobservant of the signs of discontent. But it had seemed to him even less desirable for French interests than for those of the Subadar, to march upon Puná. He resolved, therefore, to act in such a manner as at the same time to allay those discontents, and to further the interests of his countrymen. He accordingly supported the propositions in favour of peace, both openly and in private, thus alike disarming his enemies and gaining still more entirely the confidence of the Subadar.

The armistice concluded, the army returned towards Golkonda, overthrowing on the way some refractory rájás who had refused tribute. But in the course of its march an incident occurred which called for the prompt action of Bussy. The Prime Minister of the Subadar, Rájá Raghunáth Dáss, a man devoted to French interests, was assassinated by some of the Affghán soldiers of the army, whose officer the rájá had insulted. It then became necessary to arrange that a fitting person should be appointed in his place. And here Bussy for the first time allowed himself to be over-reached. He had met at the court of the Subadar a nobleman of ability and skilful address, Saiyid Lashkar Khán. This man had divined the designs of the French, hated their persons, and dreaded their influence. Nevertheless, in order the better to counteract their plans, he dissembled his sentiments, and pretended for Bussy in particular the greatest devotion and esteem. He hoped by his means and by his influence to obtain office under the Subadar, intending, after he should have obtained it, to use all his power to thwart the French policy and to undermine the position of the French leader. Bussy was completely taken in. Believing Saiyid Lashkar to be the man he represented himself to be, he recommended him to the Subadar as a fit successor to the deceased rájá, and obtained for him the appointment.

There was, however, much for Bussy to effect before the intrigues which Saiyid Lashkar instantly set on foot should have time to work. Ghází-ud-dín yet lived and threatened. So far indeed from abating his pretensions in consequence of the defeat of Báláji, he had stirred up the Bhonsla to attack the Dakhan in the north-east, whilst he himself, with Malhar Ráo Holkar to assist him, should enter it through the gate of Aurangábád. The threatened invasion of Hindustan by Ahmad Sháh

Abdálí had, indeed, combined with the hostile attitude of the Rohillas, and the consequent intrigues at the court of Delhi, to detain Gházi-ud-dín at that capital longer than he had anticipated. By degrees, however, the difficulties in the way of his departure were removed, and in the month of September, 1752, he reached Aurangábád with an army computed at 150,000 men.

Then began those intricacies of intrigue such as are seen only in an oriental court. There were assembled at Aurangábád, Gházi-ud-dín, whose real and avowed object was to obtain the sovereignty of the Dakhan, and to obtain which he was ready to sacrifice a portion of it to the Maráthás; on the side of that people, Báláji, supported by Holkar and the Bhonsla, was endeavouring to persuade each of the rivals to offer him a higher bid than the other. Salábat Jang had there no avowed representative, although his minister, Saiyid Lashkar, was present at the conferences. This man, however, the better to carry out his plans, had persuaded his master to connive at the fiction that he had been dismissed from the office of Diwán, and had, therefore, proceeded as a discontented noble to the confederates. In this way, he urged, he could better worm out their secrets. His real object, however, was to cement to the utmost of his power the alliance between the Maráthás and Gházi-ud-dín, with the view of expelling Salábat Jang, and, with him, the French general and his troops.

The right of Gházi-ud-dín, as the eldest son of his father, gave him in this dispute a moral influence, which was not without its effect on the nobles of the Dakhan, and which very much disturbed Salábat Jang himself. It is possible that under the circumstances, and in the face of the Marátha alliances, which Gházi-ud-dín had at length cemented by the offer of a considerable sacrifice of territory, he might have been inclined to listen to a compromise, when an event occurred which

CHAP. VIII.
1751.

removed the necessity for further negotiations. Living at Aurangábád in the ancient palace of the Subadars was one of the widows of Nizám-ul-Mulk—she who had borne him but one son, the next in order to Salábat Jang, Nizám Alí. All the hopes of this lady were concentrated in the ardent desire to see this son sitting on the viceregal seat of his father. Between that wish and its accomplishment there were however two obstacles. One of these, Salábat Jang, was out of her reach; the other, Gházi-ud-dín, was at Aurangábád. To thrust him out of the path she wished her son to follow she had no scruple as to the means by which such a result might be obtained. She accordingly invited Gházi-ud-dín to a feast, and in a dish of which she persuaded him to partake, telling him truly that it had been prepared with her own hands, she poisoned him. Ghazi-ud-dín died that night.

The commission of this crime left Salábat Jang without an avowed competitor for the office of Subadar of the Dakhan. He had still, however, before him the whole force of the Maráthás, not only the army of the Peshwá, but, united with it, those of Holkar and the Bhonsla. The ruler of the Muhammadan state of Búrhánpur, who had before declared for Gházi-ud-dín, now announced his intention to stand by his engagements with the Maráthás. There remained then to Salábat Jang the alternative of a murderous and doubtful war, or the resignation to the Maráthás, offered by Gházi-ud-dín, of the territory west of Bírar from the Tapti to the Godávarí. The decision was left by the Subadar to Bussy, and he regarding a solid peace on such conditions as more favourable alike to the interests of the French and the Subadar than a doubtful war, recommended compliance with the terms offered, stipulating only that the Bhonsla should retire beyond the Waingangá river. This stipulation was agreed to, and peace was proclaimed.

These arrangements having been completed, Saiyid Lashkar returned, unsuspected, to his office of Diwán, and the Subadar, who, accompanied by Bussy and his army, had been moving in the direction of Aurangábád, set out for Haidarábád, destined thenceforth to be the capital of the Dakhan. This was in the early part of 1753. During the year that had passed, Bussy in addition to his own duties had been in constant communication with Dupleiz, had watched and lamented over the incapacity of Law without being able to draw him from his embarrassment, and had shown in every letter his own readiness to be employed for the best advantage of France. In the course of it he learned the decline and death of Chanda Sáhib, at the same time that he received from Dupleix intimation as to the utter unfitness of him who should have been his successor. Under these circumstances he applied himself with untiring zeal to use his position at the court of the Subadar for the benefit of France. How, he thought, could this be more strenuously carried out than by the appointment of Dupleix himself to be Nawwáb of the Karnátik. This appointment had indeed been conferred upon Dupleix by Muzaffar Jang, but, from motives of policy, Dupleix had made over the dignity of the office to Chanda Sáhib. On the death of this latter, was it to revert to Dupleix, for him either to administer the office himself or to appoint a deputy in his place, or was he to suffer it to be bestowed upon some possible enemy of the French power? To such a question there could be but one reply. By his influence with the Subadar, with whom the nomination legally rested, the confirmation only of the court of Delhi being required, Bussy procured the issue of the patent for the investiture of Dupleix, the receipt of which at Pondichery we noticed in our last chapter.

We have now described to our readers the manner in which Bussy was employed during that trying period,

CHAP. VIII.
1753.

when the unassisted genius of Dupleix had to contend against the steadfastness of Lawrence and the genius of Clive. Although the scene of his action continued to be still distant from Pondichery, yet his movements were so intimately connected with the policy of Dupleix, that we propose to continue the account of them up to the moment when, in an evil hour for the interests of the French, their greatest proconsul was recalled to be another victim to the besotted Government he had served but too well.

The year upon which he was now entering, 1753, was to see Bussy exposed to many trials; to witness his successful over-riding of the dangers and artifices peculiarly calculated to test the qualities of a statesman; to show how vain are troops and resources and strong military positions, when there is not a real man to command them. In the month of January, just after peace had been concluded with the Maráthás, and whilst the Subadar was on his return march to Haidarábád, Bussy, worn out by fatigue and exposure, was suddenly prostrated by sickness. So severe was the attack, that, unwilling as he was, at a moment so critical, to relax his grasp of the threads of the various negotiations in which he was engaged, he was nevertheless forced, in obedience to the directions of his medical advisers, to consent to proceed for change of air to Machhlipatan. The reluctance with which he allowed himself to be persuaded was due mainly to his conviction, that, just at that precise period, the maintenance of the influence of the French depended almost wholly on his own presence at the court of the Subadar. He had no one near him to whom he could intrust those delicate negotiations; not a single officer in whose judgment, even in whose ability to maintain discipline over his troops, he could place any confidence. His second in command, M. Goupil, was a man of the most ordinary abilities—one of those simple characters whose want of imaginative power constantly exposes them to the machinations of intriguers. To leave the force in his hand, even had Bussy possessed, as he supposed, a devoted friend in Saiyid Lashkar, was indeed a risk: to leave it with him, when that Diwán was his determined though secret foe, was to expose it to almost inevitable disgrace. Fortunate was it for Bussy, that in the state of weakness to which his malady had reduced him he never once suspected the secret object to which all the machinations of Saiyid Lashkar were directed. It is scarcely too much to suppose that the shock of such a discovery and the endeavour to counteract its effects would have been fatal to him. But, though not suspecting it, the prospect of his departure caused him terrible uneasiness. But there was no help for it, he must have rest and change and relaxation or he must die. With a heavy heart, then, he set out, leaving his place to Goupil, his counsels to the Subadar and Saiyid Lashkar, and promising to all a speedy return, little imagining the form and fashion which that return would take.

No sooner had the Subadar reached Haidarábád after his departure, than the Diwán commenced the secret machinations, by means of which he hoped to effect a permanent breach between the Subadar and the French, to rid the country, in a word, of the latter. In this course the weakness and indecision of Goupil came greatly to his aid. We have before adverted to to the strict discipline which, from the time of his arrival at Aurangábád, Bussy had introduced into his army, and we have pointed out how the exact and rigorous order which he enforced had contributed to the confidence of the people, even to their affection for their European allies. General as such feelings were among the population, they were far more deeply implanted in the breast of the Subadar himself. Salábat Jang had not been a careless spectator of the fate of his relatives. The fact that his own brother, Nasir

Jang, and his nephew, Muzaffar Jang, had both been treacherously slain by their own vassals, had impressed him with the advantage of having in his immediate vicinity a body of men unconnected with his nobles, upon whom he could fully and entirely rely, whose support would enable him to make a successful stand against the worst form of rebellion. He had determined, therefore, at the outset, never to separate himself from the French. To them he ad been indebted for his quasi-regal position; depending upon them only he felt that he could maintain it. These resolutions in their favour had been confirmed and strengthened by the signal services rendered by Bussy in the war with the Maráthás, not less than by the exact discipline which he had maintained amongst his men.

On the departure of Bussy, however, the Subadar not only lost the man with whom alone, of all the French, he was accustomed to hold confidential intercourse, but he witnessed likewise, very soon after, a marked change in the conduct alike of officers and soldiers. Goupil, in fact, was not even a disciplinarian; he was simply good-natured and weak. The regulations which Bussy had so rigidly enforced, were by him one by one set aside. The consequence was that the troops who had been, under the one, the preservers of public order, became, under the other, its persistent infringers. Drunkenness and licentiousness took with them the place of sobriety and discipline. This change of conduct on their part was naturally followed by a change of feeling on the part of the people, until by degrees the alienation became marked, and the dislike to the foreigners intensified. Saiyid Lashkar had not only watched this change of conduct with an eager eye, but he had, by many means in his power, encouraged it. The most effective of these means was the withholding from the French their monthly pay. Not only did he hope thus to incite them to some acts of indiscipline such as would embroil them with the people, and exhibit them in an odious light to the Subadar, but he trusted to it likewise as the charmed weapon by which he would procure the removal of their headquarters from Haidarábád, and their final expulsion from the Dakhan. He set to work, however, with great caution and with all the appearance of friendship. When he informed the French officers that he possessed not the funds to pay them, he accompanied this avowal with numberless professions of the most profound regret, laying the blame on the tributaries who had neglected to send in their imposts. When, some time afterwards, the French officers, beset by their soldiers for want of money and themselves seriously inconvenienced on the same account, again complained to him on the subject, he went a step further. The state of affairs, he said, as to the non-receipt of the public revenue, remained the same, but, he added, the French were at liberty to take the law into their own hands, by moving against the refractory tributaries. These, in different parts of the country, distant from one another, he indicated; nor did he fail to point out to the French officers the pecuniary advantages which might result to them personally from such a mode of collecting the revenue. This proposition, apparently so fair and even considerate, completely deceived Goupil and his officers, and some detachments were at once sent out. Under other circumstances it might perhaps have been difficult to obtain the consent of the Subadar to their departure, but the acts of violence and disorder recently committed by the French had even scandalised Salábat Jang, and he offered no opposition to the plan.

But though the force had been thus diminished, Saiyid Lashkar determined to divide and weaken it still more. He persuaded the Subadar to return to Aurangábád—the city in his dominions most distant from the seat of the French power—accompanied only by a small detachment of French soldiers and sipáhis, leaving the remainder at Haidarábád, the governor of which city received at the same time the most positive instructions to make them no advances of pay. He determined at the same time to disembarrass himself and the court of the presence of M. Goupil, who, imbecile as he was, yet by virtue of his commission as commandant *ad interim* of the French forces, occupied a position which, when the plot was ripe for execution, might give him sufficient influence with the Subadar to defeat it. This part of his scheme he managed with an adroitness the coolness of which is worthy of admiration. He went to Goupil, told him of the intended movement to Aurangábád, intimated the intention of the Subadar to take with him but a small escort of French troops, and then begged that he would command it. Goupil, unsuspicious, replied that his duty was to remain with the bulk of the force, and that as the escort was to be so small, it would suffice if it were commanded by an officer of inferior rank. He accordingly remained at Haidarábád, sending M. de Janville, an officer of but little weight or experience, to command the escort accompanying the Subadar.

Determined from the outset to leave no stone unturned to accomplish his end, Saiyid Lashkar had likewise entered into a correspondence with the English, offering to aid them with the whole power of the Dakhan, if they would assist him in his schemes for the expulsion of the French. This proposition coincided entirely with the wishes of Mr. Saunders, but, engaged at the time in a deadly struggle with the French before Trichinápallí, he was able to lend only a moral support. He entered, however, into an active correspondence with Saiyid Lashkar, and encouraged him to persevere in his great undertaking. Towards the end of April, 1753, the plot seemed on the verge of success. The

SAIYID LASHKAR'S PLOT DEVELOPS ITSELF.

French were scattered all over the country; their main detachment at Haidarábád had been starved into a condition bordering upon mutiny; in attendance upon the Subadar was a young officer without influence or ability. It seemed natural to Saiyid Lashkar that troops, so high-spirited as the French, thus starved and neglected, would be but too glad to accept a free dismissal from the country in which their presence seemed to be so unwelcome. So completely, indeed, did Saiyid Lashkar count upon the success of this policy, that he wrote at that period to Mr. Saunders, telling him to have no fear for the result, "for," he said, "I have arranged the mode in which to rid myself of your enemies. The plan is in action, and with the assistance of Providence, the result will be what you wish. I expect to be with you by the end of the rains, and to arrange then everything in a satisfactory manner."

Meanwhile, the French at Haidarábád were in want of everything. The governor of that city, Muhammad Husén Khán, had carried out only too well the orders he had received, and had refused the French troops and sipáhis even the smallest supplies. Nor were their detachments better off in the provinces. Separated from the main body and from one another, they were not in a position to effect anything in the presence of the silent opposition that seemed everywhere to rise up against them. They fell at once into despondency; every thought turned towards Bussy; had he been on the spot, they argued, this dilemma would never have occurred; he alone could extricate them from it. Such were their thoughts, and, thus thinking, they despatched messenger after messenger to their old leader.

When Bussy received these messengers and the letters they carried, he was lying still sick at Machhlipatan. The sea-breezes of the coast had indeed contributed somewhat to the restoration of his strength, but prudence counselled him a longer intermission from the harassing duties of official life. But almost simultaneously with the letters from Haidarábád there came from Pondichery a communication which decided him. That confidential letter from Saiyid Lashkar to Mr. Saunders, from which we have extracted, happened to be intercepted by French agents. By them it was carried to Pondichery, and handed over to Dupleix.

Dupleix received this letter at a time when he was meditating those proposals to Mr. Saunders for peace, which he essayed in July of the same year, and to which we shall refer in their proper place. To this course Bussy, from his sick bed at Machhlipatan, had long urged him, advising him to renounce the old policy of empire he had so long followed. To make proposals for peace with any effect, however, it was necessary for Dupleix that he should be paramount in at least one province of India. Hitherto he had trusted that his prestige in the Dakhan would make up for his losses in the Karnátik. But now, this letter showed him that his prestige in the Dakhan was waning, his power about to be anihilated. He comprehended all in an instant. He saw at once how it had happened, how it was to be remedied. With him to think strongly was to act vigorously. He at once despatched to Bussy a letter, written in the most emphatic terms, urging him, even though his health might not be completely re-established, to set out immediately for Haidarábád. The manner in which Bussy acted on receipt of this letter is thus recorded by Dupleix himself: "Le sieur de Bussy," he writes, "was too zealous a patriot not to sacrifice even health itself for the benefit of the State." Without delaying a day he issued orders to all the detachments in the district to unite at a place near Haidarábád, where he proposed to join them at the end of that month.* Setting out then himself, he found all his troops, amount-

* May, 1753.

ing to 500 Europeans and 4,000 sipáhis, assembled there. His first step was to re-establish the relaxed discipline of his little army, the next to restore their confidence: this done he marched upon Haidarábád. The governor of that place, intimidated by his prompt action, and seeing that the scheme of his chief had missed fire, consented, after some demur, to liquidate the arrears of pay, without, however, engaging to make any stipulation for the future.

Meanwhile, a letter from Dupleix to the Subadar had made Saiyid Lashkar aware of the interception of his letter to Mr. Saunders. He knew then that the mask had fallen from his visage, and that the keen glance of the ruler of Pondichery had read all the thoughts of his heart. Still he seemed resolved to trust to the chapter of accidents to carry him through his hazardous game. Still he refused to advance the necessary sums to Janville's detachment. Still he ordered Muhammad Husén Khán to temporise and gain time. He thought most probably that at Aurangábád, in the extremity of the Dakhan, in close contiguity to the almost impregnable fortress of Dáolatábád, he was safe even from the scorn of Dupleix and the vengeance of Bussy.

But he was not. The communications of Bussy with Muhammad Husén, and the shifting and prevaricating conduct of the latter, very soon convinced the French leader that, under the circumstances of the case, but one course of action remained to him. He must march at once to the city which the advisers of the Subadar had selected as the place whence to offer to himself and his French these repeated insults; he must push these traitors from their seats, and re-establish with the Subadar his old bonds of confidence and amity. Every preparation accordingly was at once made for a march upon Aurangábád on the conclusion of the rains.

An undertaking more hazardous, more difficult, more daring, it is not easy to conceive. From Haidarábád to

Aurangábád is a distance of five hundred miles. The officials of the entire country were under the sway of Saiyid Lashkar. The equipment of the force for such a march was a matter of no small consideration. No money for that purpose was forthcoming from Muhammad Husén, and the expenses, not only of the equipment, but likewise of the supplies had to be met and provided. But besides this, the possible attitude of the Subadar and his advisers had to be looked to. There was no means of knowing what Saiyid Lashkar, wielding as he did the resources of the province, might not attempt in such a conjuncture. There was the possibility, indeed, that the handful of Frenchmen might have to fight their way to Aurangábád, surrounded by enemies, with no resources but their own brave hearts and the courage and capacity of their leader.

Nevertheless, Bussy, not only found means to equip the force, but no sooner had the rain ceased to fall than he set out. The mere fact of his march completed the confusion that reigned in the mind of Saiyid Lashkar. It unnerved and unstrung him. As abject and depressed as he had before been haughty and confident, he despatched letters of submission to Bussy, tendering his resignation, confessing his fault, and requesting the French general to appoint another in his place. This submission, however, did not stop Bussy. He still marched forward until he arrived within a few miles of Aurangábád. He then altered his plan. Feeling himself master of the situation, he was unwilling that the terms which he resolved to impose should seem to be the result of force or compulsion on his part. He resumed then at once the old character of the submissive ally of the Subadar. He claimed nothing, but hinted at everything. Sometimes he flattered Saiyid Lashkar, at other times he whispered the faintest indication of a menace. The result answered his expectations. Having allowed his wishes to be penetrated, everything that he coveted was granted, and Saiyid Lashkar, who had exhausted intrigue in order to rid the Dakhan of this French warrior, was forced to sign his name to a treaty which rendered that same Frenchman independent of ministerial influence; which severed from the Dakhan to add to the government of Pondichery four of the finest provinces on the eastern coast of Southern India.

On December 4, all preliminaries having been arranged, Bussy was met by Saiyid Lashkar and other lords of the court, and conducted into the presence of Salábat Jang. This interview, which was of a purely formal character, having been concluded, Bussy signed with Saiyid Lashkar the articles of agreement by which the French alliance was thenceforth to be regulated. The principal of these provided that the four provinces Mustafanagar, Ellúr, Rájámahendri, and Srikákolam, should be made over to the French for the support of their army so long as a certain strength should be maintained in the Dakhan, they receiving the rents then due on account of them; that the French troops should have the sole guardianship of the person of the Subadar; that he should not interfere in the affairs of the Karnátik; and that the other affairs of the State should be conducted with the concurrence and by the advice of M. Bussy. In return for this Bussy engaged to support Saiyid Lashkar in the office of Diwán.

By this treaty there accrued to the French 470 miles of sea-coast, from the Chilka Lake to Motupili; stretching inland to a distance varying from 30 to 100 miles, watered by such rivers as the Krishná, the Gundlakamma, and the Godávarí, and—including the headland of Divi and the districts previously ceded—containing the important districts of Gánjam, Vizágapatan, Godávarí, Yanaon, and Krishná, containing many important towns and trading stations. This united territory, afterwards called the Northern Sirkars, possessed

CHAP VIII.

1753.

an area of about 17,000 geographical miles, and yielded an annual revenue of about £400,000 sterling. The forests within its limits abounded in teak; one part of the country was famous for its manufacture of cloth, another for its growth of rice. Nor was it wanting in capabilities of defence. Resting on the sea, it was separated from the inland by a chain of mountains running, at unequal distances, nearly parallel with the coast. These mountains were covered with forests possessing only three or four passes, capable of being defended by a hundred men against an army. To use the language of the English historian, " these territories rendered the French masters of the greatest dominion, both in extent and value, that had ever been possessed in Hindustan by Europeans, not excepting the Portuguese, when at the height of their prosperity."*

Was not such a prize worthy of the struggle? Did not this important cession of a rich, a defensible, country, justify to some extent the pertinacity with which Dupleix continued to struggle, the obstinate retention of Bussy in the Dakhan? What impartial observer, looking at the position of the French and that of the English in the month of December, 1753, would hesitate to affirm that the main advantages rested with the French? The English of that period could not help seeing and admitting it. Had it been possible for Dupleix at this period to have waived something of his high pretensions, to have given up his scheme in its shadowy outline in order to be the more secure of its substantial proportions, his policy might yet have ultimately triumphed. But it was not to be possible. When we do revert to the history of the negotiations that he inaugurated, we shall, we fear, be forced to allow that the sentence pronounced by the French historian† upon one

---

* Orme, from whom this account of the Northern Sirkars has been mainly taken.

† M. Thiers, *Histoire du Consulat et de l'Empire.*

of whom in the greatness and versatility of his genius Dupleix was in many respects the type and forerunner, may be applied also to him, and to admit, that if in war he was guided by his genius, he was sometimes impelled, to too great an extent, in politics by his passions.

The first act of Bussy after receiving the patents for the transfer of the four provinces, was to send thither a body of 150 Europeans and 2,500 sipáhis to take possession of and to protect them; that force being placed under the order of the French agent at Machhlipatan, M. Moracin. There is conclusive authority for stating that the mode in which these provinces were administered by the French was such as to do them great honour. "The rent was moderate, enforced without rigour, accurate accounts were prepared, and most of the hereditary officers, if not those possessing rent-free lands, were confirmed in their property." *

But although thus foiled, notwithstanding that his efforts to expel the French had resulted in the aggrandisement of that nation, Saiyid Lashkar Khán did not in the least relax his endeavours to get rid of them. He was still left minister, and of the minister there were abundant opportunities of whispering calumnies into the ears of a credulous prince. Once more, therefore, he resolved to play upon the fears of Salábat Jang. He represented to him that it had ever been the policy of the French to make the accession of a new ruler an occasion for their own profit and advantage; that to this end they had supported Muzaffar Jang against Nasir Jang, and on the death of the former had preferred him, the present Subadar, to the legitimate heir of Muzaffar Jang; he added, that out of all these transactions the French had made a profit, and that now, having obtained all that was possible from the reigning sovereign, they

* Grant Duff.

would be prompt to listen to the ambitious offers of his brothers. He therefore urged the Subadar at once to place his brothers in confinement. He did this in the hope that Bussy, knowing the innocence of the two princes, would at once intercede in their favour, and that this intercession, interpreted by the Subadar to his discredit, would instil into his mind suspicions which must tend to his speedy disgrace.

With the Subadar, indeed, this scheme produced the desired result. He issued prompt orders for the incarceration of his brothers. But Saiyid Lashkar had mistaken the character of Bussy. The able officer at once recognised the right of the Subadar to an uncontrolled supremacy in his own family. The imprisonment of the two princes did not affect French interests. Notwithstanding, therefore, that several of the nobility and many friends of Saiyid Lashkar urged him to intercede in their behalf, he held himself studiously aloof. To all their importunities he replied that he respected the orders and secrets of the Subadar and his ministers, and that he did not wish to mix up in State affairs which did not concern the interests of his nation. This prudent conduct on his part convinced the Subadar of the groundlessness of the suspicions with which his minister had endeavoured to poison his mind. As to Saiyid Lashkar, he was so disconcerted at the result of this second intrigue, that he sent in his resignation and retired into private life. He was succeeded in his office by Sháh Nawáz Khán, a nobleman of high character and position, believed by Bussy to be attached to French interests. Opportunity was taken at the same time to remove from office all the adherents of the fallen minister, and to replace them by others professing devotion to the French.

This change had the happiest results. From the time of its taking place to that of the recall of Dupleix in August of the same year, the condition of the French troops remained unaltered. It is true that Jánují Bhonsla, son of the famous Raghují, made an attempt to invade the dominions of the Subadar. No sooner, however, had he learned that it was Bussy who was marching against him, than he hastened to conclude a peace.* Another attempt of some stray Marátha bands to disturb the French occupation of the Northern Sirkars was dissolved by the fire of the French artillery; the disaffected noble who had incited it being forced to throw himself on the mercy of Salábat Jang. In other respects, thanks to the prudence of Bussy, to the confidence which he inspired in all about him, everything continued tranquil. The French troops, well housed and regularly paid, showed their ancient discipline and recovered the lost confidence of the people. In the month of April, Bussy accompanied the Subadar to Haidarábád. After remaining with him there for two months, he set out for Machhlipatan to settle the affairs of the four new provinces he had obtained for France on a regular basis. The day before his departure an incident occurred which is worthy of being recorded. The Subadar summoned for that day a grand council of his ministers, and invited Bussy to be present at it. On his entering the hall of audience, the Subadar and his nobles hastened to assure him that as they felt, one and all, that to him and to French valour alone they owed their present peace and prosperity, they wished, before he left for the coast, to swear to him an inviolable attachment and an eternal gratitude, requiring from him a solemn oath on the sacred book of the Christians to continue to them his protection, and to return to their aid when they should be menaced by an enemy. A Testament was then produced, and in the presence of all Bussy took the required oath. Then, leaving behind him officers whom he could trust, he set out for

* April, 1754.

Machhlipatan. Here he was when the arrival of M. Godeheu at Pondichery, on the 1st August following, gave him the first intimation of the fatal blow which France herself had dealt to her own struggling children in the East.

CHAPTER IX.

THE FALL OF DUPLEIX.

IT is now time that we should return to Dupleix. We left him at the end of 1752, disappointed indeed in his views on the Karnátik, but still maintaining a bold front before his enemies; still hopeful of the future, especially hopeful of the action of Bussy in the Dakhan: not having resigned one of his daring schemes, nor faltered in the prosecution of his far-seeing plans of empire; still cool, determined, resolute; confident in himself, confident in the fortunes of France. He had likewise this consolation, that the great Genius who had delivered the English at Trichinápallí had left India for Europe, and he was himself daily expecting the arrival of 700 men under a leader who had proved his steel. It was not, alas! for him to imagine that those troops and the gallant de la Touche would meet with the most terrible of the deaths* on the broad ocean, and that he would have again to parry, with diminished resources and without a general, the powerful attacks of Saunders and Lawrence.

The number of European troops which Dupleix had at his disposal at the beginning of 1753 did not exceed 360. To support these were 2,000 trained sipáhis and 4,000 Marátha horse under the command of the versatile Murárí Ráo. Major Lawrence, on his side, was able to bring into the field not less than 700 Europeans aided by 2,000 sipáhis and 1,500 horsemen

---

* A body of 700 men under de la Touche left the Isle of France for Pondichery in a vessel called the "Prince," in 1752. She, however, was destroyed by fire with nearly all on board.—*Orme*.

in the employ of Muhammad Ali. With respect to the cavalry arm, therefore, the French had the superiority both in the number of the troops and the material of which they were composed. But in the number of Europeans, the nerve and mainstay of an army, the English had immeasurably the advantage.*

But notwithstanding this real inferiority, Dupleix determined to make up by the rapidity of the movements of his force for its inequality in the matter of Europeans. In the leader of the Marátha, Murárí Ráo, he met with a man willing and able to second him in this mode of warfare. With him it was concerted that whilst the Maisurians under their Dalwai (prime minister) Nandaráj, should press the city of Trichinápallí—upon which Dupleix had renounced none of his views—he, with his own Maráthás cavalry and the entire available French infantry, avoiding a pitched battle, should so occupy Major Lawrence and the English, that no opportunity should be afforded them of assisting the beleaguered garrison of that city. The fall of that place would, it was hoped, at once ensure the overthrow of Muhammad Ali and the supremacy of the French.

In pursuance of this plan, the allied force of French and Maráthás, under the command of Murárí Ráo and M. Maissin, marched from Valdávur on January 14, and intrenched themselves on the river Panár, near Tiruvádí, seven miles from Fort St. David, and in close vicinity to the spot in which d'Auteuil had defeated Cope and Muhammad Ali in July, 1750. From this place, which they fortified very strongly, they commenced a series of harassing movements against the English, cutting off their supplies, capturing their forage parties, and rendering it most difficult for the

---

* The statements in this chapter are based on the memoir and correspondence of Dupleix, the narrative of Colonel Lawrence, and the histories of Mr. Orme and Colonel Wilks.

garrison of Tiruvádí to hold any communication with the garrison of Fort St. David, or with the inhabitants of the surrounding country. In vain did Lawrence attempt to bring them to action; the allies on his appearance in force invariably drew up behind their intrenchments. To such a state of distress was he reduced at last, that he found himself compelled to use his whole force as an escort to the convoys whose arrival was necessary for the support of his troops. This service wearied and dispirited his army, besides entailing upon it many losses from the Maráthá skirmishers, who never failed to hover about and harass his line of march.

For three months this state of affairs continued, the French and Maráthás constantly issuing from their impregnable position to annoy and damage the enemy. On April 12th, in particular, the English force returning to Tiruvádí from Fort St. David with a convoy was surrounded by the whole body of the enemy, and but for the ability of Lawrence and the misconduct of the French battalion, which hastily abandoned a defile which it ought to have held, would have been in great danger. The same day, however, Lawrence having been joined by 100 English and 100 Swiss from Madras, determined to endeavour to put an end to the unsatisfactory state of affairs, by storming the French intrenchment. He accordingly made a strong reconnaissance in its direction the next day, and mounted two 24-pounders on a battery whence he might bombard it. The little effect, however, which the fire from these two pieces produced on the enemy's defences, as well as an examination of their strength, determined Major Lawrence to desist from the attempt as one that was beyond his power.

The three months during which the main force of the English was thus kept employed on escort duty at Tiruvádí had been used meanwhile to a very different purpose by the contending parties at Trichinápallí. This city, after the surrender of Law, had been left by the English commander under the charge of Captain Dalton, having under him a force of 200 Europeans and 1,500 sipáhis. An abortive attempt on the part of the Dalwai of Maisur to surprise the city after the departure of Major Lawrence, had resulted in his retiring with his troops to Srirangam. Here he entered into correspondence with Dupleix at the same time that he continued to profess friendship for Muhammad Ali and the English. When, however, the junction of his ally, Murárí Ráo, with the French, and his stoppage of the supplies necessary for the English, left no doubt as to his hostile intentions, Mr. Saunders resolved no longer to keep terms with him, but sent instructions to Dalton to treat him as an enemy.

The twelve months of renewed warfare before Trichinápallí, of which we are about to give a general description, were fraught with the most important consequences to both the rival European nations then struggling in India. We shall see the genius of the two peoples displayed in the form for which each has for centuries been remarkable. The daring of the French, their activity, their courage, their devotion, will be found not less conspicuous than the obstinacy, the perseverance, the coolness, the intrepidity under difficult circumstances, of the English. We shall have to admire not less the address and versatility of Dalton and the vigour and presence of mind of Lawrence, than the skill of Astruc and the dash of Mainville. In one point, and that an essential one, the English had the advantage at the outset. Their European soldiers were superior in number; they, too, had shared in all those conflicts which had terminated in the surrender of Law; they had served under Clive and under Lawrence, and had learned under their able leading to believe in their own invincibility. The French soldiers, on the other hand, were, at all events, for several months, not only fewer, but they were dispirited by defeat, and had ceased to place the smallest confidence in their leaders.

The campaign opened on January 3 by an attempt on the part of Dalton to drive the Maisurians and Maráthás by a night-surprise out of Srirangam. Night-surprises with a force composed to a great extent of native troops are always more or less hazardous, and this one proved no exception to the rule. Dalton made good way at the outset, but the darkness of the night caused amongst his men a confusion, which the repeated charges of the Marátha cavalry converted into disorder. The attack was consequently repulsed, and Dalton was forced to retreat into Trichinápallí with a loss in killed and wounded of 70 Europeans and 300 natives. Far from being cast down by this defeat, Dalton exerted himself with success to foil all the attempts of the Maisur leader to take advantage of his victory; and when, at last, this latter succeeded in establishing 8,000 of his best troops at the Fakír's Tope—a strong position, about four miles south of Trichinápallí—Dalton availed himself of his personal acquaintance with the character of their commander—one Viráná—so to play upon his fears, that he abandoned of his own accord his impregnable position, and left it still feasible for Dalton to communicate with the open country beyond.

But before this had happened, Dalton had ascertained from personal inspection that but three weeks' supplies remained to him in Trichinápallí. At the time he made this discovery, the position of the Dalwai of Maisur in Srirangam, and of Viráná to the south of the town, had effectually barred from him all communication with the country, and ignorant then how far he might be successful in his attempts to frighten the latter, he had despatched an express messenger to

CHAP. IX.

1753.

Major Lawrence begging him to march to the relief of the city.

Major Lawrence received this intelligence on the 1st May, not quite three weeks after he had proved the inutility of attempting the French position on the Panár. His part was instantly taken. Leaving 150 Europeans and 500 sipáhis under Captain Chace for the defence of Tiruvádí, he marched with the remainder of his troops, amounting to 650* Europeans and 1,500 sipáhis for Trichinápallí by way of Chelambram, Kundúr, and Tanjúr. He took with him no tents, and only the quantity of baggage absolutely necessary. As he approached Trichinápallí the plain was crowded with the 5,000 cavalry and 3,000 infantry that formed Viráná's force. They, however, offered him no opposition, retiring into Srirangam, as he, on the 17th May, entered Trichinápallí.

But this movement on the part of the English did not escape the eagle eye of Dupleix. Conjecturing at once that the destination of their force could be no other than Trichinápallí, he instantly despatched 200 Europeans and 500 sipáhis to Srirangam to reinforce the hundred men he had sent thither at the beginning of the year. The command of this force he confided to M. Astruc, a promising officer though untried in command, and he directed him to proceed by the Volkondah and Utátur route, already familiar to us from the movements of the previous year. In the intrenched camp on the Panár, there remained 160 Europeans and 1,500 sipáhis under the command of M. Maissin.

Hostilities between the rival powers before Trichinápallí commenced on May 21, by a daring attempt on the part of Major Lawrence to drive the enemy out of

---

* Major Lawrence had with him at the beginning of the year 700 Europeans; he was joined in April by 200 more, as stated in the text; deducting from these the 150 left behind and 100 as casualties, there would remain 650. Of these he sent 100 into hospital on arrival at Trichinápallí, and his force was further thinned by desertions.

Srirangam. In this, however, after operations which lasted twenty hours, he was foiled.* He accordingly withdrew his troops, who had suffered but slightly, and moved to the Fakír's Tope, the old position of Viráná, four miles south of the town. Despairing then of driving the French out of Srirangam, he set to work to supply the city with provisions. Owing, however, to the numbers of the Maráthá horse and the intrigues of the enemy with his allies, he found this a work of greater difficulty than he had anticipated. Nevertheless, as its accomplishment was of primary importance, he devoted to it all his energies, though it compelled him rigorously to avoid hostilities for the five weeks following his repulse from Srirangam.

This time had been well employed by Dupleix. No sooner had he ascertained the small number of troops left behind by Lawrence at Tiruvádí—a number liable to be diminished by the necessity of providing supplies for that garrison and for Fort St. David—than he sent instructions to Maissin to spare no efforts to storm it. Maissin, in consequence, attacked the place first on May 3, and, failing, renewed the assault some days later. He was, however, once more repulsed, but when the English, not content with repelling the attack, sallied forth to the number of 60, accompanied by 300 sipáhis, into the plain, they were surrounded by the Marátha horse, and cut to pieces to a man. From this success resulted the capitulation of Tiruvádí with all its remaining garrison, the capture of Chelambram, and a movement on the part of Murtizá Ali, the Nawwáb appointed by Dupleix, to recover the strong places of the Karnátik. Accompanied by fifty French soldiers and a considerable native force, this chieftain did indeed cause considerable alarm to the partisans of Muhammad Ali, completely defeating on one occasion

---

* Mr. Orme attributes this failure less to the skill of M. Astruc than to the want of perception on the part of Captain Polier, a Swiss officer in the English service. He admits, however, the ability of Astruc.

the troops of that Nawwáb commanded by his brother, although aided by a party of forty English, most of whom, after a gallant resistance, were slain in the encounter.

The Karnátik thus once more cleared of active enemies, Dupleix again bent all his energies to the capture of Trichinápallí. The troops that had been on the Panár were accordingly despatched to reinforce those in Srirangam—a measure by which the French force in that island was raised to 450 Europeans and 1,500 drilled sipáhis. Their arrival at that place combined with the inaction of Lawrence to incite Astruc to vigorous measures. Marching out of Srirangam, therefore, he crossed the Kávarí, and took up a position to the south of Trichinápallí, a little to the north of the English camp.

Learning next morning that Major Lawrence was confined to the city by ill-health, Astruc profited by his absence to take possession of some heights about a mile south of and commanding the English camp. These heights, known as the Five Rocks, being guarded only by sipáhis, Astruc easily carried. He at once diligently set to work to fortify them, and succeeded so well that when Lawrence, hearing of their loss, moved out to endeavour to recover them, he was repulsed and compelled to retire to a position about a quarter of a mile nearer the town out of reach of the enemy's fire.

This bold and successful manœuvre on the part of Astruc gave an immense advantage to the French. Their position at the Five Rocks was not only unassailable, but it was the key of the surrounding country. It enabled them to intercept all the supplies destined for the garrison, and to bar a passage to the enemy's convoys. The advantage they possessed in cavalry seemed to render any movement on the part of Lawrence impossible. Nor did the idea of a general action present to the mind of the English leader any impression that it would better his position. Sickness and exposure had worked with such effect upon his garrison, that he was unable to bring more than 500 Europeans into the field. To support these he had but 1,300 sipáhis and 100 horse—the rest of his native allies remaining in the city out of dread of an encounter with the Maráthás. On the other side, Astruc commanded 400 French soldiers and 1,500 sipáhis, supported by 8,000 Maisur horse, 1,200 foot, 3,500 Maráthá cavalry, and 15,000 irregular infantry. Was it likely, was it even probable, that the small superiority in the number of Europeans, or that the superior ability of their leader, should make up for the general numerical superiority possessed by the French and their allies?

The position of the English was indeed gloomy, and it seemed as though a few days' patience on the part of Astruc must compel them either to attack an impregnable position or to capitulate. To precipitate matters, however, Astruc resolved to force the enemy to take refuge within the city itself. This, he saw, must be the result of the capture of another eminence called the Golden Rock, about a mile nearer to the city than his own position, and on which there was only a sipáhi guard. This rock taken, there was no position between it and Trichinápallí which could afford shelter to the English force.

We see now clearly the position of the hostile armies. On the one side Astruc, with a force on the whole overwhelmingly superior, though in one particular, that of European troops, inferior by one-fifth;— Astruc with this force possessing an almost inaccessible position, barring supplies from the garrison, and needing only the possession of another height, one mile nearer the city, to insure its downfall; on the other side Lawrence, sick and weakly, in a defensive position unable to attack with any chance of success, with no

CHAP. IX.

1753.

native allies, dependent solely on his Europeans, and well aware that the capture of the Golden Rock, from which they were but a mile distant, by the French, was alone wanting to insure his ruin. Such was the position. It will be patent to all that it only remained for the English leader to await with what calmness he could, command the attack of the French.

After some days' mingled dread and expectation it came. On the morning of the 7th July, watching the moment when a large number of the English sipáhis had been detached to receive their rations, Astruc sent forward a select body of his grenadiers and best sipáhis to attack the Golden Rock, whilst he himself supported their onslaught with his whole army. The advanced party moving with the dash and celerity peculiar to French soldiers, clambered up the heights, and after a vigorous resistance carried the post. Meanwhile Lawrence, who was in camp, had no sooner noticed the movements of the enemy against the rock, than he hastily collected all his available force, amounting then to 420 Europeans and 500 sipáhis, and hastened to support his men on the rock. So much time, however, had been lost in turning out, that he had scarcely covered half the distance between his camp and the rock, before the position had been carried by the French. Scarcely, too, had he endured the mortification of seeing the flag of France waving over its summit, when the fire of the French artillery from either flank of the base of the rock, showed him that the whole force of the enemy had arrived to repel any attack that might be made to recover it.

The loss of the rock and the extraordinary danger of his own position, became evident to the mind of Lawrence at one and the same moment. What was he to do? To retire was to expose himself to almost certain destruction, for his retreat would be harassed and impeded by the crowds of Marátha horsemen who were even then threatening his battalion. To advance was to advance in the face of a triumphant enemy, possessing a strong position, vastly superior in numbers. It appeared indeed but a choice of deaths. Thus seemed to think Lawrence. For a moment he halted, though but for a moment only. That brief interval was sufficient to bring him to a resolution worthy of himself, worthy of the nation to which he belonged. Under all doubtful circumstances to attack is a principle which, in India, should be stamped upon the mind of every commander. Especially when retreat and attack present alike sombre aspects should the general recollect that the one encourages, the other demoralises; the one insures defeat, the other at least offers a chance of success; it is, at the very worst, better to die advancing than retreating, to command the respect of the enemy rather than to afford him an opportunity for the display of his contempt, with its concomitant encouragement to his soldiers.

It is probable that some such thoughts coursed through the mind of Lawrence, as after that momentary halt he detached a chosen body of grenadiers and sipáhis to storm the hill on its front, whilst he himself moved rapidly against the main body of the French, drawn up on the left of its base. It was a heroic resolve, heroically carried out. The grenadiers and sipáhis clambered up the hill without pulling trigger, and reaching the summit charged the French stationed there with so much vigour and impetuosity, that they drove them headlong down on the opposite side. Meanwhile Astruc, noting the advance of Lawrence, but not the movement of the grenadiers, had drawn up his men with their right resting on the left spur of the rock which, he deemed, covered his flank. Opposing thus his own line to the English, who by this time were within fifty yards of him, he ordered the Marátha horse and his native allies to move up and take them in flank and rear. Their destruction seemed to him to be, beyond question, inevitable. But just as his arrangements were about to take effect, the fire of the English grenadiers from the rock on his right flank startled and discomposed his line, and before they could recover from their surprise, a volley from the English followed by a bayonet charge completed their confusion. The French officers, and conspicuously amongst them Astruc himself, exerted themselves to restore the battle, but it was in vain. Completely panic-stricken by the suddenness of the surprise at the moment when victory seemed certain, the French soldiers hurried from the field, leaving it to Murárí Ráo and his Maráthás to cover their retreat. This service was performed by these famous horsemen with their usual gallantry. They even, indeed, attempted to dispute the field with the English, when, three hours later, Major Lawrence moved off to his old position with the two French guns —the trophies of the day—which he had captured. But the little body of Englishmen, formed in a moving square, repulsed every attack, and, finally halting, poured in so continuous a fire upon the masses, that they broke and fled in all directions.

It is impossible to over-estimate the service which Major Lawrence rendered his country on this eventful day. But for his unsurpassed coolness and presence of mind Trichinápallí would have fallen, and with it all the hard-earned conquests of the previous year. Fortunate indeed would he have been if in the presence of the swarming Marátha cavalry, and the French troops, flushed with victory, he had escaped the fate of Law. His merit on this occasion was the greater, because the French leader, Astruc, committed no glaring mistake. His plan was well conceived and well executed. He could not imagine that his soldiers would give up the place they had won almost without a blow. He acted throughout with courage and judgment; and though forced to succumb, it was in consequence of an event which it had been impossible to foresee, and against which he could not have provided. The greater honour is on that account due to the Englishman, who, in a sudden and dangerous crisis, elected to dare all in the face of an overpowering enemy, rather than to yield to him in the field!

CHAP IX.

1753.

Nor is it possible to leave this subject without a word with respect to those gallant troops who followed him so nobly. Those men had been trained by Clive and by Lawrence himself to the same state of perfection attained many years later by the veterans of Wellington. They were men who could be trusted to perform any service—men who regarded neither difficulties nor numbers, who asked merely to be shown the position of the enemy and to be told to attack it. No finer feat of arms has been performed in any part of the world than the assault by a handful of grenadiers of the Golden Rock, held by an enemy that had just conquered it, and whose army was formed up at its base! The attempt alone was sufficient to intimidate an enemy whose *morale* was inferior, who had not learned by experience that the one way to conquer was to move straight on. It was, in fact, one of those deeds of heroism which deserve to be recorded in the archives of a nation's history, never to be suffered, as has been the case with this, to fall into oblivion and neglect.*

The French, after their defeat, retreated to the Fakír's Tope, thence to continue the system of blockade

---

* The story is told at length by Mr. Orme, Colonel Wilks, and by Major Lawrence. Their works, however, published at intervals from upwards of half a century to nearly ninety years ago, are scarcely available for the general reader. Mr. Mill describes the whole campaign of 1753 in nineteen lines, and makes no particular allusion to this action. Baron Barchou de Penhoen is more just to his adversaries than Mr. Mill to his friends. He writes: "Lawrence knowing how much he could depend upon his troops, marched boldly against the French, and, after an obstinate and bloody combat, remained master of the field of battle." It will not then be denied that this gallant action has, with modern historians, fallen into "oblivion and neglect."

which they had inaugurated. Astruc after his defeat resigned his command, and proceeded to Pondichery. His successor, M. Brennier, determined to attempt to effect by blockade the object that force had failed to compass. He succeeded in reducing the townspeople to extremities: the price of rice speedily rose to one rupee the pound; of firewood there was an absolute want; the city became rapidly deserted by its inhabitants, who preferred even the risk of attack from the enemy to death from starvation. In his chief object, however, Brennier had no better fortune than his predecessor, for Lawrence, determined to employ every possible means to avert disaster, moved with the main body of his army in the direction of Tanjúr, leaving Dalton to defend the city.

On learning this movement on the part of Lawrence, Brennier proposed to himself two plans: the first to storm Trichinápallí whilst so weakly guarded; the second, to move upon Lawrence with his whole force and destroy him. But, unfortunately for his own purposes, he allowed his mind to rest upon both objects at the same time, instead of concentrating all his energies upon one. Thus, the better to carry out the first, he sent into the town a devoted Frenchman, named de Cattans, who engaged to act the part of a deserter, and whilst so employed to make drawings of all the internal defences, and to indicate the weak parts of the fortifications. It happened, however, that de Cattans was discovered, and obtained a promise of his life solely on the condition that he should indicate to the French leader the strongest parts of the fortress as those which were the weakest and least guarded. This was accordingly done.* So much time, however, had passed in the interval that before these papers reached Brennier he was entirely engrossed by the other plan—the inter-

---

* De Cattans was nevertheless hanged as a spy in sight of the French force, on the return of Major Lawrence to the city.—*Orme.*

ception and attack of Major Lawrence, who, he heard, was escorting a large convoy of provisions from his camp near Tanjúr into Trichinápallí. It was of the utmost consequence to the French that this movement should not succeed.

Accordingly, on the morning of the 18th August, Brennier moved from his camp, and took up an extended position stretching from Waikánda on the south-west to the French Rock on the south-east of the city—the points the French occupied in force being Waikánda itself, next to that the Golden Rock—the scene of the defeat of Astruc, but of which in the absence of Lawrence they had taken possession;—the Sugarloaf Rock, distant about a mile and a half from it, and the French Rock. Their infantry and artillery were strongly posted at the Golden and Sugarloaf Rocks; the space between the Golden Rock and the French Rock was filled by swarms of cavalry; there was a small detachment at Elmiseram; Waikánda was held by sipáhis, the intervening spaces being filled by masses of irregular troops, whose line stretched even to the banks of the Kávarí. In this position, occupying all the strong posts, Brennier believed he could intercept and destroy the English force, burdened as it was with a large convoy.

But the English had advantages that he knew not of. It was true that their force was burdened with a convoy, but it was not less so that whilst encamped near Tanjúr, Lawrence had received a reinforcement not only of 5,000 Tanjurians, but of 170 Europeans, and 300 sipáhis from Fort St. David. But that was not all. By means of the high tower in the centre of the city, Dalton was able to observe all the movements of the French, and to communicate them to Lawrence. This he did not fail to do on the present occasion. The English leader marched to the attack, therefore, not only at the head of a body of Europeans considerably larger than that of the enemy, but with almost as perfect a knowledge of his movements as if he had been an officer on Brennier's staff.

It will have been noticed that the two rocks, called the Golden and Sugarloaf, formed the key of the French position. The Golden Rock was, however, by far the most important of the two, as it commanded the entire country between it and the city, and Brennier ought to have held it at all costs. Lawrence, knowing its importance, determined, after depositing his convoy in safety, to direct on it his main attack. The better, however, to delude Brennier, he halted his troops in front of the Sugarloaf Rock, and made all his dispositions as if to attack it. Brennier, completely deceived, believing that he was to be attacked on the Sugarloaf Rock by Lawrence's whole force, sent hurried orders that the greater part of the force on the Golden Rock should be despatched to reinforce him. Lawrence gave him plenty of time to carry out this movement, but it had no sooner been effected than he detached his grenadiers and 800 sipáhis to seize the Golden Rock. This they did without much difficulty. Before, however, it had been accomplished, Brennier noticed the movement. Then, too late, perceiving his error, he sent a detachment to preserve or to recover it. This detachment finding the rock lost did not attempt to recover it, but taking up a position on some high ground between the two rocks, opened a very galling fire on the English. Lawrence, noticing this, conceived the idea of cutting off and destroying this detachment before it could be assisted by the main body, which, after making a slight forward movement, remained as if paralysed on the slopes of the Sugarloaf Rock. He accordingly detached 500 men, natives and Europeans, for this purpose. They advanced without guns in the face of a heavy fire of artillery which mowed down many of them. This caused a hesitation on the part of their leader, but Lawrence, perceiving it, ran out to them himself, and led them to the charge. At this moment, also, Dalton, who from the tower within Trichinápallí had watched the progress of the fight hastened to the ground with his detachment and two field-pieces, and attacked the French in rear. Separated from their main body, which all this time remained in an extraordinary state of inaction, the French detachment retreated to Waikánda, not however till they had inflicted and suffered heavy loss. Brennier, whose earlier movement might have saved the day, no sooner beheld the retreat of his detachment, than, seeming to recover himself, he advanced with his main body to attack the victorious English. It was, however, too late; for his troops, disheartened by the retreat of their comrades, and by the sight of the English in force on both flanks, declined the combat, and retreated, as fast as possible, to the Five Rocks, and thence followed their comrades in disorder to Waikánda. The Tanjurian cavalry, which might have handled them severely, feared, even in their retreat, to attack the soldiers of France. They contented themselves with reducing Elmiseram, which was but slightly guarded.

This second battle before Trichinápallí cost the English 140, the French 100, Europeans, and proved not less than the first the superior generalship of the English leader, and the higher *morale* of his soldiers. It is difficult to imagine conduct more imbecile than that exhibited by Brennier. He allowed himself to become the dupe of the most transparent stratagem, and its success so confounded him that he seemed incapable of giving any orders until it was too late to retrieve his vanished fortunes. It is not surprising that the French soldiers should display their want of confidence in such a leader.

Meanwhile, after the action, the French concentrated

CHAP. IX.
1753.

in Waikánda threw up intrenchments, as though prepared to defend it. Lawrence, whose supply of provisions had become again exhausted, advanced, a few day later, to the Five Rocks, and on September 4 made as if he would attack Waikánda. Brennier, totally demoralised, did not even attempt the defence of the place, but retreated hurriedly and in disorder to Mutáchalinur, on the banks of the Kávarí, a position which assured his communications with Srirangam. Here, to his surprise, he was joined by an important reinforcement of 400 Europeans, 2,000 sipáhis, and six guns, under M. Astruc, and 3,000 tried Marátha cavalry. Astruc at once re-assumed the command of the French force.

This reinforcement ought to have changed the fortune of the campaign. The French soldiers, of which it was partly composed, were men who had but recently arrived from the Isle of France, and who had been engaged during the few subsequent weeks in overrunning the Karnátik. They were free from the discouragement that had fallen on the others, and should have been employed on the offensive before they had become inoculated by the despondency that reigned in the camp. But previous ill-success had made Astruc overcautious. The third day after the junction he led the combined force towards the south, and took possession of the Five Rocks, and the Golden and Sugarloaf Rocks, recommencing that system of blockade which had twice before brought the English to great straits. Lawrence on his part moved towards Elmiseram, alike with a view to cover his convoys, and to effect a junction with a fresh reinforcement of Europeans then shortly expected. In such a position it was the policy of the French to avail themselves of their superior numbers to attack the English. The occasion was favourable; Murári Ráo in particular urged it upon them; but their councils were divided, and Astruc himself was averse to appeal to the arbitrament of the sword. He confined himself, therefore, to intercepting supplies and attacking convoys, whilst he hurried on the defences he was throwing up at the Golden and Sugarloaf Rocks. This was acting the policy of Lawrence. This officer remained in the open plain, amusing the French by feigned attacks, till September 27. On that date he was joined by 237* Europeans and 300 sipáhis. As bold as his adversary was cautious, he at once determined to attempt the storm of the French intrenchments before they should be quite finished. Astruc had, like Brennier before him, placed the greater part of his force on the Sugarloaf Rock, the intrenchments of which had been completed on three sides; to the Golden Rock he had detached 100 Europeans, 600 sipáhis, and two guns, intending to fortify that also. The space between the rocks and all around them was occupied by the Maráthás and Maisurians. Astruc hoped, by holding an impregnable position here, to blockade the English on three sides, whilst Dupleix should induce the Rájá of Tanjur to renounce their alliance. This would complete the investment, and insure the fall of Trinchinápallí.

Such was the state of affairs when, on September 27 the detachment under Captains Ridge and Calliaud joined Lawrence. That officer resolved to attack with as little delay as possible. Moving, accordingly on the morning of October 1 to the Fakír's Tope, he drew up his men and offered battle. Astruc, however, having declined it, he encamped on the ground on which he was drawn up. But before break of day on the following morning, he advanced at the head of 600 Europeans, six guns, and 2,000 sipáhis towards the Golden Rock, assaulted it in three columns before he had been

* One of the officers with these was Captain Calliaud, a man subsequently famous in Anglo-Indian warfare.

perceived, and carried it without giving the French leisure to fire their two guns, which were captured loaded. Only waiting to re-form, Lawrence then advanced quickly towards the Sugarloaf Rock, his men shouting and drums beating, the Maisurians fleeing before them. Here, however, in front of the unfortified face, the French were drawn up to receive him, with a strong body of sipáhis on their left. These men, however, would appear to have been disheartened by the sight of the fugitive Maisurians escaping from the English, as well as by the shouts of the latter, for they gave way without striking a blow. The right division of the English, following them up, discovered the left flank of the French unguarded. They, therefore, wheeled to the left, and took their line in flank at the same moment that the two other divisions charged it in front. Stationary as they were, the French could not stand this double attack. In vain did Astruc exert himself to restore the battle. The English pressed on so hotly that rallying was impossible. Broken and divided, fleeing in disorder and dismay, the scattered remnants of the French force made no halt till they had placed the waters of the Kávarí between themselves and their pursuers.

This great victory, gained by the superior boldness and daring of the English leader, was decisive. Eleven pieces of cannon, 111 prisoners—amongst whom were M. Astruc and ten officers, 200 killed and wounded, testified to its importance. On their side the English lost but 40 men. Nor were its results on Trichinápallí less favourable to the English. That city was at once delivered from the horror of scarcity. For whilst the main body of the French took refuge, cowed and paralysed, in Srirangam, Major Lawrence, sweeping their detachments from the country south of the Kávarí, poured supplies into the city, and then moved himself with the main body of his troops to Koiládí, on the north bank of the Kávarí, within the territories of Tanjur. In this position we must leave the hostile parties—the French beaten and dispirited, without confidence in themselves or in their leaders; the English proud of themselves, proud of the general who had three times led them to decisive victory, proud likewise of their achievements, confident and secure as to the future; here we must leave them, to return once again to the action of the Governor whose great plans had thus been so strangely baffled.

Whilst these tremendous conflicts were going on in the vicinity of Trichinápallí, Dupleix, continuing to feed and to strengthen his armies before that place, had been exerting himself to the utmost to restore peace to the Karnátik. To this course he had been moved by several concurring reasons. The Directors of the Company of the Indies and the French Ministers had never ceased to urge it upon him. The continued warfare, from which so much had been expected, drained the pockets of the shareholders, a result ill calculated to satisfy those who looked only for dividends. The contest which Dupleix had declared over and over again could not possibly last long, and could not end but in the elevation of France to a pitch of unprecedented glory, seemed to the Directors likely to be spun out indefinitely, and to end in humiliation rather than in advantage. In that august body, the want of immediate success on the part of Dupleix had produced the usual results. Those who had long been envious of his success now joined the faction that was really alarmed, to agitate for an end to such a state of things. The longer the war lasted, the more powerful and persistent became the adherents of the party in favour of peace at any price.

But that was not the only reason. Dupleix was himself most anxious for peace with the English, if only to give him time to consolidate his arrangements with the native powers, to obtain from his European rivals an acknowledgment of his right to the territories conceded to him by the representatives of the Mughal. He had previously, in February, 1752, addressed Mr. Saunders with this object, but the answer he received not having been of a nature to encourage him in the hope of a successful result, he had allowed the subject to drop. In the July of the following year, however, urged by the considerations to which we have adverted, as well as by the pressing solicitations of Bussy, who, by an engagement to become his stepson, had but just acquired a fresh right to advise him, he attempted to renew the negotiation. Saunders met him in what may be termed a conciliatory spirit, if we have regard only to the main object proposed to be attained. But the course of their correspondence soon showed that, though they equally wished for peace, the rival powers held very different ideas as to the conditions on which that peace was alone attainable. Dupleix insisted on the recognition by the English of himself as Nawwáb of the Karnátik, an office which had been bestowed upon him by the Subadar, and been confirmed, he asserted, by the Court of Delhi. The English Governor, on the other hand, loudly asserted the claims of Muhammad Ali. Under these circumstances it would appear that whilst both governors continued to negotiate, they felt alike strongly that the terms of the treaty would be decided, not by their arguments or protests, by the validity of the parchments they displayed, or of the patents promulgated in their favour, but by the armies which were then contending for the possession of Trichinápallí. This fact alone is sufficient to account for the perseverance, constancy, and energy displayed by Mr. Saunders in sending reinforcements to Lawrence, and by Dupleix in the despatch of every available soldier to strengthen the forces of Brennier and Astruc.

It will readily be conceded, we think, that having regard to the number of European troops he despatched to the scene of action, and the largely preponderating force and superior excellence of his native allies, Dupleix had good reason to hope for a decided success before Trichinápallí. He, at least, had strained the resources of Pondichery to assure himself of such a result, and it was not for him to anticipate that a fatality would continue to be inseparable from the operations of the French leaders before that place. He was not a man to be easily discouraged. He had replied to the first and second battles of the Golden Rock by pouring in fresh reinforcements, and urging his generals to renewed exertions. When even the news reached him of the third and most fatal defeat on that fatal ground he did not despair. That information, on the contrary, only nerved him to make another vigorous effort, conducted with more subtlety, more daring, than any of the others. His plan was, whilst still continuing to negotiate with Saunders, to send secretly to Srirangam the last reinforcements he had received from Europe, with instructions to their commander to use them at once to attempt the storm of Trichinápallí, whilst Lawrence was resting, with the main body of his forces, at Koiládí, fifteen miles distant.

In pursuance of this determination, 300 Europeans and 1,200 sipáhis were despatched from Pondichery early in November under the command of M. de Mainville.* They arrived at Srirangam on the 21st. The better to conceal his intentions Mainville endeavoured, and very successfully, to keep his arrival secret from the English garrison and from Lawrence. He did not even endeavour to intercept the supplies of the garrison, but employed his whole time in preparing for the meditated enterprise. At length, on December

---

* All the English writers state that M. Maissin commanded on this occasion; but the records show that only after the arrival of Godcheu was the command made over to Maissin.

8, all his arrangements having been made, without any suspicion existing on the part of the English, Mainville determined to put his plan into execution. His orders were clear and precise; 600 Europeans supported by 200 more and the sipáhís, were to attack and carry the work covering the gateway known as Dalton's battery. As there were here but fifty sipáhís, Mainville anticipated that this could be accomplished easily and without firing a shot. He, therefore, gave the strictest orders to abstain from firing. This work carried without alarming the garrison, it was determined to dash round the traverses, of which there were two, and apply a petard to the gate of the town, or should that fail, to attempt to escalade—the walls here being but eighteen feet above the rock;—for this purpose ladders had been prepared.

Following this arrangement Mainville crossed the Kávarí at 3 o'clock on the morning of the 9th, and succeeded in reaching the base of the outwork without having been perceived. The 600 Frenchmen escaladed this place and surprised the sipáhís, whom they found mostly asleep. Had they then but pushed forward, had they obeyed Mainville's instructions to abstain from firing, nothing could have saved Trichinápallí. But instead of thus acting, their evil genius prompted them to turn two of the 12-pounders which they had captured and found loaded against the walls of the town. They accompanied this fire by a volley of small arms and by shouts of *Vive le Roi*.

The effect of this fire was to rouse the garrison. Under orders received from Captain Kilpatrick, the commandant, detachments instantly proceeded to their respective alarm posts ready to receive the enemy. Meanwhile the French, after their insane and useless volley, pressed along the passage round the traverses, and under the guidance of an English deserter followed closely by two men carrying petards, had arrived within a short distance of the gate—the exact locality of which, however, was known only to the deserter. Whilst they were advancing, the English had hurried to the gate, and had commenced an indiscriminate fire into the passage leading up to it. The night was dark, and they could take no aim; nevertheless, their first fire killed the English deserter and the two petardiers when within a few paces of them. The others, not knowing exactly what had happened, began, after some little confusion, consequent on the darkness, to attempt the escalade. Their ladders, however, had suffered so much from the enemy's fire and from other causes, that they had but a small number available. Those that they had were nevertheless boldly planted, and an officer preceded by a drummer and followed by his men led the way up one of them. The drummer, however, was killed, the officer pulled into the town, and the ladder thrown back. Others were similarly treated, until, having lost all their ladders, without ropes or any means to retreat down the rock they had ascended, exposed to the fire of the enemy without being able to return it, the French were driven to despair. They could not even make known to the garrison their wish to surrender. For some hours longer, hiding themselves as best they could, still exposed on the least movement to a continued fire, they were left in the most pitiable position. When at last day dawned, it was only that the greater part of this large force, which had set out with such hopes of victory, which had had victory within its grasp, might surrender, *en masse*, prisoners of war. Of the entire body of 600 men, eight officers and 364 men were taken prisoners, many were wounded, one officer and 40 men were killed; the remainder, nearly 200 in number, jumped down from the rock into the ditch, and though several of them were maimed in the attempt, were carried off by their comrades.

It would seem, in sober truth, that a fatality did attend

all the French operations against Trichinápallí! This enterprise, well planned, up to a certain point well executed, certain then under the conditions of ordinary prudence to succeed—why did it fail? What was it that prompted that ill-timed and useless volley? The second query is an answer to the first; to the second itself it is beyond our power to reply. We must content ourselves with remarking that that foolish act of a few foolish men changed entirely the face of events. It not only by its consequences took away from the French the hope of ever gaining Trichinápallí;* it not only gave all the triumphs of the campaign to the English, but it was the main cause of that humiliating treaty, in which, but a few months later, France gave up the labour of years, renounced the right even to aspire to dominion in the territories of Southern India. What a lesson does not this story convey to soldiers—what a lesson to mankind in general! What a lesson never to turn, when in the pursuit of a great end, either to the right or to the left, to allow no lighter thoughts, no ideas of vain glory, to move a man off the direct path by following which with singleness of purpose he can alone hope to reach the desired goal!

To the views of Dupleix, the author of the plan, although not responsible for any part of its execution, the blow was fatal. Nor had it, unfortunately for him, come entirely unaccompanied by other disasters: Murtizá Ali had a little before been defeated before Trinomali, and Muhammad Kumal, another French partisan, before the pagoda of Tirupati. But this was the finishing stroke; this it was that convinced Dupleix of the necessity of at least entering into negotiations with the English Gover-

---

* Major Lawrence writes: "The scheme was well laid, and had not French petulance made them too soon discover themselves, they, perhaps, might have had time to execute their designs." Mr. Orme writes that the assault "exposed the city of Trichinápallí to the greatest risk it had run during the war." Colonel Wilkes: "If the orders prohibiting firing had been obeyed, the place must in a few minutes have been in possession of the French."

nor. Far better for him to come to terms, even though they might be disadvantageous, than to see his best-laid plans thwarted and ruined by the want, on the part of those who were to execute them, of ordinary prudence and the commonest self-command.

Accordingly, and with the hope rather than the expectation that some practical result might arise from the meeting, Dupleix proposed that commissioners should be appointed, armed with full powers, to treat regarding an accommodation. To this the English Governor acceded, and the little town of Sadras belonging to the Dutch, nearly equidistant from Madras and Pondichery, was fixed upon as the seat of conference.

The English commissaries, Messrs. Palk and Vansittart, arrived at this place on the 30th December; the French—M. de Kerjean, M. Bausset, and Father Lavaur, the principal of the Jesuits—delayed by the non-arrival of passports from the English Governor —not till the 21st of January. The next day the conference held its first sitting. The English commissaries began by declaring that they had no propositions to make, and none to listen to, which did not comprehend the acknowledgment of Muhammad Ali as sole and legitimate master and Nawwáb of the Karnátik, or which did not guarantee to the Rájá of Tanjur the full and entire possession of his kingdom.

The proposals of the French commissaries were, in words, much more moderate. They suggested that Madras should be quit of the annual ground-rent due to the government of the Karnátik; that Púnamath, a town in the Chengalpat district, and its dependencies should be ceded to the English Company; that all the expenses of the war on the part of the English should be defrayed; that the French Company should give to the English Company the necessary securities for freedom of commerce; and that in consequence of these cessions, the English Company should evacuate the countries and fortified places dependent on the Karnátik; that for Muhammad Ali there should be provided a suitable governorship in some part of the Dakhan under the mutual guarantee of the French and English Companies; that he should be considered quit of all monies due by him to the treasury of the Dakhan; and that the Rájá of Tanjur should be maintained in the possession of his territories under the guarantee of the two Companies. Such were the French propositions, extremely moderate, even conciliatory, in their outward form, but in reality no less favourable to French, than were the counter-proposals to English, interests. The French scheme, in fact, must be examined rather with reference to what it omitted than to its contents. We find in it no mention of the Subadar of the Dakhan, none of the Nawwáb of the Karnátik. But, the rival candidate for the last-named appointment being in it provided for, the intention was clear to take it for granted that Salábat Jang would be acknowledged as Subadar and his nominee, Dupleix, as Nawwáb of the Karnátik. Exactly then as the English proposition claimed all that the English had been contending for, so did this of the French ask everything that Dupleix had demanded from the very beginning. The English commissaries received the French propositions in silence, but at the next meeting of the conference they declared that their instructions forbade their even discussing any articles, until the two which they themselves had presented should have been subscribed to by the French deputies. To this the French would by no means agree. They challenged Mr. Vansittart and Mr. Palk to show them any patent conferring upon Muhammad Ali the office of Nawwáb of the Karnátik; they showed them that it was not an hereditary office; that the father of Muhammad Ali had been appointed by the Subadar of his day; and that his successors had, on his demise, given the office, originally to Chanda Sáhib, and secondly to Dupleix: and they produced several patents granted to the latter, and a letter from the Great Mughal confirming all that Salábat Jang had granted in favour of Dupleix. The English to this replied, that Muhammad Ali had received his appointment from Nasir Jang, and afterwards from Gáhziu-d-dín, but that the patents were at Trichinápallí; the letter from the Great Mughal they treated as a forgery. Something more was said, but little to any purpose. That meeting was the last held by the conference. Finding it impossible to agree even upon preliminaries, the English commissaries left on February 5 for Madras; the French, three days later, for Pondichery.

Dupleix was the less inclined to abate any of his pretensions on this occasion, for whilst the conference was sitting he received from Bussy the intelligence of that gift of the four Sirkárs to the French Company, the history of which we have already recorded. The possession of these rich provinces rendered him quite independent of English wishes. Better, he argued, to maintain war than to give up one iota of his just claims. He opposed no obstacle, therefore, to the breaking up of the conference, but throughout the written communications which followed, he adhered, without renouncing a single article, to the rigid programme he had dictated to his agents at that assembly. When Saunders even yielded so far on his side as to concede in substance every claim of the French, with the exception of that which referred to the Nawwábship of the Karnátik; when even he agreed so to modify his claims in this respect, as to leave that office vacant, on the understanding that Muhammad Ali should be appointed to it, under the protection of the two Companies, by Salábat Jang, whom the English would then acknowledge, Dupleix haughtily rejected the proposal, and insisted only the more strenuously on the validity of his own titles.

In the course of our history we have had many occasions to point to the versatility of intellect, the untiring energy, the varied resources under all circumstances, the self-denial, the persistence, the patriotic devotion of this illustrious Frenchman. All these qualities he united indeed to an extent such as is seldom found in one man. But the same candour, which has forced us to admit and to admire these great virtues, compels us to lament the fatal obstinacy which influenced his conduct throughout this memorable negotiation. Too clear it is, alas! that on this occasion he was guided, not by his genius, but by his passions. His pride would not allow him to take that one retrograde step which he, more than most men, would have known how to make the prelude of a further advance. He had fought so long so openly and so persistently for this empty title, therefore he would not lower himself by giving it up now—now especially, when the influence of Bussy at Haidarábád and the possession of the four Sirkárs seemed to make him virtual master of the Dakhan. Blind and fatal reasoning! His successes in the north ought to have made him more compliant, more yielding, more anxious to conciliate. He should have been content to bide his time. There would not always be a Saunders and a Lawrence at Madras. England had had its Morses, its Floyers, its Copes, and its Gingens, and might have them again. He too, who had influenced every native with whom he had come in contact, who had so bent to his will a Muzaffar Jang, a Chanda Sáhib, a Murtizá Ali, as to make them like clay in the hands of the potter, who had won the daring spirit of Murárí Ráo, was he to despair of gaining a Muhammad Ali? Once independent, free from the clutches of the English, as by this treaty he would have become, and Muhammad Ali would speedily have fallen under the sway of that potent influence, that irrefragable will. Whilst then, as Englishmen, we cannot but rejoice at the unyielding pride which preferred to risk everything rather than to yield one small portion of its pretensions, we cannot but lament, regarding the question abstractedly, that so vast a genius should have been marred by this one great failing. In similar circumstances Napoleon acted similarly. In 1813-14 he too preferred the risk of the sacrifice of his throne to the certain sacrifice of the smallest of his pretensions. The reason which prompted both these great rulers was the same. It was simply, we repeat, this, that on an occasion requiring peculiarly a cool judgment and clear discrimination, they were both alike influenced by their passions!

Meanwhile, hostilities did not cease in the Karnátik Even before Trichinápallí the temporary success of the French arms seemed almost to justify Dupleix in his policy of haughty persistence.

After the failure of his attempt to surprise Trichinápallí, Mainville had withdrawn his parties within Srirangam, and there awaited reinforcements. These Dupleix, with his usual promptitude, had sent him.

On their arrival, Mainville resolved to strike another blow at his enemy. He had observed that the guards which escorted convoys periodically sent in to the city had gradually become smaller. Formerly Lawrence had made a point of attending them with his whole army, but convinced apparently that all the steel had been taken out of the French, he had latterly remained himself in camp, sending only a much smaller party with the convoys. Having noted this, Mainville determined to surprise and attack the next convoy regarding which he might receive tidings. Intelligence having reached him very soon afterwards, that a particularly large convoy, escorted by only 180 Europeans, 800 sipáhis, and four guns, would endeavour to make its way into the city, from Kilákotá, a small fort on the south of the Kávarí, about twelve miles from Trichinápallí, on the early morning of February 26, he made the following preparations to intercept them. Between Kilákotá and the village of Kutápárá, a distance of five miles, the ground, covered with trees and underwood, afforded cover for a large body of men; here accordingly, he sent 12,000 horse under Murárí Ráo and Innis Khán, with instructions to lay in ambush about two miles beyond Kutápárá, and not to attack the convoy until at least half its length should have passed them, and it should have been attacked in front by the French. He himself, with 400 French and 6,000 sipahis, took post in front of Kutápárá, at the point where the wood debouches into the plain. These dispositions having been made on the evening of the 25th, he anxiously watched the result.

The morning of February 26 had already dawned, and yet no convoy had appeared. Half an hour later, however, a small platoon was seen advancing, followed by the carts and bullocks in single file, the soldiers marching also singly and unsuspicious of danger, on either side. They reached the point where Murárí Ráo was posted, they passed it even, not making, though they had seen some native horsemen in the woods, any change in their disposition. The French, however, were still two miles off, and Murárí Ráo, anxious that the surprise should be complete, noting too the negligent manner of marching, and fearing lest something might occur to give the alarm before the convoy should reach the French, determined to anticipate his orders. He accordingly sent to the parties he had posted in the wood to hold themselves in readiness to charge. He then gave the signal. The effect was electric. The English, without order or cohesion, their small body stretching along a long line of carts, could offer no effectual resistance. They could only die at their posts. The Maráthás, galloping amongst them, attacked all who opposed them. The English still resisted, however, until the French troops arriving offered them quarter. This was accepted; of the whole force 50

TRANSIENT SUCCESS OF THE FRENCH.

were killed, 138—of whom 100 were wounded—were taken prisoners.*

This, however, was but a transient gleam of success. On May 23, a French force, 700 strong, supported by a large body of sipáhis and Maráthás, was repulsed near the Sugar-loaf Rock by a body of English, much inferior in numbers, on one of those occasions when a victory on the part of the French would have terminated the war in those parts. Again, however, the tide turned. Mainville, prompted by Dupleix, took the sudden resolution of abandoning his position before Trichinápallí, and of carrying the war into the enemy's country. Moving eastward, accordingly, he attacked and took Kílákotá, then possessed himself of Koiládí. Here he caused the waters of the Kávarí to be diverted into the channel of the Kolrun, with a view to distress the people of Tanjur. Having seen this done he moved back to Trichinápallí, and took up the position at the Five Rocks, whence he could best intercept the supplies destined for that city. Murárí Ráo, about the same time, completely defeated the army of the Rájá of Tanjur. To cover the capital of that country, Major Lawrence had left his position near Trichinapállí, leaving it feasible for Mainville to make the movement we have recorded. He was, at the time we are writing, wistfully watching from Tanjur the movements of Mainville at the Five Rocks, whilst —such is Oriental diplomacy—the secret agent of Dupleix had more than half succeeded in detaching the Rájá whose country he was protecting from the English alliance!

It will be seen then that Dupleix had at least some reason for maintaining his pretensions in his negotiations with the English. Had he been an absolute prince we can scarcely doubt but that in the end his policy would

* Amongst these men was the famous battalion of grenadiers which had borne the brunt of all Lawrence's battles.—*Lawrence*.

have triumphed. The last ally of the English, the Rájá of Tanjur, was ready to abandon them, and notwithstanding the reverses of 1753, he still, in the middle of 1754, held a stronger position than ever before Trichinápallí. The famous grenadiers, who had borne the brunt of all the victories of Lawrence, had been killed or made prisoners, and his own troops, resuming the offensive, and victorious in more than one skirmish, were threatening the possessions of the English and their allies on every vulnerable point. It had become, in fact, a question with the latter whether the English alliance was worth maintaining at so great a risk to themselves, at the cost of so heavy a drain on the resources of their country.

But when the state of affairs was thus favourable, there came into action those other circumstances upon which Dupleix ought to have, but had not, sufficiently counted. The success of Bussy in the north, of Mainville and his partisans towards the south-west, were of little moment so long as he did not also possess the confidence of his masters in France. In those days, when a communication to the Home Government could not reach France in a less period than six or eight months, Dupleix ought to have been prepared for the effect which the disasters of the previous year would probably have on a corporation in which a large minority was, as he well knew, already hostile to himself. It was the consideration of the consequences likely to follow a long record of disasters, all burdensome to the finances of the Company, that should have powerfully influenced him in his dealing with the English Governor. It is the more strange that he should have neglected to allow such a consideration to weigh with him, because he well knew the jealousy to which his proceedings had given birth, and he was aware that by success alone in India he could maintain his position with the Directors in France. Perhaps it was that he felt, as did the illustrious Wellesley of his masters, the scorn of a great genius for men inferior to him in all respects; perhaps also he did not reckon to its fullest extent the extreme length to which human meanness and human ingratitude would not hesitate to have recourse. Conscious of his own deserving, he did not fear the result of any scrutiny. He had to deal, however, as we shall see, with men to whom consciousness of deserving was but a phrase, when the conduct which accompanied it did not exactly dovetail with their own paltry notions and petty ideas.

A party amongst the Direction in France had, indeed, been endeavouring for some time to compass his downfall. So far back as 1752 the complaints of Governor Saunders and his friends to their own Company, regarding the boundless ambition and enormous views of Dupleix, had found an echo in the heart of the French Direction. It was in consequence of this that it had that same year despatched M. Duvalaer to London, charged with full powers to negotiate, in concert with the French ambassador at the Court of St. James', with the English Ministers, regarding a basis upon which to settle affairs in the East. Both parties vehemently declared that they wished for peace; that their one aspiration was to engage in commercial operations, to abstain from all interference in the affairs of the natives of India.

In the course of these negotiations, the English Ministers, instructed by the India House, which again received its inspiration on this point from Governor Saunders and his friends, never ceased to attribute all the evils of which the two Companies complained to the one man who ruled at Pondichery. But for him, they declared, there would have been no contests, no ruinous expenditure, no interference with commercial undertakings. He alone was responsible for all. These complaints, constantly repeated, could not fail to work upon the credulity of certain members of the French Company's Direction. These were simple enough to believe that their most deadly enemies and rivals were capable of giving them purely disinterested advice; that they wished for the removal of Dupleix as much for the advantage of the French as of their own Company. We need scarcely observe that those tactics ought to have made the French more reluctant to part with the man whom their rivals would have removed. Passion, however, never reasons; it seeks rather excuses wherewith to a cloak its own darling plans. In this instance it so worked upon the French Directors, that a majority was gradually brought round to the idea that French and English interests would be alike consulted by removing from his post the man who was the firmest supporter of the former, the most determined foe of the latter.

It was not, however, all at once that they fell into this snare. For a long time, indeed, Duvalaer continued to defend Dupleix, and to retort against Saunders the accusation which they piled upon the head of the French Governor. But not the less insidiously did the poison work. Not the less did the impression gradually become disseminated that Dupleix was the sole obstacle to a good understanding. The prudent boldness of the English Ministry favoured this view. Without actually declaring that they saw no hope of a cessation of hostilities so long as Dupleix should remain Governor, yet letting it plainly appear that such was their belief, they equipped four ships of war, embarked a full regiment on board, and despatched them ostentatiously under the orders of Admiral Watson to the East Indies.

Well would it have been for Dupleix, well for France herself, if the Company of the Indies had been able to answer this demonstration by an assurance that peace had already been concluded between the two

Governments on the spot; that there was no need for further negotiations. At any moment from July to December, 1753, it had been in the power of Dupleix to have expedited such a message. None however came, and the French Directors were brought at last to the determination to sacrifice this one man for, they professed to believe, the benefit of the whole nation. They accepted, therefore, a proposition made by the English Commissioners, to the effect that both the Governors, English as well as French, should be recalled, and that in their place two Commissaries should be nominated, one by each nation, to proceed direct to India, there to place matters on such a footing that future warfare between the two settlements, so long as their principals remained at peace, should be impossible. In consequence of this resolve, the French Ministry nominated M. Godeheu, at one time member of Council at Chandranagar, to be Commissary of the King to conclude peace, and to verify and examine the accounts of his predecessor. From the Directors the same Godeheu received likewise his commission as Governor-General of the French settlements. The English, more astute, made no fresh nomination, but sent out the necessary powers to Governor Saunders and the members of his Council.

The first intelligence received by Dupleix of these proceedings was contained in a letter from Godeheu himself from the Isle of France, announcing his early departure from that place to co-operate with him as Commissary of the King and of the Company in India. The letter was written in a modest and submissive tone, the writer lamenting his own inexperience, and expressing his earnest desire to be guided by the advice of his old friend. Whatever may have been the feeling of Dupleix on receiving this communication, it can scarcely be doubted but that its friendly tone and his personal knowledge of the writer must have tended to reassure him. He had known Godeheu since his early youth, and had ever befriended him. He had been his superior at Chandranagar, where he had ever been treated by the young councillor with marked deference and respect. He had even, on one occasion, been the means of saving his life. After his departure from Chandranagar, Godeheu had become a director of the Company of the Indies, and in that capacity had corresponded closely and intimately with Dupleix. He had ever evinced towards him a devotion and an admiration that were quite unbounded.

The appointment of a man so befriended, so devoted, to act—as Dupleix then believed—solely as Commissioner to bring about peace, could have in it nothing to alarm the French Governor. He did not know—in fact he had had no opportunity of knowing—that this man, seemingly so devoted, was one of those miserable vermin who seek to raise themselves by fawning on and flattering great men. He did not know that all the time this Godeheu had been writing to him letters full of the most fulsome professions of friendship, he had been intriguing amongst the Directors for his downfall, in the hope to be himself appointed his successor. He did not know that so far from desiring to aid him, or to profit by his advice, this Godeheu had asked for authority to send him home in disgrace and arrest, but had been overruled by the Directors, who had especially forbidden him to use force or restraint, except in the improbable event of the resistance on the part of Dupleix to lawful authority. How could he know such things; how, even, could he divine them? A noble and generous nature invariably revolts from the very suspicion of baseness. It appears to him too horrible, too unnatural, a degradation of intellect below the range of even the animal creation? Endowed himself with a lofty sense of honour and a warm, sympathising nature, how could Dupleix imagine that one whom he had treated as a friend and as a confidant, could use that friendship and that confidence to betray him.

But Dupleix was not suffered to remain long in his self-deception. On August 1, the ship, "Duc de Bourgogne," having Godeheu on board, arrived in the roadstead of Pondichery. A letter was at once sent off to Dupleix announcing his arrival, and intimating that one other ship was accomanying him, and that three more with 2,000 troops on board would follow in a few days. Dupleix at once went to meet his ancient comrade. His reception, however, was most frigid. Godeheu declined to become his guest, or even to land until a house should have been fitted up for him. He made over to Dupleix, however, three documents:—the first a letter from himself containing profuse professions of anxiety to make his situation as little painful as possible; the second a demand for a full report on the state of affairs in French India; the third an order from the King containing his recall. The first letter was probably written with the intention of diverting Dupleix from offering, as he feared he might, armed resistance to his authority, for on landing the next day in great pomp and splendour, received with all deference by Dupleix on the quay, he curtly informed him that he expected him to sail at once with his family for Europe. He then proceeded to the Council Chamber, and had his commission read out. The silence which followed this reading was interrupted by Dupleix himself, not indeed by querulous complaints or undignified protests, but by the loyal cry of *Vive le Roi!*

On August 2, 1754, Dupleix made over to Godeheu the command of that vast extent of territory on Indian soil, which partly in actual tenure, partly by means of the influence he exercised, he had gained for his country. Ten weeks later, October 14, Dupleix and his family bade a last adieu to the land to which he had

CHAP. IX.
1754.

devoted a lifetime. The public acts by which that interval was distinguished belong to the career of M. Godeheu, and we shall treat of them under that head. Of the conduct of Dupleix during that period we will merely state that it was distinguished by a loyalty, an abnegation of self, a devotion to the interests of the Company which had cast him off, of which the history of the world gives few examples. It was replied to, on the contrary, on the part of Godeheu, by a spiteful arrogance, an anxious desire to wound and annoy; a determination, if possible, to ruin and dishonour the ex-Governor, such as could only have emanated from a mean and paltry spirit. Not only did Godeheu, as we shall see when discussing his public acts, reject advice by following which he would have established French domination on a secure basis, but he ordered his commanders to preserve an inaction which saved the enemy from destruction, simply because action would have justified the long-pursued policy of Dupleix. But it was in his treatment of the pecuniary claims of Dupleix on the Company, that he showed the greatest malevolence. Unable to detect a single flaw in his accounts, finding that even the private invitation on his part of accusations against the ex-Governor failed to bring against him a single tenable charge; disappointed in the hope he had indulged of sending him home in chains, he resolved at all events to ruin him in his private fortune, and to dismiss him a dependent and a beggar. To a man so utterly unscrupulous the means were not wanting. The examination of the accounts of the Company at Pondichery showed an amount due by it to Dupleix of between 6,000,000 and 7,000,000 francs (£240,000 to £280,000). As soon as Godeheu ascertained this fact, he forbade the commissaries he employed to proceed with the question of accounts, compelling them merely to sign a certificate to the effect that the vouchers produced by Dupleix had reference to the public accounts. By this subterfuge he avoided placing on record an acknowledgment of the sums due to Dupleix. But this was not all. We have before stated that Dupleix had been in the habit of advancing to his native allies his own private fortune for the expenses of the war. These advances had been made on the security of certain districts in the Karnátik, from the revenues of which they were repayable. In fact, the agent of the native princes, by name Papiapoulé, had at this time in his possession an order to make over to Dupleix the revenues of those districts in payment of the sums due to him. At the time of Godeheu's arrival, some of these advances had been repaid; others, however, to the amount of 22,000,000 francs (£880,000), were still standing over. At the rate, however, at which they were then being paid in, this sum would have been reimbursed during the following year, 1755. But Godeheu, seeing in this a means of enriching the State at the expense of Dupleix, chose to consider these advances as sums irregularly laid out by his predecessor for his own private advantage, and not for the benefit of the State. He, therefore, suddenly seized Papiapoulé in his own private house, placed him in confinement* under circumstances most insulting to Dupleix, deprived him of all his papers, and farmed the revenues of the districts to another native for the sole benefit of the Company. In addition to this, he refused to allow a bill drawn by the Company itself in favour of Dupleix, to the amount of 422,606 francs (£16,904), to be cashed in Pondichery. Having thus effectually ruined him, having exposed him to the claims of those who were his creditors, solely because on the credit of his character they had lent their money to the State, Godeheu allowed to depart—beggared though not dishonoured, blasted in his fortune, cheated out of the fruits of his then ripening labours—this by

* He remained in irons till released by Lally, in 1758.

far the most illustrious of the illustrious men whom the France of Louis XV. produced, only to show how unworthy she was, in her then degraded state, of a progeny so deserving.*

"England," says a recent French writer,† "has been much admired and often cited for having solved that great problem of how to govern, at a distance of 4,000 leagues, with some hundreds of civil functionaries and some thousands of military employés, her immense possessions in India. If there is much that is wonderful, much that is bold and daring, much political genius in this idea, it must be admitted that the honour of having inaugurated it belongs to Dupleix, and that England, which in the present day reaps from it the profit and the glory, has had but to follow the paths which the genius of France opened out to her." Yes, indeed! Now that the lapse of more than a century has cleared away the passions and prejudices of that exciting period; now that from the basis of accomplished facts we can gaze at the ideas and conceptions of the men who were the pioneers of European conquest on Indian soil, there lives not a candid Englishman who will deny to the great French Governor the credit of having been the first to grasp the necessity of establishing European predominance in Southern India—to show practically how that predominance could be established and maintained. The work of Dupleix did not indeed last, because it was his misfortune to be born at a season when his country was sunk in the lowest abyss of profligacy and misgovernment; when all the offices of the State had become the patronage of a licensed harlot; when virtue and honour and truth were openly scoffed at and derided. It did not last, because the besotted Government he served recalled him at the beck of the immemorial enemies of France, just at the

---

* The account of the treatment of Dupleix by Godeheu is based on the official report of the auditors and others published by Dupleix.
† M. Xavier Raymond.

GREAT QUALITIES OF DUPLEIX.

moment when his schemes were about to blossom into golden fruit. But the effect of those schemes survived him. The ground he had so well watered and fertilised, the capabilities of which he had proved, was almost immediately after his departure occupied by his rivals, and occupied with the immense result which is one of the wonders of the present age.

Nor can we doubt that if Dupleix had had but two years more to mature his great schemes, the rich heritage of Bengal would have fallen to him instead of to his rivals. The possession of the Sirkars gave him an excellent basis from which to operate with the Subadar of Bengal, Bihár, and Orísa. Who can doubt but that had Chandranagar been under his control in 1757, he would have hesitated to unite with Siráj-a-dáola to crush the English settlement on the Húglí, or that he would have crushed it? Clive acted then as Dupleix with the prior opportunity would have acted before him. In this as on many subsequent occasions the spirit of the great Frenchman ruled in the camp of his rivals and successors.

It is impossible to deny to Dupleix the possession of some of the greatest qualities with which man has ever been endowed. He was a great administrator, a diplomatist of the highest order, a splendid organiser, a man who possessed supremely the power of influencing others. He had an intellect quick and subtle, yet large and capable of grasping; an energy that nothing could abate; a persistence, a determination, that were proof against every shock of fortune. He possessed a noble, generous, and sympathising nature; he was utterly incapable of envy or jealousy;* and was endowed besides with that

---

* We have placed in its true light the real reason of the quarrel between Dupleix and La Bourdonnais, and have vindicated the character of the former from all the charges which the hatred and prejudices of the hour had heaped against him, and which subsequent writers had repeated, without examining them. No one ever charged him with being jealous of Bussy; yet Bussy had a far greater influence in India than La Bourdonnais.

equanimity of temper that enabled him to bear the greatest reverses, the most cruel injustice towards himself, with resignation and composure. He was not indeed a general. He did not possess the taste for leading armies into the field. Yet he showed on many occasions—notably on the occasion of the siege of Pondichery by Boscawen—that he could not only stand fire, but could defeat by his unassisted and natural skill all the efforts of the enemy. The character of his government and the influence of his own presence are attested to by the English historian of that epoch, writing, as he was, under the spell of the prejudices of the period. "All his countrymen," writes Mr. Orme, "concurred in thinking that his dismission from the Government of Pondichery was the greatest detriment that could have happened to their interests in India."

When we think indeed how much he had accomplished—how he had built up the French power, how he had gained for it an unparalleled influence and an enormous extension of territory;—when we reflect that with half the two thousand men that Godeheu brought out with him, he could have crushed the English, already reduced to extremities at Trichinápallí—we cannot but marvel at the blindness, the infatuation, the madness, that recalled him. The primary cause was, no doubt, as we have stated, the degraded condition of the France of Louis XV. But there was yet, we believe, another reason, not entirely dependent upon the state of his country, for we have seen it act under other rulers than Louis XV., and under other Governments than France. To borrow the words of the French historian,* " Dupleix had against him that crime of genius, which so many men have expiated by misery, by exile, and by death."

* *Histoire de la Conquête de l'Inde par l'Angleterre*, par le Baron Barchou de Penhöen.

HIS TREATMENT IN FRANCE.

It was on October 14, 1754, that Dupleix bade adieu to the country of his greatness. Baffled as he had been in his large schemes, ruined as he was known to have been by the measures of Godeheu, he was yet, in spite of the declared hostility of that personage, followed to the place of embarkation by the principal officers and *employés* of Pondichery, and by all the common people. Their generous hearts spoke out in the universal feeling of regret at his departure. Their grief was far more eloquent, infinitely more expressive, than would have been the smiles of a Pompadour!

Very briefly we propose to follow the disgraced Governor to his last hour. Before he had landed in France, the Minister, Machault, fearing, in the then state of European politics, the result in India of the recall of Dupleix, and hoping it might not have been actually accomplished, had sent to Dupleix a despatch in which he affected to treat him as Governor, Godeheu merely as Commissary of the King to make peace. This despatch reached Pondichery after Dupleix had left it, though it had been expedited by the Minister in the hope that it would prevent his departure. His arrival, therefore, in France was looked upon in the light of a misfortune, and it appeared for some time not improbable that he might even be re-instated in his post. He was, therefore, well received and flattered with hopes of a settlement of his claims. As soon, however, as the intelligence of the disgraceful peace made by Godeheu—to which we shall presently refer—reached France, and the disagreements with England were consequently regarded as settled, the Ministry at once began to treat Dupleix as a man from whom nothing more could be hoped, but who, on his part, would importune them with claims. They, therefore, or rather, acting with them, the Directors of the Company, at once changed their manner towards him, and absolutely refused to take his accounts into consideration. In vain did he remonstrate. In vain did he point out that he was persecuted by creditors who were simply creditors, because, on his security, they had advanced their funds to the Government of Pondichery. In vain did he write a memoir, setting forth, in a modest but graphic style, all he had done, the sums of money he had advanced. For seven years he urged and pressed his claims, supporting them by incontestable proofs. He received not even the shadow of redress. Nay, more. Many of those whom he had befriended in his prosperity, and who had advanced sums to the Pondichery Government, sued him for repayment. Even Bussy, who was to have been his stepson, deserted him in his extremity, broke off the marriage, and appeared in the list of claimants against him. To such a state of misery was he reduced, that, three months before he died, his house was in the occupation of bailiffs. Three days before that sad event, he thus wrote in his memoir: " I have sacrificed my youth, my fortune, my life, to enrich my nation in Asia. Unfortunate friends, too weak relations, devoted all their property to the success of my projects. They are now in misery and want. I have submitted to all the judiciary forms; I have demanded, as the last of the creditors, that which is due to me. My services are treated as fables; my demand is denounced as ridiculous; I am treated as the vilest of mankind. I am in the most deplorable indigence; the little property that remained to me has been seized. I am compelled to ask for decrees for delay in order not to be dragged into prison." Thus wrote, three days before he died, the man who had done for France more than all her Kings, beside whose exploits the deeds of her Condé, her Villars, her Turenne, sink into insignificance. The founder of an empire treated as the vilest of mankind, his just claims unattended to then, unsettled even to this day*; the man who acquired for France territories in the East larger than France herself, treated as an importunate imposter! Not long could even his brave spirit endure such a contest. He died on November 10, 1764. †

Not the less will he rank with posterity as one of the greatest of Frenchmen; not the less will even the descendants of his rivals in Southern India place him on the same pedestal as the greatest of their own heroes—on the pedestal of Clive, of Warren Hastings, and of Wellesley!

* Strange it is that, considering the mutations France has herself gone through, she should still have allowed these claims to remain unsettled. The Republic, the first Empire, the Restoration, the Orleanists, the second Republic, and the second Empire, must divide with the Bourbons the shame of this great scandal. We append an extract from the letter of the Paris correspondent of the *Globe* of May 17, 1866, showing that even up to the time of his last descendant these claims had been neglected:

"Another death, which is worthy of record, is that of the last descendant of the great Nabob Dupleix, the celebrated Governor of Pondichery. The coat of arms granted him by Louis XV., for the diplomatic triumphs gained by him over the English in India, glittered for the last time over the portal of Saint Philippe du Roule, as the modest coffin which contained the remains of the last Dupleix was borne out to the cemetery. Of the great siege of Pondichery, of the glory and magnificence of Dupleix, of his riches and his disgrace, of his humiliation. his poverty and miserable death, nothing is remembered now. Even the *fête* which he had instituted at Pernan, his native place, to celebrate the raising of the siege of Pondichery, has long been discontinued for want of the funds which he had intended to be annually devoted to the dower of one of the village maidens. He died in the most abject poverty, after having had at his command whole multitudes of men and millions of rupees; and the faithless agent charged by him with the settlement of the perpetual fund for the good work of which he had been dreaming for years beneath the hot scorching sun of India, and amid the strife and bloodshed by which he was surrounded, never having sunk the money, the celebration of the one glorious souvenir of his life—that too has passed away, and his very name is now no more. When the *Ministère des Finances* was entered by the mob in 1830, the last appeal of Dupleix, imploring a settlement of his claim of 13 millions against the Government, was thrown out amongst other papers scattered to the winds. It fell into the hands of the professor of philosophy at the college Louis le Grand, who had it framed and glazed, and hung up in his class-room, where it afterwards served as illustration to many and many a lesson on the vanity of riches and the varied conformation of the wings they make to themselves when they flee away."

† He died in a house in the Rue Neuve des Capucines, on the site till recently occupied by the Foreign office, within a few doors of the official residence of the Company.

CHAPTER X.

GODEHEU AND DE LEYRIT.

CHAP. X.
1754.

BEFORE his departure from Pondichery, Dupleix had laid before his successor a detailed account of the military and other operations that had taken place in the Dakhan, in the Karnátik, and before Trichinápallí, and had indicated at great length the measures which he, had he continued at the head of affairs, would have adopted, in order to insure the triumph of the French arms. He advised him to maintain Bussy at the court of the Subadar, Moracin in the ceded districts, Mainville at the head of the army before Trichinápallí. He counselled that to this last the reinforcements then landing should be sent without delay, and that he should be instructed to use them effectually before Admiral Watson's fleet, then shortly expected, should arrive off Madras. He laid special stress on the retention of Mainville at the head of the army, not only because he had shown energy and capacity, but likewise because he had gained the complete confidence of the French allies—the Dalwai of Maisur and Murárí Ráo.

For some time Godeheu made no sign. To Governor Saunders, indeed, he forwarded proposals of accommodation, and as an earnest of his sincerity, restored to him, that they might be used against France, the Swiss soldiers captured by Dupleix during the previous year. But neither to Bussy, to Moracin, nor to Mainville, did he give the smallest indication of his policy. He contented himself with cutting off from Mainville those supplies of money with which he had been till then liberally furnished by Dupleix for the maintenance of his army.

This policy of negation, if indeed it was a policy at all, and not, as we believe it to have been, the natural inaction of an undecided mind, had the worst possible effect. The air was at once filled with rumours, all injurious to the French. The English, flushed with joy at the recall of Dupleix, made no secret as to the means by which that recall had been obtained, and as to the consequences that were to follow from it. Their stories, spread everywhere by their agents, were universally credited, and their effect exaggerated tenfold. The partisans of the French alliance were everywhere overwhelmed with shame, with mortification, and with fear.

At the court of the Subadar these feelings showed themselves in the fullest strength. "Your nation," wrote Salábat Jang* to Bussy, on the arrival of messengers from Pondichery informing him of the assumption of authority by Godeheu, "your nation has supported and succoured me till now. I have recognised to the utmost of my power the services it has rendered me. I have given to my uncle, M. Dupleix, the government of the Karnátik, and I have ever hoped that he would gain the upper-hand over his enemies. It is with the greatest chagrin that I have heard of his recall. To the messengers who were intrusted with my letters for him the new Governor said: 'Tell the Subadar, your master, that I am sent here by my sovereign, who has forbidden me to interfere with the Múghal Government, and that he must defend himself as best he can.' They

---

* The correspondence quoted in this chapter has been translated from the originals appended to the memoir of Dupleix. On that correspondence, on the histories of Orme, of Wilks, and of Grant Duff, on the narrative of Colonel Lawrence, and on the Sër Mutákharin, the other statements contained in it are based.

have also reported that the prisoners have been restored to Muhammad Ali, that Murárí Ráo and the Maisurians have abandoned you. All this proves to me that the English have gained completely the superiority over your nation." The Diwán, Sháh Nawáz Khán, writing to the Muhammadan governor of Haidarábád, thus expressed himself: "I cannot recover from the surprise which the news of the recall of the Governor Bahádur has caused me. I cannot imagine what the French are at; but by that act they will lose their honour and their territories. I cannot conceal from you that we can arrange nothing with the new governor, who has not the least knowledge of our affairs. Besides, it appears that the French are neither so powerful nor so generous as they would have us believe, and that the English have the absolute mastery over them. I will not hide from you then that I am about to negotiate with the English and Muhammad Ali."

The letters of the French officers themselves were not at all more cheerful. "I foresaw," wrote Moracin to Bussy, from Machhlipatan, " in the same sense as yourself, what would be the effect of the arrival in India of the King's Commissary. I wrote to him a fortnight ago, and I believe I gave him an opinion similar to your own. It is fit that I should inform you of the contents of the letters from Madras which our native bankers have shown me. In these it is stated that the King of England has forced the King of France to recall M. Dupleix from Pondichery, under a threat of war; and that the King of France, in sending out the new governor, said to him: 'Go and make peace in India; restore to the Nawwáb the territories which he has given to the Company; I will not keep them, because to do so would annoy my brother, the King of England.'" Both Bussy and Moracin felt at this time the utter hopelessness of their position so completely, that nothing but the earnest exhortation of Dupleix to them to continue to serve France, no matter by whom she was represented, induced them to remain at their posts. The answer of Bussy to this earnest exhortation deserves to be recorded. "I reply," he wrote, under date August 23, "to the letter with which you favoured me on the 4th. Your departure for Europe is a thunderbolt which has confounded and alarmed me. You, who are leaving, exhort me to continue to serve the nation, and to support a work which is on the brink of destruction. Do you sincerely believe that I shall not be enveloped in the same disgrace as yourself? The blow is perhaps deferred, or suspended only to be struck with the greater force. But however that may be, I have ever considered it my duty to defer to your counsels, and to follow your reasoning. Under no circumstances shall I ever depart from that respectful and inviolable attachment, which has been till now my happiness and my glory, and which will always remain so. I await M. Godeheu's replies to determine myself, although, like you, I am persuaded that I ought to await in India the replies of M. de Conflans. If, nevertheless, in the post which I occupy I am not to be allowed liberty to act, if they shall endeavour to fetter me by the ideas of ignorant people and men without experience, my work will perish in my hands; and it will be concluded, either that I have destroyed it in pique, or that it was neither so splendid nor so well established as you and I have declared it to be. On the one side I declare that if the confidence with which you have honoured me is continued by M. Godeheu, I shall not refuse to devote myself to the service of the nation and the Company; it is not that I expect that my services will be recognised or even acknowledged; but I shall have, like yourself, the advantage of having served my country, without any emolument but the glory of having been useful to it, and the consolation of attributing its neglect and ingratitude only to the factiousness of the envious, themselves too wanting in merit not to seek to obscure that of others. . . . . Do me the favour to inform me if you can of the views of M. Godeheu regarding the Dakhan. Personally I am disposed to abandon all and to retire to France. But I wait your answer and your advice. I am so overwhelmed that I cannot apply myself to business. The army is crying out from hunger;—no one pays,—and I am forbidden to act."

Such was the state of matters in the Dakhan and in the Sirkars. Before Trichinápallí it was worse. We left the French army under Mainville occupying the Five Rocks, completely shutting in the city; Lawrence absent at Tanjur, with the king of which country Dupleix continued up to the last to be in secret communication. Very shortly after the arrival of Godeheu, the 2,000 troops that sailed with him from France landed at Pondichery. These should have been sent, as Dupleix strongly urged, to reinforce Mainville, who could then have made sure of the city for which the French had been so long struggling. But far from so acting, Godeheu sent only petty reinforcements; he cut off also from his army the supplies of money it had been in the habit of receiving; he stopped the transport of provisions; he sent no orders; the letters and remonstrances of Mainville he left unanswered. The consequence was that a portion of the army mutinied, and the revolt was only suppressed by the loyal exertions of the officers. The letter written by Godeheu to Dupleix on hearing of this outbreak serves to illustrate the character of the new Governor,—to show in a striking light the crime committed by the French Government in sending out such a man to supersede Dupleix. "What resources would you have," wrote he, "in the same case? You were in a position to make advances from your purse and on your credit; I can do neither one nor the other."

POLICY OF GODEHEU.

But this was not all. The new Governor seemed determined to sacrifice not only the territories acquired by Dupleix, but even the honour of France to the one great object of making peace with England. So transparent was this intention, so patent to all, that it produced in the French settlement and in the French army, a discouragement and a despondency fatal to the life of a people. It is not too much to affirm that, had Governor Saunders himself been appointed successor to Dupleix he could not have more effectually injured French interests than did this nominee of the French Direction and the French Crown. He began by changing the superior command of the army. Mainville having been recommended by Dupleix as the most capable officer, as the man of all others the most acceptable to his native allies, Godeheu took an early opportunity of superseding him, appointing in his stead M. de Maissin,—a man remarkable for his little capacity and his want of resolution. Not the less, however, did he suit the purposes of Godeheu. It would not be credited were there not evidence to prove it,* that, at a moment when the English garrison at Trichinápallí was sorely pressed by famine; when the French army had only to hold the position at the Five Rocks and the dependent posts to prevent the possibility of the ingress of any convoy; Godeheu instructed his new general to connive at its re-victualment, to offer no real obstacle to the retention by the English of that all-important city. As at this time, as before, the result of the negotiations with the English still depended on the fortunes of the campaign, we can easily conceive how the interests of France suffered in the hands of her representative. To that campaign we purpose now to refer.

Mainville made over the command of the French army to Maissin on August 16, 1754. It had long

* Mainville's *Report*, "Letter from the Dalwai of Maisur, to his Agent at Pondichery." *Vide* also Orme.

been known that the English commander, Major Lawrence, had been waiting only the conclusion of an arrangement for native assistance with Mafauz Khan, elder brother of Muhammad Ali, to endeavour to escort supplies into Trichinápallí. Of the movements of this convoy Mainville had had the most certain intelligence, and he had made all his arrangements to cut it off. Only three days after he had delivered up his command to Maissin he learned that the convoy, escorted by 1,200 English troops, 3,000 sipáhis, and fourteen field-pieces, with a native contingent of 5,500 men and several guns, had arrived at a village six miles to the east of Elmiseram, and that it would endeavour to force its way the next morning between the Sugar-loaf and the French Rocks. Mainville, who had employed the previous two months in reconnoitring this ground, at once informed his successor of the intended movement, and strongly urged him to move out at once and take possession of a watercourse running out of the Kávarí, the near bank of which commanded the country beyond. He indicated to him also the names of two officers, MM. Gaudart and Aumont, who were thoroughly acquainted with the country, and to whom Mainville himself, when in command, had confided his intentions. Maissin listened to the communication with apparent pleasure, and set out with the avowed intention of putting it into execution. No sooner, however, had he reached the Sugar-loaf Rock, than, obedient to his secret instructions, he drew up his army close to a tank in front of it, and, leaving the watercourse unguarded, waited the approach of the enemy. When Lawrence did appear,— his convoy defiling on his right,—marching as much at ease as on a field day, and opened fire from a battery he had erected on the high bank of the watercourse, Maissin declined an action, and retired without even firing a shot.* Whilst this was going on, a Maisurian officer,

* M. de Mainville says, "il se retira sans qu'il y eût une amorce de fusil brûlée."

named Haidar Naik (the Haidar Ali afterwards so famous), moving round the English force, fell upon the rear of the convoy, and captured thirty-five carts all laden with supplies and stores. This attack diverted the attention of Major Lawrence from the French, and offered them a good opportunity to assault with advantage. In vain did the Dalwai urge Maissin to use it; in vain did he point out that one charge would finish the campaign; Maissin was deaf to every representation; reposing on the secret instructions of his superior, he moved quietly back to his position at the Five Rocks. Meanwhile, not only Lawrence's convoy, but others from different parts of the country, poured into Trichinápallí.

A few days later, Maissin retired to Mutáchélinur on the Kávarí, abandoning his posts around Trichinápallí. He had not the firmness to remain even here when, some few days later, Lawrence appeared before the place—which nevertheless was strongly fortified—but retreated precipitately into Srirangam. The English, satisfied with this success, proceeded to house themselves for the rainy season in the Wáriúr pagodas, nearly due west of Trichinápallí.

Meanwhile, Godeheu, by his unskilful efforts to bring about peace at any price, had been working the most effectual damage to French interests in the eyes of the native powers. His lieutenants were everywhere left in a state of the most painful uncertainty. After wavering long as to whether he should withdraw his support from Salábat Jang, or leave Bussy with diminished influence and restricted powers at his court, he wrote on September 16, that he was convinced of the necessity of not abandoning the Subadar. To Moracin, however, the administrator of the Sirkars, he threw out hints in the same letter regarding his projected renunciation of the territorial acquisitions of the Company, on the ground that "he preferred a safe and extended com-

CHAP. X.

1754.

merce to any other advantage."* It was in vain that Moracin assured him, in reply, that whoever had persuaded him that the peace and security of one part of the French possessions would be best maintained by the abandonment of another part, could know nothing either of the map of the country, the locality, or the interests of the Company. It was to no purpose that he warned him that such an act would be but the prelude " to our total and proximate expulsion from this part of the Dakhan."† Godeheu's mind was made up. To undo the work of Dupleix, to make peace with the English, the honour and interests of France were but light sacrifices.

Negotiations had, meanwhile, been pending with the government of Madras. Mr. Saunders had indeed been recently reinforced by the arrival of Admiral Watson's fleet, having on board Her Majesty's 49th regiment, and several recruits for the Company. This advantage was, however, to a certain extent counterbalanced in the mind of Mr. Saunders by the fact that Colonel Adlercron, who commanded the 49th, superseded the tried and gallant veteran who had so often led the English forces to victory. As the French had just before received reinforcements certainly not inferior in number, it was still a question as to which of the contending parties, in the event of a continuation of the war, would have the advantage. But the folly of Godeheu had given Saunders a moral superiority, of which he did not fail to make the fullest use. The wise forethought, likewise, of the English Government, in despatching a fleet to influence the negotiations for peace, produced a wonderful effect. Saunders was not insensible, however, to the advantages to be derived from the feverish impatience of Godeheu, and he readily acceded, on October 26, to a truce for three months, during which commissioners should meet at

* Letter to Moracin, September 16, 1754.　† Reply of Moracin, dated October 9, 1754.

Pondichery to discuss the conditions of a permanent peace. The principal articles of this truce declared, that, till January 11, 1755, no act of hostility should ensue between the French and English, or between their allies; that commerce should be free to both nations in the Karnátik; that there should be a mutual, but *ad valorem*, exchange of prisoners; and that commissaries should be appointed on both sides to see that the conditions of the truce were not infringed.

Two months later, a treaty of peace was agreed to, so far only provisional, that it required the ratification of the East India Companies of France and England. The first condition of this treaty laid down that the two Companies should "renounce for ever all Múghal dignities and governments, and should never interfere in the differences that might arise among the princes of the country"; the second and third, that the English should possess Fort St. George, Fort St. David, and Dévikotá; the French, Pondichery and a limited settlement at Nizámpatnam, it being arranged, that to the French should be allotted either a territory between Nizámpatnam and the river Gundlákámma, to compensate for the inferiority of Kárikál to Dévikotá; or that the districts of Pondichery should be made equal to those of Fort St. George and Fort St. David, the French in that case abandoning the country about Nizámpatnam. The fourth clause abandoned for the French their claims on Machhlípatan and the adjoining districts, it being arranged that equal territories should be there assigned to the rival Companies. The fifth, sixth, and seventh clauses regulated the navigation of certain rivers, and the possession of certain other minor territories, on the same principle. The eighth provided for the prolongation of the truce till the confirmation of the treaty should arrive from Europe. The ninth, for the non-construction of any ports or obtaining any new grants of territory during the truce. The tenth, for the principle of *uti possidetis* till the treaty should be confirmed from Europe; and the eleventh, for some future plan of indemnification for the expenses of the war.

When we commented on the conditions of peace which the agents of Dupleix submitted to the Conference of Sadras in the autumn of the previous year, we noticed that the French proposals were remarkable more for their omissions than for what they contained. The same observation is applicable, in one particular point, to the treaty of which we have here given an outline. No mention is made of Muhammad Ali; not a single reference to the office of Nawwáb of the Karnátik. It was not, however, the less clear from this omission, that the English had gained, in this particular, all for which they had been contending. The clause which forbade either nation to accept office or government from the native authorities was an unmistakable renunciation on the part of Godeheu of all the dignities and governments which the Subadar had conferred upon his predecessor. The French competitor for the office of Nawwáb having thus resigned his claims, on whom but on the rival competitor, Muhammad Ali, would the vacated government devolve? For five years had the French and English battled for this single point; to maintain the French view, Dupleix had risked and lost his semi-regal seat in the Council of Pondichery, he had refused substantial offers of territory which did not include this concession. His successor tamely renounced it, without, however, obtaining those substantial advantages which alone could make it palatable.

But the third and fourth clauses, and especially the fourth, contained concessions not only damaging to French interests but disgraceful to French honour. The third, under the pretext of giving to each nation equal possessions on the Koromandel coast, kept indeed

ITS SHAMEFUL PROVISIONS.

"the word of promise to the ear," but only "to break it to the hope." Kárikál was not the equivalent of Dévikotá as a place of commerce. But—what was worse, what was even insulting—to bring about on another part of the coast this declared equality, the English proposed, and the French agreed, to take a district which actually belonged to the French, which was their own, their property, and to give them only a small portion of it, restoring the rest to the native powers. We allude to the agreement to form a settlement to be confined rigidly to the country between Nizámpatnam and the river Gundlákámma, at a time when the entire coast from Nizámpatnam to Jaggannáth was French—French by gift, French by actual possession. The alternative proposal, to make the districts of Pondichery equal to those of Fort St. George and Fort St. David together, was even more dishonouring and insidious, for the effect of it would be, to agree to abandon for ever, though without special mention of them, those Sirkars which the genius and policy of Bussy had gained for his country.

But of all the clauses, the fourth was the most directly injurious to French interests. This actually proposed that the city of Machhlípatan, with certain districts round it, and the highland of Divi, both actually French property, should be divided between the rival powers. The carrying out of this proposition would alone entail a sacrifice, on the part of the French, of a fixed annual revenue of 4,000,000 francs (£160,000). The fifth, sixth, and seventh articles dealt likewise with French territory to the advantage of their rivals.

The remaining articles of the treaty, especially those which referred to the native allies of the two powers, were equally one-sided. The English had but one ally, the Rájá of Tanjur; for Muhammad Ali was but their helpless tool, the puppet in whose name, and under the shadow of whose usurped authority they had endeavoured to overthrow French influence. The French, on the contrary, had the Maráthás, the Maisurians, and the Subadar. These knew not a word of the treaty. The effect of it, therefore, was to impose English law, not alone upon the French, but upon the independent princes of India; to force Salábat Jang to accept, as Nawwáb of the Karnátik, a man whom he had frequently declared to be a rebel and an outlaw; to compel the Maisurians and Maráthás to desist from their views on the city which they already regarded as their own. As a climax to this condition, the French, the allies of these princes, were to guarantee that they would execute it.

Such was Godeheu's treaty—a treaty in which he renounced all that the French had been contending for. He gave up the office of Nawwáb of the Karnátik; he practically renounced the northern Sirkars; he abandoned his allies; he surrendered French influence and French honour. Could there have been a greater contrast to Dupleix? To him the English had offered to guarantee the possession of all his territories, provided he would resign the position and office of Nawwáb of the Karnátik. His successor not only renounced that office, but with it those material advantages which France had secured, the undisputed possession of which would still have left her, under any circumstances, infinitely more powerful than her rival. It is certainly not too severe a sentence, not too extravagant a criticism, to pronounce such a treaty to have been, in a French point of view, disgraceful. It was disgraceful to France, disgraceful to the man who made it. To his timorous love of peace, fostered by the mean and unworthy desire to undo the work of his predecessor, Godeheu sacrificed—and sacrificed knowing what he was sacrificing—the very foundations of an Indo-French empire.

For, indeed, great as were the material advantages

given up, they were less important than the abnegation of moral influence, of the prestige of superiority which their renunciation implied. The treaty, in fact, was an announcement to the native princes of Southern India that thenceforth France was not strong enough to contend with England on the soil of Southern India, that she gave up the struggle; that she abandoned her allies to their fate. The impression produced by the rival of Godeheu upon the bankers of Machhlípatan has been already quoted Damaging as that was, this confirmation of the views then entertained, and declared by Moracin and others to be exaggerated, was a hundred times more injurious. We shall see, as we proceed, the fatal effects produced upon the princes of India by this policy of abnegation.

In striking contrast to the conduct of the French Governor was the action of the Englishman, Saunders. If the empire of Hindustan is an appanage of which the English have reason to be proud; if the possession of India has brought with it solid advantages to Great Britain, then do his countrymen still owe to the memory of Mr. Saunders a debt which was never fully acknowledged to himself. It was his constancy and resolution, his determination, when the English fortunes were at their lowest, to support Muhammad Ali, in order that through him he might stop the progress of Dupleix; that, more than any other circumstances, changed the face of events; that tended, by a slow but certain procedure, to lower the pride of France, to exalt the fortunes of England. Never did he despair, never did he hesitate in his determination to oppose those pretensions which, if submitted to, would, he felt, have overwhelmed the English settlement in ruin. True it is that he was fortunate; true, that he enjoyed the rare advantage of having a Clive and a Lawrence at his disposal. But it is not too much to affirm, that but for his stubborn policy even these advantages would have ultimately availed nothing; that but for his promptitude in recognising and employing merit, Clive might even have languished in obscurity. Nor was his tact inferior to his determination. He would have treated with Dupleix,— Dupleix being absolute master of his Presidency—on better terms than he offered Godeheu; for he could not but feel that if France were to support Dupleix, a prolongation of hostilities must end in an increase of French territory. He was prepared, therefore, to give up everything but that one point he considered necessary to the safety of the English, viz.: that the Nawwáb of the Karnátik should not be a French nominee. But with Godeheu he pursued a different treatment: he saw that from the fear and malice of such a man he could wring almost anything; he squeezed him, therefore, to an extent that left him powerless and exhausted.

That, whilst doing justice to the merits of Saunders, and vindicating the policy of Dupleix, we have not wronged the memory of Godeheu, is clear from the recorded sentiments of that functionary. What, indeed, but a feverish desire for peace at any price, and a mean jealousy of Dupleix, could have prompted him, on January 11, to sign the ignominious treaty to which we have referred, when, on December 17 preceding, the terms of the treaty having been virtually settled, and the truce still existing, he had written these words to Moracin at Machhlípatan: "Prepare everything with all promptitude to the extent of your ability, so as to make yourself safe from a *coup-de-main*, for it is quite possible you may be attacked before the end of January. It is by such sudden enterprises that the English begin to declare war!"[*] He thus prepared Moracin for an attack on the Sirkars at the end of December; and yet, on January 11 following, virtually resigned them up to the English.

Not long did he remain in India to watch the working

[*] This correspondence is attached to the memoir of Dupleix.

of his treaty. On February 16, 1755, after holding office little more than six months, he embarked for Europe, leaving the affairs of the French settlement to be administered by a secret committee, composed of MM. Barthélemy, Boileau, and Guillard, until the arrival of the officer nominated to be his successor, M. Duval de Leyrit. His departure was hailed by the colony as a national benefit. That alone, of all his acts, produced a good effect for French interests throughout Southern India, for it gave rise to the rumour, artfully encouraged by Bussy, that it was but the prelude to the return of Dupleix.

But the recall of that statesman had had more than a transient effect. The members of the secret committee, having before them his example, and ignorant of the political views of M. de Leyrit, would do nothing. Writing to Bussy, who pressed the Pondichery government for instructions as to the course of conduct he should adopt in the difficult circumstances we shall have to record, they could only reply that they had received all the letters he had addressed to M. Godeheu; that they had not answered them, because certain points in them were of too delicate a nature to allow them to arrive at a fixed decision; but that M. de Leyrit, on his arrival, would probably explain himself fully upon all the questions at issue.* The same conduct was pursued in every other subject of importance, the consequence being, that from February 16, the date of the departure of Godeheu, to the arrival of de Leyrit on March 25 of the same year, the government of French India was but a blank.

De Leyrit, though a very ordinary man, was an improvement on the secret committee. He too had been trained in India in the civil branch of the service, and had been a contemporary of Dupleix. At the time of the expedition of La Bourdonnais, he had been the

* M. Barthélemy to Bussy, February 28, 1755.

French agent at Mahé, and he had succeeded Dupleix as Director-General of Chandranagar in 1741. He would have made probably an excellent head of a purely trading corporation, for he was well versed in mercantile operations; but he was most unfit for the conduct of the delicate policy by which the relations of Pondichery with the native chiefs required to be guided; equally was he wanting in the firmness of purpose and determination of will by which alone the aggressive policy of the English could be stayed. In a word, though well-meaning and laborious, he was slow, undecided, wanting in forethought and energy.

Yet at that time, if at any, French India required other qualities in her chief ruler. Godeheu had not even quitted the scene of his inglorious labours, scarcely dry was the ink with which he and the English Commissioners had signed the treaty,—one clause of which provided that the English and French "should never interfere in any difference that might arise between the princes of the country,"—when the English began to equip a force to assist their ally, Muhammad Ali, in his endeavours to coerce the petty rulers of Madura and Tinivellí, his right over whom was simply the right of the strongest. Although the English were actuated in this policy by purely mercenary motives, hoping to obtain from those districts the means of re-couping themselves for the expenses of the war just closed, there can be no doubt but that it was a glaring infraction of the treaty. That it was attempted is a clear proof of the contempt with which the power of the French on the Koromandel coast had come to be regarded.

In the beginning of February, under orders received from Madras, an English force under Colonel Heron, of H.M.'s 49th foot, was detached from Trichinápallí on this service. Whatever might have been the apparent success of this enterprise—and Colonel Heron did

STRAINED RELATIONS BETWEEN THE TWO COUNTRIES.

succeed in occupying both Madura and Tinivellí—it must not the less be regarded as a failure. The English soldiers, commanded by an officer ignorant of the country, were allowed to insult the religion and to deride the prejudices of the people; the money gained in the foray was not sufficient to pay the expenses of the expedition;* and, worse than all, an example was given of the little respect entertained by the government of Fort St. George for the most solemn engagements when its own interests were concerned. De Leyrit had not been an inattentive spectator of this action on the part of the English. No sooner had he landed than he addressed to the Madras Government a strong remonstance on the infraction of the treaty. It was replied to him, however, that Colonel Heron's expedition was not an act of war in any sense of the word; that the Nawwáb was simply engaged in the collection of his rents. However specious this reply might have appeared, de Leyrit was for the moment forced to be content with it; for Admiral Watson was on the coast, and de Leyrit, new to the scene, felt that it would be impolitic to inaugurate his career as Governor by a renewal of hostilities. He determined, therefore, to rest satisfied with his protest, inwardly resolving, however, to follow the example so imprudently set him. Accordingly when, some few weeks later, he found that the rents due from the lands west of Utatur and south of the Valaru river, known by the name of Tirur, and in which the French had been empowered to act as agents of the Rájá of Maisur, were not paid into the Pondichery treasury, he sent Maissin at the head of 500 Europeans and 1,000 sipáhis to make arrangements which should be satisfactory for the future. The English made no opposition to this movement. But when the French, succeeding in Tirur, were tempted to move against the more

CHAP. X.

1755.

* Colonel Heron, on his return to Trichinápallí in June, was ordered to Madras, tried there by a court martial and found guilty of malversation.

G G

CHAP. X.
1755.

eastern lands nearer Palamkotá, stretching almost from the Valaru to the Kolrún, and which the English chose to regard as feudally dependent on the Nawwáb, orders were sent to Calliaud to oppose the movement, if necessary, by force. If the French had persisted in their pretensions, war was then inevitable. But de Leyrit, still unprepared, yielded and withdrew his troops. Nevertheless, a precedent of interference had been established on both sides, and before Godeheu reached Europe, the treaty which he carried with him had been violated in that part which was alike its main principle and its only possible justification—by the English in acting as allies of Muhammad Ali, by the French as agents of the Maisurians.

De Leyrit indeed had not been long at Pondichery before he became convinced that the theory of non-interference, on which Godeheu had based his policy, was, in the actual state of India, simply impossible. Both the rival powers on the Koromandel coast having armies and strong places, both brought constantly into contact with possessors of territory whose weakness they had proved, and who were continually tempting them with offers, it was impossible that either should have the virtue on every occasion to abstain, always to restrain its hands. Excuses were found to justify, at least to their Directors in Europe, every infraction of the treaty. It is clear from the correspondence of de Leyrit with Bussy and with Dupleix,* that this feeling on his part grew stronger every day, and that he became more and more convinced of the insensate folly of Godeheu in consenting to divide a portion of the Sirkars with the English. Of these, however, the French still held possession, and were empowered to hold possession, till the ratification of the treaty should arrive, that is, till about the middle of 1756. As de

---

* De Leyrit to Bussy, July 29 and August 17, 1755; to Dupleix, October 16, and other letters.

Leyrit saw clearly that war would then be inevitable, all his foreign policy was directed to nurse the resources of Pondichery, to avoid committing himself to a contest, until his own private knowledge of the confirmation of the treaty should render it advisable for him to provoke hostilities on other grounds. Should the treaty not be confirmed, war would naturally ensue.

This exposition of the views of de Leyrit will enable us to comprehend and account for the cautious policy he continued for some time to follow. We shall understand why it was he continued to support Bussy at Haidarábád, why, when the English again infringed the treaty, he confined himself to threats and to protests, until, learning that the treaty had been confirmed by his Directors, he made the aggression of the English a pretext for renewing hostilities, endeavouring thus to retain for France permanent possession of the ceded Sirkars. It was undoubtedly, in theory, a sagacious and able policy, but to succeed it required the possession of greater energy and vigour in action than de Leyrit and his subordinates, always excepting Bussy, possessed.

Opportunities for protesting were never wanting to either party. In the autumn of the same year, 1755, the French having taken possession of some lands contiguous to Sadras, midway nearly between Pondichery and Fort St. George, the English remonstrated, and the dispute only terminated by an equal division of the contested territory.* But in the following year affairs took a turn which could not fail to embroil the two nations.

The English had always been jealous of the position held by Bussy at the court of the Subadar. The influence which thus accrued to the French could not fail to make itself felt on both shores of Southern

---

* A truly European mode of settling a dispute, the lands in question having belonged to native princes who were parties to the treaty.

CHAP. X.

1756.

India, at the court of the Peshwá, as well as with the various petty chieftains in the Karnátik. In the treaty concluded with Godeheu, no special mention had been made of Bussy, and there had been a tacit understanding that it had no reference to the affairs of the Subadar, who indeed had never committed hostilities against the English. Unable, then, to demand as a right the expulsion of Bussy, the English were yet desirous to weaken the influence he was able to exercise by his position at Haidarábád, either by undermining him with the Subadar, or by gaining new possessions for themselves on the western coast. The manner in which the first was attempted, and how it succeeded, will be related when we have to refer to the operations of Bussy. But, before that, the return to India of Clive, with the commission of Lieutenant-Colonel and Governor of Fort St. David, gave the English an opportunity of trying the second. Clive, under orders from the Court of Directors, had been sent in the first instance to Bombay, in order that he might be ready to co-operate in an expedition which they contemplated in concert with the Peshwá against the northern parts of the Dakhan. Colonel Scott, the officer appointed to command the English contingent, dying in Bombay, his place was at once occupied by Clive, and it needed but the orders of the Bombay Government to enter upon the contemplated movement. The members of that Government, however, regarding Godeheu's treaty as prohibitory of any such undertaking, hesitated to embark in it, until at least they should have received the opinion on that point of the Madras authorities. These had no such scruple. And, although they were ignorant of the views of the Home Government regarding the disposal of Clive's force; although, indeed, they were not destined, at the time, to be enlightened—the ship which conveyed the despatches of the Bombay Government having been wrecked—yet no sooner had they heard of the arrival of Clive at Bombay, than they sent to suggest the mode in which his force could be best used—a mode almost identical with the plan of the Court of Directors. But before their despatch could reach Bombay, the Government of that Presidency, more cautious than that of Madras, had determined to employ Clive's force and Admiral Watson's fleet for the reduction, in conjunction with the Maráthás, of the Fort of Ghériah, the principal stronghold of the famous pirate Angria.

It forms no part of this history to give the details of this expedition, unconnected as it was with French interests. It will suffice to say that it was attended with complete success; that Ghériah was taken, Angria's fleet destroyed, and the ten lakhs of prize-money captured divided on the spot amongst the English— the Maráthás being excluded* from all participation therein, notwithstanding that it was to them, and not to the English, that Angria surrendered.

This expedition terminated, Clive and Watson returned to the coast of Koromandel, the former taking up his Government at Fort St. David, the latter repairing to Madras. He reached this place on the 16th May, and began at once to concert with Governor Pigott† a scheme which the expulsion of Bussy by Salábat Jang seemed to facilitate for replacing French by English influence in the Dakhan. But just two months after his arrival, accounts were received of the capture of Kásim-bazar, and, three weeks later, of the taking of Calcutta by the Subadar of Bengal. Clive was instantly summoned from Fort St. David to take part in the deliberations having for their object the

---

* Before the expedition left Bombay, the English had agreed amongst themselves that the Maráthás were to be excluded from all participation in the prize-money; nay more, although it had been previously agreed that Ghériah should be given up to the Maráthás, the English determined to keep it. This was not perhaps the most effectual mode of inducing a hearty co-operation against the Subadar.—*Grant Duff.*

† Governor Pigott succeeded Governor Saunders at Madras in 1755.

recovery of the English settlement in that province. In the presence of such a calamity it appeared advisable to give up the projected expedition into the Dakhan, even to allow Madras to shift for herself, in order to concentrate the undivided energies of the Presidency on the recovery of Calcutta and the punishment of the Subadar. After some discussion, Clive was appointed to the land command, subordinate to the commander of the naval operations, Admiral Watson. On the 16th October they sailed, taking with them 900 Europeans and 1,500 sipáhis, on that enterprise to which, in so far as relates to its connexion with Chandranagar, we shall have presently to refer.

Meanwhile the English had not been idle in the Karnátik. Their protégé, the Nawwáb, being still in want of funds, and being thus unable to settle the claims they had against him, it was determined at Madras to make another attempt to extract money from some of the subordinate princes of the Karnátik. Murtizá Ali, Governor of Vellur, was selected for this purpose. It will be recollected that Murtizá Ali had been set up by Dupleix, on the death of Chanda Sahib, as Nawwáb of the Karnátik. As soon, however, as the fall of Dupleix appeared imminent, Murtizá Ali had hastened to disclaim all pretensions to the title, and had made his submission to Muhammad Ali. By this means he hoped to be allowed to remain unmolested in his possessions. But it was not to be. He suffered under the great misfortune of passing for the richest man in the Karnátik, a crime that could only be atoned for by the surrender of his property. It was easy to find a pretext to attack him. Some old story about arrears of tribute was raked up; and, almost without warning, a force of 500 Europeans and 1,500 sipáhis, under Major Kilpatrick, appeared before Vellur on the 30th of January.

Vellur had the reputation of being the strongest

fortress in the upper Karnátik. Its walls were built of large stones, and were strengthened by bastions and towers. It was surrounded by a deep and wide ditch cut out of the rock, and always filled with water swarming with alligators. It commanded the high road to Maisur, and was in other respects a very important position. De Leyrit would have been weak indeed had he allowed such a place to fall into the hands of the English. Nor did he. No sooner then had he heard of the movements of Kilpatrick than he despatched a messenger to Madras to intimate that he would regard an attack upon Vellur as an infraction of the treaty, and that he should oppose it with all his available force. Not content with that, he ordered 300 Europeans and 300 sipáhis to march instantly in the direction of that fortress, supporting them two days later by a reinforcement of 400 of the former and 1,200 of the latter, the whole taking up a position between Jinjí and Chittapét. This demonstration so far succeeded that it prevented an attack upon Vellur. There was no Dupleix, however, at Pondichery to improve the occasion to the advantage of France; no persuasive eloquence to induce Murtizá Ali to admit French troops into Vellur. That chieftain feared his allies probably as much as his enemies; and after a negotiation of three weeks, he was glad to purchase the retirement of the latter by the payment of 400,000 rupees.

The departure in October of the English armament for Bengal, following that of 320 French to aid Bussy in the July preceding—the circumstances relating to which belong properly to the account of that officer's proceedings—left the rival powers in the Karnátik almost too powerless to cause one another effectual injury. The English, however, experienced to its fullest extent the inconvenience of having placed at the head of the affairs of the Karnátik a man such as Muhammad

Ali, without personal resources and without ability. In January, 1757, they found themselves once more compelled to levy contributions from Madura and Tinivellí; and Calliaud, who then commanded at Trichinápallí, was directed to proceed with the greater part of the garrison into those districts. He accordingly marched at the head of 180 Europeans, and 1,000 sipáhis, and six pieces of cannon to Tanjur, to endeavour to obtain from the Rájá succours for his purpose. The Rájá, however, and his ministers, tired of contributing to successes which brought only advantage to their allies, practically refused his aid; whereupon Calliaud, hearing that some petty insurgent chieftains were ravaging the district, moved without delay to Tinivellí. Here he was detained for some time by difficulties regarding supplies and money, and it was not till April 10 that he was able to march towards Madura. At three o'clock on the morning of May 1 he attempted to take this city by surprise, but, being repulsed, took up a position on the south-east face of the town, there to await the arrival of two 18-pounders he had sent for from Trichinápallí. Instead of these guns, however, he received at three o'clock in the afternoon of the 11th the startling intelligence that the whole French army, taking advantage of his absence, was attempting Trichinápallí! Intelligence of the same nature recalled to Madras Colonel Forde, who at the head of 100 Europeans, 56 Africans, 300 sipáhis, and 10,000 auxiliaries, had, till then unsuccessfully, been attempting the reduction of Nellor, held against Muhammad Ali by his brother.

The time had indeed arrived when de Leyrit felt himself empowered to put into execution the schemes he had been long meditating. On May 17, 1756, war, which for two years previously had been impending between France and England, was formally declared. Intelligence of this event reached de Leyrit at the end

HOSTILITIES RECOMMENCE.

of 1756, accompanied, however, by the intimation that France was about to make a tremendous effort to recover her waning influence in India, and that he was to attempt nothing till the armament then fitting out should arrive. But de Leyrit, knowing that the few English troops in the Presidency were occupied before Madura and Nellor, having himself, too, just welcomed the annual detachment from Europe, under the command of the veteran d'Auteuil, thought the moment too opportune to be neglected. On the 6th April, therefore, he despatched 200 Europeans and 1,000 sipáhis into the interior, having given secret instructions to their commander, d'Auteuil, to feign to be entirely occupied by an attack upon the fort of Elvasanur—a few miles north of the river Panar, and on the high road between Jinjí and Trichinápallí—and other strongholds in its vicinity, whilst he should secretly collect all his forces for a combined attack upon the city which had so long bid defiance to French arms. De Leyrit justly argued that the English, engaged with their own plans, would care little about so unimportant a place as Elvasanur; that they would the rather on that account believe that no intention existed to attack Trichinápallí.

It turned out as de Leyrit had imagined. D'Auteuil was allowed, unmolested, even unsuspected, to capture Elvasanur and other places in its vicinity. His action there tended, as de Leyrit had hoped, to make the English feel all the more secure regarding Trichinápallí. Suddenly, however, d'Auteuil massed his forces, amounting to 1,150 Europeans, 3,000 sipáhis, and ten field-pieces, and on the 12th May occupied the island of Srírangam. To enable him to collect so large a force of Europeans not a single soldier fit for duty had been left in Pondichery.

The garrison of Trichinápallí at this time consisted of but 165 Europeans, 700 sipáhis, and 1,000 native auxiliaries, the whole commanded by Captain Joseph

Smith. But guarded within the walls were 500 French prisoners, and d'Auteuil naturally hoped that these, if they could not openly aid him, would, at all events, draw off the attention of a great part of the garrison. On the morning of the 14th, the French leader, crossing the river, took up a position at the Wariur pagodas, nearly three miles west of the city; from this place he opened a fire of shot and shell, and continued it to the 20th, when he sent a summons to Smith to surrender. This summons was, however, answered by defiance.

It had been the intention of d'Auteuil to attempt an assault on the morning of the 21st, but he received during the day intimation that Calliaud, at the head of 120 Europeans and 1,200 sipáhis, was in full march from Madura to relieve Trichinápallí. He deemed it, therefore, advisable to defer his attack in order the better to intercept this force. Instead, however, of massing the greater portion of his troops, leaving a few only to watch Smith, and moving out to crush Calliaud on the road, he resolved to follow the old plan,— dear, we must suppose, from its repeated failure,—of occupying the strong places to the south and east of the town. Like Astruc and Brennier before him, he marched to take up a position stretching from the Five Rocks to the French Rock, occupying, besides those two, in considerable force, the Fakír's Tope and the Golden and Sugar-loaf Rocks. He thus shut out Calliaud from Trichinápallí on the only side on which he could hope to gain it; should the English attempt to force in their way between any of the rocks indicated, it would, he calculated, be in his power to crush them at a blow. The better to acquaint himself with the movements of the enemy, he had arranged that several spies should join them, and with these he had settled an efficient mode of communication.

But this was, after all, but a gouty mode of carrying on war. To sit still, and to depend on spies for information, was to give full play to the activity of an enemy who had hitherto shown himself not wanting in expedients. If d'Auteuil thought at all on the subject, he could not have believed that Calliaud was so wanting in ordinary perception as to run his head against the positions he occupied. A strong reconnaissance on the Madura road would have compelled Calliaud to fight. But if governments will intrust the command of their armies to gouty octogenarians, they must refrain from expecting that activity of movement, that watchful and daring vigour, which are almost synonymous with success.

D'Auteuil, well satisfied with his arrangements, received information early on the evening of the 25th, that Calliaud had just reached Aour, a village ten miles south-east of Trichinápallí, and that he intended, a few hours later, to force his way between the Five Rocks and the Sugar-loaf Rock under cover of the darkness of the night. He instantly massed his forces about half a mile in front of the Golden Rock, denuding even the other positions in order to concentrate every available man against the enemy. All night long he remained in a state of anxious expectation; day dawned, yet there was no appearance of an enemy; at last, the sun itself appeared gilding the horizon; still not a soldier was to be seen; but scarcely had the entire disk become visible to the still expectant d'Auteuil, when a triumphant *feu de joie* from the walls of Trichinápallí announced to him the terrible fact, that he had been out-witted and out-manœuvred, and that Trichinápallí had been relieved!

It was too true. Fortunately for the English, their commander was still young, hale, and active, fully impressed with the necessity of using all his faculties, mental and bodily, when he had a great end to pursue. Breaking up from Madura on the 11th, Calliaud had marched at the head of the small force we have indicated, without tents, baggage, or artillery. On the morning of the 25th, arriving at Eliapur, nineteen miles from Trichinápallí, he had learned from Captain Smith the disposition made by d'Auteuil. The same evening he marched, as truly reported by the spies, to Aour. Here he halted, giving out that he intended in half an hour to force his way through the space between the Five Rocks and the Sugar-loaf Rock. The time fixed for this march being so close, the spies instantly made their way to the French camp, and reported it to d'Auteuil, with the result we have seen. Calliaud, half an hour later, did actually commence his march, but on arriving within two miles of the Five Rocks, he struck off to the right till he came opposite Elmiseram. The ground here being entirely under water on account of the rice cultivation, the French had supposed it impassable for troops, and had neglected to guard it. It was indeed heavy and swampy; but it was Calliaud's best chance, and, strictly enjoining silence, he attempted it. The distance was about nine miles. In seven hours he had accomplished only seven. But by this time the day had dawned, and the sight of the city inspired the gallant band to new efforts. Still struggling on, Calliaud himself supported by two grenadiers, they entered Trichinápallí in time to be welcomed by the rising sun. A salute was at once fired to convey to the Frenchman the notification of the defeat of his plans.

We will not stop to dwell on the mortification of d'Auteuil. So badly had his position been taken, all his troops concentrated upon one narrow point, that it would have been possible, as it turned out, for Calliaud to have marched in under the very shadow of the Sugar-loaf Rock. A body of sipáhis he had sent to make a false march in that direction, in the hope to persuade the French that he himself was moving that way, were able to convert it into a real one, advancing under the lee of the rock without once having been challenged. The course followed by d'Auteuil after this check was not inspired by greater wisdom than his previous strategy. It is, however, always useless to endeavour to analyse the motives of a man who is himself incapable of thinking. Had he been other than he was, d'Auteuil would have recollected that notwithstanding the reinforcement brought by Calliaud, he still outnumbered the English with his Frenchmen by four to one. But it would not appear that such a thought occurred to him. Utterly discouraged, he crossed the Kávarí the same evening, and proceeded next day to Pondichery.*

Meanwhile the Madras authorities, not trusting entirely to the efforts of Calliaud, had ordered every available man into the field. These, forming a force of 430 Europeans and 800 sepáhis under Colonel Adlercron, had already reached and captured Uttámatur when they heard of the relief of Trichinápallí. As the French garrison of Uttámatur had thrown itself into Wandiwash, one of the most important towns in the Karnátik, sixty-four miles south-west of Madras, Colonel Adlercron marched forward with the apparent intention of besieging that also.

Meanwhile, de Leyrit had been neither unskilfully nor unsuccessfully employed in other parts of the coast. No sooner had the news of the fall of Chandranagar—the account of which will appear in its proper place—reached him, than he ordered Moracin to take possession of the English factories on the Godávarí, and sent instructions to Bussy to attack that of Vizágapatam. Both these officers acquitted themselves of this service without any difficulty—the garrison of Vizágapatam surrendering to Bussy on June 25. Whilst thus satisfying himself regarding his territories in the north, by a policy which gave him uninterrupted possession of the coast from Gánjám to

* *Vide* Orme and Lawrence.

Machhlípatan, de Leyrit was not neglectful of the south. He had hoped to avenge the fall of Chandranagar by the capture of Trichinápallí; and though disappointed of that by d'Auteuil's unaccountable strategy, he still endeavoured to use the troops he commanded to some satisfactory purpose. On the return of d'Auteuil to Pondichery, therefore, he removed him from the command, and replaced him by M. Saubinet, reputed to be a man of capacity. To him he gave instructions at once to concentrate his army, which lay scattered at Jinjí, at Tiruvádí, and at Pondichery, and to march to the relief of Wándiwásh, then threatened by Adlercron.

When Saubinet, at the head of 600 Europeans and about 200 sipáhis, arrived before this place on June 1, he found Adlercron in possession of the town, and preparing to batter the fort. The approach of the French, however, combined with orders he received from his own Presidency to return, induced Adlercron at once to quit this enterprise and to retreat towards Madras. Before doing this he very barbarously and very unnecessarily set fire to the town, thereby injuring only the unoffending inhabitants. Saubinet instantly followed him upon the Chengalpat road, whilst he despatched 200 Europeans and 500 sipáhis to attack Kánchipúram, a most important town with a strongly fortified pagoda, only forty-six miles from Madras. This detachment was, however, repulsed from Kánchipúram, and retired, after following the example of the English, by burning the town. The main body, after recapturing Uttámatúr, retired to Wándiwásh, and intrenched themselves about a mile in front of that town. Here they were followed to within four miles by Adlercron, under whom Lawrence, now a lieutenant-colonel, had consented to serve as a volunteer. For six weeks the two armies, nearly equal in numbers, remained facing one another, the English anxious for a decisive action before the expected reinforcements of the

French should arrive, the French on that account desirous to avoid it. Finding their efforts to force a battle unavailing, the English army broke up on July 26, retiring, the greater part towards Kánchipuram, the remainder to Chengalpat and Karangoli. Saubinet, thus left master of the campaign, remained at Wándiwásh till the middle of September. Learning then that a considerable squadron, having on board the Chevalier de Soupire with the regiment of Lorraine, fifty artillerymen and twenty siege guns,—the advanced guard of the force destined for the conquest of India under the Count de Lally—had reached Pondichery, Saubinet made a sudden attack upon Chittapett. Capturing this after a desperate resistance, he moved against Trinomali. Not this only, but several other forts in the Karnátik fell into the possession of the French, who were thus enabled to collect contributions from all parts of the province. It was not, however, until the arrival of Count Lally, on April 28 in the following year, that the French ventured to carry out the scheme originally intended to be commenced by de Soupire—a scheme beginning with the intended capture of Fort St. David, as a preliminary to the entire rooting out of the English from the Karnátik. We shall see, when we come to that exciting portion of our history, how it was that de Soupire delayed this attack; we shall notice likewise the prompt and energetic action inaugurated by Lally himself. We leave the Karnátik, on the eve of his arrival, overrun by French troops; all its strong places, with the exception of Arkát, Vellur, Kánchipuram, Chengalpat, and the two English seats of government on the coast, in their hands; the English shut up in Madras and Trichinápallí, sensible of the storm about to burst over their heads, and conscious of having no efficient means to protect themselves against its downpouring. We leave them thus, whilst we proceed to trace, on the one side, the fate of the French settlement in Bengal; on the other, the still eventful action of Bussy, ever gathering new triumphs, till recalled by the new Lieutenant-General of the armies of France from the scene of his brilliant successes to take part in the enterprise which, he fondly hoped, was to sweep the English into the sea.

CHAPTER XI.

CHANDRANAGAR AND THE DAKHAN.

CHANDRANAGAR, after the departure of Dupleix in 1741 to take up the Governor-Generalship of French India, had not long continued under the influence of the impulse which he had given to it. Whether it was that his successors were restricted in their powers, or were too indolent; that the duties on commercial enterprise amounted almost to a prohibition of trade; that it was neglected by the Home Government; or, more probably, from a combination of all these causes; it is certain that its once flourishing trade had decreased, that it was burdened with debts, and that it was being maintained at a loss. In 1756, the Chief of the settlement was M. Renault de St. Germain, whilst the dependent factory of Kásim-bazar came early in the year under the charge of M. Law. The garrison in the former place consisted of 146 Europeans and 300 sipáhis.* Law had with him about a score of European and sixty native soldiers.

The calamity which had overwhelmed Calcutta in

---

* All the English historians give the number of the French garrison as at least 300 Europeans and 300 natives. That Clive and Watson believed these to have been their numbers we cannot doubt, nor equally, that the same impression prevailed amongst the English in India generally. It is nevertheless incontestable that the numbers given by us in the text are correct. In the official despatch sent by M. Renault to Count Lally regarding the events connected with the loss of Chandranagar we find the following statement:—"In every letter we used the strongest and most touching language to demonstrate the absolute necessity of sending us such assistance as would place this settlement beyond the chance of similar misfortunes" (such as had happened to the English). "We received 67 sipáhis and a detachment of 61 Europeans, of whom 45 were invalids, which added to the 85 Europeans we then had, made 146 Europeans. We expected then every day to learn that war had been declared against England, and there was preparing at the time a considerable armament to re-take Calcutta." This extract is decisive as to the number of Europeans.

H H

1756 had left Chandranagar uninjured. When the first-named city was threatened by Siráju-dáola in that year, the English, despairing of assistance from their own people, had invited the Dutch of Chinsurah and the French of Chandranagar to make common cause with them against the enemy. Whilst the Dutch had positively refused, the French, more courteous, had offered the English protection within the walls of Chandranagar. This offer, which would seem to have been made in good faith, was, however, regarded as an insult by the English, and declined. Certain it is that when themselves threatened with the full weight of the Subadar's anger in case they should refuse to assist him in his operations against the English, the French resolutely declined to aid him,—and this, although they knew well that the extermination of the English, if unavenged, would probably be only a prelude to an attack upon their own settlement. It happened, indeed, that after the capture of Calcutta and the flight of the surviving English to Falta, the Subadar, recognising the loss of revenue caused by their expulsion, appeared disinclined to take hostile measures against the other European settlements on the Huglí. Contenting himself with quelling the disaffection which had appeared in other parts of his government, he apparently forgot his European enemies, and lulled himself into a too confident security.

Such was the state of Bengal, when the fleet and army under Watson and Clive, which, preceded by a detachment under Major Kilpatrick, had arrived at Falta at intervals between October 16 and December 20, left that place on December 27 with the intention of recovering Calcutta by force of arms. But the instructions given to these two leaders permitted them to look to something more than the mere recovery of Calcutta. They were directed, should they deem it necessary, to attack the Subadar in his own capital; especially were

CLIVE'S DIFFICULTIES.

they exhorted, in case the news of the declaration of war between France and England, then expected, should reach them whilst they had so strong an armament in Bengal, not to fail to use it for the destruction of the rival settlement of Chandranagar.*

The action fought at Bajbaj; the surrender to the English of Calcutta on January 2, 1757; and the capture and storming of the town of Huglí eight days later, are incidents which belong solely to the history of the English settlements; it will therefore be sufficient here to record the bare facts. But it was during the march to Huglí that Clive received the long-looked-for intimation of the declaration of war by France against England. To him and to all the members of the Calcutta Council it seemed that this intelligence reached them at the most opportune moment. They could not but congratulate themselves that the French had not learned it before the success of the operations of Clive and Watson against Calcutta had been assured. It came to them just after the difficulties of the river navigation had been overcome, when Calcutta had surrendered, and when they did not doubt that the attack upon Huglí would produce a strong moral effect on the natives of Bengal.

Still, however, the situation of Clive, in itself one of great difficulty, could not bear to be compromised by a too early manifestation of hostile intentions against the French settlement in Bengal. He could not but feel that the Subadar of Bengal would not leave unavenged the expulsion of his troops from Calcutta, and that he would not easily pardon the raid against one of the principal stations of his province. He could not shut his eyes to the possibility that the French, learning that war between the two nations had been declared, might

---

* Orme. The account here given of the fall of Chandranagar is based upon the histories of Orme and Broome, the journal of Dr. Ives, the official report of M. Renault, and the extracts from the public records, communicated to the writer by M. Derussat, the administrator in 1866-8 of the French establishments in Bengal.

yet unite with the Subadar and, by this union, not only baffle his designs on themselves, but crush the attempt permanently to re-occupy Calcutta. It was not, therefore, the time to publish to his enemies all that he had in his heart. It was his part rather, under such circumstances, to temporise, to watch carefully the course of events, and to suffer no opportunity to escape him.

The Subadar, meanwhile, furious at the loss of Calcutta and the destruction of the town of Huglí, hastily assembled an army of 10,000 foot and 15,000 horse, and marched to recover the retaken city of the English. He sent at the same time to the French chief, M. Renault, and invited him in the most pressing terms to join with him in crushing the nation that was as much the enemy of the French as of himself.

Renault, for his part, was in a situation of very great perplexity. He knew too well that war had broken out,* but it was a question, and a most difficult one, whether with his 146 Europeans, of whom 45 were invalids, he should aid the Subadar, or endeavour to arrange a treaty of neutrality with the English. The former course would lead, in the case of the Subadar's failure, to the certain capture of Chandranagar; he had, besides, received the most positive orders from de Leyrit in no case to attack the English. Would it not then, he argued, be a sounder policy to endeavour to win

---

* Professor H. H. Wilson conjectures that the French may not have known that war had been declared. His conjecture, however, is entirely unfounded. Through the courtesy of M. Derussat, the chief in 1867 of the French establishments in Bengal, we are able to present to our readers the translation of an extract from the registers of the proceedings of the "Conseil de Fabrique" for 1757, which is decisive as to the fact that the French knew of the declaration of war on January 2, 1757, the date on which it was first known to the English. The minutes of the proceedings run as follows: "Thus things remained till the beginning of January, 1757. Then M. Renault and his council, *learning that war had been declared between France and England,* fearing to be attacked and to lose the place by means of the church and the parsonage which commanded it, assembled a council of war *on January* 2, in which it was resolved and decreed to begin the demolition of both on that very day, and that until the new house and the new church should be fit for use, they would," &c., &c. There cannot then be the shadow of a doubt that the French knew of the declaration of war on January 2, 1757.

from the fears of the English, who had then a great respect for the power of the Subadar, and greatly dreaded his junction with the French, the neutrality which should place Chandranagar beyond the reach of danger? After much deliberation, feeling keenly the loss of the opportunity which the indolence and want of enterprise on the part of de Leyrit* compelled him to forego, Renault sent a proposition for neutrality during the European war to the Council in Calcutta.

To Clive and Watson, believing as they did that the European troops at Chandranagar amounted to 300 men, and that Law had nearly 100 at Kásim-bazar, this proposition was like a message from heaven. From their previous experience in forcing their way up the river Huglí, they had been inclined to rate the soldiers of the Subadar as infinitely superior, in fighting capabilities, to the levies of Muhammad Ali and Chanda Sahib. They knew that the Subadar, full of anger, was marching against them, and they looked upon the result of a battle with him alone as by no means certain. Were he to be reinforced by the 300 French soldiers whom they believed to be at Chandranagar they would have but little hope of success. Great, therefore, was their relief when they received this message from Renault, proposing neutrality during the war with Europe.

Instantly they acceded to it; the French Chief was even requested to send deputies to Calcutta to arrange regarding the conditions. This was at once complied with. The French deputies came to Calcutta; the conditions were discussed and agreed upon; the treaty itself was written out fair and was ready for signature, when, instead of signing it, Clive and Watson inti-

* De Leyrit excused himself vaguely by asserting the difficulty of sending reinforcements into Bengal at a time when he expected the arrival of an English fleet; yet Law with his 61 Europeans, who did not leave the Sirkars till November or December, arrived there in safety: why then could not 300?

mated their intention of proceeding with their whole force for the reduction of the settlement whose representatives they had been thus amusing. Events, in fact, had effaced from the minds of the English commanders all fear of the Subadar, and had left them free to act as they wished.

There can be no question, in fact, that Clive had accepted the proposition of M. Renault in the first instance, solely because he saw in that a means of preventing the dreaded junction of the French with the Subadar. But, on February 4, he attacked the army of the Subadar before Calcutta, and, though surprised himself, had made a demonstration which utterly disheartened Siráju-Dáola. On the 9th he concluded with him a treaty. Thus free from his principal enemy, the thought came into his mind that such an opportunity for crushing the French at Chandranagar would probably never occur again; that it would be feeble policy to neglect it; that there was yet time to do it, as notwithstanding that he and they were mutually agreed upon the terms of the treaty, the treaty itself had not been signed. There was but one obstacle. He did not deem himself strong enough to attack Chandranagar whilst there should yet remain a chance of his being assailed by the Subadar. He therefore, on various pretexts, detained the French deputies in Calcutta whilst he should endeavour to obtain the permission of the Subadar to attack their settlement.

The Subadar refused it. Nevertheless, fortune favoured Clive. Satisfied by the Subadar's refusal that an attack upon Chandranagar would be too dangerous to attempt, he prepared to sign the treaty. When, however, on the point of so doing, he met with an unexpected scruple on the part of Admiral Watson, who declined to sign on the ground that the settlement of Chandranagar not being an independent settlement, but under the orders of the Pondichery authorities, the treaty would require

RESOLVES TO ATTACK CHANDRANAGAR.

ratification at that city. The Calcutta Government, he argued, was an independent Presidency. For it to agree to a treaty with a dependent settlement was to agree to a treaty liable to be upset. He therefore refused to sign. Clive placed before him the only other alternative, that of attacking Chandranagar. This, however, he refused to attempt without the consent of the Subadar.

But it was written that Chandranagar was to fall. The very next day a messenger reached the Subadar with the news that Ahmad Sháh Abdálí had taken Delhi. Seeing in his own mind the Affghans marching upon Bengal, the terrified Subadar at once wrote to Clive offering him 100,000 rupees a month if he would march to his assistance. Two days later a boat from Híjlí arrived off Calcutta with the intelligence that three English ships of war with three companies of infantry and one of artillery were at its mouth, and that another, the "Cumberland," was off Baleswar. These two items of intelligence removed any apprehension that Clive might have had regarding an attack from the Subadar's army; they appeared likewise to silence the scruples of Watson.* Was it considered that in giving them this increased force, and in paralysing for the time the movements of the Subadar, the voice of Providence had spoken out too clearly to be misunderstood?

Meanwhile, Renault, having heard from his agents the acceptance of the terms of the treaty, had regarded the matter as settled, and had ceased to disquiet himself as to the possible movements of the English. His surprise then may be imagined when his deputies, returning, brought him, instead of a signed treaty, the

---

* We are aware that Watson based his final acquiescence on a letter from the Subadar, abounding in Oriental imagery, and which was interpreted as a permission to act as he chose. But the receipt of a letter the next day from the Subadar, positively forbidding him to attack Chandranagar, whilst it revealed to him the real mind of the Subadar, did not stop his preparations.

terrible intelligence that the English fleet and army were on their way to Chandranagar. However indignant he might have felt, however much he may have reproached his superior at Pondichery for exposing him to such a danger, Renault yet prepared, on its approach, to meet it with courage and vigour. Chandranagar possessed many capabilities of defence. The square fort, called Fort d'Orléans, situated at an equal distance from either extremity of the town, immediately on the river bank, mounted ten 32-pounders on each of its bastions. On the ramparts, at regular intervals between the bastions on the river and southern faces, were an equal number of 24-pounders; the south-western curtain angle was covered by a ravelin, on which were eight 32-pounders; whilst the flat terrace of the high church within the fort, and which over-topped its walls, had been converted into a battery and armed with six guns. An outer ditch and glacis were being constructed, though all the houses on the proposed glacis had not been demolished at the time. Beyond this glacis, however, especially on the river and southern face, several batteries had been thrown up, commanding all the approaches to the fort. The garrison consisted, as we have said, of 146 European troops and 300 sipahís, but nearly 300 Europeans were collected from the inhabitants and sailors, and were armed for the defence. Prominent among these last was Captain de Vigne, the commander of one of the French ships, to whom the defence of the bastions had been consigned by Renault.

But it was not alone in their fortifications that the French confided. The river Huglí at Chandranagar was not, even in those days, easily navigable by ships of heavy burden. There was in fact but one practicable channel, and this could be blocked up by sunken ships. Here, accordingly, Renault ordered several ships to be sunk, about a hundred and fifty yards south of the fort, and on this point the guns of one of the batteries outside the fort were directed. In this operation an artillery officer named Terraneau co-operated.

The English force, numbering 700 Europeans and 1,500 natives, marched from Haurah on March 7, 150 artillerymen with their guns following in boats, escorted by Admiral Watson's fleet.* On the 14th Clive came with his little force in sight of Chandranagar. Avoiding the batteries in front of the western and southern faces, he took possession of the high road on its northern side, and then changing direction towards the fort, occupied the houses on the north-west, the French skirmishers retiring, as he approached, to a battery on the road commanded by the north-west bastion. From the houses he kept up all night a strong fire, which compelled the French to evacute the battery and retire within the fort. The abandonment of this battery necessitated the abandonment of all the batteries, except those on the river face. The following day the English strengthened their position in the houses, suffering but little from the fire of the fort. On the 16th, the guns were landed, and for the next five days a mutual cannonade was kept up, on the whole to the advantage of the garrison, the fire from whose heavy guns told with tremendous effect on the brick-built houses which the English had improvised as batteries.

It was not, however, Renault well knew, on the shore that the fate of Chandranagar was to be decided. Could he but beat off those powerful men-of-war, who were making their way slowly and cautiously through the intricate channels of the Huglí, he would care but little for all the efforts of the English troops on the mainland. He could at least hope that the Subadar,—to whom he had sent a pressing appeal for assistance, and part of whose army was then marching towards the town of

---

* This fleet was composed of—
"The Kent," 64 guns, Capt. Speke;
"The Tiger," 60 guns, Capt. Latnam;
"The Salisbury," 50 guns, Capt. Knowler, and other smaller vessels.

Huglí,—would speedily operate on their rear. Meanwhile, however, the English ships approached. On the 20th, they neared the place where the ships had been sunk. This, however, did not stop them. The French artillery officer, Terraneau, to whom we alluded as co-operating in this work, had in consequence of some quarrel with Renault, deserted to the English, and had sold them the secret that the channel had not been entirely closed by the ships, but that there was way for a passage round them.* This information proved to be correct. The task was then easy. On the morning of the 23rd, the "Tiger," having Admiral Pocock on board, sailing up till opposite the ravelin, compelled its evacuation; she then proceeded on and anchored opposite the north-east bastion. Admiral Watson's ship, the "Kent," was not so fortunate. Assailed by a tremendous fire from the south-east bastion when about to anchor opposite the ravelin, her captain was killed, and the ship, drifting down, anchored, stern foremost, below the bastion. One consequence was that the "Salisbury" was unable to come up, and could exercise but a slight influence on the attack.

The French, by this time, had abandoned all their outside batteries and were concentrated within the fort. Here they were under the orders of de Vigne. But with a limited garrison, many of them civilians, exposed for the first time to fire, the Governor could make no effective opposition. He was handicapped, moreover, by having to defend the land face against Clive. It very soon became apparent that resistance was hopeless. After defending the place with great

---

* It may not be generally known that this Terraneau sent a portion of the price of his treason to France, for the use of his father, who was poor and old. It reached the old man safely, but as soon as he learned the means by which it had been acquired, he refused to touch or to make use of it. This information is on record at Chandranagar. The same story is also related by the translator of the *Seir Mutakherin*, who adds that, in despair at the style of his father's letter, Terraneau hanged himself at his own door with his own handkerchief.

spirit * for three hours, and having lost 110 men, including the inhabitants, in killed and wounded, Renault determined to surrender. The white flag was therefore hoisted, the firing at once ceased, and at 3 P.M. conditions of capitulation were agreed upon.

By these it was arranged that the chief of the settlement, his councillors and civil officers, should go where they would, taking with them their effects; the Jesuits were permitted to take away their church ornaments, but the garrison remained prisoners of war. A few days after, the party at Kásim-bazar under the command of Law, reinforced by some fifty of the garrison of Chandranagar, who had managed to escape when surrender was no longer doubtful, retired to Bhágalpur. Thenceforth they may be regarded rather as adventurers taking service under native princes than as an integral portion of the French power in India. It will be sufficient only to state that, to the last, Law remained true to his character for feebleness; that he remained at Bhágalpur whilst Plassey was being fought; that when a forward movement after that battle would have saved Siráju-dáola, he did not make it; and that, finally, he was taken prisoner after the battle of Gayá in 1761, fighting gallantly it is true, atoning to some extent by his personal valour for his many faults as a general and a leader.

The capture of Chandranagar was not less a seal to French dominion in Bengal than it was the starting-point of British supremacy in that province. It was necessary for the schemes of Clive. With the example he had had before him of the constant warfare between

* Dr. Edward Ives, surgeon of Admiral Watson's ship, and who was present at the attack, writes thus in his journal regarding the behaviour of the French: "It must be acknowledged that the French made a gallant defence; for they stood to their guns as long as they had any to fire. We never could learn how many of their men were killed and wounded on the whole, though they confessed they had forty dead carried from the south-east bastion. The north-east bastion was also cleared of its defenders twice."

CHAP.
XI.

1757.

the French and English in the Karnátik, he dared not hesitate, when he had the means in his power, and when the occasion was propitious, to prevent for ever the possibility of similar contests in Bengal. He crushed Chandranagar, just as, we believe, had Dupleix been at that settlement, Dupleix uniting with the Subadar, would have striven to crush him. It was unfortunate for France that at such a crisis her interests were so feebly appreciated, that her representative at Pondichery possessed neither the foresight nor the energy to provide Chandranagar against a contingency that was always possible. The misfortune was fatal to her. Clive, freed from apprehension as to French rivalry, speedily overthrew the native powers in the country, not pausing till he had completed the conquest of the richest province in all India; till, from Calcutta to Allahábád, the law of the English ruler was undisputed. Chandranagar, on the contrary, received her death-wound. Though restored to France, it has only been that she might drag on an existence replete with memories of former greatness; that she might witness, powerless to prevent it, the exaltation and supremacy of the nation with which, for eighty-one years, from 1676 to 1757, she had contested the trade of Bengal. This was but one result of the policy of a nation which could remove a Dupleix to replace him by a man who succeeded too surely in infusing his timid and feeble spirit into his subordinates.

1754.

We left Bussy at Machhlípatan, engaged in settling the affairs of those four Sirkars, which the policy of Dupleix and his own great ability had added to the districts previously ceded to the French. There he was, and there he continued till the close of that year (1754). Godeheu, after many hesitations, had resolved to walk in the steps of Dupleix so far as to maintain Bussy and the French contingent at Haidarábád. "I feel," he said in a letter to Moracin,* "all the necessity of not abandoning Salábat Jang in the position in which he now is, and I have, therefore, ordered M. de Bussy to rejoin him as soon as possible." In consequence of these instructions, Bussy, after settling the revenue administration of the ceded districts, and seeing French authority enforced from their most northern to their southern point, returned to Salábat Jang, and resumed his old position at his court.

It very soon appeared, however, that the recall of Dupleix and the substitution in his place of one so imbued with *doctrinaire* principles as was Godeheu, had made a profound impression upon the Muhammadan nobles in the Dakhan. To them, up to this point, the very name of Dupleix had had a magic sound; they had regarded him with respect, with veneration, with a sort of dread. He had combined in their eyes all the energy and daring of the Northern race with the tact, the subtlety, the management of the Eastern. Feeling that he was their master, they yet had not chafed under the yoke. Affection was mingled with their respect, and reverence with their dread. The Subadar himself had always addressed and spoken of him as his uncle. By all he was regarded as the leader who could not fail. And now, suddenly, he was dismissed—dismissed too with every mark of ignominy—dismissed to be replaced by one who openly declaimed against warlike enterprises, and declared that the mission of the French nation in Southern India was purely commercial! This declaration sounded strange, indeed, in the ears of the proud nobles of the Dakhan,—the descendants of the men who had followed Akbar, who regarded commerce as the pursuit of an inferior race and of inferior men.

* The narrative of Bussy's achievements in the Dakhan, from 1754 to 1758, is based upon the histories of Orme, Wilks, and Grant Duff, the official correspondence attached to the memoir of Dupleix, and the *Seïr Mutakherin*.

CHAP. XI.

1754.

Little likely were they to consent to remain subordinate for long to the representatives of such a policy! When we recollect too that with these accounts came also details of the triumphs of the English both on the field and in negotiation, we shall be able to understand how it was that a feeling of doubt and distrust began to undermine the confidence and regard which Bussy till then had known how to evoke towards himself and his nation.

1755.

Nor was this feeling lessened by the communication made by Bussy to the Subadar, almost immediately after his return to Haidarábád in January, 1755, of the details of the treaty concluded between Godeheu and Saunders at the end of that month. In the course of an interview granted for the purpose of hearing this communication, the Subadar, instructed beforehand by his advisers, inveighed bitterly against the new policy that had been inaugurated at Pondichery. "Your sovereign," said he, "promised to support me against my enemies, to establish my authority, and to make it respected. Of this you yourself have given me assurances on which I have always depended. Yet I now hear everywhere that it is the King of England who specially concerns himself with the affairs of India, even with those which affect me." Bussy endeavoured to put the best possible gloss upon the proceedings of Godeheu. The Subadar and his ministers heard him but without being convinced. They were indignant that the fate of the Karnátik should have been settled without reference to the Subadar, its liege lord. "You have put me," said Salábat Jang, "in the balance against Muhammad Ali; you have allowed to be placed at the head of one of my tributary provinces a man whom I have never employed, who has always rebelled against my authority. Nay more, if I were to proceed to the Karnátik to drive him out of it, the English would support him, and you, on account of this truce, would hold back; you, who are engaged to support me on all occasions, would aid me neither against the English nor against Muhammad Ali." The Subadar concluded with these significant words—words the more significant in that they were prophetic; in that the necessity for the ruler of the Dakhan to lean upon a stronger power, clearly seen then, has been admitted by all his successors. "You know," he said, "that the state of my affairs necessarily demands the support of a European power; on this condition I am able to govern; either you must remain here, or I must enlist the English in my interest. Are you disposed to render me the services which you have rendered hitherto? I must do you the justice to say that I am grateful for them; but it would appear now that you have neither the power nor the inclination."

To these questions, the natural result of the impressions produced on the native mind by the abnegation policy of Godeheu, Bussy could only reply generally. He declared that the French nation possessed the power, and would ever be influenced by the ardent desire, to be of use to him; and that he would promise him beforehand that he would be as much satisfied with the future services of the French, as he had been with those he had so cordially acknowledged. An opportunity soon presented itself to Bussy of giving a practical indication of his sincerity, of endeavouring by means of it to chase from the mind of Salábat Jang the thoughts regarding the English to which he had given utterance. As representative of the Mughal, the Subadar of the Dakhan possessed, in theory, feudal authority over all the countries south of the Vindhya range. This authority never embraced, and never was intended to embrace, more than the right of levying an annual tribute, the token of the supremacy of the Delhi Emperor. Its execution, even its recognition, depended solely on the power of coercion in the hands of the Subadar. Thus, theoretically, the rights extended over the Marátha country; yet, so far from their being exercised in any of the territories occupied by them, that freebooting people not only kept their own revenues to themselves, but were in the habit of extorting one-fourth of the yearly revenue due to the Mughal government from many villages and districts in the Dakhan. Maisur was equally liable in theory to the imposition, yet it was never acknowledged or paid, except when the Subadar was able to enforce it. For many years prior to the date at which we have arrived, Maisur, aided by the Maráthás, had been comparatively strong, whilst the Dakhan, torn by internal factions and foreign invasions, had been powerless for aggression. But in 1755, Salábat Jang found himself undisputed master, at peace with his neighbours, and with a body of French in his pay. Maisur, on the contrary, had sent all her available forces to Trichinápallí, which her Dalwai had pledged herself to reduce. It was nothing to the Subadar that the Maisurians were also allied with the French; Bussy was bound to support him in all his enterprises. The opportunity likewise was too tempting to be foregone. A few days, therefore, after the interview we have recorded, the Subadar intimated his plans to the French leader, adding that he should require his co-operation.

Bussy felt all the difficulty of the situation. To march against the Maisurians might be to dissolve their alliance with the French; to augment immensely, by throwing them into their hands, the influence of the English. To refuse to march, would be to annihilate French influence at Haidarábád, to impel the Subadar to summon the English to his aid. But in this crisis, the tact and ability for which Bussy had ever been remarkable did not fail him. He entered with apparent heartiness into the scheme of the Subabar, whilst he wrote at the same time to the Dalwai of Maisur, warning him of the danger, and advising him to satisfy the claims urged against him. Meanwhile, the army

THE SUBADAR MOVES ON MAISUR.

marched, Bussy, at the head of his 500 French, really directing the operations.

Dév Ráj, brother of Nandaraj—who had conducted the operations of the Maisurian army before Trichinápallí—would willingly have paid the tribute demanded by Salábat Jang, but his treasury was empty, and he was unable even to promise compliance. Trusting, therefore, to the anticipated slowness of the movements of the Mughal army, he despatched a messenger to his brother before Trichinápallí, requesting him to take the enemy in flank whilst they should be marching upon Seringapatam. The celerity of Bussy's movements, however, rendered such a manœuvre impossible. His very name struck terror into the Maisur soldiers, and disposed them to regard opposition as hopeless. The only fort that did not at once open its gates to him, Kúngal, he stormed. Between that place and Seringapatam, a distance of fifty-four miles, there was nothing to oppose his progress. He rapidly traversed it, and appearing before Seringapatam on the third day, summoned it to surrender. It deserves to be recorded, that throughout this march, rapid as it was, he carefully guarded the interests of the Maisurians, protecting them as much as possible from plunder and damage; the main object he had in view being to paralyse, by the celerity of his march, all chance of opposition, and to bring the operations to a close with the least possible delay.

An event happened soon after his arrival at Seringapatam, which tended very much to bring about this desirable result. The Peshwá, Bálájí Bájí Ráo, had not witnessed unmoved the Muhammadan invasion of Maisur, but he had deemed it more advisable to endeavour to share in the spoils of that country, rather than to send his squadrons to be repulsed by the invincible Bussy. He accordingly invaded Maisur from the side of Puná. No sooner did intelligence of this invasion reach Dév Ráj, than, to avoid the danger of

CHAP. XI.
1755.

being entirely swallowed up, he determined to agree to the demands of Salábat Jang. After some discussion, it was arranged that the Rájá of Maisur should acknowledge himself a tributary of the Mughal, through his agent, the Subadar of the Dakhan, and that he should pay to that officer, as arrears of tribute, fifty-two lakhs of rupees. Salábat Jang, on his side, engaged to rid Maisur of its Marátha invaders. To carry out his part of the contract, his treasury being empty, Dév Ráj was compelled to strip the Hindu temples of their ornaments, and to give up all the jewels of the royal family. Even then he collected but one-third of the amount demanded; for the remainder he induced the Subadar to accept bills.* Bussy, on his side, persuaded Báláji to retire with the booty he had collected. The army then quitted Seringapatam, in April, and returned to Haidarábád in the July following.

For the remainder of that year peace and quietness reigned in the Dakhan. Whilst de Leyrit was occupied in endeavouring to maintain in the manner we have described, and not wholly unsuccessfully, French influence in the Karnátik, Moracin in the Sirkars, and Bussy at Haidarábád, found their position easier than at the beginning of the year they had dared to anticipate. This was no doubt owing to the success that had attended the French arms against Maisur. In a letter† to Dupleix, alluding to Bussy's conduct on this occasion, de Leyrit had written as follows:—"The position of M. Bussy in the Dakhan is as brilliant as ever. It may even be affirmed that since the expedition to Maisur his influence has increased. He escorted Salábat Jang into that country, and he managed matters so well between him and the Rájá of Maisur, who was also our ally, that even whilst extorting fifty-two lakhs of rupees from the

---

* These bills were never paid; the bankers who were securities for them mostly languished and died in prison.—*Wilks.*

† Dated 16th October, 1755.

latter, he satisfied both. He is even now in correspondence with the Grand Vizier, and has lately received very flattering letters from the Great Mughal!" In the same letter may be traced the determination of de Leyrit to have recourse to any expedient rather than carry out the partition system agreed to by Godeheu. Nevertheless, notwithstanding this determination and these favourable reports, it soon became every day more evident that the recall of Dupleix, the triumph of the English, as evinced by the installation of Muhammad Ali as Nawwáb, and the policy of non-interference announced by Godeheu, had been working with a fatal effect on the minds of the proud Muhammadan chieftains of the Dakhan. Of those who regarded the late occurrences as surely indicating the predominance of the English, the most considerable was the Prime Minister, Sháh Nawáz Khán, a man who owed his elevation to Bussy, and upon whom Bussy believed he might surely count. But this chieftain had another reason for his action. Like Saiyid Laskhar before him, he had become jealous of the influence exercised by Bussy in the councils of his master; he could not but see that in all important matters the wishes of the French were consulted, their advantage was mainly studied. In his quiet oriental manner he took care that every transaction tending to bring out this feature should come under the notice of the Subadar, nor were insinuations wanting as to the drift of all the public measures proposed by the French statesman.

An opportunity soon offered which enabled him to confirm in the mind of the Subadar the vague impressions to which his insinuations had given birth. In the month of February, 1756, the Haidarábád Government resolved to send an expedition against the Nawwáb of Sávánur, the successor of one of the four Affghan chiefs who had conspired against Nasir Jang at Jinjí, and against Muzaffar Jang at Kadapah. This Nawwáb had

CHAP. XI.
1756.

steadily refused to acknowledge the supremacy of Salábat Jang, relying on the friendship of the Maráthás. At the same time, Murárí Ráo, the Marátha, had occupied the state of Gutí, and maintained it against his superior, the Peshwá, relying upon the protection of Salábat Jang. But in 1756, the Subadar and the Peshwá, being on good terms, resolved each to renounce the protection of the dependents of the other, and to compel them to submission to lawful authority. In accordance with these views, the armies of both nations, Bussy accompanying the Subadar, moved against Sávánur.

Murárí Ráo showed on this occasion that he united to the capacity of a warrior the spirit of a statesman. Knowing that an attack on Gutí would inevitably follow the reduction of Sávánur, he resolved to make common cause with the Nawwáb, and to defend his own possessions behind the walls of the chief city of his Muhammadan ally. He accordingly threw himself into Sávánur. But he no sooner beheld Bussy and his French, backed up by the army of Salábat Jang, with that of the Peshwá ready to follow, than he recognised the futility of resistance. Having made his own terms with the Nawwáb, he secretly opened negotiations with Bussy. It happened that for his services before Trichinápallí he had received from the French authorities a bond which the policy of Godeheu had deprived them of the power of redeeming. In his communication to Bussy, he now proposed to give up this bond, on condition that Bussy would use his good offices to obtain for him from the Peshwá the cession in perpetuity of the district of Gutí, in subordination, however, to the chief of the Maráthás—the Nawwáb of Sávánur at the same time acknowledging the supremacy of the Subadar. Bussy, who had received from Salábat Jang full powers to treat, accepted these conditions, and did effectually carry them out—he, according to the secret agreement, receiving back the French bond. It was impossible, however, to keep such an arrangement long concealed from the watchful enemies of the French leader. The transaction had scarcely been concluded, before all the details connected with it were in the possession of Sháh Nawáz Khán. The Diwán instantly communicated them to Salábat Jang; he painted in its blackest colours the "crime" committed by Bussy; pointed out that he had deprived the Subadar of the treasures which the capture of Sávánur would have gained for him, merely to put this bond into his own pocket; called attention to the fact that notwithstanding that a Frenchman had been appointed Nawwáb of the Karnátik, no rents had been received from the French; he intimated that now was the time for their expulsion, now, when the Subadar was at peace with the Maráthás, when Báláji himself would support him in his action, now, when Bussy was on the borders of the Maráthá country, cut off from the ceded provinces, from Haidarábád and Pondichery. All these arguments, artfully urged and supported by a large party amongst the nobility, so worked upon the feeble mind of Salábat Jang, that he was at last prevailed upon to sign an order dismissing Bussy and his corps from his service, and directing them to quit his territories without delay: to this was added a proviso, not intended to be kept, that they should not be molested on their way, except in case of their commencing hostilities.

The blow once struck, Sháh Nawáz prepared to follow it up effectually. He instantly despatched a special messenger to the Madras Government, giving full details of the operation, and requesting that the English would at once send a body of troops to aid in the expulsion of the French; to the Peshwá the proposition was of a different nature—he suggested the assassination of Bussy.

Both these applications failed, though from different

CHAP. XI.
1756.

causes. The English, who had nothing more at heart than the expulsion of the French from the Dakhan; who, in the early part of this very year, had sent a force to the Bombay coast with the hope that it would be employed with Bálájí against the Subadar; received, indeed, the application of Salábat Jang and his Minister with extraordinary pleasure, and at once transmitted to him a most favourable reply. A force of 300 Europeans and 1,500 sipáhis was ordered into the field; it was on the point even of setting out, when there arrived from Bengal that disastrous intelligence of the capture of Calcutta, which compelled them to send every available man in that direction. From the English, therefore, Sháh Nawáz received no aid.

Nor was he more successful with the Peshwá. Bálájí, indeed, received the project for assassination with disdain; but he did not the less, for his own secret ends, encourage Sháh Nawáz to procure the dismissal of Bussy. He felt, in fact, that as long as the Subadar should have in his service a leader so capable and troops so brave and disciplined, so long would the Dakhan be proof against the ambitious designs he had formed upon it. He was anxious, therefore, not only that the Subadar should dismiss Bussy, but that, the dismissal having been effected, he might secure his services for himself. He, therefore, congratulated the Subadar on his policy in dismissing Bussy, but did no more.

The conduct of Bussy on receiving this abrupt and contemptuous dismissal from the service of the Subadar deserves to be studied and admired. Of all the courses open to him, he chose the wisest and most prudent, that which marked him as a man who knew thoroughly how to keep all his passions under efficient control. He was well aware of his own strength. He knew that with the 600 European infantry, 200 European cavalry, and the 5,000 drilled sipáhis of whom his force was composed, he could bid defiance to all the efforts of the

Subadar; that he could force him to dismiss from his service, and submit to condign punishment, all those who had plotted against him; he knew that it needed but the faintest whisper to Báláji to pour a Marátha army into the Dakhan. But he was guided by other considerations than by a mere desire for vengeance, or by an anxiety to replace himself by force. He could not forget, in fact, that his position at Haidarábád had been the consequence of the earnest requests of the Subadar; that he had thus ever been regarded, at least by the outer world, as conferring a favour by his stay; he could not forget that, though he might forcibly reinstate himself, the very resort to force would entirely change his position: that from being the invited protector, he would become the hated subjugator; nor that, sooner or later, under such circumstances, his fall would become inevitable. He knew, on the other hand, the facile disposition of the Subadar; he knew that he was acting merely from the influence of others; that in a little time he would feel the want of the counsels to which he was accustomed, the worthlessness of his new advisers. Under these circumstances he felt that it was his policy to act, as he had ever before acted, as the faithful servant of the Subadar; to obey his orders and instructions, leaving it to time to bring about that change which he distinctly saw looming in the future. No sooner then had he received the order dismissing him, than he prepared to march to Haidarábád, there to await the course of events.

No sooner had he set out (the 25th May), than he received a messenger from Báláji, conveying his congratulations on having quitted "so perfidious and ungrateful* a nation as the Mughals, and offering him at his own court the same positions, the same emoluments, and the same allowance to his troops that had been granted at

---

* Orme, who says, "these were his expressions."

the court of the Subadar. But Bussy knew well the difference between acting as auxiliary to an able and capable leader, the head of the rising power of India, and being the moving spring of all public matters in the Dakhan. To have accepted the Peshwá's offer would have been to isolate himself from his own people at Pondichery, and to throw the Subadar definitively into the hands of the English. Pleading, therefore, the necessity of first obtaining orders from Pondichery, Bussy, though with many expressions of friendship and goodwill, declined the proffered alliance and continued his march. Bálájí, to ingratiate himself still more with one whom he so highly honoured, and knowing the hopes and intentions of Sháh Nawáz Khán, despatched 6,000 horse under the command of one of the greatest of the Marathá leaders, Malhar Ráo Holkar, to escort the French troops until they should be out of reach of pursuit on the part of the Subadar. In this, doubtless, he had a double object, for any attack made on the French whilst Malhar Ráo should be with them, would give him just grounds for interfering in the affairs of the Dakhan, and he would then find himself fighting side by side with the French.

But Bussy was not to be entrapped into hostilities. He accepted the escort, but at the end of eight days he dismissed it with many presents and protestations of regard.

Scarcely, however, had the intelligence of this occurrence reached the camp of the Subadar, than Sháh Nawáz, who, from the fear of embroiling himself with the Maráthás, had hitherto restrained his longing desires, despatched 25,000 men, under the command of one of his best generals, Mir Jafar Ali, with orders to attack and destroy the French. Instructions were, at the same time, expedited to all the governors and officers of the provinces to obstruct in every possible manner the retreat of the French; to hover around them; to remove all supplies from their path : to make, in fact, their march through the disturbed country, with an enemy hanging on their rear, absolutely impossible.

The position of Bussy had thus become both difficult and dangerous. From the south-west extremity of the Dakhan, he had to make his way to Haidarábád in its centre, thence possibly to the Sirkars on the western coast; this too, through a hostile population, in a difficult country, with the Krishná to cross, and pursued by a large army! He was not, however, appalled by any one of these consideration. His great object was to push on so as to reach the Krishná whilst it should be fordable. He did not doubt then that he would gain Haidarábád.

Fortune favoured him, as she almost always does favour those who are bold, self-reliant, and courageous. Arriving on the banks of the Krishná, though after many skirmishes with the levies that sprung up on the order of the Minister all around him, he found that the rains, though threatening, had not fallen, and that the river was fordable. No sooner, however, had he crossed it than the waters commenced to swell, and for fifteen days imposed an impassable barrier between himself and his pursuers. At ease regarding his men, he marched them leisurely to Haidarábád. There he resolved to make a stand. Policy counselled no further retreat. At Haidarábád he was in the centre of the kingdom, at no impossible distance from Pondichery, within easy communication with Machhlípatan ; to have retreated to that place would have been to abandon the Dakhan. Time also was with him; for he could not doubt that the Subadar, a man of a fearful and timid nature, surrounded by men whom he distrusted, would soon feel the want of that firm support that had never failed him in the time of need. Urged by these varying considerations, he resolved to await at Haidarábád the reinforcements which, he doubted not, would be sent him from Pondichery. As, however, the city was in itself too extensive to be defended by so small a force, he took post in the plain bordering the viceregal garden of Chár Mahall, a walled enclosure about 500 yards square in the northern suburb, separated from the city by the bed of the river Músí. This garden contained buildings capable of lodging his soldiers, it had a tank in its centre, and Bussy had well supplied it with provisions. It is a signal proof of the influence he possessed with the natives of the city, that, before even he entered it, when the governor had notified everywhere his own hostility to the French, and when it was known he was being hunted out of the province by order of the Subadar, he was able to raise from the native bankers, on his own credit, a sufficient sum to settle the arrears of his army, and even to have a supply in hand. It deserves to be noted, that upon his sipáhis, even thus early, he found he could place little dependence, for they began, after his arrival at Haidarábád, to desert him in great numbers. Bussy, nevertheless, remained in the open plain referred to, continually skirmishing with the enemy, whose detachments arrived fifteen days after him, till he had completed his arrangements regarding the Chár Mahall. He then moved into it, but slightly molested, on July 5.

Four days after Bussy's entry into the Chár Mahall, Jafar Ali and the bulk of his army arrived, and for the following five weeks Bussy was exposed to their incessant attacks. His sipáhis almost entirely abandoned him. Sháh Nawáz Khán had hired a native soldier of fortune, one Muzaffar Bég—who in previous campaigns had commanded the sipáhis under Bussy, and who had obtained over them very great influence—to debauch them from their allegiance. He succeeded only too well; on the occasion of every sortie, whole bodies of them went over to the enemy. Their conduct at length determined Bussy, notwithstanding that he had gained several brilliant successes in the field, to confine himself to the defence of the garden.

Meanwhile, intelligence of some of these events had reached de Leyrit at Pondichery and Moracin at Machhlípatan. The action of both of these officers was prompt and energetic De Leyrit at once detached 320 Europeans, 400 sipáhis, and six field-pieces in the ship "Favourite" to Machhlípatan. But before they could arrive Moracin had collected the scattered garrisons of the Sirkars, amounting in all to 160 Europeans and 700 sipáhis, placing them under the orders of M. Law, and had directed him to force his way to Haidarábád, there to effect a junction with Bussy.

This was the same Law* whom we met, six years earlier, combating against Clive and Lawrence before Trichinápallí, and forced, through his own bad generalship and incapacity, to yield himself and his force prisoners of war. Exchanged in due course by the English, Law was at once placed under arrest for his conduct pending orders from France; but he was ultimately released, though with the intention of not employing him again in important military commands. On the arrival of Godeheu, he had been sent into the Dakhan to act under the orders of Bussy, who, on his own departure for Sávánur with the Subadar, had sent him to Moracin. It thus strangely happened that the measures which had been taken to prevent his being employed in command, were the actual cause of his being placed at the head of so important an expedition as the relief of Bussy.

Law set out from Machhlípatan at the head of his 160 Europeans, 700 sipáhis, and five guns, on July 16, and reached Bezwádá, a town on the north bank of the Krishná, on the 20th. The excessive rains and the inundations of the Krishná fortunately detained him

---

* The reader will observe that the events here recorded are of a date prior to that on which Law surrendered at Gayá.—*Vide* p. 461.

CHAP.
XI.

1756.

here several days, for, meanwhile, the "Favourite" had arrived at Machhlípatan, and the troops she brought with her, under the command of M. d'Aramburé, a most capable officer, were able to join him before he was in a position to move forwards. Law, as the senior officer, at once assumed command of the whole party, and leaving Bezwádá on the 3rd, arrived on the 10th at Megnapárá, about fifty-two miles from Haidarábád.

Up to this point Law had met with no enemies. But his troubles were only now to commence. Salábat Jang himself had reached Haidarábád on August 1st, and it was believed by the French in the Chár Mahall that his arrival would be celebrated by an attempt to storm their position. Wiser counsels, however, prevailed near the Subadar; and it was resolved, instead of storming the place, to adopt the surer plan of intercepting and destroying the party marching to the relief of Bussy. This, it was believed, would render his destruction inevitable.

Under ordinary circumstances, due consideration being had to the character of the officer commanding the relieving party, this might have been quite possible; and considerable credit is due to Sháh Nawáz Khán for preferring such a plan to the more showy scheme of an assault upon the Chár Mahall. But in dealing with Bussy he had to do with a man who was not accustomed to be foiled, and whose resources were inexhaustible. It must not be supposed that when Sháh Nawáz persuaded the Subadar to dismiss Bussy, he was supported by the entire voice of the nobility of the Dakhan. He had, indeed, at the moment, from various causes, a considerable party at his back, probably a numerical majority, but there were many, some of them very considerable men, who had remained thorough partisans of the French connexion. These were unable at the time to show their sentiments in any other manner than by communicating to Bussy all that passed in the camp of the

Subadar. But there were others who were able to render him still greater service. In the employ of Salábat Jang were two Marátha chieftains, tributaries bound to follow him in the field, Rámchandr Jadáo and Jánují Nimbalkar; they commanded 6,000 horse, and, up to the time of which we are writing, had been conspicuous for the efficiency and gallantry of their action. On one occasion, indeed, Jánují had intercepted a corps of 600 Arabs and Abyssinians on their way to join Bussy from Surat, and, killing fifty, had made the rest prisoners. With both these men Bussy had come to an understanding. He arranged with them that in the projected attack upon Law, they should only feign to take a part, and they had promised to hang out distinctive banners as an indication to the French leader that from them he had nothing to fear. Due intimation of this was at once despatched to Law.

Meanwhile, that officer, ignorant as yet of the means taken by Bussy to save him, had moved on the 11th from Megnapárá, and entered a country, hilly and wooded, full of defiles, offering abundant opportunities to an enemy to retard his progress. In advance were 400 sipáhis, under the command of Mahmud Khán; then came the main body of French, with the remainder of the sipáhis in the rear. After marching nine miles, some parties of the enemy appeared on the road, upon which the 400 French sipáhis, who had been already corrupted by the intrigues of Muzaffar Bég, went over to them in a body. The French were immediately attacked by the enemy, who harassed them by constant firing and desultory charges as they threaded their way through the defile. At length, however, they came to an open plain, in which the French drew up and halted for the night. The enemy, whose powder had been damped by a heavy rain that had fallen, retreated to a little village at the foot of a hill. Before daybreak, the French marched against this village, and, though surrounded by the Maráthá cavalry, they pushed on—the body of horsemen commanded by Jánují and Rámchandr acting against them only in appearance. Another chieftain, however, not in league with Bussy, made a sweep upon Law's cattle and baggage-carriage, and carried them all off. This was a serious loss; nevertheless, as their only hope lay in advancing, Law pushed on to the village, and resting there all day, forced his way in the night to Meliapur, through a very difficult country, every inch of which he had to contest with the enemy. During the day he received from Bussy the letter sent to inform him of the arrangements made with the Marátha chiefs. At Meliapur, which was about seventeen miles from Haidarábád, he put up in a ruined mud-fort near the town.

Hitherto Law had shown an amount of dash and energy, such as those who had studied his previous career would not have been prepared to witness. So long as he was moving on, the mere action of advancing, and the example set by his lieutenant, d'Arambure, sustained him. But he had scarcely seen his men safely within the mud-fort of Meliapur before the old Srirangam spirit came over him. Not that his losses had been heavy, only two men had been killed and but three wounded; but they were all exhausted by fatigue; the Marátha cavalry had swept off their bullocks, and their carriage had been rendered nearly useless. The next march, too, was more difficult than any of the marches preceding it.* Law decided, therefore, to halt where he was, till at least the men should have recovered from their fatigue. It was not a wise resolve. Asiatic troops can bear anything but the onward march of Europeans, that at once unnerves them; but let the Europeans halt, and the power of the Asiatic is increased by one-half—let the Europeans falter or show a disposition to retire, then, man for man, the Asiatic is

------

* Orme, from whom the details of this march are mainly taken.

his equal. The greatest European generals who have served in India have succeeded because they understood this—because they never hesitated to act upon it. Law, who was not a great general, neither understood nor conformed to it.

Law halted. With that halt, the dangers of his position, on which, in action, his mind would have had no time to dwell, became exaggerated tenfold to his mental vision. He began by degrees to lose sight of the great end for which he had set out from Machhlípatan. His mind fell gradually under the conviction that it was for Bussy to relieve him, not for him to relieve Bussy. His situation assumed the most deplorable hues; all appeared lost. The other officers caught the infection from their leader; and, in a council of war, it was resolved to send a letter to Bussy, intimating the impossibility of further advance.

Bussy received this letter on the night of the 12th of August, on his return from a successful night attack on the enemy's camp, made solely by his Europeans. It perplexed him exceedingly; but knowing that the detachment was strong enough to force its way to Haidarábád, neutralised as had been the opposition of two of the Maráthá chieftains, he sent Law a despatch, conveying, " in the name of the King," a categorical order to march forward at once and under all circumstances. At the same time, to paralyse any further movement on the part of the enemy, he marched out of the Chár Mahall at the head of 150 Europeans and 300 sipáhis, crossed the bridge over the Músí, and pitching his own tent, known to everyone in the Dakhan, on the other side, encamped there.

This single act on the part of Bussy showed not less courage and daring than a profound and intimate knowledge of the native character. He knew the impressionable minds, the light and credulous nature of the people of the Dakhan. He knew that the fact of his tent being pitched outside the Chár Mahall would of itself be

CHAP. XI.
1756.

sufficient to magnify tenfold the number of men by whom he was accompanied; that it would keep the entire force of the enemy on the *qui vive*, expecting an attack, not daring to make one. He knew that it would have the effect of preventing a single man being sent to reinforce the party that had been detached against Law. The result proved the clearness and excellence of his judgment. Not only did Sháh Nawáz Khán make every preparation against attack, but he even recalled the troops that he had detached the previous day to assist in the destruction of Law.

Meanwhile, that leader, on receiving Bussy's letter, had given the order to march. At 9 o'clock on the evening of the 14th, he set out, leading the advance himself; leaving the rear, the post of honour, to d'Arambure. The country between Meliapur and the little river Kingoram consisted of a long and difficult defile of four miles in length, which, during their four days' rest at Meliapur, the enemy had considerably strengthened. This defile led into a thick copse, between which and the river the country was comparatively open; between the river and the town of Haiatnagar, a distance of six miles, the country bore the same open character. Once arrived at that place, nothing could prevent their effecting a junction with Bussy.

During that long night the French laboured vigourously to burst through the four miles of defile. In endeavouring to effect this movement, the brunt of the action fell upon d'Arambure; for Kandagla, the Marátha chieftain who had not been gained over, entering the pass with his cavalry and infantry, took every opportunity of harassing and charging their rear-guard, whilst the party in advance, slowly and with difficulty, surmounted the obstacles in front of them. These obstacles consisted of felled trees, strong positions occupied by the enemy, sharp turns in the rock round which the guns had to be moved amid a continued fire. So great were they, that when day dawned, the French had advanced but three miles. There remained now only one more mile of the defile. But with break of day the attacks of the enemy redoubled in intensity. D'Arambure plied the two fieldpieces he had with him, no less than the small arms of his Europeans, with unabated vigour, but the enemy rode right up to the muzzle of his guns, and attacked with unwonted daring. At last, as the sun rose, the French emerged from the defile into the plain. Then, forming up, they allowed a party of the Maráthás to follow them, but no sooner had these appeared in sufficient numbers, than they opened out a heavy fire from all their pieces in the direction of the mouth of the defile. This had the effect of dispersing the greater part of the cavalry. Many, however, rode round to gain the river before the French, to dispute with them its passage. The little river runs in a deep clift between two high banks, the further of which was occupied by the enemy. It was necessary, therefore, that Law should keep the nearer bank in his own possession, till with a part of his men he should have driven the enemy from that on the further side. It was arranged, accordingly, that whilst he crossed with the infantry, d'Arambure, with all the guns, should cover his passage and keep off the enemy, who were collecting in large bodies in the rear. This service was performed by d'Arambure with great skill and gallantry. From the eastern bank of the river he maintained a simultaneous fire on the enemy on the western bank, and on the enemy behind him. Having thus ensured Law's safe passage, he crossed his guns, one by one, still keeping up a fire on the enemy; the guns as they crossed being placed in position on the other side to cover his final movement. In this manner he effected the passage in safety, the Maráthás never daring to come very near him.

The river crossed, the way was comparatively easy. Haidarábád was near, and the knowledge cheered the hearts of the tired soldiers. Though surrounded and harassed, they pushed on, favoured considerably by the merely feigned action of Jánují and Rámchandr. It was not, however, till 5 P.M. that they reached the town of Haiatnagar, having thus marched twenty-two hours without intermission, overcoming obstacles which alone were most difficult, but which were increased tenfold by the unceasing attacks of the enemy. Their losses had not been light: 25 Europeans, two of them officers, had been killed, 65 wounded; the sipáhis, who were more in number, had likewise suffered more. Of the enemy it was calculated that upwards of 2,000 were killed; no wonder, when we find that the French fired 40,000 musket cartridges, besides their field-pieces.*

Four hours later Bussy heard of the arrival of the detachment at Haiatnagar. He at once sent out a party he had before organised, consisting of 140 Europeans, 1,000 sipáhis, with a large proportion of carriage for the sick and wounded, and with provisions, to bring them in. To prevent any attack being made upon this party, he availed himself of the opportunity to beat up the Subadar's camp with his remaining forces. Everything turned out as he had wished, and at ten o'clock the next morning Law's detachment entered Haidarábád without having seen an enemy between that place and Haiatnagar.

The arrival, an hour later, of a messenger from the Subadar with proposals for an accommodation, showed Bussy that he had not ventured in too sanguine a spirit to maintain his post at Haidarábád. He felt again, as he had felt before, at Aurangábád in 1753, that he was absolute master of the situation. Again, too, he evinced his unsurpassed tact and judgment, in not insisting too strongly on concessions, which his position as master would have enabled him to enforce. He wished to return to his post on the invitation of the Subadar, to

* Orme. *Vide* also the "Sëir Mutakherin."

efface by his own dutiful conduct every recollection of the past three months; that alone excepted which fixed in the mind of the Subadar the conviction of French invincibility, of the absolute necessity of their presence as supporters of the viceregal throne. He therefore imposed no terms beyond the abandonment of Muzaffar Bég and the deserter Mahmúd Khán; he did not even stipulate for the removal of Sháh Nawáz Khán; he himself was to be received only in his former position as the officer in the Dakhan whose authority was second only to that of Salábat Jang himself. On these conditions a reconciliation was effected, and on August 20th, just three months after his dismissal, Bussy was publicly reinstated by the Subadar in all his titles, dignities, and honours.

Never, perhaps, had any statesman been subjected in a similar period to a harder trial. It is scarcely too much to say that one false step would have ruined him. Yet, however narrowly we may examine all the movements of Bussy in this critical period, we shall be unable to detect the faintest impress even of a turn in the wrong direction. From the very first he did what was right, though exposed to numerous temptations to do what was wrong. His refusal alike of the Marátha alliance and the Marátha aid; his march on Haidarábád; his determination to wait there instead of moving on to the Sirkars; his requests to the governments of Pondichery and Machhlípatan to order the reinforcements, not to cover his retreat to the latter place, but to meet him at Haidarábád; his positive order to Law to move on; his own choice of the Chár Mahall; the means he adopted to employ the main army while Law should be approaching; his firm consistency in refusing every offer to treat, except upon the condition of absolute reinstatement—all these acts stamp him as a general and a statesman of the very first order. We can no longer wonder at his great influence, his greater reputation; we cease to be surprised that his name should have been invoked by all the principal opponents of English progress in Bengal as the name of one who was invincible, who would paralyse their onward march, and at some unexpected moment hurl them into the sea. We can but admire the tact, the judgment, the coolness, the address, and the valour displayed, not in the heyday of prosperity, but under circumstances most difficult and most trying: not when he had leisure to deliberate, but when the pressure of events was at its strongest, when upon the decision of the moment depended glory or shame.

Yet, successful as he was, triumphing as he did over difficulties almost unexampled and dangers apparently overwhelming, it is impossible that a critical observer should fail to remark the immense importance to England of the events of those three months. When we recall to mind that the English were at that very time preparing for the re-conquest of Bengal; that their operations against Calcutta did not have effect till the end of December, nor against Chandranagar till the middle of the following March; that meanwhile Madras was denuded of troops, and many of the strong places in the Presidency were left to fall into the hands of the French; that the news of the declaration of war reached Pondichery in November; we can easily imagine the effect which Bussy, trusted by the Subadar and his court, secure of his position at Haidarábád and in the Sirkars, could have produced either in Bengal or at Madras. There would have been nothing to prevent him from co-operating with the Pondichery authorities against Madras itself, or from moving rapidly with 800 or 1,000 veteran Europeans through Orísá into Bengal. From making one or other of these attempts he was prevented by this three months' campaign in the heart of the Dakhan, and by that alone. Though victorious in that campaign, his confidential intercourse with the

THE INCIDENT LOSES HIM GREAT OPPORTUNITIES.

Subadar and his ties with the other chiefs had been, in the interval, rudely shaken ; and not only that, but the native chieftains established by himself in the Sirkars, seized the opportunity to endeavour to rid themselves of the rule of France, and to establish their independence. Instead, therefore, of operating against the chief possessions of the English, and of crushing them in Bengal or at Madras, the events consequent upon his sudden dismissal from the service of the Subadar compelled Bussy to forego that grand opportunity, in order to devote all his efforts to the re-establishment of French power in the provinces ceded to Pondichery. Who shall say then how much the English were not indebted to that abortive effort of Sháh Nawáz Khán?

From the 26th August to the 16th November Bussy continued at Haidarábád, interfering as little as possible with the affairs of the Subadar, but engaged in arranging for the prevention of the possibility of being subjected in any future time to a similar danger. Having effected this, so far as it was possible for him to effect it, he proceeded on the last-mentioned date towards the Sirkars, at the head of 500 Europeans and 4,000 sipáhis, there to re-establish his authority. With the Subadar, who was about to proceed to Aurangábád, he left 200 Europeans and 500 sipáhis under a trusted officer.

It is unnecessary to enter into minute details regarding the successful march of Bussy throughout these provinces. His principal object was to reward those who had remained faithful to the French in their hour of difficulty, to punish the chiefs who had evinced disaffection or who had rebelled. Nowhere, except at Bobilí, did he meet with any real opposition. At this place, however—the Rájá of which had a private quarrel with one of Bussy's most trusted feudatories—the resistance was so determined, that the defenders stabbed their wives and children, and then threw themselves on the bayonets of the French, rather than surrender. From these districts, by order of de Leyrit, he had despatched Law with 61 men into Bengal, to strengthen the garrisons at Chandranagar and at Kásim-bazar. It had been his own intention to follow him as soon as the pacification of the Sirkars had been concluded. This, however, could not be brought about until April; he was then preparing to set out, when the fatal tidings reached him of the surrender of the French settlement on the Huglí.* Considering it too late then to start upon such an expedition, he proceeded to the reduction of the English factory of Vizagapatam. This he accomplished, the garrison surrendering at discretion on the 25th June. The English factories of Madapollam, Bandarmalanka, and Injirám, situated on the three arms of the Godávarí, near its mouth, surrendered likewise to his detachments. Whilst thus engaged, however, the intrigues of Sháh Nawáz Khán had once more brought the affairs of the Dakhan to the verge of a revolution. Intelligence of this reached Bussy at the end of the year, just after he had completed the pacification of the ceded provinces, and forced him to set out, without any delay, for Aurangábád. It will be necessary, before we accompany him, to give a brief outline of the events which thus called him from his post.

It will be recollected that the former Diwán, Saiyid Lashkar Khán, had endeavoured to instil into the mind of the Subadar suspicions of Bussy, and had persuaded him to imprison his two brothers, thinking that the French leader, interceding on their behalf, would convert these suspicions into certainty. We have seen likewise how the conduct of Bussy completely frustrated

* It it clear from this that but for the three months' campaign, the events of which we have recorded, and their consequences in the ceded provinces, Bussy would have marched to Bengal in time to prevent the capture of Chandranagar by the English The struggle for empire would then in all probability, have taken place in Bengal.

AFFAIRS AT AURANGÁBÁD.

this intrigue. The confinement of the princes did not long follow the fall of Saiyid Lashkar, for the Subadar, completely reassured as to Bussy, and following his advice, almost immediately released them, giving them each a liberal income, but without any administrative or political power. Thus they continued till the period of Bussy's dismissal in May, 1756. Then it was that Sháh Nawáz Khán, dreading the facile character of Salábat Jang, and fearing that he would recall the French, hoping more from the determined character of the next brother, Nizám Ali, persuaded the Subadar to confide to him the government of Barár, and the Basálat Jang, the younger, the government of the territory of Adoni in the district of Bellári. The possession of some power would not fail, he knew, to induce them to aspire to more.

The success of Bussy at Haidarábád delayed for some time the plans that Sháh Nawáz had formed, but as the French leader did not interfere after his own reinstatement with the arrangements made by Salábat Jang regarding his brothers, Sháh Nawáz took advantage of the subsequent march of Bussy to the Sirkars to renew them. In the month of May following, affairs appeared to him ripe for a movement. He took advantage, then, of the death of his predecessor,* Saiyid Lashkar, to summon the fortress of Daolatábád, in which the treasures of the deceased minister, computed at nearly a million sterling, and which of right reverted to the Subadar, were stated to be concealed, and which the governor refused to deliver up. At the end of a month Daolatábád surrendered, and was immediately taken possession of by Sháh Nawáz, the office of governor being bestowed upon a dependent of his own. His object was to take an early opportunity of confining the Subadar in Daolatábád, of then proclaiming Nizám Ali, and of expelling the French from the Dakhan. The

* May, 1757.

more effectually to carry out this plan he invoked the assistance of the Maráthás,* who, the better to aid him, were to appear under their ordinary guise of enemies.

No sooner was it known that the Maráthás under the son of the Peshwá, Wiswás Ráo, were approaching Aurangábád, than Sháh Nawáz, under the pretext of massing all the forces of the province to oppose him, summoned Nizám Ali to that city.† Basálat Jang had preceded him. Immediately there was formed a whole network of intrigue, which, balancing now to one side now to the other, ended in the investiture of Nizám Ali with the administrative work of the province, the title of Subadar only being left to Salábat Jang. Basálat Jang was at the same time appointed keeper of the great seal. So entire was the transfer of power that but for the presence of the 200 French troops, the life of Salábat Jang would probably have been sacrificed; certainly he would have been effectually deprived of his liberty.

Such was the state of affairs when Bussy, marching quickly from the Sirkars, arrived at Aurangábád. He found Nizám Ali in command of the army, Basálat Jang his nominated minister, Salábat Jang a cypher, Sháh Nawáz Khán in possession of the fortress of Daolatábád—all waiting for the movement which should deprive Salábat Jang of even the shadow of power. It is curious to notice how all these intrigues were disconcerted by the presence of Bussy. Having by a stratagem possessed himself of Daolatábád, he imposed his law upon the brothers of the Subadar. Basálat Jang he proposed to attach, as Minister, to the interests of Salábat Jang, Nizám Ali to invest with the government of Haidarábád, where he would be easily accessible to the French. All these arrangements had been concluded, when, on the eve of his departure for Haidarábád, Nizám Ali enticed the Diwán of M. Bussy, by

* Grant Duff considers it probable that the Peshwá himself designed the plot.
† December, 1757.

name Haidár Jang, into his own tent, and caused him to be assassinated. In the tumult that followed, Sháh Nawáz Khán was killed, whilst Nizám Ali fled for his life to Burhánpur, one hundred and fifty miles north of Aurangábád. The flight of Nizám Ali simplified the arrangements that had been proposed, and which were in no other way altered than by his removal from the government of Haidarábád. An attempt, indeed, was made to pursue him, but it was speedily countermanded, and Bussy, more secure than ever in his position, prepared to accompany the Subadar and his new Minister to Haidarábád. Here he arrived on July 15, and found waiting for him a letter from the Count de Lally, dated June 13, ordering him to repair at once to Arkát, leaving no French with the Subadar, and only so many in the Sirkars as would be sufficient to maintain them. He was instructed to make over the command of these troops to M. de Conflans, an officer recently arrived from Europe, and who had but just joined him on the march, and to bring with him Moracin, who had hitherto administered the affairs of Machhlípatan.

This letter was like a thunderbolt to Bussy as well as to Salábat Jang. It called upon the former to renounce at once the work of the past seven years and a half, to give up the province to maintain which Dupleix had not hesitated to risk the loss of the Karnátik, and Bussy had devoted, to an extent bordering on the superhuman, his never-tiring energies. He had however only to obey.* But the Subadar, who had leant so long upon Bussy, who had so recently ex-

* In his reply, dated the 15th July, Bussy writes :—"I reply at once to the letter you have done me the honour to write to me on the 13th June last, which I received yesterday evening at 9 o'clock. There is one thing, Sir, which I have always known how to do better than anything else; it is to obey; and although your orders throw me into the greatest perplexity, considering the fearful situation in which I am, I proceed to execute them with the utmost promptitude." The remainder of his letter is taken up in explaining the state of affairs as they affected him and the projected movement.—*Mémoire pour Bussy.*

perienced the advantage of his alliance, could not but regard it as a fatal blow. "He took leave of Bussy," writes Mr. Orme, " with the utmost despondency, called him the guardian angel of his life and fortune, and forboded the unhappy fate to which he should be exposed by his departure." But there was no help for it. Bussy endeavoured, indeed, to cheer him up by the promise of a return in which he himself at the time really believed. Five days later, at the head of all his troops, he set out, and reached Waiúr on the north of the Krishna on August 3. Here having been joined by Moracin, he made over the government of Machhlípatan to M. de Conflans, then turned for ever his back on the provinces he had gained for France, to join, with 250 Europeans and 500 sipáhis, the new commander whose exploits we purpose to record in our next chapter.

CHAPTER XII.

THE LAST STRUGGLE FOR EMPIRE.

THE new commander, Thomas Arthur, Count de Lally and Baron de Tollendal, upon whom the hopes of France in her struggle with England for supremacy in the East now rested, was regarded at the time of his appointment as the most eminent and promising of all the younger officers of the armies of Louis XV. The son of an Irish exile, Sir Gerard O'Lally, who had entered the service of France after the capture of Limerick in 1691, Lally, born nine years later, had, from his earliest days, been initiated in war. When a mere youth he had served under his father at Gerona and Barcelona, and he was not yet nineteen when he obtained the command of a company in the regiment of Dillon, one of the regiments of the Irish Brigade. During the French-Austrian war of 1734, he distinguished himself greatly at Kehl and Philipsburg. Nor, when peace followed, did he show himself less capable of achieving diplomatic success. Sent into Russia to negotiate a secret alliance between France and that country, he acquitted himself so well as to gain the favour of the Czarina, though the timid policy of Cardinal Fleury rendered his mission resultless. On the breaking out of the war of the Succession, Lally served with distinction, but it was at Fontenoy that he gained his spurs. To him, it is said, was due the idea of that famous charge on the flank of the English column, terribly galled by the artillery in its front,

CHAP. XII.

1758.

which decided the day. Certain it is that for his conduct on this occasion he was appointed by Louis XV., on the field of battle, Colonel of the regiment of Dillon, and that he was personally thanked by Marshal Saxe. From this time his reputation was made. Passing over to England after Fontenoy he exerted himself to the utmost to aid the cause of Charles Edward, but, sent to the south after the battle of Falkirk, in which he had served on the Prince's staff, he was compelled, mainly in consequence of the despair and denunciations that followed Culloden, to return to France. He there rejoined the army in the Netherlands; was present at Laffeldt, and at Bergen-op-Zoom, where he was taken prisoner. He was, however, soon released, and was rewarded by his Sovereign for his services in that campaign with the rank of Major-General.

The treaty of Aix-la-Chapelle restored peace to Europe, and deprived Lally of any further opportunity of distinction on the field of battle. He was nevertheless regarded as a man destined to a brilliant career; as certain to occupy a very prominent position, in the event of future complications. He was looked upon as a man with respect to whom "it needed only that success should be possible for him to succeed." Voltaire, who recorded this opinion regarding him, added that he had worked with him by the desire of the Minister for nearly a month, and had "found in him a stubborn fierceness of soul, accompanied by great gentleness of manners." It is beyond question that his reputation at this period was very great, that his influence with the Ministry on military questions was unbounded; that to him the Government looked for suggestions as to the conduct they should pursue in case of war.

When, seven years after the conclusion of the peace of Aix-la-Chapelle, complications of no ordinary character ensued between France and England; when, in reprisal for French aggression in Canada, the English

LALLY APPOINTED TO COMMAND IN INDIA.

captured two French merchantmen off Newfoundland, and persistently refused to restore them, it appeared to the French Ministry that war was inevitable, Lally was, therefore, called upon for his opinion. His advice was characteristic. "There are," he said, "three courses open to you: the first, to fit out a sufficient fleet and army, and taking Charles Edward on board, to make a descent upon England; the second, to chase the English out of Canada; the third, to drive them out of India; but," he added, "whatever course you adopt, it is primarily necessary that you should think and act at the same time." The French Ministry did not at the time accept this advice, but, when, a year later, they saw three-fourths of their merchant navy swept from the seas, they concluded an alliance with Austria, Russia, and Sweden, and on May 17, 1756, the King of France declared war against England. Very soon after the issue of this declaration of war, it was resolved to make a great effort to drive the English from India, and Lally was appointed to the command of the expedition destined for this purpose.

It had been originally intended that this expedition* should consist of 3,000 men and three ships of war; but before it could set sail, it had become evident to the French Ministry that the English, more ready and more vigorous in action than they were, had appropriated to themselves one of Lally's plans, and were bent upon making a great effort to drive the French out of Canada. Almost at the last moment, therefore, they withdrew from Lally one-third of the force intended to act under him, and deprived him of two of his men-of-war. The order for the diminution of his force would, however, have arrived too late—for the expedition had already

---

* The account of French India, under Lally, is based upon the official correspondence attached to the Memoirs of Lally, Bussy, de Leyrit, and Moracin, upon those memoirs, upon the histories of Orme, Wilks, and Broome, and upon the "Sëir Mutakherin."

sailed—but that Count d'Aché, who commanded the fleet, insisted, against the advice of all his captains, on returning to the port of Brest on account of some trifling repairs he considered necessary for two of his vessels. Whilst he was lying there, the order for the reduction reached him. It happened, therefore, that whilst one half the force, under Chevalier de Soupire, left l'Orient on December 30, 1756, the other half, under Lally in person, was not able to sail till May 2 of the following year.

Those who have accompanied us thus far in our history of the attempts of the French to form an empire in India, cannot fail to have been struck by the remarkable fact of the incongruous character of the various leaders who ought to have acted together. There is, perhaps, in the entire story, no more striking example of this peculiarity than that afforded by Lally and his associates. He himself was apparently a man of hasty temper, yet possessing a ready mind, fertile in resources, and quick to apprehend; one who feared no responsibility, prompt in action, a daring soldier, fully impressed with the conviction, that, in Eastern warfare, he wins who strikes quickly and with all his force; he had too a proper idea of the point at which his blows should be directed—the expulsion of the English from the Koromandel. He was a man who, had he enjoyed the advantage of some slight Indian training and experience, would have been invaluable as a leader at Pondichery; but, not having had that, and having imbibed a supreme contempt for all who had acquired that experience, he was destined to fall into errors more than sufficient to neutralise his other many shining qualities. The second in command, de Soupire, was a man the very opposite of his chief. Indolent, unenterprising, and incapable, he was just the man to waste the time which Lally would have employed, and to lose opportunities which the other would have eagerly seized. D'Aché was even worse. It is probable that if the French armament which accompanied Lally had been commanded by a Suffren, it would have achieved at least a temporary success. Suffren himself, some five and twenty years later, did maintain on the seas the superiority which in 1758 would have enabled Lally to carry out his designs on shore. But d'Aché was the feeblest, the weakest, the most nerveless of men; the very last officer to whom the command of a fleet should have been intrusted, the most unfit man in the world to be the colleague of Lally.

The Chevalier de Soupire, sailing with nearly a thousand men of the regiment of Lorraine, 50 artillerymen, and two millions of livres (about 80,000*l*.) on December 30, 1756, anchored off Pondichery on September 9 of the following year. He arrived at a moment, which, had he been a man of action, might have been made decisive. It was at the time when the English had retired from all their conquests in Southern India—Trichinápallí, Arkát, Chengalpa, tand Kánchipúram alone excepted; when Madras was still but slightly fortified; when Fort St. David, almost in ruins, was garrisoned by but 60 invalids; when Saubinet was retaking the places which his predecessors had lost, unopposed by the English in the field, and caring little for the undisciplined levies of Muhammad Ali. It was just such a moment which Dupleix, or La Bourdonnais, or Bussy, or Lally himself would have used to the complete expulsion of the British from the Karnátik. For the French were not only masters on land; they were, up to the end of the month of April of the following year, masters also at sea.

It is obvious that in this crisis the Government of Pondichery should have directed the combined forces of Saubinet and de Soupire to proceed against the cardinal points of the English possessions—Fort St. David and Fort St. George. The first would most certainly have fallen without a blow, and its fall would have so shaken English influence in the Karnátik that it would not have been difficult—in fact, under an efficient leader, it would have been easy—to strike a decisive blow at Madras itself. For all the English troops, except those actually necessary for purposes of defence, had been despatched to assist Clive in Bengal, whilst the English fleet still remained in the waters of the Huglí.

But neither de Leyrit, nor de Soupire, nor Saubinet, was equal to the occasion. De Soupire indeed was a stranger to the country, and being a man of weak and facile character, he suffered himself to be guided by the Governor. Saubinet was simply a brave soldier in the field, and he too was entirely under the authority of de Leyrit. At this important crisis, therefore, of the fortunes of France, everything depended upon the decision arrived at regarding military operations by the civil governor, a man sufficiently well-meaning, but utterly deficient in those higher qualities which mark the practical statesman. To de Leyrit, indeed, it occurred, as it occurred to all around him, that in the advantageous position in which he found himself, consequent upon the arrival of de Soupire's reinforcements,* an expedition against Fort St. David presented the most tempting opportunity. But other considerations crowded themselves at the same time into his mind. He could not forget that Fort St. David had successfully resisted all the attacks made upon it by Dupleix, and that the repulses received before that place had given to the English the encouragement which had enabled them gradually to attain a position of at least equality in the Karnátik. Then again, the reported character of Lally, described as haughty, imperious, violently prejudiced against all Franco-Indians, influenced him not

---

* Col. Lawrence, in his Memoirs, states that the English authorities were "surprised that they (the French) should remain inactive for so many months after the taking of Chitápét." Chitápét is a town in Southern Arkát district, 30 miles south of Arkát.

a little. He could not foresee that Lally would be nearly twelve months on his way; he did not even know that he had put back; he believed, on the contrary, that he had left France six weeks after de Soupire, and he thought therefore that it might be regarded as presumptuous on his part, and that it would certainly be rash, were he to attempt any considerable object before the arrival of the Commander-in-chief. A third reason * likewise weighed with him; he dreaded lest the English fleet in the Huglí should at any moment bear down upon the Koromandel coast and regain the superiority at sea. He could not then know the great things to which the conquest of Chandranagar had given birth in the heart of Clive.

Instead, therefore, of attempting to strike at either of the vital points of the English position, de Leyrit resolved to content himself with the reduction of the various forts in the Karnátik, and with subjecting the country under the influence of those forts to the sway of men devoted to the Pondichery Government. In this view he joined the soldiers of de Soupire to Saubinet, and employed them, in the interval between the arrival of the former and the close of the year, in the capture of Trinomáli and other places in the vicinity of Chitápét and Jinji.† But from the beginning of the following year till the arrival of Lally on April 28th, the precious moments were frittered away in inactivity, in delusive negotiations with Haider Ali, or in abortive attempts to induce a rising amongst the French prisoners in Trichinápallí.

Meanwhile d'Aché's squadron had been slowly pursuing its course. Throughout the whole voyage the Admiral himself had never ceased to display his weakness and folly, to show how utterly unfit he was for such a command. He had picked up on the way a small English merchant ship, and, to preserve this ship, which was not worth 1,600*l*., he had not hesitated, despite the remon-

* Orme.   † Chapter XI.

strances and even the threats of Lally, to lie to every night. More than that, arriving at Rio de Janeiro, he actually remained six weeks in port in order to dispose of the cargo of that vessel, and to reload her; to avoid the Cape during the equinox, he steered for six weeks out of his course; to avoid the second equinox he took the longest course from the Isle of France to Pondichery. So timid was he, that on the appearance of a sail in the daytime he altered his course by night, and took in his sails whenever there was the smallest gust of wind. He took a course, in fact, which—to use Mr. Orme's graphic expression—it would be useful to know, in order to avoid it. And this, whilst the English fleet was following in his wake; whilst the possession of India depended upon the rapid movements of those ships whose course he was thus hindering. If, indeed, there is one person than another more responsible for the fatal result of Lally's expedition, that individual is undoubtedly Count d'Aché. A little more haste on his part, the curtailment of the delays with the merchant ship and of the long sojourn in Rio de Janeiro, and Lally, with the cold weather before him, with d'Aché's squadron unopposed to aid him, could not have failed to capture both Fort St. David and Madras. He himself was sanguine that under such circumstances he would have been able to expel the English from Bengal.

At length, on April 28th, the fleet anchored off Pondichery, and Lally, with some of his principal officers, arrived. Amongst these were the representatives of some of the great aristocratic families of monarchical France. There were under his command a d'Estaing, descended from him who saved the life of Philip Augustus at the Battle of Bovine, and who transmitted to his family the coat of arms used by the Kings of France; a Crillon, great-grandson of Crillon, surnamed the brave, worthy of the love of the great Henry IV.; a Montmorency; a Conflans, of ancient and illustrious family; a La Fare, and many others of the first rank.* Besides these there were Breteuil, Verdiére, Landivisiau, and other officers of good family and of the highest merit. A singular circumstance, which occurred before the landing, did not fail to be regarded by many, especially by the sailors, as of very evil omen. On the arrival of Lally in the Pondichery roads becoming known to the authorities of that city, it was directed that a salute should be fired in his honour. By accident —it could hardly have been by design—some of the guns set apart for firing the salute were loaded; by a greater chance still, five shots fired struck the "Comte de Provence," the vessel on board of which was Lally, three of which went right through the hull and two damaged the rigging. It was a strange greeting for the new Commander-in-chief, and gave him, it would appear, some impression of the hostility he might expect to meet from the authorities.

Lally had come out armed with very extensive powers. He was appointed Commander-in-chief and Commissary of the King for all French possessions in the East; he was to command as well the inhabitants of Pondichery and the other French settlements as the officers and clerks of the Company; "likewise the governors, commanders, officers of the land and sea forces of the Company who now are, or who hereafter may be there, to preside in all the Councils, as well superior and provincial, both those that are already, and those that may be hereafter, without making any innovation, however, in the settled order for collecting the votes." All the governors, counsellors, commanders, officers, soldiers, land and sea forces and all servants of the Company, and all the inhabitants of the French settlements, were directed to recognise Lally as Commissary of the King and Commander-in-chief, " and to obey him in everything he may command, without any

* Voltaire's Fragments.

contravention whatever."* It will thus be seen that Lally in a way superseded de Leyrit, the latter, however, still retaining the rank and position of governor. This position, combined with his local influence, and added to the restriction relative to the votes, gave the latter, as Lally was destined soon to discover, very considerable power.

Lally had sailed prepared to find fault. Before he left France, the Directors had themselves placed in his hands a memorandum, in which their principal officers on the Koromandel coast, Bussy alone excepted, were painted in the most unfavourable colours. But this was not all. It had been likewise intimated to him, as well by the Directors as by the Ministers of the Crown, that corruption was rampant at Pondichery, and that they looked to him to check it. He had been informed that the farming out of lands, the supply of artillery cattle, the provisioning of the sipáhis, the purchase and re-sale of goods drawn from the magazines of the Company, and—the most important of all—the conducting of treaties with native princes, were matters which required thorough and searching investigation, inasmuch as it was believed that they were made the means of enriching private individuals to the great injury of the shareholders of the Company. To such an extent had these points been pressed upon his attention whilst in Paris; so incontestable apparently were the proofs that had been placed before him—that Lally had left France with the conscientious conviction on his mind that he was coming out to uproot a nest of robbers and extortioners. He had, he believed, a double mission—to root out those robbers, and to throw the English into the sea.

He landed, as we have stated, with a few of his officers, on April 28. He at once set himself to work to inquire as to the condition of Madras and of Fort St.

---

* This order is dated December 31, 1756; signed by Louis XV., and countersigned by the Minister Machault.

SENDS TROOPS AGAINST GUDALUR.   517

David, regarding the fortifications of Gudálur, and the number of English troops on the coast of Koromandel. To his surprise, de Leyrit could give him precise answers to none of these questions; nor could he even afford him any definite information as to the route to Gudálur, or the number of rivers to be crossed; he could only offer guides. Lally, impatient for action, was not, however, deterred by this ignorant and apparent want of interest from following the policy, which, in his belief, ought to have been attempted eight months earlier, but sent off, that same evening, a detachment of 750 Europeans and some sipáhis, under the command of the Count d'Estaing, to Gudálur, following himself the next day. Whilst on his way to join, he learned to his mortification one of the first results of the slowness and unfitness for command of his naval colleague. Commodore Stevens, who had left England three months after d'Aché had left France, had, by pursuing a direct course, arrived at Madras five weeks before d'Aché had reached Pondichery. Uniting himself there to Admiral Pocock, who had returned from Bengal on February 24, the two squadrons had sailed from Madras on April 17 to intercept the French fleet, and had come up with it at noon on April 28 off Nágápatan.

CHAP. XII.
1758.

The English fleet consisted of seven ships of war* ranging from fifty to sixty-six guns each. These ships, all belonging to the royal navy, had just been placed in the best condition possible for sea,† and were unencumbered by troops. In this respect they had a considerable advantage over the French squadron, which had

* These were : The Yarmouth   64 guns, Captain John Harrison,
                ,, Elizabeth   64   ,,   ,, Kempenfelt,
                ,, Cumberland 66   ,,   ,, Brereton,
                ,, Weymouth   60   ,,   ,, Vincent,
                ,, Tiger   60   ,,   ,, Latham,
                ,, Newcastle   50   ,,   ,, Legge,
                ,, Salisbury   50   ,,   ,, Somerset,
                and two store ships.
† Colonel Lawrence's narrative.

arrived that very day after a long voyage, crowded with soldiers, and but one of the ships composing which belonged to the royal navy of France. At the time he was seen by the English Admiral, d'Aché* was standing up towards Pondichery from Nágápatan, seven of his ships being in line, and two cruising in the offing. The English Admiral at once formed his line, between three and four o'clock in the afternoon, bore down on the " Zodiaque," and, as soon as he came within half-musket shot, made the signal to his captains for close action. Meanwhile the ships of d'Aché's squadron had opened a hot fire on the approaching enemy, though without receiving any in return. About four o'clock, however, the action became general, the two admirals sailing close to, and directing their fire at, one another. But the French ships experienced in this sort of engagement all the disadvantage of want of regular training and of overcrowding. Their fire was slow and badly directed, whilst the well-aimed discharges of the English made terrible havoc on their crowded decks. It is due, however, to d'Aché to state that he fought his ship, the " Zodiaque," with great skill and gallantry, and it was only after the " Sylphide," the " Condé," the "Duc de Bourgogne," the " Bien Aimé," and the " Moras," had been forced to quit the line, that d'Aché, with the remainder of the squadron, bore up to follow them. Meanwhile the " Comte de Provence "† and the " Diligente " had come out from Pondichery to assist the French. Towards them therefore d'Aché directed his course, intending, with their aid, to renew the engage-

---

* His ships were: Le Zodiaque 74 guns, of the French Navy.
,, Vengeur 54 ,,
,, Bien Aimé 58 ,, ⎫ belonging to the Com-
,, Condé 44 ,, ⎪ pany of the Indies, and
,, Saint Louis 50 ,, ⎬ built to serve, when re-
,, Moras 44 ,, ⎪ quired, as men-of-war.
,, Sylphide 36 ,, ⎭
,, Duc d'Orléans 50 ,,
,, Duc de Bourgogne 60 ,,

† Carrying 74 guns, the Diligente, 24.

ment. But the rigging of the English ships had been so shattered by the ill-directed fire of the French, that Admiral Pocock, anxious as he was to complete his victory, was forced to renounce the pursuit, and to haul down the signal for action. The French squadron, thereupon, with the exception of the "Bien Aimé," which, by the parting of her cable, was driven on shore, ran into the roadstead of Alumpárva,* and five or six days later reached Pondichery. The English Admiral bore up to Madras to refit.

Such was the intelligence that reached Lally on April 29, whilst on his way to join the detachment he had sent towards Gudálur, the previous evening, under Count d'Estaing. He was little, if at all, daunted by it, resolving to atone, so far as was possible, for a defeat at sea, by the celerity of his movements on land. The detachment under d'Estaing, though misled by its guides, appeared before Gudálur on the 29th; it was followed the next day by a portion of the regiment de Lorraine and some heavy guns: on May 1, Lally himself appeared before the place, and summoned it to surrender.

To such an extent had the spirit of neglect and unconcern made way in the Pondichery Government since the departure of Dupleix, that, although a year and more had elapsed since it was known that war between France and England had been declared; although the question of attacking Gudálur and Fort St. David had, in that interval, been considered by de Leyrit and his colleagues, not one of them had taken the trouble to ascertain the military condition of those places, or the provision, if any, that had been made for defending them. Lally was compelled, by this culpable indifference on the part of the Franco-Indian authorities— strongly confirmatory as it was in his mind of the character he had received of them from their own

* A town in the Chengalpat district.

CHAP. XII.
1758.

Directors in Europe—to find out everything through his own officers. Count d'Estaing, who first appeared before Gudálur, found it fortified on three sides ; he did not know, nor did anyone in the force know, although the Pondichery authorities ought to have known, that it was open towards the sea. Lally, on his arrival, was no better informed. He agreed therefore to accept the capitulation offered by the garrison for the third day, although had intimation been given him of its defenceless state on the fourth side, he would probably have forced its surrender at once.*

Still, on May 4, Gudálur surrendered. With that surrender began Lally's first difficulties—none of them, it is proper to observe, of his own creation. Surely he had a right to expect that de Leyrit, who for eight months had postponed the expedition against Fort St. David on the main plea that it was proper to await the arrival of the Commander-in-Chief, would in the meanwhile have taken the precaution to procure carriage for movements he must have known to be inevitable. The two finest regiments of the French army, still less the most rising of all the generals in the French service, had not come out to Pondichery merely to sit there at their ease. De Leyrit was well aware of this, yet up to the hour of the landing of the new general he had not made a single preparation. Although large sums were charged in the Pondichery accounts for carriage cattle, none were available; there were no coolies, no means of transport, not even guides. The difficulty was not so much felt in the first march to Gudálur, though even then Lally, determined to move, and left entirely unaided by de Leyrit, had not hesitated to impress the native inhabitants of the town. It was when Gudálur was taken, when the siege of Fort St. David was immi-

---

* Gudálur was garrisoned by 30 European infantry, 25 European artillerymen, 400 sipáhis, and some lascars. The garrison was allowed to retire to Fort St. David.

DIFFICULTIES ENCOUNTERED BY LALLY.

nent, when it had become necessary for the army to sit down before that place, dependent upon Pondichery for supplies, and for the carriage of supplies, that the culpable indifference of de Leyrit and his colleagues began to make itself keenly felt.

Lally, seeing the utter impossibility of carrying on a siege until he had first organised a system of supply, aware also, in consequence of the presence of the victorious English fleet at Madras, of the absolute necessity of promptitude, returned, immediately after the taking of Gudálur, to Pondichery, with a view to rouse the authorities there to a sense of their duties and of their position, and to make, at all costs, proper arrangements for supplies. At Pondichery, however, Lally found nought but apathy and indifference. To every request that he preferred he was answered by an " impossible." He did not find there, although he had sent 100,000 francs to make preparations, resources that were worth 100 pence.* It can scarcely be wondered at if Lally attributed this conduct to something more than indolence or apathy. He says himself, in his memoirs, that he saw very clearly how ill-will lay at the bottom of it all. It is little marvellous then, if he, ignorant of India, knowing nothing of the distinction between castes, left to himself by those who should have aided him, and whose duty it was to have prevented this necessity, should, rather than abandon his enterprise, have insisted on a wholesale conscription of the native inhabitants to carry the loads necessary for his army. True it is that such a course was a fatal blunder; true it is that it would have been wiser far to have aban-

---

* The extent to which Lally felt this is shown by the following extract of a letter he addressed to de Leyrit, dated the 15th May, and which runs thus:—" The Minister (at Paris) will find it difficult to believe that you awaited the disembarkation of the troops on board the first vessel of our squadron, before you employed the money at your disposal in preparations for an enterprise of which you had had eight months' warning. I sent you 100,000 francs of my money to aid in the necessary expenses; I have not found on my arrival resources of 100 pence in your purse or in that of your Council."—*Official Correspondence in Lally's Memoirs.*

doned his enterprise, to have re-embarked even for Europe, than to adopt a line of action so repugnant to the feelings and the ideas of the class without whose hearty co-operation nothing of permanent importance could be achieved; but whilst we blame him for that, let us not forget the wilful neglect of the Pondichery authorities, his own ignorance of Indian customs, the grounds he had for disbelieving all the assertions of the Franco-Indians. He was doubtless culpable, but they were ten thousand times more so.

Some sort of a system having been established by these unwise means, and by others, more legitimate, to which the employment of these compelled de Leyrit and his colleagues to have recourse, Lally returned to Gudálur, and on May 16 opened fire on Fort St. David. This fort is situated at the southern angle of an island nearly three quarters of a mile long and about half the breadth. On two sides of that angle it was guarded by the backwater connecting the Gaddilám and Paravánar rivers. On the base it was protected by four small masonry forts, nearly a quarter of a mile from the covered way, each supporting the other. It was necessary to take these before trenches could be opened. The garrison of the fort consisted of 619 Europeans,* of whom 83 were pensioners, and of about 1,600 sipáhis and lascars. The fortifications, especially those of the two exterior forts, had been repaired and greatly strengthened during the eight months that had intervened between the arrival of de Soupire and the investment. The troops under the command of Lally consisted of 1,600 Europeans and 600 natives of all arms.

The four forts already alluded to were the first objects of Lally's attack. These were stormed—notwithstanding that the guns and mortars sent him from Pondichery, and on which he depended for success, unaccountably failed him—sword in hand, on the night of the 17th.

* Of these 250 were sailors.—*Orme.*

On the evening of the following day trenches were opened at a distance of less than 400 yards from the glacis. From this date to June 2 the siege continued, under great difficulties on both sides. In the French camp there was a scarcity of money, of provisions, of guns, of ammunition, and of carriage; the most angry letters passed between Lally and de Leyrit, the one accusing and threatening, the other constantly asserting that his resources were exhausted. In the fort, on the other hand, discipline was relaxed, desertions were frequent, and defence had become hopeless, unless it were from the English fleet. Under these circumstances the feelings of Lally may be imagined when on May 28th he received intimation that the English fleet had appeared before Pondichery, making apparently for Fort St. David, whilst the French sailors had unanimously refused to embark on board their ships, on the pretext that faith had not been kept with them regarding their pay, and that d'Aché had thereupon announced his intention to moor his ships in the roadstead of Pondichery under the protection of the place.

However much Lally felt that his presence before Fort St. David was necessary for the carrying on of the siege, this intelligence of the determination to yield the sea to the English forced him to return at once to Pondichery, taking with him 400 Europeans and 200 sipáhis. Assembling, on arrival, a council, he ordered 60,000 francs to be paid out of his own funds to the sailors, embarked them and the 600 men he had brought with him on board the ships of the fleet, and persuaded d'Aché to proceed at once to sea. He then returned to his post before Fort St. David. The result corresponded to his anticipations. The French fleet, putting to sea, effectually prevented any communication between the English Admiral and the besieged fort; the latter, thus left to itself, and hardly pushed by Lally, capitulated on June 2, the garrison surrendering as prisoners of war. The fortifications were immediately razed to the ground.

Thus, in less than five weeks after his landing, had Lally, notwithstanding difficulties unheard of and almost inconceivable, certainly entirely unexpected, carried out one part of his programme. He had driven the English from one of their principal settlements—from that one indeed which for a long time had remained their seat of government, which had defied the efforts of Dupleix, and whence Lawrence and Clive had sallied to baffle the French arms at Trichinápallí. But he did not stop here. The very day of the surrender, the Count d'Estaing was detached to Dévikótá, which the English garrison, counting only 30 Europeans and 600 sipáhis abandoned on his approach. Whilst this expedition was in course of progress, d'Aché landed at Fort St. David, and dined with Lally, who seized the occasion to open to him his new designs. Now was the time, he said, to attack Madras. The place was unfortified, the garrison weak, the Council discouraged by the capture of Fort St. David. Let but d'Aché agree to act with him, to take his army on board, and to land it either at Madras itself or at least on the high land of Alumpárva, already occupied by the French, and success, he said, was certain. But, to his chagrin, d'Aché refused him his support. Acting in the same spirit which had animated him when he had delayed his voyage to India in order to keep and dispose of the little merchant ship which he had captured, d'Aché alleged that it devolved upon him to cruise off Ceylon to intercept the stray merchant ships of England. To all the remonstrances of Lally he replied only by urging the deficiency of provisions and the sickness of his crews—reasons which appeared equally to apply to their cruising off Ceylon. Unable to shake his resolution, Lally, rejoined by the detachment under d'Estaing, returned to Pondichery, into which he made a triumphant entry—a *Te Deum* being celebrated in honour of the capture of Fort St. David. Still, however, bent more than ever on the practical, he lost no time in vain rejoicing, but summoned a council to which he invited d'Aché. Again he urged his reasons for instant action against Madras, but again was he met by the dogged and obstinate refusal of his naval colleague. It was a hard trial to see the fruits of his victory thus snatched from his grasp by the stolid stupidity of the man whose indecision and delays had already cost him so much, and who happened to be the only official not subjected to his orders. But hard as it was, Lally was forced to bear it, and to see the fleet that might, he believed, have carried him in triumph to Madras, leave the roadstead of Pondichery, on an uncertain and profitless cruise, carrying with it the 600 troops he had lent its commander.

Still, notwithstanding the defection of d'Aché, Lally was very unwilling to renounce his designs on Madras. With the *coup d'œil* of a real soldier he saw, as La Bourdonnais had seen before him, that there the decisive blow was to be struck. Yet he was helpless. He had not the money to equip his army, and de Leyrit and his colleagues persisted in declaring that it was impossible for them to raise it. Out of this difficulty, the local chief of the Jesuits, by name Father Lavaur, one of the most influential of the residents at Pondichery, suggested an escape. It so happened that amongst the prisoners taken at Fort St. David was that same Sahújí, ex-king of Tanjúr, who had been twice expelled from that country in 1739, and who, taken up by the English for their own purposes, in 1749, and thrown aside when no longer of use to them, had continued ever since a pensioner on their bounty.* The arrival of Sahújí in Pondichery suggested to the mind of the

---

* Chapters III. and VI.

Jesuit that he might be made use of to frighten the Rájá of Tanjúr, his nephew, upon whom the French had a claim for fifty-five lakhs of rupees in consequence of a bond given to Chanda Sáhib, and made over by his son, Rajú Sáhib, to Dupleix. "Thus," added Lavaur, to Lally, "you will obtain, at easy cost, the means of equipping your force for Madras, and gaining at the same time a considerable augmentation of influence." Lally did not like the plan. His mind was bent upon Madras. Any object that would delay the movement against that place was to him unpalatable. The Tanjúr expedition was a diversion from the direct line he had marked out for himself, and of which he never once lost sight—the expulsion of the English from India. But he was helpless. Unsupported by the authorities of Pondichery and by d'Aché he could not march towards Madras. Unwillingly, therefore, and solely as a means whereby he could eventually carry out his own plans, he consented to move upon Tanjúr.

Meanwhile d'Aché had sailed on his projected cruise, and had arrived on the 16th (June) off Kárikál, which it had been his intention to leave the next day. But a curious fatality attended all the counsels of the French at this epoch. Had d'Aché left Kárikál, as he intended, on June 17, he would almost certainly have intercepted two English ships which were conveying to Madras a portion of the annual supplies of *specie* from England. This supply would have been more than sufficient to enable Lally to equip his army and to march to Madras. Unfortunately for him, however, and for the French cause, the members of the Council of Pondichery were so alarmed at the idea of being left exposed by the contemplated absence of Lally, to an attack from the English fleet, that they sent a pressing message to d'Aché to return. This message reached him on the 16th. More pliable to the wishes of the Council than to those of Lally, he suffered himself to be persuaded,

FATALITY ATTENDING D'ACHÉ.

renounced his intended cruise, and returned to Pondichery. The two English vessels, which could not have escaped him had he proceeded in a southerly direction, arrived safely at Madras.

On the following day Lally started for Tanjúr, at the head of 1,600 European troops and a proportion of sipáhis, leaving 600 Europeans and 200 sipáhis under de Soupire in an intrenched camp between Alumpárva and Pondichery. So powerful a force in point of numbers had never before invaded the dominions of a native prince, but it was wanting in every particular which tends to make an army useful and efficient.

It marched without organised carriage, without provisions, without money, without even a sufficiency of ammunition. All these supplies, even the ammunition, were to be obtained on the road, an arrangement which could not be carried into effect without relaxing to a dangerous extent the discipline of the army, and, what was of even more importance, alienating the people of the country. It is difficult to exaggerate the sufferings the soldiers endured.* At Dévikóta they had nothing to eat but rice in the husk, and it was not till they reached Kárikál, 100 miles by the road from Pondichery, that they really had a meal. Even here Lally found only twenty-eight oxen and a small quantity of meal, the remainder of the supplies having been consumed by the squadron. But he received the next day from the Dutch at Tranquebar and Nágápatan both ammunition and food.

The difficulties of his march, the suffering of his

---

* From Dévikotá, which they reached on the second day, without finding wherewith to satisfy their hunger, Lally wrote thus to de Leyrit: "J'attends dans la nuit les bœufs qui traînent l'artillerie afin de les faire tuer. . . . . J'ai envoyé a Tranquebar pour y acheter tous les chiens-marrons (dog-fish) et bœufs que l'on pourra rencontrer, ainsi que la raque à quelque prix que ce soit : voilà, à la lettre, l'horreur de la situation dans laquelle vous nous avez mis, et le danger auquel vous exposez une armée, que je ne serais point surpris de voir passer à l'ennemi pour chercher à manger."— *Lally's Correspondence with Pondichery.*

CHAP. XII.
1758.

troops, and the obstacles thrown in his way upon every occasion, had affected the disposition of Lally to such an extent, that, from the moment of his entering into the Tanjúr territory, he began to indulge in acts of harsh and unreasoning severity, most detrimental to his cause. He plundered the town of Nágar, ransacked all the Brahman temples he met with on his route, and finding six Brahmans lingering about his camp, he blew them away from guns. Such was the license he allowed his army, and so wide was the terror caused by his approach, that we cannot wonder that he should have written that he met with scarcely an inhabitant on his route, and that the country through which he marched was "like a barren desert."*

At length, on July 18th, the French army found itself close to Tanjúr. Lally had previously sent a requisition to the rájá requiring payment of the fifty-five lakhs of rupees, but to this he had received an evasive reply, it being the object of the rájá to delay him until assistance could be obtained from the English. In the negotiations that followed it is probable that Lally might eventually have reaped some advantage had he conducted himself with ordinary prudence. But the violence of his temper ruined him. When he had brought the rájá to an undertaking to pay five lakhs and the value of three or four lakhs in the shape of supplies, his suspicions induced him to regard an accidental failure in the fulfilment of one of the stipulations into a deliberate breach of faith. Completely carried away by his violence, he at once sent the rájá a message in which he threatened to transport him and all his family as slaves to the Isle of France. This was too great an indignity to be endured, and the rájá, supported by the promises of the English and some trained sipáhis sent him by Captain Calliaud from Trichinápallí, bade defiance to his enemy. Lally upon

* Mémoire pour Lally page 67.

this determined to try the effect of an assault. Two batteries were opened on August 2nd, a breach was effected on the 7th, and the attack ordered for the 8th. On the morning of that day, however, intelligence reached the camp that d'Aché had been attacked by the English, been beaten and driven off the coast, and that the English were threatening Kárikál, which formed the base of the French operations against Tanjúr. At the same time advices were received from de Soupire to the effect that Pondichery was threatened by a corps of 800 English from Madras, and that he, having only 600, was preparing to evacuate his position.

When this intelligence reached Lally, he had in camp supplies for but two days, and the Tanjurian cavalry effectually prevented him from procuring any more; his small arm ammunition was almost entirely exhausted, and for cannon-shot he depended on those fired by the enemy. Still the breach had been effected, and both d'Estaing and Saubinet were eager that the assault should be delivered. But the consideration that after the fort was taken it would be necessary to attack the town, which was itself strongly defended, that the attack upon the fort would exhaust all his ammunition, and, if that attack were unsuccessful, his men would be, as it were, an unarmed multitude, determined Lally, on the advice of the council of war he assembled, to retreat. Instead, therefore, of delivering the assault on the 8th, he sent off a detachment of 150 men, escorting the sick, the wounded, and the siege stores, in the direction of Kárikál, on the 9th, intending to follow himself with the main body on the evening of the 10th.

Early on that morning, however, the Tanjurians, gaining courage from the reported intentions of Lally, attacked his camp suddenly. They were repulsed, indeed, with considerable loss on their side, but, meanwhile, a Jámadár and fifty horsemen had ridden up to the pagoda in which Lally was sleeping, giving out that they were deserters. Lally, who was still in his night-dress, went, on hearing of their approach, to the door of the pagoda, but they had no sooner come up, than their leader, instead of making his submission, struck at Lally with his sabre. The French general warded off the blow with a stick, but it was about to be repeated, when the Jámadár was shot dead by one of Lally's followers. The conspirators then made successive charges on the French guard, which had turned out on witnessing these events, but they were each time repulsed, twenty-eight of their number being killed. Disheartened by this loss, the remainder endeavoured to escape, but galloping by mistake into a tank, they were destroyed to a man. The general attack made on the other part of the camp was, as we have said, easily repulsed.

That night Lally broke up from before Tanjúr, having subsisted for two months on the country. Of *specie*, his great want, he had succeeded in wringing from the rájá but little. The three pieces of heavy cannon which had constituted his siege battery he spiked, breaking up their carriages for want of cattle to drag them. He then marched in two columns, the baggage and carriage for the sick being in the interval between them, two pieces of artillery preceding and two being in rear of the force. The retreat was executed in the finest order. Lally left nothing behind him but the three spiked guns. Unfortunately, however, hunger was the constant attendant of his camp. He had exhausted all his supplies, and the Tanjurian cavalry effectually prevented him from gaining any from the country. Arriving at his first halting-place, after marching from midnight till nine o'clock in the morning, he could serve out to his soldiers nothing but water. Hungry and faint, they marched on to Trivalur, twenty-four miles, where provisions had been sent for them from Kárikál. From this place the enemy, abandoning the pursuit, returned to Tanjúr; from here, too, Count d'Estaing was sent to Pondichery to endeavour once more to persuade d'Aché, who had signified his intention of returning to the Isle of France, to make a combined attack on Madras. After a halt of three days at Trivalur, the army continued its retreat, and arrived on the 18th at Kárikál, which they found blockaded by the English fleet. A few days later Lally marched with part of his force to Pondichery, arriving there on the 28th.

Meanwhile d'Aché, leaving the Pondichery roadstead on July 28th, had encountered the English fleet off Tranquebar on August 1st, and after a severe engagement of about two hours, in which he lost many men and was himself wounded, had been completely worsted, and had saved himself only by the superior sailing qualities of his ships. Bearing up for Pondichery he arrived there the next day, and learning that the Dutch at Nágápatan had allowed a French ship to be captured in their roadstead by the English squadron, he seized in reprisal a Dutch vessel lying in the Pondichery roads, on board of which were three lakhs of rupees in gold and merchandise. Apprehensive of an attack from the English, he then brought to his squadron under the guns of the town.

He was in this position when Lally, on August 28th, arrived. Great was the indignation of the French general at what he considered the pusillanimous position taken up by his naval colleague; greater still his fury, when he found that all the remonstrances of d'Estaing had availed nothing, and that d'Aché was resolute, not only to decline all further contests with the English, but to abandon the coast. In vain did Lally offer to strengthen his fleet with as many of his soldiers as he might require, with a view to his again encountering the English, whilst Lally himself should march upon Madras: in vain did the Council, for once unanimous, urge upon him the necessity of at least remaining some time longer on the coast. He was obstinate to run no further risk; the utmost he would do, and that he did, was to land 500 of his sailors to augment the land forces of the settlement. He then—on September 2nd—sailed for the Isle of France. The English squadron, now without an opponent, remained for three weeks longer before Pondichery, and then sailed for Bombay.

The capture of the Dutch vessel, however indefensible in itself, had at least supplied Lally with money. He employed the time, therefore, after his return to Pondichery in making preparations for his darling design upon Madras. As a preliminary to this expedition he despatched Saubinet to retake Trinomali—which had been recaptured by the adherents of the English—; de Soupire against Karangúlí; de Crillon against Trivátúr; appointing all these detachments to meet him at Wandiwash. Here, too, Bussy, to whom, as we have seen, he had written on June 13th,* joined him, having preceded his troops left under the orders of Moracin. The three expeditions having been successful, and the troops having reunited, Lally marched towards Arkát, which the native commandant, who had been gained over, surrendered to him at once. There now remained between the French and Madras, in occupation of the English, the posts of Chengalpat and Kánchipúram, neither of them adequately garrisoned, and both almost inviting attack. Upon these, more especially upon Chengalpát, the position of which on the Palar made it of great importance to the English, it was his obvious duty to march without delay. He himself declares that he could not move because his money was exhausted, and the sipáhis refused to march unless they were paid. But it is difficult to believe that he could not have detached the divisions of Saubinet or d'Estaing to besiege a place which, at the time of his entry

---

* In that letter Lally had opened his whole heart to Bussy. After stating his designs upon Madras he had added—" I will not conceal from you, that, Madras once taken, I am determined to proceed to the Ganges, either by land or by sea. . . . I confine myself now to indicate to you my policy in these five words; *no more English in India*" (*plus d'Anglais dans le Péninsule*).

into Arkát (October 4th), was guarded only by two companies of sipáhis, and the capture of which would have ensured him at least supplies. It would appear that it was not until the English had strengthened the place considerably, and supplied it with an adequate garrison, that he became sensible of its importance. But it was just at that moment that, in the view of the chance of a protracted siege, the absolute necessity for a further supply of money came home to him. Unable to procure that supply by means of a letter to the Council, he left his army in cantonments, and proceeded with Bussy and other of his officers to Pondichery, in the hope to be able to come to some definite arrangement by means of which the expedition, not only against Chengalpat, but against Madras itself, might be made feasible.

The deliberations at Pondichery succeeded better than Lally had dared to hope. At a meeting of a mixed council the expedition against Madras was resolved upon, the military and some of the civil members expressing their opinion that it was better to encounter the risk of dying from a musket-ball on the glacis of Madras than of hunger in Pondichery. De Leyrit alone dissented, alleging that he had no money whatever. But this article was not altogether wanting. Moracin had brought with him not only 250 European troops and 500 sipáhis, but 100,000 rupees; the superior officers and members of Council, instigated by the example of Lally himself,* added contributions from their private purses. Still notwithstanding the considerable sum thus raised, it was very much reduced by the necessary preparations, and when, on November 2nd, Lally started to join his army, his treasure-chest contained but 94,000 rupees, whilst the monthly expenses of the army alone were not less than 40,000.

The meeting between Lally and Bussy had been ap-

* Lally subscribed 144,000 livres, Count d'Estaing and others 80,000 livres in plate. According to Lally, Bussy gave nothing.

parently friendly. Lally had not only expressed his sense of the advantage he would derive from the great Indian experience of his subordinate, but on their arrival at Pondichery, had paid him the compliment of inviting him to a seat in the Supreme Council. Nevertheless the secret feelings of the two men for one another were far from cordial. Lally, whose one great idea was the expulsion of the English, could not enter into the plan of a French Empire in the heart of the Dakhan, dependent on English weakness and English forbearance. Aware besides that Bussy, whilst maintaining the fortunes of France at Haidarábád, had gained not only a great name but an enormous fortune, he could not forbear from connecting the one circumstance with the other, nor from secretly including Bussy amongst the self-seekers* whom he had found so numerous at Pondichery. On the other hand, Bussy, distrusting Lally's capacity from the first, and noticing the dislike which the other could not conceal, bound too by ties of friendship and long service with the de Leyrits and Desvaux and other councillors of Pondichery, gradually and insensibly fell into opposition. Nor were his first proceedings calculated to make matters better. He used every effort in his power to induce Lally to send him back to the Dakhan with increased forces; every day he presented to him letters from the Subadar to the same effect. This was the course best calculated to confirm the suspicions and sharpen the indignation of Lally. A mind constituted as was his, bent eagerly upon one point, could not tolerate a proposition, which so far from tending to aid him, went precisely in the opposite direction, and instead of strengthening, would have weakened, his force. He came therefore to regard the requests of Bussy and Moracin as part of the general

---

* The Jesuit, Father Lavaur, had more than once impressed upon Lally, that in India, the officials worked for something more than the glory of the King.

OPPOSITE OPINIONS OF BUSSY.

plan to thwart him, as sure and certain proofs that they too regarded only their own interests and not the interests of France. So far from giving in to them, he the more firmly insisted that Bussy should accompany him. All this time he treated him with outward politeness, but in reality he regarded him as a most ordinary and over-rated man.*

But if Lally had this opinion of Bussy, far different was the impression made by the trusted lieutenant of Dupleix on the officers under his command. They were not slow in recognising his ability, his large views, his acquaintance with the country and the true mode of managing the people. To such an extent did they display their confidence in his talents and his devotedness, that on the eve of the expedition to Madras, six of their number,† including the chivalrous d'Estaing, who had already made a reputation, signed a request to the Commander-in-chief, that Bussy, the Company's general, might be placed over their heads, and occupy the position next to de Soupire. Lally was unwilling to comply; he attributed even this request to the effect of Bussy's money;‡ but he could not well refuse, and the order was issued accordingly.

At length, in the beginning of November, Lally collected his forces, amounting to 2,000 European infantry, 300 cavalry, and 5,000 sipáhis, and marched upon Madras. These were divided into four brigades, commanded by de Soupire, d'Estaing, Crillon, and Saubinet. Bussy held no actual command, but he was present with

---

* The memoirs of Lally and Bussy abound with proofs of the little estimation in which each, in his heart, held the other.

† These were MM. d'Estaing, Crillon, de la Fare, Verdiére, Breteuil, and de Landivisiau.

‡ Lally asserts that to secure the good offices of some of these noblemen Bussy lent or gave or offered to them the following sums: to Count d'Estaing, 100,000 crowns; to the Chevalier de Crillon, 2,000 louis d'or. Crillon, however, refused them. Lally adds that Bussy offered him 460,000 livres to be sent back to the Dakhan, and stated that he was ready to advance 240,000 livres for the service of the Company, provided Lally would be his security. Lally states that he declined both offers.—*Mémoire pour Lally.*

the force as Brigadier, with an authority superior to that of all the other officers, de Soupire and Lally excepted. Taking possession of Kánchipúram on the 27th, the army marched from there on the 29th, and reached the plain in front of Madras on December 12. The strong position of Chengalpat, which, two months before, Lally might have taken with little loss, he now, with regret, left in his rear. Retaining that, the English had been, and were still, able to procure abundant supplies from the surrounding country.

The English garrison of Madras consisted of 1,758 Europeans, 2,220 sipáhis, and 200 horse; there were besides within the walls 150 Europeans, who were likewise employed in various ways in the defence. The Governor was Mr. George Pigot, afterwards Lord Pigot, a man of ability and discrimination, and who had the good sense to make over all the arrangements of the defence to the veteran Colonel Lawrence, who found himself within the walls. Under Lawrence were Lieutenant-Colonel Draper, the conqueror of Manilla,* Major Calliaud of Trichinápallí renown, Major Brereton, and other good officers. Chengalpat was garrisoned by 100 Europeans and 1,200 sipáhis, commanded by an active leader, Captain Preston. It will thus be seen that in the number of Europeans—the backbone of an army in India—the French did not possess a very overwhelming advantage over the enemy that they had come to besiege. The defence was confined mainly to Fort St. George, although three fortified posts were left in the Black Town.

Lally, as we have seen, reached the plain in front of Madras on the 12th. The van of his little force was commanded by the chivalrous d'Estaing, and consisted of 300 European infantry, 300 cavalry and two guns, he himself following with the main body. On the 13th the army encamped in the plain, whilst Lally employed

* The same who engaged in a controversy with Junius.

the day in reconnoitring the Fort and the Black Town. Having done this to his satisfaction, he detached the Chevalier de Crillon with the regiment of Lally to take possession of the Black Town, an enterprise which succeeded with but little loss on the side of the French, the posts being evacuated as they advanced. The conquest, however, gave rise to great relaxation of discipline, for the town was rich, and the camp-followers, of whom there were 10,000, would not be restrained, nor had Lally a sufficient number of troops to enforce obedience, in this respect, to his orders. An indiscriminate pillage was consequently the result; the value of the property seized being computed at 15,000,000 of francs (£600,000).* To the military chest, however, there resulted from the capture of the town a gain of but 92,000 francs or less than £3,700, being the contributions of an Armenian whom Lally had saved from plunder, and of the Hindú chief of Arní.

The town having been occupied, the Lorraine brigade and the brigade of Company's troops were posted on its right near the sea, the brigade of Lally and the sailor brigade establishing themselves in some buildings belonging to the Capuchins on the rising ground on the left of the town. About ten o'clock on the following morning, whilst Lally, accompanied by Bussy and d'Estaing, was engaged in reconnoitring on the left of the Black Town, intimation was brought him that the English were making a strong demonstration against his right—an intimation quickly confirmed by the firing of small arms. Though separated from the brigades which formed the right by a marshy plain about 200 yards in width and by a little stream, d'Estaing at once started in full haste to join in the combat. He had approached the scene of action, when, noticing some troops dressed in scarlet, he rode up to put himself at their head, believing them to be the volunteers of

* Mémoire pour Lally.

Bourbon, who wore a uniform of that colour. It was not until he found himself a prisoner amongst them that he discovered them to be English. Bussy, who had followed him, returned, on noticing his misfortune, to the regiment of Lally, whilst the general, accompanied by his aide-de-camp and orderly officer, succeeded in gaining the scene of action. They found that the officers of the regiment of Lorraine had duly noticed the approach of a body of 500 men under Colonel Draper, supported by 150 under Major Brereton, with two guns, but, mistaking them, as d'Estaing afterwards did, for their own men, had made no dispositions to oppose them. They had only become aware of their error when the English guns opened on their left flank. Completely surprised, they had fallen into confusion, and, abandoning their guns, had sought refuge under cover of some houses that were near. Had the English then advanced the guns might have been carried off and the siege ended that very day. But their troops likewise fell into confusion amongst the houses, and their native buglers having run away, a part of the force became separated from the rest. Two officers of the regiment of Lorraine, Captains Guillermin and Sécati, noticing this, rallied their men with great spirit, and advanced with fixed bayonets to support their guns. It was now the turn of the English to fall back. Their position was a dangerous one; not only were they in the presence of a superior force, recovered from its surprise, but to regain the fort they had to cross the marshy plain and the small bridge of which we have spoken, and to which the regiment of Lally, burning for action, was nearer than they were. It will thus be seen that the fate of the English depended on the conduct of the officer of that regiment.

There are some critical moments decisive of the fate and fortunes of individuals and nations; moments which offer golden opportunities not to be flirted with, but to be seized at once if success is to be achieved. This was one of them. The regiment of Lally had but to advance, and the fate of Madras would have been sealed. For not only would these 650 men have been slain or captured, but the effect upon their comrades within the walls would, according to the testimony of their commandant, have been decisive.* It was a great opportunity—let us see how the French used it.

We have said that after the capture of d'Estaing, Lally had proceeded to the right of the position, where the action was going on, whilst Bussy galloped back to his post on the left. Lally arrived at the scene of action after Guillermin and Sécati had rallied their men, and the English in their turn had begun to retreat. He at once directed a movement whereby eighty of the latter were cut off from their comrades and made prisoners, at the same time that he ordered a vigorous pursuit of the remainder; on the other side the Chevalier de Crillon, who commanded the Lally brigade, saw the English retreating towards the bridge, in disorder, and pursued by the Lorraine and Indian brigades. The thought at once came into his mind that by occupying the bridge on which that detachment was retreating, he might cut it off to a man. As, however, he did not command in that part of the field, Bussy being on the spot, he went up to that officer, and asked his permission to make the movement with his corps. To his intense mortification Bussy refused. In vain did other officers crowd round him; he was obstinate and obdurate.† So sensible, however, was Crillon of the

---

* Colonel Lawrence states in his Memoirs that the previous retrograde movements of the English had greatly discouraged his men, and that this sortie had been determined upon, because "it appeared necessary to do something immediately to restore the spirits of the garrison." Had the men composing the sortie-party been killed or taken, it would undoubtedly have tended to the still further discouragement of those remaining within the walls.

† The conduct of Bussy on this occasion has been hotly contested. The following points, however, are clear: 1st:—That if the bridge had been occupied by the regiment of

CHAP. XII.
1758.

immense value of the opportunity, that he started forward himself with fifty volunteers and gained the bridge. Such a force was not, however, sufficiently strong to prevent the passage of the enemy, which soon became an accomplished fact, though with a loss at the bridge itself of several killed and thirty-three prisoners.

Thus was the opportunity suffered to escape, and the remains of the English party succeeded in regaining the fort. Their loss, however, was heavy. It amounted, by their own statement, to more than 200 men and six officers, 103 of whom were taken prisoners. The loss of the French was, however, even more severe. It is true that in actual killed and wounded they did not lose more than 200 men; but two of their best officers were placed *hors de combat*. One of these, as we have seen, was the gallant d'Estaing, the other the no less daring Saubinet, who was mortally wounded. He was an officer in the service of the Company of the Indies, of great and improving talents, ever foremost in danger.

Lally, the retreat of the English would have been cut off; 2nd, that the regiment of Lally could easily have occupied the bridge; 3rd, that Bussy was with that regiment or near it at the time. We have adopted in the text the account given by Lally himself. To this account Bussy, in his lifetime, demurred, stating, 1st, that he had no command, being a simple volunteer; 2ndly, that he was thanked for his conduct by the Pondichery Government; 3rdly, that on the field of battle Lally conferred on him the command of the Lorraine brigade vacant by the capture of d'Estaing. He also added that he remembered on passing by the Lally brigade after the capture of d'Estaing, he recommended them to bring up two pieces of field artillery, as the enemy had none, that he then passed on to the brigade commanded by the Chevalier de Poete, to whom he said that having neither rank nor command, he had come to fight with him; further that he had never heard of the story until after he had left India.

The statement of Bussy seems, however, inconsistent with the facts that he had rank in the army next to de Soupire, that rank having been conferred upon him before leaving Pondichery; that having that rank, it became his duty to exercise its functions; that the statement of Lally was confirmed, on his trial, by the Chevalier de Crillon, the witness who was best qualified to speak. In the state of feeling between Lally and the Pondichery Council the thanks of the latter are of little weight; whereas the conferring the command of the regiment on the field of battle may be accounted for on other grounds. Certainly the balance of evidence is against Bussy.

Mr. Orme states that Bussy gave other reasons for his conduct. Bussy does not, however, state them in his Memoirs. Mr. Orme gives them. They are, however, so little satisfactory, that were they really Bussy's they would but confirm our opinion of his conduct on this occasion.

THE SIEGE BEGUN.

The loss of these two able officers far outweighed in importance the loss of the rank and file.

The same day Lally established his headquarters in the Black Town, and waited impatiently for his heavy guns. But before they arrived the expenses of the campaign had begun to exhaust the sums raised by the capture of the town. At this crisis, however, the frigate "La Fidéle" arrived at Pondichery having on board one million of francs (£40,000). She ought to have brought to Pondichery two millions, but, having touched at the Isle of France about the time of the arrival there of d'Aché from Pondichery, that unpatriotic and inefficient officer had appropriated one million for the service of his squadron, sending the frigate on with the remainder. She arrived at her destination on December 21st, just in time to determine Lally, not merely to content himself with devastating the country round Madras, but to besiege that place in form. The arrival of his heavy guns about the same time enabled him to complete his arrangements. His artillery then consisted of twenty pieces of 12, 18, and 24-pounders, and of ten mortars, 8 and 12-pounders. These were soon placed in position and a fresh parallel opened at a distance of 500 yards from the place. He had decided to attack the fort on the side immediately opposite the position he had taken up, although in appearance it was the strongest. He satisfied himself partly on the ground that though the fort might be the stronger on that side, the aproaches to it could be more easily made; and partly, because, as had been proved on the 14th, the intricacies of the Black Town afforded a means of defence against sorties, such as bade defiance to an enemy.

But Lally soon found how impossible it was to effect anything great with officers the majority of whom were bad, and with an army disorganised and disaffected. The difficulties and obstacles which he had to encounter during the first twenty days of the siege were sufficient to break the spirit of any ordinary man. Very many of the soldiers, instead of working in the trenches, employed themselves in searching for treasure in the deserted houses of the Black Town and in making themselves drunk with the proceeds. Several of the officers, far from checking their men, or doing their duty in the field, were themselves engaged in guarding the contents of the shops which they had appropriated. Multitudes from Pondichery swarmed into the Black Town, many of them forging the general's signature in order to obtain boats wherewith to carry off their plunder. Even the artillery cattle were employed by some officers in conveying furniture and property to Pondichery. It was impossible for Lally alone to put a stop to this state of things. In fact, the paucity of skilled officers rendered it necessary for him to be always in the trenches. Of five engineer officers who had come out with him from France but two remained; one of these, the senior, was idle and useless; the other had, under Lally, the charge of the trenches. Of six officers of artillery, three were killed in the first three weeks of the siege; of the others, two were with the artillery park, and the third was a boy. The superior officers of the army were engaged with their several brigades. Upon Lally, therefore, devolved the main charge of directing the operations of the siege, and he devoted himself to it with a zeal and energy that could not have been surpassed. For he had, it must be remembered, other matters to attract and engage his attention. The English had not been slow to use the advantages offered to them by the possession of Chengalpat. The force that guarded that post issued frequently into the field to attack the French in their flanks and rear, and to disturb their communications with Pondichery; and not only this, but Major Calliaud, sent to Tanjúr, succeeded in obtaining from the Rájá, and bringing into the field

600 men, one half of whom were cavalry. Muhammad Isuf, a partisan, brought 2,000 more. These various parties, hovering about Lally's position, kept him in a continual state of alarm. They might be driven away, but, like wasps, they returned to annoy. Lally's difficulties were still further increased by the fact that even the powder necessary for carrying on the siege had to be brought from Pondichery, through a country swarming with partisans, who carried their depredations to the very gates of that city. Besides these outer enemies there were within the walls of Madras 200 French deserters. These constantly mounted the ramparts, holding in the one hand a bottle of wine, and in the other a purse, and calling out to the French soldiers to follow their example. Scarcely a day passed but missives from these men were discharged by arrows into the besieging camp, all tempting the soldiers to desert. At length, on January 2nd, after overcoming innumerable trials and conquering difficulties seemingly insuperable, two batteries, called, from the brigades to which they belonged, the Lally and the Lorraine, opened their fire. This they continued almost incessantly for forty-two days, a great portion of the army being at the same time engaged with varying success almost daily with the enemy's partisans, with the troops under Calliaud from Tanjúr and under Preston from Chengalpat, and with the numerous sorties from the garrison. At length the crisis approached. The garrison received intimation, early in February, that Admiral Pocock's fleet was on its way from Bombay, and would infallibly arrive off Madras in a few days. On the other hand, a breach had been effected in the walls, and Lally, who knew how much depended on the promptitude of his proceedings, determined to deliver the assault. At this moment, however, he found all his designs shattered by the backwardness of his officers. Those of the engineers and artillery declared that although the breach was quite

practicable, yet that, " having regard to the situation of things, to our force compared with that of the enemy," an assault would cause the destruction of a great many soldiers, and would end in nothing. These officers, not content with writing this to the general, made no secret of their opinion in the camp, intimating that to try an assault would be to march to certain death. But Lally, though disappointed at this opinion, sensible how great was the responsibility of acting on such an occasion against the written advice of his scientific officers, yet feeling persuaded that they were wrong, and that his soldiers would follow him, did not renounce his determination. He waited only for the wane of the moon to deliver the assault, and had intimated to Crillon, charged with the chief attack, that he was to hold himself in readiness to make it on the evening of February 16th, when to his intense disappointment, he saw Admiral Pocock's squadron sail into the roadstead on the afternoon of that very day.

The situation of the besieging army was now desperate. For the past twenty days the troops had had no pay, and the officers had been on soldier's rations; there remained but 20,000lbs. of powder in the artillery park, and only a similar supply at Pondichery. For three weeks not a single bomb had been fired, that species of ammunition having been exhausted; the native troops, unpaid, had melted away, and even the European cavalry threatened to go over to the enemy. Pondichery, too, had but 300 invalids left to guard it. Under these circumstances, the arrival of the English fleet, at once relieving Madras and threatening Pondichery, made the raising of the siege inevitable.

On the night of February 17th, this operation took place. Sending all the wounded who could be moved from St. Thomé by sea, and burying his cannon-shot, he left in the trenches, from want of cattle to take them away, five pieces of cannon, and in the pagoda, used as a hospital, thirty-three wounded incapable of being moved, and a surgeon in charge of them. These he commended in a letter to the care of the Governor of Madras; then, taking with him all his baggage, he retired umolested, but full of rage * and mortification, by way of St. Thomé to Kánchipúram.

Thus failed the great enterprise on which Lally had set his heart—to which he had devoted every energy of mind and body. It has been said, indeed, that that failure was owing as much to his own infirmities of temper, to the manner in which he trampled on the cherished feelings of others, as to any other cause. But, after a careful examination of the facts of the case as shown in the correspondence between himself and de Leyrit, we cannot resist the conclusion that, great as were those infirmities of temper, violent and excitable as was his manner towards others, those who allowed themselves to be betrayed by that behaviour on his part into a neglect of their duty towards France were, infinitely more than Lally, the authors of the failure. Lally, at least, behaved like a soldier; he gave every thought, every exertion to his country. But the Council of Pondichery did the reverse. Mortified and enraged at the rough hand with which Lally had un- veiled and exposed abuses, as well as at the style in which he had pointed out to them that their first duty was to their country, they gave him no assistance ;

---

* The rage of Lally was directed against those whose self-seeking and corruption, by hindering and alto- gether keeping back the supplies of which he stood in need, had con- tributed to the unfortunate result of his expedition. In a letter to de Leyrit, dated February 14, he thus recounted some of the iniquities that were taking place under his eyes, and forcibly expressed his own opinion of the conduct of some of his officers: "Of 1,500 sipáhis," he said, "who are with our army, I calculate that nearly 800 are employed on the road to Pondichery, laden with sugar, pepper and other goods; as for the coolies, they have been employed on the same account ever since we have been here." In concluding the letter he renounced all interference with the civil administration of Pondichery, "for," he added, "I would rather go and command the Káfars of Mada- gascar, than to remain in that Sodom (Pondichery), which the fire of the English, in default of the fire of Heaven, will, sooner or later, inevi- tably destroy."

the money sent out to them for the purpose of the war they often squandered on themselves. More than that, they took a pleasure, which they scarcely attempted to conceal, in thwarting his designs. To such an extent did they carry their ill-feeling, that they allowed their hatred of the individual so far to conquer the remnants of their patriotism, that the retreat from Madras was the signal for the manifestation in Pondichery of the most indecent joy. Is it credible that men who thus rejoiced over the reverses of the French arms, because those reverses humiliated Lally, would have made the smallest self-sacrifice to attain an opposite result? On them, therefore, mainly, and not on Lally, must rest the responsibility of the failure of the siege.

Meanwhile, in another part of the coast reverses had likewise attended the French arms. We have seen how Lally, immediately after his arrival in Pondichery, had recalled Bussy and Moracin from the Dakhan and the Sirkars, and how these two, unwillingly obeying, had made over the government of Machhlípatan and the ceded provinces to the Marquis de Conflans in the month of August, 1758. The troops left with Conflans consisted of about 500 men, a number which, under a commander so experienced as Bussy would have been sufficient to keep the entire country in subjection. But Conflans had neither the ability, the tact, nor the knowledge of his predecessor. He was ignorant of the country, the language, of the mode of dealing with its feudal lords. Many of these latter, no longer sensible of a master's hand, noting the diminution in the number of European troops, determined to strike a blow to rid themselves of the French yoke, not calculating that by so doing they would in all probability exchange it for the English. It is possible, indeed, that looking at the balanced state of both powers in the Karnátik, they deemed it might not be an impracticable policy to play one against the other. However this may have been, it is certain that, three months after the departure of Bussy from the Dakhan, Rájá Anandaráj, ruler of the Sríkákolam and Rájámahendrí, raising the standard of revolt, took possession of Vizágapatam, plundered the factory, confined the French agent, hoisted English colours, and wrote to Madras for assistance. Threatened as Madras then was by Lally, aid from it was impossible; whereupon the Rájá appealed in despair to Clive. No one knew better than Clive how to seize an opportunity, no one was more acquainted than he with the advantages which the possession of the Sirkars would infallibly bring in its train. Overruling the advice of the Calcutta Council, who regarded interference in that quarter as little short of madness, he wrote to the Rájá promising speedy support, and despatched by sea on October 12, Colonel Forde at the head of 500 Europeans, 2,000 sipáhis, and eighteen guns. The fact that, by the despatch of this force, he left himself in Bengal with little more than 300 Europeans at a time when a hostile feeling had risen in the mind of Mir Jáfar, and when Bihár was threatened by the united forces of the son of the Emperor of Delhi, and by the Nawwáb Wazir of Oudh, testifies in no slight degree to the strong, fearless, and intrepid character of the founder of the British Empire in India.

Meanwhile, Conflans was acting in such a manner as to facilitate the plans of the English. Instead of marching rapidly upon Vizágapatam and crushing the rebellion in its bud, before the rebels could receive assistance from outside, he contented himself with sending repeated applications to Lally for support, whilst he moved leisurely against Rájámahendrí. He occupied that town, and was still encamped on the northern bank of the river of the same name, when intelligence reached him that an English force had, on October 20, landed at Vizágapatam. To him intelligence of that nature ought not to have been very alarming. The troops under his command were the most seasoned and the best disciplined of all who served the French Company in Southern India. They were the men before whom the famed Marátha cavalry had been scattered, and who, but a short year before, had forced their way through opposing hosts to relieve Bussy at Haidarábád. They had never yet shown their backs to a foe, and they might well have been counted upon, under efficient leadership, to defend the ceded provinces against even a larger force than that which then threatened it. Under these circumstances, and as they were supported by about 4,000 trained sipáhis, and by some of the native princes of the country, it would seem that it should have been the policy of Conflans to advance, to give to his men that spirit of self-confidence which a movement to the front always inspires; by that he would undoubtedly also have encouraged his native allies. It is the more strange that he did not do this, as a rumour had reached him, in which he entirely believed, that Colonel Forde's force was composed of raw troops, whom, therefore, it would be good policy to attack. He preferred, however, to adopt the course, which, in India, has but rarely proved successful—of waiting the attack of the enemy in the position he had chosen. He accordingly moved his force to the village of Kundúr, forty miles north of Rájámahendrí. Near this he was encountered, on December 8, by Colonel Forde, enticed out of his strong position, out-manœuvred, and completely defeated—losing his camp, his guns, and several of his men. He himself, fleeing on horseback, found refuge in Machhlípatan that same night.* Forde, pursuing his victory, occupied Rájámahendrí with a part of his force on the 10th.

---

* A detailed account of this battle and of all the actions of the campaign is to be found in the author's " The Decisive Battles of India " 3rd (new) edition, pp. 77-115.

His difficulties, however, were not over. The long connexion of the French with Salábat Jang, the intelligence that the principal settlement of the English was being besieged, combined to render the position of Forde dangerous and difficult. To the incapacity of his adversary was it alone due that it was not made fatal. Though virtually abandoned by his native allies, Forde, who thoroughly understood the conditions of Indian warfare, continued to advance towards Conflans, and notwithstanding that the French leader was enabled, by recalling troops from his garrisons, to bring a superior force of Europeans into the field, he actually besieged him in Machhlípatan. Rightly judging of the importance of moral force in war, he would not allow himself to be moved from this position even by the recapture of Rájámahendrí, nor by the intelligence that Salábat Jang was marching with 15,000 horse and 20,000 foot to overwhelm him. Nevertheless, as time advanced, his position became such as would have tried the nerves of the strongest leader. In the beginning of April it even seemed desperate. Before him was Conflans with a superior force, occupying Machhlípatan, which he was himself besieging; on his right, at Bézwádá, forty miles distant, was the army of the Subadar, ready to overwhelm him; on his right rear, a French corps of 200 men under M. du Rocher, prepared to cut off his communications. Under such circumstances, a weak leader would probably have endeavoured to retreat, though retreat would have been disgraceful and fatal; but Forde, being a strong man, preferred the chance of death in the attempt at assault to such a movement. Not knowing even that the breaches were practicable, but only in the hope that they might be so, he ordered his troops under arms at 10 o'clock on the night of the 7th, and delivered the assault in three divisions at midnight. He met with the success which a daring dashing leader can always look forward to over an unenterprising and hesitating adversary, for, after a fierce struggle, he not only captured the fort, but forced Conflans with his whole army to surrender.

The consequences of this unsurpassed act of cool and resolute daring were most important. Less than a week after, Moracin,* ordered to Machhlípatan by Lally on receiving the first message from Conflans, arrived with three hundred troops off the place. Finding it occupied by the English, he proceeded to Gánjám. There, however, he effected nothing: indeed, the place was abandoned, and his whole party dispersed by the end of the year. But the most important result was the treaty concluded with Salábat Jang. Struck by the unexpected defeat of the French, and annoyed at the time by the pretensions of Nizám Ali, the Subadar hastened to conclude with Forde a treaty whereby he renounced the French alliance, agreed never to allow a French contingent in the Dakhan, and ceded to the English a territory yielding an annual revenue of four lakhs of rupees. Before the end of the year, those districts, the possession of which constituted one of the triumphs of the administration of Dupleix, passed entirely into the hands of the English, and thenceforth the fate of French India was sealed.

Meanwhile Lally, retreating from Madras, had taken post at Kánchipúram. Thence, leaving his troops under the command of de Soupire, he set out for Arkát to arrange for the provisioning of the army. At Arkát he received a strange account of the proceedings of de Leyrit. Profiting by the absence of Lally with the army, de Leyrit had summarily, and against the protest of four members of his Council,† put a stop to an

---

* Moracin was indeed at once ordered to Machhlípatan, and had he obeyed, he would have arrived in time to have placed Forde in a position from which even his skill and daring could with difficulty have extracted his force; but, the ally of the French intriguers at Pondichery, he endeavoured for a long time to evade the order, and did actually delay so long, that he only arrived in time to share in the ruin in which the force of Conflans was involved.

† The names of the protestors were MM. Barthélemy, Boileau, La Selle, and Nicholas.

inquiry ordered to be instituted by Lally into the accounts of M. Desvaux, the head of the department of excise at Pondichery, and who had been accused of embezzlement. Other abuses, tending to the individual profit of the servants of the Company,* to the great detriment of the Company itself, which Lally had ordered to be abolished, had been restored. On March 8, therefore, Lally left Arkát for Pondichery, with a view to put a stop to these disorders, as well as to make new plans for a campaign.

During his absence, the French army under de Soupire had been followed to Kánchipúram by an English force of about equal numbers, under Major Brereton, who had succeeded to the command which the gallant Lawrence had but then resigned. De Soupire's orders restricted him to fight only if attacked, and as he occupied a strong position, the English leader was careful not to risk a defeat by assailing him at a disadvantage. For three weeks the armies remained in face of one another, when Brereton, rightly conjecturing that to threaten his communications would be the surest mode of dislodging the enemy, broke up from before Kánchipúram, and, passing it, moved on Wándiwásh, and opened ground before it. De Soupire, pressed for money and supplies, marched then to Arkát, twenty miles from Wándiwásh, and took up a position on the Palar. This was the opportunity Brereton had wished for. He hastily decamped from Wándiwásh, marched rapidly on Kánchipúram, and stormed it before de Soupire had any idea that it was in danger.

This was the intelligence that reached Lally, whilst,

---

* For instance: the members of the administration were in the habit of issuing treasury bills, instead of cash in payment of their liabilities; but they purpesely issued these in such numbers, that they became greatly depreciated in value, and a bill for 100 francs was purchaseable for 20 francs in cash. The members of the administration, after paying the troops and the subordinate functionaries in these notes, set to work to buy them up for their own profit, thus realising more than eighty per cent.—*Mémoire pour Lally.*

CHAP. XII.
1759.

after a stormy altercation with the Council of Pondichery, he was on his way at the head of 350 men, to rejoin his army. It was his desire to proceed at once to retake Kánchipúram, but the low state of his military chest, the absolute want of all resources, and the bad spirit evinced by many of his officers, would not permit him to attempt any forward movement. He was compelled, therefore, to place his army in cantonments on the Palar, until the arrival of d'Aché, then shortly expected with supplies of money and stores, should place him in a position to resume the offensive. The English army followed his example. Lally himself returned to Pondichery, but he had scarcely arrived there, when the fatigue and excitement to which he had been exposed combined, with the disappointment he had suffered, to bring on a serious illness. This, however, did not prevent him from carrying out an enterprise which he had designed against Elmiseram; succeeding in this, the leader of the party, M. Mariol, moved suddenly against Thiágár, a strong fortress about fifteen miles distant. The English guarding this were surprised, and the fort was captured on July 14. Amongst the prisoners were forty English soldiers.

But although planning such enterprises as these, Lally was unable from the state of his army to undertake anything really great. No doubt his soldiers had to submit to very great hardships, but these they would readily have borne, had they been left alone. The spirit of personal dislike to Lally, however, which prevailed in the Council Chamber of Pondichery, had penetrated to the Franco-Indian section of his forces—those in the immediate service of the Company of the Indies—and the example set by these had not been without its effect on the royal troops. Matters were brought to a very dangerous crisis by a measure which in itself was a matter of the most ordinary detail. It happened, that after the raising of the siege of Madras, the English and French

Governments agreed upon an exchange of 500 soldiers on each side. Most of those received by the French, in virtue of this agreement, were the men belonging to the French Company's forces, who had been taken before Trichinápallí when serving under Astruc, Brennier, Mainville, and Maissin. Some of these had been five years in confinement, well fed and well cared for. To fill up the gaps in the regiment bearing his name, Lally transferred to it two hundred of these men. But, by them, the scanty fare, the rigorous discipline, and the hard work of camp-life, were, after their five years of idleness and inaction, scarcely to be borne. They made no secret of their discontent, and even endeavoured to spread it among their comrades. The first result of this baneful influence appeared on July 7, when the small French force occupying the fort of Kávaripák, well capable of being defended, evacuated it on the first summons of the English army. But, four weeks later, the grand explosion took place. Instigated by the two hundred ransomed prisoners, the regiment de Lally, with the exception of its officers, its sergeants and corporals, and about fifty old soldiers, suddenly mutinied, and marching out of Chitápet, declared that they were going over to the English. On hearing this, their officers instantly went after them, and by threats, entreaties, by the payment of some of their arrears, and the promise of more, persuaded all but sixty to return to their allegiance. These sixty, all belonging to the Trichinápallí prisoners, persisted in going over to the enemy.* Lally, meanwhile, was making every possible exertion to collect provisions and stores. Despairing of every other means, he had despatched one of the Pondichery councillors to Kárikál with 36,000 francs belonging to himself to purchase rice for the troops. When, however, his hopes were at the lowest, his spirits were cheered by the arrival of the frigate, "La Gracieuse,"

---

* We have preferred Lally's own account of this mutiny to that given by Orme.

CHAP. XII.
1759.

conveying the hopeful intelligence that she was but the herald of the arrival of Count d'Aché's fleet, reinforced by three ships which had joined him at the Isle of France. The frigate also brought instructions to the French commander to exercise a still tighter hand over the financial administration of Pondichery—instructions which had the ill effect of still more embittering the feeling between himself on the one side, and de Leyrit and the other members of the Council on the other.

At length, on September 10, d'Aché arrived. Since leaving the coast on September 3 of the previous year, this officer had been to the Isle of France, had there met the three ships under M. d'Egville, from whom, as we have seen, he had taken, for the service of his own squadron, one million of the two million francs d'Egville was bringing out for the colony. The rest of the time d'Aché had employed in refitting, re-arming, and re-victualling the ships of his squadron. Having accomplished this, he sailed from the Isle of France on July 17, and arriving on September 10 off Fort St. David, found himself suddenly in sight of the English fleet, which likewise had been strengthened and reinforced.

D'Aché, who possessed at least the merit of physical courage, showed no inclination to decline the combat which Admiral Pocock at once offered him. He had eleven ships, though but four of them belonged to the French navy, whilst Pocock had nine ships of the Royal navy, two Company's vessels, and a fire-ship.*

* The English squadron consisted of:

The Yarmouth	66 guns	Capt.	Harrison	
The Grafton	68	,,	,,	Kempenfelt
The Elizabeth	64	,,	,,	Tiddeman
The Tiger	60	,,	,,	Brereton
The Sunderland	60	,,	,,	Colville
The Weymouth	60	,,	,,	Sir W. Baird
The Cumberland	66	,,	,,	Somerset
The Newcastle	50	,,	,,	Michie
The Salisbury	50	,,	,,	Dent

All King's ships.

And two Company's ships, the number of whose guns is not given. The French had—

About a quarter past two o'clock in the afternoon, the action took place, the crews of both fleets standing manfully to their guns and cannonading one another with great fury. For two hours the battle was undecided. By that time several of the ships on both sides were greatly crippled, and some of those of the French leaving the line for the purpose of refitting, the officer who commanded the "Zodiaque," her captain having been killed, put his helm up to follow them. D'Aché, running to reverse the order, was struck in the thigh by a grape shot and fell senseless. There was no one left to correct the error, and the other ships of the French squadron, following what they believed to be their Admiral's order, hauled out of action, and made sail to join their consorts, the English being too crippled to follow them. On the 16th, d'Aché anchored in the Pondichery roadstead. He had brought with him a seasonable supply of between three and four lakhs of rupees in diamonds and piastres, but he sensibly diminished the pleasure which his arrival had caused by the startling announcement of his intention to return at once to the Isle of France. Knowing well what must result from such a desertion, the English fleet being still on the coast, Lally, unable from sickness to move himself, sent MM. de Leyrit, de Bussy, and de Landivisiau, accompanied by other councillors, to remonstrate with the admiral. But d'Aché, brave in action, had neither moral courage nor strength of character. He could not dismiss from his

Le Zodiaque	74 guns.	(Name unknown, killed)	French Royal Navy.
L'Illustre	64 ,,	M. de Ruis	
L'Actif	64 ,,	M. Beauchaire	
La Fortune	64 ,,	M. Lobry	
Le Centaur	74 ,,	M. Surville	Company's ships.
Le Comte de Provence	74 ,,	M. La Chaise	
Le Vengeur	54 ,,	M. Palliere	
Le Duc d'Orleans	50 ,,	M. Surville, Jr.	
Le Saint Louis	50 ,,	M. Johanne	
Le Duc de Bourgogne	60 ,,	M. Beuvet	
Le Minotaur	74 ,,	M. d'Egville	

CHAP. XII.
1759.

mind the idea that he had been beaten in the late action, and that he would infallibly be beaten again. He had done, he believed, his duty by bringing to Pondichery the supplies of which it stood in need, and he would do no more. It was in vain that the commissioners in person, and that Lally in writing, pointed out to him that the English fleet had suffered more than his, and that his departure would inevitably lead to the fall of Pondichery; in vain did they beg him to stay at least till the movements then going on in the neighbourhood of Wándiwásh should have been concluded; in vain did the Council send to him a protest signed by every one of its members, fixing upon him the responsibility for the loss of Pondichery, and threatening to make his conduct the subject of a special representation to the Crown. In vain. D'Aché, usually so irresolute and doubting, was firm on this point, and despite their representations, sailed, never to return.* Meanwhile, the English, reinforced by the arrival of 300 men belonging to the battalion of Colonel Eyre Coote, then being conveyed out in four ships commanded by Rear-Admiral Cornish, determined to beat up the French cantonments on the Palar. With this object Major Brereton, massing about 2,000 Europeans, made a dash on September 16 at Tripatur, captured in it thirty men, and then moved quickly on Wándiwásh. M. Geoghegan, an officer of Irish extraction who commanded there, on learning the first movements of Brereton, hastily collected 1,100 men, and posted them in such a manner as best to meet any attack that might be delivered. On the night of the 29th, Brereton, bringing up his men, made a gallant attempt to carry

---

* He sailed, as he said he would, on the 17th, but the protest was sent after him, and reached him at sea. Upon this he returned to Pondichery, but after staying there five days, he again set off as stated in the text. Lally mentions that the day after his return, the English fleet passed Pondichery in disorder, gave d'Aché a good opportunity of attacking it, but that he abstained.

the place, and had at first some success. Soon, however, as Geoghegan had anticipated, his troops became entangled in the narrow streets which lay between the town and the fort, and were exposed to a heavy fire from the latter, as well as from the French troops under cover. They being thus checked, Geoghegan determined to turn the repulse into a defeat. At daybreak, therefore, he assaulted the English in the positions they had gained in the night-time, and after a fight of two hours' duration, drove them completely out, with a loss of eleven officers and 200 men. The French loss was scarcely less severe in point of numbers; amongst their dead was M. de Mainville, the whilom commander before Trichinápallí. The victory might have had important results, but the illness of Lally, the indiscipline of the army, the absence of d'Aché, not less than the early arrival of Colonel Coote with the remainder of his regiment, combined to render it abortive. After the repulse, the English cantoned themselves in the neighbourhood of Kánchipúram, there to wait the expected reinforcements.

Meanwhile Lally, hopeless of aid from any other source, had felt himself impelled to seek alliances in the quarter in which he had at first laughed them to scorn. Ever since the departure of Bussy from the Dakhan, affairs had taken a turn in that locality most unfavourable to French interests. In the first instance, Nizám Ali, the brother next in order to Salábat Jang, had once more resumed his pretensions, and was again grasping at supreme power. Salábat Jang, faithful, so long as the French possessed the ability to aid him, to his old alliances, had, as we have seen, marched into the Sirkars to assist them, only on their defeat to transfer the right to those provinces to the English, and to conclude with them a solid treaty. Nizám Ali, having ever shown himself a hater of the French, was not to be thought of; and Salábat

Jang* had, as we have seen, thrown over the French. These circumstances presented to Lally the importance of endeavouring to attach the third surviving brother, Basálat Jang, to French interests. Bussy, therefore, who by the recent orders from Europe had received a commission as second in command of the army, proposed to Lally to tempt Basálat by the offer of the office of Nawwábship of the Karnátik. Lally was at first unwilling, as he had already conferred the appointment on the son of Chanda Sáhib, but, very desirous not to lose a chance in his then distressed circumstances, he directed Bussy to proceed at once to Wándiwásh, and to make the best arrangement in his power with Basálat Jang.

Ever since the siege of Madras, Bussy had remained at Pondichery, suffering from various disorders. On receiving, however, Lally's instructions, he started for Wándiwásh, where he arrived the day after the repulse of the English. His orders were to cause himself to be received at Wándiwásh as second in command of the forces, to remain there only four-and-twenty hours, then, taking with him all the European cavalry and three companies of infantry, to go to the camp of Basálat Jang, there to arrange with him the terms of an alliance. But the account of the repulse of the English reached him on arrival, and caused him to deviate somewhat from these instructions. He thought that the English might possibly be disposed to meet him in the open plain, and he hailed the prospect of thus operating against them on his own account. Collecting, then, all his forces, he marched, the third day after his arrival, on Tripatur, and took it. But as he soon discovered that the English had retired to Kánchipúram, he sent back the army to Wándiwásh, and proceeded with his appointed escort to Arkát. But here the rains and

---

* It may be interesting to those who have so far followed the fortunes of Salábat Jang, to know that he did not long survive the abandonment of the French alliance. He was imprisoned by Nizám Ali in 1761, and murdered by his order in 1763.

MUTINY OF THE FRENCH ARMY.

other causes detained him another week, and when, at last, he did set out for the camp of Basálat Jang, who all this time had been anxiously awaiting his arrival, it was only to be recalled by the distressing intelligence that the army at Wándiwásh had mutinied. It was too true. At daybreak, on October 17, the European portion of the French army, at a given signal, took possession of the field artillery, and, leaving their officers and colours, marched six miles in the direction of Madras. Here they halted, and elected officers from amongst their sergeants, in the place of those they had abandoned, one La Joie, Sergeant-Major of the regiment of Lorraine, being appointed Commander-in-chief. The new officers, having first made every disposition for the order and defence of the camp, then drew up and despatched a letter to Lally, in which they expressed their willingness to allow him four days for reflection, and for the payment of the arrears due to them ; on the expiration of that time, should these demands not be complied with, they would proceed to extremities.

The fact was that the soldiers, themselves ten months in arrear, had been deceived by the reports, industriously circulated, as to the amount hoarded by Lally himself, and despatched by him in a frigate to France. It fortunately happened, however, that the Sergeant-Major La Joie, thoroughly well-disposed towards his general, had only accepted the office with a view to bring the revolters promptly to their duty. His endeavours in this respect were seconded by the prudent conduct of Lally. As soon as the intelligence of the revolt reached him he assembled the Council, and appealed to the patriotism of its members to assist him in this urgent need by their subscriptions, he himself heading the list with a donation of 20,000 rupees. Many of those present, including Father Lavaur, M. Boileau, and the Chevalier de Crillon, responded heartily to the call. De Leyrit, not content with

CHAP. XII.

1759.

holding back himself, affirmed that the public funds could supply nothing, because the diamonds and piastres, brought by d'Aché, had not then been converted into silver. Nevertheless, a sufficient sum to distribute six months' pay was collected, and with this sum the Adjutant-General of the army, Viscount de Fumel, was sent to negotiate with the troops. As, however the revolted soldiers would not listen to this officer, Lally sent Crillon, whose influence over them had always been very great, in his place. After some conversation, the soldiers agreed to accept six months' pay down, and the balance on November 10; they demanded at the same time a complete amnesty for the past, and requested that their officers would come and place themselves once again at their head; they added that " they were one and all imbued with sentiments entirely French, and that they were ever ready to fight for their country and for the honour of their king and to submit to their superiors."* Thus did the troops return to their duty. Their revolt, however, had had the effect of dissipating any hopes that might have been formed from the combined action of Basálat Jang. For this chieftain, already impatient of waiting for Bussy, retreated, on hearing of the revolt, in the direction whence he had come. Bussy indeed followed him, after appeasing the discontent which had already arisen amongst his own troops, but, by the time he arrived in his camp, the turn French affairs had taken had entirely indisposed Basálat Jang to the alliance. Bussy therefore contented himself with raising money and troops amongst his former friends, and with these he returned on December 10 to Arkát, with what effect will be seen.

Meanwhile Lally, on the mutiny being quelled, determined to put in force a project which nothing but the direst necessity could have justified. This was to divide his force and to send a portion of it to alarm the Eng-

* Mémoire pour Lally, p. 142.

lish for Trichinápallí. It seemed, indeed, a rash measure to weaken the force with which he would have to encounter, in the then ensuing cold weather, the reinforced army of the English, and as such it was considered by de Leyrit and others of the Council. But Lally was in very great perplexity. He had not money enough to pay all his troops, and he had a very strong idea that a certain portion of them—the Europeans in the service of the Company—were not worth paying. He conceived, then, that he would facilitate his own movements by sending away troops in whom he had no confidence, at the same time that he alarmed the English for the safety of a city they had held so long, and confined their garrison within its walls. Taking advantage of a repulse sustained by the English before Dévikótá, he despatched Crillon at the head of the battalion of India, and three companies of grenadiers, to Srirangam. Crillon carried this island by assault on November 21, then leaving the battalion of India to keep the garrison in alarm, he rejoined Lally with his grenadiers.

Whilst Crillon was engaged on this expedition, Lally, recovered from his illness, had proceeded to Wándiwásh, and had marched thence with his army to Arkát. Here, on December 10, he was joined by Bussy, at the head of 350 Europeans and 2,000 native irregulars. The commandant of these last had, however, fortified himself with claims upon the French Government for considerable sums of arrears of pay. These he had lost no opportunity of presenting, and did so to such an extent, that, to use the expression of Lally, he and his followers resembled more a troop of creditors than a troop of auxiliaries. To provide himself with native cavalry indispensable to his campaign, Lally succeeded, after some negotiation, in making an arrangement with Murárí Ráo for 2,000 horse.*

* These men were engaged at the rate of 25 rupees each per mensem.

CHAP. XII.

1759.

The campaign on which the rival nations were now about to enter, promised to decide for a time the possession of the Karnátik. A defeat in the field would be fraught with disaster to either, but more especially to the French, who had not the command of the sea, and whose resources were almost exhausted, whilst it was in the power of the English to fall back upon Bengal, or at all events to await the certain return of their fleet after the monsoon. Under these circumstances, it would have seemed to be the policy of Lally to wait; to avoid an engagement; and to harass the communications of the English, compelling them, if they were determined to fight, to fight at a disadvantage. This at least was the opinion of Bussy. But Lally was scarcely in circumstances to act according to the rules of war. Owing to the absence of many of his men at Srirangam, he had been compelled to witness, without being able to prevent it, the capture of Karangoli and Wándiwásh by the English. This inaction had produced its natural effect on the minds of his men. To follow, too, the other course, it was necessary that he should have supplies and money, and he had neither. It was absolutely indispensable, it appeared to him, that he should act with

1760. decision and vigour. No sooner then had he been joined by Crillon from Srirangam, on January 10, than feigning a retiring movement in the direction of Pondichery, he divided his army into two columns. Placing himself at the head of one, he changed its direction during the night, crossed the Palar, and moved rapidly upon Kánchipúram. Without attempting the pagoda, he plundered the town, captured 2,000 bullocks and other stores, and rejoining the other column, which had moved to support him, marched the next day to Tripatúr. Having by this movement drawn Colonel Coote and a portion of his army to Kánchipúram, and obtained supplies for his men, he set out on the 14th at the head of 600 Europeans and some native troops to recover Wándiwásh, leaving the bulk of the army under Bussy at Tripatúr.

The fort of Wándiwásh was surrounded by the town of the same name, and this was protected by a wall flanked by small towers, and bordered by a hedge, a great part of it being further protected by a ditch. It was Lally's plan to surprise and gain the town, then, under cover of the narrow streets, to plant a battery within a short distance of the fort, so that it might be breached and carried before the English, whom he had lured off to Kánchipúram could come up. It was a plan, bold, well-considered, and feasible, but it required in its execution the utmost promptitude and daring. These qualities, it will be seen, were not exhibited. On the night of the 12th he divided his troops into two columns, one under M. de Genlis to make a false attack, whilst he should make a real one. But de Genlis's party, consisting mostly of sailors, having been seized with a panic, fell back upon the other column, the soldiers of which, mistaking them for enemies, fired into them. The night attack thus failed. Its failure, however, only made Lally more furious. "Since," he said, "they had failed in the night, he would teach them to carry it by day." Re-placing de Genlis by de Verdière, he ordered the same dispositions as on the previous evening. One party he despatched close to the wall, and made them lie on their faces, whilst Colonels de Crillon and de Poëte ran in front to fathom the water in the ditch. The fire, however, was so hot, that the men of the column hesitated to follow them, until Lally, who came up at the moment, waving his sword, and telling them that now was the time to show their good will towards him, dashed forward into the ditch. His soldiers followed him and carried the town.

Now was the time for despatch. To establish a battery *en barbette*, and to open a fire as soon as it should be constructed—this was Lally's design. But his chief

CHAP. XII.
1760.

engineer, M. Durré, insisted on proceeding as if he had been engaged in a regular siege. "The soldiers," wrote Lally, "said openly, that it seemed as though they were about to attack Luxemburg." It resulted from these methodical tactics, that four days were wasted in the construction of batteries; two more in rectifying its defects; on the seventh day, the English appeared advancing to the relief of the place.

The great blow, well contrived, having thus failed in consequence of the absence of the two qualities essential to its success, there but remained now to Lally the chances of a battle. By the arrival of Bussy, who joined him on the evening of the 20th, he was able, after leaving 150 Europeans and 300 sipáhis in the batteries, to bring into the field 1,350 European infantry, about 200 of whom were sailors, and 150 cavalry. He had besides about 1,800 sipáhis, and 2,000 Marátha cavalry; but of the former, all but 300 refused to be led into the field, whilst but 60 of the Maráthás were present, the remainder being engaged in foraging for the army. The force led by Colonel Coote, on the other hand, consisted of 1,900 Europeans, of whom 80 only were cavalry, and 3,350 natives.* On hearing from the Marátha scouts that the English were approaching, Lally hastened to draw up his men in a single line. His left, thrown forward, resting on a tank, and, supported by an intrenchment on the other side of it, formed an obtuse angle with his line, and commanded the ground over which the enemy must pass. This intrenchment was manned by the sailors and armed with a couple of guns. His centre rested on nothing, but about 400 yards in its rear were two defiles, protected by a dyke, and guarded by fifty men and two guns. These fifty men were drawn up in front of the head of the defiles, so as to have the appearance

* The number of the French here given has been adopted from Lally's reports: that of the English has been taken from Orme.

of a reserve destined to support the first line. Between the intervals of the regiments were posted the guns, sixteen in number. The cavalry were on the right. Lally himself commanded in the centre, and Bussy on the left.

Meanwhile Coote, who by a series of able manœuvres had obtained a position which enabled him to force an action, no sooner beheld the disposition made by the French than he drew up his men in order of battle and advanced. He himself led the first line, consisting of his own regiment and a battalion of sipáhis; the two Company's regiments came next, Colonel Draper's regiment on the left. As he approached the French, to whose position his own was oblique, the guns from the intrenchment near the tank opened upon him, and Lally, thinking he noticed some confusion in the English left, in consequence of this fire, deemed the moment opportune to charge with his cavalry. He galloped up, therefore, to the right of the line, and placing himself at the head of his horse, gave the order to charge. Not a man, however, stirred. Attributing this to the ill-feeling of the commanding officer, Lally displaced him on the spot, and ordered the second in command, M. d'Aumont, to follow him. But d'Aumont having likewise refused, Lally placed him under arrest, and addressing himself to the men in a body, ordered them to charge. M. d'Heguerty with the left squadron at once advanced, and Cornet Bonnessay calling out that it would be shameful thus to abandon their general, the others followed. Lally, having thus induced them to move, made a *détour* so as to sweep down on the left flank of the English force. He had already arrived within 100 yards of it, driving the English horse before him, when Draper, whom the delay caused by the refusal of the French cavalry to charge had warned of the danger, brought up two pieces of cannon loaded with grape, and opened them on the French horse. The fire was so well directed, that about fifteen men in the front line were disabled, and, although had the French persisted, the English would not have had time to reload, the effect was to cause a panic amongst them. They, therefore, fled, leaving their leader alone. Lally, thus deserted, galloped towards the infantry in the centre, upon which the English guns in the other part of their line had already opened. He found them eager for an advance. Placing himself at their head, he formed them in column and marched against the English line. Regardless of the fire which thinned its rank as it advanced, the French column charged, and by its superior weight broke that part of the English line which it attacked. The unbroken part of the English line, however, immediately formed up on its flank, and threw the column into disorder. The men on both sides becoming then mingled together, a hand-to-hand contest ensued, which was yet undecided, when a fatal occurrence on the left of the French line determined the fate of the day.

The extreme left of the French constituted the *point d'appui* of Lally's position. It rested, as we have said, on a tank, in front of which and forming an obtuse angle with his line, was an intrenchment, from which two pieces of cannon played on the advancing English. So long as Lally held this firmly, the occurrences in the other part of the line were of secondary importance, for the English, even if successful, could not follow up an advance without exposing their flank. But it happened, unfortunately for him, that whilst his centre was engaged in desperate conflict with the English centre, a shot from the artillery on the enemy's right blew up a tumbril in the intrenchment, killing the Chevalier de Pöete, and placing eighty men *hors de combat*. Nor was this the extent of the damage it occasioned; for such was the panic caused by the explosion, that the sailors ran out of the intrenchment, abandoning the

THE FRENCH DEFEATED AT WÁNDIWÁSH.

guns, and not stopping till they had taken refuge behind the right. Coote, noticing this, ordered Brereton to carry the intrenchment. But, before he could reach it, Bussy, who commanded on the French left, hastily collected some fifty or sixty men of Lally's regiment, and led them into the intrenchment. They reached it just in time to fire a volley at the advancing English, which mortally wounded Brereton, but did not stop his men, who, coming on with a rush, carried the post. Whilst the key of the French position was thus carried, the English left, freed from the hostile cavalry, had marched to the aid of its centre and fallen on the right of the Lorraine brigade. This body, attacked in front and on both flanks, noticed the loss on the left of the position, and fell back in disorder, not, however, till it had lost its commandant and many officers, and had covered itself with glory. Bussy, meanwhile, after the loss of the intrenchment, had brought up the Lally brigade to recover it, and if possible to restore the battle. But whilst leading on his men to a bayonet charge, his horse was shot, and he, falling to the ground, was taken prisoner. The brigade having thus lost its leader, opposed in front by a superior force, whose artillery then played upon it, threatened also on its right flank by the victorious centre and left of the enemy, fell back in its turn, and abandoned the field. At this conjuncture, the cavalry, recovered from its panic, advanced to the front, and interposing itself between the retiring infantry and the advancing English, effectually put a stop to pursuit. The French were thus enabled to rally at a distance of less than a mile from the field of battle, and to carry off also the party they had left before the fort of Wándiwásh.

Such was the battle of Wándiwásh—a battle which, though the numbers on each side were comparatively small, must yet be regarded as a decisive battle, for it dealt a fatal and decisive blow to French domination in

CHAP. XII.

1760.

India. It shattered to the ground the mighty fabric which Martin, Dumas, and Dupleix had contributed to erect; it dissipated all the hopes of Lally; it sealed the fate of Pondichery. By it, the superiority in the field, which during that war had rested mainly with the French in the Karnátik, was transferred entirely to the English. It was the proximate cause why Lally, who had himself acted as besieger before Madras, should, in his turn, suffer the misfortune of being himself besieged in Pondichery.

The conduct of Lally in this action, the dispositions that he made, the fact of his fighting a battle at all, have been severely condemned by his enemies. The candid military critic is, however, bound to do him justice on all these points. His plan was the best he could have adopted. Drawing Coote by a skilful manœuvre from the line of the Palar, he assaulted Wándiwásh, took the town, and had he been well served, would have taken the fort also. Baffled in this, he determined to accept a battle on ground which he had reconnoitred and chosen. No doubt to deliver a battle, defeat in which must be ruin, is very dangerous policy. But with Lally it was unavoidable. He had not the means of attempting a war of manœuvres. Straitened as were his resources, such a policy must have resulted in a retreat to Pondichery to be followed by a siege there. This result being unavoidable, he was surely right in attempting to ward it off by a direct blow.

Then, again, as to his conduct in the action. He, at least, is not to be blamed for the behaviour of his cavalry. Had they followed him, he would, he says, have thrown the left of the English force into disorder so great that an advance of the infantry must have changed it into an overthrow. He is not to be blamed, for, he could not have foreseen, the accident in the intrenchment which caused its evacuation, and lost him the battle. His dispositions were good. The intrenchment served as the pivot whereon to move his army; had that been held, he could not have been beaten. Accidents not very dissimilar have before this decided the fate of greater battles, without that prejudice and passion have fixed the blame on the commander.

The remainder of the campaign may be told in a few words. The next day Lally fell back to Chítápét, taking with him all his wounded; thence, sending the Maráthás and native troops to Arkát, he retreated to Jinjí, but as at that point the English were nearer than himself to Pondichery, he made a cross-march to Valdávur, fifteen miles from that city. In this position he was able to cover Pondichery, and to receive supplies from the south. He was fortunate in being able to do so much, for had the English only followed up their victory with vigour, they would have reached Pondichery before Lally, and that place, destitute of provisions and of troops, would probably have surrendered on the first summons. The English leader, however, preferred the slower method of reducing the subordinate places held by the French—a policy which the absence of d'Aché and the utter abandonment of Pondichery by the mother-country allowed him to carry out unmolested. In pursuance of this resolution, Coote carried Chítápét on January 28 and Arkát on the 9th of the following month. Timerí, Dévikótá, Trinomalí, and Alampárva fell about the same time; Kárikál surrendered on April 5; on the 15th, Lally was constrained to retreat from Valdávur to within the hedge that bounded Pondichery; and on the 20th, Chelambram, and a few days later Gúdalúr—the last important place except Thiágar and Jinjí held by the French in the Karnátik—fell into the hands of the English. It is not to be supposed that all these places were lightly given up. Some of them, indeed, Lally would have done well to evacuate, so as to carry with him the garrisons; but Kárikál, so long in the possession of the French, their second seaport, he made a great effort to preserve.* But what could he do? He found the enemies he met with inside the walls of Pondichery worse than those he had to combat without; he found self-interest everywhere, patriotism nowhere. The inhabitants refused even to don the soldiers' uniform, though only for the purpose of making a show before the enemy. Sedition, cabals, and intrigues—everyone striving to cast upon Lally the discredit of the inevitable ruin that awaited them—everyone thwarting his wishes, and secretly counteracting his orders—each man still bent on saving for himself what he could out of the wreck—this was the internal condition of Pondichery—these the men with respect to whom it might be said that an appeal to patriotism was an appeal to a feeling that, long deadened, had now ceased entirely to exist. "From this time," says Lally, "Pondichery, without money, without ships, and without even provisions, might be given up for lost." Yet though he could not be blind to the impending result, Lally himself used every effort to avert the catastrophe. He treated with the famous Haidar Ali, then commander of the Maisur armies, for the services of 10,000 men, one half of them horse, transferring at once to Haidar the fortress of Thiágar, and promising him, in case of a favourable issue of the war, to make over to him Trichinápallí, Madura, Tinivelli, and all the places he might conquer in the Karnátik. In pursuance of this agreement, Makhdúm Ali arrived at Thiágar on June 4, and at Pondichery a few days later. The intrigues of the councillors rendered this treaty partially abortive, but this did not prevent Makhdúm Ali from attacking, on July 18, a corps of 180 English infantry,

---

* The commandant at Kárikál was M. Renault de St. Germain, the same who had surrendered Chandranagar to Clive. At Kárikál he made so poor and faint a resistance, that he was brought to trial, and sentenced to be cashiered. Lally says he deserved death.

50 hussars, and nearly 3,000 native troops, inflicting upon them a severe defeat, and forcing the survivors to take refuge in Trívádí.* But it was not alone by such attempts at native alliances that Lally endeavoured to turn the tide of misfortune setting in so strongly against him. Weak as he was in European infantry, he determined to make one bold stroke to rid himself of the besieging enemy. To understand the plan he adopted it will be necessary to state that, after the retirement of the French within the bound-hedge which forms the limits of Pondichery, the English had taken up a position, their right resting on the fort of Villanúr, and their left at the base of the hill of Perimbé, the space between covering an extent of about a mile and a half. In front of Perimbé they had, moreover, thrown up a redoubt, armed with three pieces of cannon, whilst the centre was covered by a house in a garden surrounded by a hedge, connected by a tree-avenue with the town. The plan which Lally arranged, and which was so skilfully devised as to deserve success, provided that, whilst his right column should surprise the redoubt in front of Perimbé, and the centre the hedge-bound house, the left, which was stationed on the other side of the river Ariákupum, should cross that river, and fall upon the rear of the enemy, who, it was calculated, would be thrown into utter confusion by the diversity of the attacks. To guard against mistakes, Lally the day previous accompanied the commander of the left column, M. d'Arambure, over the ground he was to take, indicating the point at which he was to cross the river, and the exact direction he was then to pursue.

But a fatality seemed to attend all the operations of Lally. The surprise indeed was complete—for having given no intimation of the intended movement to his councillors they were unable to betray him: the right assault completely succeeded, the redoubt being quickly

* Wilks; Orme.

carried; the centre attack was desperately contested. The French never fought better. Colonel Coote, on his side, seeing the importance of the place, brought up his best troops to defend it. But notwithstanding all his efforts, the French, though in the regiment of Lally alone they had lost eight sergeants besides several privates, still persisted, hoping to hear every minute the sounds of the assault on the enemy's rear. Just as these hopes were at their highest, d'Arambure and his men appeared, not in ths rear of the enemy, but between the assaulting columns and the town! This officer, who on other occasions had behaved so well, would appear to have lost his head; he crossed the river at a far lower point than had been poined out to him, and brought his men to the attack in exactly the opposite direction to that indicated by Lally. By this false move, he rendered impossible a success which, if attained, would have deferred, if it had not altogether prevented, the catastrophe that was to follow.

The end was now near at hand. On September 16, Monson, who had succeeded Coote in the command of the English force, delivered an assault on the Ulgáral post, and compelled the French to quit the defence of the bound-hedge, and to retire under the walls of the place. This attack, however, cost the English many men, and Monson was so severely wounded, that Colonel Coote returned to take up his command. Notwithstanding this movement, which shut out all supplies from Pondichery, Lally determined to continue the defence, and prohibited all mention of surrender. Every measure that could be adopted to procure sustenance for the troops was taken; contributions were levied; grain was dug out of places where it had been buried for concealment; taxes were imposed;* the idle sections of the native inhabitants were turned adrift: no pre-

---

* From the operation of these latter the European inhabitants of the town were specially exempted by the Council, de Leyrit presiding.

caution in fact was neglected to prolong the defence of the town till the arrival of d'Aché, whose squadron was even then daily expected. But, on December 24, there remained in the magazines but eight days' full rations for the soldiers. It had become necessary to reconsider the position. Under these circumstances, Lally, who for the three weeks preceding had been confined to his bed by sickness, directed the assembly of a mixed council to take into consideration the terms which should be offered to the English. The members of the party opposed to Lally, unwilling to take upon themselves any share in the responsibility of a capitulation, evaded this order. But an event occurred which rendered their evasion of the less consequence. On the 31st the roadstead of Pondichery was visited by one of those storms not uncommon at that season on the Koromandel coast. The effect of this on the English fleet was most disastrous. Three large ships were driven on shore two miles below Pondichery; three others, having on board 1,100 Europeans, foundered; all the remainder were severely injured. Nor did the siege works escape. All the batteries and redoubts raised by the besiegers were destroyed. Soldiers, unable to carry their muskets, had thrown them away in despair; all the ammunition, except that in store, was rendered useless; every tent had been blown down; so great was the confusion that had a sortie been made by the garrison, not a hundred men could have been collected to resist it. The question of a sortie was indeed mooted in Pondichery, and though such a movement would, owing to the still raging wind and the inundation caused by the storm, have been attended with great difficulties, it ought certainly, even as a last despairing blow, to have been attempted. But who was there to organise such a movement? Lally lay helpless in his bed; his orders canvassed and cavilled at rather than obeyed. With the enemy at their gates, the citizens of Pondichery thought more of combining to thwart the general they hated, than of effectually opposing the foe, who threatened them with destruction. No sortie, therefore, was made.

Nevertheless, the storm had at least the effect of reopening the door of hope to Lally and the garrison. If d'Aché or, failing d'Aché, if even five French ships were to arrive, the damaged English fleet could be destroyed. With the destruction of that fleet, deliverance, and with it the command of the seas for at least twelve months could be obtained.* It became, therefore, an object with Lally to provide subsistence for his men for another fortnight longer. To effect this, he sent to the Jesuit, Lavaur, and informed him of his intention to search his convent for grain, which he had reason to believe was stored there. The reply to this was an agreement on the part of Lavaur to subsist the garrison till January 13.

How terribly each day passed, how the expectation of the arrival of d'Aché, eager and stimulating to action at the outset, became gradually more and more faint, till it finally disappeared, can be better imagined than described. The English, on their part, were not idle. One week after the storm they had nine ships in the roadstead ready for action, and they had erected new batteries in the place of those that had been destroyed. Further defence was then impossible. The French had but one day's supply of food remaining. On January 14, therefore, Lally summoned a council of war, to debate regarding the terms of surrender; whilst de

---

* There is no stronger proof of the incapacity of the Government of Louis XV., than that offered by the idleness of d'Aché at this conjuncture. On the mere rumour that the English Government were debating a plan for an attack upon Bourbon, the Cabinet of Versailles sent orders to d'Aché not to leave that island, or should he have left it, to return to it instantly. Thus, on the strength of a mere rumour, the French Ministry did not hesitate deliberately to sacrifice India. They withheld the fleet from the point threatened by an army and ships of war, to keep it in the quarter that was menaced only by report.—*Memoirs of Count Lally: Voltaire's Fragments.*

SURRENDER OF PONDICHERY.

Leyrit, though invited to that council, assembled in opposition the Council of Pondichery to draw up articles of capitulation for the inhabitants.

On the following day, the 15th, a deputation from Pondichery was sent to the English camp. The terms proposed by Lally were virtually terms of unconditional surrender, for although he declined to give up the town, as not having authority to do so, and because arrangements between the two Crowns placed Pondichery, as he pretended, out of risk of capture, yet he declined further to defend it, and agreed to yield himself and his troops as prisoners of war, stipulating only for the proper treatment of the inhabitants, the religious houses, and for the safety of the mother and sister of Rájú Sahib. In reply to these propositions, Colonel Coote, declining to discuss the question of the agreement between the two Crowns, offered the French commander terms identical with those offered by Admiral Watson to M. Renault at Chandranagar, and by Lally himself to the commandant of Fort St. David. These provided that the garrison and inhabitants should surrender, unconditionally, as prisoners of war. Coote would only promise, in addition, to give the family of Rájú Sahib a safe escort to Madras, and to treat the garrison favourably.

On the following morning the English troops entered the Villanúr gate of the town, and in the evening took possession of the fortifications. The scene immediately preceding that last act is thus described by the English historian of the war, himself a contemporary, and a member of the Madras Council. "In the afternoon," writes Mr. Orme, "the garrison drew up under arms on the parade before the citadel, the English troops facing them. Colonel Coote then reviewed the line, which, exclusive of commissioned officers, invalids, and others who had hid themselves, amounted to 1,100, all wearing the face of famine, fatigue, or disease. The grenadiers of Lally and Lorraine, once the ablest-bodied men in the army,

CHAP. XII.

1761.

appeared the most impaired, having constantly put themselves forward to every service; and it was recollected that from their first landing, throughout all the services of the field, and all the distresses of the blockade, not a man of them had ever deserted to the English army. The victor soldier gave his sigh (which none but banditti could refuse) to this solemn contemplation of the fate of war, which might have been his own."

The scenes that followed the surrender were little creditable to the Franco-Indian officials of Pondichery. When Lally, directed by the victorious General to proceed under an escort of English soldiers to Madras, was leaving the town in a palanquin, he was insulted by a mob of some eighty of the principal adherents of de Leyrit, two of them members of his Council. These ruffians, who had openly avowed their wish to despatch him, were only prevented from executing their design by the presence of the escort. But when, two minutes later, Dubois, the intendant of the French General, and who had in his possession some most valuable documents, proving the corruption that had reigned within the town, attempted to follow his chief, he was assailed with the most furious menaces. Dubois, who, though almost seventy years old and nearly blind, was a man of spirit, turned round to reply to these invectives, drawing his sword as he did so. He was immediately attacked by one Defer, and run through the body. His papers were at once secured by the conspirators. Well might the French historian,* relating this incident—this crossing of the two French swords on the threshold of the city that had been lost to France by French dissensions—forcibly describe it as " a fit image and striking *résumé* of the history of the last three years of the French in India."

We may be pardoned if for a few short sentences we leave the direct thread of our history to follow Lally to his last end. Sent from Madras to England, he found

---

* M. Xavier Raymond.

on arrival there, that the hatred and fury with which he had been regarded in India had followed him to France. Allowed by the English Government to proceed to Paris on his parole, he attempted to bring home against de Leyrit and his Councillors the charges with which he had threatened them in India. This movement on his part had the effect of uniting against him all the different parties criminated by his statement. Bussy and d'Aché, de Leyrit and Moracin, Father Lavaur and the Councillors of Pondichery—all made common cause against him. So great was the effect of the converging assertions of these different partisans, that even the Duke of Choiseul, one of the most powerful noblemen in France, advised Lally to seek safety in flight. But he, conscious of innocence, preferred to meet all the charges against him before the tribunals of his country. The proceedings were yet languishing, when, in 1763, Father Lavaur died. This intriguing monk, to make sure of his own position, had written two memoirs of the events that had happened at Pondichery, the one favourable, the other inveterately hostile, to Lally. His papers, however, having fallen into the hands of the promoters of the accusation against the General, the favourable memoir was suppressed, and the other given to the world.* Strange as it may seem in the present day, this memoir was actually received by the Parlement of Paris as evidence against Lally, and was mainly decisive of his fate. Refused all legal aid by his judges, he was, after three years of lingering agony—fit sequel to his struggles in India—convicted, by a majority, of having betrayed the interests of the King and of the Company, and sentenced to be beheaded. A request, made by Marshal de Soubise "in the name of the Army," for commutation of the sentence, was coldly refused, and on May 9, 1766, transferred from his prison to a dung-cart, gagged and guarded, Lally was led forth to the scaffold—a striking example of the fate which, in the

* Voltaire; Orme.

CHAP. XII.
1761.

France of Louis XV., awaited those who, though they had given all their energies to their country,* and whose faults were faults natural to humanity, had the misfortune to be unsuccessful. Revolutionary France annulled the sentence which the France of the Bourbons passed upon Lally, and restored his place in the annals of his country. Whilst there are few, who, whilst they regret a fate so untimely and so undeserved, do not recognise the justice of the reversal of the sentence pronounced upon Lally, none care to inquire after those whose combined incapacity, corruption, and malevolence forged the bolt by which he was struck down. No memoir records the last hours of the palsied de Leyrit, or of the irresolute, mindless d'Aché. Of Bussy—Bussy who promised so well, whose performances up to a certain point were so splendid—yet who deserted Dupleix in his misfortunes, and who joined in the cabal against Lally—of Bussy it is only known that, after living luxuriously † on the enormous wealth he had acquired in India, he returned twenty years later, at the head of a fine army, to the Karnátik, there to lose his reputation and to die! The very Company which had connived at his fate—which had shown itself on every occasion timorous, narrow-minded, and unjust—which had ruined and persecuted to death the most illustrious of the proconsuls it had sent out to India—the Company did not long survive the execution of Lally. It died in 1769!

* "No one," wrote Colonel Coote after the capture, "has a higher opinion of Lally than myself. He has fought against obstacles which I believed invincible, and he has conquered them. There is not another man in all India, who could have kept on foot for the same length of time an army without pay, and receiving no assistance from any quarter."
Another English officer wrote at the time from Madras:—"It is a convincing proof of his abilities, the managing so long and vigorous a defence in a place where he was held in universal detestation."

† Not only Bussy, but de Leyrit and all the Councillors of Pondichery, took home with them large fortunes. Even that arch-intriguer, the Jesuit Lavaur, carried off with him 1,250,000 francs, besides diamonds and bills of exchange to a large amount. Yet to such an extent did he carry his duplicity, that he pretended poverty and actually petitioned to the Government for a small pension for his subsistence.—*Voltaire, Orme.*

FINAL COLLAPSE OF THE FRENCH.

The fall of Pondichery was the natural precursor of the capture of the other places yet remaining to the French in Southern India. On February 4, Thiágar surrendered to Major Preston, and on the 13th, Mahé to Major Munro. Jinjí presented greater difficulties than either of those places to an attacking force, but on April 5, the garrison, seeing the helplessness of its condition, surrendered on favourable terms to Captain Stephen Smith. Of the French troops in the service of the Company, 300 who were on detached duty at the time of the siege, under MM. Alain and Hugel, took service with Haidar Ali; 100 were embodied in the English army, in which, however, they showed themselves as mutinously disposed as when commanded by their own countrymen; the remainder became prisoners of war.

We have now brought to a conclusion the history of that stirring episode, adorned with so many brilliant names, and boasting of some of the most original and striking achievements ever performed on Eastern soil. Beginning with small means, then suddenly astonishing the world by its dazzling promise, the venture of the French in India was destined to end thus early, in humiliation and failure. It was the sad fate of France, in this, the most unfortunate of her wars, to be disgraced on the Continent, and to lose simultaneously her possessions in the East and in the West. First, in endeavouring to save Canada, she lost the best chance she ever had of conquering Southern India, for it cannot be doubted, but that the troops, the ships, and the money, which the French Government diverted at the last moment from Lally's expedition, would have sufficed to make him victorious everywhere on the Koromandel coast, might possibly even have enabled him to carry out his meditated designs upon Bengal. The diversion, whilst it caused the failure of the blow struck at English India, did not save Canada. After Canada had fallen, sound policy would have dictated the strengthening of Lally's hands in the Karnátik, but the troops and the money which might still have enabled him to carry out his original designs, were frittered upon the armies of the nominees of Madame de Pompadour—the Soubises, the Richelieus, the Contades, and the Broglios, with their legions of opera-dancers and hair-dressers.* To keep up those costly armies—which nevertheless were barely able to make head against a lieutenant of the King of Prussia—and their more costly contingents, French India was left without money sufficient to carry on a campaign, without reinforcements, without even the few ships that might have sufficed to save her. However much, then, the candid Frenchman of the present day may lament the corruption that was rampant amongst the officials of Pondichery—however he may mourn over the want of unanimity in her Council, and the intrigues of her Councillors—however much he may condemn the absence of patriotic devotion that contributed to her fall—he will still be forced to lay the chief blame at the door of France, on the shoulders of the sensual monarch under whose rule the resources of the kingdom were so lavishly wasted and misdirected. Whilst English India received plentiful supplies of men and ships in abundance, and thought herself hardly-used, because, in the last year of the war, she did not also receive her annual supply of money, French India, after the arrival of Lally's troops, received from the mother-country scarcely more than two millions of francs! There could be but one result to such a mode of supporting a colony, and that result appeared on January 16, 1761.

We do not hesitate thus to fix the date of the final

---

* The reader is referred to Carlyle's graphic description of the followers of the armies of Soubise and Riche- lieu, given in his *Frederick the Great*.

failure to establish a French Empire in India, because up to the moment of the actual capitulation, it was always possible that the fall of Pondichery might be delayed, and a chance afforded to the French of again asserting their supremacy. United counsels and energetic action so late even as January 1, 1761, might have caused the annihilation of the besieging army; the arrival of d'Aché up to the 6th would have forced the English to raise the siege, and might even have insured the destruction of their fleet. But the events of January 16 made French supremacy in the Karnátik for ever impossible. It is true that the Peace of Paris restored to France, in 1763, Pondichery and her other dependencies in Southern India; but they were restored dismantled and defenceless, with their trade annihilated, with their influence gone, with the curse of defeat and failure stamped upon their habitations; they were restored at a time when England, using well the precious moments, had rooted herself firmly in the soil. The difference in the power and position of the rival settlements was shown clearly in 1778, when on the breaking out of war between France and England, Pondichery was at once invested and captured by a British army.* It is true, indeed that during that war, the French made a desperate effort to profit by the misfortunes of England in America, by sending out 3,000 men under Bussy and a fleet under Suffren to assist Haidar Ali, then alone almost a match for the few English in Madras. But whilst, on sea, the splendid achievements of the greatest of French admirals covered with a halo of glory this last effort on the part of France to expel the English from the Karnátik, on land the campaign was productive of little but disaster.†

---

* Pondichery was restored to France by the Peace of 1783, captured again in 1793, restored by the Peace of Amiens, captured again in 1803, and finally restored in 1814 and 1815.

† For an account of this war the reader is referred to the supplementary work of the author, entitled "Final French Struggles in India."

CHAP. XII.
1761.

Thenceforth the attempt was renounced, and partisans and adventurers represented France at the courts of native princes, and endeavoured, though in vain, to accomplish by their means the result, which at the period we have described, had been indeed possible, but which, after January 16, 1761, was for ever illusory and hopeless.

But was there not, it may be asked, something due to the different characters of the rival nations, that contributed to a result so disastrous to France? Much, very much, in our opinion. England, doubtless, in the greater wealth of her East India Company, in the greater influence of its Directors with the government, and in her free parliamentary system, possessed advantages which were denied to France. We believe that the fact that the Directors of the East India Company were often members of parliament, and as such possessed considerable influence with the Ministry of the day, tended not a little to that prompt action of the latter, to that despatch of royal fleets to defend the Company's possessions, which acted so favourably for English interests. Under the despotic system of France such action was but seldom taken; the Company was, except in rare instances, left to defend its possessions with its own ships alone. Whilst England, working in unison with its East India Company, saw clearly that imperial interests required her to use imperial means to defend the settlements of the Company, the France of Louis XV., throughout the epoch of which we have written, but once raised herself to the height of regarding India from an imperial point of view, and then, as we have seen, displayed a want of a resolute and decided policy, which rendered success impossible. But, though this circumstance mainly caused the fall of French India, there were other circumstances dependent on the character of the agents on the spot, that contributed much to the same result. We confess that before we had studied the public documents which form the basis of this history, we could not understand how it was that characters so brilliant, so energetic, so enterprising, as Dupleix, La Bourdonnais, Bussy, and Lally, should have failed, opposed as they were by men, who, with the exception of Clive and Lawrence, must be regarded as inferior to them in capacity. But the solution of the question becomes after examination easy. Those four French names shine out as bright lights among a crowd of flickering satellites. It is they, or rather—for he stands out far above the others—it is Dupleix, the lustre of whose great name reflects the struggles of his countrymen for empire in the East. He did it all. He was unsupported except by Bussy. He it was who caused the fame of the French nation to resound in the palaces of Delhi, who carved out a policy which his rivals seized and followed. He did not succeed, because he was not properly supported at home, because he was alone amongst his countrymen in India. Those contests for the possession of Trichinápallí showed that, even under the most favourable circumstances, his soldiers would not win battles. He could do everything but imbue them with his own spirit. He was in fact alone—in everything supreme, except as a soldier in a field.

If we examine, on the other hand, the conduct of the English, we shall see numberless instances of the pertinacious character of her people. Not counting Clive, who was but for a limited period on the scene, there was not a man in the English settlements equal in genius to Dupleix. But, again, there were many, very many among them, far superior to any of the subordinates of Dupleix, Bussy alone excepted. The daring of Lawrence, the dogged pertinacity of Saunders and his Council, the vigour and ability of Calliaud, of Forde, of Joseph Smith, of Dalton, and of many others, stand out in striking contrast to the feebleness, the incapacity, the indecision, of the Laws, the d'Auteuils, the Brenniers, the Maissins, and others whom Dupleix was forced to employ. Never was England better served than during that struggle. Never was there more apparent, alike amongst her civil and military agents, that patriotic devotion to duty, which ought to be the highest aim of every servant of his country. In the French settlement this feeling burned far less brightly. The efforts of the greatest amongst her leaders were marred and thwarted by the bickerings and jealousies of subordinates. We see La Bourdonnais sacrificing the best interests of France to his greed for money and to his jealousy of Dupleix; Godeheu, owing to the last named feeling, undoing the brilliant work of his predecessor; Maissin refusing to annihilate the English at Trichinápallí; de Leyrit and his Council thwarting Lally; the very Councillors scrambling for illegal gains, and dabbling in peculation; those energies which should have been united against a common enemy employed to ruin one another. Under such circumstances the result could not have been long deferred. Sooner or later it was inevitable. But for one man the stake for which the two countries played would never have been so great. It was Dupleix who made French India, it was France who lost it. If, in the present day, there exist amongst her citizens regrets at the loss of an Empire so vast, so powerful, so important, inhabited by a people who were civilised when we were naked savages, and who possess so many claims to the sympathy and attachment of every intelligent European, it will be impossible for France herself—however much she may condemn the action of her Government of those days, and lament the infatuation and misconduct of her countrymen—to suppress a glow of pride at the recollection that it was a child of her soil who dared first to aspire to that great dominion, and that by means of the impulse which he gave the inhabitants of Hindustan have become permanently united to their long-parted kinsmen—the members of the great family of Europe.

THE END.

APPENDIX A.

PROOFS OF THE BRIBING OF LA BOURDONNAIS.

I.

In the first edition of this work I appended a note to the page referring to the bribing of La Bourdonnais, which ran as follows:

"It was charged against La Bourdonnais in his lifetime, that he had accepted a present from the English of 100,000 pagodas (about four lakhs of rupees) as the price of the ransom-treaty made with the English.

"The charge was brought forward separately by M. Deprémesnil and M. de Kerjean. The first said that he had heard M. Dupleix affirm that an Englishman had told him that 100,000 pagodas had been given to La Bourdonnais for the ransom. He added that he had done his best to ascertain the truth of the fact, but had been able to learn nothing.

"The second, M. de Kerjean, asserted that he had heard a Jew, retired to Pondichery, affirm, that the English had given M. de La Bourdonnais 100,000 pagodas, as an acknowledgment of the good treatment they had received at his hands, and that he, the Jew, as his share of this payment, had been taxed at 7,000 pagodas, which amount he had not paid.

"Le Bourdonnais's reply to these assertions, was, in substance, that they emanated from two men, one the nephew, the other the son-in-law, of Dupleix, that he had avoided the last farewell to the English-governor because he heard that he intended to offer him a present; that had he received such a present, he would not have placed himself in the position of being obliged to restore it, by deferring the evacuation of Madras from October to January; that it was not probable he would have been received with such distinction in London by two members of the Madras Council, if they had known as if it had been true they must have known, that the ransom had been the result of a bribe.

"Here the matter dropped for a time, it being considered that the charge had fallen through. It was revived, however, in 1772, by an English gentleman, Mr. Grose, who wrote an account of his voyage to, and residence in, the East Indies. He states as follows:—'The governor and Council settled the price of the ransom with the French commodore (La Bourdonnais) at 1,100,000 pagodas, or £421,666 sterling, *besides a very valuable present to the commodore, who was willing to evacuate his conquest upon these terms*, and leave the English in full possession of their Presidency.'" Grose's "East Indies," vol 2, p. 29.

"In 'Mill's India,' 5th edition, vol. 3, pp. 37, 38, we have evidence to the same effect. Professor H. H. Wilson affirms that 'a letter to a proprietor of East India Stock, published in 1850, by a person who was evidently concerned in the Government of Madras at the time, describes discussions which took place at home, in regard to the payment of certain bonds given by the Government of Madras to raise money to the extent of 100,000 pagodas, which, it is intimated, were presented to the French commander as the price of his moderation.' But there exists proof of the fact, far more clear and positive. Papers, now in the India House (Law case, No. 31, dated March 3, 1752), show that the Directors of that day were convinced, on the testimony of Madras members of the Council, that La Bourdonnais was promised by bond, 100,000 pagodas (about £40,000) over and above the 1,100,000 pagodas stipulated in the bond given him for public use, in consideration of restoring Madras to the English. This, we think, is conclusive.

"The evidence of this Law Case was first made known to the writer by Sir Walter Morgan, Chief Justice of the High Court of Agra. The nature of its contents was subsequently verified on the spot by his friend, Professor Fitz-Edward Hall, librarian of the India House."

II.

For twenty-three years, so far as I am aware, this note remained unnoticed. Its conclusions were accepted by all the reviewers, even in France, in which country a translation of the work was published in 1871. I had heard that Sir George Birdwood had not accepted my conclusions, and had threatened to publish a refutation of them, but I had seen nothing of his actually published on the subject until at the end of 1891 I stumbled upon a work of his entitled, *Report of the old Records of the India Office, with supplementary note and appendices, second reprint*, 1891. In one of the notes to that work I read a long statement challenging the conclusions I had arrived at twenty-three years before. The note seemed to me to be the work of a man who had bent all his energies to make a bad cause appear a good one. Apart from its facts, every one of which told against the writer,

APPENDIX A. 589

it indulged mainly in conjecture, and went so far as to lecture me for unearthing a story which told against the fame of La Bourdonnais. That I may not be accused of exaggeration I append Sir George Birdwood's note in full detail. In the next section of this appendix I shall submit it to a cruical examination.

The note (page 242 of Sir George Birdwood's book) runs as follows:—

"The subject of La Bourdonnais's (Bernard François Mahá de la Bourdonnais, b. at St. Malo, 1699) bribery has always had an interest for minds given to searching out mean and sordid causes for the great results of history. Having carefully read through the 'Law Case, No. 31, of 3rd March, 1752,' the only original document in this country, I believe, in the matter, and cited by Colonel Malleson, *History of the French in India*, page 157, note, I have been led to the opinion that it affords no conclusive evidence of the truth of the charge. The capture of Madras by La Bourdonnais, its abortive ransom by Governor Morse and his Council which, according to the charge against him La Bourdonnais was induced to accept by a bribe of 100,000 pagodas (£40,000), and the annexation of the town by Dupleix, and its final restoration to the English, formed an unconsidered episode of the war of the Austrian Succession, 1744-1748. That war at once brought England and France into conflict; and the first hostile act of each country was to fit out a naval expedition for the destruction of the other's mercantile settlements in the Indian Ocean.

"The English fleet was the first to arrive in the Bay of Bengal in 1745, when Dupleix, the Governor of Pondichery, in great alarm sent a large present to the Nawab of the Carnatic, who replied, as desired, by forbidding the English, who up to that time were his tributaries, from engaging in hostilities within any part of his dominions. The English fleet in consequence left the 'Bay and Coast,' in 1746. They had no sooner disappeared than La Bourdonnais with the squadron he had collected together with extraordinary energy from the Isles of France and Bourbon, entered it; and now Morse, the Governor of Madras, 1744-1749, in his turn applied to the Nawab of the Carnatic to restrain the French, as he had previously restrained the English, from hostilities, but, as Morse neglected to send a present with his application, it was left without an answer. In consequence, on 18th August, 1746,* (as this interesting Law Case, in correction and amplification of the

---

* *Note by Colonel Mallcson.* The fleet on this occasion was commanded, not by La Bourdonnais, but by M. de la Portbarré. The date was August 29th, new style, which I have followed in my history. This corresponds to the date quoted by Sir G. Birdwood, 18 August, old style. The new style was adopted in England in 1751.

vague statements of our standing histories, inform us) La Bourdonnais, with eight ships under his command, appeared before the town of Madras, and fired a few shots in the Fort St. George, and some broadsides into the *Princess Mary*, one of the English Company's ships then in the roads, and afterwards lay to in the offing, or cruised up and down the Coromandel coast, in sight of the town and people of Madras. On 3rd September, Morse and his Council heard that La Bourdonnais had landed his men somewhere down the coast, and was marching on Madras; and the next day he opened his attack on the town. On the 10th of September, Morse and his Council, excepting Mr. Fowke, came to a resolution to capitulate, and treat for the ransom of the place; and for that purpose Mr. Monson who was next to Morse in Council, and Mr. Hallyburton, an English gentleman of Madras, who spoke French, were deputed to wait on 'Monsieur La Bourdonnais,' and settle terms with him. These, in brief, were that the town should pay 1,100,000 pagodas for its ransom; and the charge of bribery and treason against La Bourdonnais is that he agreed to this ransom in consideration of a further sum of 100,000 pagodas, to be given to him for his own private use and gratification. Dupleix quashed the treaty and confiscated all the Company's property in Madras, and all private property, excepting only personal apparel and jewelry, and carried off the chief people of the place prisoners to Pondicherry, and annexed Madras (appointing Paradis Governor) to the French possessions on the Coromandel coast.

"Had La Bourdonnais stood loyally by Dupleix at this conjuncture (after the example of our English officers in the early days of the Company's adventures in India) the future dominion of India would, as far as we can now judge, have passed away from us altogether, and 'the trade, navigation, and conquest of the Indies' fallen into the hands of the French. But La Bourdonnais, in a huff, set sail from Madras, 29th October, 1746, leaving Dupleix in the lurch; thus throwing to the winds the greatest opportunity the French ever had of establishing their Empire in the East. Dupleix fully understood this; and that La Bourdonnais did not, is the true secret of his strange conduct; and not that he took a bribe; or if he took it as a mere complimentary present (dusturi) that he was in the least influenced by it.

"After this the operations of the French and English against each other dragged on in an ineffective manner for a year or two more; and on the conclusion of the treaty of Aix-la-Chapelle in 1748, Madras was restored to the English Company.

"On his return to France La Bourdonnais was at once thrown into the Bastille, on the charge of collusion with the English in the matter

APPENDIX A. 591

of the ransom of Madras; but after a trial extending over three years (1748-51), was fully acquitted and set free. He died broken-hearted in 1755. His acquittal by his own Government, which was inspired by the deepest resentment against him, is a strong fact in his favour; and Colonel Malleson, a soldier as well as a historian, should at least have himself read the records of the case, not only in the India Office but in the French Admiralty, before reviving so scandalous a charge against one of the noblest ornaments of the French Navy. La Bourdonnais acted with the gravest indiscretion, and that sufficiently accounts for his strange, and in a political sense, culpable conduct. That he was a traitor is, for anyone who is acquainted with his character, an impossible assumption. He was a brave, ardent, and adventurous sailor, whose only idea, in fitting out his expedition from Bourbon and Mauritius, was to harry the English trade in Indian waters, and exact war prizes. Dupleix, on the contrary, was a calculating, prescient statesman, with a constitutional contempt for fighting (which, he used to say, "confused his thoughts"), whose far-reaching policy was directed to the complete expulsion of the English from India, and the raising of a great French Empire on the foundations we had laid. From the moment, therefore, that these two men met they were in direct antipathy with each other, and in all these transactions at Madras in the autumn of 1746, La Bourdonnais's perverse part from the first was to withstand and disconcert Dupleix's political plans. He acted after the manner of all French leaders in India in the last century, and it is the commonplace moral of history that it was in this manner they lost India.

"But to return to the evidence offered by Law Case, No. 31, of the 3rd March, 1752. Colonel Malleson merely refers to it without quoting it. I will now quote every material passage bearing on La Bourdonnais's alleged bribery and treason; premising that the case arose from the objection of the Court of Directors of the East India Company to meet the bonds on which the sum required for the ransom of Madras was raised, on the ground that, in part at least, the bonds had been given, not to save the Company's property, but the private property of the Governor and his Council. Morse and the rest, excepting Fowke, examined by the Court, were really on their own defence, and it may be said that the only impartial evidence incriminating La Bourdonnais to the extent of his receiving a complimentary gratification (dusturi) is that of Fowke.

"*Folio* 3.—Mr. Morse, late Governor of Fort St. George, in a letter to a Committee of the Court of Directors (18th January, 1748) . . . . says, 'I take this occasion to advise you, apart, that in that transaction (ransom of Madras), we were under the necessity for applying a further sum besides that publicly stipulated by the articles (of ransom) which affair, as it required privacy, was by the Council referred to myself and Mr. Monson to be negotiated.'

"Mr. Monson, in a letter to the Court of Directors (21st December, 1748) says: 'I am to acquaint you that, in treating for the ransom of the place, we were soon given to understand that a further sum was necessary to be paid beside that to be mentioned in the public treaty. You will easily imagine from the nature of the thing that it required to be conducted with some degree of secrecy. There was, however, a necessity for acquainting the Council with it, though for form's sake and to preserve appearances with the person (we were) treating with, it was referred to Mr. Morse and myself to settle the matter with him; I can, nevertheless, with great truth assure you that all the gentlemen of the Council were constantly faithfully acquainted with every step that was taken in the matter, except Mr. Edward Fowke, who, from the beginning of the treaty about the ransom, declared that he would not join us in any of these measures, which by all the rest were thought absolutely necessary at the juncture. . . . . . . It remains for me to acquaint you that we had no possible means for raising the money but by giving the Company's bonds for it; and this negotiation was not kept secret for those who supplied the money on this occasion, as they were to a man informed of the use it was borrowed for, before they lent it, and thought by lending it they did a meritorious piece of service to the Company; bonds were accordingly given for so much as we could borrow under the Company's seal and signed by Mr. Morse and the rest of the Council, except Mr. Edward Fowke. Part of the money thus borrowed was actually paid to the person treated with, and the rest was disbursed in defraying the charges of the garrison until the French broke the capitulations and turned us out of the town.'

"*Folio* 4.—Mr. Monson in his letter (3rd May, 1748). . . . after excusing himself from declaring to whom . . . . this money . . . was given, says: 'I hope I shall stand excused if I declare no further than that part of the money was appropriated to pay six months' salary and two months' diet to your covenant servants, with a month's arrear to the garrison, besides sundry payments to the officers and sailors of the *Princess Mary*, to your officers and military that were going to Cuddalore, and some little advances we judged necessary towards our future re-establishment, the rest of the money, with the diamonds, was actually and *bona fide* applied to the purpose already mentioned (the payment of that person) which in the opinion of those concerned in the business would have redounded very much to the honour, the credit, and the real advantage of the Company.'

APPENDIX A.

"*Folio* 5.—Mr. Edward Fowke . . . . speaking (letter of the 25th of December, 1746) of the ransom . . . . says: 'In regard to ransoming of the town, afterwards when Monsieur la Bourdonnais told us we might march out with our swords and hats, I thought it (going out with swords and hats) much more to your interest than to accept the terms that were agreed upon. . . . I could have consented so far as five or six lacs . . . . Madras is but a tributary town . . . . therefore for your Honours to be loaded with such a monstrous sum, and the Native Government not to feel any part of so severe a blow, would, I am afraid, in future have a very bad effect, especially with a little money laid out among the great men, which the French know pretty well how to place.'

"Again, 3rd March, 1748, 'I can assure you, gentlemen, notwithstanding I may have appeared so lukewarm in defence of your town . . . . I would rather have sacrificed my life than to have acceded to those terms of agreement, I thought them as directly opposite to your interest, honour and credit, as others thought them for it. In the same letter he says one of the bonds was brought to him to sign; and he wrote on it:—'I acknowledge Mr. George Jones to have brought me the above-mentioned bond to sign, but as I do not approve the ransom, nor do I know whether I am now legally authorised (being a prisoner of La Bourdonnais) to take up money on the Company's account, I refused to sign it.'

"*Folio* 10.—In the examination (1753 ?) of the bond creditors by interrogatories, Messrs. Abraham Franco, Jacob Franco, Aaron Franks *inter alia*, say: 'That they heard and believe that the then President and Council of Fort St. George did, after the 10th of September, 1746, agree to give and pay to Monsieur de la Bourdonnais 88,000 pagodas, but they did not know and believe that the said 88,000 pagodas, or any part thereof were so agreed to be paid in order to free or exempt the goods and effects of the merchants and inhabitants . . . . and particularly the goods and effects of the said Governor in Council, or the said Solomon Solomons (one of the bondholders) in their private capacity from being seized, taken, or plundered, but that the same was agreed to be given or paid to the said Monsieur de la Bourdonnais, as a *douceur* or present on behalf of the said East India Company, with the view to reduce the amount or value of the ransom insisted on by the said Monsieur de la Bourdonnais.'

"And the same further say (*Folio* 11), 'They do believe in their consciences that . . . . the same and said present of 88,000 pagodas, as agreed to be given to the said Monsieur de la Bourdonnais, was entered into for the benefit and interest of the East India Company.'

"*Folio* 12.—Francis Salvadore, executor to Jacob Salvadore, says:

He don't know, but hath heard and believes that the said President and Council did after the said 10th day of September, 1746, agree to give and pay to or to the use of the said Monsieur de la Bourdonnais the sum or value of 88,000 pagodas, as at present,* but whether . . . . in order to exempt or free the goods and effects of the said Governor and Council in their private capacity, or the said Edward and Joseph Fowke, or the said Jacob Salvadore, ... he don't know nor has been informed.'

"*Folio* 21.—In reply to certain interrogatories, Mr. Monson says; He, the said Mr. Monson, having afterwards (after the treaty of ransom had been settled) heard from Monsieur de la Bourdonnais that they must pay him down 100,000 pagodas, if they expected performance of the agreement, he communicated such his information to the Council, who, after deliberation agreed to pay it, but says this money was not demanded for granting the 15th and 16th articles.'

" Again :—' No receipt was taken or required for the money privately paid, nor could any be insisted on in such a transaction, nor was any agreement made for returning the 88,000 pagodas in case the treaty was rejected by the Governor and Council of Pondichery; and can't say whether the Governor and Council of Pondichery were ever informed of this private transaction.'

"*Folio* 23.—Mr. Fowke, in answer to the interrogatories, says ' He is a stranger to the payment, but don't doubt the money being paid.'

" In *Folio* No. 11, Francis Salvadore, executor to Jacob Salvadore, seems to prove that Mr. Morse and Messrs. Edward and Joseph Fowke advanced money on the Council bonds for the ransom; but I should like someone better acquainted with the phraseology of money dealings to examine this passage, before relying on it as of any pertinence in the present question.

" In the whole case the extract from *Folio* 23 seems to me the only evidence that any money was ever paid to La Bourdonnais by way of *dusturi.* Excepting Fowke, all the rest of the Council are out of Court, *and so would Fowke be, if, while he disapproved of the capitulation, he yet joined with Solomons, Salvadore, Franco, and the rest of these extortioners, in advancing money on the Council bonds he would not himself sign.* Indeed, if Edward Fowke was personally interested, as a sleeping partner with his brother Joseph, in the prospective profits of an usurious advance of this kind, this of itself would be a sufficient explanation of his refusal to join with Messrs Morse and Monson in signing the bonds

---

* *Note by Colonel Malleson.* Sir G. Birdwood writes in the printed volume "at present," but as those words convey no meaning, I presume that he intended to write " a present."

APPENDIX A.

for the amount, on the plausible pretext of his disapproving of a capitulation that could not possibly have been prevented. Besides, if anyone who advanced the money knew for what it was intended, Dupleix, through his half-caste wife, to whom he owed, so much of the success of his intrigues in India, would easily have obtained sufficient evidence against La Bourdonnais to convict him when he was put on his trial for corruption and treason on his return to France. On the face of the case also very little of the 88,000 pagodas could have gone to La Bourdonnais; and what Colonel Malleson states is that he received 100,000.* La Bourdonnais was probably quite capable of accepting a *douceur* or *dusturi*. It was the universal custom of his time. It was one of the perquisites of public office. But this document, cited without quotation by Colonel Malleson, affords no evidence for reviving the charge of corruption and treason against La Bourdonnais after his acquittal by his own Government. It seems to me very probable that, in consideration of La Bourdonnais's 'politeness and generosity in exempting Madras from pillage' (I am quoting from the case from memory, for I cannot trace the passage), 'The Governor, Nicholas Morse, and his Council, agreed to make him a private present, and raised 88,000 pagodas for the purpose; that this sum was mostly otherwise expended; and that difficulty having arisen with the Court of Directors about refunding this and other sums embraced in the ransom, it was plausibly pleaded that this particular sum was paid to La Bourdonnais to secure the execution of a treaty of ransom which was never exercised but disvowed by Dupleix."

III.

Such is the case which Sir George Birdwood has submitted to the public to disprove my contention that La Bourdonnais was offered, and received, a considerable sum of money, probably 100,000 pagodas, for negotiating the ransom of Madras.

My contention, the reader will recollect (pages 160-2), was that whilst Dupleix did not desire that Madras should be ransomed, La Bourdonnais persisted in negotiating to ransom it in order to gain a large sum of money for himself. I now contend that not only is my argument proved to the hilt, but it is proved by the evidence which Sir George Birdwood has provided. His method is certainly a queer method. He

---

* *Note by Colonel Malleson.* In the first edition, page 157, Colonel Malleson wrote in the note: "It was charged against La Bourdonnais in his lifetime that he had accepted a present from the English of 100,000 pagodas (about four lakhs of rupees) as the price of the ransom treaty made with the English." In the text, also page 157, Colonel Malleson wrote: "That he did receive a considerable sum is undeniable."

APPENDIX A.

makes a great display of force; he poses as the pure and upright man who is incapable of "searching out mean and sordid causes for the great results of history." He then marshals his witnesses, men some of them of distinction in their time; the only men whose evidence could throw any light on the subject; and then, when he finds that their evidence tells against his theory, and establishes beyond a doubt the statement that La Bourdonnais did negotiate for and accept a bribe for the ransom of Madras, he asks the reader to disbelieve them because "they were really on their own defence." They were not on their own defence more than a member of Council of the present day would be who might be asked to narrate certain transactions in which, by virtue of his office, he had taken a prominent part. Who but Mr. Morse and Mr. Monson could have revealed the negotiations between themselves and La Bourdonnais? It is conceivable why their evidence is very disappointing to Sir George Birdwood, for it proves my contention; therefore he can find no other method of getting rid of it than by summarily putting the witnesses out of court. But, I would ask, is that fair argument? I am wrong to call it argument at all; it is the resource of a mind driven to its last shift to avoid a palpable issue. The then late Governor of Madras and his senior member of Council, state that La Bourdonnais insisted on negotiating for and accepting a bribe (vide *Folio* 3, 4, and 21, quoted by Sir George Birdwood), they formed the committee to which the negotiation was intrusted; and their statement is practically confirmed by the men to whom they applied to raise the money (vide *Folio* 10.) Their colleague, Mr. Fowke, although a stranger himself to the transaction, expresses "his belief that the money was paid."

So much for the facts of the case. But Sir George Birdwood, fighting against conviction, states that after a trial of over three years in France La Bourdonnais was acquitted of this very charge. He was acquitted simply because the evidence on which he now stands condemned had not then been taken. La Bourdonnais captured Madras and negotiated for the ransom in 1746; he was tried in France in 1748-51; the date of the case in which the evidence regarding him is recorded in England is 1752. Who can doubt but that if that evidence had been in existence during 1748-51, and had been produced before the court which tried La Bourdonnais in France, he would have been condemned? There is no getting away from that evidence. And here I would call attention to the fact that it entirely satisfied the distinguished judge who first brought it to my notice, and who subsequently became Chief Justice of the High Court of Madras.

But I have not yet done with Sir George Birdwood. Beaten at all points, and forced at last to admit that La Bourdonnais may have

APPENDIX A. 597

received some money, he suggests that it may have been by way of *dastúrí* or *douceur*, and that the former was one of "the perquisites of public office." Further, that the members of Council may have given it out of their private purse in consideration of the politeness and generosity of La Bourdonnais in exempting Madras from pillage. Let us examine these suggestions for a few moments.

Let me recall the attention of the reader to the position of La Bourdonnais. He had captured Madras from the English. His superior, the Governor of Pondichery, wanted to keep Madras, and ordered La Bourdonnais not to ransom it, but to make it over to officers whom he nominated. If La Bourdonnais had obeyed him he would have received no private money for himself. He, therefore, negotiated with the two senior members of the English Council for the ransom of the place. The witnesses prove that as the negotiations proceeded La Bourdonnais made known that he must have something for himself. Whether he called it *dastúrí*, or *douceur*, or present, or bribe, is absolutely immaterial. All four words meant the same thing. They meant the transfer of about 100,000 pagodas to La Bourdonnais' pocket. Did that sum constitute, as Sir George Birdwood contends, " one of the perquisites of public office." A high official negotiating, against the orders of his superior, for the ransom of a town, to accept *dastúrí*, that is percentage on the amount of ransom, for disobeying his own superior officer at Pondichery because it was "the universal custom of the time?" The thing is incredible. La Bourdonnais demanded the money, because it was money. It certainly was not "the universal custom of that time" for an officer to demand a sum of money from a beaten enemy that he might fill his own pockets, whether he hid his demand under the form of *dastúrí* or *douceur*, or any other form. And it is because it was not the universal custom that those living at the time, and posterity afterwards, have cried shame on it.

As to the other suggestion of Sir George Birdwood, that the members paid the sum demanded out of their own pockets, it is too childish to treat seriously. It shows the straits to which Sir George Birdwood is reduced to establish a contention which is absolutely baseless. It is contradicted by the purport of all the evidence, and, logically, by Sir George Birdwood himself in the last four lines of the paragraph in which he suggests the possibility.

But I need say no more. It is always bad policy to "slay the slain," so I shall omit the comments which naturally suggest themselves. But I cannot part from Sir George Birdwood without thanking him most sincerely for placing on public record the evidence which proves my case. After all, his fate is not at all uncommon. The man who dug a pit for another and fell into it himself; the engineer who was hoisted with his own petard; the prophet who set out with the intention of cursing, and finished by blessing; and now Sir George Birdwood himself, presents examples of the danger a man incurs by basing his actions on purely personal sentiments. Sir George Birdwood started to convict me of error: he has simply convicted himself of that which is worse than mere error.

G. B. MALLESON.

London, March 16, 1893.

INDEX.

ACH

ACHE, Count d', appointed naval colleague to Lally, 511. His character, 511. He wastes time on the passage out, 514. Is beaten off Nágápatan, 503. Refuses to act against Madras, 536. His indecision and ill-luck, 536. Is defeated off Tranquebar, 531. Sails for the Isle of France, 532. Appropriates for the fleet money intended for Pondichery, 541. Arrives in the Indian waters, 554. Is beaten by Pocock, 555. Abandons Pondichery, 557. Becomes the accuser of Lally, 581

Adlercron, Colonel, commands a force in the Karnátik, 466. Retreats towards Madras, 467

Ahmad Sháh, Abdáli, effect of his invasion of India on the movements of Clive, 475

Ahmad Sbáh, becomes King of Delhi 234

Aix-la-Chapelle, treaty of, effects of, in India, 229

Alemanava, acquired by the French, 281

Anvria, surrenders to the English and Marathas, 454

Arnadaráj, Rájá, revolts against the French. 549

Anwaru-din, Nawwáb, appointed to administer the Karnátik, 106. Nominated Nawwáb, 106. Appealed to by Dupleix, 106. Responds, 107. Refuses to restrict the movements of the French against Madras, 143. Threatens the French, 150. His impatience at the French occupation of Madras, 189. Sends troops there under Mafauz Khán, 190. Comes to terms with the French, 205. Declares against the French, 224. Opposes Chanda Sáhib, 237. Is killed in battle, 238

AUT

Arambure, M d', reinforces Law, 487. His brilliant conduct, 489. Bears the brunt of the action, 491. His skill and gallantry, 594. His fatal mistake at Pondichery, 570

Arkát, its capture by Clive, 294

Ariankupum, its situation, 217. Is fortified, 217. English repulsed at, 225. Abandoned by the French, 225

Asiatic, the, his peculiarity as a soldier, 491

Astruc, M., appointed to command before Trichinápallí, 387. Repulses an attack on Srirangam, 387. Crosses the Kávari and occupies the Five Rocks, 389. Attacks and carries the Golden Rock, 391. Has victory within his grasp, 393. It is snatched from him by Lawrence, 385. Resigns his command, 395. Resumes it, 400. His caution, 400. Is attacked by Lawrence, 401. Is defeated and taken prisoner, 402

Aumont, M. d', his shameful conduct at Wándiwásh, 537

Aurangábád, entered by Salábat Jang and Bussy, 279. Occupied by Gháziu-d-din, 368. Bussy marches on, 380

Aurangzeb, his plans on the Dakhan and death, 348

Auteuil, M. d', commands the French force, 237. Is wounded, 238, Wins the battle of Ambur, 239. Takes command at Valdávur, 251. Vainly tries to stop the mutiny in his army, 252. Resolves to retreat, 253. Repulses the Maráthás, 254. Brought to trial by Dupleix, 255. Is restored to command, 256. Detaches a party to attack Násir Jang, 257. Moves on Tiruvádi, 258. Defeats Muhammad Ali, 258. Aids in the capture of

INDEX.

BAL

Jinji, 264. Leads a force towards Trichinápalli, 284. Defeats Gingens at Volconda, 286. His gout and apathy, 286. Follows up the English, 287. Shuts them up in Trichinápalli, 287. Relieved of his command, 289. Sent to supersede Law, 316. Attempts to reach the Kolrun, 320. Retires from Utátur, 324. Surrenders to Clive, 324. Appointed to command a force against Trichinápalli, 450. His faulty method of warfare, 451. Its ill-success, 453. Replaced by Saubinet, 454

BALESHWAR, factory at, founded, 33

Baláji Báji Ráo, the Peshwá, receives two lakhs from Salábat Jang, 280. Promises to support Ghaziu-d-din, 349. Enters the Dakhan, 356. Hastens to bar the road to Puná, 356. Is defeated by Bussy, 359. His intrigues, 360. Forced to fly for his life, 360. Is again beaten, 361. Opens negotiations with Salábat Jang, 363. And concludes an armistice, 364. Offers himself to the highest bidder, 365. Agrees to peace with Salábat Jang, 368. Invades Maisur, 477. Retires, 478. Refuses to assassinate Bussy, 481. His anxiety to gain Bussy, 482. Endeavours to propitiate him, 483
Búrá Sáhib, defeated and slain by the Maráthás, 90
Barnet, Commodore, charged to destroy the French settlements, 101. Appropriates the plan of La Bourdonnais. 120, *note*. Dies, 126
Barneval, Mrs., daughter of Dupleix, writes to La Bourdonnais, 147
Baron, M., Director of Surat, 20. Besieged in St. Thomé, 22. Visits Martin at Pondichery, 23. Returns to Surat and reports to the Company, 23, *note*
Barthélemy, M., appointed Councillor at Madras, 157. Protests against La Bourdonnais, 164. Appointed member of secret committee, 444
Basálat Jang, appointed keeper of the great seal to Salábat Jang, 499. Nominated his minister, 499. Declines the French overtures, 557
Battles, of Damalcheri, 82. Off Nágápatan, 127. Near Madras, 194. Near St. Thomé, 196. Of Ambur, 238. On the Panar, 260. Near Jinji, 268. Of Volconda, 285. Of the Arni, 304. Of

BUS

Kávaripák, 304. Of Vicravandi, 336. Of Bahur, 337. Near Beder, 358. Of Rájápur, 360. Near Korigaon, 373. Of the Golden Rock (first), 390. Of the Golden Rock (second), 395. Of the Sugarloaf Rock, 399. Off Nágápatan, 509. Off Tranquebar, 531. Of Kondur, 549. Off Fort St. David, 555. Of Wándiwásh, 567
Bausset, M., appointed Peace Commissioner, 410
Beaulieu, Captain, joins Commodore de Nets in an expedition, 6. Commands one of his own, 7. Returns to France, 7
Bijápûr, succumbs to Aurangzeb, 23, 24
Boileau, M., appointed member of secret committee, 442
Bonnessay, Cornet, obedient among the disobedient, 565
Boscawen, Admiral, his lineage, 219. Appointed to command the expedition against Pondichery, 219. His abortive attack on the islands, 221. Is repulsed at Ariánkupum, 222. Occupies it and closes on Pondichery, 224. His great efforts and their failure, 226. Raises the siege, 226. Leaves for England, 247
Bourbon, Isle of, *see* Isle of France.
Bouvet, M., Governor of Bourbon, sails for Pondichery, 214. Out manœuvres the English admiral, 214. Returns the coast, 228
Brennier, M., succeeds Astruc in command, 397. His two plans, 397. Determines to intercept Lawrence, 398. His mistakes and defeat, 399. Retreats to Mutachelinur, 401. Resigns command to Astruc, 401
Brereton, Major, supports a sortie against the French, 536. Storms Kánchipúram, 551. Takes Tripatur, 554. Is repulsed at Wándiwásh, 554. Is mortally wounded, 564
Bruyère, M., appointed a Commissioner under De Bury, 165.
Bury, General de, appointed to execute the orders of Dupleix against La Bourdonnais, 165. Hands over to La Bourdonnais a letter from the Council, 166. Is arrested with his companions, 168. Appointed to command the force against Fort St. David, 201. Marches thither, 202. Is surprised and beaten, 204
Bussy, M. de, is present at the battle of Ambur, 239. Gains the day, 239. His lineage, 262. Sent to attack Jinji,

INDEX.

BUS

264. His success, 265. Is attached to Muzaffar Jang, 277. His conduct at Kadapah, 278. His address after the death of Muzaffar Jang, 279. Appoints Salábát Jáng to be Subadar, 279. Accompanies Salábat Jang to Aurangábád, 279. His wise arrangements there, 351. Hears of the movements of Gháziu-d-din, 356. His advice to the Subadar, 357. Moves upon Beder and threatens Puná, 359. Defeats the Peshwá, 360. Again, 361. Again, 362. Moves the Subadar to make peace, 367. Procures the nomination of Dupleix as Nawwáb of the Karnátik, 362. Falls sick and proceeds to Machhlipatan, 368 Learns the treacherous conduct of Saiyid Lashkur, 376. His prompt action, 376. Marches on Aurangábád, 379. Obtains the cession of four provinces, 380. Agrees to maintain Saiyid Lashkur, 380. Takes possession of the four Sirkars, 382. Accompanies the Subadar to Haidarábád, 384. His touching farewell on setting out for Machhlipatan, 384. His mortification, but noble resolve, on the recall of Dupleix, 435. Is ordered by Godeheu to rejoin Salábat Jang, 474. The language used to him by the Subadar, 476. Marches against Maisúr, 479. Returns to Haidarábád, 468. Moves against Sávánur, 481. Enters into a secret agreement with Murári Ráo, 482. Is dismissed from the service of the Subadar, 483. His statesmanlike conduct, 484. Receives overtures from Báláji, 485. Resolves to make a stand at Haidarábád, 487. Occupies the Chár Mahall, 487. Gains over two Maráthá chiefs, 490. Sends intimation to Law, 490. Orders Law, in the name of the King, to advance, 492. His own daring action, 492. Sends to bring in the sick, 495. Is reconciled to the Subadar, 484, Remarks on his conduct, 496. Marches into the ceded districts, 498. Despatches Law into Bengal, 499. Disperses the Aurángábád conspirators, 501. Is ordered to join Lally, 502. Makes over charge to Conflans and sets out, 503. Joins Lally at Arkát, 529. His real opinion of Lally, 531. The high opinion entertained of himself by the other French commanders, 533. Is appointed to rank next to de Soupire, 534. Is with Lally before Madras, 535. Is implored to

CHA

cut off the English, 538. His refusal and its consequences, 538-9, and note. Goes to Wándiwásh, 557. His abortive negotiation with Básálat Jang, 559. Is taken prisoner at Wándiwásh, 565. Cabals against Lally, 575. His own fate adverted to, 576-7

CALCUTTA, captured by the Subadar of Bengal, 452. Recaptured by Clive and Watson, 465
Calliaud, Captain, joins Lawrence at Trichinápallí, 404. Ordered to Madura, 443. Receives startling news, 456. His rapid march to Trichinápallí and his success, 459. Operates against the French before Madras, 540
Caron, M., his origin, 14. His treatment in Batavia, 14, and note. His command of a French expedition, 15. His success, 15. Quarrels with Marcara, 19. His attack on Galle and Trinkamali. 17-18. Is recalled, 18. His ship founders, 19
Cattans, de, employed as a spy, 399. Is hanged, 400
Chace, Captain, in command at Tiruvadi, 390. Repulses the French twice, 392-3. Is cut up with all his men, 393
Chandranagar founded, 33. Its improvement under Dupleix, 70. Its state when he left it, 96. Its decline after his departure, 464. Its defences, 471. Attacked by Clive and Watson, 473 Surrenders, 472. Reflections on its capture, 473
Chanda Sáhib, his character, 74. Takes Trichinápallí, 75. Offers to assist Dumas, 78. Takes the fort of Kikan Garhí, 81. His dilatoriness, 81. Sends his family to Pondichery, 85. Visits Pondichery, 89. His proceedings at Trichinápallí, 90. Surrenders Trichinápallí and is sent prisoner to Satára, 91. His release, 237. Allies himself with Muzaffar Jang, 239. And with Dupleix, 241. Shares in the battle of Ambur, 242. Becomes Nawwáb of the Karnátik, 243. His reasons for not following Muhammad Ali, 245. Marches from Pondichery, 247. Turns off to Tanjur, 249. Is deaf to the remonstrances of Dupleix, 250. Retreats in disorder, 250. Casts in his lot with the French, 254. His gallant contest with Murári Ráo, 255. Regains his position, 261. Marches

CHI

towards Trichinápallí, 284. His slow procedure, 286. Gains a victory at Volkonda, 287. Misuses it, 287. Is repulsed by the English, 289. Takes possession of Sriraṅgam, 289. Detaches a force to re-take Arkát, 296. Vainly urges Law to vigorous measures, 318. Accompanies him into Srirangam, 320. Surrenders to Mánakjí, 327. Is stabbed by his order, 328, 329

Chicacole (Srikákolam) ceded to the French, 381

Clive, Robert, escapes in disguise from Madras, 200. His gallantry before Pondichery, 227. Serves under Captain Gingens, 284. Sketch of his earlier career, 290. His daring plans, 292. He proposes them to Mr. Saunders, 292. Marches on, and captures Arkát, 294. His gallant defence of that place, 296. Repulses the enemy, 297. Beats the French at the Arni, 302. And at Káveripák, 303. Destroys the town built by Dupleix, 305. Marches to relieve Trichinápallí, 305. Sent to cut off Law from Pondichery, 307. Is misled by an intercepted letter, 322. And surprised at Samiaveram, 323. His splendid conduct, 324. Avoids an action with Law, 325. Forces d'Auteuil to surrender, 326. Goes to Fort St. David for his health, 335. Takes Kóvlaon and Chengalpat, 340. Proceeds to England, 340. Returns to India, 449. Is employed in the attack on Gériah, 450. Hears of the capture of Calcutta, 451. Sails for Bengal, 451. Re-captures Calcutta, 463. His designs on Chandranagar, 463. He temporises, 453. Accepts Renault's proposal to be neutral, 465. Resolves to break the agreement, 466. Marches against Chandranagar, 469. Captures it, 470. Results to him of the capture, 471. Despatches Colonel Forde to the ceded districts, 544

Colbert, M. de, his capacity, 10. Forms a Company of the Indies, 11. Supports the enterprise against Galle, 17

Committee, Secret, appointed by Godeheu on his departure, 446. Will do nothing, 446

Company of the Indies, founded by Henri IV., 6. Coalesces with some merchants of Rouen, 6. Sends out two expeditions, 7. Another raised by Richelieu, 8. Attempts to colonise Madagascar, 9. A third raised by Col-

COU

bert, 11. Its attempts on Madagascar, 19. Sends Caron to the East, 15. Gives up its rights to the Company of St. Malo and others, 39. Its privileges extended, 41. Revoked, 46. Is united to the Company of the West, 47; and styled the Company of the Indies, 48. The mode of its formation, 48. It takes upon itself various functions of the State, 49. Acquires the monopoly of Tobacco, 50. The Royal Bank united to it, 55. Entitled the 'Perpetual Company of the Indies,' 56. Severed from the Royal Bank, 56. Its capital, 59. Its great expenses, 60. Its action on the Pondichery government, 68. Suspends and restores Dupleix, 68. Its economical restrictions, 98. Its approval of Dupleix's conduct 100. Apprises him of the war about to ensue with England, 101. Its timid policy, 115. Refuses to accept the resignation of La Bourdonnais, 120. Warns Dupleix of war between France and Holland, 173. Writes a letter of thanks to Dupleix, 227. Urges him to peace, 274. Expresses satisfaction with his conduct, 335. Again urges him to peace, 404. Is dissatisfied with him, 415. Sends Duvalaer to London to negociate, 415. Resolves to sacrifice Dupleix, 417. Appoints Godeheu to succeed him, 417. Its selfish and ungenerous treatment of Dupleix, 420. Its own fate adverted to, 578

Conference for peace meets, 410. Breaks up, 412

Conflans, M. de, appointed to succeed Bussy, 502. Takes over charge of the ceded provinces, 503. His unfitness for his position, 543. Awaits the English attack and is beaten, 546. Capitulates to Forde, 547

Coote, Colonel Eyre, is out-manœuvred on the Palar, 562. Beats Lally at Wándiwásh, 564. Recovers all the places in the Karnátik, 569. Moves against Pondichery, 569. Repulses Lally's sortie, 571. Resigns and reassumes his command, 571-2. Captures Pondichery, 585. His opinion of Lally, 576 *note*

Cope, Captain, leads the English against Dévikótá, 244. Is forced to retreat, 245. Advises Muhammad Ali, 259. Marches to defend Trichinapállí, 285. Unsuccessful at Madura, but enters Trichinápallí, 285. Is mortally wounded, 302

Courchant, M. Beauvallier de, Governor

CRI

of Pondichery, 58. Improves the town, 60
Crillon, M. de, arrives at Pondichery, 510. Takes Tripátur, 528. Implores Bussy to cut off the English, 537. Brings back the soldiers to their duty, 558. Sent by Lally to Srirangam, 561. Storms it and rejoins, 561

DAKHAN, the, description of, 350
Dalton, Captain, tries to rally the English, 292. Joins Lawrence before Trichinúpallí, 316. Beats up Law's quarters, 321. Captures Elmiseram, 323. Sent to attack d'Auteuil, 327. In command at Trichinápallí, 397. Fails in an attempt to drive the French out of Srirangam, 389. Operates on the fears of Virana, 389. Applies to Lawrence for relief, 389. Observe the movements of the French, 400.
Daud Khán, Nawwáb of the Karnátik, his demand on Mr. Pitt, 141. Enforces it, 142.
Dauphine, Isle, named by the French settlers, 12. Massacre at, 13.
Day, Mr., founds Madras, 141.
Desforges, M., appointed councillor at Madras, 156
Desprémesnil, M., appointed to command at Madras, 163. Protests against La Bourdonnais's usurpation of authority, 164. Replies to La Bourdonnais, 168. Succeeds him at Madras, 181. Threatened by Mafauz Khán, 192. Sends a detachment to drive him off, 194. Recalled to Pondichery, 199
Dev Ráj, his helplessness against the French, 479. Pacifies the Subadar, 481
Dévikótá, the English retreat from, 245. Stormed by them, 239. Taken by the French, 520. Retaken by the English, 566
Dordelin, M., senior naval officer at Pondichery, 181. Ordered to Pulikat, 181. Succumbs to La Bourdonnais, 181. Sails with four ships to Achén, 184. Arrives at Pondichery, 202. Proceeds to Goa, 206. Thence to the islands, 214
Dost Ali, Nawwáb of the Karnátik, grants permission to Dumas to coin money, 73. Is defeated and slain, 81
Draper, Colonel, the Conqueror of Man-

DUP

illa, 534. Heads a sortie against the French, 536. Is repulsed, 536. His able conduct at Wándiwásh, 554
Dubois, M., Intendant of the French Army, is assassinated, 565
Dulaurent, M., appointed Councillor at Madras, 157. Protests against La Bourdonnais, 164
Dulivier, M., succeeds Martin as Governor, 41 *note*. Is succeeded by Hebert, 41 *note*. Holds the appointment again for two years, 41 *note*
Dumas, M., appointed Governor of Pondichery, 71. His earlier career, 71. Obtains permission to coin money, 73. Aids Sáhuji, 76. Is deceived by him, 77. Sends troops to occupy Kárikál, 79. Obtains a grant of it from Partáb Singh, 80. Prepares to defend Pondichery, 82. Receives the families of Dost Ali and Chanda Sáhib, 84. His replies to Rághuji Bhonslá, 85. Receives Sufdar Ali and Chanda Sáhib, 88. Applies for aid to the Isle of France, 90. His wise behaviour towards Rágbuji, 92. The honours showered upon him, 92-93. Character of his administration, 93
Dupleix, M., his early career, 67. Appointed chief of Chandranagar, 69. Improves its trade, 70. Succeeds Dumas as Governor of Pondichery, 94. Its state on his arrival, 97. His policy of ostentation, 98. Is crippled by the Company, 98. His bold and self-reliant measures, 99. Is thanked for his disobedience, 100. Proposes to Mr. Morse to be neutral during the war, 102. His defenceless position, 100. Applies to Anwáru-din, 106. His friendly correspondence with La Bourdonnais, 130. States his views regarding Madras, 129. Protests against the plan of La Bourdonnais, 135. Sends intimation to him at Madras, 146. Again, 147. His agreement with Anwáru-din, 150. Intimates the same to La Bourdonnais, 150. The reasons for his policy, 154. Writes sharply to La Bourdonnais, 157. Sends him a touching letter, 165. Appoints an executive commission to carry out his orders, 166. His feelings on learning the arrest of the deputies, 169. He protests, 169. Receives overtures from La Bourdonnais, 171. His dilemma, 168. Is strengthened by the arrival of a squadron, 172. The instructions

DUP

he received, 173, and *note*. Offers conditions to La Bourdonnais, 174. His disinclination to attend to the new proposals of La Bourdonnais, 182. Reasons for supposing him to have been sincere, 190. His difficulties regarding Madras, 192. Resolves to retain it, 193. Sends instructions to Desprémesnil, 194. Orders Paradis to relieve Madras, 195. Appoints Paradis Governor of Madras, 198. Resolves to drive the English from Fort St. David, 200. Is forced to appoint de Bury to the command, 203. Orders Dordelin to the coast, 206. Makes overtures to Anwáru-din, 206. Fails to surprise Gúdalúr, 206. Orders Dordelin to Goa, 207. His apparently fatal mistake, 208. Appoints Paradis to command, 208. His unaccountable inaction, 210. Its consequences, 206. His perplexity, 212. Sends Dordelin to the isles, 213. Attempts again to surprise Gúdalúr, 214. Is repulsed, 215. Fortifies himself against attack, 217. His grief at the death of Paradis, 223. Takes the conduct of the defence upon himself, 220. His skill, 225. Compels Boscawen to raise the siege, 225. Announces his triumph all over India, 228. Is forced to restore Madras, 229. Allies himself with Chanda Sáhib and Muzaffar Jang, 238. Exhorts the former to march on Trichinápalli, 241. Advances funds to him for that purpose, 245. Remonstrates with him, 248. His plans defeated, 249. Though perplexed prepares others, 251. His mortification at the behaviour of his army, 254. Punishes the officers, 255. Intrigues with the native chiefs, 256. Orders active measures, 257. Sends an expedition to Machhlipatan, 257. Negotiates with Nasir Jang and his chiefs, 266. Sends precise orders to de la Touche, 268. Which arrive too late, 268. His joy at the victory of de la Touche, 269. Is visited by Muzaffar Jang, 272. His conduct at the famous durbar, 274. Founds a city, 270. Is disposed to peace, 275. Negotiates with Muhammed Ali, 277. Resolves to send Bussy into the Dakhan, 280. His acquisitions from Salábat Jang, 281. His great position, 281. His policy, 282. Is outwitted by Muhammad Ali, 284. Sends a force against Tri-

DUT

chinápalli, 284. Sends men against Arkát, 29b. His well-planned policy, 299. His mortification at Clive's victories, 307. His anger with Ráju Sahib, 307. His graphic instructions to Law, 308. His anger at Law's folly, 314. His still greater amazement, 315. Sends d'Auteuil to reassume command, 317. His conduct on learning the surrender of Law, 331. Negotiates with the native allies of the English, 333. Succeeds in bringing over two of them, 333. His plans to destroy Kinneer, 335. Captures a company of Swiss mercenaries, 337. Is formally appointed Nawwáb of the Karcátik, 337. Appoints Ráju Sáhib, and afterwards Murtizá Ali, as his lieutenant, 338. Is created a Marquis, 338. Sends a force to blockade Fort St. David, 338. Wins over the Maisurians and Maráthás, 340. His position at the close of the campaign, 340. His designs on the Dakhan, 354. The excuse for his policy, 356. His prompt orders to Bussy, 375. Triumph of his policy, 379. The means at his disposal, 383. Sends Astruc to Trichinápalli, 388. Exerts himself to obtain peace, 402. Makes proposals to that effect to Saunders, 402. His policy accounted for, 403. His secret trust in the fortune of war, 403. The fatal blow to his views, 407, Re-opens negotiations, 408. Will not yield his pretensions, 410. His fatal mistake, 410. Sends reinforcements to Mainville, 412. Is represented as the cause of hostilities, 418. And is superseded by Godeheu, 418. His false impression as to Godeheu's character, 419. The latter's behaviour towards him, 419. His generous conduct, 420. The injustice perpetrated towards him, 421. The probable result of his policy if he had been supported, 424. His character, 424. He returns to France, 427. His shameful treatment there, 428. His last words, 428. His death and place in history, 429. Stands alone among his countrymen in India, 580
Duquesne, M., commands the French levies with Chanda Sáhib, 246. Adopts vigorous measures against Tanjur, 248. Dies, 253
Durré, M, thwarts Lally's plans by his want of dash, 561
Dutch, the, recapture Trinkamali, 18.

INDEX.

DUV

Take St. Thomé, 21, Capture Pondichery, 28. Restore it, 34. Intrigue against the French, 75. Inform the French regarding Peyton's squadron, 134. Join Admiral Boscawen, 220. Furnish Lally with supplies, 525 Duvalaer, M., sent to London to negotiate a peace, 415

ELMISERAM, occupied by Law, 316. Captured by Dalton, 319. Occupied by the French, 404. Again, 550
Elore, ceded to the French, 378
English, the, their fleet repulsed off Nágápatan, 125. Surrender Madras, 147. Retire to fort St. David, 199. Resolve to defend it against Dupleix, 201. Their plans for that end, 199. Their success, 205. The strange inactivity of their fleet, 203. It arrives at Gúdalúr and forces Paradis to retire, 211. Defeat the attempt of the French to surprise Gúdalúr, 215. Determine to retaliate on Pondichery, 219. Futile reconnaisance of the French Islands, 220. Besiege the French in Pondichery, 221. Are repulsed, 226. Determine to aid Sáhuji, 229. Repulsed at Dévikótá, 241. Storm it, 241. Abandon Sáhuji, 244. Reinforce Muhammad Ali at Trichinápalli, 247. Retire to Fort St. David, 259. Driven from Volkonda, 285. Shut up in Trichinápalli, 287. Capture Arkát, 294. Beat the French on the Arni, 302. Again at Kávaripák, 303. Relieve Trichinápalli, 317. Force Law to surrender, 327. Their opinion of the French leaders, 329. Beaten at Vicravandi, 334. Denounce the capture of the Swiss mercenaries, 334. Beat the French at Bahur, 337. And at the Golden Rock, 393. Splendid qualities of their soldiers, 394. Again beat the French at the Golden Rock, 395. And at the Sugarloaf Rock, 397. Repulse the French at Trichinápalli, 408. Are cut up at Kontajárá, 413. Repulse the French at the Sugarloaf Rock, 414. Try in London to effect the removal of Dupleix, 416. Despatch Admiral Watson to the East, 417. Succeed in their designs, 417. Conclude a treaty with the French, 436. Infringe its provisions, 444. Ill-success of their expedition to Madura, 445.

FRE

Jealous of the influence of Bussy with the Subadar, 449. Attack and capture Ghériah, 450. Send an expedition to Bengal, 452. The necessities of their position, 452. Invite the Dutch and French to assist them, 462. March to attack Chand ranagar, 469. Capture it, 469. Are unable to assist Sháh Nawáz Khán, 481. Their obligations to him, 496. Beat the French off Nágápatan, 514. Again off Tranquebar. 526. At Condore, 543. Off Fort St. David, 552. Capture Karangoli and Wándiwásh, 560. Beat the French at Wándiwásh 562. Their fleet severely damaged by a storm, 570. Is quickly refitted, 572. Capture Pondichery, 574. Reflections on the character of the nation in India, 581.
Estaing, Count d', arrives at Pondichery, 513. Is ordered to Gúdalúr, 516. Takes Dévikótá, 522 Advises an attack on Tanjur, 527. Taken prisoner by the English, 537.

FLEURY, Cardinal, his conduct to La Bourdonnais, 113. His assent to his plan, 115
Floyer, Mr., Governor of Fort St. David, acknowledges Chanda Sáhib as Nawwáb of the Karnátik, 237 note. Refuses to detain Boscawen, 244
Forde, Colonel, is despatched to the ceded districts, 544. Defeats Conflans, 545. His brilliant and daring conduct, 546. Obtains the Four Sirkars for the English, 547
Fort St. George, vide Madras.
France, declares war against England, 100. War declared between, and England, 455. Declares war against England, 506. Reflexions on the Government of, 576
France and Bourbon, Isles of, natives of Madagascar transported to, 9. Discovery by the Portuguese, and occupation by the Dutch and French 13. History of, to the time of La Bourdonnais, 102. Improvements effected in, 214. Advantages of their position, 214. Warn off Admiral Boscawen, 220
François I., invites his subject to trade, 5
French, the, occupy Madagascar, 12. Also the Isles of France and Bourbon, 13. Arrive at Surat, 15. Form a factory at Machlipatan, 15, 31

INDEX.

FRE

Repulsed from Galle, 17-18. Take Trinkamali, 18. Lose it, 18. Settle at Pondichery, 22. Surrender to the Dutch, 28. Abandon Surat, 31. Found Chandranagar and its dependencies, 33. Conquer Mahé, 64. Obtain Karikal, 78. Repulse the English fleet off Nágapatan. 126. Take Madras, 147. Defeat Máfauz Khán near Madras. 194. Again at St. Thomé, 196. Repulse him at Sadras, 202. Are surprised and repulsed at Gúdalúr, 205. Attempt again to surprise it, but in vain, 206. Take and miss prizes, 208. Move against Gúdalúr, 209. Are forced to retire, 210. Attempt again to surprise Gúdalúr, but are beaten, 215. Are besieged in Pondichery, 221. Repulse the besiegers, 224. Their position in 1749, 229. Win the battle, of Ambur, 238. Officers mutiny at Valdavur, 250. Surprise the camp of Murári Rao, 256. Repulse Muhamad, 258. Defeat Muhamad Ali, 259. Storm Jinjí, 262. Beat Násir Jang, 268. Obtain great increase of territory, 272. Beat the English at Volkonda, but fail to follow up their victory, 286. Shut up the English in Trichinápalli, 287. Are beaten by Clive, 302. Again, 303. Retreat into Srirangam, 318. Surrender to the English, 327. Beat the English at Vicravándi, 332. Beaten by them at Bahoor, 335. Defeat the Maráthás, 358. Again, 359. Again, 360. Driven to desperation at Haidarábád, 369. Obtain the cession of four provinces, 375. Defeat Captain Chace at Trivádi, 386. Are defeated at the Golden Rock, 390. Again, 395. Again at the Sugarloaf Rock, 398. Take refuge in Srirangam, 398. Are repulsed at Trichinápalli, 404. Causes of the repulse, 404. Surprise the English at Kutápárá, 409. Repulsed near the Sugarloaf Rock, 411. Make peace with the English, 433. Refuse to aid Siráj-u-daola against the English, 459. Beaten off Nágápatan, 509. Take Gúdalúr. 512. And Fort St. David, 515. Repulsed from Tanjur, 524. Beaten off Tranquebar, 525. Beaten at Kondúr, 542. Beaten off Fort St. David, 549. Army mutinies, 552. Returns to its duty, 554. Beaten at Wándiwásh, 560. Surrender Pondichery, 578. Reflections on the character of, in India, 575,

GUD

579. The consolation that remains to them, 579

GEOGHEHAN, M., repulses Brereton at Wándiwásh, 554
Gingens, Captain, co-operates with Muhammad Ali's levies, 284. Marches to intercept Chanda Sáhib, 285. Is repulsed from Volkonda, 287. The panic of his men, 287. His little self-confidence, 302. Is left in command of the troops, 333
Gháziu-d-dín, eldest son of Nizámu-l Mulk, prefers to remain at Delhi, 235. Allies himself with the Maráthás, 348. Threatens the Dakhan, 363. Arrives at Aurangábád, 363. Is poisoned, 364
Godeheu, M., commissioned by Dupleix to explain his case, 92. Appointed to succeed Dupleix, 417. His real character, 420. His meanness towards Dupleix on landing, 421. Refuses to settle the accounts of Dupleix, 423. His importunate spite, 423. The advice he received from Dupleix, 424. Restores the Swiss soldiers to the English, 427. Cuts off supplies from the army, 431. Replaces Mainville by Maissin, 432. Whom he instructs to connive at the English movements, 432. Resolves on peace at any price, 433. Obtains one, 434. Its disgraceful conditions, 429. He abandons all the French conquests, 439. His strange warning to Moracin, 441. Embarks for Europe, 442. Good effect of his departure, 443
Goens, Commodore Ryckloff van, drives the French from Trinkomali, 20. Ordered to attack St. Thomé. Takes it, 21
Golkhondá, King of, aids the Dutch against St. Thomé, 21. Succumbs to Aurangzeb, 24
Goupil, M., commands a French detachment, 248. Acts for Bussy at Haidarábád, 362. His weakness and indecision, 368. Consents to divide his forces, 371
Griffin, Admiral, arrives with his fleet off Cuddalore, 209. Outwitted by M. Bouvet, 213. Returns to England, 220
Guillard, M., appointed member of the secret committee, 441
Gúdalúr, plundered by the Maráthás, 90. Its situation, 197. The French

HAI

are surprised at, 197. Abortive effort of the French on, 205. The French repulsed at. 214. Taken by Lally, 513. Retaken by the English, 567.

HAIDAR ALI, falls upon the English baggage, 436. Enters into engagements with Lally, 566
Haidar Jang, murdered, 500
Haidarábád, Lussy's stand at, 485
Hallyburton, Mr., offers to treat for the surrender of Madras, 145. His part in the surrender, 149 *note*
Hóbert, M., Governor of Pondichery, 41, *note*
Heguerty, M. d', sets an example to the French cavalry, 562
Henri III. invites his subjects to trade, 5
Henri IV. forms a company to trade to India, 6
Heron, Colonel, commands an expedition to Madura, 446. Is found guilty of malversation, 446, *note*

INNIS KHAN, is disgusted with Captain Gingens, 300. Aids in surprising the English at Kutápárá, 464

JÁNÚJI, Rájá, makes overtures to Muhammad Ali, 275
Jánújí Bhonsla, invades the Sirkars and retires, 378
Jánújí, Nimbalkar, gained over by Bussy, 488. Feigns action against Law, 489
Janville, M. de, commands the escort of the Subadar, 375
Jinjí, taken by Sivají, 25. Attacked by Aurangzeb, 127. Its strength, 261. Stormed by the French, 261. Surrenders to the English, 569

KANDAGLA, harasses the French, 492.
Kadapah, Nawwáb of, the intrigues of Dupleix with, 246. Shoots Nasir Jang, 267. Conspires against Muzaffar Jung, 277. Is wounded and flies, 280
Kárikál, taken by the French, 77. Made over to them, 79. Description of, 79 *note*. Lally retreats on, 527. Surrenders to the English, 566.
Kásim-bazar, lodge at, founded, 32. Law stationed at, 461

LA BOU

Karnúl, Nawwáb of, is gained over by Dupleix, 254. His treachery towards Násir Jang, 268. Conspires against Muzaffer Jung, 277. Is hacked to pieces, 278
Karnúl, Fort of, stormed, 279
Kerjean, M. de, accuses La Bourdonnais of being bribed, 159 *note*. Defeats the English at Vicravándi, 334. Is sent to blockade Fort St. David, but retreats towards Pondichery, 335. Is outmanœuvred and beaten, 337. Commissioner at the Conference, 408
Kilpatrick, Captain, moves to assist Clive at Arkát, 294. Repulses the French from Trichinápalli, 401. Appears before Vellur, 446. Retires, 447
Kinneer, Major, sent back to attack Jinjí, 332. Is wounded and defeated, 334
Kondaoir, ceded to the French, 279

LA BOURDONNAIS, M. de, his early career, 64. His attack on Mahé, 65. His subsequent proceedings, 107. Appointed Governor of the Isles, 107. His energetic proceedings, 110. He returns to France, 112. His proposals to Fleury, 114. His departure for the isles, 115. The reversal of his orders, 117. He relieves Mahé, 117. Sends back his ships, 118. Resigns, but resignation not accepted, 119. Prepares "to conquer the impossible," 120. His difficulties, 121. Sails for Pondichery, 122. His losses and their repair, 123. Meets the English off Ceylon, 125. Fights Commodore Peyton, 126. Repulses him, 127. Offers battle again, 127. Anchors off Pondichery, 129. Friendly correspondence with Dupleix, 129. His designs regarding Madras, 131. Applies for more guns, 130. His irresolution, 133. Cruises off Karikal, 134. Contrast- the ships of the King with those of the Company, 135. Appeals to the Council, 135. The burden of all his letters, 137. Orders the squadron to leave, 138. Sets out for Madras, 139. Attacks Madras, 144. His alarm, 145. Forces the place to surrender, 146. Writes to Dupleix regarding the capitulation, 147. Declares that he had been authorised to dispose of the place, 147. Explains his reasons to Dupleix, 150. Gives Dupleix credit

608 INDEX.

LAH

for his success, 152. His real position, 153. His anger at the assumption of authority by Dupleix, 156. Disavows his subordination and agrees to ransom Madras, 156. The reasons of his behaviour, 157. His acceptance of a bribe, 159, and Appendix. Other reasons that prompted him, 160. His difference with Paradis, 162. Receives the deputation from Pondicherv, 165. Replies to the letter of the Council, 165. Assembles a council of war, 166. Repulses the Pondichery deputies, 166. Gets rid of the Pondichery contingent by a ruse 167. Arrests the deputies and denounces Paradis, 167. His real feelings, 168. Makes overtures to Dupleix, 169. Sneers at the instructions of Dupleix, 172. Receives his reply, 173. His fleet encounters a storm, 175. His losses, 176. Announces his intention to leave the coast, 178. Signs the treaty and sends it to Pondicherv, 178. His energy, 179. Leaves Madras, 180. Influences Dordelin, 180. Arrives at Pondichery, 181. Makes proposals to Dupleix, 181. Refuses to land, but obeys the Council, 182. Leaves Pondichery, 183. Brief review of his proceedings, 184. Proceeds to the isles and thence to Martinique, 185. His reception in England, his treatment in France, and his death, 185-6

Lahaye, Admiral, commands 'the fleet against Galle and Trinkamali, 17. Declines a contest with the Dutch, 18. Besieged in St. Thomé, 21. Visits Martin at Pondichery, and returns to Surat, 22 *note*

La-Joie, Sergeant Major, appointed commander-in-chief by the mutineers, 555. His prudent conduct, 556

Lally, Count de, orders Bussy to Arkát, 502. His antecedents, 503. His advice to the French Ministry, 405. Is ordered to India, 505. His character, 509. His strange greeting on arriving at Pondichery, 513. His extensive powers, 513. His idea of Franco-Indians, 514. Moves against Gúdalúr, 516. Experiences the neglect of the Pondichery authorities, 516-8. Takes Gúdalúr, 519. Besieges Fort St. David, 519. Impresses the natives, 520. The fault rather that of the Pondichery authorities, 520. Takes Fort St. David, 522.

LAW

Exhorts d'Aché to act with him, 523. Unwillingly consents to move against Tanjur, 524. The sufferings of his soldiers, 525. His violence and want of judgment, 527. Is attacked by a Tanjurian, 528. Retreats from Tanjur, 528. His letter to Bussy, 530 *note*. Fails to act against Chengalpat, 531. Raises money at Pondichery, and joins the army, 531. His real opinion of Bussy, 533. Takes Kánchipúram, and attacks Madras, 534. His assertions regarding Bussy, 534 *note*. Repulses the English sortie, 537. His difficulties, 526. The misconduct of his officers, 541. Is forced to raise the siege, 543. The reason why, 544. Returns to Pondichery, 550. His great difficulties, 551. Hears of d'Aché's arrival, 553. Orders Bussy to treat with Basálat Jang, 556. His prudent conduct on learning the mutiny of his army, 558. Brings it back to obedience, 559. Divides his force, 559. Joins the army at Wándiwásh, 560. Loses Karangolí and Wándiwásh, 561. Retakes Wándiwásh, 562. The dilatoriness of his chief engineer, 562. Fights at Wándiwásh, 563. Is beaten, 566. Is justified for fighting, 567. Negotiates with Haidar Alí, 567. His bold stroke, and its ill-success, 569. Resolves to hold out at Pondichery, 571. Takes no advantage of the storm, 572. Hopes for the arrival of d'Aché, 572. Surrenders, 573. His treatment by his countrymen, 576. Proceeds to France, 576. His condemnation and death, 577. The reversal of his sentence, 577

Lavaur, Father, a Jesuit, commissioner at the Conference, 407. Persuades Lally to act against Tanjur, 521. Subscribes to pay the arrears of the soldiers, 554. Engages to feed the troops, 569. His baseness and death, 578. His hypocrisy and wealth, 575 *note*

Law, John, of Lauriston, forms the General Bank, 42. Its success, 43. Establishes a Company of the West, 44. Converts the General into the Royal Bank, 44. Unites all the Companies into one Company of the Indies, 45. His system, 47. Raises the Government notes to par, 49. Attempts to extinguish the public debt, 50. Large sums made under his auspices, 51. Appointed Con-

INDEX.   609

LAW

toller General, 52. Attempts to prop up his scheme, 53. Fails, 54.
Law, Captain, appointed to command at Ariákupum, 217. His early success, 221. His sudden collapse, 222. Succeeds d'Auteuil before Trichinápallí, 288. His energetic commencement, 289. His pride and indecision, 298. His bad arrangements, 299. His want of energy, 300. His utter folly, 306. His unmilitary plans, 307. Their failure, 304. The feebleness of his next measures, 310. Their defeat, 311. Resolves to retreat into Srirangam, 313. His panic when the English were in his power, 315. Retires into Srirangam, 317. Attempts to surprise Clive, but fails, 323. Marches against Clive, but does not fight, 323. His despair, 324. Makes terms for Chanda Sáhib, 325. Surrenders with his whole force, 326. Is in charge of Kásím-bazar, 458. Retires to Bhagulpur, 468. Is captured, 469. Is detached to aid Bussy, 486. Is reinforced by d'Arambure, 487. Displays some energy, 489. Collapses and writes to Bussy for aid, 490. Is ordered forward, 490. Arrives at Haidarábád, 493. Despatched into Bengal, 497
Lawrence, Major, repulses the French at Gúdalúr, 213. Taken prisoner at Ariákupum, 220. Commands the second expedition to Dévíkóta, 241. Conquers it, 242. Joins Násir Jang, 247. Leaves for England, 258. Returns, 302. Outmanœuvres Law, 307. Effects a junction with the garrison, 308. Repulses Law, and enters Trichinápallí, 310. His share in the death of Chanda Sáhib, 325, and *note.* Forces Law to surrender, 326. Leaves the force, 342. Reassumes command, and marches against Kerjean, 335. Outmanœuvres and beats him, 336. His opinion of Dupleix, 339. The means at his disposal, 380. Harassed by the French and Maráthás, 382. Desists from his attempts against them, 382. Marches to relieve Trichinápallí, 384. Is repulsed from Srirangam, 385. Is attacked by Astruc, 389. His perilous position and heroic resolve, 390. His great victory, 391. Moves to Tanjur, 393. Outmanœuvres and beats Brennier, 395. Defeats Astruc, 399. Covers Tanjur, 413. Revictuals Trichinápallí, 433. Appointed to command in

MAD

Madras during the siege, 530 Resigns the command, 545.
Lenoir, M., Governor of Pondichery, 55. Pays off the debts of the company, 57. His difficulties, 57. Governor for the second time, 58. His disagreement with Dupleix, 67. Is succeeded by Dumas, 70
Leroy, Gerard, employed in the service of the French Company, 6
Leyrit, M. Duval de, appointed successor to Godeheu, 444. His service and character, 445. Protests against the English movements and follows their example, 446. Yields to their threats, 447. Is convinced that a non-interference policy is impossible, 448. His crafty policy, 448. Forces the English to retire from Vellur, 452. His design to capture Trichinápallí, 454. Orders the seizure of the English factories on the coast, 458. His excuse for not reinforcing Chandranagar, 465 *note.* His opinion of Bussy, 478. Detaches troops to aid Bussy, 486. Delays action till Lally's arrival, 509. His unpatriotic conduct, 528. Shelters the corrupt councillors and others, 545. Combines against Lally, 572. Earns the contempt of posterity, 573
Louis XII., two ships fitted out for the East in the time of, 5
Louis XIV., declares trade to India not derogatory to a man of noble birth, 12 *note.* Dies, 42

MACHAULT, M., appointed Controller General of French finances, 170
Machhlipatan, factory of, founded, 1 31. Seized by Násir Jang, 256. Recovered by Dupleix, 257. French possessions there increased, 279. Taken by Forde, 545
Madagascar, discovered by the Portuguese, 8, 9. Visited by the French, 9. Who settle there, 9. Visited by the Company of Colbert, 12. Abandoned by the Company, 13
Madras, its first occupation, 139. Its government in 1744,141. Its defences, 141. Attacked by La Bourdonnais, 146. Surrenders, 146. Articles of capitulation of, 146. Storm at, 175. Threatened by Mafauz Khán, 180. Paradis appointed to administer, 196. Saunders Governor of, 291. Succeeded

R R

MAF

by Pigot, 450 *note*. Invested by Lally, 533. The siege of, raised 540 Mafauz Khán, eldest son of Anwarudín, advances against Madras, 190. Defeated by the French, 193. His masterly movements afterwards, 193. Is beaten by Paradis, 194. Attacks Paradis and is repulsed, 200. Surprises de Bury, 203. Visits Dupleix at Pondichery, 205. Taken prisoner at Ambur, 238
Mahé, attacked and taken, 65. Name of, changed, 65. Relieved by La Bourdonnais, 117. Taken by the English, 577
Mahmú Khán, is gained over by Muzaffar Bég, 490
Mainville, M. de, appointed to command at Srirangam, 402. Attempts to surprise Trichinápallí, 403. The folly of his troops and his failure, 403. Surprises the English, 411. Repulsed near the Sugar Loaf Rock, 413. Floods the country, 413. His supplies stopped by Godeheu, 427. Replaced by Maissin, 432. His strong recommendations to his successor, 432. Is killed, 551
Maissin, M., in command of a body of French, 382. Makes two abortive attempts on Tiruvádí, 387. Occupies it, 387. Takes command from Mainville, 432. Connives at the revictualling of Trichinápallí, 434. Retreats into Srirangam, 435
Maisur Dalwai of, his treachery to Násir Jang, 269. Generals of, enter into negotiations with Dupleix, 333. Waver, 338. Finally join the French,' 338 *see* Nandaráj.
Makhdum Ali, cuts up a corps of English, 565
Malhar Ráo Holkar, negotiates with Ghaziu-d-dín, 348. Assists him, 366. Accompanies Bussy, 481
Mánakjí, promises to spare the life of Chanda Sáhib, 326. Orders him to be stabbed, 327
Maráthás, the, invade the Karnátik and defeat Dost Ali, 81. Retire, 85. Take Trichinápallí, 90. Plunder Portonovo and Gúdalúr, 91. Evacuate Trichinápallí, 104. Their treachery to Násir Jang, 268. Beaten by Ráju Sáhib, 302. Coquet with Dupleix, 332. Again waver, 338. But join the French, 338. Their peculiar power, 359. Are defeated by Bussy, 360. Acquire territory, 367. Excluded from participation in Angria's booty, 449 *note*

MOR

Marcara, M., associated with Caron, 15. Proceeds to Golkhonda, 15. Establishes a factory at Machhlipatan, 15. Quarrels with Caron, 16. Is supported by Colbert, 17. Goes to Java, 17 *note*
Mariol, M., takes Thiagar and Elmiseram, 548
Martin, François, his early career, 19, Sent to the province of Jinjí, 20. Buys a plot of land on the coast, 20. Returns to St. Thomé, 20. Proceeds with sixty men to his plot of land, 22. Lends money to Shér Khán Lodí, 22. Founds Pondichery, 23. Describes it to the Directors, 23. Applies to be allowed to have native soldiers, 24. Obtains further cessions from Shér Khán, 26. Is allowed to fortify Pondichery, 26. Is attacked by the Dutch and surrenders, 28. Retires to France, 33. Returns and strengthens Pondichery, 35. Dies, 37. His system, 36, 38.
Martizu Ali, his lineage, 72-3. Murders Safdar Ali, 104. Flees to Vellur, 104. Engaged in the murder of Seid Muhammad Khán, 105. Appointed to act under Dupleix, 335. Makes some captures in the Karnátik, 386. Defeated at Trinomali, 405. Renounces his title and submits to Muhammad Ali, 448. Threatened by the English, 450. Buys them off, 450
Mauritius, *see* Isle of France.
Mir Asad, taken prisoner, 80. His advice to Safdar Ali, 84. His enmity to Chanda Sáhib, 411 *note*
Mir Japar Ali, detached to attack Bussy, 485. Arrives at Haidarábád, 486
Monson, Mr., offers to treat for surrender of Madras, 145
Monson, Colonel, assumes command before Pondichery, and is wounded, 568
Moracin, M., appointed to command in the Sirkars, 377. His alarm at the recall of Dupleix, 428. Remonstrates with Godeheu, 435. Receives a strange warning from him, 441. His position easier than he had anticipated, 476. Detaches men to aid Bussy, 485. Joins Bussy, 500. His disobedience and its consequences, 543, and *note*
Morse, Mr., Governor of Madras, rejects the proposal of Dupleix for neutrality 101. His character, 141.

INDEX. 611

MUH

Applies for aid to restrain the French, but is refused, 143. Is abandoned by the fleet, 144. Signs a convention with La Bourdonnais, 156. And a capitulation, 180
Muhammad Ali, defeated at Ambur and flees, 238. Joins Násir Jang, 249. Appointed by him Nawwáb of the Karnátik, 254. Reinforced by Násir Jang, 257. Repulsed by the French, 258. Separates from the English and is defeated by the French, 259. Flees to Trichinápallí, 276. Affects to agree to the terms offered by Dupleix, 276. Throws off the mask, 284. Quarrels with his allies, 332. His reply to Dupleix, 341. Embarrassment of the English from being associated with, 449
Muhammad Husén Khán, secretly distresses the French, 372. He temporises, 374
Muhammad Issuf, operates against the French before Madras, 536
Muhammad Komal, defeated at Tripatí, 408
Muhammad Sháh, Emperor of Delhi, confers honours on Dumas, 93. Dies, 234
Murárí Ráo, accompanies Rághújí Bhonsla, 79. Appointed Governor of Trichinápalli, 89. Joins Násir Jang, 249. Attacks the French in their retreat, 252. Surprised by de la Touche, 257. Resolves to join the English, 297. Concerts measures with Dupleix, 384. Harasses Lawrence, 385. Covers the French retreat, 393, Surprises the English at Kutápárú, 413. Is threatened by the Subadar, 478. Enters into a secret understanding with Bussy, 479. Allies himself with Lally, 556
Mustafanagar, ceded to the French, 376
Muzaffar Jang, nominated successor to Nizamu-l-Mulk, 233. Meets and allies himself with Chanda Sáhib, 234. Appointed Subadar of the Dakhan, 237. Turns off towards Tanjur, 245. Surrenders to his uncle, 252. Released and recognised as Subadar, 269. Visits Pondichery, 271. Shows his gratitude to Dupleix, 273. Applies for a contingent of French troops, 275. Conspiracy against him, 276. Is killed, 278
Muzaffar Bég, a soldier of fortune, hired by Sháh Nawáz Khán, 485. Corrupts the French sipáhis, 487

PAR

NARSAPUR, acquired by the French. 280
Násir Jang, succeeds Nizámu-l-Mulk in the Dakhan, 233. Moves an army towards Pondichery, 249. Appoints Muhammad Ali Nawwáb of the Karnátik, 254. Loads Muzaffar Jang with irons, 254. Refuses the terms proposed by Dupleix, 255. Surprised by the French, retires to Arkát, 256. Seizes Machhlipatan and Yanaon, 256. Reinforces Muhammad Ali, 257. His carelessness, 260. He takes the field, 265. Negotiates with Dupleix, 267. The conspiracy against him, 268. Is surprised and slain, 269
Nets, Commodore de, commands an expedition to the East, 7
Nizám Ali, younger brother of Salábat Jang, 364. Invested with the administration of the Dakhan, 493. Murders Haidar Jang and flees, 494. Obtains the upper hand over his brother, 547. Deposes and causes him to be murdered, 54, *note*
Nizamu-l-Mulk, confers honours on M. Dumas, 92. Enters the Karnátik, 104. Enters Trichinápallí, 104. Dies, 184
Nizámpatnam, acquired by the French, 279
Nandráj, Dalwai of Maisur, 382. Tries in vain to surprise Trichinápallí, 384

ORLEANS, Duke of, Regent of France, 41. Patronises Law, 42
Orry, M., Controller General, authorises La Bourdonnais to retain his fleet, 117. Succeeded by Machault, 170

PALK, Mr., Commissioner at the Conference, 407. Leaves it, 408
Paradis, M., commands at Karikal, 135. Is the bearer of a letter from Dupleix, 152. Appointed Councillor at Madras, 156. His difference with La Bourdonnais, 162. Appointed a Commissioner under de Bury, 164. Denounced and arrested, 167. Liberated and sent to sound Dupleix, 16. Sent towards Madras, 193. Defeats Máfauz Khán at S. Thomé, 195. Appointed Governor of Madras, 197. Escorts the plunder of Madras to Pondichery, 199. Repulses Máfauz Khán, 199. Jealousy entertained regarding, 201. Appointed General, 207. Marches against Gúdalúr, 208. Is forced to

INDEX.

PAR

retire, 210. Sent to fortify Ariákupum 216. Appointed chief engineer at Pondichery, 217. Heads a sortie and is killed, 223.
Pardaillan, M. de, attacks Mahé, 62. Takes it, 65
Partáb Singh, his lineage, 74. Becomes Rájá of Tanjur, 79. Makes over Karikal to the French, 79. And Dévikótá to the English, 244. Attacked by Chanda Sáhib, 247. His wiliness, 247. Attacked by Lally, 519-22.
Pereira, M., his operations at Karikal, 78
Peyton, Commodore, fights La Bourdonnais and is repulsed, 126. Sails to Trinkamali, 126. Abandons Madras, 144
Pigott, Mr., succeeds Saunders as Governor of Madras, 448. Appoints Colonel Lawrence to command during the siege, 530
Pitt, Mr. Thomas, Governor of Madras, demand made upon, 140. Forced to comply, 141
Pocock, Admiral, engaged in the operations against Chandranagar, 470. Sails from Madras, 513. Beats d'Aché, 514. Again, 516. Again, 551
Pondichery, founded by Martin, 23. Threatened by Síváji, 25. By the Dutch, 26. Captured, 28. Restored, 34. Fortified, 34. Becomes the seat of the French Government, 35. Description of, 36. Its declension under the successors of Martin, 41. Reduced to financial extremities, 57. Further account of, 60. Its fortifications strengthened, 81. Visited by Safdar Ali and Chanda Sáhib, 86. Its state on the arrival of Dupleix, 98. Its new defences, 217. Besieged by Admiral Boscawen, 223. Who raises the siege, 224. Grand Darbár held at, 272. Besieged by Colonel Coote, 564. Storm in the roadstead of, 568. Surrender of, 571. Fate of the garrison of, 575. Its surrender, the doom of the French, 578
Pondichery, Council of, how constituted, 60. Appealed to by La Bourdonnais, 135. Its reply, 136. Serves a summons on La Bourdonnais, 138. Appoints a Council for Madras, 163. Supersedes La Bourdonnais by Desprémesnil, 164. Replies to La Bourdonnais' letters. 175. Sends sealed orders to Dordelin, 183. Refuses to entertain the new scheme of La Bour-

SAF

donnais, 183. Dealings of with Lally 510 and onwards.
Portebarré, M. de la, takes the French squadron to Madras and returns, 137. His want of skill, 143.
Preston, Captain. commands at Chengalpat, 531. Operates against the French before Madras, 538
Provostière, M. de la, Governor of Pondichery, 56

Raguji Bhonsla, invades the Karnátik, 79. Threatens M. Dumas, 84. Moves suddenly on Trichinápalli, 88. Defeats Bárá Sáhib and takes it, 89. Threatens Dumas, 89. His wife's love of Nantes cordials, 91. He retires, 92. Engages to support Gházu-d-dín, 367. Agrees to retire beyond the Waingangá, 369
Ragunáth Dass, Dáwán of the Subadar, is assassinated, 363
Rájámahendri, ceded to the French, 379
Ráju Sáhib, moves upon Arkát, 295. Proposes to Clive to surrender, 296. Assaults Arkát, 297. Is repulsed and retires, 297. Defeats the Maráthás and is beaten by Clive, 302. Beaten again, 305. Is disgraced by Dupleix, 307. Is too slothful for the views of Dupleix, 337
Rámchandr Jádao, gained over by Bussy, 487. Feigns action against Law, 489
Rám Rájá, his reply to the Dutch overtures, 27
Renault, M. de St. Germain, Chief of Chandranagar, 457. Invited to join the Subadar against the English, 459. Proposes neutrality to the English, 459. His surprise at their conduct, 463. Defends himself with vigour, 464. Surrenders Chandranagar, 465. Surrenders Karikal and is cashiered, 563 *note*
Richelieu, Cardinal de, forms a new Company of the Indies, 8
Rouen, two merchants of, begin the trade to the Indies, 5. Two others amalgamate with the Company, 6
Ryswick, effects of the treaty of, 34

Safdar Ali, his character, 73. Commands an expedition against Trichinápalli, 78. His dilatoriness, 81. Sends his mother to Pondichery, 83. Visits Pondichery, 87. Grants privileges to M. Dumas, 88. Proceeds

INDEX. 613

SAH

to Arkát, 88. Confers honours on M. Dumas, 93. Is murdered, 104 Sáhújí, becomes Rájá of Tanjur, but is expelled, 75. Allies himself with M. Dumas, 75. Recovers Tanjur, 76. Refuses to fulfil his engagements, 77. Is again expelled, 79. Appeals to the English to aid him, 233. Is supported by them, 244. Is abandoned and pensioned, 244. His name used by the French, 519
Salábat Jang, appointed by Busy Subadar of the Dakhan, 278. His concessions to Dupleix, 278. Is invested at Aurangábád, 279. Ratifies the engagement of his predecessor, 281. The state of his viceroyalty, 347. His facile nature, 352. Accompanies Bussy in his expedition against Puná, 360. Is anxious for peace, 364. Concludes an armistice with Báláji, 365. Makes peace with him, 366. Cedes four provinces to the French, 376. Swears eternal gratitude to Bussy, 386. The effect on him of the recall of Dupleix, 428. Inveighs against the policy of Godeheu, 471. His prophetic language, 471. His feudal authority in Southern India, 472. Requires Bussy to march against Maisur, 473. Dismisses Bussy from his service, 478. Arrives at Haidarábád, 485. Sends to propose a reconciliation, 492, His grief at Bussy's departure, 498. Marches to assist the French, 543. Concludes a treaty with the English, 543. His deposition and death, 554, *note*
Saubinet, M., appointed to command the French force in the Karnátik, 450. Overruns the Karnátik, 451. His character, 508. Advises an attack on Tanjur, 522. Takes Trinomali, 525. Is mortally wounded, 536
Saunders, Mr., Governor of Madras, enters into the plans of Clive, 292. Exerts himself to relieve Arkát, 296. Agrees to a conference, 408. His liberal proposals to Dupleix, 410. Influences the English ministry, 416. Accedes to Godeheu's wish for a truce, 436. And to a treaty, 436. Its conditions, 437. The debt due to him by England, 440. Succeeded by Pigott, 449 *note*
Sávánur, Nawwáb of, overtures made to by Dupleix, 254. His treachery, 267. Conspires against Muzaffar Jang, 276. Is killed, 277
Sávánur, Nawwáb of, son of the preced-

ST

ing, rebels against Salábat Jang, but submits, 478
Seid Muhammad Khán, succeeds Safdar Ali 104. Is murdered, 105. Again occupied by the French, 401. Again, 432. Stormed by them, 556
Shán Nawáz Khán, succeeds Saijid Lashkar as minister of the Subadar, 378. His surprise at the recall of Dupleix, 428. Intrigues against the French, 469. Denounces Bussy to the Subadar, 479. Suggests his assassination, 480. Stirs up the country against him, 483. Hires a soldier of fortune, 485. Determines to intercept Law, 486. Is cowed by Bussy's boldness, 491. Though he loses the game, his measures greatly assist the English, 494. Continues his intrigues, 495. Summons Nizám Ali to Aurangábád, 498. Is killed, 498.
Sher Khán Lodi sells a plot of ground to Martin, 20. Borrows money from him, 22. Allows Martin to maintain native soldiers, 24. Is defeated by Siváji, 25. Grants lands to Martin, 25
Siváji takes Bijapur and Golkhonda, 24. Defeats Sher Khán Lodi, 25. Threatens Pondichery, 25. Takes Surat, 31
Siváj-u-daola, Subadar, threatens Calcutta, 460. Is disinclined to attack the French and Dutch, 460. Marches against Calcutta, 462. Offers to engage Clive in his service, 464
Sirkars, the four, ceded to the French, 375. Some account of, 375-6. Conquered by and transferred to the English by the action directed by Clive, 545
Smith, Captain Joseph, commands in Trichinápallí, 452
Soupire, the Chevalier de, arrives at Pondichery, 428. His character, 504. His indolence, 506. Takes Karangoi, 526. Is outmanœuvred by Major Brereton, 546
Srirangam, island of, occupied by the French, 287. The French retreat into, 319. Are cooped up there, 319 Surrendered to the English, 327
St. David, Fort, the English retire to it from Madras, 198. Its situation and early history, 198. Receives reinforcements, 207. Besieged and taken by Lally, 518
St. George, Fort, *see* Madras
St. Thomé, taken by the French, 18 Taken by the Dutch, 21. Lally retreats by, 539

ST

St. Malo, ships of, seized at Surat, 31. Company of, trades to India, 40
Stevens, Commodore, joins Admiral Pocock, 512
Surat, is visited by Caron, 15. Taken by Síváji, 30. Abandoned by the French Company, 31. Ships seized a*, 32. Lenoir pays the debts of the French Company at, 58

TANJUR, its early history, 74. Attacked by Chanda Sáhib, 247. By Lally, 523. Who retreats, 525
Terraneau, M., assists in blocking up the channel of the Hugli, 468. Betrays the secret to the English, 469. His fate, 470 *note*
Tiruvádí, taken possession of by the French, 256. Action at, 259. Occupied by the English, 381. By the French, 387. By the English, 568.
Touche, M. de la, surprises Murári Ráo's camp, 254. Surprises and defeats Násir Jang, 267. Returns to Europe, 276. Is burnt with 700 men in the *Prince*, 381 *note*
Trinkumali, taken by the French, 18. Retaken by the Dutch. 18
Tricbinápallí, taken by Chanda Sáhib, 74. Muhammad Ali flees to, 275. English shut up in, 287. Description of, 287. Relieved by Lawrence, 311. Attempted by Nandoráj, 382. Effect of Lawrence's victory on, 398. French attempt to surprise, repulsed, 430. Revictualled by Lawrence, 432. D'Auteuil's attempt upon, 451. Defeated, 454

ZUL

VANSITTART, Mr., Commissioner at the conference for peace, 408. Leaves it, 409
Vellur, Murtizá Ali flees to, 103. Again, 104. Description of, 452. Threatened by the English, 452. Who retire, 452
Vigne, Captain de, commands the defences of Chandranagar, 468. His brave defence, 470 and *note*
Viráná, a Maisurian general, is frightened out of an impregnable position, 385
Volkondah, attacked by the English, 285. Who are repulsed, 286. D'Auteuil surrenders at, 325

WATSON, Admiral, ordered to the Indies with four ships, 417. Arrives in India, 436. Employed in the attack on Ghériah, 448. Recaptures Calcutta, 461. Concurs in accepting the French proposition of neutrality, 463. Refuses to sign the agreement or to attack Chandranagar, 464. His scruples are silenced, 465, and *note*. Sails against Chandranagar, 466. Attacks it, 468
Wiswás Ráo, son of Bálájí Bájí Ráo, advances on Aurangábád, 497

YANAON, seized by Násir Jang, 256. Restored, 272

ZULIKÁR Khán, his ability, 344. His death, 345

Works by the Same Author.

THE DECISIVE BATTLES OF INDIA, from 1746 to 1849 inclusive. With a Portrait of the Author, a Map, and Three Plans. 8vo. 18s. London: W. H. Allen & Co. 1883.

Notices of the First Edition.

"All these battles are narrated with Colonel Malleson's usual power, combining a scientific understanding of the military events with a clear appreciation of the political situation; while his literary ability enables him to present a mass of compressed information in a pleasant and readable shape. In speaking of political events, especially, he is as outspoken and uncompromising as ever; never, as a soldier, so dazzled by the brilliancy of a victory as to be blind to any wrong-doing or injustice that may have paved the way for it; never, as a politician, so overborne by the success of any scheme as to be silent when it seems to him that the process by which it was gained deserves unsparing exposure, or stern and even harsh reproof."—GUARDIAN.

"Colonel Malleson's book is simply the story of how we won India. . . . Differences of opinion may exist as to the relative importance of the several actions which he recounts; but nobody can rise from a study of them without being convinced that the English Infantry in those days were the first soldiers in the world, and that the system under which they were reared must have been admirably suited to the material of which they were composed."—ST. JAMES'S GAZETTE.

"As to the manner in which the author has accomplished his task, it is sufficient to say that the work before us is not unworthy of Colonel Malleson's deservedly high reputation as a writer on Indian subjects."—ATHENÆUM.

"We know of no book so well calculated as is the one we are noticing for giving the student a clear and comprehensive knowledge of the successive steps taken in conquering for ourselves the Empire of Hindostan. It is not simply the story of so many decisive battles. The causes which led to each one are set forth, and the connection between each successive

WORKS BY THE SAME AUTHOR.

war is clearly shown. The author has consulted 'as far as possible original documents, or the writings, published and unpublished, of contemporaries'; and, to judge by the list of such given, the labour of composing this excellent work must have been considerable."—SATURDAY REVIEW.

"Colonel Malleson's narrative is vivid, but unexaggerated; and even the non-military reader will be able to form from his pages a lively idea of the events described. What, too, is a commendable feature in his book is that, whilst he makes us honestly proud of the glorious deeds of our own countrymen, he teaches us to respect the valour and determination of those whom they conquered."—FIELD.

"This is just the sort of book we should like to place in the hands of boys—if there are such—whom the influence of æsthetic or luxurious mammas may be in danger of rendering milksops. The annals of the Roman Proconsulate do not contain a more stimulating story of endurance, daring, and the manlier virtues generally, than that told in Colonel Malleson's twelve chapters. Almost every page shows traces of original research."—SPECTATOR.

"A book just published, 'The Decisive Battles of India,' is well fitted to minister to what is, after all, a healthy appetite. The records of stirring adventure—of those 'fierce wars' which with 'faithful loves' make up the romance of history—must always have the deepest interest for men who have not lost their manhood; and no more thrilling story has ever been told than that of the English conquest of India."—TIMES, Leading Article.

"Colonel Malleson's history will be read with interest now and in the future, and will be always valuable for reference and a companion to the history of our Great Empire in the East."—MORNING POST.

THE BATTLE-FIELDS OF GERMANY, from the Outbreak of the Thirty Years' War to the Battle of Blenheim. With Maps and Plans. London: W. H. Allen & Co., 13, Waterloo Place. 1884.

"Colonel Malleson is all along thoroughly in sympathy with his subject. His pages reflect not only the deep delight of the soldier in recounting the brave deeds of brave men, but the keen relish of the scientific student, in unravelling the subtleties of successful strategy. His analysis of the operations of either army, whether they resulted in success or defeat, is always so thoroughly terse and lucid that even readers who have not the slightest comprehension of military matters will find themselves following the details with a deep and intelligent interest; and he is always scrupulously fair to all parties. . . . This volume must have cost great research and patient industry to collect the materials which are digested in its pages. But the author may well be rewarded by the consciousness that he has produced a

WORKS BY THE SAME AUTHOR.   iii.

thoroughly good book, and one in which, from beginning to end, it is scarcely possible to find a single word that is either superfluous or misapplied."—THE GUARDIAN.

"Colonel Malleson has already given us a valuable series of volumes on Indian history, and among them one of great interest on the 'Decisive Battles of India.' In the present book he has turned to Western history, and has treated some of the most famous battles fought on German soil in the masterly fashion conspicuous in his former works. While writing as a scientific soldier, Colonel Malleson has by no means produced a merely professional book. Although he does not profess to deal with political history, he gives a clear and satisfactory account of the events connected with the battles which form the avowed object of his work, and exhibits no small degree of literary skill as well as of historic perception in his selection and treatment of them. . . . We hope we may receive two more volumes of the Battle-fields of Germany as delightful as the one he has already given us."—SATURDAY REVIEW.

"Colonel Malleson has shown a grasp of his subject and a power of vivifying the confused passages of battle in which it would be impossible to name any living writer as his equal. In imbuing these almost forgotten battle-fields with fresh interest and reality for the English reader he is reopening one of the most important chapters of European history, which no previous English writer has made so interesting and instructive as he has succeeded in doing in this volume."—ACADEMY.

"The intense realism of the author's narrative is very fascinating; his thorough understanding of everything, his keenness in fathoming hidden motives for action, and his unsurpassed talent in imparting lively interest to dry-as-dust details, make his books as universally entertaining as instructive. . . . His life-like account of martial exploits is worthy to be read with pleasure like that to be derived from the perusal of old Greek and Latin historians, who in sonorous poetry and flowing prose recorded heroic deeds and consummate feats of generalship."—THE WHITEHALL REVIEW.

LOUDON: A SKETCH OF THE MILITARY LIFE OF GIDEON ERNEST, FREIHERR VON LOUDON, some time Generalissimo of the Austrian Forces. London: Chapman & Hall (Limited). 1884.

"Colonel Malleson has had a difficult task in describing Loudon's eventful career, on account of the vast amount of incidental matter which he was compelled to introduce in order to make his narrative intelligible. This obstacle he has, however, overcome triumphantly, and has produced a military and historical essay that is at once concise and interesting."—ATHENÆUM.

WORKS BY THE SAME AUTHOR.

"How great a soldier Loudon was may be pleasantly learned from the volume Colonel Malleson has contributed to the series of military biographies. . . . Loudon's had been, indeed, a great career, and Colonel Malleson has described it not unworthily."—SATURDAY REVIEW.

"Colonel Malleson has narrated his hero's career most ably, and produced a book which will not only possess a professional value, but in its vigorous and vivid description of the affairs in which Loudon was engaged, is singularly interesting even for the general reader."—FIELD.

FOUNDERS OF THE INDIAN EMPIRE: CLIVE, WARREN HASTINGS, WELLESLEY. Vol. I.—Lord CLIVE. With a Portrait and Four Plans. Price 20s. London: W. H. Allen & Co.

"It would not be possible to find in any other work a more faithful or vivid word-picture of the work accomplished by this great soldier and statesman, or of the manner in which he performed it."—SCOTSMAN.

"To Colonel Malleson and to Mr. W. W. Hunter in our own day is chiefly due that rehabilitation of India as a source of literary interest which was begun by Lord Macaulay. And the book before us continues the good work by giving the purely Indian aspect of Clive's doings; while by an excellent style and attractive treatment it shows, further, that this aspect is one to which men may turn their eyes without danger of being sent to sleep. . . . The book is one of undeniable value."—ACADEMY.

HISTORY OF THE FRENCH IN INDIA, from the Founding of Pondichery in 1674 to the Capture of that place in 1761. Second Edition. 8vo. 16s. London: W. H. Allen & Co.

"Colonel Malleson has produced a volume alike attractive to the general reader, and valuable for its new matter to the special student. It is not too much to say that now, for the first time, we are favoured with a faithful narrative of that portion of European enterprise in India which turns upon the contest waged by the East India Company against French influence, and especially against Dupleix."—EDINBURGH REVIEW.

"It is pleasant to contrast the work now before us with the writer's first bold plunge into historical composition, which splashed everyone within his reach. He swims now with a steady stroke, and there is no fear of his sinking. With a keener insight into human character, and a larger understanding of the sources of human action, he combines all the power of animated recital which invested his earlier narratives with popularity."—FORTNIGHTLY REVIEW.

WORKS BY THE SAME AUTHOR.   V.

FINAL FRENCH STRUGGLES IN INDIA AND THE
INDIAN SEAS. Including an Account of the Capture of the
Isles of France and Bourbon. London: W. H. Allen & Co.
1878.

" How India escaped from the government of Prefects and Sub-Prefects to fall under that of Commissioners and Deputy-Commissioners ; why the Penal Code of Lord Macaulay reigns supreme instead of a Code Napoleon ; why we are not looking on helplessly from Mahe, Karikal, and Pondichery, while the French are ruling all over Madras, and spending millions of francs in attempting to cultivate the slopes of the Neilgherries, may be learnt from this modest volume. Colonel Malleson is always painstaking, and generally accurate ; his style is transparent, and he never loses sight of the purpose with which he commenced to write."—SATURDAY REVIEW.

HISTORY OF THE INDIAN MUTINY, 1857-58. Commencing from the close of the Second Volume of Sir John Kaye's History of the Sepoy War. In Three Volumes. Demy 8vo. Price 20s. each Volume. Cloth. London: W. H. Allen & Co. 1878.

" It need only be remarked that Colonel Malleson wields his pen with so much skill that while giving a realistic account of all important operations, passing over no really noteworthy act of talent or heroism, and acutely criticizing everything which demands criticism, he abstains from overlaying his narrative with details which would have increased the bulk of his book beyond all reason. Another characteristic of Colonel Malleson is that he never hesitates to condemn conduct of which he disapproves, or to draw attention to errors which he conceives were committed, whatever the rank or position of those who are the objects of his criticism. The result is that many of the actors in the drama will find their laurels somewhat injured, while others, who from official prejudice have not yet received full credit for their exploits, obtain from the author due praise for their services. The rewards given for the Mutiny were liberal, but it is distressing to find that some of them were undeserved, while, on the other hand, many able and gallant men have received no recognition at all. . . . There are many highly-placed officials whose fame is sadly tarnished by the frank, truthful criticisms of the fearless, uncompromising author of the book before us."—ATHENÆUM.

" A brilliant narrative, in which a great number of threads of history are taken up and combined with singular skill. We have never read a volume in which this merit is more conspicuously displayed : and a history which, in unskilful hands, might have become confused to the last degree, is made remarkably clear and intelligible."—SPECTATOR.

vi.   WORKS BY THE SAME AUTHOR.

"A work as fearless in its criticism of men and warlike operations as it is remarkable for vigour and picturesqueness of style."—TRUTH.

"The second volume of Colonel Malleson's 'History of the Indian Mutiny' is quite equal to the first in every respect. The style is as eloquent, the grasp of the subject as firm, the arrangement as clear, and, above all, there is the same evidence of industry, the same evident desire to be impartial."—TIMES.

"It is difficult, in speaking of a living writer, to give expression to the unqualified praise which we hold Colonel Malleson's work to merit. It is not less remarkable for its literary beauty and its loftiness of diction than it is for the research and careful inquiry which are perceptible on every page. Posterity will recognize in this book a great and true exposition of one of the crises through which his countrymen have fought their way, by characteristics truly British, to wider empire and to greater fame."—EXAMINER.

AN HISTORICAL SKETCH OF THE NATIVE STATES OF INDIA IN SUBSIDIARY ALLIANCE WITH THE BRITISH GOVERNMENT. With Notices of the Mediatized and Minor States. In One Volume. 8vo. With Six Maps. Price 15s. London: Longmans & Co. 1875.

"Colonel Malleson is recognized as one of the masters of Indian history; and his acquaintance with the vast vicissitudes, as well as the actual state of the Feudatory States of Hindostan, could not easily be surpassed."—THE TIMES.

"We cannot conclude without again expressing a sense of the value of the present publication. Colonel Malleson set himself a most difficult task, even though it was only one of compilation, as he modestly styles it; he has kept himself strictly within the limits of the work prescribed for himself, has consulted only the very highest authorities, and has, in addition, brought his own extensive knowledge and reading to bear on his subject, the result being that his history is a valuable and useful one in the sense he intended it to be, compendious in volume and style, and yet replete with all that is important and material to a proper understanding of the scenes and events brought before us."—LIVERPOOL ALBION.

A HISTORY OF AFGHANISTAN, from the Earliest Period to the Outbreak of the War of 1878. 8vo. With Map. 18s. Second Edition. London: W. H. Allen and Co. 1879.

"The charm, vivacity, and dramatic force of Colonel Malleson's narra-

WORKS BY THE SAME AUTHOR. vii.

tive style are not less conspicuous in this book than in his continuation of Kaye's 'History of the Indian Mutiny.' With rare skill and literary judgment he has disentangled the facts of Afghan history from the various chronicles and records, and has put them into the form of a clear, continuous narrative."—SCOTSMAN.

"The name of Colonel Malleson on the title page of any historical work in relation to India or the neighbouring states is a satisfactory guarantee both for the accuracy of the facts and the brilliancy of the narrative. An Italian critic has lately spoken of one of his recent books as combining the attractiveness of a romance with the higher qualities which we naturally look for in such works. The author may be complimented upon having written a History of Afghanistan which is likely to become a work of standard authority."—MELBOURNE ARGUS.

"Even those who differ from his final view of the case will at least admit that his statements are fairly made on each side of the question, and that he has supplied much valuable information on a subject which at the present moment occupies no small share of public attention."—MORNING POST.

HERAT, THE GRANARY and GARDEN OF CENTRAL ASIA. One Volume. 8vo. Price 8s. London: W. H. Allen & Co. 1879.

"This volume is a perfect arsenal of facts and authoritative opinions as to the extreme importance of the fortress city and district of Herat; whilst the deductions drawn by the writer from these facts and opinions are conclusive as to the necessity, incumbent upon ourselves, not to risk the presence of Russia upon its western frontier, or perpetuate the misfortunes of the Afghans by leaving them, as heretofore, a helpless prey to Muscovite perfidy and inter-tribal strife. . . . If there be still any who affect to doubt that the citadel of Herat commands Afghanistan and Khorassan, and that the possessor of it will be the paramount power in those countries, we cannot suggest a more speedy and definitive settlement for his doubts than the perusal of Colonel Malleson's volume."—MORNING POST.

STUDIES FROM GENOESE HISTORY. One Vol. Crown 8vo. London : Longmans. 1875.

"Colonel Malleson has done well in preferring to give us rather a series of pictures of the salient points in Genoese history than a mere methodical narrative or a succinct epitome. The sketches of Jacobo Donfadio and of the Doria are specimens of literary work of a high order."—THE WORLD.

WORKS BY THE SAME AUTHOR.

THE REFOUNDING OF THE GERMAN EMPIRE. One Vol. Seeleys. 1893.

"Colonel Malleson has succeeded in giving within the compass of a book of three hundred pages a very interesting and instructive account of the events between 1848 and 1871 which culminated in the refounding of the German Empire. His account of the military operations of 1866 and 1870-71 is much the best, on a moderate scale, that we have seen. It is painstaking, clear, and for its limits very full and complete."—SPECTATOR.

W. H. Allen & Co.'s Recent Works.

THE LAND REVENUE OF BOMBAY. A History of its Administration, Rise, and Progress. By ALEXANDER ROGERS, Bombay Civil Service, Retired. Just published. 2 vols. demy 8vo, with 18 Maps, 30s.

" A very elaborate survey, at once comprehensive and detailed, of a very important branch of Indian Administration. . . . To students of Indian institutions Mr. Rogers' volumes will be full of interest."—TIMES.

" An immense mass of information, which gives a high, though of course special, and indeed technical, value to his elaborate work. To the practical student of Indian affairs his volumes cannot fail to be of the greatest utility."—GLASGOW HERALD.

OLD RECORDS OF THE INDIA OFFICE, with supplementary Notes and Appendices. By SIR GEORGE BIRDWOOD, M.D., K.C.I.E., C.S.I., LL.D., ETC., ETC. Demy 8vo, with Illustrations. By W. Griggs, and Maps, 12s. 6d. London: W. H. Allen & Co., Limited, 13, Waterloo Place.

" No one knows better than Sir George Birdwood how to make a 'bare and shorthand' index of documents attractive, instructive and entertaining, by means of the notes and elucidatory comments which he supplies so liberally, and so pleasantly withal, from his own inexhaustible stores of information concerning the early relations of India with Europe."—THE TIMES.

" Full of readable and instructive matter."—SCOTSMAN.

" Ought to be in every public Library."—LEEDS MERCURY.

X.   W. H. ALLEN AND CO.'S RECENT WORKS.

MAHÂBODHI; OR, THE GREAT BUDDHIST TEMPLE UNDER THE BODHI TREE AT BUDDHA-GAYÂ. By MAJOR-GENERAL SIR ALEXANDER CUNNINGHAM, R.E., K.C.I.E., C.S.I. Royal 4to. Cloth, with 51 Illustrations, £3 3s. net.

"The author gives an elaborate account, illustrated with numerous photographs, of the results of the excavations and restorations recently undertaken at the Great Buddhist Temple of Buddha-Gayâ. All Oriental archæologists will recognise the importance of these remains and the value of Sir A. Cunningham's monograph upon them."—THE TIMES.

"Sir A. Cunningham is the greatest authority on the ancient monuments of India, and his volume, historical, descriptive, and illustrative of the *Mahâbodhi* is a work of unusual interest and value. . . . The work is illustrated by a series of beautifully executed plates, and these, together with the letterpress, give us a very clear and complete idea of this famous temple."—SCOTSMAN.

"This handsome volume will increase the deservedly high reputation of its author."—MANCHESTER GUARDIAN.

HISTORY OF INDIA. From the Earliest Times to the Present Day. For the Use of Students and Colleges. By H. G. KEENE, C.I.E., HON. M.A. Oxon., Author of "The Fall of the Moghul Empire." Two vols. Crown 8vo, with Maps, 12s. London: W. H. Allen & Co., Limited, 13, Waterloo Place.

www.ingramcontent.com/pod-product-compliance
Lightning Source LLC
Chambersburg PA
CBHW071352300426
44114CB00016B/2033